The Collected Writings of Walt Whitman

The frontispiece is an oil study of Walt Whitman made by Thomas Eakins, probably in 1887; reproduced courtesy of the Museum of Fine Arts, Boston (Helen and Alice Colburn Fund).

WALT WHITMAN

The Correspondence

VOLUME IV: 1886–1889

Edited by Edwin Haviland Miller

NEW YORK UNIVERSITY PRESS 1969

The frontispiece is an oil study of Walt Whitman made by Thomas Eakins in 1887. Reproduced by courtesy of the Museum of Fine Arts, Boston (Helen and Alice Colburn Fund).

LIBRARY OF CONGRESS CATALOG CARD NUMBER: 69–19259
MANUFACTURED IN THE UNITED STATES OF AMERICA

The Collected Writings of Walt Whitman

GRATEFUL ACKNOWLEDGMENT IS MADE TO

Mr. Charles E. Feinberg,

WHOSE ASSISTANCE MADE POSSIBLE THE ILLUSTRATIONS
IN THIS VOLUME AND WHO ALSO MADE
AVAILABLE TO THE PUBLISHER THE RESOURCES
OF THE FEINBERG COLLECTION.

Preface

Like its predecessors this book owes much to other people, particularly to librarians unknown to me in the New York Public Library and its Annex, Harvard University, the Boston Athenaeum, the American Antiquarian Society at Worcester, Massachusetts, and the New York University libraries.

I have always drawn freely upon the vast knowledge of my colleague, Gay Wilson Allen. To the following curators and librarians I express my gratitude: to the late Dr. John D. Gordan and his staff in the Berg Collection at the New York Public Library; John Alden of the Boston Public Library, Mrs. June Moll of the Miriam Lutcher Stark Library at the University of Texas, and John H. Reed of the L. A. Beeghly Library at Ohio Wesleyan University. My former student, Professor Harold Jaffe, assisted in preparing the index of this volume.

What I owe to Charles E. Feinberg, who has assembled the greatest Whitman collection in existence, I cannot adequately express.

In the preparation of this manuscript I received assistance from the Arts and Science Research Fund at New York University and from the Guggenheim Foundation.

I am indebted to the following institutions for permission to print Whitman letters in their collections: Barrett Literary Manuscripts Collection, University of Virginia; Henry W. and Albert A. Berg Collection, New York Public Library; Boston Public Library; British Museum; Brooklyn College; Brown University; Mark Twain Papers, University of California at Berkeley; Columbia University; Royal Library of Copenhagen; Cornell University; Estelle Doheny Collection of the Edward Laurence Doheny Memorial Library, St. John's Seminary; T. E. Hanley Collection, University of Texas; Harvard University; Henry E. Huntington Library; Huntington (New York) Public Library; Iowa State Education Association; Knox College; Library of Congress; Oscar Lion Collection, New York Public Library; Mills College; Missouri Historical Society; Pierpont Morgan Library; New Jersey Historical Society; Museum of the City of New York; New York Public Library; Northwestern University; Oberlin College; William D. Bayley Collection, Ohio Wesleyan University; University of Pennsylvania; The Carl and Lily Pforzheimer Foundation, Incorporated, on behalf of The Carl H. Pforzheimer Library; Phillips Exeter Academy; Princeton University; University of Richmond; Rutgers University; University of Southern California; Stanford University; Syracuse University; Trent Collection, Duke University; Vassar College; Whitman House, Camden; Widener Collection, Harvard University; and Yale University.

The following individuals have allowed me to print letters in their possession: Professor Gay Wilson Allen, Roger W. Barrett, the William E. Barton Estate, Mrs. Louis Broido, Mrs. Charles Cridland, Dr. R. J. H. DeLoach, Paul J. Eisel, Charles E. Feinberg, Mrs. Ward Greene, Mrs. Barbara Halpern, John Z. Katz, Professor Harold D. Kelling, George McCandlish, Gilbert S. McClintock, John S. Mayfield, Mrs. Doris Neale, Charles Norton Owen, Bernard Sarrazin, Professor Rollo G. Silver, Professor Cora E. Stafford, the Louis E. Stern Estate, Robert H. Taylor, Mrs. William R. Weber, and James S. Wroth.

E. H. M.

CONTENTS

PREFACE *vii*

INTRODUCTION *1*

A LIST OF WHITMAN'S CORRESPONDENTS *7*

ABBREVIATIONS *11*

The Correspondence

1886 *15* 1889 *139*

1887 *62* 1888 *260*

APPENDICES:

A. A List of Manuscript Sources *411*

B. A Check List of Whitman's Lost Letters *424*

C. A Calendar of Letters Written to Whitman *428*

D. Chronology of Whitman's Life and Work *442*

INDEX *447*

Introduction

Before the last "So long" was said, the man who had celebrated the body electric was forced to watch his own body atrophy and disintegrate. This singer of athletes and of manliness gradually became more and more an invalid. In the last seven years of his life—the autumn that gradually but inevitably became a winter of physical pain and of confinement to the rooms of his Mickle Street "shanty"—Walt Whitman reluctantly accepted the constant attendance of a nurse. The mail that he received became his avenue to an outside world which he rarely entered. The visits of Horace Traubel nightly relieved the monotony of his days, and famous callers created a brief flurry of excitement.

Contraction was the rule. As his health deteriorated, he zealously, within the limitations of his reduced physical energy, supervised publication of the final editions of *Leaves of Grass* and of collections of minor scribblings in *November Boughs* and *Good-bye My Fancy*. Although Traubel was delegated to act as his agent, all decisions of consequence were Whitman's: to the very end he supervised the details of publication from the selection of type face to the binding itself, as he had done over thirty years before when the anonymous *Leaves of Grass* appeared in Brooklyn. He continued to write but mostly "pot-boilers," and he continued to lament, as he had done all his life, that editors refused to print his poems. Which, to be blunt, was scarcely a half-truth, since he was well remunerated for poems and prose pieces of little merit. Poems that appeared in American magazines and newspapers were almost always copied in England, in the *Pall Mall Gazette* and *The Review of Reviews*.

The martyr pose that he and his followers indulged in concealed two important facts. Friends of Whitman were associated with important newspapers in Philadelphia (Talcott Williams of the *Press*), Boston (Sylvester Baxter of the *Herald* and William Sloane Kennedy of the *Evening Transcript*), and New York (Julius Chambers of the *Herald* and later of the *World*). The Gilders printed almost everything he sent to *The Critic*, and Joseph M. Stoddart of *Lippincott's* and Richard Watson Gilder of *Century* were active partisans. In England, William T. Stead devoted a great deal of space to the American poet in *Pall Mall Gazette* and later in *The Review of Reviews*. If a list of articles by and about Whitman were made, as the notes in this volume indicate, it would immediately become apparent that Whitman received an enormous amount of attention in magazines and newspapers. What he was not accorded was universal admiration, but no artist to my knowledge has enjoyed (or could endure) unanimous adulation.

Although death's shadow hovered over him during the last four years, he continued to send off his characteristically chatty, unadorned letters and post cards. At times Richard Maurice Bucke tried to goad him to apocalyptic statements, to personal revelations, but Whitman maintained that curious integrity which he announced in letters to uneducated soldiers during the Civil War. A letter was a personal document: it was not autobiography, it was not an excuse to state esthetic theories, and it was not written for posterity. The revelations and oracular utterances were in the poems, his recollections of his past appeared in prose articles, and *Specimen Days* recorded his delight in the natural environment. Of course he knew that his friends kept and cherished his letters; after all, he gave rough drafts of the early letters to Traubel when they turned up in the debris that littered his rooms. When Traubel informed him in 1889 that Bucke had "seven or eight hundred" letters in his possession, he observed: "That is doing pretty good for a fellow who prided himself on writing few letters—for one whose early printer predilection for a letter on one sheet only and one side only of that sheet still persists." Upon learning in the same conversation that Ellen M. O'Connor had kept the letters and cards written to her husband, he remarked: "So that is the case? I'm only sorry they are not more worthy. They are all so short, so empty—so much the result rather of a desire to write than of any feeling of anything particular to say."[1] Although he expected his literary executors to publish his writings, the tone of his letters never changed, even when he sent greetings to a correspondent "as f'm a flickering well-burnt down candle, soon to be all out."[2]

In his letters Whitman sought the warmth of personal relationships, the kind of empathic family which he had not known at first hand. He said as much on one occasion to Traubel:

> A man's family is the people who love him—the people who comprehend him. You know how for the most part I have always been isolated from my people—in certain senses have been a stranger in their midst. . . . Who of my family has gone along with me? Who? Do you know? Not one of them. They are beautiful, fine: they don't need to be apologized for: but they have not known me: they have always

1. Traubel, v, 129, 130. 2. Letter 2586.

> missed my intentions. Take my darling dear mother: she and I—oh! we have been great chums: always next to each other: always: yet my dear mother never took that part of me in: she had great faith in me—felt sure I would accomplish wonderful things: but Leaves of Grass? Who could ever consider Leaves of Grass a wonderful thing: who? She would shake her head. God bless her! She never did. . . . But she would put her hand in mine—press my hand—look at me: all as if to say it was all right though in some ways beyond her power to explain.[3]

As "a stranger" he reached out his hand in his letters to strangers like the Australian poet whom he never met, Bernard O'Dowd, to say: "what we hold to & pass each other is pure sentiment, good will &c. (am not sure but such things are the best proof of immortality)."[4] In one of his last letters, on November 1, 1891, he wrote to the same correspondent: "The doctor says I have *progressive paralysis*, wh' is eligible to have a fatal termination any hour—so you must all take my letters & conveyances of friendship & affection (strangers as we are face to face) as my last missives."[5]

Although Whitman accepted (and perhaps needed) the veneration he received from the idolators, he did not place an aura around the personal man in his letters. He was willing to make large claims in unsigned newspaper notices, he overreacted to criticism, and he generally minimized the actual physical and emotional state in print. But in his letters, like Huckleberry Finn, he pretty much told it as it was. He did not conceal his constipation from his two English admirers, J. W. Wallace and Dr. John Johnston, although they concealed his candor by removing the references to bowels when they printed his letters after his death. And Bucke made no attempt to include the hundreds of letters he had received in the ten-volume edition of *The Writings of Walt Whitman.* Of these letters Whitman said quite rightly, "They are all about my bowels, head, symptoms, diet—the professional facts which a doctor knows what to do with."[6] Whitman's preoccupation with the decaying shell he inhabited was in part perhaps hypochondriacal, and it certainly made the hero-saint of the admirers all too human, but the role of the hero-saint was the preoccupation of his idolators, not of the poet. Although he occasionally postured in public, he was not self-deceived. Geniuses rarely are.

Correspondents wrote flatteringly about Whitman's ability to endure the agony of his final illnesses and commended in reverent tones his serenity. It is true that only infrequently did he allow the boredom of his enforced isolation to show through even in a message to a friend. The

3. Traubel, III, 525–526; and see IV, 473–474.
4. Letter 2461. 5. Letter 2671.
6. Traubel, I, 446.

following passage is not representative: "Pretty dull—If I did not have naturally good spirits I dont know what would become of me, run in here like a rat in a cage day in & day out—But I must not growl—it might be so much worse."[7] Whitman was always in control of his art and his life. The artistic discipline was evident in the careful revisions of his poems, and the self-discipline, which rabid followers usually did not recognize, kept him from wearing his heart on his sleeve. The admirers sometimes fell apart in their ecstasies, but Whitman always remained of a piece. One of his favorite expressions was, "Hold your horses." He kept his own seething emotions under tight rein. As he once said to Traubel when they were discussing the poet's serenity, "If I let myself go I'd wear out my resources at once."[8] He phrased it better in that celebrated letter to John Addington Symonds in which he fathered himself with six children: "One great difference between you and me, temperament & theory, is *restraint* — I know that while I have a horror of ranting & bawling I at certain moments let the spirit impulse, (?demon) rage its utmost, its wildest, damnedest — (I feel to do so in my L of G. & I do so)."[9] Whitman knew that no artist can squander randomly his creative and emotional energies.

His optimism also rested on the same protective device. Traubel reported the following conversation:

> "I do not worry: I determine not to worry—let come what may come. Resignation, I may call it: peace in spite of fate." I broke in: "Peace at any price?" Laughed. "Almost that: what the religious people call resignation: the feeling that whatever comes is just the thing that ought to come—ought to be welcomed."[10]

He made a similar comment to Bucke in a letter: "Don't be uneasy ab't me in any respect — nature has not only endowed me with immense emotionality but immense bufferism (so to call it) or placid resignation to what happens."[11] Yet few people appear to be aware that one of the stabilizing forces in Whitman's life was his realistic acceptance of an ancient truism — whatever is, is. That this position — this "immense bufferism" — was at odds with some of the declarations in his poetry he probably never considered. Like Emerson, Whitman was not a philosopher but a poet.

On another occasion he observed to his Boswell, "I am not a scintillator, I am not a fire-worksy man: I take better to quietude, to the inertia of large bodies."[12] Our insistence upon referring to the "yawp" has often kept us from recognizing the validity of the poet's own evaluation. His was a deli-

7. Letter 1533.
8. Traubel, IV, 148.
9. Letter 2278.
10. Traubel, IV, 148–149.
11. Letter 2133.
12. Traubel, IV, 441.

cate sensibility both in the poetry and in the letters. Seldom did he compose a scintillating sentence in a letter. But some of the quiet effects testify to the keen ear and eye of an invalid artist who found riches in physical impoverishment: "the wind is sighing & singing & piping around the house as I write"; "splendid effect f'm electric light shining in on big bunch of snowy white chrysanthemums"; or "our dear friend [William D. O'Connor] is buried & all has gone like tracks on the shore by sea waves washed away passing."[13] His canary became the subject of a poem and eventually a museum piece when it was stuffed and sent to Wallace and Dr. Johnston. In 1888 he described the bird: "my little bird sits hunch'd up in a lump, & sings not — but spring weather is coming & early summer & I will write a little poem ab't it to warm me up."[14] The "little poem"—"Soon Shall the Winter's Foil Be Here" — was sent off on the following day to the New York *Herald.* On another occasion the canary became part of his aural environment: "The bird is singing — the cars are puffing & rattling, & the children of the neighborhood are all outdoors playing — So I have music enough."[15] Few can create such a lovely symphony out of commonplace sounds unheard by ordinary ears.

As death became an almost daily possibility the language in the letters not unexpectedly recalled the language of the poetry, particularly the water imagery in "As I Ebb'd with the Ocean of Life," "Out of the Cradle Endlessly Rocking," and the carol in "When Lilacs Last in the Dooryard Bloom'd." A breeze "laves" him. He is "at low ebb . . . perhaps the waters may come in again — perhaps *not* — it will be all right either way." He observes "a gradual depression & defection like an ebb tide every month." For he is "a wreck at best, but lolling on easy seas just at the passing moment."[16] There is something strangely appropriate that the creator of "Out of the Cradle Endlessly Rocking" spent the last few days of his life on a water bed. Life has a way of confirming art.

The "burial house" which he had constructed in the last year of his life recalls the tomb described in "When Lilacs Last in the Dooryard Bloom'd." Unlike the buildings he constructed with his father before the appearance of the first edition of *Leaves of Grass*, this "house" was made of Massachusetts granite and placed in the side of a little hill in Harleigh Cemetery. Whitman spoke vaguely of inspiration from one of William Blake's poems, but more mythically in another passage: it "will probably be the rudest most undress'd structure (with an idea) — since Egypt, perhaps the cave dwellers."[17] It matters little whether the completed

13. Letters 1652, 2152, and 2043.
14. Letter 1671. 15. Letter 1537.
16. Letters 2611, 2533, 2615, and 2635. 17. Letter 2548.

structure resembles Egyptian tombs: the intent was to create a "house" that evoked the past and would outlast the present. It was to be part of the cosmic continuity he spoke of. But cosmic continuity is an intellectual concept, valid but somewhat chilling. The more meaningful continuity was established when he decided to collect in the tomb the remains of his parents. Then, and only then, were the estranged mother and father depicted in "There Was a Child Went Forth" and "As I Ebb'd with the Ocean of Life" reunited with the stranger-child "who went forth every day, and who now goes and will always go forth every day."

A LIST OF WHITMAN'S CORRESPONDENTS

This alphabetical list includes all the recipients of extant letters written between 1886 and 1889. The name is followed by the letter number.

Alden, Agnes Margaret, 1416
Aldrich, Thomas Bailey, 1977
Alexander, John White, 1381
Baxter, Sylvester, 1459, 1546, 1566, 1582, 1590, 1616, 1883
Bennerman, Mr., 1711
Bennett, James Gordon, 1732.1
Biddle, Mrs. Noble T., 1473
Brainerd, Erastus, 1589.1, 1593
Brown, Arthur Newton, 1968, 1978
Brown, Leonard M., 1631
Bucke, Richard Maurice, 1490, 1500, 1511, 1529 1540, 1578, 1587, 1600, 1634, 1637, 1645, 1649, 1651, 1653, 1661–1662, 1668, 1671, 1675–1677, 1679, 1684, 1686–1687, 1691, 1693, 1697, 1700, 1705, 1712, 1716, 1718, 1720–1721, 1723–1724, 1726, 1729–1731, 1733, 1736–1737, 1744–1746, 1749, 1753–1754, 1758–1759, 1761, 1764, 1766–1768, 1771, 1773, 1775, 1777, 1779, 1781, 1784, 1786, 1790, 1794, 1798–1799, 1802, 1806, 1810, 1812–1813, 1816, 1821, 1823–1829, 1831–1832, 1840, 1842–1843, 1845–1847, 1849–1850, 1852–1853, 1855–1857, 1859, 1861–1862, 1865–1867, 1871–1872, 1874–1875, 1877–1879, 1881–1882, 1884, 1887, 1890, 1892, 1894, 1896–1897, 1899, 1902, 1904, 1906, 1908, 1910, 1913–1915, 1918, 1921, 1925, 1927, 1937, 1967, 1971, 1974, 1976, 1981, 1983–1984, 1986, 1988, 1992, 1994, 1998–1999, 2002, 2004, 2007, 2009, 2012, 2015, 2019, 2021–2022, 2027, 2029, 2031, 2033, 2035, 2039, 2044–2045, 2047, 2049, 2051, 2054–2056, 2061, 2065–2066, 2068–2069, 2071, 2073–2075, 2077, 2079–2082, 2085–2086, 2088–2089, 2091–2093, 2095, 2098, 2101–2103, 2105–2106, 2108, 2111, 2113–2115, 2120–2121, 2123–2124, 2126, 2128, 2130, 2132–2137, 2139–2145, 2148–2153, 2155, 2157, 2159, 2161, 2163, 2166, 2168–2169
Burroughs, John, 1383, 1392, 1452, 1465, 1490, 1500, 1511–1512, 1515, 1529, 1540, 1583, 1600, 1621, 1646, 1667, 1704, 1742, 1760, 1776, 1807, 1813, 1820, 1846, 1919, 1939, 1948, 2036, 2043, 2075, 2099, 2117
C., V. S., 1713
Carey, William, 1609, 1613, 1626, 2063
Carnegie, Andrew, 1659

Carpenter, Edward, 1399, 1504, 1536, 1851, 1891, 1895, 2048
Century Illustrated Monthly Review, 1414, 1417, 1424, 1800–1801
Chamberlin, Jessie C., 1468
Chambers, Julius, 1639, 1681, 1732.1
Channing, Dr. William F., 1574
Chatto & Windus, 1454, 1466
Child, Josiah, 1836
Childs, George W., 1373
Clemens, Samuel, 1562
Colles, Richard W., 1434, 1455, 1657
Contemporary Club, The, 1670
Conway, Moncure D., 1503
Cook, Kenningale, 1380
Cosmopolitan, Editor, 1692
Costelloe, Mary Smith, 1397, 1401, 1420, 1429, 1442, 1449, 1457, 1463, 1474, 1483, 1495, 1501, 1560, 1570, 1576, 1607, 1618, 1625, 1722, 1727, 1732, 1735, 1743, 1763, 1780, 1804, 1818, 1841, 1934, 2011, 2060, 2090, 2129, 2138, 2160
Cox, G. C., 1563, 1610, 2064
Critic, The, 1405, 1464, 1472, 1508.1, 1552, 1628
Deaf and Dumb Callers, 1901
Dick & Fitzgerald, 1674
Donaldson, Thomas, 1387, 1394, 1425, 1447, 1453, 1893.1, 2058
Dowden, Edward, 1437, 1839
Eldridge, Charles W., 1509, 1530, 1539, 1569, 1599, 1932, 2076
Garland, Hamlin, 1819, 1834, 1893
Gilchrist, Herbert, 1433, 1445, 1461, 1510, 1620, 1683, 1696, 1748
Gilder, Jeannette L., 1485, 1531
Gilder, Joseph B., 1435, 1485, 1502
Gilder, Richard Watson, 1458, 1525
Gould, Elizabeth Porter, 1552
Gunther, Mr., 1390
Harned, Thomas B., 1626.1, 1633, 1699, 1734, 1888, 2037, 2059
Harper's New Monthly Magazine, 2100
Hartmann, C. Sadakichi, 1472.1
Hemenway, O. O., 2118
Hempstead, O. G. & Company, 1704.1
Houghton, Mifflin and Company, 1664
Hughes, Harry D., 1484
Ingram, William, 1604, 1688, 1789, 2104
Johnson, Robert Underwood, 1632
Johnston, Alma Calder, 1496, 1772, 1954
Johnston, Dr. John, 1550
Johnston, John H., 1497, 1521, 1527, 1601, 1614, 1701, 1954
Johnston, Katherine, 1869
Kennedy, William Sloane, 1389, 1393, 1396, 1404, 1406, 1410, 1412, 1419, 1421–1423, 1426–1428, 1430, 1432, 1440, 1446, 1451, 1462, 1469–1470, 1480, 1486–1490, 1492, 1498–1500, 1507, 1511, 1514, 1518–1519, 1523, 1526, 1529, 1532, 1534, 1540, 1543, 1545, 1547, 1549, 1556, 1559, 1561, 1567, 1573, 1575, 1577–1578, 1579, 1580–1581, 1587, 1591, 1600, 1603, 1608, 1615, 1619, 1622, 1629–1630, 1636, 1638, 1643, 1647, 1654, 1656, 1660, 1666–1667, 1669, 1673, 1685, 1687, 1689–1690, 1697, 1700, 1706, 1715, 1728, 1738, 1756, 1778, 1795, 1805, 1808, 1814–1815, 1820, 1846, 1858, 1863, 1876, 1885, 1899–1900, 1907, 1912, 1923, 1928, 1941, 1943, 1946, 1963,

1969, 1975, 1995, 1999, 2006, 2016, 2026, 2032, 2038, 2041, 2046, 2052, 2062, 2070, 2084, 2107, 2109, 2119, 2122, 2125, 2127, 2131, 2146, 2164
Klein, Jacob, 1785, 1793
Knortz, Dr. Karl, 1402, 1505, 1538, 1564, 1788, 1889, 1929, 2000, 2024
Linton, William J., 1791
Loftus, J. P., 1641
McClure, S. S., 1565, 1571, 1592, 1602, 2158
McKay, David, 1709, 1811, 1817, 1870, 1873, 2162, 2170.1
Morris, Charles, 1415
Morse, Sidney H., 1678, 1796
New Orleans *Picayune*, 1477
New York *Herald*, 1640, 1783
Norman, Henry, 1475
North American Review, The, 1471
O'Connor, Ellen M., 1586, 1594, 1672, 1682, 1860, 1864, 1880, 1909, 1926, 1957, 2034, 2040, 2067, 2087, 2097, 2110, 2112, 2116, 2147, 2156, 2165
O'Connor, William D., 1374, 1377–1378, 1385, 1388, 1391, 1398, 1431, 1436, 1456, 1623–1624, 1634, 1648, 1652, 1655, 1695, 1698, 1702, 1707, 1710, 1714, 1719, 1725, 1739, 1747, 1757, 1762, 1765, 1797, 1803, 1809, 1813, 1822, 1830, 1833, 1837, 1846, 1854, 1898, 1903, 1905, 1911, 1920, 1922, 1924, 1930, 1933, 1935–1936, 1938, 1940, 1942, 1944–1945, 1947, 1949–1953, 1955–1956, 1958–1962, 1964–1966, 1970, 1972–1973, 1979–1980, 1982, 1985, 1987, 1989, 1991, 1993, 1996, 1999, 2001, 2003, 2005, 2008, 2010, 2013, 2018, 2020, 2023, 2028, 2030
Oldach, Frederick, 1817.1, 1844, 1848, 1931, 2042
Palmer, Courtland, 1650
Philadelphia *Press*, 1409
Pond, Major James B., 1522, 1528
Potter, Edward T., 1644, 1741
Price, Arthur, 1479
Price, Helen E., 1694
Redpath, James, 1411, 1413, 1418
Rhys, Ernest, 1384, 1450, 1482, 1558, 1598, 1755, 1792, 1868, 2078, 2096
Rossetti, William Michael, 1400
Sarrazin, Gabriel, 2025
Schmidt, Rudolf, 2167
Smith, Alys, 2014
Smith, L. Logan, 1642
Smith, Logan Pearsall, 1572, 1596
Smith, Robert Pearsall, 1513, 1542, 1584, 1605–1606, 1617, 1708, 1751
Spielmann, M. H., 1663, 1665
Stafford, George, 1703, 2083
Stafford, Harry, 1533, 1585, 1838, 1917
Stafford, Susan, 1375–1376, 1379, 1382, 1408, 1448, 1478, 1493, 1506, 1508, 1516, 1524, 1537, 1544, 1548, 1554, 1557, 1573.1, 1579.1, 1589, 1611, 1644.1, 1658, 1703, 1740, 1750, 1752, 1769, 1774, 1782, 1787, 1916, 1997, 2017, 2083, 2094
Stead, William T., 1597
Stedman, Edmund Clarence, 1990
Symonds, John Addington, 1407
Tilton, John W., 1886
Tooley, Sarah A., 1578.1
Traubel, Horace, 2050
Wallace, J. W., 1551, 2053
Westminster Hotel, Proprietor, 1520

Whitman, Jessie Louisa, 1441, 1443, 1494
Whitman, Louisa Orr, 1770, 1835, 2057, 2072
Whitman, Thomas Jefferson, 1438–1439, 1441, 1443–1444, 1447.1, 1491, 1517
Wilkins, Edward, 2170
Williams, Talcott, 1395, 1403, 1481, 1553, 1595, 1635, 1680
Williamson, George M., 1612
Wilson, General James Grant, 1460
Woodruff, Edwin H., 1467
Wroth, James Stewart, 1588
Wormwood, R. F., 2154

*

Additional Letters Not by Whitman

Tennyson, Alfred Lord, 1476, 1627

ABBREVIATIONS

AL	*American Literature*
Allen	Gay Wilson Allen, *The Solitary Singer* (1955)
Allen, *Handbook*	Gay Wilson Allen, *Walt Whitman Handbook* (1946)
Asselineau	Roger Asselineau, *L'Évolution de Walt Whitman* (1955)
Barrett	Clifton Waller Barrett Literary Manuscripts Collection, University of Virginia
Barrus	Clara Barrus, *Whitman and Burroughs — Comrades* (1931)
Berg	Henry W. and Albert A. Berg Collection, New York Public Library
Blodgett	Harold Blodgett, *Walt Whitman in England* (1934)
Bolton	County Borough of Bolton (England) Public Libraries
Bucke	Richard Maurice Bucke, *Walt Whitman* (1883)
CB	*The Commonplace-Book*
CHAL	*The Cambridge History of American Literature*
Corr.	*The Correspondence of Walt Whitman*, ed. by Edwin Haviland Miller. In Coll W
Coll W	*The Collected Writings of Walt Whitman*, in progress: New York University Press, 1961–
CP	*Prose Works 1892*, ed. by Floyd Stovall, 2 vols. (1963–1964). In *Coll W*
CRE	*Leaves of Grass: Comprehensive Reader's Edition* (1965), ed. by Harold W. Blodgett and Sculley Bradley. In *Coll W*
CT	Complete Text
CW	*The Complete Writings of Walt Whitman* (1902), 10 vols.
DAB	*Dictionary of American Biography*
DNB	*Dictionary of National Biography*
Doheny	Estelle Doheny Collection of the Edward Laurence Doheny Memorial Library, St. John's Seminary
ESQ	*The Emerson Society Quarterly*
Furness	Clifton Joseph Furness, *Walt Whitman's Workshop* (1928)

Gilchrist	Herbert Harlakenden Gilchrist, *Anne Gilchrist: Her Life and Writings* (1887)
Gohdes and Silver	Clarence Gohdes and Rollo G. Silver, eds., *Faint Clews & Indirections* (1949)
Hanley	T. E. Hanley Collection, University of Texas
Harned	Thomas B. Harned, ed., *The Letters of Anne Gilchrist and Walt Whitman* (1918)
Holloway	Emory Holloway, *Whitman — An Interpretation in Narrative* (1926)
Huntington	Henry E. Huntington Library
Kennedy	William Sloane Kennedy, *Reminiscences of Walt Whitman* (1896)
LC	The Library of Congress
LC #	*Walt Whitman — A Catalog Based Upon the Collections of The Library of Congress* (1955)
Lion	Oscar Lion Collection, New York Public Library
Livezey	Livezey Collection, University of California at Berkeley
Manchester	The John Rylands Library, Manchester, England
Morgan	Pierpont Morgan Library
NAR	*The North American Review*
NB	*November Boughs* (1888)
N & Q	*Notes and Queries*
NEQ	*New England Quarterly*
Nonesuch	Emory Holloway, ed., *Walt Whitman — Complete Poetry & Selected Prose and Letters* (1938)
NYPL	New York Public Library
Pennsylvania	University of Pennsylvania
PT	Partial Text
SB	*Studies in Bibliography*
Syracuse	Syracuse University
Traubel	Horace Traubel, ed., *With Walt Whitman in Camden* (1906–1964), 5 vols.
Trent	Trent Collection, Duke University
UPP	*The Uncollected Poetry and Prose of Walt Whitman* (1921), 2 vols., ed. by Emory Holloway
Visits	John Johnston and J. W. Wallace, *Visits to Walt Whitman in 1890–1891 by Two Lancashire Friends* (1918)
WW	Walt Whitman
WWN	*Walt Whitman Newsletter*
WWR	*Walt Whitman Review*
Yale	Yale Collection of American Literature

The Correspondence of Walt Whitman

VOLUME IV: 1886–1888

1886

1373. *To George W. Childs*[1]

TRANSCRIPT.

328 Mickle Street, Camden, New Jersey,
Jan. 3, 1886

Thanks for the $50, which has reached me safely.

Walt Whitman

1374. *To William D. O'Connor* [*1.4.1886*][2]

ENDORSED: "Answ'd Jan. 21/86." ADDRESS: Wm D O'Connor | Life Saving Service | Washington | D C. POSTMARK: Camden | Jan | 4 | 4 PM | 1886 | N.J.

Camden | Monday p m

All ab't the same with me—I took dinner with the Scovel family Sunday & a ride with my old nag & rig in the afternoon[3]—So you see I have not utterly stopt *moving*—but I feel exceeding heavy & lethargic & stir only with great effort.

I send you Kennedy's note rec'd to-day—Have you seen his pamphlet-essay on poetry?[4]—A dark persistently rainy warm day here.

W W

1886

1. On January 1, WW received $50 from George W. Childs, co-owner of the Philadelphia *Public Ledger* (CB, and see 900). He had received a similar amount on January 13, 1885 (CB). In "Personal Recollections of Walt Whitman," *Scribner's Magazine*, LXV (1919), 685, William R. Thayer, in discussing WW's slyness in money matters, stated that for the last six or eight years of the poet's life Childs and Horace Howard Furness subscribed "an annual sum," and paid a young man to act as his driver and valet.

2. January 4 fell on Monday in 1886. This note was written on the verso of Kennedy's undated letter.

3. Later that year, on August 24, WW lent $50 to Colonel James Matlack Scovel (CB, and see 774.1), who, on September 16, thanked his "dear old friend" (Feinberg). In 1888 Scovel reported "some ultra-intimate suspicions to Kennedy about W.'s private life," which "shocked" the poet (Traubel, I, 278–279).

4. *The Poet as A Craftsman* (see 1354). In his letter Kennedy spoke of Edmund Clarence Stedman's reaction to his book and to WW's poetry—"a dwarf walking round a giant, a pigmy measuring a god" (Berg).

1375. *To Susan Stafford*

ADDRESS: Mrs: Susan M Stafford | Kirkwood (Glendale) | New Jersey. POSTMARK: Camden | (?) | 7 | 7 AM | N.J.

328 Mickle street | Camden
Wednesday Even'g Jan. 6 | '86

My dear friend

I am sitting here in my little front room down stairs writing this—a good fire in the stove—It is cold & cloudy outside, & the day is drawing to a close—Two visitors from Phila: have been to see me—two youngish middle-aged ladies, one an artist & the other a writer (I knew her years ago in Washington—Marie Le Baron then)—the latter married to her second husband, (the first one dead) now Mrs: Urie, a little bit of a body, but a great talker, full of life & good sense & good nature (like the best goods done up in small parcels)—

I have not been out all day—wish I could just come in & spend the evening & take supper with you all. If it is any thing like fair weather next Sunday, shall be down ab't the usual time—but if it is storming or very cold, don't look for me—Ed, I gave your gloves to Billy,[5] ten days ago, to take to you, so I suppose you have them long before this—Went to dinner New Years to Dr. Shivers[6]—had a first rate time—& Sunday to Col & Mrs. Scovel's also to dinner—Have not heard any thing further from Herbert—Often think of Mrs. Gilchrist—(I have a good photo. of her)—Do you remember that day—last of May '77 I think—she & her two daughters came down to see us, & me down at the pond, under the old oak tree?[7]—Ah that old pond & the banks, & the old lane—I shall never forget them—Shall never forget you & George, & all of you, either—Love to you all, & God bless you—

Walt Whitman

Shall be down Sunday if the weather is tolerable—if not *not*—

5. Probably William H. Duckett, WW's young driver.

6. Dr. C. H. Shivers lived in Haddonfield, N. J.; WW also dined with him on October 13, 1885 (*CB*).

7. Mrs. Gilchrist had died on November 29, 1885 (see 1356). WW did not

1376. *To Susan Stafford* *1.9–10.* [*1886*]

ADDRESS: Mrs: Susan Stafford | Kirkwood | Glendale | New Jersey. POSTMARK: (?) | Jan | 10(?) | 8 PM | 1886 | N.J.

Saturday afternoon Jan. 9.

As I shall not get down to Glendale to-morrow I will write a few lines & send Edward Carpenter's letter, rec'd this morning,[8] which may interest you—As I look out, the ground is all cover'd with snow, a foot deep, & the wind blowing quite a gale—& freezing cold—But I have a good fire—Mrs. Davis has gone out to market, & shopping—So I am alone in the house—One of my Quaker girls Alys Smith[9] from Germantown has been over to see me to-day—I told her I considered it indeed a compliment to pay a visit to a fellow such weather—she said she liked the snow & breeze—liked to whack around in it—

Sunday Jan 10—noon—

Cold, cold, & snow everywhere outside—bad luck all around—the fire goes out, the clock stops, & the water-pipe bursts in the bath room—but the sun shines, the bird sings away, & Mrs. Davis is in jovial humor—Susan, I wish I had something interesting to write you—but I havn't—the Lord be with you all[10]—

W. W.

1377. *To William D. O'Connor* *1.22.* [*1886*]

ENDORSED: "Answ'd March 23/86." ADDRESS: Wm D O'Connor | Life Saving Service | Washington | D C. POSTMARKS: Camden | Jan | 22 | 5 PM | 1886 | N.J.; Washington, Rec'd | Jan | 23 | 7 AM | 1886 | 5.

328 Mickle street Camden | Jan: 22 noon

Dear friend

Yours of 21st rec'd this forenoon, with slip from *Nation* (herewith enclosed, returned)—*I am glad you sent it me*, as I do not see the N.—The eye-works have resumed operations pretty nearly same as before

record either in his letters or in CB a visit of Mrs. Gilchrist and her daughters, Beatrice and Grace, to Kirkwood in May 1877.

8. This letter is apparently lost.
9. The daughter of Robert Pearsall Smith.
10. In CB, WW noted the birth of Dora, the first child of Harry and Eva Stafford.

—I see out of *both* now & a great blessing in my imprisoned condition—A friend has sent me Stedman's book, & I have looked it over[11]—it seems to me a dissertation & biographies on very grand themes & persons by an amiable "clerk with a pen behind his ear"—as Warren Hastings or Macaulay, or Canning or Sheridan or somebody said—("By God, sir, if I am to have *a master*, don't let it be a mere clerk with a pen behind his ear")—I heard from John Burroughs ten days since—he was well & every thing right—I hear from Dr Bucke pretty often—he is not well himself—(though not *down*)—& there has been bad sickness in his family & the hospital staff—his last letter rec'd yesterday is dated at Sarnia, Canada[12]—

I am getting along comfortably—the weather has been bad as can be & the traveling ditto, for three weeks past, my old nag has nearly given out too, & I have not been out of the house—which tells on me—great torpor of the secretions—I am very clumsy & can hardly get up or down stairs—

The English "offering" (through Rossetti and Herbert Gilchrist) will am't to over $500—the principal part of which has been already sent me[13]—& on which I am really living this winter—write oftener—My last half-annual return of royalties for both my books just rec'd—$20.71cts[14]—the death of Mrs. Gilchrist has been a gloom to me, & has affected me ever since—I am not sure but she had the finest & perfectest nature I ever met—Glad to hear ab't the Channing's[15]—Give them my love—I am scribbling in my little front room down stairs—the parrot has been squalling & the canary singing—I write hardly at all—

W. W.

11. *Poets of America* (1885), which contained Stedman's article on WW.

12. Neither Burroughs' letter nor Bucke's is extant.

13. On January 25 WW received the fourth instalment from Rossetti—£33 16*s.* 6*d.* (*CB*). See also 1353. In a letter on January 5 Rossetti mentioned that he had inserted in *The Athenaeum* on January 2 "a reminder to any well-wishers" who might want to contribute to the offering (Feinberg; Traubel, II, 291). An identical notice appeared in *The Academy* on the same day. Commenting on Rossetti's letter, WW said to Traubel: "Rossetti is the kind of friend who never forgets the market basket" (Traubel, II, 291).

14. WW received this sum from McKay on December 1, 1885 (*CB*).

15. O'Connor's brother-in-law, Dr. William F. Channing, had recently moved to Pasadena, Calif., according to O'Connor's letter on January 21 (Feinberg; Traubel, III, 74).

16. WW delivered his "Death of Abraham Lincoln" lecture at a banquet of the

1378. *To William D. O'Connor*

ENDORSED: "Answ'd March 23/86." ADDRESS: Wm D O'Connor | Life Saving Service | Washington | D C.

Elkton Maryland | Feb. 3 '86

I came down here yesterday to deliver a lecture, which came off all right last evening—Return to-day. Tho't you would like to know I move around yet[16]—

W W

1379. *To Susan Stafford*

ADDRESS: Mrs: Susan Stafford | Kirkwood | (Glendale) | New Jersey. POSTMARK: Philadelphia, Pa. | Feb | 3 | 1886 | 4 PM | Transit.

Elkton Maryland | Feb 3 '86

I came down here yesterday to deliver a lecture, which came off all right, last evening—I am going back to day—Shall come down the first Sunday the weather & travelling are good[17]—

W W

1380. *To Kenningale Cook*

328 Mickle street | Camden New Jersey
U S America | Feb: 11 '86

My dear K C[18]

I send you the two Volumes, same mail with this, (same address as this note)—The price is one pound two shillings, which please remit me

"Pythian Club" on February 2, for which he received $30 (*CB*). Folger McKinsey (1866–1950) was responsible for the invitation. McKinsey, then a railroad clerk in Philadelphia, began to call on WW in 1884, as indicated by his letter of June 10 (Feinberg) and the reference to his occasional visits in *CB* on June 17. In 1885 McKinsey became the editor of the Elkton (Md.) *Cecil Democrat*, in which he printed an interview with the poet on December 12. On March 12, 1886, the newspaper termed WW's lecture "a failure." See Rollo G. Silver, *N & Q*, CLXX (1936), 190–191, and Ernest J. Moyne, "Walt Whitman and Folger McKinsey," *Delaware Notes*, XXIX (1956), 103–117. Later McKinsey became the editor of the Baltimore *Sun*.

17. Apparently WW was unable to visit the Staffords before March 7 (*CB*).

18. Cook ordered books from WW in 1876; see his letter on February 29, 1876 (Feinberg). On April 23, 1877, he asked the poet's permission to print some verses in the *Dublin University Magazine* (Feinberg; Traubel, II, 219).

in post office order—I am ab't as usual of late, bodily disabled, but in good heart.

Walt Whitman

1381. *To John White Alexander*

328 Mickle Street | Camden Feb: 20 '86

Dear Sir[19]

Yours of 19th rec'd—Yes, Monday will suit me—will be ready for you by 10 1/2 a m—

Walt Whitman

1382. *To Susan Stafford* *2.24. [1886]*

328 Mickle st. Camden | Wednesday p m Feb: 24

My dear friend—

Thanks for your good letter, which the carrier bro't this morning, & I was glad to get word from you all.

An artist from New York, from the *Century* Magazine, has been here the last three forenoons, painting a big portrait of me—he has finished all he wants here, & has just boxed it up & taken it off to N Y by express—he is a first rate young fellow, a good talker, & has already travelled a good deal over the world—& he made it all very interesting, telling me this, that, & the other.

I am middling well, but very heavy & nerveless—it is nearly two months now I have been in the house most altogether—I am bad enough —but I wonder I a'nt worse than I am—Yes, if the weather & roads are any thing like fair I want to come down next Sunday & shall come—my nag is about the same as ever—(lame in hind foot ab't a week ago)—I keep him here in the stable yet[20]—the weather has been pleasanter of late

19. For three days beginning on Monday, February 22 (*CB*), WW sat for a portrait by Alexander (1856–1915). On April 17, 1891, Alexander informed WW that one of the poet's admirers had purchased and presented the painting to the Metropolitan Museum of Art: "I am delighted to have been the means of giving to future generations a portrait of you that is certainly one of my best works" (Feinberg). Burroughs, however, termed the portrait "a Bostonese Whitman—an emasculated Whitman—failing to show his power and ruggedness" (Barrus, 261). WW himself was not impressed (Traubel, I, 132, 284).

20. According to entries in *CB*, WW paid a Mr. Bennett $18 monthly to take care of his horse.

& I get out a little occasionally to the cars or down to the ferry, but I am getting more & more clumsy & stupid.

I got a letter from Herbert G[ilchrist] ab't three weeks ago—nothing new of any importance—they are getting up a little book, Life and Letters of Mrs. G.[21]—I suppose you rec'd Edward Carpenter's letter to me which I enclosed to you some time ago[22]—

Every thing goes on as well as could be expected with my affairs &c. We get along the same as ever here, & very comfortable considering. I wish when you come up you would stop here—& tell George so too—I wonder when he comes up & is going around Camden he don't stop here—Tell Ed too—Mrs. Davis is an old-fashion'd Jersey woman, & has been to sea—& as to me, you know what I am—

Well I am call'd to dinner—the parrot is yelling away as I close—

Love to you & George—& all—

W W

1383. *To John Burroughs*

328 Mickle Street | Camden New Jersey |
March 18 '86

Dear friend

I send to-day by mail the three Vols. of your Emerson so long detained—deepest apologies for not returning them before[23]—I don't know that I have any thing to tell you of any account. I am not writing any thing. Have a small screed of three or four pages to appear in A T Rice's forthcoming *Reminiscences of Lincoln*, but I consider it unworthy the theme.[24] James Redpath, who manages things for A T R, has been very good to me—persistently so—& it is to his urgency I have responded—

Have not yet finished the *Army Hospital* article for the *Century*, but intend to do so forthwith.[25] Had a violent spell of illness ab't a week ago—remained in bed all last Friday—am up since, & go out a little, but

21. In his letter of January 25, Gilchrist requested permission to quote from WW's letters to his mother (Feinberg).
22. See 1376.
23. On December 31, 1885, Burroughs had asked WW to forward the Emerson volumes, which WW had borrowed during the Washington years (Feinberg; Traubel, II, 86–87). Burroughs noted receiving the volumes on April 3 (Feinberg; Traubel, II, 549).
24. See 1358.
25. See 1282.

dont feel even as half-well as usual.[26] Beautiful here to-day & I am enjoying the sunshine, sitting here by the window, looking out—

Have read my *Death of Abraham Lincoln* paper *twice* this spring, on applications ($25 and $30)[27]—got along with it rather slowly, but didnt break down, & seems to have given a sort of satisfaction—

Want to scoop up what I have (poems and prose) of the last MSS since 1881 and '2, & put in probably 200 page book (or somewhat less) to be called perhaps *November Boughs*—

I am getting along comfortably enough here—spirits generally good —my old horse has quite given out[28]—we have a canary bird, dog, & parrot—all great friends of mine (& teachers)—

Best love to you & 'Sula—not forgetting the little boy—

Walt Whitman

1384. *To Ernest Rhys*

328 Mickle Street | Camden New Jersey
U S America | March 20 1886

My dear Ernest Rhys

Thank you for the little volumes—three copies have reached me[29] —they look very well, & I am pleased with them, & with prefatory notice —I am here, ab't the same as of late years—Keep up pretty good spirits & buoyancy—that makes the best of it all—Give my respects to the Walter Scott folk—& dont forget to write to me soon, to let me know how the Vol. goes—I much hope to reach the working men, & guilds of the British Islands—especially the young fellows—& trust the W. S. vol. will forward that object.

Walt Whitman

26. In CB on March 12 WW recorded "bad spell sickness—stomach & head—in bed all day—(better & up next day)." He had bad spells on March 16 to 18 and 20 to 23.

27. WW gave the lecture for the second time in 1886 on March 1 at Morgan Hall, Camden, and was paid $25 (CB).

28. On March 16 WW wrote in CB: "The nag Frank seems to me *played out.*" On March 28 he bought a new horse named "Nettie" from Edwin Stafford for $152.50.

29. *The Poems of Walt Whitman.* [*Selected.*], with an introduction by Rhys, was printed in The Canterbury Poet Series, published by Walter Scott. WW noted receipt of the volumes on March 18 in CB. A presentation copy in the Feinberg Collection reads:

1385. *To William D. O'Connor* 3.26. [*1886*]

ENDORSED: "Answ'd May 25/86." ADDRESS: Wm D O'Connor | Life Saving Service | Washington | D C. POSTMARK: Camden | Mar | 26 | 4 PM | 1886 | N.J.

328 Mickle st—Camden—March 26

Am ab't the same as usual—Had a bad spell two weeks ago, but am now around after my sort, nearly the same (a letting down a little peg, if no more, every time)—Yes I have had superb treatment from my English friends—Yours of 23[?]d rec'd[30]—I dont know whether I told you that a young Englishman who came into a fortune not long since, sent me 50 pounds[31]—then the *Nineteenth Cent* paid me 30£ for the little poem[32]—

W W

1386. *To an Unidentified Correspondent*

328 Mickle Street | Camden New Jersey |
March 26 1886

Dear Sir

Yours of 26th rec'd—I send my heartiest thanks to the members, individually & collectively, of the *Northwestern Literary and Historical Society*—

Walt Whitman

1387. *To Thomas Donaldson*

TRANSCRIPT.

Camden, April 8, 1886

[WW wrote about an engagement on April 15 at the Chestnut Street Opera House in Philadelphia, where he was to deliver his Lincoln lecture.]

"Walt Whitman with Ernest Rhys's apologies & high regards. 1st March 1886."

On May 22 Rhys informed the poet that about 8,000 copies of the edition were sold, and that the publisher expected to print a second edition. In the same letter Rhys requested permission to include *Specimen Days* in a prose series called The Camelot Classics (Hanley).

30. On January 21 and March 23 O'Connor complained of an incapacitating lameness (Traubel, III, 74; IV, 413).

31. Edward Carpenter. Actually the gift came from Carpenter and the Ford sisters (see 1333).

32. "Fancies at Navesink" (see 1340).

1388. *To William D. O'Connor* *4.12. [1886]*

ENDORSED: "Answ'd May 25/86." ADDRESS: Wm D O'Connor | Life Saving Service | Washington | D C. POSTMARKS: Philadelphia, Pa. | Apr | 12 | 1886 | 7 PM | Transit; Washington, Rec'd | Apr | 12(?) | 12 PM | 1886 | 1.

328 Mickle Street | Camden,
April 12 p m

Dear friend

Rec'd yours last week & was glad as always to get letter from you[33] —Dr Bucke has been here—left this morning for N Y—sails Wednesday next for England—to stay two months—was with me Friday, Saturday & Sunday—we rode out every day—

He is pretty well—I am ab't the same as when I last wrote—am to read the "Death of Lincoln" lecture Thurs: afternoon next in the Phila: Chestnut St Opera House—the actors & journalists have tendered me a sort of benefit—Thomas Donaldson and Talcott Williams are the instigators of it all—(I am receiving great & opportune Kindnesses in my old days—& this is one of them)[34]—

The printed slip on the other side I just cut out of my Phila: *Press* of this morning[35]—I am looking for your little book[36]—Good weather here—

Walt Whitman

33. O'Connor, according to his notations on WW's letters, did not write to the poet between March 23 and May 25. Either O'Connor was in error or WW had a lapse of memory.

34. On April 15 WW received $370 from Donaldson and $304 from Williams (Feinberg). In *CB* WW noted receiving an additional $13 at an unspecified date. The total, according to WW, was $687, but in Donaldson's book the amount is given as $692 (107–108). The discrepancy apparently stems from the amount of Donaldson's share: he gave it as $375, WW as $370. Williams forwarded an additional $8 on June 11 (Feinberg).

WW read his lecture for the fourth time this year in Haddonfield, N. J., on May 18, "without pay, for the benefit of a new Church, building fund, at Collingswood" (*CB*). For an account of the sparsely attended lecture, see *WWR*, IX (1963), 65–66.

35. The item, pasted on the first page of the letter, includes the following: " 'William D. O'Connor,' says the New York *Commercial-Advertiser* of a former Philadelphian, 'is one of the very few clever writers who do not write enough. The reason may be that, having a Government position in Washington, the salary of which supports him, he has not the need, and without the need the desire for composition is perhaps absent.' The same paper, saying that 'Carpenter' is the best of Mr. O'Connor's stories, adds: 'It is a story of which Walt Whitman is visibly the idealized hero, and it is singularly

1389. *To William Sloane Kennedy* 4.17. [*1886*]

Camden New Jersey | April 17—noon—

I have rec'd the *Indexes*—thanks—I send you a paper—I read my *Death of Abraham Lincoln* screed in Phila: Thursday last—best turn out & most profit to me yet.

I am about as usual—but certainly gradually slipping down every year. Dr Bucke has gone to England for two months. Love to you[37]—

W W

1390. *To Mr. Gunther* [*4.19. 1886*]

ENDORSED (in unknown hand): "April 19, 1886."
TRANSCRIPT.

328 Mickle Street, Camden, New Jersey.

I have received from W. Bushell $5.00 (for Mr. Gunther) for MS page furnished him by me.[38]

Walt Whitman

interesting and rememberable.' "

36. O'Connor's *Hamlet's Note-book*. On January 21 O'Connor reported to WW that "the New York publishers have uniformly refused to publish my Baconian reply to R. G. White, even at my expense" (Feinberg; Traubel, III, 74). On March 23 he said that the book was to be published by Houghton, Mifflin & Company (Syracuse; Traubel, IV, 414).

37. According to the Philadelphia *Press* on April 16, the lecture at the Opera House was preceded by a concert; the house was filled with guests, including Dr. S. Weir Mitchell, George W. Childs, Richard Watson Gilder, and Horace Howard Furness. With the lowering of the footlights, the stage was "in a half darkness save where in the centre the glow of the rose-globed study lamp cast its mellow light upon the august head of the poet as he bent over his pages." After the lecture Whitman read "O Captain! My Captain!" and "the audience remained seated until the poet dismissed them with an inclination of his massive head."

Although Kennedy was writing enthusiastically about a book he proposed to do on the poet, WW evinced little interest. With his usual canny patience he bided his time until Kennedy "interpreted" his silence to mean that he wanted to see the manuscript. See 1406.

38. On May 28 WW sold Bushell twenty copies of the 1876 edition of *Leaves of Grass* and *Two Rivulets*, and received $80 on June 5 (CB). The receipt for this transaction is in the Whitman House, Camden.

1391. *To William D. O'Connor* [*4.19. 1886*][39]

ENDORSED: "Answ'd May 25, /86." ADDRESS: Wm D O'Connor | Life Saving Service | Washington D C. POSTMARKS: Camden | Apr | 19 | 8 PM | 1886 | N.J.; Washington, Rec'd | Apr | 20 | 7 AM | 1886 | 1.

328 Mickle St—Camden | Monday—p m

Your little book has come & I have been sitting here by the open window, looking it over the last hour. It is a wonderful specimen, first of typographical beauty & solid excellence—then I find it interesting, absorbing in quite a devouring degree—

Walt Whitman

I am ab't as usual—the lecture netted me $674—Dr Bucke is half-way to England—I have rec'd John Burroughs' new book[40]—warm sunny day here—I am going out with my horse for two or three hours—

1392. *To John Burroughs* 4.20. [*1886*]

TRANSCRIPT.

April 20

Your book has come so nice and fresh like a new pot-cheese in a clean napkin—I have read the first piece—"Look Out"[41]—all through and thought it fully equal to anything in the past, and looked over the rest of the pages—doesn't seem to me to deserve the depreciatory tone in which you speak of it.

Dr. Bucke went to England April 14—I rec'd a letter from Wm. O'C[onnor], and his little book.[41.1]

I am much the same as of late—made out very handsomely with my lecture April 15th—$674—have seen Gilder[42]—Early summer here—I have a new horse—very good—

39. The date is established by the postmark (April 19 fell on Monday in 1886) and by the reference to *Hamlet's Note-book* as well as to the Lincoln lecture. The presentation copy of the book in the Feinberg Collection reads: "Walt Whitman from his friend W. D. O'Connor, Washington, D. C., April 17, 1886."

40. *Signs and Seasons* (see 1361).

41. The title of the first chapter in *Signs and Seasons* is "A Sharp Lookout." In sending the book to WW on April 3, Burroughs commented: "I do not think much of it—the poorest of my books, I think" (Feinberg; Traubel, II, 550).

1393. *To William Sloane Kennedy*

328 Mickle st. | Camden New Jersey |
April 27, p m '86

I send you Dublin magazine with an article in you may like to run your eye over[43]—After you are through with it, mail to Wm D O'Connor, Life Saving Service, Washington, D C—

I am ab't as usual—went down to the sea-shore three days since & had a rousing dinner of shad & champagne with some friends[44]—

W W

1394. *To Thomas Donaldson*

ADDRESS: Thomas Donaldson | 326 North Fortieth Street | Philadelphia. POSTMARKS: Camden | May | (?); Received | May 6 | 9 PM | Phila.; (?) | May 7 86 | 6 AM

328 Mickle Street | Camden New Jersey
May 4 '86

I have been going for two weeks to write special letters of thanks &c. to you & T[alcott] W[illiams] for your kindness & labors in my lecture —& raising in it $674 for me.[45] I appreciate it all, & *indeed thank you.* It is the biggest stroke of pure kindness & concrete help I have ever rec'd—But all formal letters must just fizzle down to this card—whose duplicate I send to T W—

Walt Whitman

1395. *To Talcott Williams*

328 Mickle Street | Camden New Jersey
May 4 '86

I have been going for two weeks to write special letters of thanks

41.1. *Hamlet's Note-book;* WW admitted to Traubel in 1888, "I have never read it myself" (II, 2).

42. Richard Watson Gilder attended the lecture; see note 37 above.

43. H. Rowlandson's review of Carpenter's *Towards Democracy* appeared in the *Dublin University Review* in April. The article was actually written by T. W. H. Rolleston; see his letter to WW on August 8, 1885 (Feinberg; Traubel, III, 487).

44. On April 24 WW had a "planked shad & champagne dinner at Billy Thompson's" (*CB*).

45. See 1388.

&c to you & T[homas] D[onaldson] for your kindness & labors in my lecture, and raising in it, $674 for me—I appreciate all, & *indeed thank you*—It is the biggest stroke of pure kindness & concrete help I have ever rec'd—But all formal letters must just fizzle down to this card—whose duplicate I send to T D—

Walt Whitman

1396. *To William Sloane Kennedy* 5.4. [*1886*]

328 Mickle Street | Camden May 4 p m

The wine has arrived, has been tried, & proves delicious[46]—best & many thanks—warm, dry, growing weather here—I am going out for a two-hours evening drive—go out most every day—Dr Bucke is in England—Burroughs is going to jaunt through Kentucky.[47]

W W

1397. *To Mary Smith Costelloe* 5.11. [*1886*][48]

ADDRESS: Mrs.: B F C Costelloe | 40 Grosvenor Road | Westminster | London S W | England. POSTMARK: Camden | May | 11 | 3 PM | 18(?) | N.J.

328 Mickle St. Camden New Jersey | May 11—noon—

I am still here & nothing very new or different—I suppose you rec'd the *Press* with a brief report of my Lincoln lecture in Phila: April 15—I go out every day with my mare & rig—sometimes to Phila.—Alice[49] comes often, was here Saturday.

Has Dr Bucke arrived?—& you too I haven't heard from you in a long time—I am sitting here in the little front room down stairs—

Walt Whitman

46. Kennedy sent elderberry cordial on April 19 (Feinberg).
47. On May 5 WW had a "visit from John Burroughs, en route for Kentucky" (*CB*). Of this visit Burroughs observed in his journal: "He was not very well, and I was myself dull" (Barrus, 262).
48. Mary apparently married Benjamin F. W. Costelloe early in 1886.
49. Alys or Alice Smith.
50. O'Connor sent the powder for WW's constipation, and reported, "My special trouble now is what they call *sclerosis*—an induration of the lower part of the spinal cord,

1398. *To William D. O'Connor*

ENDORSED: "Answ'd August 17, /86." ADDRESS: Wm D O'Connor | Life Saving Service | Washington | D C. POSTMARK: Camden | May | 2(?) | 3 PM | 188(?) | N.J.

328 Mickle Street | Camden New Jersey
Thursday noon | May 26 '86

Dear friend

Your letter came yesterday—also the liquorice powder—I have no doubt the powder will be good for me.[50] I have already begun it—I am as well as usual with me—up, and at my window, as now—get out with the horse & wagon every afternoon but shall not to-day—nothing new in my affairs—get along quite comfortably—have some visitors—a canny Scotchman, a literary man, but a good jovial fellow, elderly with a humorous turn, & much reminiscence, has been in this forenoon to see me—I like to have him—It is a raw, dark, rainy day—I wish I could have you here to eat a bite of dinner with me, & chat for the afternoon—Several of my friends have had your little book,[51] lent them by me—Scovel (with his lawyer's head) said to me after reading it, "there can be no doubt of it"—i e that B[acon] is the true author—

W. W.

1399. *To Edward Carpenter*

ADDRESS: Edward Carpenter | Millthorpe | Chesterfield | England. POSTMARKS: Camden | May | 29 | 3 PM | 86 | N.J.; Philadelphia | May | (?) | 1886 | (?).

328 Mickle Street | Camden New Jersey
U S America | May 29 1886

Thanks, thanks indeed, dear friend—to yourself, Mr Roberts, Bessie and Isabella Ford, C R Ashbee, Wm Thompson,[52] & brother &

a bequest of the inflammation caused by the nervous prostration" (Syracuse; Traubel, IV, 283).

51. *Hamlet's Note-book.*

52. R. D. Roberts had a master's degree from Cambridge, and Charles R. Ashbee was a Cambridge undergraduate; see Carpenter's letter of May 17 (Feinberg). On May 10, 1883, WW sent three copies of *Leaves of Grass* and *Specimen Days* to William Thompson in Nottingham, England (CB). The Ford sisters had given WW £50 in 1885 (see 1334). On this date WW noted receipt of $216.75 from Carpenter and $145.58 from Rossetti (CB).

sister, for the kind & generous birthday gift—for your letter with the £45 which has just reached me—

We have fine weather here, & I am enjoying it—My health remains nearly as usual, but there is a little decline & additional feebleness every successive year—as is natural.

The Staffords are all living and well—I drive down there Sundays & they often speak of you. Harry (at Marlton, New Jersey)—and Ruth[53] (in Kansas) are some time married, & have children.

Love to you & to B[essie] and I[sabella] F[ord]—

Walt Whitman

1400. *To William Michael Rossetti*

328 Mickle Street | Camden New Jersey
U S America | May 30 1886

My dear friend

Yours of May 17, enclosing the fifth instalment £29.18.3 is just now safely received, making altogether—

September 1885	£	22. 2.6
October 20 "		37.12.
November 28 "		31.19.
January 25, 1886		33.16.[54]
May 17 "		29.18.3
	£	155. 9.9

for which I indeed, indeed thank you, and all—We have beautiful sunshiny weather here, & I am sitting by my open window writing this—If Herbert Gilchrist prints the circular you spoke of, send it me—send me three or four copies. I send best respects & love to my British contributor-friends—they have done me more good than they think for.[55]

Walt Whitman

53. Ruth (Stafford) Goldy and her daughter Amy had returned to Topeka, Kansas, on March 23 (*CB*).

54. The entry in *CB* for this date lists the sum as £33.16.6.

55. Rossetti distributed a facsimile of this letter to the donors, eighty or more of whom are listed on the verso with their contributions. Among the donors were Henry James, Robert Louis Stevenson, John Addington Symonds, George Saintsbury, and Edward Dowden.

1401. *To Mary Smith Costelloe*

ADDRESS: Mrs: Costelloe | 40 Grosvenor Road | Embankment Westminster | London S W | England. POSTMARK: Camden | Jun | 1 | 4 30 PM | 1886 | N.J.

328 Mickle Street | Camden New Jersey—
U S America | June 1 '86—

Best love & greeting to you, & to Mr C[ostelloe]—also to Dr Bucke[56]—I have rec'd Dr's good letter, with your good note enclosed—Nothing new with me—I am ab't as usual—no very warm weather here yet—Am sitting here by the open window—great bunches of roses, pinks & mignonette near me—

W W

Best love to your father, mother & Logan[57]—I to-day enter on my 68th year—fine sun and air to-day—

1402. *To Dr. Karl Knortz*

ADDRESS: Dr Carl Knortz | 540 East 155th Street | New York City. POSTMARK: Camden | Jun | 14 | (?) PM | (?) | N.J.

328 Mickle Street | Camden New Jersey |
June 14 '86

Dear Sir

Yours rec'd & I send you a few names I would like to have the address forwarded to.[58] I am ab't as usual in health. I wish you to keep me posted of any thing that occurs—& I will you.

Walt Whitman

Edward Carpenter, Millthorpe, near Chesterfield, England
W S Kennedy, Belmont, Mass:
T W Rolleston, Editor University Magazine[59] Dublin Ireland

56. On May 13 Bucke had written to WW enthusiastically about his visit with the Costelloes (Feinberg).
57. Mary's brother, Logan Pearsall Smith.
58. Knortz's lecture: *Walt Whitman. Vortrag gehalten im Deutschen Gesellig-Wissenschaftlichen Verein von New York am 24. März 1886* (1886).
59. On August 8, 1885, Rolleston had informed WW that he was the editor of the *Dublin University Review*, which "aims at introducing Nationalist thought amongst the upper classes in Ireland" (Feinberg; Traubel, III, 487).

Wm M Rossetti, 5 Endsleigh Gardens, Euston Square, London n w England
(Dante Rossetti is dead)
Mrs: B F C Costelloe, 40 Grosvenor Road, Westminster, London S W England
Ernest Rhys, 59 Cheyne Walk, Chelsea, London S W England
J Addington Symonds, Davos Platz, Graūbünden Switzerland
E C Stedman 45 E 30th St New York City
Prof: Edward Dowden, Temple Road, Winstead, Rathmines Dublin Ireland

1403. *To Talcott Williams*

328 Mickle street | Camden June 16 '86

My dear friend

Enclosed I send my piece in Thorndike Rice's just issued *Lincoln Reminiscences*[60]—I don't know whether you will want it—but I do know you like to have earliest copies of any thing. Should you print it, I leave the head-lines & introductory to you—& dont forget to give Rice's book the due credit. Should you print, I wish you would send me here 25 copies paper.

I am ab't as usual—just going to drive down 12 miles to visit a poor young fellow, Walter Borton,[61] very low with consumption. Love to Mrs. W. and the sister.

Walt Whitman

If you cant use it, return the enclosed proof to me.

60. See 1358 and 1383. A lengthy review of Rice's volume with an extract from WW appeared in the Philadelphia *Press* on June 28.

61. In *CB*, WW noted that he visited Walter Borton at Clementon, N. J., on May 23, June 4, and June 16.

62. *Art and Life: A Ruskin Anthology* (1886). In an undated letter to WW written about January 2, Kennedy had disparaged his own work: "Am hard at work on a Ruskin Anthology for Pirate [John B.] Alden, & feel rather knavish over the job" (Berg). Kennedy called on the poet on June 3 and 6 (Kennedy, 4–9).

63. This note to *The Critic* was written on the verso of a letter from W. I. Whiting to WW on June 14, in which he noted that at a recent auction a first edition of *Leaves of Grass* had brought $18 and an autographed letter $80 (Feinberg). The magazine printed a notice of the sale on July 3.

64. Apparently Kennedy was encouraged to undertake a longer study after WW's praise of *The Poet as A Craftsman* (see 1354). Kennedy's letter of February 5 had been filled with ambitious plans: "The book on you that I had been contemplating for some years is coming bravely to the birth. It has burst from me as from a ripe pomegranate, its seeds come from me with throes. I have been 2 weeks in a fever of parturition. . . . Knortz has been at me twice to make this book, & I hope you will not be displeased. . . . Dr. Bucke's book is invaluable, but it lacks profundity & literary knack in its treatment of

1404. *To William Sloane Kennedy* *6.17.* [*1886*]

Camden—June 17—p m

I have rec'd the Ruskin "Art" booklet[62]—thanks—Am ab't as usual in health—hot weather here to-day—

W W

1405. *To the Editor*, The Critic

ENDORSED (in unknown hand): "See *Critic* Lounger July 3."

Camden N J | June 17 '86

Dear Sir

I send you this note just rec'd—as you might possibly care to make an item from it—Please return it to me[63]—

Walt Whitman

1406. *To William Sloane Kennedy* *6.20.* [*1886*]

June 20—Evn'g

Dear W S K

I send you a note of introduction to J A Symonds—whom I think most likely & valuable, for the purpose you spoke of—(if I rightly understood it)—Symonds has leisure, has long been a reader of L of G.—& I have heard has for some time been wanting to have something to say in print about it—If possible send him at first a copy of your complete book, in proof from the types, or type-written in slips, complete[64]—In fact get

the work (analysis) & estimate of the problems involved. In fact I find it quite inadequate in these respects" (Feinberg). Kennedy, of course, did not know that Bucke's book was really WW's book.

On April 19 Kennedy again lauded his book ("Walt Whitman, the Poet of Humanity"): "I have completed (rough finish) my seven chapters on you. They are the most stunning eulogy & defence a poet ever rec'd I do believe—260 pp—Have done for you what Ruskin did for Turner" (Feinberg). On July 10 Kennedy spelled out the contents of his seven chapters: "Enfans d'Adam," "Whitman's Title To Greatness," "The Style of Leaves of Grass," "Analytical Introduction To Leaves of Grass," "Democrat & Comrade," "Passage To India," and "Walt Whitman and His Friends," to be followed by an appendix, conclusion, and bibliography (Feinberg).

Without consulting WW, Kennedy had begun negotiations for publication. Frederick W. Wilson, the Scottish publisher of *Leaves of Grass*, was not willing to undertake publication when he wrote to Kennedy on April 24, 1886, because the trade "is so terribly depressed that all enterprise is knocked on the head" (Trent). This manuscript was the first of several drafts of what became two books, *Reminiscences of Walt Whitman* (1896) and *The Fight of a Book for the World* (1926). Part of the manuscript with WW's corrections is in the Trent Collection. For WW's conflicting opinions of Kennedy's study, see Traubel, I, 165; II, 157–158; IV, 145.

two or three such copies, & send me one in advance—No doubt I would see many important corrections to be made—or additions—or elisions—Maybe (though may-be *not* too)—J A S would like the chance of giving his say, in such introduction—I dont think well of requesting any thing from Dowden[65]—

W W

Your Ruskin book has been rec'd & I have been reading it all day—

1407. *To John Addington Symonds*

ADDRESS: John Addington Symonds | Am Hof Davos | Platz Graūbünden | Switzerland.

from 328 Mickle Street | Camden New Jersey
U S America | June 20 1886

My dear Sir

I write a line to introduce & authenticate a valued personal & literary friend of mine, Wm Sloane Kennedy, who will send you this. He is every way friendly & rapport with "Leaves of Grass" & with me.

Walt Whitman

1408. *To Susan Stafford* *6.21.* [*1886*]

ADDRESS: Mrs. Susan Stafford | Kirkwood | (Glendale) | New Jersey. POSTMARK: Camden | Jun | 21 | 12M | 1886 | N.J.

Camden—June 21—noon

All ab't the same with me—the mare was quite lame, sprain of right hind foot, was the reason I didn't come down yesterday—I miss'd the jaunt & was grum & dull all day—I got a letter from Dr. B[ucke] this morning—he had spent a day & took dinner with Herbert Gilchrist &

65. On June 17 Kennedy had requested a letter of introduction from WW to Dowden (Feinberg). Since Dowden always wrote sympathetically, WW's remark is somewhat puzzling. On June 19 Edward T. Potter sent an extract from Dowden's most recent reference to WW (Syracuse; Traubel, IV, 311–312); see "The Interpretation of Literature," *The Contemporary Review*, XLIX (May, 1886), 701–719.

66. Duckett (see 1349, *n.* 86) was a neighbor of WW, living at 534 Mickle Street, and often acted as the poet's driver. On December 12, 1885, he moved to Westmont, near Haddonfield, N. J. On May 1, 1886, he came "to 328 [Mickle Street] to board" and "left in early June" (*CB*). On July 18 he became a "news agent" on the railroad train, but was

Edward Carpenter—all well—Delightful weather here as I write by the open window—but I am disabled worse than ever & can't get out—can hardly get across the room—tell George if he wishes it I will get a 7 hat in place of that 6⅞—

W W

1409. *To the Philadelphia* Press

328 Mickle street Camden N J | June 22 '86

Dear Sir

Is there any situation in the *Press* establishment, (counting-room or writing staff,) that could serve for my young friend, William H. Duckett,[66] who was with me the afternoon of the lecture? He is used to the city, & to life & people—is in his 18th year—has the first Knack of Literature—& is reliable & honest—

Walt Whitman

1410. *To William Sloane Kennedy* 6.23. [*1886*]

Camden June 23d—p m

Yours of 21st rec'd—acknowledging mine containing note of introduction to Symonds. I suppose you rec'd the big MS of yours, (concordance of criticisms &c)—*I returned some ten days ago*—but you havn't acknowledged it—all right & satisfactory the way you propose. Take your time, & follow out & fulfil what the spirit moves you to make. I will authenticate statistics &c—

W W

When you address me, always write the *New Jersey* out in full on envelope. I am not at all afraid of my handwriting appearing on the printer's copy—

laid off early in September for a short period of time (*CB*). About this time he began to make notes about WW's activities, and on December 27 he asked Bucke whether he wanted "my collection of notes about him." In his jottings Duckett observed that WW "was entirely free from indelicacy or any unchastity whatever"; he struck out the phrase "in any form" which originally followed "unchastity." On November 28 he noted that he had driven to the cemetery "where the poets beloved mother and little nephew are buried. It was his costume to visit there graives every few days" (Feinberg). There is a picture of WW and Duckett in October 1886 in Donaldson (172). See 1910 for WW's later difficulties with the young man.

1411. *To James Redpath*

TRANSCRIPT.

Camden, June 29, 1886

I send you "How I made a Book—or tried to"—If you can use it I think it should be in the Review[67]—It makes 3300 words, & would take from 7 to 8 pages Rev.—The price is $80, & I should want 100 proof sets on slips.

1412. *To William Sloane Kennedy*

328 Mickle Street | Camden New Jersey
July 8 '86

Dear W S K

I have returned from my jaunt to the Jersey sea shore[68]—& have rec'd yours of the 1st—Don't exactly know the scope, draft, *spine* of your proposed book ab't me, but entertain full faith that it has a reason-for-being, & that it will fulfil that reason—

I see in your letter, you have crossed out the "Walt" in the name—I like best to have the *full name* always if possible instead of merely "Whitman"[69]—Give both words, & don't be afraid of the tautology. I will help you & suggest or criticise freely & candidly, leaving the decision to you of course—hope you understand this, as it is.

Very hot weather here—I am quite comfortable, though—Have you rec'd Dr Knortz's German lecture?[70]—Burroughs is home from his Kentucky trip[71]—Dr Bucke will be back from England next week[72]—

Love to you—

Walt Whitman

67. WW sent the article to Redpath, of *The North American Review*, on June 29 (*CB*), and it evidently appeared in the Philadelphia *Press* and other newspapers associated with Rice's syndicate on July 11. He received $80 from Rice on July 10 (*CB*). This article, with "A Backward Glance on My Own Road," "How Leaves of Grass Was Made," and "My Book and I" became "A Backward Glance O'er Travel'd Roads" in *November Boughs* (1888), 5–18.

68. WW stayed at the "Minerva House" in Sea Isle City, N. J., from July 3 to 6 (*CB*).

69. Kennedy, on July 1, in citing the title of his "literary chef-d-oeuvre" as "Whitman, the Poet of Humanity," had stricken "Walt" from his tentative title

1413. *To James Redpath* *7.10. [1886]*

328 Mickle Street | Camden N J July 10 Noon

My dear J R

By an announcement in the Phil: *Press* this morning I suppose you have used my "How I made a Book" &c for the newspaper syndicate[73]—All right. What I am somewhat concerned ab't is that I have not seen the proof (which is always an important point with me)—& my 100 slips—What I mainly write now for, is to say, if possible, to have the slips run off from your type if still standing, & sent me here—Thanks for the prompt pay—

Walt Whit[man]

1414. *To The Editor*, Century Illustrated Monthly Review

ADDRESS: Editor | Century Magazine | Union Square | New York City. POSTMARKS: Camden | Jul | 15 | 8 PM | 1886 | N.J.; P.O. | 7–16–86 | 6 A | N.Y.

328 Mickle Street | Camden N J July 15 '86

Thanks for the three slips. I shall keep them carefully in my own hands until I see "Father Taylor" printed in the Magazine[74]—If I am indebted, as I fancy, to the printing office, for the courtesy of the slips please send this card there if convenient—

Walt Whitman

(Feinberg).

70. On July 10 Kennedy praised Kurtz's tract unstintedly (Feinberg).

71. Burroughs had commented on his trip to Kentucky on June 28. He also noted his visit with O'Connor, who "has probably got that horrible disease called *progressive locomotor ataxia*" (Feinberg).

72. Bucke came to Camden on July 18: "We go down to Glendale" (CB). Writing from England on June 9, Bucke had urged WW to spend the summer with him in London, Canada (Barrett).

73. The Sunday issue of the *Press* was not available for confirmation.

74. "Father Taylor and Oratory" appeared in February 1887.

1415. *To Charles Morris*

328 Mickle Street | Camden New Jersey |
July 20 '86

Dear Sir

I hereby give you permission to include any of my pieces you desire in your "Half Hours"[75]—

Walt Whitman

1416. *To Agnes Margaret Alden*

ADDRESS: Agnes Margaret Alden | Care Consulate General | U S America | Rome Italy. POSTMARK: Camden | Ju(?) | (?) | 1886 | N.J.

328 Mickle Street | Camden New Jersey
U S America | July 23 '86

I have to-day sent to Mr de Bosis the Volume "Leaves of Grass"[76]—

Walt Whitman

1417. *To The Editor*, Century Illustrated Monthly Review

TRANSCRIPT.

Camden, July 26, 1886

I send you the Hospital article at last.[77] I have preferred to give human cases, with their emotional accompaniments, sketched in on the spot, to any statistics. . . . the price of the article if you want it is $150. . . .

Walt Whitman

75. Charles Morris (1833–1922) wrote to WW on July 19 (Feinberg) requesting permission to include "Song of the Redwood-Tree" in *Half-Hours with the Best American Authors* (1886–1887), 4 vols. The poem appeared with a prefatory comment upon WW's "lack of the spiritual element of thought" (II, 489–494).

76. This copy of *Leaves of Grass* was intended for "Sig: Adolfo de Bosis, Villa d'Este, Tivoli: Rome, Italy." For it WW received "85 cts" (CB).

77. "Army and Hospital Cases," which WW had begun in 1884 (see 1282), appeared in *Century* in October 1888. WW received $150 from the magazine on August

1418. *To James Redpath*

328 Mickle Street | Camden New Jersey |
July 28 '86

My dear Redpath

Yours of 26th rec'd—All right & no harm done—But I mortally hate to have any thing with my name signed go to press without my seeing proof—Also I wanted the slips—Yes I will furnish you the (ab't) seven page article you request, & soon[78]—My health much as usual—better this summer so far than last—

Walt Whitman

1419. *To William Sloane Kennedy*

328 Mickle Street | Camden New Jersey |
July 30 '86—a m

Yes, I am ready for the MS[79]—Send it on.

W W

1420. *To Mary Smith Costelloe*

ADDRESS: Mrs: Costelloe | 40 Grosvenor Road | Westminster | London England. POSTMARK: Camden | Aug | 2 | 3 PM | N.J.

328 Mickle Street | Camden New Jersey
U S America | Aug: 2 '86

A pleasant forenoon as I write, here by the open window. I remain ab't as usual—a little pull'd down by the heat perhaps. Your letter came, & was welcome, as always—Alys's "circular"[80] came, & now one from Romsey arrived this morn'g—I had a letter from Dr B[ucke] two days ago—all well—

Walt Whitman

7, 1886 (*CB*).

78. See 1413. On August 6 WW sent Redpath "Robert Burns As Poet and Person," for which he received $70 (*CB*). WW returned the proof on August 31 (*CB*). The essay appeared in *The North American Review* in November 1886.

79. "Walt Whitman, the Poet of Humanity."

80. Alys had sent a "circular" letter to her friends. It reached WW in a letter on July 30 from Mary Grace Thomas, a young student at Bryn Mawr College (Feinberg).

In her article in the *Pall Mall Gazette* on December 23 Mrs. Costelloe combined the texts of this card and 1429.

1421. *To William Sloane Kennedy* 8.4. [*1886*]

328 Mickle Street | Camden Aug: 4—noon—

Your MS book has not arrived yet—I am ab't as usual—Cool & sunny weather as I write—

W W

1422. *To William Sloane Kennedy* 8.4. [*1886*]

328 Mickle Street | Camden New Jersey | Aug 4—Evn'g—

The MS Book has reach'd me safely—I will read it at once—will carefully have an eye to it—

W W

1423. *To William Sloane Kennedy*

Camden, Aug 5 '86

I have looked over the 2d piece "Jay Charleton's"—& it is the silliest compound of nonsense, lies & rot I have ever seen—Not a line but has an absurd lie—The paper of Conway is not much better[81]—

If you want to keep your book from *foulness* & ridiculous misstatements you had better leave both pieces out.

W. W.

1424. *To The Editor*, Century Illustrated Monthly Review 8.10. [*1886*]

ADDRESS: Editor | Century Magazine | Union Square | New York City | attention of | C C Buel. POSTMARKS: Camden | Aug | (?) | 3(?) PM | N.J.; P. O. | 8–10–86 | (?) | N.Y.

328 Mickle Street | Camden New Jersey Aug: 10

I sent the revised & added *Copy* of the *Hospitals article*[82]—also the

81. *Pen Pictures of Modern Authors* (1882), 161–177, included a reprint of Conway's article in *The Fortnightly Review* in 1866 (see 197) and "a flashy bit of Bohemian literature by 'Jay Charlton,' " the pen name of J. C. Goldsmith (see Kennedy, *The Fight of a Book for the World*, 55). Kennedy on August 18 agreed to omit both articles (Feinberg).

82. According to CB, WW sent the copy of "Army and Hospital Cases" and a receipt on August 8.

83. With this letter is a copy of the Lincoln lecture with directions to the printer; WW had corrected a newspaper account of the presentation of the lecture on April 15,

signed receipt. Send me a line acknowledging them, as I have a little uncertainty ab't my P O messenger.

Walt Whitman

1425. *To Thomas Donaldson* *8.11. [1886]*

ENDORSED: "Rec'd | August 12 – 1886 | Thos Donaldson." ADDRESS: Thomas Donaldson | 326 North 40th Street | Philadelphia. POSTMARK: Camden | Au (?) | 1(?) | 3 PM | 188(?) | N.J.

328 Mickle Street | Camden Aug: 11—noon

My dear friend

I send enclosed a full report of my Lincoln lecture for our friend Bram Stoker, as you request[83]—

Nothing very new with me—I am standing the summer pretty well, so far, go out with the rig every day—Hot here as I write, by the open window.

I have finished the *Army Hospitals* article for the *Century* & sent it on, & it has been accepted & handsomely paid for. (Will not be out I think for several months)—W Sloane Kennedy, of Belmont, Mass. (near Boston) has written a book ab't me—supplementing Dr Bucke's—has something to say ab't you[84]—& full of contemporary statistics—Send me word what day to come over—say from 2 to 5 p m—& have a chat with you—

Walt Whitman

1426. *To William Sloane Kennedy* *8.11. [1886]*

TRANSCRIPT.

Camden Aug. 11 Evn'g.

I may keep the MS a few days longer—two or three—I find upon

1880 (see 951).

On March 26, 1885, WW gave copies of *Leaves of Grass* to Donaldson for Henry Irving and Bram Stoker (CB). On December 22, 1887, Stoker, accompanied by Donaldson, called on the poet, who presented them with pictures and copies of *As a Strong Bird on Pinions Free* for themselves as well as for Irving and Ellen Terry (CB). Miss Terry thanked WW for the book on January 4, 1888 (Feinberg; Traubel, I, 5).

84. On July 10 Kennedy had confessed, "I hardly dare to state here on paper the uncertainties I feel about [Donaldson]" (Feinberg). Kennedy, in short, was not sure that Donaldson deserved to be called a friend (or idolator) of the poet.

taking it up to-day, it has a wonderful tenacity—of course a capital sign—I will send a few suggestion[s]—notes.

W. W.

1427. *To William Sloane Kennedy* 8.13. [*1886*]

Camden N J 4½ P M | Aug: 13—

I have just sent the MS book package to Adams' Express office, en route for Belmont—You ought to get it by Monday 16th—We are having a hot spell here, & it pulls me down—

W. W.

1428. *To William Sloane Kennedy* [*8.13(?). 1886*]

Have look'd over the whole MS. pretty well—with an eye to correction of dates & statistics—have a very few times made my own comments & suggestions (from my own point of view, or feeling, or knowledge)—you follow the suggestions or not, as you think best[85]—

1429. *To Mary Smith Costelloe* 8.15. [*1886*]

ADDRESS: Mrs: Costelloe | 40 Grosvenor Road | Westminster | London | S W | England. POSTMARKS: Camden | Aug | 15 | 6 PM | N.J.; Philadelphia | Aug | 15 | 1886.

Camden—Aug: 15 | Sunday afternoon

Nothing particular to write about—but I tho't I would send you a line—Am standing the hot season pretty well so far—have written several pieces (the War Hospital article for *Century* among the rest) which have been accepted & paid for—will send them to you when printed—Alys's letter rec'd—heard from Dr B[ucke] yesterday.

W W

85. This note to Kennedy may have been attached to the manuscript itself, which, as the preceding note indicates, was returned on August 13.

86. O'Connor sent on the previous day a clipping from *The Nation* of August 12 containing "a cheering review" of a book by Hutcheson Macaulay Posnett entitled *Comparative Literature* (1886), in which WW was referred to; see also O'Connor's

1430. *To William Sloane Kennedy* *8.18.* [*1886*]

Camden, Aug: 18

I send O'Connor's letter, with the clipping from the *Nation*—if you care to look at them. I have not heard whether you rec'd the MS. book—I sent it hence by Adams' Express, last Friday afternoon. I remain ab't the same in health—as I write (Wednesday forenoon) it is cloudy and sufficiently cool here, & I am sitting by the open window downstairs as usual—am comfortable. I have of late-past been writing several pieces (as I believe I told you before)—they are to appear in time in N A Rev:—Century—& Lippincott's—have been paid for—

W W

1431. *To William D. O'Connor* *8.18.* [*1886*]

ENDORSED: "Answ'd Dec. 11/86." ADDRESS: Wm D O'Connor | Life Saving Service | Washington D C. POSTMARKS: Camden | Aug | 18 | 10 30 AM | N.J.; Washington, Rec'd. | Aug | 18 | (?) PM | 1886 | 2.

Camden Aug: 18 noon

Yours of yesterday, with clipping from the N[ation] rec'd—thanks[86]—(Always so glad to hear or get letters from you, dear friend)—

I am getting along pretty well physically, have stood the summer well so far—digestion matters better—have been writing somewhat busily for me the past three or four weeks—articles, generally ordered ones—Century—N A Review—and Lippincott's—a little bit about Shakspere in last Critic[87]—

Walt Whitman

1432. *To William Sloane Kennedy* *8.19.* [*1886*]

Camden Aug: 19 P M

Yours of yesterday rec'd. I approve of the Chatto & Windus plan, & of the three (or two) years' guarantee.—I am glad you are going to let me have printed proofs (say second proofs, after the *first* is read by copy

comments on December 10 (Syracuse; Traubel, IV, 129). In the letter of August 17 O'Connor wrote: "Life seems to have almost stopped still with me. I earnestly wish I could get well, or else peg out suddenly" (Yale).

87. "A Thought on Shakspere" appeared in *The Critic* on August 14. The magazine printed Kennedy's "The Procession of the Poets" on September 4.

& corrected) & shall count on receiving them—All ab't same as usual with me—

W W

1433. *To Herbert Gilchrist*

ADDRESS: Herbert H. Gilchrist | 12 Well Road | Hampstead | London | England. POSTMARK: London, N.W. | 7 U | Sp 3 | 86.

328 Mickle Street |
Camden New Jersey U S America | Aug. 23 '86

Dear Herbert

Thank you for the remittance of the £2 from Prof. Dowden—(& I deeply thank him also)—Of the *Circular*—Should you have them to spare, I should like a dozen copies[88]—I have had a pretty good summer, so far—better than last summer—I drove down yesterday (Sunday) to Glendale & staid four or five hours—took dinner there—In general, matters there ab't as usual—Mrs. Stafford up & around, but not near as healthy & strong as I would like to see her—the rest all well—We talked of you—Address *Wm D. O'Connor*, *Life Saving Service*, *Treasury Department*, *Washington D. C.*, U S America—

I get letters from Dr. Bucke, who is home in London, Canada[89]—I send enclosed a ¶ for your consideration for the book[90]—I send my best love & thanks to you & Wm Rossetti.

Walt Whitman

1434. *To Richard W. Colles*

ADDRESS: Rich'd W Colles | 122 Tritonville Road | (?) Sandymount | Dublin Ireland. POSTMARKS: Camden | Aug | 24 | 12 M | 1886 | N.J.; Dublin | 4 | Se 7(?) | 86.

328 Mickle Street | Camden New Jersey
U S America | Aug 24, '86

Yours of Aug. 8 rec'd—I send (same mail with this, same ad-

88. The "Circular" was a facsimile of WW's letter to Rossetti (see 1400).

89. On September 10 Gilchrist wrote: "What I wrote about Dr B[ucke] sings discordantly in my ears—but in truth I was and am angry at his cool request to hand over your letters (& mothers) to him: his *injudicious* literary zeal does you and every body else harm" (Feinberg).

90. This paragraph appears in Herbert's preface to his biography of his mother: "I do not know . . . that I can furnish any good reason, but I feel to keep these utterances exclusively to myself. But I cannot let your book go to press without at least saying—and

dress) a copy of John Burroughs's book & can send another "Leaves of Grass," author's special ed'n & "Specimen Days"—would be £1—s2 (one pound, two shillings, the two vols.) Sent best by post office order to me here.[91] Before you decide to reprint J B's little book write me—there are several things I sh'd like to post you up on.

Walt Whitman

1435. *To Joseph B. Gilder*

ADDRESS: Joseph B Gilder | *Critic* office 20 Astor | Place | New York City. POSTMARKS: Camden | Aug | (?) | 12 M | N.J.; D | 8–24–86 | 7 P | N.Y.

328 Mickle Street | Camden New Jersey Aug 24 | '86

Thanks for the $10, which came last Sunday as pay for the "Thought"[92]—Thanks for the slips & for the copies of the paper—came this morning—

Walt Whitman

1436. *To William D. O'Connor* *8.24. [1886]*

ENDORSED: "Answ'd Dec 11/86." ADDRESS: Wm D O'Connor | Life Saving Service | Washington | D C. POSTMARKS: Camden | Aug | 25 | 6 AM | N.J.; Washington, Rec'd. | Aug | 25 | 2 30 PM | 1886 | 4.

328 Mickle Street | Camden New Jersey Aug. 24 p m

Charles Eldridge was here yesterday noon—a pleasant 3 hour visit—went to Atlantic City in the 5 p m train en route for Boston—

Nothing very different with me—I get quite a good many letters from Europe (some buyers)—rec'd a German (Wisconsin) paper with a long notice of L of G. & me, to-day—Fine weather here, & I am alone.

Love to you—

Walt Whitman

wishing it put on record—that among the perfect women I have known (and it has been my unspeakably good fortune to have had the very best, for mother, sisters and friends) I have known none more perfect in every relation, than my dear, dear friend, Anne Gilchrist." Apparently in a lost letter Herbert had asked permission to include his mother's letters to the poet. See also 1445.

91. Colles was probably one of the many students of Dowden who became fervid admirers of WW. On September 18 the poet sent the two books, and on October 18 he forwarded copies of Mrs. Gilchrist's essays (*CB*). See also 1455.

92. "A Thought on Shakspere."

1437. *To Edward Dowden*

ADDRESS: Prof: Edw'd Dowden | Temple Road | Winstead Rathmines | Dublin | Ireland. POSTMARKS: Camden | Aug | 26 | 12 M | N.J.; Philadelphia, Pa. | Aug | 26 | 1 PM | 1886 | Transit.

328 Mickle Street | Camden New Jersey | U S America | Aug: 26 '86

My dear Edward Dowden

Herbert Gilchrist has sent me £2 from you, as your annual donation, wh' I rec'd yesterday, & hereby rec't & thank you for. I am still living here, not much different from formerly—in good spirits, & getting along, hearty & fat and red, but clumsy & debilitated more & more.

I think of collecting together my prose & verse of the last five years, & printing a little Vol: under the title of "November Boughs"—also of bringing out a complete budget of *all* my writing in one book.[93] I remember you with much love—

Walt Whitman

write, when at leisure & give me the news over there—also your exact address—

1438. *To Thomas Jefferson Whitman*

Camden Sept 6 '86

I hardly know what to say to you and Jess in your fearful affliction—will not attempt any of the usual consolations[94]—

I suppose Lou is there, as she wished to start Saturday night—& I havn't heard since. Dear, dear Hattie—

I am ab't as usual—have got thro' the summer pretty well—

Walt Whitman

93. Apparently one of the first references to *Complete Poems and Prose of Walt Whitman, 1855–1888*.

94. Mannahatta (Hattie) Whitman, the poet's niece, died on September 3 and was

1439. *To Thomas Jefferson Whitman* 9.7. [*1886*]

Camden Sept: 7 p m

I think every hour of the day, (& night too when awake) of Hattie—& of how it must be there with you & Jess—but keep on much the same, with my doings & affairs—I know well enough, dear brother, how gloomy & blank all must be to you & Jess—I wish I could do something to help—

W W

1440. *To William Sloane Kennedy* 9.7. [*1886*][95]

Camden Tuesday p m | Sept 7

Yours rec'd. Herbert Gilchrist's address is | 12 Well Road, | Hampstead | London England | —I am ab't as usual—Fine weather here—(to-day a little warmer)—I send a paper—

W W

1441. *To Thomas Jefferson Whitman and Jessie Louisa Whitman* 9.8. [*1886*]

Camden Sept: 8

Dear Brother | & Dear Jess

Our hearts out here are with you more than you probably think at this gloomy time. I hope & trust you both bear up under it, & that the "God help us" of your telegraphic message will be fulfilled—I find myself better than toward the conclusion of former summers—am still living here at 328 Mickle st—& comfortable—I am anxious to hear whether Lou got there all right—am sitting here down stairs by the open window as I write—warm here for two days.

Walt Whitman

buried three days later (*CB*). George Whitman's wife Louisa went to St. Louis to be with Jeff and his daughter Jessie Louisa.

95. September 7 fell on Tuesday in 1886.

1442. *To Mary Smith Costelloe*

ADDRESS: Mrs: Costelloe | 40 Grosvenor Road | Westminster | London England. POSTMARK: Camden | Sep | 10 | 3 PM | 1886 | N. J.

328 Mickle Street | Camden New Jersey
U S America | Sept: 10 '86

The summer is drawing to a close, but we are having a warm spell here—(now the fourth day of it)—I am ab't as usual in health—my locomotion however giving out pretty fast—I shall be looking for Logan before long—Love to you, Alys, & all—

Walt Whitman

1443. *To Thomas Jefferson Whitman and Jessie Louisa Whitman* *9.11. [1886]*

Camden—Saturday, near noon | Sept: 11—

Dear Brother | & Dear Jess—

The days slip away, & one's sorrow—though it does not cease—seems to mellow & spread with the lapse of time—I continue ab't as usual in health—but it is very monotonous & lonesome, as I can hardly get around at all—often remain in the house all day, most of my time in the big chair by the window—afternoons are the worst & most tedious—happily my spirits keep pretty good, & I write some, though nothing but "pot-boilers"[96] [*incomplete*]

1444. *To Thomas Jefferson Whitman* *9.13. [1886]*

Camden Sept 13

I still think of Hattie—have been trying to find her picture—for I

96. Two "pot-boilers" were rejected: *Baldwin's Monthly* declined "Lafayette in Brooklyn," which WW sent on August 25 (CB), and Alden, of *Harper's Monthly*, refused "Some War Memoranda. Jotted Down at the Time" on September 20 (Feinberg; Traubel, II, 226). The latter was sent early in October to Redpath, who, on October 5, informed WW that Rice's syndicate "is dissolved," but that possibly he might put the piece into *The North American Review* (Feinberg; Traubel, II, 226), where it appeared in January, 1887. WW received $60 (CB).

97. WW mounted a newspaper clipping containing these lines from the conclusion of Longfellow's fourth sonnet in a group entitled "Three Friends of Mine." The second and third lines are run together, and should read: "Beneath this roof at midnight, in the days | That are no more, and shall no more return. . . ." The final line should read

have it, (& several copies I think)—but did not find it yet—How pretty these lines of Longfellow—

> Good night! Good night! as we so oft have said
> Beneath this roof, at midnight, in the days
> that are no more
> And will no more return.
> Thou hast but taken thy lamp and gone to bed,
> I stay a little longer, as one stays
> To gather up the embers that still burn.[97]

I had my long drive of 10 miles & back yesterday—was caught in the gale & heavy rain, (rain much needed)—but got home all safe—am ab't as usual—weather changed to quite cool to day here—Love to you & Jess[98]—

W. W.

1445. *To Herbert Gilchrist*

ADDRESS: Herbert H Gilchrist | 12 Well Road | Hampstead | London England. POSTMARK: Camden | Sep | 14 | 4 30 PM | 1886 | N.J.

328 Mickle Street | Camden New Jersey
U S America | Sept. 14 '86

Yours rec'd—The anecdote ab't Sir E[dward] T[hornton] at Washington is substantially correct.[99] (He knew who the lady was). You are all wrong in your literary estimate of Dr. B[ucke]—but I am glad you refused the letters for publication—They were strictly private[1]—

Walt Whitman

Don't forget my circular specifying all the English subscribers—love & thanks to W M R[ossetti]—

"cover up," not "gather up."

98. On November 9 Jeff wrote to his brother: "We are jogging along as best we may. . . . I find both for [Jessie] and myself there is nothing like the open air—the out doors. . . . It is pretty hard on Jess to leave her alone (with servants of course) in the house yet at times (for a short time) this does occur, and of course she gives way to her feelings, poor child, but I am doing my best to counteract it all I can do" (Feinberg; *Missouri Historical Society Bulletin*, XVI [1960], 112).

99. Sir Edward Thornton (1817–1906) was the English envoy at Washington from 1867 to 1881. According to the anecdote, Sir Edward, upon observing an intoxicated lady surrounded by jeering people in the streets of Washington, descended from his carriage and escorted her home (Herbert Gilchrist, *Anne Gilchrist*, 233).

1. See 1433.

1446. *To William Sloane Kennedy* *9.14. [1886]*

Camden Sept. 14

Know nothing of such an issue of L of G by any "antique bookseller" in Boston[2]—Doubt if it is worth tracing out, or noting—All goes on with me much the same—perfect weather here—I have been reading Cowley—well pleased—

W W

1447. *To Thomas Donaldson*

TRANSCRIPT.

Camden, N. J., September 15, 1886.

As I sit here by the open window, this cloudy warm forenoon, I feel that I would just like to write a line (quite purposeless, no doubt), sending my love and thanks to you and yours. Do you know this is the anniversary day of my receiving the present, through you, of the horse and wagon? And much good has it done to me. I remain in health much as usual of late. Shall come over and spend a couple of hours with you soon. Shall send you a postal, day before.

Walt Whitman.

Shall get the tintype of horse and wagon, etc., for you first opportunity.[3]

1447.1 *To Thomas Jefferson Whitman* *9.15. [1886]*

ADDRESS: Thos: J Whitman | 2437 2d Carondelet | Avenue | St Louis | Missouri. POSTMARK: Camden | Sep | 15 | 5 30 PM | N.J.

Camden Sept 15 noon

Lou got home last night all safe—She & George came here ab't 10 last night—She told me many little particulars I was glad to hear, though

2. Kennedy had learned from Trowbridge of "a seller of antique books in Boston who consented to put his imprint on a small edition of Leaves of Grass" (see Kennedy, 17*n*). See also Gohdes and Silver, 74*n*.

3. A picture of the horse and buggy was taken in October (Donaldson, 172).

all is so sad—Nothing special in my affairs—I am writing some—have just sent off a piece to Harpers[4]—(they may take it, & may *not*)—I have written a piece ab't "War Hospitals" for the Century—which they have taken & paid me for—(Both mag's pay handsomely)—I send you & Jess a letter just rec'd from Hannah—We have had several inquiries here about dear Hattie's death—two ladies call'd yesterday who had seen Hattie here at Lou's. Love to you, dear brother—Love to you, Jessie dear—

Walt Whitman

1448. *To Susan Stafford* *9.21. [1886]*

Camden Tuesday noon | September 21

I sent Harry the Doctor's address (131 South 15th street)[5] last Sunday evn'g, so he must have got it next day—We had a fine visit Sunday, & I enjoyed the drive very much—& you dont know how much good I have had out of *that chicken*—I have had three meals out of it—a bit broiled—& am to have the rest stewed for dinner to-day—it was sweet & tender—

I am ab't as usual—havn't been anywhere (though several invitations)—I keep good spirits, but grow clumsier & clumsier, & my sight is giving out—I enclose one of Herbert's last letters[6]—(I had written to him over a month ago, when you were not very well)—By it, he is not likely to come to America this fall—Cool & bright weather as I write—Love to you & George & Ed—

Walt Whitman

1449. *To Mary Smith Costelloe*

ADDRESS: Mrs: Costelloe | 40 Grosvenor Road | the Embankment | London | S W | England. POSTMARK: Camden | Sep | 27 | 1 30 PM | 1886 | N.J.

Camden New Jersey | U S America Sept 27 '86

Yours from Etretat rec'd & welcomed warmly—also the picture—

4. See note 96 above.

5. According to an entry in CB, this was the address of Dr. William Osler, whom WW had consulted about his health in 1885 (see 1349, *n*.85).

6. Gilchrist wrote to WW on September 10 (Feinberg).

Logan and Alys have arrived[7]—I have not seen them, but shall soon no doubt—I remain much as usual—I drove out a long jaunt Sunday—Yes, dear M, I have no objection to your writing or collating the "reminiscences" you speak of—actual occurrences, anecdotes, conversations, delineations, personalities, *plus*—criticisms *minus*[8]—

W W

1450. *To Ernest Rhys*

ADDRESS: Ernest Rhys | 59 Cheyne Walk | Chelsea | London England. POSTMARK: Camden | Oct | 13 | 8 PM | 1886(?) | N.J.

328 Mickle Street—Camden New Jersey |
U S America—Oct. 13 1886

First I ought to apologize for not answering your letters before—I am always glad to get them—Nothing specially new or different with me —I am willing you should print "Specimen Days" in your series—let W[alter] S[cott] send me what he thinks he can afford, & I shall want 10 copies of the book.[9] I should advise you to leave out the Appendix—If you want it further cut down, let me furnish you with a prepared copy—

Walt Whitman

1451. *To William Sloane Kennedy*

328 Mickle street | Camden N J
Oct: 16 '86 | P M

Yours of 14th rec'd by midday mail—*Good roots* (as the N Y boys used to say) *to your venture*[10]—I havn't heard from O'C[onnor] in quite a while—I fear he is, medically, in a bad way—I am sailing along ab't as usual—have just had my light dinner—Cool & raw weather here—my canary is singing blithely, as I write—

Walt Whitman

7. Logan called on September 26, but WW was not in. Robert Pearsall Smith and Alys visited the poet on October 9 (CB).

8. Mrs. Costelloe's article about WW's "Camden entourage" appeared in the *Pall Mall Gazette* on December 23: "Walt Whitman at Camden. | By One who has been there."

9. On November 26 Rhys spoke frankly: "Thanks very much for letting me have it! I will get as much as I can out of the publishers; for as Walter Scott is one of the largest railway contractors, as well as a publisher, & well stocked with money, I have no scruple on that score. It is not easy in any case to get much out of him, unfortunately. For my own sake, as well as yours, I wish it were!" (Feinberg; Traubel, IV, 229). On January 19, 1887, he informed WW that Scott was willing to pay ten guineas for *Specimen Days*,

1452. *To John Burroughs* *11.5. [1886?]*[11]

ADDRESS: John Burroughs | West Park | Ulster County New York. POSTMARK: Camden | Nov | 5 | 8 PM | N.J.

Camden Nov. 5 P M

Yours rec'd to-day, & glad to get it—I had a bad week last week, gastric & head troubles, but am much better—(Every time lets me down a peg.) I hear nothing from O'C[onnor] but fear the prospect is gloomy. Dr. B[ucke] is well & busy—I was out driving to-day, 11 to 1—Nothing definite done to my "November Boughs"—May be out in a year—I believe Kennedy has finished his book—

Walt Whitman

1453. *To Thomas Donaldson*

Camden Nov. 6 '86—noon

I think of driving over, with Billy,[12] to-morrow, Sunday, to be with you from 1 to 4, if the weather is favorable—

Walt Whitman

1454. *To Chatto & Windus* *[11.18. 1886]*

DRAFT LETTER.

I would like to exchange with you—I to send you my two volume Centennial Ed'n Leaves of Grass and Two Rivulets, (half leather, pub. at $10)—& you to send me two copies your late Ed'n *Leaves of Grass*. If you agree, mail the copies, & I will mail mine to you by return.[13]

the same amount he had paid for the right to print *The Poems of Walt Whitman. [Selected.]* (Feinberg, and see 1350).

10. Probably a reference to Kennedy's plan to submit his study of WW to Chatto & Windus (see 1432). Kennedy's letter is not known.

11. The year is conjectural, though WW began in 1886 to plan for the publication of *November Boughs;* Kennedy, of course, was actively at work on his book.

12. William H. Duckett.

13. According to *CB*, a letter was sent on November 18 to Chatto & Windus, the English firm which had just printed the second edition of Rossetti's *Poems by Walt Whitman.* On December 13 WW received six copies of the new edition, and on December 19 he sent two copies of the 1876 edition (*CB*, and see 1466).

1455. *To Richard W. Colles* [*11.18. 1886*]

ENDORSED: "letter sent to R W Colles, Dublin | Nov: 18 1886."
DRAFT LETTER.

Yours of 31st and 1st rec'd. I send the two Vols: of '76 Ed'n. I should accept with thanks from your hands any contribution from my Irish friends (Prof. Edw'd Dowden has already contributed liberally, & should not be solicited any further)—Take leisure and ease ab't it & let it amount to what it may—*or naught at all, if Destiny so disposes.*[14]

Yes, I should like to see the article in the *Quarterly*.[15] My late bad spell of sickness seems to have passed over—I was out driving yesterday the three sunny midday hours, & enjoyed them much.

Send me word if the two Vols. reach you safely. The price is £2,[16] which please remit me by P. O. order.

1456. *To William D. O'Connor*

ENDORSED: "Answ'd Dec 11/86." ADDRESS: Wm D O'Connor | Life Saving Service | Washington | D C. POSTMARKS: Camden | Nov | 19 | 12 M | 1886 | N.J.; Washington(?) | Nov | 19 | 10 PM | 1886 | 6.

328 Mickle Street | Camden New Jersey
Nov. 19 '86

Dear friend

If you feel like it write me soon as convenient after rec'ing this, as it is quite a while since I have heard from you, & I am getting anxious.[17] Nothing very different with me—I go out by my own volition not at all, as my power of walking &c. is quite gone. I only get from one room to another in the house, with effort & very slowly—I drive out fair mid-days —Sleep tolerably—appetite good—digestion so-so—

14. On November 9 Herbert Gilchrist sent a gift of ten shillings from Colles with the following excerpt from Colles's letter: "You will kindly consider it annual & I hope not only to increase the sum but have the great pleasure of sending it for many years" (Feinberg). See also 1461.

15. *The British Quarterly Review* for October contained an article on "American Poets" in which WW, according to O'Connor, received a "glorious tribute" (Traubel, IV, 129).

16. WW struck out "$10."

17. O'Connor did not reply until December 10 because "the difficulty of managing pen and ink is indescribable, and only equalled by the difficulty of putting even the simplest expressions together" (Syracuse; Traubel, IV, 128).

I write (prose pieces) from time to time yet—have one ab't "Burns" in *N. A. Review* for November—(they pay quite well, & Redpath is very good to me)[18]—Have a paper "My Book & I" in *Lippincott's* for Jan. next[19]—will send it you in printed slip—Shall probably get ready my little concluding book "November Boughs" this winter or next spring—I enclose Dr Bucke's last, just rec'd—the *Heine* extract it is possible I rec'd from you, but think not[20]—I found it very interesting. Best Love as always—

Walt Whitman

1457. *To Mary Smith Costelloe*

ADDRESS: Mrs: Costelloe | 40 Grosvenor Road | the Embankment | London | S W | England.
POSTMARK: Camden | Nov | 23 | 3 PM | N.J.

Camden U S America | Nov. 23 '86—2 p m—

I am ab't as usual—took a long drive by myself midday yesterday —basked in the sun & drove slow—Have just had my dinner & enjoyed it.

Your last rec'd yesterday—(a sweet newsy, cheery letter, dear M)[21]— Your father comes occasionally—is well & hearty—So you are at the *reminiscences* are you—Heaven help you. Love—

W. W.

1458. *To Richard Watson Gilder* (?)[22]

328 Mickle Street | Camden New Jersey | Dec 1 '86

My dear Gilder

If entirely convenient have the magazine sent me by mail here— have the Nov. and Dec. no's sent. I am ab't as usual—in good heart but badly paralyzed.

Walt Whitman

18. WW received $70 for this article (*CB*).
19. WW returned the proof of this article on November 1 (*CB*).
20. WW enclosed "Heine's Last Days," a reprint of an article in the *Pall Mall Gazette*.
21. On October 21 Mrs. Costelloe had informed the poet that she and her husband were about to go as delegates "to the great Liberal Convention at Birmingham. . . . The great event will be Mr. Gladstone's speech—wh. is to be *phonographed!*" (Feinberg; *Smith Alumnae Quarterly* [February 1958], 87).
22. Probably this note was sent to Richard Watson Gilder, the editor of *Century Illustrated Monthly Magazine*. The first two instalments of "Abraham Lincoln: A History," by John G. Nicolay and John Hay, appeared in November and December.

1459. *To Sylvester Baxter*

328 Mickle Street | Camden New Jersey
Dec 8 '86

Dear friend

Your kind letter of Dec. 6, rec'd—& much welcomed[23]—

I thank you deeply & Mr Lovering also—but do not consent to being an applicant for a pension, as spoken of—I do not deserve it—Send word to Mr Lovering, or show him this—I thank him deeply—

I am living here in my shanty, in good spirits, but sadly disabled physically—(have a hard job to get from one room to the next)—Am occupied in getting ready the copy of a little book—my last—to be called "November Boughs"—the pieces in prose and verse I have thrown out the last four years—

Best love to you & to all my Boston friends—

Walt Whitman

1460. *To General James Grant Wilson*

328 Mickle street | Camden New Jersey
Dec: 8 '86

Dear Gen: Wilson[24]

I have been quite unwell, or I should have ans'd you sooner. Yours of Nov. 26th, with check for Twenty Dollars, ($20) (herewith returned) was duly rec'd—Thank you most fervently, my friend—But I don't feel at all like writing a notice or biography of Halleck[25]—(nor indeed capaci-

23. Baxter, the Boston journalist, had outlined the pension plan on December 6: "I have been thinking very often of you lately, and wishing that something might be done to lighten life for you. The Nation is deeply in your debt for the services you rendered in the war, not to mention its deeper debt to you as a poet which will be appreciated more and more as the years go on. Hon. Henry B. Lovering, the Member of Congress from my district, 6th Massachusetts, and influential member of committee on invalid pensions, tells me that you are fully entitled to a pension and that he will be very glad to be instrumental in securing it, as he has a high appreciation for you. He would not like to do it, however, without consulting your wishes in the matter, and therefore I write to ask if I may not tell him to go ahead. The act would be purely voluntary on the part of Congress, and not in response to any petition from you" (Feinberg).

At the conclusion of Baxter's letter WW wrote: "Answer'd & sent on at once peremptorily declining, & forbidding the pension application W W."

Kennedy had mentioned the possibility of a pension to WW as early as January 7, 1885: "If this humbug government were worth a copper spangle it wd have settled a handsome pension on you, an honorary life salary—as a recognition of your unparalleled services during the war. But it wd probably be odious to you to even have the subject whispered of?" (Feinberg).

In his letter Baxter also referred to a "Whitman Society" that he was forming with

tated for it)—I met H. once in Park Place, N. Y. & remember his looks & talk—but I dont think I can write ab't him—Thank you & the Messrs: Appleton—Please send me word of the rec't of this—

Walt Whitman

1461. *To Herbert Gilchrist*

ADDRESS: Herbert H Gilchrist | 12 Well Road | Hampstead | London England. POSTMARK: Camden | (?) | 5 PM | (?) | N.J.

328 Mickle Street—Camden New Jersey | U S America | Dec. 12 1886

Yours of Nov. 29. with the P. O. order 14s-6d-rec'd—(the three sums, £2 10s, £5, & 14s 6d safely rec'd)[26]—Fervent thanks—(I wish I could return them personally)—I have been quite unwell for a week, but am easier to-day—have eaten a bit of breakfast for the first time in many days—A long cold snow-storm here—My bird is singing gaily as I write—

Walt Whitman

1462. *To William Sloane Kennedy*

328 Mickle Street—Camden | New Jersey | Dec. 12 '86

Have had a bad spell of illness again but am better to-day—Have just eaten a bit of dinner for the first time in over a week—(stewed rabbit,

John Boyle O'Reilly, Truman Howe Bartlett, and Mrs. Charles Fairchild, and to his article, written with W. Q. Judge, "Poetical Occultism: Some Rough Studies of the Occult Leanings of the Poets," *The Path*, I (December 1886), 270–274, a discussion of WW's mysticism.

24. See 920. In 1888 WW said: "I knew Wilson very well—he was a cordial and convincing character. . . . Wilson belongs to the conventional literary old guard in New York" (Traubel, II, 135). On April 8, 1887, Wilson invited the poet to stay with him during his New York visit (Feinberg; Traubel, II, 135).

25. General Henry Wager Halleck (1815–1872) was Grant's chief of staff. This was apparently not the type of "pot-boiler" WW was willing to write.

26. These sums are explained in Herbert's letter of December 23: he had sent £2.10 for Richard Colles (see 1455); £5 from Leonard M. Brown (see 1631); and 14*s.* 6*d.* from Cambridge friends. Herbert was hurt: "You make no allusion to my Book or my little confidences thereon! do you care for a copy?" (Feinberg). Undoubtedly he was referring to the fact that WW had not replied to his letters of September 10, October 16, and November 9 (Feinberg), in which he recounted his difficulties in publishing the biography of his mother. In the letter of November 9 he observed: "I am so sorry that I have finished my labour of love, the doing of the Biography has been the greatest imaginable comfort and solace to me,—in a sense it has given me another year of her companionship."

with a piece of splendid home-made buttered bread, covered with the stew gravy)—Every thing from you rec'd & welcomed—dull weather, the ground covered with snow—(but my little bird is singing as I write)—

Walt Whitman

1463. *To Mary Smith Costelloe*

ADDRESS: Mrs: Costelloe | 40 Grosvenor Road | the Embankment | London England. POSTMARK: Camden | Dec | (?) | 4 30 PM | 18(?) | N.J.

328 Mickle Street—Camden | New Jersey—
U S America | Dec. 13, '86—

Here I am, still, dear friend, & nothing new or special—the last week I was quite ill again, but am on the mend yesterday and to-day—Your good father comes to see me often,[27] & Logan paid me a nice visit yesterday—Your letter of Nov. 12 has been read & re-read, & quite gone the rounds—much admired—I send you "My Book & I," in print—

Walt Whitman

1464. *To The Editor*, The Critic *12.15. [1886]*

Camden | Wednesday Evn'g Dec. 15

I think I should like to write a bit about Tennyson & the new Locksley Hall, &c:[28]—intended for your first page if you wish—ab't the usual length of my pieces—Will probably send it to you by or before Sunday next—

Walt Whitman

27. On December 22 WW noted in *CB*: "Kind visits from R P Smith—liberal & kind gifts."

28. "A Word about Tennyson" appeared in *The Critic* on January 1, 1887. See also 1472. According to an endorsement by Jeannette L. Gilder, editor of *The Critic*, on May 19, 1902, this letter was in her possession at that time.

29. O'Connor's gloomy account of his health in his letter of December 10 (Syracuse; Traubel, IV, 128–130). Bucke sent the letter to Burroughs, who returned it to WW on December 21 (Yale; Traubel, IV, 130) and observed: "'Tis a pity he sits down and lets this thing creep over him. He could do much to fight it off or keep it at bay." WW concurred: "William is not of the despondent but of the hypochondriac turn: he hasn't

1465. *To John Burroughs*

ADDRESS: John Burroughs | West Park | Ulster County | New York. POSTMARKS: Camden | Dec | 19 | (?) | N.J.; Philadelphia, Pa. | Dec | 9 | 6 P(?) | (?)886 | Transit.

328 Mickle Street | Camden Dec 19 '86

Send you a paper, slip, &c. you must have got, (or soon will)—O'C[onnor]'s last letter to me, I sent to Dr. B[ucke].[29] I am ab't as usual & comfortable—have had two bad spells already this winter—been outdoors to-day, first time in two weeks—Am writing some—

W W

1466. *To Chatto & Windus*

ADDRESS: Chatto & Windus | Publishers &C | 214 Piccadilly | London | W | England. POSTMARK: Camden | Dec | 21 | (?).

328 Mickle Street | Camden New Jersey |
U S America Dec. 21 '86

Thanks for the six copies of your beautiful Edition of my Poems, wh' have safely reach'd me.[30]

Walt Whitman

1467. *To Edwin H. Woodruff* *12.21 [1886?]*[31]

ADDRESS: Edwin H Woodruff | Cornell University Library | Ithaca | New York. POSTMARKS: Camden | Dec | 21 | 8 PM | 188(?) | N.J.; (?) | Dec | 22 | 7 PM | Paid.

328 Mickle Street | Camden New Jersey |
Dec 21—

Thanks for your good letter & contents—wh' I have rec'd all right.

Walt Whitman

made the fight just as I have" (Traubel, IV, 130).

30. See 1454.

31. The year in which WW's postcard to Woodruff was written is conjectural, but 1886 seems plausible. Woodruff (1862–1941), then a member of the staff of the Cornell University Library, was introduced to the poet by Hiram Corson in a letter of March 26, 1886 (Feinberg; Traubel, I, 286–287). Two days later he was in Camden (*CB*). Earlier, on June 4, 1882, Woodruff had sent WW a poem written under his influence and printed in the *Cornell Era* (Feinberg). Later Woodruff became a professor of law and was dean of the Cornell Law School from 1916 to 1921. See *Cornell University. Faculty. Necrology of the Faculty, 1941–1942*, 5–7.

1468. *To Jessie C. Chamberlin*

ADDRESS: Jessie C Chamberlin | Sage College | Ithaca | New York. POSTMARK: Camden | Dec | 23 | 6 PM | (?).

328 Mickle Street | Camden New Jersey | Dec: 23 '86

Dear J C C[32]

Your good letter has reached me, with the generous contents—hearty thanks—

Walt Whitman

1469. *To William Sloane Kennedy* *12.23.* [*1886*]

Camden Dec. 23

I send you three little French pamphlets & one Scotch—When through reading them (no hurry) send the whole to Wm D O'Connor, Life Saving Service, Washington D C[33]—I am ab't same as usual again—Merry Christmas to you & Mrs. K—

Walt Whitman

1470. *To William Sloane Kennedy*

Camden Dec. 28 '86

I am ab't as usual & in good spirits & condition—Have been out driving to-day, & have eaten a good dinner (oysters &c)—Have a Tennyson *blaat* in the forthcoming Critic of Dec. 31[34]—Happy New Year!

Walt Whitman

32. Miss Chamberlin was a student at Sage College from 1885 to 1887. For this information I am indebted to Josephine M. Tharpe, Reference Librarian at the Cornell University Library.

33. Apparently these were the (unnamed) pamphlets O'Connor sent to WW on December 21 (Feinberg).

34. See 1464.

35. Since "Some War Memoranda. Jotted Down at the Time" appeared in the January issue of *The North American Review*, this note was probably written in December 1886.

36. This note appears at the top of the manuscript of "A Word about Tennyson"

1471. *To The Editor*, The North American Review

[12?.(?). 1886][35]

TRANSCRIPT.

If the War Memoranda piece is in Jan. number, please send me three numbers.

Walt Whitman
Camden, New Jersey

1472. *To The Editor*, The Critic *[12.(?). 1886]*[36]

—follow copy—punctuation &c—If possible send me a proof Saturday night—which I will return Sunday night—

WW—Camden New Jersey

1472.1 *To C. Sadakichi Hartmann* *[(?).(?). 1886?]*[37]

TRANSCRIPT.

Yours rec'd—With many thanks—

Walt Whitman

(Trent).

37. Hartmann includes this transcription at the conclusion of his section recounting his conversations with WW in 1886: "I never corresponded with Whitman; the only communication I received from him is a postal card acknowledging receipt of some money for several of his books I had bought" (*Conversations with Walt Whitman*, 34).

According to my tabulation, based upon his letters and his entries in CB, WW's income in 1886 amounted to at least $2,289.06: royalties, $120.21; lectures, $742.00; sales of books, $203.35; payments for articles and poems, $360.00; and gifts, $863.50. (The figures on book sales are to some extent conjectural, since I have had to assume that he charged a uniform price.)

1887

1473. *To Mrs. Noble T. Biddle*

ADDRESS: Mrs. Noble T Biddle | San José | California. POSTMARKS: Cam[den] | Jan | 2 | (?) | 1887; Philadelphia, Pa. | Jan | 2 | (?) | Transit.

328 Mickle Street | Camden New Jersey | Jan. 2 '87

I mail you the two Vols. (same address as this card)—When rec'd, please kindly send me a card notifying me—The Vols. are fully paid for.[1]

Walt Whitman

1474. *To Mary Smith Costelloe*

ADDRESS: Mrs: Costelloe | 40 Grosvenor Road | the Embankment | London England. POSTMARK: Camden | Jan | (?) | 6 PM | 1887 | N.J.

Camden Jan. 3 '87—P M

Henry Norman, of the *Pall Mall Gazette*, has sent me £81 over, in a very kind & good letter—enclosing some printed slips from paper—one written by you ab't my Camden *entourage*—very satisfactory & right to me—In the Reminiscences stick as much as possible to personal descriptions, anecdotes, & sayings—*&* *don't make me too good*—I am no angel by a long shot[2]—

Walt Whitman

1887

1. When he sent the books, WW apparently enclosed the following note: "I will also send you a late photo-lithograph portrait W W" (Feinberg).

2. On January 17 Mrs. Costelloe wrote to WW: "I am afraid by a curious fatality all thy biographers want to make thee out *too good* for thy liking! Has thee never thought of expanding the *Specimen Days* into Autobiographical sketches? Then thee could tell the world thy wickedness to the full, which thy friends are so uncomprehending as not to see!" (Feinberg; *Smith Alumnae Quarterly* [February 1958], 87. See also 1449).

3. According to CB the amount was £81.6.6 ($393.61), which WW deposited in the bank on January 11. Norman was acting for the editor of the newspaper, William T. Stead (1849–1912); see *AL*, XXXIII (1961), 68–69, and also 1597. On February 3 Norman protested to WW the citation in the Philadelphia *Press* of the names of three donors: Sir Edward Malet, the English ambassador in Berlin; Lord Ronald Gower; and A. Gerstenberg (Feinberg).

1475. *To Henry Norman*

TRANSCRIPT.

Jan. 3, 1887 328 Mickle Street |
Camden New Jersey U S America

Friend

Your kind letter of Dec. 23, with the £81 over, has safely reached me. I thank you, dear *Pall Mall Gazette*, & deeply thank the donors of the gift[3]—It is accepted, I am sure, in the same spirit in which it is conveyed —And I must add that (while I am not at all in actual want, and have generous and attentive friends here) a money aid like this comes most opportunely to me under the circumstances, and helps "keep the wolf from the door" indeed.

I am almost entirely physically disabled, but remain in good spirits and fairish health. Almost every week I write a little for pay and publication. Winter is at its height and bitter cold here now, the earth hard and covered with ice and snow, as I sit by my window well blanketed, writing this offhand letter of acknowledgement.

God bless my British friends assisters—(from the first they have come in when most wanted)—

Walt Whitman

1476. *Alfred Lord Tennyson To WW*

Farringford | Freshwater | Isle of Wight

Dear old man,

I the elder old man have received your Article in the Critic, & send you in return my thanks & New-Year's greeting on the wings of this

Pall Mall Gazette devoted a great deal of space to WW in 1887: January 10, excerpts from "My Book and I"; January 20, lengthy extracts from "A Word about Tennyson"; April 27, a quotation from WW's "Additional Note" for the English edition of *Specimen Days;* May 6, an excerpt from a private correspondent about gifts of Americans to WW (see 1597); June 2, an account of WW's birthday with quotations from the *Daily News;* July 9, "The Dying Veteran"; July 30, a summary of Swinburne's attack upon WW; August 3, 4, 6, and 11, comment, editorial and personal, on Swinburne's article; September 6, a defense of the American poet. In addition, letters from WW were reproduced on January 25 and August 30 (see 1597).

The endorsement of the draft letter (Barrett) reads: "Sent to Henry Norman | Pall Mall Gazette | London | Jan 3 '87."

The only significant difference between the newspaper text and the draft is the substitution of "this offhand letter of acknowledgement" for "this letter of thanks" at the conclusion of the second paragraph.

East-wind, which, I trust, is blowing softlier & warmlier on your good gray head than here, where it is rocking the elms & ilexes of my Isle of Wight garden.[4]

Yours always

Tennyson

Jany 15th/1887

1477. *To The Editor, New Orleans* Picayune

ADDRESS: Editor Picayune | newspaper | New Orleans | Louisiana. POSTMARKS: Camden | Jan | 17 | 8 PM | 1887 | N.J.; Philadelphia, Pa. | Jan | 17 | 9 PM | 1887 | Transit.

Camden Jan 17 '87—P M

The "Press" newspaper of Philadelphia has just sent over to say to me that they would like to have the article "New Orleans in 1848"[5] (MS. sent on by me) to print it in their columns—with your permission—Jan. 25, giving you due credit, & saying it appears in *your* columns that day—So if agreeable *send them an early proof*, for that purpose—address "R. W. Kerswell, "Press" newspaper Philadelphia"—(I have just promised Mr K to write the foregoing)—

Walt Whitman

1478. *To Susan Stafford* *1.18.* [*1887*]

Camden Jan 18—noon

Dear friend

I will send Herbert's letter,[6] just rec'd this morning & add a word myself, tho' I have nothing new to say particular—I am comfortable & ab't the same generally in health, (but slowly going down hill I suppose.) Ed was here an hour or so last evening, & we were glad to have him. Wish *you* would come & spend the day here—wish George would come, & you &

4. Of this letter WW observed: "Tennyson is an artist even when he writes a letter: this letter is protected all round from indecision, forwardness, uncertainty: it is correct—choice, final" (Traubel, I, 36).

5. On January 11 WW had received a request from the *Picayune* for an account of his experiences in New Orleans, which was to appear on January 25, the newspaper's "fiftieth year edition" (*CP*, 605). The poet sent the article on January 16 and received $25 (*CB*).

he have dinner here with us—Can't you fix a day soon? Mrs. Davis would be glad too—As I write the little bird is singing gayly in his cage—first rate cheer & company for me, for I am here mostly alone—Sun shining to-day here, but cold enough outside [&] frozen hard—

"O why hast thou bleach'd these locks, old Time
Yet left my heart so young"?

Love to you & George, Harry & all—

Walt Whitman

1479. *To Arthur Price*

ADDRESS: Arthur Price | Woodside | Queens County | New Yo[rk]. POSTMARKS: Camden | (?) | 25 | 6 PM | 1887 | N.J.; New York | Jan 26 | 1 AM | 87 | Transit.

328 Mickle Street | Camden New Jersey |
Jan: 25 '87—noon

My dear friend Arthur[7]

The box (Oranges) has just come, (the letter came two hours ago) & I hasten to acknowledge them, without opening the box, but I thank you heartily & know I shall enjoy the fruit. I am here not much different from usual late years, but older, more broken & paralyzed—I have a little old cottage of my own in which I live, & have a good young woman, a widow, for cook & housekeeper—I am fearfully disabled, yet retain good spirits—have just been out for a drive—Often think of Helen (dear Helen) and you & all—Is this letter address'd right?—I should occasionally send H. a letter or paper, but am doubtful ab't the address—

Walt Whitman

1480. *To William Sloane Kennedy*

Camden—Jan. 26 '87

Your card, acknowledging paper, came—Sylvester Baxter (back'd by Mr Lovering) opened the pension proposal five weeks ago—I immedi-

6. In a letter dated January 6, Gilchrist informed WW that he had included in the biography of his mother an account of some conversations at the Stafford farm (*Anne Gilchrist*, 239–242). He also asked specifically about Mrs. Stafford. In the same letter Gilchrist sent a gift of £3 from Miss R. E. Powell of Guildford, England (Feinberg). The poet visited the Staffords on January 23 when the weather was milder (CB).

7. The son of Mrs. Abby H. Price (*Corr.*, I, 10). His sister Helen contributed an article to Bucke's *Walt Whitman*. See also 1158.

ately wrote to S B positively prohibiting it[8]—the next thing I hear of is Mr. L's bill—I have finally concluded to let the thing take its course—I do *not* expect the bill to pass—I am ab't as usual—a bodily wreck—did you get "My Book & I" slip?

W W

1481. *To Talcott Williams(?)*

TRANSCRIPT.

328 Mickle Street | Camden Jan. 31 '87—P.M.

Dear friend

I have been somewhat *down* for days, even weeks past, but am better now—have been out a little to-day, driven in the phaeton. Come over very soon & see me. Nothing particular, but it will cheer me up. Bring anybody you like with you.

Walt Whitman

Put this in the "Personal" col. Feb. 1.[9]

1482. *To Ernest Rhys*

ADDRESS: Ernest Rhys | 59 Cheyne Walk | Chelsea | London England. POSTMARKS: Camden | Feb | 4 | 3 PM | 1887 | N.J.; Philadelphia, Pa. | Feb |4 | 1887 | Paid.

328 Mickle St Feb: 4 '87 |—Camden
New Jersey U S America

I find that the whole book "Specimen Days & Collect"—as I sent it to you—338 pages (without the Appendix)—makes about as much as y'r

8. See 1459. In CB, on January 19, WW noted the introduction of Lovering's bill, which was to grant the poet a pension of $25 a month. On February 4 he replied to a letter from Lovering (CB); both letters are apparently lost.

9. The Philadelphia *Press* dutifully printed the following on February 1: "Yesterday was Walt Whitman's best day for a long time. He went out phæton-riding in the mid-day sun and enjoyed it. Yesterday, too, he received a warm letter from Alfred Tennyson commencing 'Dear Old Man.' Life continues tenacious and cheery with Whitman, but he is very feeble."

10. The correct title was *The Romance of King Arthur.*

11. See 1450. WW had sent the copy of *Specimen Days* on February 2 (CB). On February 15 Rhys wrote: "I must not decide off-hand about the *Specimen Days*,—that is, whether to make two vols. as you suggest, or to try & get the whole into one. In the latter case, the book would be rather crowded. . . . No! I would not think of putting the copy of *Specimen Days* with your corrections into the printers' hands and will get copies from Wilson of Glasgow, carefully following all your deletions & so on. It is one of the greatest prizes I possess, & someday a sense of its value will inspire me, I'm afraid, to beg you to send me a copy of *Leaves of Grass* too with your name in it, (& mine, as proof of ownership,) & some further inscription as well" (Morgan). On January 19 Rhys wrote at

"History of King Arthur" Volume[10]—If you & the publisher prefer to pub. it all in *one volume*, you can do so.[11]

Walt Whitman

1483. *To Mary Smith Costelloe*

ADDRESS: Mrs: Costelloe | 40 Grosvenor Road | the Embankment | London England. POSTMARK: Camden | Feb | 11 | 8 PM | 1887 | N.J.

Camden—Feb. 11 '87

Nothing very new or special with me—As I write toward latter part of afternoon the weather is warm & dark & wet here. I go out hardly at all, the roads are so bad—(the winter will soon be beginning to break)—I havn't heard from you now in some time[12]—Dr B[ucke] writes often[13]—I am to be taken over to the "Contemporary Club" Phila. in a few evenings to talk to them[14]—

Best love—

W W

1484. *To Harry D. Hughes*

TRANSCRIPT.

328 Mickle Street, Camden, Feb. 12, 1887

[WW thanks Hughes for an article about himself in *Leisure Moments*.][15]

Walt Whitman

length about a kind of epiphany which he had experienced at the seashore; WW termed it "a wonderful letter" (Feinberg).

12. On January 17 Mrs. Costelloe had written: "Thee can't think what a refreshment to soul and body it is to read 'Leaves of Grass' or even to think of thee, in the midst of this artificial town life" (Feinberg; *Smith Alumnae Quarterly*, 87 [February 1958], 87).

13. The only extant item in the correspondence between WW and Bucke at this time is the latter's letter of February 20 (Feinberg).

14. On February 23 the Philadelphia *Press* reported that on the preceding evening "the venerable poet spoke at length concerning his poetry, and in the course of his address repeated extracts, among which were 'The Mysterious Trumpeter' and 'Two Birds' in 'Pauman Oak' " ["The Mystic Trumpeter" and the section beginning 'Once Paumanok . . ." from "Out of the Cradle Endlessly Rocking"]. The meeting was attended by Horace Traubel and Dr. Daniel G. Brinton, a professor at the University of Pennsylvania, who on February 28 formally conveyed to WW the gratitude of the club (Feinberg). For the reading he received $20 (CB). See Traubel's account in *In Re*, 130–131.

15. Hughes wrote in superlatives of "Walt Whitman's Prose Works" in *Leisure Moments*, II (February 1887), 17. For a photocopy of the article I am indebted to the Historical Society of Pennsylvania.

1485. *To Jeannette L. and Joseph B. Gilder* [*2.14. 1887*]

ADDRESS: J L & J B Gilder | *Critic* office | 743 Broadway | New York City. POSTMARK: Camden | Feb | 14 | 6 PM | 1887 | N.J.

No errors—all correct—if convenient send me 8 or 10 proof-slips like this[16]—

Whitman
Camden New Jersey

1486. *To William Sloane Kennedy*

ADDRESS: W. Sloane Kennedy | Belmont | Mass:. POSTMARK: Camden | Feb | 17 | 3 PM | 188(?) | N.J.

Camden Feb. 17 '87 | 2 p m

I continue much the same. Shall make up a little budget (perhaps trunk or box) of what MS memoranda or relics I think may be worth while—for you[17]—Fine sunny weather here to-day, & I have been out in it with my horse & wagon by myself, two hours—O'Connor has gone to Southern California—the poor fellow I fear is in a bad way[18]—Write often—

W W

1487. *To William Sloane Kennedy*

Camden Feb. 21 '87 p m

Dear WSK—

Yours of 19th came (always welcome) with Rhys's letters (herewith returned) & the *Transcript*—Thanks—for your warm words, y'r affectionate personal & literary extra appreciation—always—thanks for writing & sending—I am kept in here quite all the time & was glad you sent R's letters—Poor dear noble O'Connor's ailment is I fear *locomotor*

16. This note was written on a proof of "Five Thousand Poems," which appeared in *The Critic* on April 16.

17. Material for Kennedy's study of the poet.

18. WW was informed on February 11 by Eldridge of O'Connor's trip to California, where he was staying with his brother-in-law, Dr. Channing (Barrus, 262–263). Dr. Bucke wrote to WW about O'Connor's illness on February 20 (Feinberg).

ataxyia—induration of the spine—I have heard nothing further—time only can decide—but I have serious apprehensions—

Nothing new with me—am glad your book over there is under Ernest Rhys's management & overseeing—He makes the impression on me of a deep true friend of L of G & of myself—What is that ab't Trowbridge?[19] I do not understand. Had a drive yesterday thro' a splendid snowstorm—

Walt Whitman

1488. *To William Sloane Kennedy*

Camden Feb 22 '87—noon

Nothing further from O'Connor. See pp. 39 and 40 in Dr Buckes book ab't the wife & their hospitality to me—they had two children, a boy died in early childhood—the girl died not long since aged 22 or 3[20]—a fine girl—I knew her quite well—I cant get over what you say ab't Trowbridge—tell me the particulars—I am sitting here in the little front room writing this—

Walt Whitman

1489. *To William Sloane Kennedy*

TRANSCRIPT.

Camden, Feb. 25, '87—Noon

Dear W. S. K.

It is of no importance whether I had read Emerson before starting L. of G. or not.[21] The fact happens to be positively that I had *not.* The basis and body and genesis of the L[eaves] differing I suppose from Em[erson] and many grandest poets and artists[—]was and is that I found and find everything in the *common concrete*, the broadcast materials, the flesh, the common passions, the tangible and visible, etc., and in *the average*, and that I radiate, work from, these outward—or rather hardly wish to leave here but to remain and celebrate it all. Whatever the

19. See 1489.

20. Jean O'Connor died in May 1883 (see 1220, *n.*65), about the time Bucke's *Walt Whitman* was being printed.

21. In *Reminiscences of Walt Whitman* Kennedy records at length conversations with Trowbridge in which the latter avers that "Emerson inspired the first poems of Whitman," and that WW had confided to him in 1860: "My ideas . . . were simmering and simmering, and Emerson brought them to a boil" (79–83).

amount of this may be or not be, it is certainly *not Emersonian*, not Shakspere, not Tennyson—indeed, the antipodes of E. and the others in essential respects. But I have not suggested or exprest myself well in my book unless I have in a sort included them and their sides and expressions too—as this orb the world means and includes all climes, all sorts, L. of G.'s word is *the body*, *including all*, including the intellect and soul; E.'s word is mind (or intellect or soul).

If I were to unbosom to you in the matter I should say that I never cared so very much for E.'s writings, prose or poems, but from his first personal visit and two hours with me (in Brooklyn in 1866 or '65?)[22] I had a strange attachment and love for *him* and his contact, talk, company, magnetism. I welcomed *him* deepest and always—yet it began and continued *on his part*, quite entirely; HE always sought ME. We probably had a dozen (possibly twenty) of these meetings, talks, walks, etc.—some five or six times (sometimes New York, sometimes Boston) had good long dinners together. I was very happy—I don't think I was at my best with him—he always did most of the talking—I am sure he was happy too. That visit to me at Sanborn's, by E. and family, and the splendid formal-informal family dinner *to me*, next day, Sunday, Sept. 18, '81, by E., Mrs. E. and all, I consider not only a victor-event in my life,[23] but it is an after-explanation of so much and offered as an apology, peace-offering, justification, of much that the world knows not of. My dear friend, I think I know R.W.E. better than anybody else knows him—and loved him in proportion, but quietly. Much was revealed to me.

Walt Whitman.

1490. *To William Sloane Kennedy, John Burroughs, and Richard Maurice Bucke*

TRANSCRIPT.

Camden, Feb. 25, '87, P.M.

Am sitting here by the window in the little front room down stairs, well wrapt up—for though bright & sunny it is a cold freezing day—have

22. WW meant to write "1855 or '56."

23. See 1058 and 1059.

24. The entry in *CB* on this date describes his emotional and physical state with a candor he rarely permitted himself in his letters: "Am I not having a 'happy hour,' or as near an approximation to it (the *suspicion* of it)—as is allowed?—(See p. 92—*Specimen Days* [*CP*, 133–134])—(Is it not largely or really good condition of the stomach, liver & excretory apparatus?)—I was quite ill all yesterday—(how quickly the thermometer

had my dinner (of rare stewed oysters, some toasted graham bread & a cup of tea—relished all)—am about as usual—ups & downs—had rather a bad day yesterday—lay on the lounge most of the day—now better—the worst is my enforced house-imprisonment, sometimes two weeks at a time —Spirits & heart though mainly gay, which is the best half of the battle[24] —Love & comfort to you, my friends—your wives & all—Write often as you can—(monotony is now the word of my life)—

Walt Whitman

When read send to John Burroughs, West Park, Ulster County, New York.[25]

1491. *To Thomas Jefferson Whitman*

ADDRESS: Thos: J Whitman | 4237[26] 2d Carondelet Av: | St Louis | Missouri. POSTMARKS: Camden | Feb | 27 | (?); Saint Louis | Mar | 1 | 8 AM | 1887 | Rec'd.

Camden Sunday P M | Feb: 27 '87

Rather pleasant to-day—sunny, but cold—Nothing new with me —I went over to Phila. one evening last week, & read two "Leaves" in public—pleasant ride there & back in carriage—was paid—Love to dear J[essie]—O how my canary is singing as I write—

Walt Whitman

1492. *To William Sloane Kennedy*

Camden March 1 '87 | 2½ P M

Your letter of Sunday has come, & I am glad to get those impromptu well filled yellow sheets—*write again*—I have not heard any more from O'Connor—when I do I will tell you—I write or send papers or something every day[27]—Have just had my dinner—a great piece of

slides up and down!)"

25. According to the auction record this letter was written on the verso of one from Eldridge to WW, undoubtedly the one of February 11 partially printed by Barrus, 262–263. The postscript is recorded only in the catalogue of the Anderson Gallery, November 25, 1927.

26. Corrected by another hand to read "2437."

27. Although WW made a similar notation in CB on February 25, there is no extant correspondence between the poet and O'Connor during this period.

toasted Graham bread salted & well buttered with fresh country butter, & then a lot of good panned oysters dumped over it, with the hot broth—then a nice cup custard & a cup of coffee—So if you see in the paper that I am *starving* (as I saw it the other day) understand how—I enclose Rhys's letter rec'd this morning[28]—As I understand it, Wilson is no more in the W[ilson] & McC[ormick] partnership, Glasgow, but sets up by himself—

Walt Whitman

1493. *To Susan Stafford* — *3.2. [1887?]*[29]

ADDRESS: Mrs: Susan Stafford | Kirkwood | (Glendale) | New Jersey. POSTMARK: Cam[d]en | Mar | 2(?) | 8 PM | 188(?) | N.J.

Camden March 2— | noon

Dear friend

The old story—nothing very new or different with me—Still jog along here as before—have been half sick a great part of this winter—yet every thing goes on comfortably with me—I am sitting here by the window down stairs, in my big chair, writing this—(the sun shining outside, & my little canary singing furiously in his cage in the corner)—I have occasional visitors—Wm Duckett is here yet—I don't get out much, the roads are so bad. Come up & see us & spend the day. George, stop when you come up. Susan, I enclose a letter Herbert sent me some months ago—nothing particular—Ed, I still wish to sell my mare—

W W

1494. *To Jessie Louisa Whitman* — *3.6. [1887]*

Camden March 6—12¼ P M

Just as I get ready to write you a line, Mrs. Davis calls me to dinner—So as that is important, I will put down the lap tablet on which I am writing—& finish afterwards—

Well I had my dinner, cold meat, hot potatoes, nice stew'd tomatoes & onions, & a cup of tea & Graham bread—enjoyed all—Am feeling pretty

28. Probably Rhys's letter of February 15 (Morgan), quoted in note 11.

29. 1887 appears to be a plausible date. In CB on February 25 WW wrote: "Half sick (or more than half) most of this month." However, he sold his nag and bought a mare from Edwin Stafford in March 1886 (see 1383, *n.*28); it is perhaps strange that he

well these times—a couple of Wilson Barrett's actors came over in a carriage yesterda fternoon & took me to the theatre to see "Clito"[30]—had a good aftern performance—was used tip top—Mrs Davis went with me— 't sunset thro' a snow storm—My friend Wm O'Conn way—locomotor ataxia—he is now in Los Ang

te, all white with snow—I havn't heard —but I am sure they are all right—

Walt Whitman

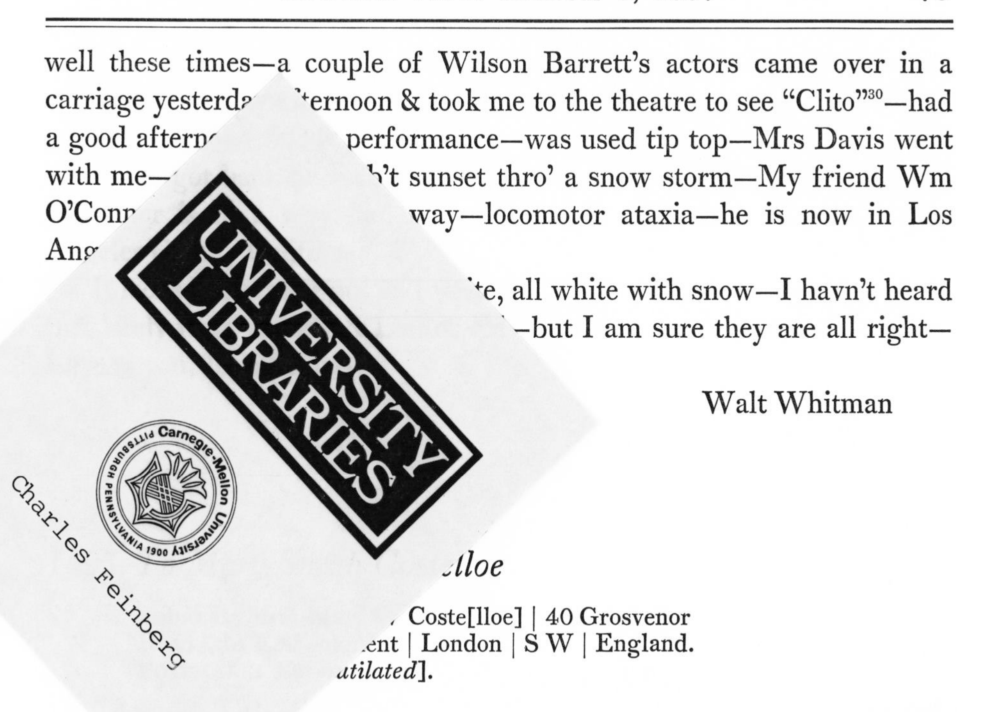

lloe

Coste[lloe] | 40 Grosvenor ent | London | S W | England. utilated].

Camden—U S America | March 6 '87

I ling fairly in health—& every thing goes comfortably these days—I went over to the theatre yesterday afternoon—had a good ride & jaunt & performance—"Clito"—Wilson Barret sent them for me—enjoyed the whole affair—have not had any letter from you now for some time—

Walt Whitman

1496. *To Alma Calder Johnston*

Camden | Sunday Afternoon March 6 '87

Am sitting here quietly—(rather dully)—to-day in the little down stairs room—nothing at all eventful or new with me—a dark sulky day outside, cold yet not quite cold enough to freeze—no visitors—have had my dinner & relished it with appetite—went over to the theatre yesterday afternoon—Wilson Barrett sent over a carriage for me & I had just a good ride, & liked the play "Clito"—Mrs. Davis went with me, & every thing

considered selling the mare a year later. The whereabouts of Duckett is not easy to trace since he held and gave up jobs frequently. On March 1, 1887, WW noted in *CB*: "W D still at Sewell practising."

30. Barrett and Miss Eastlake appeared in *Clito* at the Chestnut Street Opera House from March 2 to 5

was enjoyable—I was *made much of* & got back (thro' a snow storm) just before sunset—So you see I *do* get around some—(when I am helped—not much of my own volition)—Alma, I shall have to draw on your good nature to accept [this thin?] gossip for a letter—thank you for yours, & the girls' from Dresden, that came to me safely—Love to you & John—& Ally[31] & all—

Walt Whitman

1497. *To John H. Johnston*

ADDRESS: J. Johnston | Jeweler | 150 Bowery cor Br[oome] | New York City. POSTMARK: Camden | Mar 7 | 1887 | N.J.
TRANSCRIPT.

Camden | March 7 '87

Bless the dear baby, and all babies— Love to you & wife—

Walt Whitman

1498. *To William Sloane Kennedy* *3.9. [1887]*

ENDORSED (by Kennedy): "[1887]."

Camden March 9 noon

Much the same with me. No further news of O'Connor, (I forward the "Transcripts"[32] you send me, to him.) Rhys writes me that the Walter Scott, Eng[lish] pub's, will bring out my "Spec: Days" in one vol. & "Dem: Vistas, &c" in another.[33] I have just sent on a little preface to S D. I forward a Peora paper—when you have read it, mail to Dr Bucke. I have just had an autograph hunter visitor, but with cheery talk and presence.

Walt Whitman

31. Probably Albert Johnston (see 868). However, as the next letter indicates, the reference may be to a new child.

32. Copies of the Boston *Transcript*.

33. Rhys mentioned on February 15 (Morgan) that separate publication of the two works was about to be considered by the publisher. WW noted sending to Rhys a two-page preface to *Specimen Days* on March 8 and an "Additional Note" on March 15 (CB). In the same (missing) letter he included a receipt for the ten guineas which he had received on March 14 from Walter Scott.

34. Robert Buchanan's *A Look Round Literature* (1887) contains a chapter entitled "The American Socrates," "the wisest and noblest, the most truly great, of all

1499. *To William Sloane Kennedy*

TRANSCRIPT.

March 10, '87.

Yours came this morning with extract from Buchanan's book.[34] Thank you truly, such things are more help to me than you think. . . . Have just sent off two sets of 1876 ed'n to John Hay, of Washington, at his request.[35]

1500. *To William Sloane Kennedy, John Burroughs, and Richard Maurice Bucke* *3.16. [1887]*

ENDORSED (by Kennedy): "[Joint letter to myself, John Burroughs & Dr Bucke | sent first to me with request to forward]."
TRANSCRIPT.

Camden, March 16, A. M.

I send you the latest from our dear friend O'Connor not knowing whether you will get word directly[36]—I am having one of my bad spells, but it will probably pass over—I have had my breakfast, (two or three stewed oysters & a piece of toast)—am sitting here in the little front room down stairs—the sun is shining & my bird singing—I havent been out in many days[37]—pretty cold here—I recd a letter from J. B. Marvin,[37] his circular "Bureau of Information at Washington" &c—Washington—I am billed to read the Lincoln lecture in the Unitarian Church here, April 5—See if I can get there—God bless you all—

Walt Whitman.

modern literary men" (345): "We have a beautiful singer in Tennyson, and some day it will be among Tennyson's highest honours that he was once named kindly and appreciatively by Whitman" (346).

35. The historian (see 755, *n.*49) sent the poet $30 on March 12: "I am not giving you anything like what the writing is worth to me, but trying to give a just compensation for the trouble of copying, simply" (Traubel, III, 91). The envelope in which the manuscript of "O Captain! My Captain!" was sent is now in the Library of Congress.

36. According to Kennedy's notation on his transcription of this letter, it was written on the verso of one from Eldridge "describing the state of health of Wm D. O'Connor. Nervous prostration with a good deal of rheumatism."

37. According to CB he was able to take "a ride out" on March 21.

1501. *To Mary Smith Costelloe*

ADDRESS: Mrs: Costelloe | 40 Grosvenor Road | the Embankment | London England. POSTMARK: Camden | Mar | 18 | 6 PM | 1887 | N.J.

Camden N J—America | March 18 '87

I am under the weather again these days—(inaction, indigestion &c) but it will probably pass over with the week—Havn't seen any thing of any of your folks for many days—Logan however has just sent me a great parcel of reading matter by express—

Walt Whitman

1502. *To Joseph B. Gilder* *3.18. [1887]*

Camden March 18

Yes—I have rec'd such a letter from T[ennyson]—& do not object to your itemizing it—though it must be done carefully—Some such way as the following?

—Walt Whitman

Tennyson has written an affectionate and thankful letter to Walt Whitman on the comments of the latter—see *Critic* of Jan. 1st upon the supplementary 'Locksley Hall.' Is not this the only instance known of the English Laureate formally 'noticing a notice'?[38]

1503. *To Moncure D. Conway* *[3.19. 1887]*

ADDRESS: Moncure D Conway | care of G DeB Keim | 2009 DeLancey Place | Philadelphia. POSTMARKS: Camden | Mar 19 | 12 M | 1887 | N.J.; Received | Mar 19 | 1887 | 1 PM | Phila.

Camden New Jersey | 328 Mickle Street—
ab't 100 | rods from Federal st. ferry |
(from foot of Market St. Phila: Side)

Yes—I shall be home Sunday afternoon—Shall be glad to see you —Ab't 3 will be a good time—but suit your convenience[39]—

Walt Whitman

38. WW's letter was written on the verso of one from Gilder on March 17 in which he requested permission to mention the Tennyson letter of January 15 (Barrett; *The*

1504. *To Edward Carpenter*

TRANSCRIPT.

328 Mickle Street, | Camden, |
New Jersey, | U. S. A. |
March 22nd, 1887.

Dear E.C.,

I thought I would write you a line once more, but no particular news to send. Everything goes on much in the old way (and always has, and always will, I reckon, in this old world).

I am alive, and here, in the same locality, but pretty feeble. Wanted to thank you again, and more specifically, dear E.C., for the help you have so kindly sent me—you and my dear friends the two Misses Ford, to whom I send thanks and love.

I have just had my dinner, (buckwheat cakes, and tea, good). I am sitting here in the little front room downstairs writing this. Always love. Write.

Walt Whitman.

1505. *To Dr. Karl Knortz*

ADDRESS: Dr Knortz | 540 East 155th Street | New York City. POSTMARKS: Camden, N.J. | Mar 24 | 8 PM | 87; P.O. | 3–25–87 | 2 A | N.Y.

328 Mickle Street | Camden New Jersey
March 24 '87

I am still here, in good heart (good spirits) mainly—but almost entirely disabled & powerless to move ab't at all—Dr Bucke is well & active at his post in Canada—O'Connor is very ill, & is now in Southern California—W S Kennedy (Belmont, Mass:) has a book ab't me that is to be pub'd in Eng. soon—I am quiescent, but think of pub. in collected & revised form my pieces of last four years in a little book, "November Boughs"—

Walt Whitman

Princeton University Library Chronicle, III [November 1941], 6). On March 26, under "Notes," *The Critic* printed WW's suggested paragraph almost verbatim.

39. WW noted the visit in CB on March 20 without comment.

1506. *To Susan Stafford* 3.29. [*1887*]

ADDRESS: Mrs: Susan Stafford | Kirkwood | (Glendale) | New Jersey. POSTMARK: Camden, N.J. | Mar 29 | 6 PM | 87.

Camden March 29 Evn'g

Harry was here with me to-day[40]—He went to the hosp. to have his throat drest, & then to the RR station, to see J[oseph Browning] and D[ebbie][41] off. He is doing very well indeed.

I shall not be down next Sunday, but may the next, April 10, if it is pleasant—I am only middling.

Walt Whitman

1507. *To William Sloane Kennedy* 3.29. [*1887*]

ADDRESS: W. Sloane Kennedy | Belmont, Mass.

Camden, March 29 Evn'g

Somewhat under a cloud in physical condition & feelings these days—but will pass over I reckon—I am billed to give the "Death of Lincoln" lecture in New York, April 14—Same splurge here before the Unitarian Society April 5—A good letter lately from Rhys—Nothing further ab't O'Connor—

Walt Whitman

1508. *To Susan Stafford* [*3.31. 1887*][42]

ADDRESS: Mrs: Susan Stafford | Kirkwood | (Glendale) | New Jersey. POSTMARK: (?) | Mar (?)1 | 8 PM | 87.

Camden Thursday Evn'g

A snow-storm here as I write. I am not over my bad spell yet, but a little better perhaps—Harry is getting along very well—was up & had it dress'd & went home to Marlton in the 3' train. He is a little thin but looks well & I guess will be better than ever when it is all over—Love to you & George—

Walt Whitman

40. In CB on March 25 WW mentioned his visit to the hospital where Harry's "throat trouble" was being treated by a Dr. Westcott. On March 28 and 29 the young man stayed with the poet.

41. Deborah Browning was Harry's sister.

42. March 31 fell on Thursday in 1887.

42.1. This note was written on the galley proof of "Five Thousand Poems," which

1508.1 *To The Editor*, The Critic [*4(?).1(?).1887*]

TRANSCRIPT.

No errors. All correct. If convenient send me 8 or 10 proof slips like this.

Whitman, Camden, N. J.[42.1]

1509. *To Charles W. Eldridge*

ADDRESS: Charles W Eldridge | P O box 1705 | Los Angeles | California. POSTMARK: [Cam]den, N.J. | Apr 6 | 6 PM | 8(?); P[hila]del[phi]a | (?)r | 6 | 8 PM | Transit.

Camden New Jersey April 5 '87

Thanks, dear friend, for your letter—the third—from California & ab't William—Continue to write, for I am very anxious & look for the letters—I continue ab't the same—very feeble, but in good heart—Am to deliver the "*Death of Lincoln*" screed to-night before the Unitarians, here in Camden—& the 14th April in New York, (if I can get there,) the same lecture—Conway has been here to see me—I am writing & collating a paper ab't Elias Hicks[43]—Write soon—

Walt Whitman

1510. *To Herbert Gilchrist*

Camden—America—April 7 '87

Dear Herbert Gilchrist

The book came two days ago, & I have been looking over all of it, & reading a great part minutely—Surely it has been done well, & is a beautiful & (in one sense) sufficient memorial of the noblest mother & woman. It appeals to my printer-sense too—is a handsome & generous piece of typography & mechanical book making, with its excellent paper & press work—Thank you indeed, dear H, for sending me an early copy[44]—

George and Susan Stafford are still at Glendale—Debby and Jo have

appeared in *The Critic* on April 16.

43. In CB on February 25 WW had observed: "Am collecting 'Elias Hicks' these days."

44. WW noted receipt of *Anne Gilchrist* on April 5 (CB). On March 31 Herbert had informed the poet of the book's success in England and of his intended visit in May (Feinberg).

gone to Kansas—I was there last Sunday afternoon—they are well as usual—Harry has had a surgical operation on his throat—He now comes up from Marlton, (or Glendale) every day, to have the doctor watch & dress it—is a little reduced in flesh & blood, but is getting along well—Ed and Van and George are well—Mont is married[45]—(I went down Sunday to G[lendale] to take him (Harry) home, at his request)—I am still here in my shanty in Mickle street—probably *let down a peg or two* from when I saw you last, but not much different—mentally the same—physically a sad wreck—I am reciting my "Death of Abraham Lincoln" lecture when I get a call—(as this is the season)—go on to New York for that purpose April 14, if I can get there—had a good visit from Chas Rowley of Manchester yesterday[46]—

I am well as usual—Love to you—Spring is tardy here—My canary is singing blithely as I write—

Walt Whitman

1511. *To William Sloane Kennedy, John Burroughs, and Richard Maurice Bucke*

ENDORSED (by Kennedy): "Joint letter to Kennedy | Burroughs & Bucke."
TRANSCRIPT.

Camden | April 7 '87, | Evening.

Expect to go on to N. Y. to speak my piece [Lincoln Lecture] April 14. A friend[47] is to convoy me on—Alys Smith & other friends have been here to day.

Walt Whitman.

1512. *To John Burroughs*

TRANSCRIPT.

Camden, N. J., April 9, 1887.

Yours rec'd.—Yes, I am (expect to be) going on to N. Y. to deliver my piece April 14th. Dr. and Mrs. Bucke are not coming on—

45. Harry's brother Montgomery, according to *The Stafford Family*, married Josephine Ruff on October 28, 1886.

46. Charles Rowley came with an "introduction from Wm M Rossetti" (*CB*).

47. Robert Pearsall Smith.

48. WW's letter was written on the verso of one from Rhys dated March 29, in which Rhys informed the poet of the publishing plans for *Specimen Days* and expressed

rather think I shall return here next day. I am not very well, but much ab't as usual. Wm. O'C[onnor] is nearly the same as at last acct's—no worse.

Walt Whitman

1513. *To Robert Pearsall Smith(?)* *4.10.* [*1887*]

Camden | April 10 noon

Dear friend

I return you the cards signed—(Isn't there a mistake in the date? Ought it not to be marked right? Thursday Evn'g is the *14th*—not the 15th)—

If convenient I think I will go on from here say on the 9 a m train Thursday from the depot here—but come over to-morrow & let's have it fixed for certain—

Walt Whitman

1514. *To William Sloane Kennedy*

Camden April 11 '87—noon

Dear friend,

I send you Rhys's letter to me rec'd yesterday—Tho I suppose the disagreeable item in it, relating to the pub'n of y'r book, has been already written to you ab't by R[48]—My *under the weather spell* still continues, but with a slight let up—I expect to go on to New York to speak my "Death of Lincoln" piece, Thursday afternoon next—Probably the shake up will do me good—I drove over last evening to spend a couple of hours with my friends Mr & Mrs. Talcott Williams, Phila: & take dinner there—Enjoyed all—

I receive the *Transcripts* & look them over—then send them to O'Connor—I don't make much reckoning of the N Y performance—the best is to be borne in mind, (& warmly borne in mind) by a few dear N Y friends—Sunny & summery weather here & my canary is singing like a house afire—

Walt Whitman

gratitude for the new material included in the edition (reprinted in *November Boughs*, 93–95). *Democratic Vistas* and WW's recent prose writings were to appear in a separate volume six months later (Barrett).

Frederick W. Wilson, the Scottish publisher, informed Rhys on March 28 that he could not because of illness undertake publication of Kennedy's book at present (Trent). Rhys included the note in a letter to Kennedy on the following day and promised to look for another publisher (Trent).

1515. *To John Burroughs*

Camden April 12 '87 | A M

Dear friend

Yours of yesterday rec'd this morning—I shall leave here in the 4:30 P M Camden via Trenton to N Y train to-morrow, Wednesday, & expect to be in Jersey City by or before 7, early evening—A friend, R. Pearsall Smith, is convoying me, & I understand I am to go with him to the Westminster Hotel, for the night—Yes, meet me in Jersey City—I shall expect you—the young man Wm Duckett is coming on with me—I am feeling better than for the last two weeks, & shall go through with the lecture, according to announcement—I am to have, (according to wish & arrangement of Mr Smith) a reception at Westminster Hotel, Thursday evening—returning here Friday—Best love & thanks—

Walt Whitman

1516. *To Susan Stafford*

Camden April 12 '87.

Dear friend

I send you Herbert's last letter[49]—he expects to come over in May—He has sent me his book ab't Mrs. G—It is very interesting—Shall I bring or send it down for you to read, or have you one?

Harry left here ab't an hour ago—he went up to the Hospital to-day, & the throat was operated on again—but he feels pretty well & in good spirits—I am sorry to hear George and Ed are not well—I hope they will be over the worst of it, & indeed all right by this time—I am going to New York to-morrow evn'g, to return Friday—If I live through it all I may drive down next Sunday if it is pleasant—

Walt Whitman

49. WW wrote on the verso of Gilchrist's letter of March 31; see 1510.

50. The lecture was a tremendous success, and WW was so showered with adulation that he observed in *CB*: "If I had staid longer, I sh'd have been killed with kindness & compliments." The arrangements for the lecture were made by John H. Johnston; see his letter to WW on March 24 (Feinberg; Traubel, II, 431). The poet stayed at the Westminster Hotel in a suite once occupied by Dickens, where on April 13 he was visited by such old friends as Johnston, Burroughs, Stedman, and Richard Watson Gilder. At the Madison-Square Theatre on the next day he was escorted on stage by

1517. *To Thomas Jefferson Whitman* 4.13. [1887]

ADDRESS: Thos: J. Whitman | 2437 2d Carondelet Avenue | St Louis Missouri. POSTMARKS: Camden, N.J. | Apr 13 | 8 PM | 87; Saint Louis(?) | Apr | 15 | 7 AM | 1887 | Rec'd.

Camden April 13 12:40 P M

Am middling well—go this afternoon to New York, to deliver my lecture commemorative of "the Death of Abraham Lincoln" to-morrow afternoon there—Return here Friday—Love to you & Jess—Lou was here lately—all well—

Walt Whitman

1518. *To William Sloane Kennedy* [4.13. 1887]

ENDORSED (by Kennedy): "1887 | April 13."

Camden Wednesday 12:40 | P M

Am feeling fairly—Start in some three hours in the train for New York—to lecture to-morrow afternoon—Return here Friday—

Walt Whitman

1519. *To William Sloane Kennedy* 4.15. [1887]

New York—Westminster Hotel | April 15—a m

All went off smoothly—Lincoln lecture yesterday afternoon, (good audience) & reception last evening.[50] I return to Camden this afternoon—

Walt Whitman

1520. *To the Proprietor, Westminster Hotel*

ADDRESS: Proprietor | Westminster Hotel | Irving Place | New York City. POSTMARK: Camden, N.J. | Apr 16 | 3 PM | 87.

Camden April 16 '87

By oversight I left a book "*Poets of America*,"[50.1] by E C Stedman

William Duckett and gave his lecture before an audience that included James Russell Lowell, John Hay, Augustus Saint-Gaudens, and Andrew Carnegie. After his speech he received "two or more hundred friends" at Westminster Hotel, appearing "little fatigued," according to the New York *Evening Sun*. On the following day he sat for C. O. Cox, the photographer, and Dora Wheeler, "portrait painter" (Barrus, 264–265). A lengthy notice appeared in the *New York Times* on April 15. For this lecture WW received $600, $250 from the sale of tickets and $350 from Carnegie.

50.1. The book was inscribed "New York April 14th 1887" (Traubel, I, 70).

—in my room in the hotel, Friday last—Won't you hunt it up, & kindly send it to J H Johnston's, Jewelry store, 150 Bowery, cor: Broome st. for me?

Walt Whitman

1521. *To John H. Johnston*

ADDRESS: John H Johnston | Diamond Merchant | 150 Bowery cor: Broome St | New York City. POSTMARKS: Camden, N.J. | Apr 18 | 12 M | 87; P O | 4–18–87 | 5 (?) | N.Y.

Camden New Jersey | April 18 1887

Both yours rec'd—Major Pond has sent me $250—I came thro' Friday Evn'g in good order, & am now here—Chewing on my good time in N Y—& that every thing went off so well—

Walt Whitman

1522. *To Major James B. Pond*

ADDRESS: Major James B. Pond | Everett House | cor: 4th Av: & 17th Street | New York City. POSTMARKS: (?) N.J. | (?) | 12 M | 87; D | 4–18–87 | 5–1P | N.Y.

328 Mickle Street | Camden New Jersey | April 18 1887

Dear Sir

Yours of 16th with $250 (for my lecture of Thursday afternoon preceding) safely rec'd—& this is the receipt. Thanks—

Walt Whitman

Will write you again in a day or two—

1523. *To William Sloane Kennedy*

328 Mickle Street | Camden N J April 19 '87

Am here in my little old shanty again, & every thing ab't as usual

51. The draft of this letter (Feinberg) contains a final sentence not transcribed in the original: "I arrived [in Camden?] Friday, before suns[et—took a] carriage from the S[tation]."

—Stood it very well in N Y—it was a good break f'm my monotonous days here, but if I had stayed long, I sh'd have been killed with kindness & attention—I rec'd $250—Y'rs just come. Thanks—

Walt Whitman

1524. *To Susan Stafford* *4.19.* [*1887*]

ADDRESS: Mrs: Susan Stafford | Kirkwood | (Glendale) | New Jersey. POSTMARK: Camden, N.J. | Apr 19(?) | 8 PM | 87.

Camden Tuesday Evn'g 19 Ap

Harry has been here—is in good spirits & is surely getting along very well—I am getting over my New York spree—Count on seeing you here to-morrow.

Walt Whitman

1525. *To Richard Watson Gilder*

328 Mickle Street | Camden New Jersey
April 20 '87

Dear R W G

Yours enclosing Mr Carnegie's magnificent contribution to me (& to the Lincoln memory lecture) of $350 has safely come to hand. I thank A[ndrew] C[arnegie] from my heart—The money, of course, will help me every way & practically, & is appreciated for its source in kindest human good will.

I thank you, too, dear friend—your faithful heart & voice—I wish this note sent to Mr Carnegie with my gratitude and love.[51]

Walt Whitman

1526. *To William Sloane Kennedy* *4.20.* [*1887*]

Camden April 20 noon

Thank you specially for sending me the Mrs Gilchrist book review in Boston Herald[51.1]—send one directed *Herbert H Gilchrist, 12 Well*

According to the *Pall Mall Gazette* of May 6, Carnegie was reported to have said: "When the *Pall Mall Gazette* raised a subscription for Walt Whitman, I felt triumphant democracy disgraced" (*AL*, XXXIII [1961], 70).

51.1. A two-and-one-half column review appeared in the *Sunday Herald* of April 17.

Road, Hampstead, London Eng—Fine sunshine here as I write & I am feeling well—

Walt Whitman

1527. *To John H. Johnston* 4.20. [*1887*]

ADDRESS: John H. Johnston | Diamond Merchant | 150 Bowery cor: Broome St: | New York City. POSTMARK: Camden, N.J. | Apr | (?) | 1 30 PM | 87.

Camden April 20 noon

I am well as usual—I rec'd this morning (through Gilder) a check from Andrew Carnegie for $350 for his box, last Thursday night—making my N Y lecture recompense me $600—Love to you, Alma, Al & the dear little boys—(see *Harper's Weekly* April 23)[52]—

Walt Whitman

(I sent Mr Chandler his L of G. yesterday)[53]

1528. *To Major James B. Pond*

ADDRESS: Major James B Pond | Everett House | New York City. POSTMARKS: Camden, N.J. | Ap (?) | 12 (?) | 87; P.O. | 4–21–87 | 4–1P | N.Y.

Camden April 20, '87

My dear Major

Mr Gilder of the *Century* has just sent me Andrew Carnegie's check for $350 for his box—Making my remuneration $600 for the lecture—

Walt Whitman

52. *Harper's Weekly* for this date contained a chatty column on WW's preference for Walter Scott's poetry ("The only poetry that had nourished him"), his daily reading of the Bible, and his fondness for children who loved "Uncle Walt."

53. Arthur D. Chandler, of the Christian Union in New York, sent $3 for the book (CB).

54. According to Kennedy, whose transcription is the only available text, the letter was written on the verso of one from Eldridge to WW on April 14 discussing O'Connor's illness and his indignation over Higginson's articles in *Harper's Bazar:* "It is fortunate for Higginson that I am sick." On March 5 Higginson wrote about the "proposed pension

1529. *To William Sloane Kennedy, John Burroughs, and Richard Maurice Bucke*

TRANSCRIPT.

Camden—April 21, '87[54]

. . . I go over this afternoon at urgent request of my friend R. P. Smith—to some quarters in Arch St. provided for me, where I believe I am to be sculp'd by St. Gaudens, the sculptor.[55] I rec'd $600. for my N. Y. reading. Andrew Carnegie (thro' Gilder) paid $350 for his box. . . . I have eaten a good breakfast with zest.

Walt Whitman

1530. *To Charles W. Eldridge*

328 Mickle Street | Camden New Jersey
April 21 '87

Dear C W E

Yours came this forenoon, & was read & reread, & dispatched on the round to Kennedy, John Burroughs, & Dr. Bucke—all so anxious to get definite news from William. It somehow seems the most encouraging yet—God grant our dear friend may indeed get complete recovery—Write often as you can, dear friend. With me & my affairs no great ripple—I am worldlily comfortable & in good physical condition as usual of late—I went on to New York—was convoyed by my dear old Quaker friend R Pearsall Smith—had a success at the lecture 14th (netted $600 for my self—Andrew Carnegie gave $350 for his box)—had a stunning *reception*—I think 300 people, many ladies—that evn'g Westminster Hotel—newspapers friendly, everybody friendly even the authors—& returned here Friday 4 p m train from N Y. in good order—Am going over to Phila: this p m to be sculp'd by St Gaudiens, the N Y sculptor who has come on, to do it—Signs of spring rather late, but here—I am call'd to dinner (baked shad)—

Walt Whitman.

for Mr. Whitman, the poet; although he is not wholly an instance in point, having been a man of conspicuously fine physique, but who deliberately preferred service in the hospitals rather than in the field." On March 26, in "Women and Men. The Victory of the Weak," Higginson supported Lanier's attack upon the "dandyism" in WW's depiction of the "roughs."

55. Apparently WW did not sit for Augustus Saint-Gaudens (1848–1907), since the entry in CB on the following day made no reference to the sculptor, who had attended the New York lecture. However, he met Martha Carey Thomas (1857–1935), at this time professor of English at Bryn Mawr College.

1531. *To Jeannette L. Gilder*

ADDRESS: Miss Jeannette Gilder | *Critic* office | 743 Broadway | New York City. POSTMARKS: Camden, N.J. | Apr (?) | 12 (?) | 87; P.O. | 4–21–87 | 4(?) | (?).

328 Mickle Street | Camden New Jersey | April 21 '87

I sh'd like all the proofs—(*all* that are taken, without exception)[56] —sent to me here—I will return them, with what I have to say—Send them flat—if convenient—

Hand this note to Mr Cox—I am all right—rec'd $600 for my lecture. Andrew Carnegie sent me $350 for his box—

Walt Whitman

1532. *To William Sloane Kennedy*

Philadelphia April 22 '87

Have come over here on a few days' visit to R P Smith on Arch street—Enjoy all—Have just had my dinner—Mr S is one of my kindest friends. Y'r letters rec'd—always welcomed. The Gilchrist book seems to be making quite a ripple—Y'r comments on it I tho't tip top—

Walt Whitman

1533. *To Harry Stafford* *4.26. [1887]*

Camden Tuesday noon | April 26

Harry boy, we have missed you two or three days, & both I & Mrs D[avis] wondered & wanted you—but Ed has been here this forenoon & says you are not coming up any more to have the cut dress'd—So I hope it is healing all right & will be no more trouble—Nothing new or special with me—Sold one of my books to-day,[57] which helps along—Am not feeling quite as well as usual—(but nothing particularly bad)—Pretty

56. Apparently proofs of the pictures taken by Cox on April 15 (see 1519, *n.*50).
57. WW sent a copy of *Leaves of Grass* to Edgar R. Tratts (?) in Dublin (CB).
58. The diners included Thomas B. Harned, James Matlack Scovel, Judge Hugg, and William Duckett (CB). WW had also gone to Thompson's at Gloucester, N. J., on April 24, 1886 (see 1393).
59. Lloyd, not Logan, Smith (see 1185, *n.*11).
60. "The Good Gray Poet Is White Now," an account of the New York lecture.
61. Carpenter's letter of April 20 had the awe-stricken and confessional tone

dull—If I did not have naturally good spirits I don't know what would become of me, run in here like a rat in a cage day in & day out—But I must not growl—it might be so much worse—If the weather is good I shall be down to Glendale Sunday next—Love to E[va] and little D[ora]—

Walt Whitman

1534. *To William Sloane Kennedy* *4.29.* [*1887*]

Camden April 29 a m

Feeling pretty fair to-day. Drove down yesterday four miles to "Billy Thompson's," on the Delaware river edge, to a nice dinner, baked shad & champagne *galore*—jolly company—enjoy'd all with moderation[58] —No, the Mr Smith, my liberal & faithful Quaker friend, is R Pearsall Smith (glass manufacturer & man of wealth) father of Mrs. Costelloe, my staunchest living woman friend—the Librarian Logan Smith,[59] (now dead) was his brother—Did you see the N. Y. Eve. Sun of 15th Ap[ril]?[60]

W W

1535. *To an Unidentified Correspondent*

TRANSCRIPT.

Camden, May 2, 1887

[WW thanks his correspondent for the gift of "Every-Day Life of Abraham Lincoln."] I shall keep it by me for my own reading, & to refresh my memory of those turbulent days.

1536. *To Edward Carpenter*

ADDRESS: Edward Carpenter | Commonwealth Café | Scotland Street | Sheffield England. POSTMARK: Camden, N.J. | May 3 | 12 M | 87.

328 Mickle St—Camden New Jersey |
U S America May 3 '87

Yours of Ap: 20 just rec'd & welcomed.[61] Write oftener—The Staffords & I remember you with greatest affection & esteem—I also with

characteristic of WW's youthful admirers: "Dear old Walt—I was right glad to get your card and find you hadn't forgotten me; and that you still keep going along, fairly cheerful." Carpenter went on to relate: "I have had a baddish time the last few days, and feel tired out & sick. A very dear friend of mine—we have been companions day & night for many months now—has taken to girl whom I can't say I much care for. . . . Just now I feel as if I had lost him, and am rather dumpy—tho' I don't know that it will be altogether bad in the end" (Feinberg). WW received £25 from Carpenter on May 23 (*CB*).

deepest gratitude—I am still here in the same little old house—of course gradually sinking & dissolving—Harry S[tafford] had a surgical operation on his throat—it seems to have been properly done, & the cut is healing—He is at Marlton, New Jersey, married, has a child—I send you some papers—always best love—

Walt Whitman

1537. *To Susan Stafford*

Camden Tuesday morning | May 3 '87

Dear friend

I got home all right Sunday afternoon—had a nice enjoyable ride —enjoyed my visit anyhow—Yesterday I felt pretty dry, up in my room, & made a glass of drink, water, sugar & vinegar—from that bottle you gave me—such as I remember my dear mother[62] making sixty years ago, for my father, of a hot day, when I was a little boy—& my drink went well too—

Nothing new of any importance with me—Send you enclosed a letter just rec'd from Edward Carpenter—the dear good young man—I have just written him a few lines—told him ab't Harry—

Warm & sunny to-day & I am sitting here with my window open—Mrs. D[avis] is off to Phil. & I shall be here alone all the forenoon. The bird is singing—the cars are puffing & rattling, & the children of the neighborhood are all outdoors playing—So I have music enough—Best love to you all—

Walt Whitman

1538. *To Dr. Karl Knortz*

ADDRESS: Dr Karl Knortz | 540 East 155th Street | New York City. POSTMARKS: Camden, N.J. | May 3 | 4:30 PM | 87; P.O. | 5–3–87 | 12(?) | N.Y.

328 Mickle Street | Camden New Jersey
May 3 '87

Your letter rec'd & welcomed as always—My visit to N Y was a hasty flash only—I am more & more wretchedly physically disabled, & feel

62. On May 23 WW noted in *CB* the "anniversary of dear mother's death—1873."

63. On April 25 Pond proposed to WW a reading in Boston on May 10 (Feinberg).

64. On May 2 WW sent "November Boughs" to James Knowles, editor of

better off here in my own den—the "Anne Gilchrist" book is a wonderfully well done Vol. & interesting very to me because I knew & loved Mrs. G—but I doubt whether it contains much (or any thing) for you—I can loan you my copy if you wish—I will certainly keep you posted ab't myself, or any literary movement or change or happening of my work—

Walt Whitman

1539. *To Charles W. Eldridge*

TRANSCRIPT.

Camden, May 6, 1887

. . . After reading I send your letters to W. S. Kennedy, who sends them to John Burroughs, who sends them to Dr. Bucke. . . . I continue ab't usual—a little minus perhaps—Spring here the last week—

Walt Whitman

1540. *To William Sloane Kennedy, John Burroughs, and Richard Maurice Bucke*

TRANSCRIPT.

Camden | May 6th 1887

Major Pond has written to me fixing dates for my proposed Boston (including I believe Hartford & New Haven) lecturing tour[63]—but I am a little fearful, & have not answered & closed with him. I go out driving every day. Have just sent a poem to the *Nineteenth Century*.[64] Love to you all.

Walt Whitman

1541. *To an Unidentified Correspondent* [*5.6(?). 1887*]

DRAFT LETTER.

You must excuse the liberty I take in introducing the young man who will hand you this—a conductor on the W P City R R & a particular

Nineteenth Century, and asked £22 (CB). Knowles returned the poems on May 19 (Feinberg; Traubel, I, 28). Thereupon WW sent them on May 31 to Walsh of *Lippincott's Monthly Magazine*, where they appeared in November. WW was paid $50 (CB).

friend of mine—who will explain the reason of his call. Pray listen to what he has to say.[65]

1542. *To Robert Pearsall Smith* *5.15. [1887]*

ADDRESS: R Pearsall Smith | 1307 Arch Street | Philadelphia. POSTMARK: Camden, N.J. | May 16 | 6 AM | 87.

Camden Sunday afternoon | May 15

Am ab't as usual—get out a little, (with the horse & wagon) but not much. As I write the mocking-bird is singing over the way, & my canary—Love to A[lys] and L[ogan]—

Walt Whitman

1543. *To William Sloane Kennedy* *5.16. [1887]*

ENDORSED (by Kennedy): "87."

Camden May 16 Evn'g

Nothing different or new—I am so-so—up and around—Sidney Morse[66] from your way is here *sculping* me—(full length, seated in big chair—goes on well so far)—Fine weather here—I am seated near the open window writing this—Shall probably go out for a drive of an hour or two after supper—

Walt Whitman

1544. *To Susan Stafford* *5.16. [1887]*

ADDRESS: Mrs: Susan Stafford | Kirkwood | (Glendale) | New Jersey. POSTMARK: Camden, N.J. | May 16 | 8 PM | 87.

Camden Monday Evn'g | May 16

Nothing very new with me—I am not very well—but around as usual—Go out driving a little most every day—Herbert will soon be here.

65. This draft appears in a notebook at Yale with the following also in WW's hand: "Sir | Feeling that I am competent & determined to give satisfaction I hereby apply for an appointment under you on the road | W H Duckett | May 6 '87." Undoubtedly Duckett was expected to make a copy of the letter.

66. Morse was from 1866 to 1872 editor of *The Radical*, in which appeared Mrs. Gilchrist's "A Woman's Estimate of Walt Whitman" (*Corr.*, II, 98–99*n*). Later Morse became a self-taught sculptor. From September 7 to 14, 1876, he was in Philadelphia making a bust of WW (*CB*). On February 16, 1879, the poet noted the "head rec'd—bad

In his last letter he said he sh'd start soon[67]—Have not seen Harry for over a week—Come up & see us.

W W

1545. *To William Sloane Kennedy* *5.23.* [*1887*]

ENDORSED (by Kennedy): "[87]."

Camden May 23

Nothing very notable with me—Hot weather here—Sidney Morse continues *at me* (sculping the full-length figure, big rocking chair) & seems succeeding—I am so-so in health—

Walt Whitman

1546. *To Sylvester Baxter*

328 Mickle Street | Camden New Jersey
May 25 '87

Thanks & God bless you, my dear Sylvester Baxter, for your kind project for me—(whether it comes to a fulfilment or not)[68]—

I am feeling pretty well as I write—Should most gratefully accept & most intensely enjoy a little spot of my own to live in 6 or 8 months of the 12 in country air, so pined for by me—As it is I cannot go to a hotel, nor visiting either—although I have many & kindest invitations—I want a cheap ¼ or ½ acre & 4-or-5-room house, spot & design selected by myself—

If convenient let Sloane Kennedy & Dr Bartol[69] read this—& God bless you all—

Walt Whitman

—wretchedly bad" (CB). In 1882 Horace Traubel asked to become an apprentice, and on January 10 Morse replied: "I am only a dabbler" (Feinberg). At the time he was making cemetery monuments. Morse spent most of 1887 preparing busts of the poet; see Morse's "My Summer with Walt Whitman," in *In Re*, 367–391.

67. Gilchrist informed WW on May 27 of his arrival in New York (Feinberg).

68. Boston friends decided to raise money for what Kennedy called "The Timber Creek Cottage Project." See Kennedy, 10–11.

69. Dr. C. A. Bartol was one of the contributors to the Cottage Fund; see Traubel, II, 299.

1547. *To William Sloane Kennedy*

Camden May 25 '87

Rec'd Rhys's note ab't the book & Symonds[70]—Rec'd S[ylvester] B[axter]'s letter & project for me (or *your* project for me)—Should gratefully accept. I am well as usual—hot here—am sitting here by the window as I write—ate my dinner with appetite—heard from O'Connor day before yesterday—news unfavorable—

Whitman

1548. *To Susan Stafford*

ADDRESS: Mrs: Susan Stafford | Kirkwood | (Glendale) | New Jersey. POSTMARK: Camden, (?) | May 2(?) | 3 P(?) | 8(?).

Camden | Saturday 2 P M May 28 '87

Dear friend

I send you the within, just rec'd from Herbert G.[71]—I have an idea that he will be on here Monday or Tuesday—If the spirit moves me & the weather is fine, I may come down Sunday, (before you get this)—but possibly not—so I tho't I w'd send you the present screed—Showery & almost cool here the last two days. As I write, the sun is out, & my bird singing—I have had my dinner, mutton-stew, onions, & greens—(I used the vinegar you gave me, on 'em—good—the bottle is most all gone, & I shall bring it down to be fill'd up)—I have not felt as well as usual the last three days—we had it hot & disagreeable enough here previous—Susan, come up here & stay awhile & visit us—George too—Mrs. D[avis] would be glad too—Lord be easy with you both—

Walt Whitman

An old southern farmer, John Newton Johnson,[72] has come up here from Alabama, 700 miles, to see me, & is here now. He is the queerest,

70. Probably Kennedy sent on Rhys's letter of March 29, in which the latter spoke of writing to Symonds for his assistance in publishing Kennedy's book (Trent). See also 1514.

71. A letter from New York on May 27 (Feinberg).

72. WW's "philosophical" friend from Alabama apparently arrived in Camden about May 18 for a visit that lasted almost five weeks. WW was at first charmed by Johnson's eccentricities (see the interview in the Camden *Courier* on May 19; Kennedy, 18–19), but later became somewhat annoyed (see 1577). For a summary of Johnson's amusing correspondence with WW, see 660, *n.*18, and *In Re*, 376–378.

73. Mrs. Charles Fairchild (see 1241) was assisting in the Boston fund raising.

74. Johnston and James W. Wallace, two fervid admirers from Bolton, England,

wildest 'cutest mortal you ever saw—has a boy 12 y'rs old named Walt Whitman—

1549. *To William Sloane Kennedy* [*5.28. 1887*]

ENDORSED (by Kennedy): "May 28 | ['87]."

Camden Saturday | 3 P M

Showery & coolish here the last two days—I am now sitting here by the open window—have had my dinner, eaten with relish—Sidney Morse is still here working—You shall see a photo of the figure he has made of me soon. Herbert Gilchrist is here in America. The news from O'Connor is unfavorable. I suppose you rec'd the pictures I sent for Mrs. F[airchild][73]—

Walt Whitman

1550. *To Dr. John Johnston*

ADDRESS: John Johnston M D | 54 Manchester Road | Bolton | England. POSTMARK: Camden, N.J. | May 2(?) | 3 PM | 87.

U S America—Camden New Jersey | May 29 '87—328 Mickle Street

Your good affectionate letter, with the welcome carte pictures & the handsome birthday present, safely rec'd this morning—& thank you for all most sincerely—I am living here comfortably enough, but a paralytic bodily—As I write I sit by the open window of my room, the birds singing & summer bursting—Again thanks[74]—

Walt Whitman

wrote to WW for the first time about the middle of May and sent a birthday gift of £10 ($48.70) (*CB*). "We, two friends chiefly united by our common love of you, wish to congratulate you on your birthday, and express to you personally our very best wishes and love. To you we owe not only affection but endless gratitude and reverence. One of us, a doctor, owes to you entirely his spiritual enfranchisement and deliverance from soul-benumbing scepticism, into which—not without pain—he had gradually fallen. Your books are his constant companions, his spiritual nourishment, his continual study and delight. . . .

"The other in many obstructions and difficulties is strengthened and comforted by your example and words. In past heavy bereavement (of a mother to whom he has often mentally applied the words you use of yours) *your* words have best tallied his deepest experiences and hopes . . ." (Bolton).

1551. *To J. W. Wallace*

ADDRESS: J W Wallace | 14 Engle Street | Bolton England. POSTMARK: Camden, N.J. | May 2(?) | 3 PM | 87.

U.S. America, Camden New Jersey | May 29 '87 328 Mickle St.

Your & Dr Johnston's letter & the pictures & birthday gift have safely reach'd me, & thank you indeed from my heart—I am ab't as usual in health—& a little (but not much) engaged in writing—Your letter is indeed comforting to one—

Walt Whitman

1552. *To The Editors of* The Critic *and Elizabeth Porter Gould*

328 Mickle Street | Camden New Jersey | May 30 '87

I wish to warmly thank Elizabeth Porter Gould and yourselves for the article ab't myself & the war hospitals[75]—Nothing I have received has touch'd me deeper or been more comforting & agreeable to me.

If convenient I sh'd like to have you send this note to E P G. with my thanks and regards—

Walt Whitman

1553. *To Talcott Williams*

ADDRESS: Talcott Williams | office *Press* newspaper | cor: 7th & Chestnut | Philadelphia. POSTMARK: Camden, N.J. | May 31 | 10 AM | (?).

328 Mickle Street | Camden New Jersey May 31 '87

My dear T W

Will you do something for me, in the *Press* office, if not too much trouble? Get a certain MS of mine "A poet's 68th year" (3 or 4 pages) I

75. *The Critic* on May 28 printed her article "Walt Whitman Among the Soldiers," and on June 1 sent her a check for $8 along with WW's letter (Boston Public Library). For WW's opinion of Miss Gould, see Traubel, IV, 360–361.

76. On this date WW recorded the following in *CB*: "To day I begin my 69th year —almost altogether disabled in walking power & bodily movement—writing & composition

sent ten days ago directed "W R Merrill managing editor &c," of which no notice has been taken, & reënclose said MS to me here—

Yours as always—

Walt Whitman

Come over & see me—

1554. *To Susan Stafford* 6.1. [*1887*]

ADDRESS: Mrs: Susan Stafford | Kirkwood | (Glendale) | New Jersey. POSTMARK: Camden, N.J. | Jun 1 | 1 30 PM | 87.

Camden June 1 Noon

No Herbert yet, but he is in N Y city & I look for him every hour—Nothing new with me—Rainy & mild here this forenoon—How are you getting along?

I am not very well—Kind o' half & half—I shall be driving down (for two or three hours) soon as the roads are good[76]—

Walt Whitman

1555. *To an Unidentified Correspondent*

TRANSCRIPT.

Camden, June 2, 1887

[A letter of thanks for a birthday present.]

1556. *To William Sloane Kennedy* 6.3. [*1887*]

ENDORSED (by Kennedy): "['87]."

Camden New Jersey | June 3—P M

Yours of June 1 rec'd this afternoon—Thanks—best & joyfulest thanks to you & Baxter & all—I will write to you to-morrow, (or next

power fair—hand-writing power pretty good—appetite fair—sleep fair to middling, not markedly bad, & not really good—weigh 200 over— . . . I sit in the big arm chair nearly all the time—read & (partially) write much or rather most of the time—Sidney Morse here sculping the full length sitting figure in rocking chair from life—seems to me I like it well—O'Connor in So: California, sick—frequent visitors & some dear friends call to see me—." (A photograph of the sculpture is the frontispiece to Traubel's third volume.)

day,) after thinking it over a bit, & tell you detailedly—at present I have not settled on spot—but am fill'd with gratitude & pleasure at the prospect of having a country or perhaps sea shore shanty of my own—

Walt Whitman

1557. *To Susan Stafford* *6.3. [1887]*

ADDRESS: Mrs: Susan Stafford | Kirkwood | (Glendale) | New Jersey. POSTMARK: Camden, N.J. | Jun (?) | 4 30 PM | 87.

Camden June 3 3½ P M

Herbert has arrived & I think of driving down with him either to-morrow (Saturday) or on Sunday[77]—He is here & is just going around to a boarding house on 4th St. to see if he can get quarters. I am not well, but nothing of importance—Love to you & George & Ed & all—

W W

1558. *To Ernest Rhys*

ADDRESS: Ernest Rhys | care Walter Scott publishing | Co: 24 Warwick Lane Paternoster | row | London England. POSTMARK: Camden, N.J. | Jun 9 | 6 AM | 87.

Camden New Jersey U S America | June 8 '87

Yours of May 24 (with the printed slips Preface & Add'l Note) rec'd[78]—& welcomed, as always—nothing further rec'd, but I suppose some books will be coming soon. Thank you for the "Buchan's Ballads"[79] bro't by Herbert Gilchrist—I specially enjoy such things—I am ab't as usual (perhaps a little under a cloud, passing, I hope)—we hear from dear Mrs. C[ostelloe][80] and the birth of the child (*Rachel*—good name)—Mr S[mith] will be over there, almost with this—he is a very dear & valued friend of mine—Alys too—

Walt Whitman

77. Gilchrist went to see the Staffords on June 5, Sunday (CB).

78. Rhys informed WW on May 24 that the English edition of *Specimen Days* was now in the bookshops, and that Symonds, Mrs. Costelloe, and Gabriel Sarrazin, a young French critic, had been given copies (Feinberg; Traubel, III, 59–61).

79. Probably *Ancient Ballads and Songs of the North of Scotland* (1875), collected and edited by Peter Buchan (1790–1854).

80. Rhys had become a fervent admirer of Mrs. Costelloe. On March 29 he wrote to

1559. *To William Sloane Kennedy* 6.9. [*1887*]

ENDORSED (by Kennedy): "['87]."

Camden N J June 9 Evn'g

Your card of yesterday rec'd. Best thanks—I am feeling unwell & stupid, dont want to think or talk these times—shall emerge soon, & then define what I spoke of in my last card—Do *not* come on personally as that would not facilitate—My *Specimen Days in America* (no "Collect") is out in London in a very pretty shilling Vol—with a short Pref: & add'l note for Engl: readers—I shall have some vols. & will send you one—Tell Rhys to try Sonnenschien & Co: Paternoster Sq: to publish your book—Herbert Gilchrist & Morse are here—hot to-day—

Walt Whitman

1560. *To Mary Smith Costelloe* 6.13. [*1887*]

Camden Monday June 13 | 5½ P M

Dear Mary Costelloe

I will write you a few lines without any thing to say, but because the spirit moves me & every thing is so beautiful & peaceful in the nearly declined but dazzling sun—The little children are playing out on the walks, a mocking-bird is singing over the way, & a young just-bursting magnolia blossom, (sent me an hour ago by the grocery woman at the corner) fills the room with its spicy fragrance, from its glass of water on the window-sill—I have been somewhat under a cloud physically the last week, but feel better to day—& the best of it is a sort of consciousness (if it don't deceive me) of being better for good—at any rate for the time, wh' is as much as could be asked for—

I have written & sent a poem to *Lippincotts*—wh' has been accepted, & I have got the money for it, (& great good it does me, coming now)—Herbert Gilchrist is here—he is drawing & painting my portrait to-day—Sidney Morse has modelled a large (colossal I suppose) head of me—I think perhaps the best thing yet—Love to your father, yourself & Alys, the baby

WW: "Mrs. Costelloe impressed me most delightfully. She is one of the five or six noblest women I have come across; I say this quite deliberately. . . . Costelloe himself is of too *hard* an intellectuality, I am afraid, to give us much in common, . . . I can see that he is at any rate a very genuine & capable fellow in his way" (Barrett). On April 28 he again referred to her: "She is truly a most noble and delightful nature. She is a little afraid perhaps of your deterministic theories (further elaborated by Doctor Bucke) and non-moral apotheosis of evil; but that is natural enough" (Traubel, IV, 488).

dear, & all—as I end, after my supper, (mostly strawberries) I see glimpses of a fine sunset in the west & the boys out in Mickle Street are playing base ball—

Walt Whitman

1561. *To William Sloane Kennedy*

ADDRESS: Wm Sloane Kennedy | Belmont | Mass:.
POSTMARK: Camden, N.J. | Jun 14 | 6 PM | 87.

Camden Monday forenoon | June 13 '87

Yours of 11th just rec'd—it is a fine bright morning, just the right temperature—I am feeling better to-day—freer (almost free) of the heavy congested condition (especially the head department) that has been upon me for nearly a week—Took a long drive yesterday & have been living much on strawberries of late—Don't write much—just sold & got the money for—& it comes in good, I tell you—a poem to *Lippincotts*—(Mr Walsh editor—friendly to me)—poem called "November Boughs," a cluster of sonnet-like bits, making one piece, in shape like "Fancies at Navesink"—that ("November Boughs") is the name, by the by, I think of giving my little book, I want to have out before '87 closes—shall probably print it here in Phila: myself—it will merely give the pieces I have uttered the last five years, in correct form, more permanent in book shape—probably nothing new—I see a piece in Saturday's June 11 N Y *Times*[81] that Boyle O'Reilly is treasurer of my *summer cottage fund*—(dear Boyle, if you see him say I sent my best love & thanks)—I wish you fellows, Baxter, Mrs F[airchild], yourself &c, to leave the selection, arrangement, disposal &c of the cottage, (where, how, &c) *to me*—the whole thing is something I am making much reckoning of—more probably than you all are aware —the am't shall be put of course to that definite single purpose, & *there* I shall probably mainly live the rest of my days—O how I want to get amid good air—the air is so tainted here, five or six months in the year, at best[82] —As I write Herbert Gilchrist is here sketching in my portrait for an oil painting—I hear from Dr Bucke often—nothing now of late from O'Connor, who is still in So: Cal—My friend Pearsall Smith & his daughter sailed for England in the Eider last Saturday—

Walt Whitman

81. "A Cottage for Walt Whitman." See 1546.

82. On June 18 Baxter wrote: "Of course we shall be glad to have you take charge of the business for yourself, following your own inclinations in the way of location, plan, etc." (LC).

83. Twain attended WW's New York lecture in April. He also contributed to

1562. *To Samuel Clemens*

ADDRESS: Samuel E. Clemens | (Mark Twain) | Hartford | Conn:. POSTMARK: Camden, N.J. | Jun 14 | 10 AM | 87.

328 Mickle Street | Camden New Jersey
June 14 '87

Dear S E C[83]

I wish to send you my special deep-felt personal thanks for your kindness & generosity to me—

Walt Whitman

1563. *To G. C. Cox*

ADDRESS: G. C. Cox, Photographer, Cor: Broadway & 12th Street, New York City.
TRANSCRIPT.

June 14, 1887

["Acknowledging receipt of a note . . ."] I have no objection to either of your plans—Will sign autographically & cooperate—Send on the proofs, specimens, all of them.[84]

Walt Whitman

1564. *To Dr. Karl Knortz*

ADDRESS: Dr. Karl Knortz | 540 East 155th Street | New York City. POSTMARKS: Camden, N.J. | Jun 14 | 3 PM | 87; P.O. | 6–14–87 | 12P | N.Y.

328 Mickle Street | Camden New Jersey
June 14 '87

Yes, Doctor, I will loan you the Gilchrist book to read at your leisure[85]—Will send it on in a day or two—Go to Cox, photographer, cor. 12th St & Broadway (entrance 12th St.) & see critically some photos of me he has taken—Shall be delighted to see you here—

Walt Whitman

Donaldson's fund for the purchase of a horse and buggy (see 1346, *n.*82, and Donaldson, 174) and to the Cottage Fund (see 1616). He was reported in the Boston *Herald* of May 24 to have said: "What we want to do is to make the splendid old soul comfortable" (Barrus, 268).

84. The Cox photographs which WW autographed; see 1531 and 1601.

85. He sent *Anne Gilchrist* to Knortz on October 24 (*CB*).

1565. *To the S. S. McClure Syndicate* 6.14. [1887]

328 Mickle Street | Camden New Jersey
June 14 P M

I am inclined to say *yes* to Mr McClure's proposition. Will a week or ten days from now do, to send in the piece, if at all? Please send me Mr. McClure's address, as I sh'd like to treat with *him*.[86]

Walt Whitman

1566. *To Sylvester Baxter* 6.18. [1887]

328 Mickle street—Camden New Jersey
June 18

Dear S B—

I just send Kennedy's letter & write on it what suggests to me impromptu—Yes I am making calculation on a conveniently plann'd & built house, & garden, of my own (cheap & democratic) either in the woods, or in sight of the sea, where I can haul in & breathe a sane atmosphere, & be secure like, either for the summers, or all the time yet vouchsafed to me. I think it would be best to get all the money-fund in Mrs. F[airchild]'s, O'Reilly's, K's & your hands (& any others if any others there be)—putting it in a draught payable to my order & send it to me here—I feel as if I could suit my wants & tastes better probably deciding & directing the practicality of the whole thing *myself*—(I am sure you will all understand it.) Show this to Mrs. F and O'R—I wish them to know too how appreciatingly & gratefully I feel ab't their help—& that I appoint you to fully act as my representative & (if need be) *receiver* in the matter.[87]

As I write I am sitting here by the open window—Birds singing & fine weather—but *hot*—Herbert Gilchrist, of England, is here painting a portrait of me to take to E—

God bless you & all—

Walt Whitman

86. On June 23 WW sent McClure "The Dying Veteran" (CB), for which he received $25 (see 1571). The poem appeared in *McClure's Magazine* in June, in the Springfield *Daily Republican on July* 11, and in *Pall Mall Gazette* (London) on July 9.

87. In his reply on June 21 Baxter again agreed to give WW complete freedom in the expenditure of the funds, and enclosed a check for $373 (Feinberg; Traubel, II, 305). WW's letter was written on the verso of one from Kennedy dated June 16 (Boston Public

1567. *To William Sloane Kennedy*

Camden June 20 '87

I send you an "Academy"[88]—when you read it, send to Dr Bucke—If you wish it, I will send you (it is a handsome little Vol.) one of Eng: pub'd "Spec. Days"—Tell me in your next letter—Baxter has written me to say I can count on $800—that 600 are already subscribed—& that he has 300 in hand which he can send me soon as I say the word.[89] Nothing new—hot, hot here—Gilchrist, Morse, & J N Johnson here as I write—I am so-so—

W W

1568. *To an Unidentified Correspondent*

328 Mickle Street | Camden New Jersey
June 20 '87

Thank you, my friend, for the delicious chocolate—I have it for my breakfast frequently, & enjoy it—Please accept a copy of my little book "Specimen Days" London ed'n. which I send for the young folks.

Walt Whitman

It is just possible I have sent you a note of acknowledgment before—but I think not as I have been ill. (I suppose Pearsall Smith was the cause of your sending it to me.)

1569. *To Charles W. Eldridge*

ADDRESS: Charles W Eldridge | p o box 1705 | Los Angeles | California. POSTMARKS: Camden | Jun 2(?) | 12(?) M | 87; Philadelphia, Pa. | Jun | 21 | 1 PM | Transit.

328 Mickle Street | Camden New Jersey
June 21 '87

Yours of 13th rec'd & welcomed. I have lately sent one copy L of G (completest ed'n) to Dr C[hanning] & will send another[90]—Very hot &

Library).

88. A review of the new (Walter Scott) edition of *Specimen Days*, by Walter Lewin, appeared in *The Academy* on June 4. WW was not impressed: "It is scholarly and all that, but light weight" (Traubel, I, 445).

89. A summary of Baxter's letter of June 18 (LC).

90. According to *CB*, WW sent copies on June 21 and July 5. See also 1574.

oppressive here to-day & has been for a week—I am not well but keep up & around—I am being *gifted* by Boston friends with the means to get a shanty in the country or by the sea shore (& very welcome it is)—

Walt Whitman

1570. *To Mary Smith Costelloe*

ADDRESS: Mrs: Costelloe | 40 Grosvenor Road | the Embankment | London England. POSTMARKS: Camden, N.J. | Jun 25 | 3 PM | 87; Philadelphia, Pa. | Jun | 25 | 1887 | Paid.

Camden N J U S America | June 25 '87—*Saturday—near noon*

It is a perfect day—sunny—cool enough, & I am feeling pretty well & will write you a line—How are you getting along? & how is the baby? & how is Alys & all?—

I have written two little poems lately & sold them & got the money for them[91]—will send them to you when printed. Am better than I was—Am *sculpted* & *portraited* lately—(I like 'em)—Love—

Walt Whitman

1571. *To S. S. McClure*

ADDRESS: S S M'Clure | Tribune Building | New York City. POSTMARKS: Philadelphia | Jun | 25 | 4 PM | Transit; P.O. | 6–25–87 | 12 P | N.Y.

Camden New Jersey | June 25 '87

Yours with $25 as pay for the little piece has reach'd me—Thanks, & this is the receipt.[92]

Walt Whitman

1572. *To Logan Pearsall Smith*

Camden New Jersey | June 26 '87

Dear Logan

Nothing special to write about—yet I tho't I would send you a line —I suppose they are all over there in London, having good times—the

91. "November Boughs" and "The Dying Veteran."
92. See 1565.
92.1. July 3 fell on Sunday in 1887. According to CB the "hot spell" lasted from

baby included—dear baby! henceforth not the least among the objects of our interest—

Showery here to-day—I tho't of getting out with my horse & rig for a drive—but this prevents—I am still tied to the house & chair—a bad spell the last ten days—heat—but much less bad yesterday & to-day—Mr Morse still here *sculping* me & H Gilchrist with the portrait—both please me.

I have *born* two little poems—which you will see in due time. It is middle of afternoon—have had five of the N Y and Phila. Sunday papers, reading all day—also looking out of the window—the mocking bird over the way is singing gay & fast—God bless you, Logan boy—

Walt Whitman

1573. *To William Sloane Kennedy* 7.1. [*1887*]

ADDRESS: Wm Sloane Kennedy | Belmont Mass:.
POSTMARK: Camden, N.J. | Jul 1 | 8 PM | 87.

Camden July 1 2½ P M

Yours of yesterday rec'd—Yes I would get along handsomely with 800—(have already rec'd nearly half that from S[ylvester] B[axter]).

A hot spell here, & I am feeling it—H[erbert] G[ilchrist] is here painting—Morse is here—I shall send you a copy of S D soon—Have just had my dinner of boiled mutton & new potatoes—good—O how the sun glares—

Walt Whitman

1573.1 *To Susan Stafford* 7.3. [*1887*][92.1]

Camden | Sunday forenoon July 3

Am feeling poorly to-day—the result of the long spell of hot weather—(two poor little babies have died from it in this block the last week)—I send you and George a nice little copy of "Specimen Days"—

Love to you all—

If the weather changes, & I feel better I sh'd like to drive down & stay five or six hours, some day early the coming week—

June 29 to July 9. On Sunday, July 10, WW "drove down to Glendale—better weather." The reference is to the English edition of *Specimen Days*, which he sent to many friends at this time.

1574. *To Dr. William F. Channing*

ADDRESS: Dr W F Channing | Pasadena | Los Angeles County | California. POSTMARK: Camden, N.J. | Jul 5 | 8 PM | 87.

Camden New Jersey July 4 '87

Dear Doctor—

By request of C W Eldridge I sent a copy of author's ed'n *Leaves of Grass* June 21[93]—and now a second copy same—write me a line please to say whether they reach you safely—I send my love to you & Mrs. C and to the family, your girls & boy—Is Wm O'C[onnor] still there—Many an anxious & loving thought is wafted thither on his account—

Walt Whitman

1575. *To William Sloane Kennedy*

ADDRESS: Wm Sloane Kennedy | Belmont | Mass:. POSTMARK: Camden, N.J. | Jul 5 | 8 PM | 87.

Camden July 5 '87

Yes I sent *you* the card I ought to have sent to Baxter[94]—Can you send it to him—this one also?—To-day, Tuesday, we have the great relief of a cloudy, showery, fairly coolish day & I feel better—previously we had had a week of great heat & glaring sun & it had sapped me pretty well down—

Walt Whitman

I shall get a good 4 or 5 room shanty by the water or in the woods—

1576. *To Mary Smith Costelloe*

ADDRESS: Mrs: Costelloe | 40 Grosvenor Road | the Embankment | London | S W | England. POSTMARKS: Camden N.J. | Jul 8 | 12(?) M | 87; Philadelphia, Pa. | Jul | 8 | 1887 | Paid.

Camden U S America July 8 | '87

We have had eight days of persistent obtrusive sun, glare & heat

93. On July 29 Channing noted receipt of the volumes, and informed WW that he had accompanied O'Connor as far as Pittsburgh (*LC*).

94. See 1573.

95. George Sand's romance (1842). See Esther Shephard's *Walt Whitman's Prose*

—but as I write it is a cloudy forenoon ("for this relief much thanks") though still & warm—I am still here in Mickle Street—at this moment sitting by the open window down stairs in my big arm-chair—H[erbert] G[ilchrist] at work at the portrait (now near finished)—Loving remembrance to you all—to your father and A[lys]—I am writing a little—not much—

Walt Whitman

1577. *To William Sloane Kennedy* *7.9.* [*1887*]

ENDORSED (by Kennedy?): "'87."

Camden July 9 P M

Yours of 7th rec'd with R[hys]'s card. Tr[anscript] not rec'd—A good letter from E[rnest] R[hys] to-day—J[ohn] N[ewton] J[ohnson] is certainly crazy—a cross between Zdenko (in Consuelo)[95] & something more intellectual & infernal—Very hot weather here, continued—I am feeling it badly—yet not so badly as you might fancy—I am careful, & Mrs Davis is very good and cute—As I write it is clouded over & begins to rain—H[erbert] G[ilchrist] is still here painting—Morse here—

Walt Whitman

1578. *To William Sloane Kennedy and Richard Maurice Bucke*

ENDORSED (by Kennedy): "Quotation Fr. Joint letter to Bucke & WSK."
TRANSCRIPT.

July 11, '87

I went off yesterday on a ten-mile drive to Glendale, to my friends the Staffords' house, where I staid five hours & back in the drape of the day —a ride & all which I enjoyed greatly. . . . Two wealthy English girls, Bessie & Isabella Ford, have just sent me £20.[96]

(1938).

96. The latest gift from the Ford sisters was enclosed in a (lost) letter from Carpenter which WW received on July 11 (*CB*). Kennedy noted on his transcription that WW wrote "on back of O'Connor's last letter fr California, as he was setting out to return to Washington."

1578.1 *To Sarah A. Tooley (?)*[96.1]

Camden New Jersey | U S America |
July 11 '87

I do not object to your quoting the lines within mention'd & hereby give permission—

Walt Whitman

1579. *To William Sloane Kennedy*

Camden July 13 '87

Very hot to-day—now two weeks of it & I am pulled down by it badly—feel it to-day worse than yet—have had a few mouthfuls of dinner, & am sitting here in my big chair—after reading your letter & O'C[onnor]'s to you[97]—H[erbert] G[ilchrist] is here painting, & Morse sculping—I enclose my last little piece—a slip copy—a N Y newspaper syndicate (S S McClure, Tribune Building) vehemently solicited, & gave me $25 (far more than it is worth)—Then I have sent a three line piece "Twilight" ($10) to the "Century"[98] wh' they accepted & paid for—Hartman[99] has been in Phila ten days, but returns to B[oston]—what do you think of him & of his projected "Society"—As I close every thing is faint & still with the heat—

Walt Whitman

1579.1 *To Susan Stafford* *7.15 [1887]*[99.1]

Camden Friday Afternoon | July 15

Dear friend Susan Stafford

I should like to come down & see you & see George, but I am quite

96.1. This note was written on the verso of the following letter:
". . . copyright in that country. | May I trouble you for an early reply? I am sorry that there is no way by which I can forward postage for your letter. | Yours truly | Sarah A. Tooley | Messrs Osgood & Co." Since WW's letter had nothing to do with the fragment of Miss Tooley's, it is impossible to be certain that she was the recipient. I should guess her letter was written in September or October 1881 when WW was discussing the copyright of the Osgood edition of *Leaves of Grass* (see 1064). There are at least two possible explanations: WW wrote a draft, an unusual procedure for such a trivial matter, or he wrote a reply on a piece of paper he found in the ever-present litter in his "den."

97. O'Connor wrote on July 2 to Dr. Bucke and Kennedy (Feinberg). WW received a (lost) card from Mrs. O'Connor on July 12 (*CB*).

98. The poem appeared in the December issue.

99. Carl Sadakichi Hartmann (1869–1944), son of a German father and a

poorly & it has been such hot weather—I am quite concerned about him & w'd wish to help somehow—If you w'd wish a little money I can let you have it, as I can spare it—or if there is any thing George would like that I c'd get up here, you write me, & it w'd be a pleasure to me to get it—I send George my love & the same to you all—

Walt Whitman

1580. *To William Sloane Kennedy*

Camden Sunday Evn'g July 17 '87

Heat, heat, heat, night & day—I find Evn'g a great relief—have pass'd great part of to-day lying on the lounge, with a big palm-leaf fan—have read Fullerton in the Record and Mrs. E. in Herald[1]—best thanks to both—I suppose O'C[onnor] is in Wash'n, very poorly, but have not got word thence of his arrival[2]—I am just going to my supper (blackberries)—

Walt Whitman

1581. *To William Sloane Kennedy*

Camden Monday Evn'g July 18 '87

Am standing the weather pretty well so far—it's the hottest long spell I ever knew—I am quite comfortable as I sit here ab't sunset.

Walt Whitman

Japanese mother and author of books on religion, art, and poetry. On June 21 Baxter informed WW of a "call" from "your friend Hartmann, who is on his way back to Philadelphia from Europe" (Feinberg; Traubel, II, 305). Hartmann published in the New York *Herald* on April 14, 1889, "Walt Whitman. Notes of a Conversation with the Good Gray Poet by a German Poet and Traveller." For WW's reaction, see 2026 and also Traubel, II, 281–282.

99.1. July 15 fell on Friday in 1887. For George Stafford's illness, see 1589, *n*.8.

1. William Morlow Fullerton's eulogistic two-column review apparently appeared in the *Sunday Record* and then was reprinted on July 20 in the Boston *Advertizer* (Feinberg). Fullerton thanked WW on August 1 for some photographs and pamphlets (Feinberg). I have not identified the article by "Mrs. E.," probably Mrs. Elizabeth Fairchild. On July 5 the Boston *Herald* copied from the Providence *Journal* "The Whitman Craze," which mocked the Whitman clubs.

2. Apparently WW had a lapse of memory; see 1579.

1582. *To Sylvester Baxter*

Camden | P M July 21 '87

Yours has come with the $130—making 503 with the previous instalment sent by you—Loving thanks, dear friend, to you & all—I shall proceed immediately (from what you say) to practically suit myself & invest to the extent you speak of.

We have had a very hot (& lengthened) spell of weather—sapp'd me badly—but I have got along with it & I am quite comfortable this afternoon—It is a cloudy rainy day, here—very welcome—

I spend the time very idly—sit here by the open window in great ratan arm-chair, with a big palm leaf fan & do nothing—sleep, eat and digest middling well—pretty good spirits—am alone most of the time—bodily-getting-around-power almost entirely gone—What have you to say ab't the W W "society" project? & ab't Ch: Hartman?[3]

Walt Whitman

1583. *To John Burroughs*

ADDRESS: John Burroughs | Hobart | New York.
POSTMARKS: Camden, N.J. | Jul(?) | 12 M | 8(?); Hobart | Jul | 2(?).

Camden July 22 '87

Your letter to H[erbert] G[ilchrist] is rec'd & he has shown it to me—He is here yet painting the portrait. Wm O'C[onnor] has got back to Wash'n.—he is very poorly—nearly utterly disabled in leg-power (walking or even standing)—Eldridge is at Los Angeles to stay—Three or four weeks of fearful heat here, but I have stood it & am fairly to-day—Sidney Morse the sculptor is here[4]—I hear from Dr B[ucke][5] and Kennedy—

W W

3. Baxter replied on August 2: "Oh! about Hartmann. He was altogether 'too previous' and hardly appreciated what he had undertaken. He did not know how to go to work and appointed officers of a society which had not been organized! We all had to sit down on him and the matter is in abeyance" (Syracuse; Traubel, II, 379). According to Hartmann's *Conversations with Walt Whitman* (1895), 36, the officers were to be Bucke as president, Kennedy as vice-president, and "Your humble servant" as director. For WW's reaction, see Traubel, V, 38–39.

1584. *To Robert Pearsall Smith*

ADDRESS: Pearsall Smith | 40 Grosvenor Road | the Embankment | London | S W | England.
POSTMARK: Camden, N.J. | Jul 24 | 5 PM | 87.

Camden N J U S America | July 23 '87

Y'rs of July 8 (?)[6] rec'd—with A[lys]'s note on fourth page. All goes safely with me so far thro' the long fearfully hot spell here—It is clouded over a little to-day—some relief—I have no news to write you ab't my affairs or self. I sit in the big chair by the open window as I write this —"the same subject continued"—Best prayers & love to you all, Mary, Alys & little R[achel]—

Walt Whitman

1585. *To Harry Stafford*

ADDRESS: Harry Lamb Stafford | RR Station | Marlton | New Jersey. POSTMARKS: Camden, N.J. | Jul 24 | 5 PM | 87; Marlton | Jul | 25 | N.J.

Camden Sunday P M July 24 '87

Well, Hank dear boy, how are you standing it this hot summer? Eva, I want you to write to me & tell me. We have had it fearful hot & tainted here for over seven weeks, but I am alive & kicking yet—it is rainy to-day but warm yet—I shall drive down to your parents in a day or two—(intended to have gone to-day)—Nothing very new with me, much the same old story—H[erbert] G[ilchrist] is here yet—the sculptor Morse also—I remain in good spirits but a pretty bad case bodily. Love to you & E & the little one—

Walt Whitman

4. With his usual directness Burroughs made the following comment on the artistic work of Gilchrist and Morse: "Herbert tried to paint Walt, but it was a failure. It gave none of Walt's power. Morse made a big, shaggy sort of Homeric bust of him that had power, but he overdid it. He didn't show the womanliness there was in Walt—there was something fine, delicate, womanly in him" (Barrus, 265).

5. The only extant letter from Bucke at this time is one dated June 12 (Feinberg).

6. WW's question mark. There is no extant letter from Smith at this time.

1586. *To Ellen M. O'Connor*

ADDRESS: Mrs: E M O'Connor | 1015 O Street | Washington | D C. POSTMARKS: Camden, N.J. | Jul 26 | 8 PM | 87; Washington, Rec'd. | Jul | 27 | 7 AM | 1887 | 1.

Camden New Jersey | July 26 '87

Dear friend

Thank you for the kind postal card—Does Wm care ab't having papers (Critic, Boston Trans: &c) sent—& is he mostly at the house in O street—or to be address'd at the office? I think every day about him, & am almost feverishly anxious to do something—Would like at the least to send papers & letters to while away the time—but fear being intrusive with them—

I am living here in a little wooden house of my own, with a kind Jersey woman (a sailor's widow Mrs: Davis) for housekeeper & cook—am totally bodily disabled as to locomotion &c.—but good heart—& eating, digestion, sleep-power &c. fairly active—I am sitting here in a big arm chair by the open window as I write—hot weather here too for eight weeks—but I have stood it—

Walt Whitman

1587. *To William Sloane Kennedy and Richard Maurice Bucke*

TRANSCRIPT.

July 28/87.

Had for dinner stewed blackberries—a favorite tipple of mine—and boiled rice. . . . Sidney Morse has made a second big head—an improvement, if I dare say so, on the first. The second is the modern spirit, awake & alert as well as calm—contrasted with the antique & Egyptian calmness & rest of the first. We have decided on the second.

7. The recipient of this letter, he informs me, "was just under two years of age when this card was sent." His father, James Henry Wroth, was known as "Harry" to his intimate friends; he died in 1926. John was James Henry's brother, who had written to WW on June 2 (Feinberg). See also 1041.

8. According to a notation in *CB* on July 24 George was ill with "lung hemor-

1588. *To James Stewart Wroth*

ADDRESS: James Stewart Wroth | Care Dr. Harry Wroth | Albuquerque | New Mexico. POSTMARK: Philadelphia, Pa. | Jul 28 | (?) PM | 87.

Camden New Jersey | July 28 1887

Thanks for the good photo—dear little fellow—I too hope we shall meet personally—Best love to you—& to your parents—

Walt Whitman

John's letter rec'd, all right & welcome[7]—

1589. *To Susan Stafford* *8.1. [1887]*

ADDRESS: Mrs: Susan Stafford | Kirkwood | (Glendale) | New Jersey. POSTMARK: Camden (?) | (?) | 8 PM | 87.

Camden Monday Evn'g Aug 1

We have had three hot days right in a string but I am getting along with it all, & there is a great let up evenings & nights—Nobody here to day—I think of you & George[8] & all—H[arry] yesterday told me he was much better—good—I will be down one of these days—

Walt Whitman

1589.1 *To Erastus Brainerd* *[8(?).1(?). 1887?]*

Erastus Brainerd

News office

Dear B—

I think the enclosed or something like it might give the point of how the "Society" matter strikes me[8.1]—

hages." On August 4, when WW drove to Glendale, he found George "better."

8.1. This note apparently was sent about August 1 to Brainerd, and the item appeared in the Saturday edition of the *Daily News*, as indicated in 1593. As notes 1 and 3 above demonstrate, the Whitman Society was widely discussed at this time by WW's friends and critics. There is no extant file of the *Daily News* for this period.

1590. *To Sylvester Baxter*

Camden Aug: 3 P M '87

Dear S B

Yours has just come with $285 additional for the Cottage (making 788 altogether)—Thanks true & deep to you & to Dr Wesselhaeft[9] & *to all*—

A little let up to day & I am sitting here by the open window comfortable enough—but the three previous days here have been terrible—

Believe me, dear S B, I shall have the good of your & the friends' kind help—

Walt Whitman

1591. *To William Sloane Kennedy*

Camden Thursday noon Aug 4 '87

All going ab't as usual. I hear from Dr B[ucke] and from Rhys. O'C[onnor] is at Bar Harbor, Maine. I am feeling quite comfortable to-day. Not so hot here—S[ylvester] B[axter] has sent me nearly $800 for the cottage—I send you two Wash'n *Stars*—send them to Dr Bucke—I am going out for a long drive this afternoon—

Walt Whitman

1592. *To S. S. McClure*

ADDRESS: S S McClure | Tribune Building | New York City. POSTMARKS: Camden, N.J. | (?) | 8 PM | 87; P.O. | 8–6–87 | N.Y.

328 Mickle Street | Camden New Jersey
Aug: 6 '87

I have rec'd your kind proposition—Yes, if I compose anything fit for your purposes I will send you—but I am disabled & unwell more than half the time & cannot be relied on—Do not for the present put my name on your printed list of contributors—

Walt Whitman

9. Apparently Dr. William P. Wesselhoeft contributed $50 to the fund, since Baxter enclosed Wesselhoeft's check for that sum in his letter of August 2 (Syracuse; Traubel, II, 378). Baxter visited WW on August 11 (CB).

10. See 1589.1.

11. In a lengthy letter on August 2 Mrs. O'Connor had informed WW that her

1593. *To Erastus Brainerd* [*8.8. 1887*]

ADDRESS: Erastus Brainerd | office Daily *News* | newspaper | Philadelphia. POSTMARKS: Camden, N.J. | Aug 8 | 10 AM | 87; Received | Aug | 8 | 1130 AM | 1887 | Phila.

If you have them & to spare I wish you would send me eight copies *News* of Saturday Even'g last[10]—

Walt Whitman
328 Mickle Street
Camden N J

1594. *To Ellen M. O'Connor*

ADDRESS: Mrs E M O'Connor | 1015 O Street | Washington | D C. POSTMARKS: Camden, N.J. | Aug 8 | 3 PM | 87; Washington, Rec'd | Aug | 9 | 10 PM | 1887.

Camden Aug 8 '87

Yes, I rec'd the package of old letters all right—best thanks—also for the kind letter other—Havn't heard any thing from William at Bar Harbor (I suppose he is there)[11]—

Matters ab't as usual with me—I took a long drive yesterday—Weather pleasant here—

Walt Whitman

1595. *To Talcott Williams*

TRANSCRIPT.

August 8, 1887

If convenient I wish you would send me six copies of Press of Sunday last.[12]

husband had secretly gone to Maine in order to try the method of Dr. Kinnear for his illness. She sent "a package of letters belonging to you . . . , the Rossetti correspondence, & as a part of history valuable" (Feinberg).

12. Williams called on WW on August 3 (CB). Since Sunday issues of the Philadelphia *Press* are not available, I cannot explain WW's request.

1596. *To Logan Pearsall Smith* *8.16. [1887]*

TRANSCRIPT.

Camden Tuesday Aug: 16 PM

Dear boy Logan

Your letter has come & is welcomed—Nothing specially new with me—I have stood the hot weather pretty well & have just eaten my dinner with zest—Young Gilchrist is here yet—the portrait is ab't finished—good—he expects to take it to London for the May opening Royal Academy—I hear from your folks in London—How happy Mary must be!—Quite a good many visitors come here—they talk & I talk—as I write it is cloudy & comparatively cool & I am enjoying all. The carrier just brings me a letter from Dr Bucke—he is well & busy—comes this way early in September—Love to you, dear friend—

Walt Whitman

1597. *To William T. Stead*

TRANSCRIPT.

August 17, 1887

First thank you again for the handsome money present of some months ago, wh' did me more good than you perhaps think for—it has helped me in meals, clothing, debts, &c., ever since. My best help however has come in my old age & paralysis from the Br: Islands. The piece in yr paper (was it early in May last?) from "a distinguished American man of letters" abt me was a very large inflation into fiction of a very little amt of fact—in spirit it is altogether, & in letter mainly untrue (abt my affairs &c.).[13] My income from my books, (royalties &c.) does not reach $100 a year. I am now in my 69th year—living plainly but very comfortably in a little wooden cottage of my own, good spirits invariably, but physically a sad wreck, failing more and more each successive season, unable even to get abt the house without help—most of the time though without serious pain or suffering, except extreme weakness wh' I have a good deal—the paralysis that prostrated me after the Secession war (several shocks) never lifting entirely since—but leaving mentality unimpaired absolutely (thank God!) I have a few, very few, staunch & loving friends & uphold-

13. Stead had printed passages from a "private letter" on May 6, which detailed the American supporters of WW: George W. Childs, Carnegie, Burroughs. The author—perhaps Conway—asserted that "a rich Philadelphian told me today that he had given himself, off and on, a thousand dollars," and concluded: "All this talk of the necessity of raising

ers here in America. I am gathering a lot of pieces—uttered within the last six years & shall send them out under the name of *November Boughs* before long—a little book (200 pages or less) some new pieces—a sort of continuation or supplement. Then I think of printing a revised ed'n of complete writings (*Leaves of Grass*, *Specimen Days & Collect* & *November Boughs* all in one volume) soon. Please accept *personal thanks* from me (never mind the literary) & I know you will accept the impromptu Note in the same spirit in wh' it is written. Best thanks and love to all my British helpers, readers & defenders.

1598. *To Ernest Rhys*

ADDRESS: Ernest Rhys | Care Walter Scott publisher | 24 Warwick Lane Paternoster | Row | London England. POSTMARKS: Camden, N.J. | Aug 20 | 3 PM | 87; London E.C. | M | AU 31 87 | AD.

Camden New Jersey U S America | Aug: 20 '87

Nothing special to write—I suppose you have lately rec'd some papers from me—We appear to be thro' the long & fierce spell of hot weather—have had it very agreeable now for nearly a fortnight—John Burroughs has been here for a couple of days[14]—he is well—nothing new in my literary affairs—H[erbert] G[ilchrist] is here & is painting leisurely —he is well—I hear frequently f'm Dr Bucke and Kennedy—I drove out twelve miles & back yesterday—

Walt Whitman

1599. *To Charles W. Eldridge*

ADDRESS: Chas: W Eldridge | p o box 1705 | Los Angeles | California.

Camden New Jersey | Aug: 30 '87

Yours rec'd—thanks—Nothing specially new or different with me

money by subscriptions abroad, with the idea that he won't be taken care of at home, is ridiculous"; see *AL*, XXXIII (1961), 70. See also 1475. Because of the controversy over WW's poverty, I have summarized his annual income at the end of each year.

14. Burroughs was in Camden on August 18 and 19 and accompanied the poet to the Stafford farm on the 18th (*CB*).

—Yes, I am willing Grace[15] should go on with the Calendar—I have not heard a word from Wm [O'Connor] at Bar Harbor—

Walt Whitman

1600. *To William Sloane Kennedy, John Burroughs, and Richard Maurice Bucke*

TRANSCRIPT.

Aug 30 '87

I remain anchor'd here in my big chair—Have you read the Bacon-Shakspere résumé in the last Sunday's N. Y. *World?*[15.1] I am tackling it—take less & less stock in it.

1601. *To John H. Johnston*

ADDRESS: J H Johnston | Jeweler | 150 Bowery cor: Broome | New York City. POSTMARK: Camden, N.J. | Sep 1 | 6 PM | 87.

Camden New Jersey | 328 Mickle Street
Sept: 1 '87

My dear friend

I wish you could take half an hour if possible & go around for me to Mr Cox photographer cor: 12th St. & Broadway. He advertises (Century, Sept. number) to sell my photo, with autograph. The latter is forged, & the former illegal & unauthorized. When in N Y last April I was taken there by Miss Gilder & sat for pictures under promise that I should see them in specimens & decide wh' should be printed & put forth, & wh'

15. On July 7 Grace Ellery Channing requested permission "to bring out a Walt Whitman Calendar—of extracts from your Leaves of Grass" (Feinberg). Although she begged for an immediate response, her father reminded WW on July 29 that he had not replied (LC). On August 3, 1888, in a letter to Stedman, O'Connor observed: "I worked hard to help her to select the gnomons for it—not such an easy matter with a poet like Walt" (Feinberg). Despite the aid of Stedman, nothing came of the Calendar.

15.1. In the more "literary" days of nineteenth-century America the New York *World* on August 28 devoted its first two pages to Thomas Davidson's review of Ignatius Donnelly's *The Great Cryptogram.*

16. As letters to Cox, Carey, and Johnston later in the month indicate, WW was needlessly concerned about the sale of his photographs with a forged signature. On September 3 he noted in *CB*: "Johnston went to see Cox, photographer—J thinks 'it is all right.'" Although Johnston wrote on September 10 about a suspected forgery (Feinberg), Carey, who handled the financial arrangements (see 1614), forwarded from Cox to

not. Since, all requests to have them (proofs or specimens) sent me here have been ignored. The whole thing is *cool*, very. Go round & see if C will immediately send me copies of the pictures & follow my requests ab't them —Or will it be necessary for me to clap a legal injunction on the issue?— wh' I shall certainly do—You can show this note to Mr Cox[16]—

Walt Whitman

Take Alma with you, if she likes.

1602. *To S. S. McClure*

TRANSCRIPT.

Camden, New Jersey, Sept. 3, '87

Can you use this little poem, "Shakespeare-Bacon Cipher?" The price is $25. . . . I retain the right to print in future book. It will not be proper for you to take out copyright—but the thing is exclusively yours until after printing and publishing in your papers.[17]

Walt Whitman

1603. *To William Sloane Kennedy* *9.7. [1887]*

Camden Sept 7, Evn'g

I return S[ymonds]'s letter—All I can say ab't it is I myself like to get views from every quarter[18]—then I go on the tack that seems *to me* rightest—As I write, it is clouding up dark for a thunderstorm—I expect Dr Bucke to-morrow or next day[19]—Morse and Gilchrist still here—

Walt Whitman

WW $42 on October 3, $16.50 on November 2, and $15.50 on December 2 (CB). Note also Traubel, v, 306.

17. After McClure refused "Shakspere-Bacon's Cipher," WW sent it on September 6 to Alden, of *Harper's New Monthly Magazine*, who also rejected it. On September 13 it was submitted to *The Cosmopolitan*, which paid $20 and printed it in October (CB).

18. After Swinburne's intemperate repudiation of WW appeared in the August issue of *The Fortnightly Review*, Symonds offered what he himself termed "a temperate reprimand" in the next issue. On August 21, in a letter to Kennedy, Symonds admitted that "it is enormously difficult to write on Whitman." He continued this apologetic vein in his letter of September 17; see Kennedy, viii. The poet termed Symonds' rebuttal "a milk and water affair" (Traubel, IV, 124). The story of WW's reaction to Swinburne is well told by Harold Blodgett in *Walt Whitman in England*, 112–121.

19. Bucke accompanied WW to Glendale on September 11. Timothy Blair Pardee (see 962) apparently joined Bucke at Camden on September 13 (CB).

1604. *To William Ingram*

ADDRESS: Wm Ingram | Tea Dealer | 31 North 2d Street | Philadelphia. POSTMARK: Camden, N.J. | S(?) | (?) | 87.

328 Mickle Street | Camden Sept 9 '87

Thanks for the box of grapes wh' reach'd me safely—We have been eating them—sending plates to certain old women (sick or half sick)—& making jelly. Thanks to Mr Unger.

Walt Whitman

1605. *To Robert Pearsall Smith*

ADDRESS: Pearsall Smith | 40 Grosvenor Road | the Embankment | London S W | England. POSTMARK: Camden, N.J. | Sep 12 | 4 30 PM | 87.

328 Mickle Street Sept 12 '87 | Camden
New Jersey U S America

Dear friend

Yours (including J A Symonds's printed note) has just reach'd & been heartily welcomed by me—Thanks—I have had boxed & sent over to you, a large plaster head by Sidney Morse, the sculptor[20]—If convenient *you are to donate this head to the Royal Academy*, (or if you & Ernest Rhys feel it best, I leave it to you, where & to what public London gallery to put it)—The medallions and Emersons are your own—except that I should like one of the medallions to go to Mary & her husband with my love.

Nothing very new here—the weather is fine & has been so for many weeks—I am well, for me—drive out quite a deal—the oysters come & have come, & are invariably *good* & I thrive on them—Dr Bucke is here, continues thro' the week—Gilchrist is here, leaves on the steamer 21st—

Love to you & dear Alys—Logan has been to see me lately, he looks splendidly—

Walt Whitman

20. On August 27 WW gave Morse $70 "to pay to caster for the 10 heads." Morse brought four of the heads on September 2, one of which was sent to Bucke (*CB*).

1606. *To Robert Pearsall Smith* 9.12. [*1887*]

ADDRESS: Pearsall Smith | 40 Grosvenor Road | the Embankment | London | S W | England. POSTMARKS: Camden, N.J. | Sep (?) | 6 PM | 87; Philadel(?) | Sep | 12 | 1887 | Paid.

328 Mickle Street | Camden N. J.—
U S A. Sept: 12

In addition to what I wrote & sent off a couple of hours ago: Dr Bucke has just been in to see me & strongly suggests that the head ought to go to the *Kensington Museum* (instead of the Royal Academy, or any other place)—

W W

1607. *To Mary Smith Costelloe*

328 Mickle Street | Camden New Jersey
U S America Sept 14 '87

Dear friend

I am pretty fair in health &c of late & now—pleasant weather here for several weeks—rainy of late—Y'r nice letter from Switzerland came yesterday—one from your father also just rec'd, enclosing the J A Symonds' note in answer to Swinburne's article—(the article was not worth answering at all—I have not given it a thought)—

Dr Bucke has been here for five or six days—leaves to-night—he is well—hearty as ever & much the same—he has (in London Canada) one of the plaster heads, & is quite enthusiastic ab't it—I suppose the one I sent to y'r father has been rec'd before this—I think it had better be donated to the Kensington Museum, if they will accept it & give it a fair place—Morse is still here (in Phila)—is at work on his statuette of President Cleveland—H Gilchrist is here—he is at this moment giving some final touches on his oil painting of me—I like it—Some think it too *tame*—you will doubtless see it, as G. leaves here (NY) on the 21st on the Germania—

Phila is all agog now & for three days to come with the centennial of the Constitution (the idea is good, perhaps sublime, but the carrying out of it more or less tawdry & vulgar)—I am sitting here in the great chair,

According to the tabulation in CB, the poet paid Morse $133 in the next few months, presumably for expenses incurred in casting.

down stairs—window open—big bunches of flowers on the sill—every thing all right—had toast & a great mug of Whitman's chocolate & hot milk (*excellent*) for my breakfast—Love to Alys, to the baby, & to all—

Walt Whitman

1608. *To William Sloane Kennedy*

328 Mickle Street | Camden New Jersey
Sept: 14 '87

I am ab't as usual—have just had my dinner, a slice of cold roast beef, & a couple of cook'd apples wh' I ate with relish—Dr Bucke has been here for a week—leaves this evening—H[erbert] G[ilchrist] is here—leaves 21st on the Germani[a]. Nothing very new with me in literary matters—or anent—I sent a little poem to Harpers—(Alden)—but it came back, refused[21]—this is the 4th refusal within a few months, & I shall try no more.

Phila: is all alive with the Centennial U S Constitutional commemoration, & will be thro' the week—I have been pressingly invited, but cannot go[22]—(A crowd & hubbub are no place for me)—Fine weather here for several weeks—cloudy & rainy this week, however—I enclose J A Symonds's note—(rather flat it seems to me)—also something ab't Ruskin—How ab't the W W Society? Anything new? Yes, I shall send you a copy of English ed'n "Spec: Days"[23]—

Walt Whitman

1609. *To William Carey*

ADDRESS: William Carey | Century Office Union Square | New York City. POSTMARKS: Camden, N.J. | Sep (?) | 8 PM | 87; P.O. | 9–16 87 | 2 A | N.Y.

328 Mickle Street | Camden N J Sept: 15 '87 | Evn'g—

The package of photos. came this afternoon. Shall sign & return them to-morrow or next day[24]—all the points proposed by you & Mr C[ox] are satisfactory.

Walt Whitman

21. "Shakspere-Bacon's Cipher"; see note 17 above.
22. On behalf of the Constitutional Centennial Commission, Hampton L. Carson requested on August 3 that WW write and read a "patriotic poem commemorative of the

1610. *To G. C. Cox*

ADDRESS: G C Cox | Photographer | Broadway & 12th Street| New York City. POSTMARKS: Camden, N.J. | Sep 15 | 8 PM | 87; P. O. | 9–16 87 | 2 A | N.Y.

328 Mickle Street | Camden New Jersey |
Sept 15 '87—Even'g—

The package of Photos. came this afternoon. I will sign & return them to-morrow or next day—All the propositions of Mr Carey & yourself are satisfactory—

Walt Whitman

1611. *To Susan Stafford* *9.21. [1887]*

ADDRESS: Mrs: Susan Stafford | Kirkwood | (Glendale) | New Jersey. POSTMARK: Camden, N.J. | (?).

Camden Sept: 21 2 P M

I suppose Herb must have sail'd from N Y this morning—he was here early yesterday & took his picture & I have seen or heard nothing of him since—Mrs Davis is sick, laid up, bad—A lady friend is here, helping us—I expect to be down Sunday by 12½[25]—Am sitting here by the window in the big chair & have been all day—Weather rather pleasant.

Walt Whitman

1612. *To George M. Williamson*

328 Mickle Street | Camden New Jersey
Sept: 22 '87

Dear Sir

Yours rec'd with the $5 in advance for "November Boughs"—The book is not printed yet, but is contemplated before long. Thank you for the papers that come occasionally, always acceptable & new—I do not know

triumph of popular institutions" (Feinberg).

23. WW sent the book on September 29 (CB).
24. WW returned the photographs on September 17 (CB).
25. WW "drove to Glendale" on "Sunday afternoon" (CB).

what "letter" you allude to in a late "Tribune"—I send some scraps, MS. and autographs.

Thanks & good bye for the present—

Walt Whitman

1613. *To William Carey*

TRANSCRIPT.

September 28, 1887

["Indicating that WW had sent Carey photographs and would send more later."]

1614. *To John H. Johnston*

Camden Thursday Evn'g Sept 29 | '87

Nothing special—Am somewhat under the weather four or five days—Cold in the head or malaria—I sent Shiell's the book 16th Sept.[26] —McKay, my Phila: publisher, has just been over—paid me $77 for royalties for the last eight months—I paid the Camden taxes on my shanty to-day $26[27]—

The photos come from Cox all right, & I sign & return them—Wm Carey, at the *Century* office, seems to be managing the sale & financial part of the matter—I am satisfied with all—H Gilchrist the painter has gone back to England & taken his picture with him—Morse the sculptor is still here (in Phila)—I think the plaster head by him (the 2d head we call it) is the best thing yet. Cloudy & rainy spell of weather here—I havn't been out of the house since last Sunday—have been amusing myself with *Pepys' Diary* (McKay sent it to me, good edn. 4 vols.)—When you come again, don't forget to bring my Stedman book *American Poets*[28]—Love to Alma and Al and all of you—

Walt Whitman

26. The book was sent to Robert Shiells at the "National Bank, Neenah, Wisconsin" (*CB*).

27. McKay paid WW $76.91 on September 22; the exact amount of the city tax was $25.37 (*CB*).

28. WW had left Stedman's *Poets of America* at the Westminster Hotel (see

1615. *To William Sloane Kennedy* [*10.4. 1887*]

ENDORSED (by Kennedy): "[Oct. 4, '87]."

Camden Tuesday P M

Nothing very different with me—I am just going out for a drive—cool & bright weather—hear from Dr Bucke frequently—he is busy & well—always writes me cheerily & chipper—wh' I like, for it is pretty monotonous here—have not heard from O'Connor for several weeks—suppose he is yet at Bar Harbor—& if "no news is good news" he must be on the mend, wh' I deeply hope—

I return Symonds's letter herewith[29]—the whole matter—*this* letter & the Fortnightly note—seems to me funny.

("Perhaps there may be bairns, kind sir
Perhaps there may be *not*")

Yes, I like the little English Spec. Days, too—you keep y'r copy—I have a photo. for you soon too—One from Cox's (N Y) I call it the laughing philosopher—

W W

1616. *To Sylvester Baxter*

Camden P M Oct: 7 '87

Dear friend

Yours with the $12 has reach'd me safely—making $800 altogether sent me by my Boston friends, & now herewith receipted—Soon as convenient cant you send me a plain list of names and am'ts to this fund—so I may know definitely who have help'd me?—I am ab't as usual of late—was out driving yesterday, & shall probably go out for an hour this afternoon—Thanks to you & my Boston friends, & God bless you all[30]—

Walt Whitman

1520).

29. Undoubtedly Symonds's second letter of September 17 to Kennedy (see 1603).

30. On the following day Baxter transmitted the names of the subscribers, who included William Dean Howells, Samuel Clemens, Charles Eliot Norton, and Edwin Booth (Traubel, II, 299–300).

1617. *To Robert Pearsall Smith* *10.7. [1887]*

ADDRESS: Pearsall Smith | 1309 Arch Street | Philadelphia. POSTMARKS: Camden, N.J. | Oct 7 | 12 M | 87; Received | Oct | 7 | 1 PM | 1887 | Phila.

Camden Friday noon | Oct: 7

Welcome back[31]—your card rec'd—Come over soon—Alys too, (I suppose she has returned)—I have survived the hot seige of the summer & am all right. Drove out yesterday—I hear from Dr Bucke—he is well & busy—Gilchrist is back in Eng: with his picture—Best love & thanks—

W W

1618. *To Mary Smith Costelloe*

ADDRESS: Mrs: Costelloe | 40 Grosvenor Road | the Embankment | London | England. POSTMARK: (?) en, N.J. | (?) | (?) PM | 87.

Camden New Jersey America | Oct 10 '87

Yours from Scotland rec'd. Your father has been here twice & is evidently hearty & happy—Logan is coming home for good & the folks are most happy to have him—I authorize you to unbox the head[32]—call in the help & advice of Ernest Rhys, (if you feel so inclined) & carry out the Kensington Museum project, if you like—I however hereby give you full power in the matter, & confirm what you do whatever it is—I am ab't as usual & go out riding frequently—pleasant fall weather here—I am sitting by the open window writing—

Walt Whitman

1619. *To William Sloane Kennedy*

Camden Oct: 20 '87

O'Connor has been here visiting me on his return to Wash'n[33]—I have written an acc't to Dr B[ucke] wh' he will send you—I sh'd not wish

31. Smith had just returned from England, where he had seen his new grandchild Rachel Costelloe.

32. Morse's sculpture (see 1607).

33. O'Connor spent the afternoon and evening of October 18 in Camden—"went on to W[ashington] in the midnight train" (*CB*). The letter WW wrote to Bucke about his last meeting with O'Connor is apparently lost.

34. In Kennedy's manuscript of his projected book on WW he recorded the following which "Whitman is said to have said" to Hartmann: "E. C. Stedman is after all nothing more than a sophistical dancing master. If Hercules or Apollo should make their

any such item as that ab't my alleged opinion of Stedman to be printed[34]—I have no such opinion—My feeling toward S is one of good will & thanks, markedly—O'C says he is a good fellow, & I say so too—Nothing new with me specially—A new little piece[35] of mine out in Nov. *Lippincott's* wh' I will send you probably to-day—

Walt Whitman

1620. *To Herbert Gilchrist* *10.22–23.* [*1887*]

Camden America Oct 22 Evn'g

Dear Herbert Gilchrist

Yours of the 10th came to-day & is welcome. Every thing goes on much the same here. Quite biting wintry cold to-day after a long stormy spell. I am ab't the same as when you were here—& am sitting by the window in the big chair. Mrs. D[avis] is well. We have been feasting on some nice stewed quinces and quince jelly—a triumph of Mrs. D's cookery —we wish you were here to have some—the very color goes beyond all description.

I have no doubt the portrait fully justifies all encomiums there, and goes beyond them.[36] In a good light & in a frame it must indeed appear well—having *neither* here, & intentionally hung where it would be tested to the severest—Success to the painter of it—& to it (the nobly carnal & Shaksperian work)—I have rec'd a nice letter from Herbert Horne—have heard from Morgan Brown,[37] who is well & remains in N Y state—the Smiths are here, & come to see me—Morse is here—has been here every day this week—Mrs Stafford was here Wednesday, is well, as are all the family—But it is growing too dark to write—

Sunday forenoon early—Oct 23—The sun is shining bright—I have had my breakfast (pann'd oysters toast & coffee) & in half an hour I shall start in my light wagon & Nettie[38] for Glendale—you ought to be here to accompany me—the air is full of sheen & oxygen with a pleasant coolness —write soon again. Give my best regards to Ernest Rhys—a synopsis of

appearance, he would look at them with the eye of a dancing master" (Trent). Hartmann attributed the remark to WW in the New York *Herald* on April 14, 1889.

35. "November Boughs."

36. Gilchrist's letter of October 10 was filled with comments on his portrait, including that of "Bernard Shawe, (a delightful Irishman who reviews books in the *Pall Mall* cleverly). . . . He thought there was a joyous spirited look about its execution" (Feinberg). This portrait is now at the University of Pennsylvania, and is the frontispiece to the *Comprehensive Reader's Edition.*

37. Leonard M. Brown; see 1631, and *n.*47 below.

38. WW's mare.

his "New Poetry" lecture has been published here in the "Critic"[39]—Well I must be off—

Walt Whitman

1621. *To John Burroughs*

ADDRESS: John Burroughs | West Park | Ulster County | New York. POSTMARK: Camden (?) | Oct 26 | 4 30 PM | 87.

Camden Oct 26, '87

early P M—have just had my dinner, (plain boil'd beef, potatoes & a roast apple—all relish'd well) & am now sitting here in my big chair in the little front room—Cold & cloudy out—looks like winter—O'C[onnor] was here eight days ago, spent an afternoon & Evn'g with me—& is now in Wash'n, & at the office—He is in a pretty bad way—paralysis the Dr now calls it—(I will get Kennedy to send you on a letter giving fuller details) —The Pall Mall Gaz. letter you speak of appears to have *erased* a sentence or two (showing my gratitude & appreciation of *home* helpers)[40]—but even as it is I hope it doesn't bear the construction you speak of—I enclose my last two bits[41] tho you may have seen them before—

I have just recd letters from Dr B[ucke] and Kennedy—Herbert G went back five weeks ago, with his picture, & I have heard from him & it in London—they like the portrait—the Smiths are back in Phila—I am much as usual—but the *peg-letting down* goes on with accelerated pace—

Walt Whitman

1622. *To William Sloane Kennedy* *10.26. [1887]*

Camden Oct: 26 P M

Y'r card of 24th rec'd—I keep on ab't as usual—please send the O'C[onnor] letter of mine to John Burroughs, West Park, N Y—Letters rec'd this noon from yourself, Dr B[ucke] and J B—pleasant for me—makes up for the glum weather—

W W

39. *The Critic* of September 24.

1623. *To William D. O'Connor*

ENDORSED: "Answ'd Nov 25/87." ADDRESS: Wm D O'Connor | Life Saving Service | Washington D C. POSTMARKS: Camden, N.J. | Oct (?)8 | 4 30 PM | 87; Washington, Rec'd. | Oct | 28 | 10 PM | 1887 | 1.

Camden Oct 28 '87

Ab't the same as usual with me—Few or no visitors—have been reading Pepys & Lewes's Goethe papers—A letter from John Burroughs yesterday—he inquires particularly for you—he is at West Park again—I have just written to C W E[ldridge] & sent him a bundle of papers. My canary is singing loud & fast, as I write—Cloudy half-dripping weather, promising cold—clear skies I think before night—as I sit here by the window—

Walt Whitman

1624. *To William D. O'Connor*

ENDORSED: "Answ'd Nov 25/87." ADDRESS: Wm D O'Connor | Life Saving Service | Washington D C. POSTMARK: [*indecipherable*].

Camden Oct: 30 '87

To-day winter blowing & cold, but the sun shining & I feeling comfortable & hearty—took quite a drive yesterday afternoon & out to supper in the evening to my friends Mr and Mrs: Harned here—enjoy'd all—Have had letters from Dr B[ucke], Burroughs, H B Forman & Dr Knortz—the German—L of G. is out or ab't out, (at Zurich, Switz) Dr. K says—God bless you—

W W

1625. *To Mary Smith Costelloe*

ADDRESS: Mrs: Costelloe | 40 Grosvenor Road | the Embankment | London England. POSTMARK: Camden | Nov 1 | 8 PM | 87.

Camden U S America | Nov. 1 '87

Your good letter just rec'd & indeed welcomed—I remain ab't the same—cold weather here—no snow yet but raw & aching enough—Logan

40. See 1597.
41. "Shakspere-Bacon's Cipher" and "November Boughs."

& Alys here day before yesterday. All well—your father here lately on his way to Milville—Ab't the sculptured head, *you have full power*—I am writing a card to Ernest Rhys to-day—I was out driving Sunday, & out to supper evening—Would you like me to send you the Phila: papers—or any others?

Walt Whitman

1626. *To William Carey*

ADDRESS: Wm Carey | Century Office | Union Square | New York City. POSTMARKS: Camden, N. J. | Nov 2 | 6 PM | 87; P.O. | 11-3-87 | 1-1(?) | N.Y.

Camden Nov. 2 '87

Dear Sir

The $16.50 on acc't of photo. sales, came safely to hand & this is the receipt—with best thanks—

Herbert Gilchrist hurried off, & I did not have a chance to mention to him ab't the London agency for the photos. I should suggest however the selection of some established shop or name in London as the best place—some place where such things are in their line—

I like best Nos. 3, 6 and 8 of the photos. Would send those only—

Am ab't as usual—

Walt Whitman

1626.1 *To Mr. and Mrs. Thomas Harned* *11.7. [1887?]*[42]

Nov. 7 1½ p m

Mr: and Mrs: Harned | Dear friends

I send the two tickets for the lecture—Also a little book for Anna. Also a programme of Donnelly's "Cypher Book"—curious to look over—Also your Sunday *Tribune* wh' I pilfered last night—also a couple of *Critics*—enjoyed a happy three hours last night & am all the better for it to-day—

W W

42. 1887 appears to be a plausible date since November 7 fell on Monday in that year; the "programme" was probably an announcement of Ignatius Donnelly's *The Great Cryptogram* (1888).

1627. *Alfred Lord Tennyson To WW*

TRANSCRIPT.

November 15th, 1887.

Dear Walt Whitman,

I thank you for your kind thought of me.[43] I value the photograph much, and I wish that I could see not only this sun-picture, excellent as I am told it is, but also the living original. May he still live and flourish for many years to be. The coming year should give new life to every American who has breathed a breath of that soul which inspired the great founders of the American Constitution, whose work you are to celebrate. Truly, the mother country, pondering on this, may feel that how much soever the daughter owes to her, she, the mother, has, nevertheless, something to learn from the daughter. Especially I would note the care taken to guard a noble constitution from rash and unwise innovators.

I am always yours,

Tennyson.

1628. *To The Editor*, The Critic

Camden Nov 15 '87

Your note rec'd. I send you *Yonnondio* if you can use it. The price is $8.[44]

W W

1629. *To William Sloane Kennedy*

Camden Nov: 16 '87

Your card rec'd—I dispatch to-day by express the plaster head, directed to *care Sylv: Baxter, Herald office, 255 Washington st. Boston.* (It ought to go through to-morrow) I also mail to you at Belmont the Cox photo. we call "the laughing philosopher". The head I want given to some appropriate permanent gallery in Boston, that you & S B decide on—

W W

43. WW sent Tennyson one of Cox's photographs. The text of the letter appeared in the New York *Tribune* on November 22, apparently before WW received it (see 1634).

44. It appeared in *The Critic* on November 26.

1630. *To William Sloane Kennedy*

Camden | Nov. 17 '87 noon

I express'd the plaster head to you last evening pre-paid, address'd to you, care of Sylvester Baxter, Herald office, 255 Washington st. Boston —it is in a stout rather heavy box—I myself like the head muchly—it is what we call the 2d head—Morse made one, the 1st, with more brooding-repose & dignity, more of the antique spirit &c. wh' many like best—it *is* good, & attractive but tho' I like the 1st decidedly I am quite clear *this* is the typical one, modern, reaching out, looking ahead, democratic, more touch of animation (perhaps unsettledness) &c. &c.—not intended to be polished off—left purposely a little in the rough—

I suppose you rec'd my cards—You and S B think over what I say ab't giving the head to some Boston Art Institution or (if you prefer) other depositary, appropriate. *You & he have absolute power to dispose of it in that way*—It ought to be ready for you there at the Herald office, Friday or Saturday morning—I also sent you by mail to Belmont the Cox photo you requested—hope you will write me Tuesday (or Wednesday) ab't all, the meeting &c. details[45]—I am ab't as usual, health &c—pretty dull & heavy —M D Conway[46] has been to see me—No word from O'C[onnor]. Morse is here. I expect to see Ernest Rhys soon. I get word from Dr B[ucke] often. Sunshiny out to-day—I think of going forth with horse & rig after dinner—God bless you and wife—

Walt Whitman

1631. *To Leonard M. Brown*[47]

Camden Nov. 19 '87

Thank you & double-thank you, my dear young man, for your affectionate letter & money help $25 which came safely to-day—Every thing is going on here much the same—Mrs. D[avis] is well & busy—& I sit here each day in the big chair by the window—(slowly waning I suppose)—H Gilchrist is back in London with his picture, wh' as I

45. See 1634.

46. On November 12 WW had a "visit from Moncure D Conway with carriage, to take me over to R P Smith's for a few days. (I do not go)" (*CB*).

47. Brown, a young English schoolteacher and friend of Gilchrist, came to America in May, 1887. On March 31 Gilchrist wrote to WW: "He is an uncommonly good fellow, quiet earnest serious soul and very practical, full of solid worth, whose knowledge and attainments are sure to be valued in America. His father is a clergyman,

understand gets good opinions. I have heard from him once or twice. I am expecting Ernest Rhys here soon. Morse the sculptor is still here. Mr Eakins the portrait painter, of Phila:, is going to have a whack at me next week.[48]

Dull dark dripping day as I write. My little canary is singing blithely. I enclose you my last pieces—Yes, indeed we shall be glad to see you—Mrs D will & I will—Meanwhile love to you & God bless you—

Walt Whitman

1632. *To Robert Underwood Johnson*

ADDRESS: R U Johnson | Century Office | Union Square | New York City. POSTMARK: Camden, N.J. | Nov 19 | 4 30 (?) | 87.

Camden Nov.19 '87

My dear Sir[49]

I tho't I w'd send you word that Mr Eakins the portrait painter of Phila: is coming over here to paint me next week & I suppose will continue off & on all the current month (or more)—so you might tell Miss Wheeler[50]—Also give my best respects & remembrance to Miss W. & say I continue in the mind & promise of last summer (when it suits)—

Walt Whitman

1633. *To Thomas B. Harned* *11.22. [1887?]*

ADDRESS: T B Harned | 568 Federal Street | Camden.

Camden Nov. 22 Evn'g

Yes I shall be very glad to take dinner with you Thursday at 1. If I see Morse I will ask him to come along.

Walt Whitman

and this son of his reads Leaves of Grass silently & unobserved by the sect of his orthodox family" (Feinberg). An entry in *CB* on August 29 reads: "Leonard Morgan Brown goes back to Croton-on-Hudson—has been here ab't a week." See also 1461, *n.*26, and 2184.

48. On December 22 WW wrote in *CB:* "Thos. Eakins is here painting my portrait—it seems strong (I don't know but powerful) & realistic—very different from Herbert's—It is pretty well advanced & I think I like it—but we will see."

49. See 938.

50. Undoubtedly Dora Wheeler, the artist (see 1519, *n.*50).

1634. *To William D. O'Connor and Richard Maurice Bucke*

ENDORSED (by O'Connor): "Answ'd Nov. 25/87 | Sent Dr. Bucke." ADDRESS: Wm D. O'Connor | Life Saving Service | Washington | D C. POSTMARKS: Camden, N.J. | Nov 23 | 8 PM | 87; Washington, Rec'd. | Nov | 24 | 7 AM | 1887 | 6.

Camden Wednesday Evn'g Nov. 23 | '87

(Please send on to Dr Bucke)

May-be you will like to read Kennedy's letter—so I send it on. There was to be a meeting of the N E Womans' Club, (somewhat swell) last Monday Evn'g—at wh' Kennedy was invited to take a hand—as I & mine were to be the themes—& K requested of me to send him replicas of Morse's plaster h'd & Cox's new photo, wh' I did—furthermore see letter[51]—

A dull spell of weather here—cloudy & raw—I don't get out or around much—going out to-morrow—Thanksgiving dinner, to my friends Mrs and Mr Lawyer Harned—turkey & champagne—always have something good to drink, & plenty of it—(H. has the best whiskey in America)—& a blazing wood fire—also a charming little girl & boy—I go there quite often—

In the London budget in N Y Tribune Nov. 22, is a short letter (extract) from Tennyson to me[52]—rather curious—nothing important—I sent T. one of Cox's photos of me (the "laughing philosopher")—& this I suppose is an answer or part thereof—but how it got out & in cable is funny—

Dear O'C, I havn't heard from you in a month. Write soon, do. Dear Maurice, yours of 20th came this morning. Ernest Rhys has not arrived here yet, but I am looking for him. Morse is here to-day. Mr Eakins of Phila: has commenced painting me. A bouncing Thanksgiving week to you both—

Walt Whitman

51. WW's letter was written on the verso of one from Kennedy, who described a meeting of the New England Woman's Club at which "I swept the audience away by my electric fire" (November 18–22, Feinberg). On November 25 O'Connor forwarded WW's

1635. *To Talcott Williams*

ADDRESS: Talcott Williams | *Press* newspaper | 7th & Chestnut | Phila:. POSTMARK: Camden, N.J. | Nov 2(?) | 6 PM | 87.

Camden New Jersey | Nov: 26 '87

If convenient I wish you would send me six copies *Press* of Nov: 24.[53]

Walt Whitman

1636. *To William Sloane Kennedy* *11.29.* [*1887*]

Camden Nov. 29 latter p m

As I write I am sitting in my big chair—*cold* to-day here—sunny however—Morse is here working on a life size Emerson—(somewhat of a demand for them)—Your last letter good reading for him (& me too)—dont *push* the getting of the head into any Boston gallery ("wait for the wagon")—it must depend on its artistic merits—as a piece of modeling &c—Nothing new with me—no E Rhys yet—I have heard from O Connor—tolerable—

Walt Whitman

1637. *To Richard Maurice Bucke*

ADDRESS: Dr R M Bucke | Asylum | London Ontario | Canada. POSTMARK: Camden, N.J. | Dec 5 | 8 PM | 87.

Camden Evn'g Dec 5 '87

A pleasant day here to-day has been, after a cold spell—Ab't as usual with me—No sight of Rhys yet—the artist Eakin of Phila: comes off & on painting my portrait—it is going to be realistic & severe I think (ab't likeness, excellence &c. we will see)—Did I tell you I rec'd a letter from O'C[onnor] ten days ago, rather cheery?

W W

letter to Bucke (Feinberg).

52. See 1627.

53. "Thanks in Old Age" appeared on this date.

1638. *To William Sloane Kennedy* *12.7. [1887]*

Camden Dec: 7 P M

Yours rec'd to-day—Rhys has arr'd & in N Y—Expect him here now every day—I have just written a few lines on Whittier (by request & moderate cash) for an illustrated Phila: periodical, wh' I will send you when printed[54]—Morse decidedly likes the Art Museum as the place to put the bust (& I am inclined the same) but as I said leave it to you & B[axter][55]—Affectionate regards to Mrs. Fairchild—O'Connor is poorly—I had a letter from Mrs. O'C. I continue ab't the same—Write often as you can—Have Hartmann & the "Society" completely fizzled?[56]

W W

1639. *To Julius Chambers*

TRANSCRIPT.

Dec. 12, '87

Thanks for the invitation to write abt Whittier, which I will if the spirit moves me. . . . Cannot tell either what extent the piece (if any) would be, nor price.[57]

1640. *To The Editor, The New York* Herald(?)

TRANSCRIPT.

Camden, Dec. 16, 1887

Thanks for the handsome pay for the WHITTIER SONATA—Best regards to Mr. Bennett, Mr. Chambers & all the boys.

Walt Whitman

54. WW's greeting to Whittier ("As the Greek's Signal Flame") appeared in the New York *Herald* on December 15 and in *Munyon's Illustrated World* in January 1888. He received $10 from the latter (CB). Whittier wrote to WW on January 13, 1888 (Feinberg; Traubel, II, 8). See also note 57.

55. On December 5 Kennedy reported his reaction to Morse's bust ("a fine, nay a great, work"), and observed that although Baxter was trying to persuade the Boston Public Library to accept the work, he "preferred the Art Museum" (Feinberg). On December 29 the library declined "the proposed gift"; Kennedy noted, "They tho't it too sketchy, they said" (Trent).

56. On April 24, 1888, WW informed Traubel that "The Whitman Club in Boston has petered out"—a conclusion he approved of: "I seem to need to be studied by each man

1641. *To J. P. Loftus*[58]

ADDRESS: J. P. Loftus | Poughkeepsie | New York.
POSTMARK: Camden, N.J. | Dec 19 1887 | 4:30 PM.

328 Mickle Street | Camden New Jersey |
Dec. 19 '87

I send you same mail with this, *Leaves of Grass* and *Two Rivulets* —2 vols. Please send me a card soon as rec'd notifying me—pay rec'd—

Walt Whitman

1642. *To L. Logan Smith* [*12.22. 1887*]

ADDRESS: (not in WW's hand): L Logan Smith | 507 S. Broad St. | Phila. Pa. POSTMARK: Camden, N.J. | Dec 22 | 6 AM | 87.

328 Mickle Street | Camden New Jersey

For the present send Ernest Rhys's letters addressed here to my care[59]—

Walt Whitman

1643. *To William Sloane Kennedy*

Camden Dec. 27 '87 Evn'g

Much the same as of late with me. I was out to Christmas dinner —turkey & champagne galore—Rhys is here—Morse has gone to Richmond, Indiana—address there care of Wm B Morse—send the "Time" magazine[60] to Dr Bucke after reading it—

Walt Whitman

for himself, not by a club" (I, 63–64).

57. According to the auction record WW's letter was written on the verso of one dated December 11 from Chambers, of the New York *Herald* (formerly in the Dorn Collection). On December 14 WW sent the *Herald* "As the Greek's Signal Flame. [For Whittier's eightieth birthday, December 17, 1887.]," for which he received $25 (CB). It appeared in the Boston *Advertizer* on December 17 (CRE, 533*n*.).

58. Loftus was an instructor at Riverview Academy in Poughkeepsie in 1887. He paid $5 for the volumes (CB).

59. In CB WW noted on December 22 the arrival of Rhys, who had Christmas dinner at the Harneds' with the poet and the Traubels.

60. The December issue of *Time: A Monthly Magazine* contained "Mr. Swinburne on Walt Whitman," by Roden Noel (see 768).

1644. *To Edward T. Potter*

ADDRESS: Edward T Potter | 26 S 38th Street | New York City. POSTMARKS: Camden, N.J. | Dec 2(?) | 6 PM | 87; F | 12–30–87 | 6 A | N.Y.

328 Mickle Street | Camden New Jersey | Dec. 28 '87

Thanks, my dear friend, for your kind letter & (Christmas) contents—I am ab't as usual—

Walt Whitman

1644.1 *To Susan Stafford* [(?).(?). *1887?*][61]

TRANSCRIPT.

328 Mickle Street—Camden

Thursday—we have just had dinner & I have come in the front room by the fire—A deep snow everywhere outside, but comfortable here —the little canary bird singing blythely & I feeling pretty well for me though indeed as the hymn says—"Old age is creeping on with its great load of sin."

I havn't heard from you or seen any of you in some weeks—hope everything goes on right—Hope you or George or both of you will come here soon & spend some hours & stay to dinner—Mrs. Davis spoke of it Thanksgiving Day—& we both would be glad to have you both come yet —Everything goes now with me about as usual—have not been as well as usual the last month—send one of Herbert's last letters enclosed—Dr. B[ucke] speaks of Harry in his last and wants to know if anything has been done—Love to you and George & Ed & all—

The roads and going are dreadful at present—

Walt Whitman

61. This letter appears to have been written in December 1887. Harry Stafford, as the following letter reveals, was having throat trouble at the time.

According to my tabulations, based upon his letters and his entries in *CB*, WW's income in 1887 amounted to at least $2,575.98: royalties, $131.91; lectures, $620.00; sales of books, $95.75; payments for articles and poems, $233.00; gifts, $1,421.32; and sale of photographs, $74.00. (As noted in 1472, the figures for book sales are conjectural, since I have had to assume that he charged a uniform price.)

1888

1645. *To Richard Maurice Bucke*

ADDRESS: Dr R M Bucke | Asylum | London | Ontario | Canada. POSTMARK: Camden, N.J. | Jan 7 | 6 PM | 88.

Camden Jan 6 '88 | P M—

A quiet dull day with me—bad obstinate cold in the head, the old inveterate constipation, & bad kidney tribulation, day & night—but I am up & dressed & sitting here by the fire, & my bird is singing cheerily behind my big chair—I send you Kennedy's and Rhys's and O'Connor's last letters[1]—return me the printed *Nation* slip (wh' you may have seen before)—

Rhys is to be communicated with at present, care of Kennedy, as you will see—Morse is still at Richmond, Indiana—yours of[2] rec'd, acknowledg'g "*Time*" &c.—poor Harry Stafford's throat trouble is the same as ever—

Walt Whitman

1646. *To John Burroughs*

ADDRESS: John Burroughs | West Farms | Ulster County | New York. POSTMARKS: Camden, N.J. | Jan(?) | 6 PM | 88; New York | Jan 9 | 1 PM | 88 | Transit.

Camden Saturday Evn'g Jan 7 '88

Dear J B

Your sister Abigail[3] and Mrs Dart have just been here to see me

1888

1. WW's letter was written on one from Kennedy dated January 2, in which the latter reported that Frederick W. Wilson was willing to publish his "Walt Whitman, Poet of Humanity," and requested WW's "book of addresses" for a circular soliciting subscriptions. The letter was signed "yr faithful son, & lover" (Feinberg). Rhys wrote on January 4 from Orange, New Jersey, and described a Shakespearean masquerade at which Alys Smith, dressed as Portia, danced like "A wild Bacchantë, passionate of foot!" (Feinberg). O'Connor enclosed a review of *Anne Gilchrist* in *The Nation* in his letter of January 3 (Feinberg).

2. WW forgot to insert the date of Bucke's (lost) letter.

3. Abigail was married to Hiram I. Corbin.

& have given me the latest news I have had ab't you for a long time—Glad to get the visit & glad to hear—

I am getting along in much the same fashion as before, do not get out or around at all—but keep fair spirits & am comfortable enough—(just now under a cloud physically, bad cold in the head & kidney troubles)—bad weather yesterday & to-day, am sitting here by the fire—a parrot and canary in the room—Ernest Rhys has been here some time—is now in Boston—Morse the sculptor has gone temporarily to Indiana—Kennedys *W W book* is [to] be pub'd by Wilson in London I believe—I hear frequently from Dr Bucke, he is all right—I got a letter from O'Connor three days since—he is pretty ill yet, but I believe gets to the office—I write a little—short bits to order mostly—spend the time seated in my big chair here, quite aimlessly—

Love to 'Sula and to Julian[4]—Write when you can—

Walt Whitman

I enclose slips but you may have seen them before—

1647. *To William Sloane Kennedy*

Camden Jan 10 '88

Am sitting here by the fire alone early afternoon & will write you a few lines—have had my light dinner—(stew'd chicken & a cup of tea & enjoy'd with sufficient zest)—Feelings in general not much different—of good substantial spirits, the fund still holds out—but quite a perceptible, steadily, almost rapidly increasing weakness of limb, strength, eyesight &c.—In fact a, more or less slow, loosening & deadening of the physical machine—After a dark storm, (with snow,) nearly a week, the sun is out this afternoon & there is a half-thaw—My friend Pearsall Smith (who is very kind all along,) was here yesterday & bro't a great bundle of London literary weeklies &c. wh' I have been looking over—I like the advertisement pages ab't as well as any—I suppose Ernest Rhys is there with you—I

4. Burroughs' son.

5. Kennedy wrote on January 10 and again on the following day after receipt of WW's letter (Feinberg), and reported an impending visit with Sanborn at Concord and Rhys's lecture before the Saint Botolph Club. In a postscript on January 10 he observed: "Rhys is obeying yr injunction to show me myself. Nothing delights me more—my limitations are so many. I see chances of improvement in many directions, already—from his friendly suggestions."

6. See 1627.

7. On January 13 Burroughs wrote: "My domestic skies are not pleasant & I seem

sent him three letters yesterday enveloped to your care. I rec'd your letter —Wilson then is the pub[lisher] y'r book—If you think well of it, express the whole MS. first, to me here, that I may look over & authenticate—Put it in stout pasteboards, tie well, & direct fully & carefully, & it will easily travel & the expense will not be great[5]—

W W

1648. *To William D. O'Connor*

ENDORSED: "Answ'd Jan. 27/88." ADDRESS: Wm D O'Connor | Life Saving Service | Washington | D C. POSTMARKS: Camden, N.J. | Jan(?) | 8 PM | 88; Washington, Rec'd. | Jan 15 | 7 AM | 1888.

Camden Jan 14 '88 Evn'g

Was very glad to get y'r letter—(I return herewith the *Nation* criticism)—I have rec'd another letter from Tennyson[6]—Rec'd to-day a letter from John Burroughs. He is rather blue—the boy Julian is his great comfort—the "domestic skies" (as he terms it,) are not fair and happy[7]— I hear from Kennedy—Rhys is there with him & they take to each other muchly—I am invited (by letter from Cortland Palmer, rec'd to day) to [go] to R's lect: before the Century Club, N Y Feb 7, & say a word at conclusion—But of course cannot go—I have rec'd a nice letter from Whittier, thanking me, &c.[8] I hear from Dr Bucke regularly & often—he is true as steel—

Has been very bleak & cold here, but better & sunny to day—I am quite unwell, but keep up & around & eat my meals in moderation—(an old fellow who comes here said to me as I was eating my supper "No extremes any way—but eternal vigilance in eating & drinking is the only thing for a sick man, or an old coon.")

I want to print a little 15 or 20 page *Annex* to L of G—Also a sketch of Elias Hicks—but don't know when—

Walt Whitman

depressed & restless most of the time. . . . I dislike the winters more & more & shall not try to spend another in this solitude. Indeed I am thinking strongly of selling my place. I am sick of the whole business of housekeeping. If it was not for Julian I should not hesitate a moment. J. goes to school & is a bright happy boy, very eager for knowledge, & with a quick intelligence. He alone makes life tolerable to me" (Feinberg).

8. In a brief note on January 13 Whittier wrote: "But for illness I should have thanked thee before this for thy vigorous lines of greeting in Munyon's Illustrated World, combining as they do the cradle and evening song of my life. My brother writers have been very generous to me and I heartily thank them for it" (Feinberg; Traubel, II, 8).

1649. *To Richard Maurice Bucke*

ADDRESS: Dr R M Bucke | Asylum | London | Ontario Canada. POSTMARK: Camden, N.J. | Jan 14 | 8 PM | 88.

Camden Saturday Night | Jan 14 '88

Have had my supper (some rice pudding & a cup of tea) & am sitting here by the fire, all comfortable—Nothing very new or different—Have just written to O'C[onnor]—Have rec'd letters from Whittier, Kennedy & John Burroughs. The latter rather *cloudy*—Been a cold sunny pleasant day here—

Walt Whitman

1650. *To Courtland Palmer*[9]

ADDRESS: Courtlandt Palmer | 117 East 21st Street | New York City. POSTMARKS: Camden, N.J. | Jan 14 | 8 PM | 88; P. O. | 1–15–88 | 2–1A | N.Y.

Camden New Jersey | Saturday Night Jan 14 '88

My best respects & thanks to you, & to the Club—but I am disabled & cannot avail myself of the kind invitation.

Walt Whitman

1651. *To Richard Maurice Bucke*

ADDRESS: Dr R M Bucke | Asylum | London | Ontario Canada. POSTMARK: Camden, N.J. | Jan (?) | 6 PM | 88.

Camden PM Jan 18 '88

Yours of 16th (? or 15th) just rec'd—I am certainly no worse *in re* the late physical ailments—easier more likely[10]—ate my dinner with

9. President of the Nineteenth Century Club, freethinker, and friend of Ingersoll. On his death in July, WW observed to Traubel: "They may bury Palmer—they will bury him—and I do not feel like crying over his grave. There's only one word for some graves—hurrah is that word. Hurrah is the word for brave Palmer!" (Traubel, II, 42).

10. At nine o'clock on the same evening WW was not so optimistic in his CB entry: ". . . Cold in the head keeps on—grows worse I think—any thing like easy bodily movement will soon be impossible—it is very nearly so now—trouble in head, kidney

relish—(cold beef, potatoes & onions)—Eakins has been today painting my portrait—it is altogether different from any preceding—plain, materialistic, very strong & powerful ("A poor, old, blind, despised & dying King")[11]—

W W

1652. *To William D. O'Connor*

ENDORSED: "Answ'd Jan. 27/88." ADDRESS: Wm D O'Connor | Life Saving Service | Washington | D C. POSTMARKS: Camden, N.J. | Jan (?) | 6 PM | 88; Washington, Rec'd. | Jan | 19 | 7 AM | 1888 | 4.

Camden Jan: 18 '88

Nothing very new with me. Storms, snow & cold weather—I send the *Harvard Monthly*[12]—when thro' send to Dr Bucke. I am pottering along—certainly no worse in my late physical ailments—rather better possibly—the wind is sighing & singing & piping around the house as I write.

Walt Whitman

1653. *To Richard Maurice Bucke*

ADDRESS: Dr R M Bucke | Asylum | London | Ontario Canada. POSTMARK: Camden, N.J. | Jan (?)4 | 8 PM | 88.

Camden Jan: 24 '88

Just after 2 P M—Yours of 22d has just come—Have you rec'd a letter from J H Johnston proposing that you & Mr P[ardee] & he go to *Havana?*—very cold here now for eight days—The cold affects me unfavorably, but I think I feel somewhat better—(somewhat *plus*)—no late news of O'C[onnor]—I rec'd a letter this mn'g from N Y Herald, from J G

botheration pretty bad, joints all gone, locomotion & movement gone—mentality all right yet—& spirits far better than could be expected—appetite fair—sleep, minus to tolerable."

11. Eakins resumed work on the portrait on January 14 (*CB*).

12. The January issue of the *Harvard Monthly* included Charles T. Sempers' article "Walt Whitman and His Philosophy" (149–165). On March 3 Sempers invited WW to address the Harvard Signet Society. On the following day, in a personal communication, he informed the poet that "Prof. Wm James would like you to be his guest," and that he was making a study of WW's poetry under an unnamed English instructor (Feinberg).

B[ennett] himself ask'g me to write for the paper[13]—I have just had my dinner, corned beef & mince pie.

W W

1654. *To William Sloane Kennedy*

Camden Evn'g Jan 24 '88

The MS-package has just come, all right, freight p'd—I am perhaps better than three weeks ago—the cold pinches me—very cold here for over a week—What of Rhys?—Did he get the five letters I sent?—I have been invited (by letter of J G B[ennett]) to write for the N Y Herald—

W W

1655. *To William D. O'Connor*

ENDORSED: "Answ'd Jan. 27/88." ADDRESS: Wm D O'Connor | Life Saving Service | Washington D C. POSTMARK: Camden | Ja(?) | (?) | 8 P(?) | 88.

Camden Jan. 24 '88 | Early P M

Sunny here to-day, but very cold for over a week—I am less ill than ab't New Years—nearly my usual condition—the cold blunts me badly (& I have no margin to spare)—my dear friend, how are you getting along? I think ab't you daily. Dr B[ucke] is probably going south with his friend Pardee—but returns immediately & may call on you at Wash'n—I have just eaten my dinner with zest—

Walt Whitman

13. On January 23 Bennett suggested that contributions on "any subject whatever that may suit your fancy can be treated. The *Herald* would be very willing to pay a reasonable compensation for this work, and only as much as you desire need be signed. The stanzas need not contain more than 4 to 6 lines" (LC). Beginning on January 27 and continuing until May 27, WW submitted the following pieces, for which he received $180 (*CB*): January 27, "To Those Who've Failed"; January 29, "Halcyon Days"; February 3, "After the Dazzle of Day"; February 11, "America"; February 15, "True Conquerors"; February 21, "Soon Shall the Winter's Foil Be Here"; February 23, "The Dismantled Ship"; February 25, "Old Salt Kossabone"; February 27, "Mannahatta"; February 29, "Paumanok"; March 1, "From Montauk Point"; March 2, "My Canary Bird"; March 9, "A Prairie Sunset"; March 10, "The Dead Emperor"; March 12, "The First Dandelion";

1656. *To William Sloane Kennedy* 1.26. [*1888*]

Camden Jan: 26 late Evn'g

I have look'd over the MS &c—hardly made any emendations—Shall send it back soon—y'r card dated 24th rec'd[14]—What do you mean ab't E R[hys]?—write more fully & plainly—I am ab't as usual—very cold here—It is most 10 & I am going off to bed—

W W

1657. *To Richard W. Colles*

ADDRESS: R W Colles | 26 Oxford Road Ranelagh | Dublin | Ireland. POSTMARKS: Camde(?) | Jan (?) | 1 30 (?)M | 88; Phila[delphi]a, Pa. | Jan | 28 | 1888 | Paid.

Camden New Jersey U S America |
Jan: 27 '88

I have been waiting to get good copies of "Specimen Days" wh' I shall have shortly, & will then immediately send one—I mail "Leaves of Grass" now—the price of the two vols. is one pound, wh' I wish you to send me here by p o order (328 Mickle Street)—Nothing very new or different—arctic cold here for the last fortnight—best regards to you & my Irish friends[15]—

Walt Whitman

1658. *To Susan Stafford*

ADDRESS: Mrs: Susan Stafford | Kirkwood | (Glendale) | New Jersey. POSTMARK: Camden, N.J. | Jan (?) | 1 30 PM | 88.

Camden P M Jan. 27 '88

Quite froze up here, but ab't as usual, tho' a trifle less well than

March 16, "The Wallabout Martyrs"; March 18, "The Bravest Soldiers"; March 19, "Orange Buds by Mail from Florida"; March 20, "Continuities"; April 10, "Broadway"; April 15, "Life"; April 16, "To Get the Final Lilt of Songs"; April 23, "To-day and Thee"; May 2, "Queries to My Seventieth Year"; May 8, "The United States to Old World Critics"; May 10, "Out of May's Shows Selected"; May 14, "As I Sit Writing Here"; May 21, "A Carol Closing Sixty-Nine"; May 23, "Life and Death"; May 27, "The Calming Thought of All." (To avoid confusion I have consistently used the titles established in the last edition of *Leaves of Grass.*) WW also wrote a letter to the *Herald* on January 26.

14. Apparently lost. Since Rhys and Kennedy failed to hit it off, the letter probably referred to the impending rift; see 1683.

15. Colles replied on February 12 (Syracuse; Traubel, IV, 141–142).

common this winter—a bad obstinate cold in the head among the rest—I don't get out at all—I am writing a little to order—got up late to-day—had chocolate & buckwheat cakes with quince jelly for my breakfast—am sitting here by a good fire—How are you all?—I wish Ed or Jo would stop & tell me—

W W

1659. *To Andrew Carnegie*

ADDRESS: Andrew Carnegie | New York City. POSTMARKS: Camden, N.J. | Feb 2 | 6 AM | 88; P.O. | 2-2-88 | 10-1A | N.Y.

328 Mickle Street | Camden New Jersey | Feb: 1 '88—

Thanks for the books, (three) wh' have arrived, & will be treasured. When in Phila. come over here & see me—I have a copy of *Leaves of Grass* for you—(would mail it if I knew the right address)[16]—

Walt Whitman

1660. *To William Sloane Kennedy*

Camden Feb: 1 '88 | P M

I remain ab't the same as usual—Dr Bucke was here most of yesterday[17]—staid over in Phila: on his way to Florida with an invalid friend—Dr B to return in ab't two weeks—Shall return your MS. in two or three days or so (by express to Belmont, unless you wish otherwise)—I am writing a little for the N Y Herald *personal column*—E R[hys] is not here yet—weather more endurable—

W W

1661. *To Richard Maurice Bucke* [*2.2–3. 1888*]

ENDORSED (by Bucke?): "2 Feb 88." ADDRESS: Dr R M Bucke | of Canada | St Augustine | Florida. POSTMARK: Camden (?) | Feb 3 | 6 PM | 88.

Thursday night—9—I am sitting here in the little front room alone—Mrs D[avis] has gone to her room—I have had rather a bad

16. WW sent this postcard to "New York City"; someone added "5 West 51st St." Carnegie contributed $50 in 1889 to the fund that paid for WW's nurse (Traubel, IV,

day—uncomfortably *full* feeling & two or three brief pronounced spells of pain & dizziness in the head—but feel ab't as usual to-night—the things & note came all right last evn'g from the Phila. druggist—best thanks—Eakin[s] is here to-day painting—weather fine here—Andrew Carnegie has sent me his books with friendly inscription—

Friday noon—A fine day—Rose pretty late & have had my breakfast, buckwheat cakes & chocolate—feel pretty well—Shall try to get out a little—out doors looks so attractive—no letters this morning—took some of the bitter water when I got out of bed—no letter has come here for you —Sh'd one come I will mail it to you St A[ugustine]—Did you see O'C[onnor] at Wash'n?

Walt Whitman

1662. *To Richard Maurice Bucke*

ADDRESS: Dr R M Bucke | of Canada | St Augustine | Florida. POSTMARK: [Cam]den, N. J. | (?).

Camden Feb: 7 '88

Nothing new or special, I am ab't the same—quite frequent visitors—weather dark & moist & snowy, not very cold—I believe Rhys is to lecture to-night before the N Y Century Club—a week from to-night before the Phila: Contemporary—no letters have come here for you—I have just sent L of G. to Andrew Carnegie.

Walt Whitman

1663. *To M. H. Spielmann*

ADDRESS: M H Spielmann | Magazine of Art | La Belle Sauvage Ludgate Hill | London | E C | England. POSTMARK: Camden, N.J. | Feb (?) | 6 PM | 88.

Camden New Jersey U S America | Feb. 7 '88

Yours of Jan: 13 rec'd—Of course the little "Twenty Years" has not been hitherto publish'd & will not be until after you issue it—No word nor money from y'r American agent or any one has reach'd me up to date

435).

17. Bucke was accompanied by Pardee and Dr. Osler (*CB*).

—If convenient when the 20 is sent me, remit by P O money order, as that is most convenient to me.[18]

Walt Whitman

1664. *To Houghton, Mifflin and Company*

TRANSCRIPT.

Camden, February 9, 1888

Dear Sirs,

Thank you for the little books, No. 32 "Riverside Literature Series"—Somehow you have got a couple of bad perversions in "O Captain," & I send you a corrected sheet.[19]

Walt Whitman

1665. *To M. H. Spielmann*

ADDRESS: M H Spielmann | Magazine of Art | La Belle Sauvage Ludgate Hill | London | E C | England. POSTMARK: Camd(?) | Feb 1(?) | 8 PM | 88; London E. C. | (?) | Fe 20 88 | AC.

Feb. 10 '88—328 Mickle St |
Camden New Jersey U S America

The $20 in pay for the little piece came to me to-day from C[assell] & Co: Fourth av. N Y. Thanks—

Walt Whitman

18. "Twenty Years" appeared in the *Pall Mall Gazette* in July and in *The Magazine of Art* in August, with saccharine illustrations by Wal Paget, which, however, the poet admired (Traubel, II, 134).

19. A search in the archives of Houghton Mifflin Company reveals that RLS #32 (in the extant 1913 revision) has the following title page: "The Gettysburg Speech|and Other Papers|by|Abraham Lincoln|Lowell's Essay on Lincoln|and|Whitman's O Captain! My Captain!" Since the poem is set in a smaller type than the preceding text, WW's suggested corrections may have been made. For this information I am indebted to Marie L. Edel of the editorial staff of Houghton Mifflin Company. See also Traubel, IV, 453.

20. About this time Kennedy asked for names of potential subscribers to his study of WW. In the same letter he mentioned Howells' comment on the poet in *Harper's*

1666. *To William Sloane Kennedy* [*2.10(?). 1888*]

Will send the MS. back by express next Monday, 13th—
Put down
T B Harned
566 Federal Street
Camden New Jersey
as a subscriber to the book
C O D—(or I suppose any time)—
I will send some names[20]—

1667. *To William Sloane Kennedy and John Burroughs*

Camden Feb: 11 '88

My dear friends | WSK & JB

I send you Dr Bucke's letter from Florida just rec'd with the latest from our dear friend O'Connor (tho' I think Dr B's view is ab't as severe & dark as the case will stand)[21]—

Nothing very new or special with me—I am jogging along much the same—down hill no doubt even if slowly—this is the most nipping winter I have ever had—at present am sitting here by the fire in my little front room—have had my late breakfast (I rise late these cold days) of chocolate & buckwheat cakes with quince jelly—feel so-so fair—Ernest Rhys is here—was here last evn'g—his lecture, debate ab't, & advocacy of, L of G. last Tuesday evn'g in N Y. seems to have been quite an affair—a success—the leaning of the full dress audience (many ladies) was palpably certainly on our side—quite remarkable—Tho' little Fawcett & Rev. Lloyd had their say against L of G.[22] Rhys delivers lecture again, here in Phila. next Tuesday evn'g. I still have little bits in N Y Herald—

Walt Whitman

send to | John Burroughs | West Park | Ulster County | New York

Monthly for February (478–479)—"some colorless & diplomatically drawing-roomish talk on you & Tolstoi. Pretty good though, & worthy yr reading. H. is never profound, methinks; but is graceful & happy" (Feinberg).

21. WW's letter was written on the verso of one from Bucke (Feinberg), but the part pertaining to O'Connor is missing. O'Connor noted Bucke's "very pleasant" visit in a letter to WW on April 14 (Syracuse; Traubel, IV, 497).

22. According to the Philadelphia *Ledger* of February 9, Edgar Fawcett (1847–1904), a minor poet and novelist, "satirized Walt Whitman's poetry. Mr. Fawcett said he had heard it stated that there had been auctioneers' catalogues duller than Walt Whitman's poetry, but he attributed that to partisan bias. Rev. Mr. [William] Lloyd also condemned Whitman's poetry." For Fawcett's vitriolic rant, see Kennedy, *The Fight of a Book for the World*, 83–84. Also see *The New-York Times* of February 9, 1888.

1668. *To Richard Maurice Bucke*

ADDRESS: Dr R M Bucke | Ocean View Hotel Bay Street | St Augustine | Florida. POSTMARK: Camden (?) | (?) | 9(?) | 88.

Camden Feb: 11 '88

Yours just rec'd—I am ab't the same—sitting here as usual—Rhys is here—had quite a success at the N Y Century Club last Tuesday night advocating & debating L of G. There was quite a debate—the trend was with us—very cold again, dark & an icy rain—Morse writes me it is doubtful if he comes back here again[23]—he thinks of going to Chicago & thence south—I have just written to Kennedy & enc: y'r letter—to be forwarded to John Burroughs—

Walt Whitman

1669. *To William Sloane Kennedy*

Camden Feb. 14 '88

I send the MS. package by express to-day, prepaid, address'd same as this card. Dr B[ucke] is at St Augustine, Florida. Rhys is here—(lectures to-night before the Contemporary Club, Phila)—I continue much as usual—Sunny & comfortable weather here to-day—Your circ. appears in N Y. *Times*[24] & in *Post* here—

W W

1670. *To the Executive Committee, The Contemporary Club*
2.15. 1888

To Executive Committee | Contemporary Club:

I propose the name of Thomas B Harned, Counsellor at Law, of this city, for membership in the club.

Walt Whitman

Camden | N J
Feb: 15 '88

23. Morse's letters to WW from Richmond, Indiana, where he was staying with his mother, were filled with plans to make money through sculpture demonstrations, theatrical benefits for the Y.M.C.A., etc.

24. On February 13 *The New-York Times* noted that Kennedy's "Walt Whitman, Poet of Humanity" was to be published by Frederick W. Wilson & Brother, and that subscribers were to write directly to the author.

1671. *To Richard Maurice Bucke*

ADDRESS: Dr R M Bucke | Ocean View Hotel | Bay Street | St Augustine | Florida. POSTMARK: Camden, N.J. | Feb (?) | 4 30(?) | 88.

Camden Feb: 16 '88

Yours of 12th rec'd—cheery to have such good acc'ts of the place, the weather, & your enjoying all, & good condition—Rhys has had good success with his lectures both in N Y & in Phil.—has rec'd $75 for the two & has made many friends—he leaves here to-morrow for Boston—I will see him & tell him to write you—I rec'd a very few lines from Mrs O'Connor dated 15th this morning—O'C is poorly—seems to be worse since that ill spell—Nothing special or new with me—bitter cold just now here, but sun shining to day—My little pieces continue to come out in N Y Herald—(bits of poetry personal column)—two or three times a week—(all will appear of course in *Nov. Boughs*)—rec'd the *London Adv*—have frequent visitors—Morse still away west—the Smiths going to London early in summer—Mrs D[avis] has just been in to see to my coal & to say we are to have apple pudding for dinner—it is chilly here as I finish this—my little bird sits hunch'd up in a lump, & sings not—but spring weather is coming & early summer & I will write a little poem ab't it to warm me up[24.1]—

Walt Whitman

1672. *To Ellen M. O'Connor*

ADDRESS: Mrs: O'Connor | 1015 O Street | Washington | D C. POSTMARKS: Camden, N.J. | Feb (?) | 4 30 PM | 88; Washington, Rec'd. | Feb | 17 | 11 PM | 1888 | 1.

Camden Feb: 16 '88

Card rec'd—thanks—every word is welcom'd & appreciated—All ab't the same with me as of late—severely cold here—Dr Bucke is in Florida to return in ten days—An old Quaker has paid me a visit to-day[25] (I am yet writing my *Elias Hicks* paper)—Best love to you & William—

W W

According to the Philadelphia *Press* of February 15 Rhys delivered his lecture in Haseltine's art gallery; the discussion after the address was led by Professor W. Appleton of Swarthmore College and F. H. Williams.

24.1. On the following day he sent "Soon Shall the Winter's Foil Be Here" to the New York *Herald* (CB).

25. Probably David Newport, with whom WW had a "talk ab't Elias Hicks" on February 15 (CB).

1673. *To William Sloane Kennedy*

Camden Feb: 17 '88 | 2 P M

Yours of 15th rec'd[26]—you ought to be getting the MS—package as I sent it by Express three or four days ago—Nothing new or special with me—The severe cold has pinch'd me, but the weather is pleasanter to-day—Rhys has just left here for N Y and Boston—Dr B[ucke] returns from St Augustine in ab't a week. I am sitting here anchor'd in my big chair all day—Write when you can—

W W

1674. *To Dick & Fitzgerald*

TRANSCRIPT.

Camden, February 18, 1888

. . . I have succeeded in getting you a two vol. set . . . of Leaves of Grass and Two Rivulets, edn. 1876—shall I send the vols to you. The price is $6.66. . . .[27]

Walt Whitman

1675. *To Richard Maurice Bucke*

ADDRESS: Dr R M Bucke | Hotel San Marco | St Augustine | Florida. POSTMARK: Camden, N.J. | Feb 21 | 4 30 PM | 88.

Camden Feb: 21 '88 P M

I am perhaps essentially the same—*plus* the feebleness & lameness & clouded heavy almost constant half-pain feeling of head & brain. Much milder weather here & I shall try to get out in phaeton if I can—I have

26. Kennedy informed WW that he had sent "375 (out of the 1000) circulars" soliciting subscribers for "Walt Whitman, Poet of Humanity." One of the circulars was included in the letter (Berg).

27. WW sent the edition on February 21 (*CB*). The firm was located at 18 Ann Street, New York City.

28. In his letter of February 20 Rhys discussed his lecture in Concord at the home of Dr. Edward Emerson, which had been attended by Mrs. Ralph Waldo Emerson, Ellen Emerson, and Sanborn: "There was a general agreement with my position" (Feinberg).

29. Apparently in a lost letter Bucke informed WW that he had submitted to *The*

recd the London *Adv.* Feb. 16—Two ladies have just called & chatted, (Mrs Talcott Williams one of them)—I enclose Ernest Rhys's letter, just rec'd[28]—also two letters for you—I believe they still print my little bits in the personal col. N Y *Herald*, but do not see the paper—Do you see it there? I enjoy all you say of the balm & flowers of Florida—

Walt Whitman

1676. *To Richard Maurice Bucke*

ADDRESS: Dr R M Bucke | San Marco Hotel | St Augustine | Florida. POSTMARK: Camden, N.J. | Feb 23 | 8 PM | 88.

Camden Feb. 23 '88 | Evn'g

I continue well as usual—Signs of spring—Rhys in Boston—Shall look sharp in next *Critic*—No word lately from O'C[onnor]. Have had my supper—& all right—Your letters rec'd—

W W

1677. *To Richard Maurice Bucke*

ADDRESS: Dr R M Bucke | Hotel San Marco | St Augustine | Florida. POSTMARKS: Camden (?) | Feb 2(?) | 4 30 PM | 88; Saint Augustine | 2 M | Feb | 28 | 1888 | Fla.

Camden Feb: 25 '88

Nothing special with me. Rainy & dark to day—not cold. Yours rec'd with *Critic* letter—A letter from Mrs: Costelloe this mn'g—all well & busy, baby growing & well—I am not surprised at the refusal to publish in C[29]—the opposition & *resentment* at L of G. is probably as concentrated & vital & determined in New York (my own city) as anywhere, if not

Critic an article entitled "One Word More on Walt Whitman." About February 20 he sent the poet a letter (dated February 16) from the editors of the magazine rejecting the piece: "We have printed a great many 'words' on Whitman, & can only print 'more' when there is some specific occasion for doing so—when he issues a new book, or does something to attract general attention to his work" (Feinberg). On March 11 Bucke informed WW that he was revising his article and was considering either submitting it to *Lippincott's Monthly Magazine* or withholding it until the appearance of Kennedy's book, when he could include it in a notice of that work (Feinberg). On August 15 Bucke was still working on his article and now thought to "make it into a review of the new vol." (Feinberg). Probably it became "An impromptu criticism" (see 1875).

more vital—& I do not count the Gilders as essentially *on our side*—they are smart & polite but worldly & conventional—as to the literary classes anyhow I will get a few exceptional dips out of them—but mainly I will have to wait for another generation—But this I have long known—

I am sitting here all alone to-day—I do not eat dinner these short days —only breakfast & supper—my appetite fair—had some buckwheat cakes & raw oysters for my breakfast. Shall most probably not write you at F[lorida] again—

Walt Whitman

1678. *To Sidney H. Morse*

TRANSCRIPT.

Feb. 28, '88—Noon.

Eakins' "pict." is ab't finished—It is a portrait of power and realism, ("a poor, old, blind, despised and dying king"). Things with me ab't the same. Mrs. D[avis] is well—is in the back room working. My canary is singin' away as I write.

1679. *To Richard Maurice Bucke*

ADDRESS: Dr R M Bucke | Asylum | London | Ontario Canada. POSTMARK: Camden, N.J. | Mar 3 | 4 30 PM | 88.

Camden P M March 3 '88

Your letter from N Y has come & is satisfactory ab't the W[orthington] proceeding[30]—Nothing new or special—A bright day & several visitors. Messrs Ingram and Logue were much taken with y'r talk, impression, presence &c.

W W

30. See 1691.
31. For a list of WW's pieces in the New York *Herald*, see 1653, *n*.13
32. On March 2 WW had sent a bill to the New York *Herald* for $100 for the

1680. *To Talcott Williams* *3.6. [1888]*

ADDRESS: Talcott Williams | office *Press* newspaper | Phila:. POSTMARK: Camden, N.J. | Mar 6 | 8 PM | 88.

Camden March 6

I write a line to say—Don't forget (if convenient) to look over the Herald "personal intelligence" column for the little pieces—especially the H of last ten days, including Sunday H[31]—

W W

1681. *To Julius Chambers* *[3.7. 1888]*

ENDORSED: "sent to Mr Chambers, Herald— | March 7 '88 | proposal accepted by letter from H March 8." DRAFT LETTER.

Mr. Browning has just been here & says you wish something more specific & defined in my relations and pay[32]—If you want the little pieces continued, I would like to continue them for $40 a month, & will furnish you with say ten pieces a month—of the character and length as hitherto —this bargain to commence with the current month—

Walt Whitman

1682. *To Ellen M. O'Connor*

ADDRESS: Mrs: O'Connor | 1015 O Street | Washington | D C. POSTMARK: Camden, N.J. | Mar 1(?) | 4 30 PM | 88.

Camden March 10 '88

Have not heard from you now in quite a while—write soon as convenient—Nothing specially new or different with me—Please forward this copy of the *Transcript* (March 6)[32.1] to Dr Bucke. He is now home in Canada—Best love, as always—

W W

pieces printed in January and February (*CB*). And see 1684.

32.1. The *Transcript* of this date contained a lengthy account of Rhys's lecture on "The New Poetry" before the New England Woman's Club on March 5. In the discussion following the formal address Mrs. Spaulding spoke in "eloquent praise of Whitman."

1683. *To Herbert Gilchrist*

ADDRESS: Herbert H. Gilchrist | 12 Well Road | Hampstead | London England. POSTMARK: Camden | Ma(?) | 8 P(?) | 8(?).

Camden New Jersey U S America | March 12 '88

Dear H—

Yours of Feb 17 is rec'd all right—best thanks to Mrs[?] Rosamund Powell for continuous subscription, safely rec'd[33]—I am in good heart & still writing a little but near the end of my rope I opine—Mrs S[tafford] was here lately—& she is first rate—all the rest pretty well—Tell me the fortunes of the bust, whatever happens—Morse is still west—Rhys is in Boston[34]—

W W

1684. *To Richard Maurice Bucke*

ADDRESS: Dr R M Bucke | Asylum | London | Ontario Canada. POSTMARK: Camden (?) | Mar 15 | 8 PM | 8(?).

Camden March 15 '88

Everything continuing on ab't the same with me—was out to dinner at my friends the Harneds Sunday—Harry Stafford has been here —the throat trouble still—otherwise well—O'C[onnor] is taking massage treatment[35]—the H[erald] has paid my first bill—I continue on. Y'r letters rec'd—A terrible three days' storm & cold & gale & snow—but has not affected me particularly—

W W

33. In his letter Gilchrist enclosed a contribution of £3 from Mrs. Powell, a friend of Leonard M. Brown, as "her annual subscription (free will offering) to you" (Feinberg).

34. On March 7 Rhys reported the "very hearty reception" given to him by Harvard students (Lion; Traubel, IV, 46–47).

35. Described in a note of March 13 from Mrs. O'Connor (Feinberg).

36. Ezra H. Heywood (see 1169). On March 23 WW lent Heywood $15 (*CB*).

37. On his way back from Florida Bucke stayed briefly in Philadelphia and discussed publication of WW's poetry with J. B. Lippincott Company. On March 6 the

1685. *To William Sloane Kennedy*

Camden March 15 '88

I continue on ab't as usual. O'C[onnor] is taking massage treatment—your last *Transcript* went from me to him, & so to Dr Bucke—I still write bits for the *Herald*—they pay me quite well—& then it is a sort of spur or fillip—A fearful four-day spell of cold, snow & gale here, but I have not felt it—the sun is shining as I write—

Walt Whitman

1686. *To Richard Maurice Bucke*

ADDRESS: Dr R M Bucke | Asylum | London | Ontario Canada. POSTMARKS: Camden, N.J. | Mar 20 | 6 AM | 88; New York | Mar 20 | 10 30 AM | 88 | Transit.

Camden 9 P M March 19 | '88

I was out yesterday to my friends the Harneds, & took a 3 or 4 mile drive afterward at sunset. The weather is pleasant—seems settled—I still write bits for the H[erald]—Haywood[36] the Mass: free lover here to-day, very cordial &c. I treat him politely but that is all. I rec'd yrs: with L[ippincott]'s declination[37]—Eakin[s] has taken away his picture & I havn't seen him for ten days[38]—

W W

1687. *To William Sloane Kennedy and Richard Maurice Bucke*

Camden 2 P M March 20 '88

It is a cloudy dark wet day—raining hard outside as I sit here by the window—am feeling pretty well—have just had my dinner, raw oysters & a slice of boiled ham—enjoyed the meal—Get lots of invitations,

publisher wrote to Bucke: "We have very carefully considered the question of making a proposition for the publication of Walt Whitman's Poems, but have concluded that we could not use his works to advantage" (Feinberg).

38. Apparently Eakins brought the painting back to Camden on March 23 (CB, and see 1691). Kennedy noted that it was hanging in WW's "shanty" in May, and commented: "It is a work of fine technical merit, has power in it beyond a doubt; but the expression and pose are not liked by many. To me it has something of the look of a jovial and somewhat dissipated old Dutch toper,—such as Rubens or Teniers might have painted" (30).

applications &c. every week—(O what lots of letters for autographs)—frequent visitors—sometimes an angel unawares—invites to swell dinners (or societies &c) invariably declined—Am idle & monotonous enough in my weeks & life here—but upon the whole am mighty thankful it is no worse—my buying this shanty & settling down here on ½ or ¼ pay, & getting Mrs. D[avis] to cook for me, *might* have been bettered by my disposing *some other way*—but I am satisfied it is all as well as it is—& whatever happens.[39]

Morse is still out in Indiana with a probability of remaining—at least of not coming back here—I have not heard anything definite of O'C[onnor]—I still jog away the *Herald* bits—I enclose Mary Costello's letter just rec'd—Isn't it cheery?

Walt Whitman

Send to Dr Bucke—both letters—

1688. *To William Ingram*[40] *3.21. [1888]*

ADDRESS: Wm Ingram | Tea Store—31 north 2d St: | Phila:. POSTMARK: Camden, N.J. | Mar 21 | 4 30 PM | 88.

Camden March 21 | 2 P M

The Herald has just come—all right—

W W

1689. *To William Sloane Kennedy*

Camden March 22 P M '88

Yours of 21 & the Transcripts & the Scotch papers rec'd—thanks for all—I have written you quite copiously lately—I continue well for me

39. Undoubtedly WW was informing Kennedy that he contemplated no change in his living arrangements, and that the proceeds from the Cottage Fund were to be used (or not used) as he saw fit. Although WW's friend was loath to offer any public criticism, some of the contributors were evidently annoyed that no accounting was made by the poet. Garland, in 1889, asked Traubel "what had become of the cottage money." WW retorted quickly: "It is a question not again to be reopened" (Traubel, v, 355).

40. Ingram was a tea dealer in Philadelphia (see 1604).

41. Probably the letter from John Newton Johnson which appears in Kennedy, 19–21. See 1548. On March 29 Kennedy confessed "a good deal of sympathy for our cranky friend Johnson" (Feinberg).

—all the little *Herald* pieces will appear (with misprints corrected) in *November Boughs*—two things the reason why of this card. *Dont let your Wilson book go to press till you have read the proofs.* 2d—please enclose to me the Alabama letter, to be return'd to you[41]—dont mind its malignance—the blizzard & its immediate results all over here—dark and rainy now—I am sitting here alone in the big chair—

W W

1690. *To William Sloane Kennedy*

Camden Evn'g March 26 '88

I return Mr Johnson's letter—I do not see any thing in it more than facts or appearances warrant—as he is & as things are down there poor J is in a bad, unhappy fix—as of coffee being ground in a mill—Much relieved to know you will *yourself* see all the proofs of the Wilson book—give them a good searching reading—for with Dr Bucke's book they are to be in all probability the vignette & authority of many things in my & my works' future—the backward & contemporary reference. Nothing new in particular with me—more or less evidences of gradual physical deterioration[42]—but spirits good—appetite &c fair—& you know I begin my 70th year now in ab't two months—thank God indeed that things are as well as they are & that I & my fortunes (literary & otherwise) are—Rainy & dark & raw here all day—I was out yesterday four hours to my friends the Harneds—was taken & bro't back in my phæton—a lull in my *Herald* contributions[43]—I send you the *Kottabos*[44] from Dublin—Morse is still out in Indiana—Dr B[ucke] kindly writes to me often & you must do so too.

Walt Whitman

42. In CB on March 24 WW noted "the pulse-pains (heart?) in left breast the last 20 hours and during last night."

43. No pieces appeared in the New York *Herald* between March 20 and April 10 (see 1653).

44. According to Kennedy's *The Fight of a Book for the World*, the first issue of *Kottabos*, prepared by the classical students at Trinity College, contained "a translation by J. I. Beare into Greek anapests" of "Come Lovely and Soothing Death" (42). In his letter on March 29 Kennedy noted his request to Tennyson "to say a few words of you for the appendix to the book. Also wrote Enrico Nencioni (c/o *Nuova Antologia*, Rome) asking him to send me a statement as to 'Walt Whitman in Italy' " (Feinberg).

1691. *To Richard Maurice Bucke*

ADDRESS: Dr R M Bucke | asylum | London | Ontario | Canada. POSTMARK: (?) | Apr 8 | 5 PM | 88.

Camden Sunday noon | April 8 '88

It is very pleasant & sunny to-day & I am going out in the rig abt 1 o'clock to my friends Mr & Mrs Harned, three or four hours, & have dinner & a good generous drink of the best champagne—I enjoy everything—Nothing new with me—there seems to be some hitch in the *Herald's* publ'ng my little pieces[45]—(I hear that they have been appealed to in print to stop *such stuff*)—I feel lately as if I sh'd make a start in putting *November Boughs* in type making perhaps 150 to less than 200 pp.—some 30 pp, perhaps, of poems to go afterward as *Annex* to L of G. My health though poor is "the same subject continued"—I enc: K[enne]dy's letter from Wilson[46]—(not important)—Rhys[47] is still in Boston—Morse in Indiana—I like Eakins' picture (it is like sharp cold cutting true sea brine)—I have not heard a word of the Worthington suit in N Y[48]—not a word from my dear friend O'C[onnor] in Wash'n—

Walt Whitman

1692. *To The Editor*, Cosmopolitan

328 Mickle Street | Camden New Jersey |
April 9 '88

Dear Sir

Can you use this?—the price would be $12[49]—

Walt Whitman

45. On April 1 WW sent a bill for $40 to the *Herald* (CB). According to a note of April 7 from Bennett there was a slight error in WW's bill. Bennett requested ten more poems for April (Feinberg).

46. On March 24 Wilson informed Kennedy that he was most interested in obtaining subscribers to the projected publication (Feinberg). On March 29 Kennedy observed, "I have not much faith in the despatch of F. W. Wilson. . . . I have sent him 20 names" (Feinberg).

47. Rhys had written to WW from Boston on March 7 (Lion; Traubel, IV, 46–47) and on April 3 (Feinberg; Traubel, II, 30–31). At this time relations between Rhys and Kennedy were strained; on March 1(?) Kennedy had written to WW: "Rhys continues his schemes on society's pocket-book, & demoralizes my nerves frightfully when I see him, somehow" (Yale). WW observed to Traubel in May: "You couldn't get 'em to fit nohow. Kennedy will hardly fit anything but a chestnut burr" (Traubel, I, 168). See also Traubel, II, 515.

48. A New York lawyer, Thomas J. McKee, wrote to WW on April 7: "I received your letter but had been looking into the matter for some days previously, Dr. Bucke and Mr. Johnston having spoken to me about your claim against Worthington. The difficulty I

1693. *To Richard Maurice Bucke*

ADDRESS: Dr R M Bucke | Asylum | London | Ontario | Canada. POSTMARK: (?) | Apr 1(?) | 4 30 PM | 88.

Camden April 11 P M | '88

I send you McKee's, the lawyer's, letter[50]—Matters much the same with me—pretty miserable probably with a bad cold the last three or four days—but beginning on the mend to day (I think)—Sent three little poems, one to *Century*, one to *Lippincott's*[51] & one to *Cosmopolitan* four days since—the last returned—the first accepted & paid for—& no word yet of the L—the *Herald* pieces will be resumed & carried on (March has been paid for)[52]—the weather here dark wet & heavy—I am feeling fairly as I sit here by the window down stairs alone & finish this—

Walt Whitman

Lawyer Harned was over to the Cosmopolitan Club meeting Phila. Tuesday night—talked with Carnegie—

1694. *To Helen E. Price*

TRANSCRIPT.

April 11, 1888

Yes, I will sit to Warren Davis, the painter—w'd like to have it over within five or six sittings. . . . I am still living here & comfortable &

find is this that R. Worthington failed some time since and is now unable to do business in his own name, and the business is now run by a corporation named the Worthington Co. of which Worthington's wife or some female relative is the President. The time within which to claim a forfeiture of the plates and books (two years) has run out and we are therefore limited to our action for an injunction and damages, I am therefore quietly trying to get all the facts I can as to what the 'Worthington Co.' has been doing with reference to your book. The Company is of some responsibility and undoubtedly have possession of the plates.

"As soon as I have facts sufficient to base a sure claim I will get the injunction and money" (Feinberg). See also 985 for an account of WW's dealings with Worthington.

49. "To Get the Real Lilt of Songs" was returned, but appeared in the New York *Herald* on April 16 as "The Final Lilt of Songs." The title in *November Boughs* was "To Get the Final Lilt of Songs."

50. See 1691, *n.*48.

51. "Old Age's Lambent Peaks" appeared in the September issue of *The Century Magazine*. "A Carol Closing Sixty-Nine" was returned by *Lippincott's Monthly Magazine;* it appeared in the New York *Herald* on May 21.

52. WW received $40 (CB).

in good spirits enough but probably near the end of my rope—badly paralyzed & do not get out at all except by being toted.

1695. *To William D. O'Connor*

ENDORSED: "Answ'd April 16/88." ADDRESS: Wm D O'Connor | 1015 O Street | Washington | D C. POSTMARK: Camden, N.J. | Apr 12 | (?) | 88.

Camden Thursday Evn'g | April 12 '88

Dear W O'C

Lots of inquiries & prayers & good wishes ab't you come to me (& I hear of) that *you* never hear of. I rec'd Nelly's two brief cards over two weeks ago—but hunger for more frequent & fuller information—Hear from Dr B[ucke] & Kennedy often & from John B[urroughs] at long intervals—K's book has not yet begun the printing but is to be—is settled. All my *Herald* bits will be included in *November Boughs* & I will send an early proof of all to you—As I write I am sitting here in my big chair by the window (I have open'd it a few moments—it is near sunset—air a little tart)—I am quite *immobile* & don't get out except by being *toted*—a bunch of white lilies is in the window & my bird is singing like a house afire[53]—

Walt Whitman

1696. *To Herbert Gilchrist*

Camden New Jersey U S America | April 13 '88

Dear H G

I am still here in the little Camden shanty not much different from when you were here, but more disabled perhaps in locomotion power & in more liability to head & stomach troubles & easiness of "catching cold" (from my compulsory staying in I suppose)—Mrs Davis is still housekeeping & cooking for me—It is just past noon & I am told I am to have a

53. O'Connor responded on April 14 with characteristic fervor to WW's last sentence: "What an idyl of your room you opened to me in your flash of description—you in the big chair, the window open to the sunset, the Easter lilies on the sill, and the little bird singing his furious carol! It was quite divine. How I wish you could get active and

good rice pudding (made in a big earthenware baking dish) for my dinner—wh' suits me well—(I wish you were here to help eat it)—

I see the Staffords occasionally—Mrs S was here ab't a week ago, is well as usual—nothing very new or different with them—they are still on the old farm & store & expect to continue—I see Ed and Harry & Joe Browning occasionally—Mrs. Rogers[54] (Mrs S's sister) is dead & buried, ab't two weeks ago—

Thos: Eakins, portrait painter, has painted a picture of me—very different from yours—realistic—("a poor old blind despised & dying King")—When you write tell me ab't your pict: whether it has been on exhibition &c:—also ab't the bust Mary Costello has—whether any thing has been done with it—Morse is out in Indiana yet—Rhys was in Boston at last acc'ts—I am writing little poetical bits for the N Y *Herald*—Pearsall Smith and Mrs. S. & Alice are going to London to live—a big bunch of white lilies scents the room & my little canary is singing gaily as I finish—

Walt Whitman

If you have a chance you may show this to Mary Costelloe & Wm Rossetti—to both of whom I send my love—

1697. *To William Sloane Kennedy and Richard Maurice Bucke*

ENDORSED: "Send the letters & one | slip to Dr B. | Dr. I want Ford's & O'C's | letters returned to me."

Camden noon April 18 '88

All goes as well & monotonously as usual (No news is good news) —I got up late, ate my breakfast (two or three broil'd oysters, a Graham biscuit & cup of coffee)—& here I am sitting alone in the little front room, feeling *not discomfortable* particularly—I have rec'd from Morse a plaster cast bust of *Elias Hicks* wh' I have set up in the corner—like it—it is a little larger than life proportions—you may be sure Morse is making better work than ever—I send O'C[onnor]'s letter to me,[55] just rec'd, as I know you will wish to hear & know—also send S Ford's letter[56]—Also

well!" (Syracuse; Traubel, IV, 499).

54. Mrs. Elizabeth W. Rogers (see 1114) was buried on April 2 (*CB*).

55. The letter of April 14.

56. A letter from Sheridan Ford on April 13 invited the poet to give a series of lectures in England and Scotland in the fall (Syracuse; Traubel, IV, 496–497).

send two little slips of a *Herald* bit—you keep one & send the other with these letters to Dr B—(Maurice, I have rec'd y'r letter of 15th)—Have quite a good many visitors—Yesterday two young women, one from Ireland—a lady from Virginia (authoress)—Mr Quigley (law assistant of Col. Ingersoll)—& a young Phila. littérateur &c. &c.—Receive many invitations & some queer letters—Spirits mainly good—Best love—

Walt Whitman

1698. *To William D. O'Connor*

ENDORSED: "Answ'd May 16/88." ADDRESS: Wm D O'Connor | 1015 O Street | Washington | D C. POSTMARKS: Camden, N.J. | Apr 18 | 4 30 PM | 88; Washington, Rec'd. | Apr | 18 | 10 PM | 1888 | 4.

Camden P M April 18 '88

Dear W. O'C.

Your kind good copious letter came to-day & has been read & reread. Nothing new in the monotony of my life—I have rec'd a good plaster bust of Elias Hicks, (size inclined to colossal) wh' I have put open in the corner of my room—& I think it does me good—perhaps *needful* almost to me—Elias at the latent base was *sentimental-religious* like an old Hebrew mystic—& though I may have some thing of that kind 'way in the rear it is pretty far in the rear & I guess I am mainly sensitive to the wonderfulness & perhaps spirituality of things *in their physical & concrete expressions*—& have celebrated all that—

My writing for the *Herald* continues on—they have lately written to me to continue—they have paid me so far $165, wh' I call first rate—25 for the Whittier bit, also enclosed—The little slip enclosed (Lilt of Songs) I sent first (a week or ten days ago) to the *Cosmopolitan* N Y[57] —asking $12—it came back at once *rejected*—So I sent it to *Herald* —The *Cosm.* man stopt here last fall & urged me to send him something—but I think they now have new men—Yes I think Stedman inclined to be friendly & receptive[57.1]—(L of G. though has to fight ag't a most infernal environment there in New York)—Best love to you—Best love to Nelly—

Walt Whitman

57. See 1692.

57.1. O'Connor noted, on April 14, spending an evening with Stedman, who spoke of WW's poetry "with enthusiasm": "His face is Zion-ward, & he will be a credit to the family yet" (Syracuse; Traubel, IV, 498). To which WW responded, when Traubel read O'Connor's letter aloud: "Welcome! thrice welcome, Edmund, to our bed and board!"

58. For accounts of WW's other celebrations during the shad season at Thompson's, see 1393 and 1534. An account of the festivities in 1888 appears in Traubel, I, 80–81.

59. See 778 and 1003. On May 16 O'Connor commented on Mrs. Moulton: "Her

1699. *To Thomas B. Harned*

TRANSCRIPT.

Camden, April 19, 1888

Billy Thompson of Gloucester,[58] has just been here to invite me down to baked shad dinner at his place, Tuesday next, abt 2. Wishes me to invite you in his name & my own. You come here say ½ past 12 & we will drive down in my rig. Be back by dark. . . .

Walt Whitman

1700. *To William Sloane Kennedy and Richard Maurice Bucke*

ADDRESS: Wm Sloane Kennedy | Belmont | Mass:.
POSTMARK: Camden, N.J. | Apr 23 | 8 PM | 88.

Camden | April 23 '88

I send Logan Smith's letter—please forward this & it to Dr Bucke —I am feeling badly enough to-day—cold in the head & accompaniments —nothing very new—dull dark raw weather, inclined to rain—I am sitting in the big chair all the forenoon & day doing nothing—or reading the papers wh' is ab't the same thing—Mrs. L C Moulton[59] is coming here this afternoon—I am reading Boswell's *Johnson*[60]—My Elias Hicks plaster bust stands in the corner—it is good—

Walt Whitman

1701. *To John H. Johnston*

ADDRESS: J H Johnston | Diamond Merchant | 150 Bowery cor: Broome St | New York City.
POSTMARKS: Camden, N.J. | Apr 24 | 8 PM | 88; (?) | 4 25 88 | 5-1A | N.Y.

Camden April 24 '88

Yours rec'd with the $9—pay for the books[61]—Thanks—Nothing

fault was in being too Araminta-Seraphina-Matilda" (Syracuse; Traubel, IV, 246). WW agreed: "I can't endure her effusiveness: I like, respect her: but her dear this and dear that and dear the other thing make me shudder" (Traubel, IV, 246).

60. On April 15 WW had borrowed Boswell from Harned: "I have never so far read it" (Traubel, I, 38). The poet did not respond to Johnson's "ponderous arrogance" (I, 46), but continued to read the work "as a duty" (I, 70). He remained unimpressed when he finished the work on May 13 (I, 146).

61. Johnston had taken WW's four-volume edition of Pepys and the two-volume Forman edition of Shelley on January 20 (*CB*).

very new with me—I am just off on a ride & spree to Gloucester-shore to a planked shad & champagne dinner given me by my friend Billy Thompson—

Walt Whitman

1702. *To William D. O'Connor* *4.25. [1888]*

ENDORSED: "Answ'd May 16/88." ADDRESS: Wm D O'Connor | 1015 O Street | Washington | D C. POSTMARKS: Camden, N.J. | Apr 25 | 4 30 PM | 88; Washington, Rec'd. | Apr | 25 | 11 PM | 1888 | 5.

Camden April 25 towards noon

A pleasant day out & I am feeling better than for two weeks past—Drove down yesterday three or four miles to Gloucester, on the Delaware below here, to a fine old public house close to the river, where I had four hours & a good dinner of *planked shad* & champagne—had a good view of the picturesque sight of the great boat, 20 black men rowing rhythmically, paying out the big seine—making a circuit in the river, (here quite a bay)—enjoyed all & was driven back to Camden abt sundown—So you see I get out & have fun yet—but it is a dwindling business—

I enclose an old note from Kennedy. Mrs. Louise C Moulton was here day before yesterday—two English travelers a couple of hours later—Did I acknowledge & thank you for your good letter of a week ago?—Last evn'g came a little eng: from one of J. F. Millet's pictures—a present from Felix Adler of N Y[62]—Best love & remembrances to you both—

Walt Whitman

1703. *To George and Susan Stafford*

ADDRESS: George and Susan Stafford | Kirkwood (Glendale) | New Jersey. POSTMARKS: Camden, N.J. | Apr (?) | (?) PM | 88; Kirkwood | Apr | 27 | 188(?).

Camden p m April 26 '88

If it sh'd be quite pleasant weather Sunday my present intention is

62. Adler (1851–1933) was the founder of the New York Society of Ethical Culture and author of *Creed and Deed* (1877); later he was a professor at Columbia University.

63. WW went to Glendale on Sunday, April 29, and dined with the Harneds in the evening (*CB*).

64. Joseph Browning.

65. On April 19 Hamlin Garland (1860–1940), one of Kennedy's friends, wrote to the poet for the first time. He was giving a series of lectures entitled "Literature of

to drive down & see you[63]—be there between 12½ and 1—Want to come once more, but am getting very feeble. May possibly not feel well enough to come. No special news in my affairs—things much the same old way—Joe[64] has stopt by the window a few minutes. I hear from Herbert & his picture. Also Dr B[ucke]. Harry was here 4 or 5 days ago. Backward spring here—

W W

1704. *To John Burroughs*

ADDRESS: John Burroughs | West Park | Ulster county | New York. POSTMARK: Camden | Apr | (?) | 4:30(?) | 88.

Camden noon April 27 '88

Dear J B

I was real glad to get word—& good word—from you this morning by your postal card of 25th—the early summer has always been *your time* & it seems to keep so just the same—Dr Bucke writes often & is the same good staunch friend—he is still at his Asylum, Canada, & full of work—some lecturing—Kennedy is well, living at Belmont still, & at work in Cambridge—his book ab't me not yet printed, but I believe it is settled to come out by the Glasgow publisher Wilson—

I rec'd a good & quite copious letter from O'Connor ab't a week ago—he is still very ill, appears to be little or no real improvement—nothing critical however—has paralysis—writes with the old fire & fervor—

With me things move on much the same—a little feebler every successive season & deeper inertia—brain power apparently very little affected, & emotional power not at all—I yet write a little for the *Herald*—&c.—Mrs Louise Chandler Moulton was here a day or two ago—pleasant visit—I have lately rec'd a letter from Prof: Hamlin Garland[65] who is lecturing in Boston, wh' I enclose, with slips—Send to Dr Bucke, after reading—As I write, I am sitting down stairs in my big arm chair—My sister Lou (George's wife) has just been here—It looks like such fine & bright weather I shall try to get out in my rig.

Walt Whitman

Democracy" in which he was "trying to analyze certain tendencies of American life somewhat in accordance with the principles you have taught." Garland did not share Kennedy's gloom about WW's reception: "I am often astonished at finding so many friends and sympathizers in your work and Cause. In my teaching and lecturing I find no difficulty in getting Converts to the new doctrine and find your poems mainly irresistible in effect. True they do not always agree that they *are* 'poems' though acknowledging their power and beauty. I do not care what they call them (I say to them) and receive their allegiance just the same" (Feinberg).

As I finish I get a letter from Dr B.[66] & returning two I sent him to read—I will enclose them also in this—

1704.1 *To O. G. Hempstead & Company* [*5.2. 1888*]

To O G Hempstead & Son
407 Library street
Philadelphia

Dear Sirs:

Please treat with the bearer of this, Mr Horace Traubel, a personal friend of mine, the same as you would with me, & consider him as my fully authorized agent in the matter.[66.1]

Walt Whitman
328 Mickle st Camden

1705. *To Richard Maurice Bucke*

Camden May 7 '88

Nothing special or new with me—Still stagger under the bad cold in the head, indigestion &c—was out driving yesterday afternoon—beautiful spring—enjoyed it much—rec'd a note f'm Mr Smith to-day that he had been ill & confined for a month, mostly a badly inflamed eye, a pretty serious case—suffering badly—but is getting over it. Mrs. S has sailed for England—Donnelly's book[67] I see is out—a case of "great cry & little wool" I opine—

Walt Whitman

1706. *To William Sloane Kennedy*

Camden | May 7 Evn'g '88

Here is Rhys's last letter to me[68]—I suppose (but don't know for

66. Bucke's letter of April 25 (Yale).

66.1. This note was written on the envelope of a letter dated April 28 from Hempstead & Son notifying WW of the imminent arrival of apparel sent to him by Lady Mount Temple (Feinberg; Traubel, I, 93).

67. *The Great Cryptogram* by Ignatius Donnelly (1831–1901), a book of almost

certain) that *Union League Club New York City* w'd reach him—I have been out driving this afternoon & was out yesterday, wh' is the best indication I can give of myself—I still write a little, but almost hate to not wanting to tack on lethargy & indigestion &c to what I have already uttered[69]—Thank you for the Transcripts & the last Sunday Herald—

Walt Whitman

1707. *To William D. O'Connor*

ENDORSED: "Answ'd May 16/88." ADDRESS: Wm D O'Connor | 1015 O Street | Washington | D C. POSTMARK: Camden, N.J. | May 7 | 4 30 PM | 88.

Camden noon May 7 '88

I send you some papers to while away the time—Was out yesterday driving in the country—never did the spring impress me more—it was just the right temperature—the very sun & wind and grass with sort o' human relations—(what a beautiful object is a young wheat field! what color!)—Had a good supper, oysters & champagne, at my friends the Harneds in the evn'g—I only eat two meals a day—

W W

1708. *To Robert Pearsall Smith*

ADDRESS: R Pearsall Smith | 507 S Broad Street | Philadelphia. POSTMARK: Camden, N.J. | May 7 | 4 30 PM | 88.

Camden noon May 7 '88

Dear friend

I wish I could send you something more *medicatious* than real sympathy & sorrow for your suffering & confinement—but that heartily for want of anything better. I rec'd a note from Mary with programme of her intended lecture before London women. Rec'd a letter from Logan ab't his visit to H Gilchrist's WW Portrait blow—I am not much different

one thousand pages in which O'Connor is cited as one of the foremost Baconians (923–926).

68. Rhys was in Camden on May 15—"goes this afternoon to N Y, & thence (after visiting Dr B[ucke]) to England" (*CB*). But see 1712.

69. On May 4 WW was paid $40 by the New York *Herald* for his April contributions (Yale).

here (but the net is slowly winding & tightening round me)—Was out driving yesterday afternoon & to supper at my friends Lawyer & Mrs. Harned's—I have been reading Boswell's Johnson—(what an old octopus J was!)—the oysters come—I had 3 or 4 for my breakfast—I take no other meal till ab't 5—Lady Mount Temple has sent me a present of a beautiful vest of knit stuff, wool & silk[70]—Love to Alys—As old S J says "Let us pray for each other."

Walt Whitman

I see I have taken a sheet of paper with a rambling first draught of one of my Herald yawps[71]—but *n'importe*—

1709. *To David McKay*

328 Mickle Street |Camden Evn'g May 17 '88

Dear D McK—

The bearer Horace Traubel is a valued young personal Camden friend of mine—American born, German stock—whom I wish to introduce to you with the best recommendation—He is of liberal tendencies & familiar with printing office matters & the run of books.

Walt Whitman

1710. *To William D. O'Connor*

ENDORSED: "Answ'd June 13/88." ADDRESS: Wm D O'Connor | 1015 O Street | Washington | D C. POSTMARKS: Camden (?) | May 1(?) | 3 PM | 88; Washington, Rec'd. | May | 18 | 11 PM | 1888 | 5.

Camden P M May 18 '88

Rose late this forenoon & very miserable—half a cup of coffee for my breakfast—but found your letter waiting for me—& have been better ever since—somehow does me more good than any[72]—The illness of last

70. Lady Mount Temple sent the vest on April 18 (Feinberg). On April 28 WW was notified of the arrival of the vest by O. G. Hempstead & Son (Traubel, I, 93). The poet was somewhat annoyed: "By the time we get the thing in our hands we will have paid more than it is physically worth. . . . But we'll get the waistcoat if it takes our last cent" (Traubel, I, 94).

71. On the verso are trial lines for the little poem "Life," which appeared in the

ten days must ab't have a turn for good or bad, & I guess it is going to be the former—

W W

1711. *To Mr. Bennerman*

ADDRESS: Mr Bennerman | Printing Office cor: 7th & | Cherry Streets | Philadelphia.

Tuesday May 22 '88

To Mr. Bennerman:

The bearer of this is Horace Traubel, a young friend of mine in whom I have confidence—I want to have printed (stereotyped) a book of (probably) 160 to 200 pages[73]—may-be somewhat less—long primer—exactly same sized page as the "Specimen Days" you printed of mine six years ago—

Can you & would you like to do it for me?—*Have you some good long primer?* The copy is ready—it is all printed matter—(or nearly all)—is all plain sailing—you could commence next Monday—Sh'd want liberal proofs—

You can talk with Horace Traubel just the same as you w'd with me—I am almost entirely disabled ab't walking, or bodily locomotion—

Walt Whitman
328 Mickle Street
Camden N J

1712. *To Richard Maurice Bucke*

ADDRESS: Dr R M Bucke | Asylum | London | Ontario | Canada. POSTMARK: (?) | May 24 | 4 30 (?) | 88.

Camden May 24 '88

Your two letters rec'd—thanks—things physical somewhat less maleficent than when I last mentioned—the worst is this iron-bound indi-

New York *Herald* on April 15.

72. O'Connor's letter of May 16 confirmed WW's verdict that his friend was "a master juggler of words": now exuding confidence, then describing the devil with fanciful vigor, now attacking Donnelly's critics, and then praising Stedman—all with his old manic intensity (Syracuse; Traubel, IV, 244–247).

73. *November Boughs.*

gestion—McKay has just been over to see me—nothing particularly new —he wants an extension of the contract five years more to publish L of G. and Spec. D.[74]—I told him I would think it over—is Rhys with you?[75]—the very worst spell of weather here—dull dark drizzling & raw—two days now—I have Donnelly's book—have been looking over it—havn't tackled the cipher—

W W

1713. *To V. S. C.*

328 Mickle Street |Camden N. J. May 25 '88

Yours rec'd & as you request, I send you a picture—I am still here in good enough heart, but physically wreck'd—every month letting me down a peg—Remembrance & love—

Walt Whitman

Send me a paper & don't forget it[76]—

1714. *To William D. O'Connor*

ENDORSED: "Answ'd June 15/88." ADDRESS: Wm D O'Connor | 1015 O Street | Washington D C. POSTMARK: Camden, N.J. | Jun 14 | 6 PM | 88.

Camden Thursday Afternoon | June 14 '88

Dear friend W. O'C

Here I am sitting up in the big chair—I got up ab't noon, (& shall keep up an hour or two, & send you my actual *sign manual* to show proof) —Have been pretty ill, indeed might say pretty serious, two days likely a

74. CB added a few details: "He will sell me the plates of Spec: Days for $150—he gives consent to my using the plates of Spec. Days for my *complete works edition*—500 or 600 copies."

75. When Rhys wrote to WW from New York on May 21, he was about to leave for Canada (Feinberg; Traubel, I, 292–293). On May 27 Rhys was in Camden (CB), and on May 30 he sent birthday greetings and a poem from New York (Feinberg; Traubel, II, 31–32). He wrote again on June 7, just before he sailed to England (Feinberg; Traubel, II, 33). In New York Rhys had been hobnobbing with Stedman and Colonel Ingersoll.

76. On the first page of the New York *Daily Graphic* on June 2 were photographs of the poet and drawings of his birthplace, his Camden house, and his den, with the heading "Walt Whitman's Birthday." On a later page V. S. C. devoted a column to "The

close call[77]—but Dr Bucke was here, & took hold [of] me without gloves —in short, *Monday last* (four days since) I turned the tide pronouncedly & kept the favorable turn Tuesday forenoon—havnt since kept the good favoring turn the last two days—but the indications are still favorable (good pulse the Dr says last two days) for my getting sort abt as usual— Dr B went back to Canada last Tuesday night, R.R. train—I am half thro' on my little "November Boughs"—& am stuck of it & proofs &c—

Walt Whitman

Best love to you & to Nelly—get your good letter to-day—

1715. *To William Sloane Kennedy*

Camden Thursday Evn'g | June 14 '88

Without any doubt I am on the gain—the last three hours I am up & shall probably work back before long as I was before—Five days ago my life was not worth a dime—but what will good doctors do?—The great determined heros of humanity are the best doctors—

W W

1716. *To Richard Maurice Bucke* *6.15–16. 1888*

ADDRESS: Dr R M Bucke | Asylum | London | Ontario | Canada. POSTMARK: Camden, N.J. | Jun 16 | 8 PM | 88.

Camden Friday Evn'g | June 15 '88

Rather warm weather—moist and sweaty, suits me—I am sitting up in the big chair this afternoon—looking languidly at the proof & copy

Good Gray Poet."

77. Troubled by newspaper reports of the poet's illness, O'Connor wrote for information on June 13 (Syracuse; Traubel, IV, 499–500). The almost fatal illness during the early part of June is fully recorded in Traubel, I, 259ff. Fortunately Bucke had come to Camden on June 3 (I, 254), and Nathan M. Baker became the poet's nurse on June 10 (I, 298). At first WW resisted, but for the rest of his life he was not without male nurses. On August 10 Traubel noted: "I have started a Whitman fund—am trying to get a small monthly guarantee each from a group of people to pay for the nurse and the extras required by W.'s persistent illness" (II, 116). Among the contributors were Stedman (II, 141), Richard Watson Gilder (IV, 390), Josephine Lazarus (IV, 474), and Andrew Carnegie (IV, 435). When WW learned of the fund on March 20, 1889, "he was greatly touched: the tears came into his eyes" (IV, 390).

for the printers—they & the boss are kind & indulgent to me—so far I like them & the work—had a bowel motion this morning (took a calomel powder last night)—I eat my meals every time, one at a time (rather moderately) so far yesterday—have eaten stew'd chicken—oatmeal gruel—strawberries—&c. I had two moderate roast apples for my supper Mrs. Harned sent me—Oesler[78] was here every day—is faithful—was here two hours ago—Baker is here & devoted—is very cautious (I wanted to take a calomel powder last night, but he was not willing to do it till he had your or Oesler's authority first)—Hadn't I better take these powders ab't twice a month, following them with the bitter water—in the chronic condition I seem to be in they seem to bring better result than any thing else—

Pete Doyle was over this evening—I was real glad to see him—he only staid two minutes—Horace Traubel has been—the printers move on quite lively—I have had a pretty good hour feeling on the 9 hour turning to night—If I can get over the great debility & the bad feeling (jellity & soreness & half pain) in my head, spells frequent, *then* I shall feel I am getting on ahead—

Saturday June 16—2½ P M

It is certain I hold the main in mend & eat moderately & have another bowel movement to day—but I keep very weak—head is uncomfortable—To day is hot & stuffy, but I don't mind—

Walt Whitman

Maurice, send this to Wm O'C[onnor] and Nelly—to be return'd to you ag'n—

1717. *To an Unidentified Correspondent*

TRANSCRIPT.

Camden, June 16, 1888

I am sitting up a couple of hours at a time, pretty feeble—It looks now as though I wd drift back to abt the stage of three weeks ago—such as it was.

78. Dr. William Osler (1849–1919), at that time a professor at the University of

1718. *To Richard Maurice Bucke*

ADDRESS: Dr R M Bucke | Asylum | London | Ontario Canada. POSTMARK: Camden, N.J. | Jun (?) | 5 PM | 88.

Camden Sunday 2½ P M | June 17 '88

I am sitting up for three hours in the big chair—have had a bit of dinner—had a big bath this forenoon—Dr Osler has been to-day—his prognosis remains favorable—my weakness and bad head remain—pulse good—pretty warm weather—

Walt Whitman

1719. *To William D. O'Connor*

ENDORSED: "Answ'd July 12/88." ADDRESS: Wm D O'Connor | 1015 O Street | Washington D C. POSTMARK: Camden, N.J. | Jun (?) | 5 PM | 88.

Camden Sunday 3 P M | June 17 '88

Am sitting up at present—fearfully weak & little or no *grip* on my brain—but the doctor gives favorable clues, says pulse is vigorable—my good nurse has given me a good bath—& I have eaten a moderate dinner.

Walt Whitman

1720. *To Richard Maurice Bucke*

ADDRESS: Dr R M Bucke | Asylum | London | Ontario Canada. POSTMARK: Camden, N.J. | Jun 18 | 8 PM | 88.

Camden Monday afternoon | June 18 '88

Not much different anyway. I keep weak—brain & head uncomfortable—& very & languid & torpid for two hours earliest after day—but the theories keep favorable sufficiently markedly—pulse good—a fairly movement bowel this forenoon—& eat my meals—warm weather here—I am rather better as day advances—

Walt Whitman

Pennsylvania. His reminiscences of WW appear in Harvey Cushing's *The Life of Sir William Osler* (1926), I, 264–266.

1721. *To Richard Maurice Bucke*

ADDRESS: Dr R M Bucke | Asylum | London | Ontario | Canada. POSTMARK: Camden, N.J. | Jun 19 | 8 PM | 88.

Camden June 19 '88 | 2½ P M

Have just had the most liberal dinner for three weeks—Mrs. Harned for lean tender mutton & asparagus—her own perfect cooking—Weak yet but holding up otherways—Letter from Walter Scott, London, sending me 8 pounds 10 Shillings[79]—pleasant weather—

Walt Whitman

1722. *To Mary Smith Costelloe*

Camden June 19 '88 | 3 P M

I must send you a line breathing quite decidedly favorable—I am sitting up an hour or so—Pretty critical a week or so ago—but Dr Bucke I consider saved my life—I want to finish my little brochure "November Boughs"—it is ab't ⅓d done—Love to you, dear friend, & to all—

W W

1723. *To Richard Maurice Bucke*

ADDRESS: Dr R M Bucke | Asylum | London | Ontario | Canada. POSTMARKS: Camden, N.J. | Jun 2(?) | 6 | AM | 88; N.Y. | 6–22–88 | 2 30 PM | 1.

Camden Thursday Evn'g | June 21 '88

Continued obstinate weak & bad head feeling—constipation—then otherways, quite a strong steady pulse & fair appetite, & generally hold my own—hot weather to-day—am waiting patiently to get stronger—

Walt Whitman

79. Payment for the English edition of *Democratic Vistas*, which, according to Rhys's letter of July 9–10, was "getting many first rate reviews" (Feinberg).

80. One of the visitors whom he could not see at this time was Eakins (Traubel, I,

1724. *To Richard Maurice Bucke*

ADDRESS: Dr R M Bucke | Asylum | London | Ontario | Canada. POSTMARK: Camden, N.J. | Jun 22 | 8 PM | 88.

Camden Friday afternoon | June 22 '88

Very hot yesterday & to-day—I had a very ill & languid time this forenoon, but have a little rallied later—quite a motion bowel to-day, helpful—quite a good many visitors but I don't have them up here[80]—Dr O[sler] has been over this afternoon—

Walt Whitman

1725. *To William D. O'Connor*

ENDORSED: "Answ'd July 12/88." ADDRESS: Wm D O'Connor | 1015 O Street | Washington | D C. POSTMARK: Camden, N.J. | (?) | (?) PM | 88.

Camden June 23 '88

I send the 20 proof pages of the "Sands at Seventy" as you & Nelly may care to see them entire in "November Boughs"—After four or five days I wish you w'd send these 20 pp. to mail to Dr. Bucke—

Saturday night—Nearly free all day from the prostration weakness—better though partial—a thunder storm & rain this afternoon—Love—

Walt Whitman

1726. *To Richard Maurice Bucke*

ADDRESS: Dr R M Bucke | Asylum | London | Ontario | Canada. POSTMARK: Camden (?) | Jun 24 | 5 PM | 88.

Camden Sunday midday | June 24 '88

Very hot & sultry & oppressive—Getting along pretty well, considering—your letters rec'd—a devout Catholic *faith cure* priest (or group) has or have sent me some ardent advice over here from France, by mail[81]

367).

81. An unsigned postcard urged the recipient to pray to "Sts. Peter and Paul to cure you" (Traubel, I, 371).

—came yesterday—Bowels moved Friday and Saturday & even to some effect even this (Sunday) forenoon—

Tom Harned came back last evening, after a week at Chicago[82]—it looks at present as tho' after the chaos & row & unsettledness have all settled—for definite shibboleth & ticket—that *Blaine & American Protection* will be hung out on the outer walls & make the fight to do its best—not a bad game—Well, we'll see—

I have sent the 20 pages proofs complete to Wm O Connor—the "Sands at Seventy"—wh' said 20 pp. he will send to you in ab't three days—you will then have the first 38 pages proof—(I am inferring that O'C is better)—The new little "November Boughs" is slowly but steadily moving—Horace Traubel is invaluable to me in it—My head in preparing my copy or reading proof is poorly, dull, raw, no[82.1] weak grip, no consecutive, no racionative power—Well it is getting on in afternoon & I have sat up three hours—Havn't got out of this room yet—

Best remembrance & thanks & love to you & Mrs: B, and bearing sympathy & love to Pardee, earnestly he will have a good turn[83]—(who was the old veteran had a saying *God & Time & I against all the rest world against*)—

W Whitman

1727. *To Mary Smith Costelloe*

ADDRESS: Mrs: Mary Whitall Costelloe | 40 Grosvenor Road | the Embankment | London | England.
POSTMARKS: Camden (?) | Jun 26 | 8 PM | 88; Philadelphia | Jun 26 | 11 PM | Paid.

Camden New Jersey | June 26 '88—U S America

The doctor says I hold long substantially—wh' is the best I can send you this day—I have had a hard forenoon, bad weakness &c.—but a little better & sitting up now—fearful hot weather here—best love & remembrance to you & father—I am a little apprehensive ab't him[84]—

Walt Whitman

82. See Traubel, I, 372–373.

82.1. "No" was an interpolation which probably should not have been made since it confused the sense of the passage.

83. On June 15 Bucke mentioned Pardee's illness. In the same letter he discussed a circular to raise funds for WW: "I have found time to write the circular and give it to the printer. I will send you a *proof* early in the week—but mind *you are not supposed to see it*

1728. *To William Sloane Kennedy*

Camden Tuesday afternoon | June 26 '88

The roses came by midday mail & have been enjoy'd hours & hours —The doctor says I certainly do not lose hold—but I have had a very weak bad forenoon—the weather is hot, hot—somewhat better now & sitting up this moment & comfortable—

Walt Whitman

1729. *To Richard Maurice Bucke*

ADDRESS: Dr R M Bucke | Asylum | London | Ontario | Canada. POSTMARK: Camden, N.J. | Jun 29 | 8 PM | 88.

Camden afternoon | June 29 '88

Rainy clouded cool now all day (yesterday afternoon & all last night)—dont seem any improvement in strength or *vim*—dont yet get out at all of my room, or down stairs—but have been up & dress'd yet all day—now ½ pass'd 4—no visitors yet—have eat pretty fair dinner (a bit of roast meat)—preluded by a wine glass of medicinal wine glass of coca wine—

I have finished & formally signed & witnessed the *will & testimentary matters complete*—including the dispensating of copyrights & literary matters by a sort of trustee-board, yourself, Harned & Horace Traubel—& assigned all [of] my worldly possessions to Ed, & to my sisters[85]—the "Nov. Boughs" has got to 66th page—Have you rec'd the copy from London Eng. copy of "Democratic Vistas"? (a pretty vol)—Osler was here last evn'g—goes off for a very few days (somewhere to sea shore)—I have sufficient frequent bowel movements—had a very slim day all yesterday —a little easier to-day—but slow, slow—my head gone—no grip—shall be glad enough with "Nov. Boughs" done printed with no discredit—wish it was all done—Love—

Walt Whitman

however you may as well and perhaps you would suggest a verbal change or two—if you feel like it do so" (Feinberg). WW was incensed—"hot" is Traubel's word: "I don't approve of it—I don't want money—I have enough for all I need!" (I, 349). WW's friends, however, raised money without consulting him (see 1714, *n.*77).

84. Smith, en route to England, wrote to WW on June 20. Alys noted on the envelope: "Mr. Smith much better for the voyage" (Feinberg).

85. The will is reprinted in Traubel, I, 310–312.

1730. *To Richard Maurice Bucke* *6.30–7.1. 1888*

ADDRESS: Dr R M Bucke | Asylum | London | Ontario | Canada. POSTMARK: Camden, N.J. | Jul 1 | 5 PM | 88.

Camden Saturday afternoon | June 30 '88

The sun is out again after three days—good temperature, neither hot nor cold to-day—I neither *improve* nor really go back—Keep my room rigidly yet—have had today a bowel movement—& sit up most of the time—eat my meals sufficiently—*take no brain grip* (real writing, reading, examining proofs) definitely yet, (nor anything like it plainly as of old)—

I will very soon send proof pages onward following from "Sands at Seventy" for proof pieces of ab't 50 pages further—(you have now ab't 40 proof pages)—Of course I have for all June *stopp'd writing the Herald bits*—& the H. paper ceases by mail wh' is just as satisfactory—I have written, formally completed &c. the *will document* (witnessed by ocular witnesses as this state statute requires)[86] and the designation of my copy-rights to be supervised by you, Harned and Horace Traubel—& now when "Nov. Boughs" are completed all will be attended to, the same—

Sunday afternoon early July 1

Feeling miserably to-day so far—am sitting up—not rain, but cloudy and cool and raw—bad feeling in belly and head regions, all day so far—had the preluded coca-wine, & then my breakfast, moderate—pretty good spirits—Mrs Davis has been up ten minutes—good company, good gossip—a pretty rose bouquet from Agnes Traubel—Tom Harned ret'd last evn'g from N Y three days (likes N Y much)—I am wretchedly weak in knees & anything like *body strength*—tho' pretty good arm muscular hold as I hold on—

Love to you & to Mrs B & the childer—

Walt Whitman

1731. *To Richard Maurice Bucke*

ADDRESS: Dr R M Bucke | Asylum | London | Ontario | Canada. POSTMARK: Camden, N.J. | Jul 2 | 3 PM | 88.

Camden | Monday afternoon 1½ | July 2 '88

Thanks for your letter this morn'g—the "Sands" is intended (such

86. The witnesses were Mary O. Davis and Dr. Nathan M. Baker.

as it is) for 20 pp. of "Annex" to follow L of G. consecutively paged—I have duplicate sets of them to be properly paged for the pp. for the "Annex"—

I am probably no worse, but am to day certainly no better or strongly —the bowel movement is just right (a great favorable point daily or every other daily)—my eye sight goes badly—I enclose you Pearsall Smith's note[87] wh' is favorable & you will want to know—the [weather] remains cool & pleasant to-day—My sister Lou is here to-day. My dinner is just here & I relish it—

W W

1732. *To Mary Smith Costelloe*

ADDRESS: Mrs: Mary Whitall Costelloe | 40 Grosvenor Road | the Embankment | London England.
POSTMARK: Camden (?) | Jul(?) | 8 PM | 88.

Camden July 3 '88—P M

I am sitting up & feeling pretty well—the weather is fine now (after coolish & cloudy) & I have not retrograded—Congratulate yr father & Alys after their safe & favorable arrival wh' I have heard, & sent to Dr Bucke—As I sit early afternoon every thing is quiet & comfortable—I have not yet left my room—

Walt Whitman

1732.1 *To James Gordon Bennett and Julius Chambers*

Camden New Jersey | July 3 '88

Thanks best thanks, dear Mr Bennett & dear Mr Chambers & all you dear *Herald* boys—but have not sent you a line for a month—& probably will not any more—as I am ill from breaking out of old war-paralysis —I return the check & take my name from the roll.

Again best respects to Mr B & all of you—

Walt Whitman

87. Smith's letter of June 20 (Feinberg); see 1727.

1733. *To Richard Maurice Bucke* *7.5–6. 1888*

ADDRESS: Dr R M Bucke | Asylum | London | Ontario | Canada. POSTMARK: Camden (?) | Jul 6(?) | 8 PM | 88.

Camden July 5 '88 | 3 to 4 P M

Have had a pretty bad day—ab't one of the real bad spells (except no really *definite* spell such as that special Monday)—but giving out the last 6 or 8 hours most physical & moral energy—no action at all of bowels or water works—no eating—have just risen and eaten three or four mouthfuls—(Baker's[88] strong advise)—am now sitting here in the chair (3.40 P M)—At this moment indicates rain shower—Y'r letter rec'd—I hope Eng. ed'n "Dem Vistas &c" will come yet safely—it is the best specimen of typographic make & binding (for modest expense) yet turned out there—Suppose you've got the further proofs to page 70—mail'd them yesterday—Shall have some little mendings, changings &c. to plates.

Later Thursday—9½ p m —I am less uncomfortable—Horace Traubel has been in for a short visit, & to bring the latest print proofs &c:—All things go on & I am satisfied so far (I have just paid him, Ferguson, $50)[89]—have just swallowed a calomel powder preparatory to go to bed—we have had a slight rain—the *quiet* in comparison of the last three days & nights is very helpful to me—

Noon, Friday, July 6—No particular change in the situation—I am appreciably better—bowels voided—temperature &c. very fine—am sitting up quietly this moment—heavy rather dulness & pain head—suppose you are up to your neck with work & responsibility—well I rather envy it all, supposing & the feeling & ability & physical *plus*—Love to you all—

Walt Whitman

1734. *To Thomas B. Harned* *7.7. [1888]*

just after 12 | Saturday July 7

Tom, I wish you would say to Frank the pictures of Elias Hicks and my own bust are entirely satisfactory & I want to see what [I] can do to

88. Baker left on July 15 to resume his medical training, and was replaced as nurse by W. A. Musgrove, an older man (Traubel, II, 2).

89. WW began negotiations on May 25 with George Ferguson to set the type for *November Boughs.* Ferguson agreed to charge $1.30 for each page in long primer (Traubel, I, 205–206). The first payment of $50 was made on July 3 (I, 415).

90. Frank Harned, who began to take pictures about June 8 (Traubel, I, 283), brought them for WW's inspection on July 2 (I, 411). Despite what WW said in this

print them, so as each to illustrate in the *Nov: Boughs*—one of each[90]—Of course some one—the proper person (is it not Phila or N Y?) will have to print 1000 picts—will have to be done for ab't 3ct each—I am having a bad day—had about a bad night—

As you said—Bennett of N Y has sent the check to me *back*[91]—

Love to you & Mrs H & the childer—

Walt Whitman

1735. *To Mary Smith Costelloe*

ADDRESS: Mrs: Whitall Costelloe | 40 Grosvenor Road | the Embankment | London | England. POSTMARK: Camden, N.J. | Jul 8 | 5 PM | 88.

Camden N J America | Sunday noon July 8 '88

Well here I am all alive yet—but some thumps & bruises—but above board yet—& (though perhaps not certain) count to rally in fair time—It is now a month I have been confined to room & bed—hot weather &c. brain & stomach trouble—a paralytic attack over four weeks ago—Best love to you & all—

Walt Whitman

1736. *To Richard Maurice Bucke*

ADDRESS: Dr R M Bucke | Asylum | London | Ontario Canada. POSTMARK: Camden, N.J. | Jul 9 | 8 PM | 88.

Camden Monday P M | July 9 '88

Two letters rec'd from you to-day—(Yes I probably & have realized)[92]—am glad the Eng[lish] book[93] & the proofs came safe—Am feeling rather easy—am sitting up this moment—A rainy cloudy middling warmish weather day—Tom Donaldson here last evn'g—

Walt Whitman

letter, Traubel reports on July 4 that "W. has not seemed to like Frank Harned's pictures" (I, 420), and they did not appear in the printed book.

91. Bennett sent a check for $40 after WW stopped sending poems to the newspaper, and refused to accept the check when WW returned it; see Traubel, I, 439, 447.

92. Since there are no extant letters from Bucke between June 15 and July 9, it is not possible to explain WW's cryptic reply to Bucke's question.

93. *Democratic Vistas* (1888).

1737. *To Richard Maurice Bucke*

ADDRESS: Dr R M Bucke | Asylum | London | Ontario Canada. POSTMARK: Camden, N.J. | Jul 11 | 8 PM | 88.

Camden Wednesday P M | July 11 '88

No special change for good or worse—Bowel motion last even'g, not copious but definite (by syringe)—Warm weather to-day, pleasantish —I am trying to get the E[lias] H[icks] paper presentable—but hard work —but I keep at it obstinately (my poor brain is just an old worn out horse —you tug & tug & tug)—All are good to me—I send more proof—all alone this afternoon—

Walt Whitman

1738. *To William Sloane Kennedy*

Camden Wednesday Sunset | July 11 '88

Am setting up & have just eat my supper—The flowers rec'd this day—perfumed & delicious—before me this moment—thanks to dear Mrs: K.[94]—pretty sick yet, but I shall rally.

Walt Whitman

1739. *To William D. O'Connor*

ENDORSED: "Answ'd July 12/88." ADDRESS: Wm D O'Connor | 1015 O Street | Washington D C. POSTMARKS: Camden, N.J. | Jul 11 | 8 PM | 88; Washington (?) | Jul 12 | 7 AM | 88.

Camden Wednesday Sunset | July 11 '88

Matters hold their own mainly—I have had a bad whack, confined in this room & bed now the fifth week—& am poorly yet—but I may (probably will to extent) rally—Spirits fair—work power nil—Seize a twenty minutes soon & write me ab't yourself[95]—

Walt W

94. On July 9 Kennedy had written, "Mrs. K. will send some pinks soon" (Feinberg).

95. O'Connor—"I have felt that you and I were brothers in misfortune"—wrote an exuberant reply on the following day in which he praised WW's book, except for the inclusion of "The Dead Emperor" ("[I] find some consolation in the sweet assurance that

1740. *To Susan Stafford* *7.[11]. 1888*

ADDRESS: Mrs: Susan Stafford | Kirkwood | (Glendale) | New Jersey. POSTMARKS: Camden, N.J. | Jul 11 | 8 PM | 88; (?) | Jul | 12 | 1888 | N.J.

Camden Wednesday Sunset | July 12[96] '88

Still pretty sick here now the fifth week confined here—so weak & no *grip* on the head—but hope yet for sort of rally—Eva was here to-day—Van was here last week—Love to you & George & Deb & Ed—I have good care—

Walt Whitman

1741. *To Edward T. Potter*

ADDRESS: Edward Potter | The Cedars | Newport | Rhode Island. POSTMARK: Camden, N.J. | Jul 12 | 6 PM | 88.

Camden New Jersey | Thursday P M July 12 '88

Thanks, dear friend, y'r good letter & draught rec'd safely.[97] I have been & am badly ill, but may rally yet—any how it will be all right—

Walt Whitman

1742. *To John Burroughs* *7.12–13. 1888*

TRANSCRIPT.

Camden July 12 '88 | Thursday night after 9

It gets very tedious here—(I have now been in my room and bed five weeks)—I am sitting up in a rocker and get along better than you would think—I think upon the whole I am getting mending—slowly and faintly enough yet sort o' perceptibly—the trouble is sore and broken brain—the old nag gives out and it hurts to even go or draw at all—but there are some signs the last two days that slight ambles will justify themselves—even for old habit, if nothing else—

It was probably the sixth or seventh whack of my war paralysis, and a

he is finally damned, and can trouble earth no more!"), and mentioned the hostile reception of Donnelly's book in England (Feinberg).

96. WW should have written "11"; note the postmark and the two preceding letters.

97. Potter's letter seems to be lost.

pretty severe one—the doctors looked glum—Bucke I think saved my life as he happened to be here—Shimmering, fluctuating since, probably gathering, recruiting, but as I now write I shall rally or partially rally—only every time lets me down a peg—I hear from you by Horace Traubel[98]—I have an idea that O'Connor is a little better.

A rainy evening here, not at all hot, quiet—

Friday July 13—Just after noon—Ab't the same. I am sitting up, had a fair night—rose late, have eaten my breakfast—have rec'd a good letter from O'C—nothing very special or new—fine, clear, cool. Today my head *thicks* somewhat today. Love to you, dear friend. Love and remembrance to 'Sula, to July, too. I am on to 90th page Nov. Boughs—it will only make 20 more.

Walt Whitman

1743. *To Mary Smith Costelloe*

ADDRESS: Mrs: Whitall Costelloe | 40 Grosvenor Road | the Embankment | London England. POSTMARK: Camden, N.J. | Jul 13 | 8 PM | 88.

Camden N J U S America | '88 July 13 P M

Sometimes the best news to write is to send you have nothing to say —I still keep pretty ill, but no decided retrograde—& have good prospect of rally—Best love to you & Mr S[mith] & Alys & all—the weather is good here—Remember lovingly to Herbert Gilchrist[99]—

Walt Whitman

1744. *To Richard Maurice Bucke* *7.14–15. 1888*

ADDRESS: Dr R M Bucke | Asylum | London | Ontario | Canada. POSTMARK: Camden (?) | Jul 15(?) | 6 P(?) | 88.

Camden | '88—July 14—Saturday afternoon early

Perfect temperature—sunny—cool enough—some breeze—I am pretty comfortable while I sit quietly & dawdle over papers &c. as the last

98. Traubel's letters to Burroughs appear in Barrus, 277–280. On July 12 Burroughs tried to reconcile himself in his journal to the possibility of WW's death: "How life will seem to me with Whitman gone, I cannot imagine. He is my larger, greater, earlier self. No man alive seems quite so near to me" (Barrus, 280).

99. According to Gilchrist's letter of July 8, Mrs. Costelloe showed him WW's letters during his illness (Feinberg).

three hours—but my head more or less thick & floundering (dull ache) when I read with purpose—or write—

Two letters rec'd from you to day—Mrs Harned sent me a first rate broiled chicken for my dinner & supper yesterday—I enjoyed all—Did I tell you I rec'd a long letter from O'Connor yesterday bright & cheering as ever—nothing very special—(I think O'C is better)—I wrote last evening to Burroughs—Traubel writes him the news—Maurice, how late down to are the proof pages you have? Write me without fail in your next & I will send you at once—And how long to you get a letter hence—say [it] is mail'd here (Phila) say at 8¼ Monday night—when do you get it?—bowel dejectures quite mark'd, *twice* the last four or five days—appetite fair—4 p m—Tom Harned brings me a nice homely cake-loaf from Mrs H—young Dr Mitchell[1] is here, gives me a dose for the cold-in-the-head thickness feeling I have so much of (has something with the suppressing of the free perspiration & heat of days previously)—I have not the slightest anticipation from it—we are closing the most perfect day of this summer—I am taking some calomel this evn'g—I am feeling fairly—

Sunday, early afternoon—July 15—much the same—weather pleasant—not hot—quiet—head little thick—am sitting here in the big chair—have eaten breakfast 10½ relishing fairly—no operation yet of last evening's calomel (every thing acts very slowly & lagging on me, even a day or even two)—Have letters from friends of long ago—have just answered to an old N Y Broadway driver—also just a word to my friend Sylvester Baxter of Boston[2]—Harned has just come in with a mug of peach ice cream from Mrs. H—& Tom has just gone off with "Hamlet's Note Book"[3] to add to Donnellys Cryp[togram] with which T H is just wrestling—

Walt Whitman

1745. *To Richard Maurice Bucke*

ADDRESS: Dr R M Bucke | Asylum | London | Ontario | Canada. POSTMARK: Camden (?) | Jul (?) | 6 PM | 88.

Camden | Tuesday Early P M July 17 '88

Pleasant weather warmish but not hot—my body strength & head

1. During Osler's absence, beginning on July 8, WW was attended by Dr. J. K. Mitchell, son of S. Weir Mitchell (Traubel, I, 433). For WW's opinion of the young man, see Traubel, I, 454–455.

2. Baxter had written on July 13 (Feinberg; Traubel, II, 192–193).

3. O'Connor's *Hamlet's Note-book* (1886) argues for Bacon's authorship of Shakespeare's plays.

grip low ebb still—not much different—no going ahead & no serious ebb —a bad day yesterday, brain thick & body sluggish—but to-day quite a movement bowel quite decided—used (instigated) (by a little syringe a little longer than your small finger) a small injection of glycerine—young Dr Mitchell suggested it yesterday afternoon—I feel better I suppose as I sit here, but my head is thick yet—A good letter from John Burroughs this morning—all as usual with him—(a dear friend personal & literary)[4]—

2 o'clock P M—a good letter from you wh' I will read a second time—I turn around & eat a couple of nice California pears. I send you pp 82 to 92 inclusive proof sheets, those are all the printers given me to date —I am still sitting up—have my dinner ab't 5—(now after 3 & I got up ab't 10½)—am middling comfortable—quiet afternoon—Shall lie down on the bed—generally fair spirits—

Walt Whitman

1746. *To Richard Maurice Bucke*

ADDRESS: Dr R M Bucke | Asylum | London | Ontario Canada. POSTMARKS: Camden, N.J. | Jul 20 | 6 AM | 88; N.Y. | 7–20–88 | 11 30 AM | 1.

Camden | Thursday 2 P M July 19 '88

Ab't the same subject continued, quite a decided bowel motion at 12. A brisk rain forenoon & fair temperature—warmish—yours of 17th rec'd to-day—I wonder if you are not to be envied there—my dear mother (who enjoy'd *work*) I've heard tell how she only wanted the decks clear & some one to take charge of the young ones for five or six hours, off her care —*and then*—I am sitting here fairly.

Walt Whitman

1747. *To William D. O'Connor*

ENDORSED: "Answ'd July 25/88." ADDRESS: Wm D O'Connor | 1015 O Street | Washington | D C. POSTMARKS: Camden (?) | Jul 20 | 6 AM | 88; Washington, Rec(?) | Jul 20 | 12 M | (?).

Camden | Thursday P M July 19 '88

Every thing ab't the same—with a turn probably the good—(yet

4. Burroughs on July 16 recommended "raw clams" which "are very strengthening" and hoped that WW would be strong enough in the fall to go to the seashore with him. Burroughs was still depressed: "I try to keep absorbed in my farm operations. It is much better for me than to mope about, nibbling at literature. . . . I do no writing at all" (Feinberg).

the result uncertain)—When you look at "To-Day"[5] send to Dr Bucke—A rain here.

Walt Whitman

1748. *To Herbert Gilchrist*

ADDRESS: Herbert Gilchrist | 12 Well Road Hampstead | London England. POSTMARK: C(?) | Jul (?) | 8 AM | 88.

Camden N J—U S America | Thursday Evn'g—
July 19 '88

Have now been ill for nearly six weeks—& am yet—confined to the room—an attack of paralytic sort & of old indigestion & sluggish action —have sort of kept up yet—may come to some rally—for a sort, at any rate—Best remembrances & love to you—Morse is in Chicago—Bucke is well & hard at work—Do you see Rhys?—I am putting to press a little vol: "*November Boughs*"[6]—

Walt Whitman

1749. *To Richard Maurice Bucke*

ADDRESS: Dr R M Bucke | Asylum | London | Ontario Canada. POSTMARKS: Camden, N.J. | Jul 21 | 8 PM | 88; Philadelphia | Jul | 21 | 9 PM | 1888 | Transit.

Camden | Saturday P M July 21 '88

Rather an easier day—the Doctor, young Mitchell, has call'd—weather pleasant—bowel action very favorably for three consecutive days —(no drugs)—Mrs: Stafford visited me yesterday, very acceptable—broil'd or stewed chicken yesterday—& this morning's breakfast—"Nov: Boughs" has stretch'd to 104 pages corrected—If "Elias Hicks" fragments get into a paper it may reach to ab't 120—remain in good spirits—

Walt Whitman

5. *To-day* (London) contained Reginald A. Beckett's "Walt Whitman as a Socialist Poet" (Traubel, II, 4).

6. Gilchrist had expressed his concern about WW's illness in a letter on July 8, and informed the poet that Mrs. Costelloe was "sitting 3 days a week to me" (Feinberg).

the proofs &c don't hurt me—I don't worry them—the new nurse[7] does fairly—I have rec'd word from Rhys[8]—y'rs of 19th just rec'd—

1750. *To Susan Stafford* *7.21–22. 1888*

Camden | Saturday Afternoon July 21 '88

Rather easier to-day—am writing a little & at my proofs (the little new book "*Nov: Boughs*")—have just rec'd three letters, one from my English friend Ernest Rhys, friend of Herbert Gilchrist, and one from Dr Bucke—Nothing special, but I will enclose them all (as I believe you are entertain'd—like I am by such)—I wish you to send the three back to me in the envelope—write a line to tell how you all [got] back—I liked your visit—have enjoy'd the chicken—did you get back all right? did you get the money all right at the bank?—pleasant weather here to-day—cloudy—

Sunday noon July 22

Am sitting up by the window—a little headache, & heavy feeling—but I must take the thick with the thin—moderately cool & rainy—very bearable for July—I am comfortable—good spirits—

Walt Whitman

1751. *To Robert Pearsall Smith*

ADDRESS: R Pearsall Smith | 44 Grosvenor Road | Westminster Embankment S W | London England. POSTMARK: Camden, N.J. | Jul 2(?) | (?)P(?) | 88.

Camden N J U S America | Monday Evn'g July 23 '88

Thanks first for your good letter rec'd to day—I am better than the long obstinate siege (nearly six weeks) would warrant—I am sitting here at my booklet proofs Nov: Boughs—(only two or three days now have I felt the grip on my poor brain)—I almost envy your Wales fun—Love to you and Mary & all—

Walt Whitman

7. Musgrove.

8. Rhys on July 9–10 had informed the poet of his arrival in England (Feinberg).

9. WW's note was written on the verso of Gilchrist's letter of July 8. Rhys had mentioned in his letter of July 9–10 that Gilchrist was contemplating "another visit to America in the autumn" (Feinberg).

1752. *To Susan Stafford*

ADDRESS: Mrs: Susan Stafford | Kirkwood | (Glendale) | New Jersey. POSTMARK: Camden, (?) | Jul (?) | 8 PM | 88.

Camden Monday Evn'g | July 23 '88

Well I sent you yesterday a letter enclosing others—& here is one now from Herbert, just rec'd—as I promised—he does not allude to his visit to America, but there may be something in it[9]—

I feel better—am working a little at my booklet yesterday and to-day—my head feels easier, but the weakness especially in getting about & in my knee power is fearful—Hope you & George and Ed & Deb & Jo & the young one are jolly & sitting up—

Walt Whitman

I don't want this letter of Herbert's returned—

1753. *To Richard Maurice Bucke*

ADDRESS: Dr R M Bucke | Asylum | London | Ontario | Canada. POSTMARK: Camden, N.J. | Jul 24 | 8 PM | 88.

Camden Noon | July 24 '88

Better quite perceptibly—fluctuating considerable, with bad days or hours—but a general and prevailing improvement—

I have put together the *Elias Hicks* fragments last night & sent off the "paper" to the printer—not knowing how it will look in print—but with some fear & trembling—then three or so pages (all done now) on *George Fox*—evolutionary on the E[lias] H[icks] piece—& the *Nov. Boughs* will be *done*—will make from 120 to 130 (or possibly 135) pages—(those solid long primer pages eat up the copy at a terribly rate!)—I have not worried at it—& do not[10]—indeed it has probably been more benefit to me than hurt—I have been unspeakably helped by Horace Traubel—& by the best printers I have ever yet had—The *Century* people have just sent me

10. On July 22 Bucke had offered advice which WW, characteristically, rejected: "I wish you wd hand over the balance of the M.S. to Traubel to do the best he could with it. It is not good for you to be trying at it and failing—you ought to let it go and forget it as soon as possible. In your present state you would not do any good with the Hicks if you did go through it. Let Traubel have it and tell him to alter nothing except where necessary to make sense and connection, and let it be printed and the book brought to an end" (Feinberg).

again my *Army Hospitals & Cases* proof—I judge it is intended for the October number—bowel movements continue every day or other day—I take no drugs at all—have not moved from my room yet—Keep good spirits—young Dr Mitchell has just come—weather pleasant continued —warmish but I am satisfied—Tom Harned comes every day, often bringing his nice always welcome children—

2 p m—y'rs of 22d has come—I have enjoy'd a partial wash—

Walt Whitman

I send you proof pp 97 to 104 inclusive—as I understand you have all preceding—

1754. *To Richard Maurice Bucke*

ADDRESS: Dr R M Bucke | Asylum | London | Ontario | Canada. POSTMARK: Camden, N.J. | Jul 25 | 8 PM | 88.

Camden Wednesday P M July 25 '88

Weather perfect continued—they say yesterday was fearfully hot, but I didn't mind it—the hours rather dull but ab't as usual & no setback. *Nov: Boughs* copy done—the three letters from Rhys, Miss Bates, & our old Japanee friend I will enclose[11]—(don't want them back)—If any gaps of the proof pages up to 104 exist, mention it & I will remit—Keep my room yet—am sitting now (& in four fifths time day) in the capacious ratan-seated arm chair—my condition of feebleness & locomotive capacity is fearful—the brain works ab't as before—& muscle & grip of arms (especially right) strong & glib perhaps as ever—

Walt Whitman

1755. *To Ernest Rhys*

ADDRESS: Ernest Rhys | Care Walter Scott Publisher | 24 Warwick Lane Paternoster | row | London England. POSTMARKS: Camden, N.J. | Jul 26 | 8 PM | 88; London. E.C. | (?) | (?)Au 88 | AB.

Camden N J—U S America | July 26 '88

I am still above board & shall probably make a sort of rally—This is the 6th or 7th whack thro' the last fourteen years of my war-paralysis &

11. For Rhys's letter of July 9–10, see 1749. Charlotte Fiske Bates wrote a laudatory letter on July 19: ". . . In one sense, no other writer of any age, has, in his work, laid so far-reaching and sympathetic a grasp on the heart of the future as you have done" (Feinberg). The "Japanee friend," C. Sadakichi Hartmann, on July 24, reported

a pretty heavy one—tided over the others, tho' probably weaken'd after each—I am still imprison'd to room & bed, this the seventh week. I am finishing the little "*Nov: Boughs*"—

Walt Whitman

1756. *To William Sloane Kennedy*

Camden Friday afternoon | July 27 '88

No set back essentially but still imprisoned by room & bed—sitting up most of the day—*Nov: Boughs* is ab't done. My head (physical brain) & spirits good—legs & bodily strength *gone*.

Walt Whitman

1757. *To William D. O'Connor*

TRANSCRIPT.

Camden Friday Afternoon | July 27 '88

No particular set back but am still imprisoned by room and bed—very bad weakness of legs and body—the worst of head trouble disappeared—Thanks for your letter[12]—my little *Nov. Boughs* is ab't done (with copy)—rainy here today—I am sitting up—

Walt Whitman

1758. *To Richard Maurice Bucke*

ADDRESS: Dr R M Bucke | Asylum | London | Ontario | Canada. POSTMARK: Camden, N.J. | Jul 28(?) | 8 PM | 88.

Camden Saturday afternoon | July 28 '88

Pleasant cool, calm sunny weather—a rain quite hard, & early this morning—I mustn't shout till I am well out of the woods but I feel

his return from abroad (Feinberg).

12. On July 25 O'Connor referred only briefly to his "own bad state" and expressed his gratitude that WW was recovering (Feinberg; Traubel, II, 176–177). WW observed of O'Connor's letter: "William always has the effect of the open air upon me."

perceptibly better—took a quite elaborate wash (bath) in a way that I like —helping myself leisurely—ab't two hours ago—& handled myself decidely better than five days ago—a sort of nibble *of strength*—Yours of 26th rec'd—welcomed & cheering—I have told you ab't the facts of *Nov: Boughs*—I have just read the revised proof of "Elias Hicks"—When ready, the *publication* of N B may wait quite a long while, for reasons.[13]

My opine is that our dear O'Connor is better—jaunting at present for the time an easier road on plateau land, like—(no doubt sufferings and botherations, plenty—but no one but a sick man—seriously sick—realizes the let up of some of the heaviest burdens)—O'C (do you know?) is writing a defence & essay generally, on the Donnelly *Crypto*[*gram*]—(I predict that it will be better than the C itself)[14]—Ed Stafford has just call'd with some apples & a chicken—

Saturday Sunset

Have had my dinner, stew'd chicken & rice pudding—have not left my room yet, but shall get down a few minutes to-morrow or next day—Spirits good—A letter from Logan Smith to-day—he is a collegian & revels in it—

Walt Whitman

1759. *To Richard Maurice Bucke*

ADDRESS: Dr R M Bucke | Asylum | London | Ontario Canada. POSTMARK: Camden, N.J. | Jul 30 | 8 PM | 88.

Camden Monday P M | July 30 '88

Everything moves slow & languid but well I suppose. I am sitting here in the chair in my room yet—weather fine, rain at nights, to-day a little clouded & warmish—copious normal bowel action yesterday—fair appetite—almost no bother (nor want of grip) in the brain—

Walt Whitman

13. WW could not publish *November Boughs* until after the appearance of "Army and Hospital Cases" in the October issue of *Century;* see 1798. In his reply to this letter on August 4, Bucke offered the following suggestion: "I think myself a good idea would be to print a hundred or two hundred copies on good (and large) paper, bind them nicely and sell *yourself* for $5. or even $10. with autograph, by & by publish through McKay

1760. *To John Burroughs*

Camden Tuesday noon | July 31 '88

Dear J B

Just a line—sending Mrs O'C[onnor]'s letter to me, as the best last news of Wm—Quite certainly I am weathering—to all appearance—this ab't sixth *whack* of my war paralysis—(thanks mainly I opine to a sound strong *body heredity* from my dear father & mother)—I am still keeping my room—shall attempt a mild raid soon—take no medicines—have finished (sent in *all* copy) my little *Nov: Boughs*—Horace Traubel is a noble faithful fellow—Weather continues superb—

Walt Whitman

1761. *To Richard Maurice Bucke*

ADDRESS: Dr R M Bucke | Asylum | London | Ontario Canada. POSTMARK: Camden, N.J. | Aug 2 | 8 PM | 88.

Camden Thursday P M | August 2 '88

Yet continue weak & listless—but no set-back. I shall send you more proofs in two or three days. I am sitting up in the big chair most of the day. Spirits good. Continued pleasant weather—warmish—

Walt Whitman

1762. *To William D. O'Connor*

ENDORSED: "Answ'd Aug 31/88." ADDRESS: Wm D O'Connor | Life Saving Service | Washington | D C. POSTMARKS: Camden, N.J. | Aug 4 | 8 PM | 88; Washington, Rec'd. | Aug 5 | 7 AM | 88 | 1.

Camden Saturday noon Aug: 4 '88

Your dear letter came this morning, enclosing Dr Channing's

or another" (Feinberg).

14. *Mr. Donnelly's Reviewers* was published posthumously. On August 7 Bucke wrote: "I am glad you are getting cheerful letters from O'Connor. I trust he is not suffering so much these times. Am a little sorry he is worrying himself about the Cryptogram which I fear is more or less of a fraud though perhaps not intentionally so on Donnelly's part", Feinberg; Traubel, II, 114).

(herewith returned)[15]—Thank you & Dr. C. & dear Grace & Stedman & all —all the movements are certainly *roseate* toward me & I feel thankful & responsive—& all the confirmatory possible—

I am still kept in my room, hoping each day to get firmer & stronger, & get out—but no such day comes yet—or even the indication of it—& to-day Saturday a fearful hot & oppressive *baker & prostrater*, the worst to my feelings, as I sit here, of any yet—there is no set back, so far—but if a long spell of hot unhealthy August weather sets in "the second time of that man will be worse than the first"—

The *November Boughs* (did I tell you?) is all done *in copy*—The printing office is now all diverged on a Harrison and Morton book,[16] hurrying up—will take them a week—my *Boughs* will be at least two months before published—possibly longer—I remain in good spirits—It seems to be grow[ing] hotter & melter—

Walt Whitman

1763. *To Mary Smith Costelloe*

ADDRESS: Mrs: Mary Whitall Costelloe | 40 Grosvenor Road | the Embankment | London England.
POSTMARK: Camden, N.J. | Aug 4 | 8 PM | 88.

Camden Sunset | Aug: 4 '88

This has been the hottest day of the season—but I have got thro' fairly with it—& have just finish'd & quite enjoy'd my dinner. Not yet left my room for down stairs—

Walt Whitman

1764. *To Richard Maurice Bucke*

ADDRESS: Dr R M Bucke | Asylum | London | Ontario | Canada. POSTMARK: Camden, N.J. | Aug 4 | (?) PM | 88.

Camden Saturday P M | Aug 4 '88

Hottest & most prostrating day yet—good bowel action—I have washed all off in cool water & sit here half naked in solitude writing this—A welcome lively letter from O'Connor—Dr Channing's daughter

15. On August 3 O'Connor mentioned that Grace Channing's calendar (see 1599) had been sent to Stedman, who was to arrange for publication (Feinberg; Traubel, II, 101–102). On the same day O'Connor wrote to thank Stedman for his assistance in the projected work (Feinberg). On September 21 Stedman informed Traubel that three firms had rejected publication of the calendar (Traubel, II, 362).

Grace (& other folks) has (& have) compiled a book, "*Walt Wh—— Calendar*," & are now north seeking a publisher—Dr C has put this job (seeking a grand N Y publisher) in the hands of Stedman—& that's the way the situation stands at the present moment—dont you *sorrow* for poor Stedman?—think of such temperature as to-days!—An artist S Hollyer[17] has etched me (from a photo Mary Costelloe call'd *the Lear*)—I guess it is pretty good—I shall not forget one for you soon as I can get one—I send proofs 105 to 117 inclusive—there will be ab't 20 more—I am more comfortable than you may suppose—

Sunset

Have had & enjoy'd my dinner, roast lamb, potatoes & onions, a slice of good bread, tea & roast apples—(only eat two meals a day)—This I suppose will be *high revel* (for two or three weeks now) for excursions & vacations & country trips &c—20 cars went out in one train from here to-day—yours yesterday rec'd—

Walt Whitman

1765. *To William D. O'Connor*

ENDORSED: "Answ'd August 31/88." ADDRESS: Wm D O'Connor | 1015 O Street | Washington | D C. POSTMARKS: Camden (?) | Aug 6 | 8 PM | 88; Wash. D.C. Transit | Aug 7 | 7 AM | 88.

Camden Monday P M | Aug: 6 '88

Hot & sweltering weather here now the sixth day—No good news to send you ab't my health—but no bad either—I keep [on?]—sitting up —but have not left my room—

Walt Whitman

1766. *To Richard Maurice Bucke*

ADDRESS: Dr R M Bucke | Asylum | London | Ontario Canada. POSTMARK: Camden, N.J. | Aug 8 | 8 PM | 88.

Camden Wednesday Sunset | Aug: 8 '88

Nothing special or notable. The sweltering hot weather continues —may be two or three days before I send you the last proof pages—

Walt Whitman

16. Probably the Reverend G. L. Harney's *The Lives of Benjamin Harrison, and Levi P. Morton.*

17. Hollyer wrote to WW about April 6 to request permission to make the etching. In CB WW wrote of the etching on August 3: "I rather like it." But for more adverse opinions, see Traubel, II, 131, 144.

1767. *To Richard Maurice Bucke*

ADDRESS: Dr R M Bucke | Asylum | London | Ontario Canada. POSTMARK: Camden (?) | Aug 9 | 8 PM | 88.

Camden Thursday P M | Aug: 9 '88

Thanks for the letter of Aug: 7, came at 1.30—Rather pleasant weather to-day—rain last night & sun clouded to-day—bowel action—I sit here yet—the booklet will make 140 pages—Shall certainly have a pict: of E[lias] H[icks] & probably one of self if eng[rave]d satisfactory—

Walt Whitman

1768. *To Richard Maurice Bucke* *8.10–11. 1888*

ADDRESS: Dr R M Bucke | Asylum | London | Ontario | Canada. POSTMARK: Camden, N.J. | Aug 11 | 8 PM | 88.

Camden Aug. 10 '88 | Friday a m—

A mark'd & good & welcome change of temperature the first thing in the morning—a merino undershirt & socks—& a coat—it is just right to-day & it helps me—now past for nine days uninterrupted hot & sweltering—frequent rains (evn'gs or nights) but not the least relief—(good they say for the corn crop)—I have been the last hour and over with the proof of "Elias Hicks," the concluding paper in the *Boughs*—Shall have to wait & slowly subside into some verdict (literary & personal) for myself about it all—am not certain whether I am satisfied or no—Have just sent the *Herald* (at their request) a short poem for Sheridan's burial[18]—I expect it will be in H. 12th[19]—

Saturday—toward noon—Aug. 11.—

Delightful day—am sitting here ab't as usual—had my breakfast ab't 9—(get my dinner ab't 4 or ½ past)—nothing very notable—rec'd a letter from Mrs. Costelloe—nothing very special—but I enclose it as you might care to hear—I also send proof pages 119 to 127—part of "Elias Hicks"—In a few days shall send 118 & all the rest—I send my best

18. "Over and Through the Burial Chant" (later "Interpolation Sounds") appeared in the New York *Herald* on August 12. On August 8 the newspaper printed WW's prose "tribute to Sheridan."

19. This passage originally read: "H. Saturday 11th (possibly 12th)." On the following day WW struck out everything except "12th."

20. On August 8 Bucke noted a visit from Dr. Jack Harkness—"(you will recollect

remembrances & respects to Mr Harkness[20]—I believe Herbert Gilchrist is coming soon back to America—quiet day here—

Walt Whitman

1769. *To Susan Stafford*

ADDRESS: Mrs: Susan Stafford | Kirkwood | (Glendale) | New Jersey. POSTMARK: Camden (?) | Au 12 | 5 PM | 88.

Camden Sunday Evn'g | Aug: 12 '88

Nothing very new or different—I am still in my sick room—Sit up most of the day—write some & keep pretty good spirits—but am as weak & feeble as ever. (Sometimes I opine will remain so.) I think Herbert is coming to America soon—may be this month. It is raining all day like fury—coolish—

Walt Whitman

1770. *To Louisa Orr Whitman(?)* *[8.13(?). 1888]*[21]

I am about the same—Strangely somehow I don't get any more power in my body or legs—I feel pretty well—have written one or two pieces for the *Herald*—& they have printed as before—I have not left the room up stairs yet (now nine weeks)—the Doctor thinks it not best yet—

My little booklet *November Boughs* is ab't done—concludes with quite a long but very hurried & scratchy paper on "Elias Hicks"—done mostly when I was sickest all, & thought it best to hurry it done right off—But at present I am much as of late years, except my legs & getting around even the room—wh' I sometimes fancy is not even coming back.

Love to Jess. I have got a few lines from Jeff (in St Louis)—I am now sitting in the big chair—Spend most of the day here—had my dinner a little ago—now 5½—cool & clear & pleasant to-day—I am quite comfortable—Hope this will find you feeling well—Rain'd like fury nearly all

him at Kingston and down the St Lawrence and up the Saguenay?)" (Feinberg).

21. August 13 appears to be a plausible date. In 1769 WW wrote: "It is raining all day like fury"; and here: "Rain'd like fury yesterday." Two pieces had recently appeared in the New York *Herald* (see note 18 above). Jessie, Jeff's daughter, was staying with Louisa (see note 23). There is no extant letter, however, from Jeff, who wrote from Milwaukee on July 14 (Feinberg).

yesterday—Mrs. D[avis] intended going yesterday—I was favorable to her going—

Walt Whitman

1771. *To Richard Maurice Bucke*

ADDRESS: Dr R M Bucke | Asylum | London | Ontario Canada. POSTMARK: Camden (?) | Aug 15 | 6 AM | (?).

Camden Aug: 14 '88

Sunny & cool to-day—nothing new in my case—bowel action—my lines on Sheridan's burial were printed in *Herald* Aug: 12—(I am beginning to keep my bits & contributions, poetic spurts &c. again already—tying in a budget in stiff covers)—I enclose you page 118—having now sent, if I think right, *all* the proof pages of *Nov: Boughs* complete from 5 to 140—We wish to have real good paper & press work—& Horace & I are for binding it very neatly in stitched linen—making if successful a handsome plain, *pocketable* booklet—want it to be retail 1.25 or better still $1—who or when the publishers & bro't out still undecided—not before than October anyhow—I still have the design of making a 900 page Vol. my *complete works*, the paper & printing uniform & a few typos corrected—Will see how the cat jumps—I am writing sitting here up stairs yet—am comfortable—

Walt Whitman

1772. *To Alma Calder Johnston*

ADDRESS: Mrs: Alma Johnston | Care John H. Johnston | Diamond Merchant | 150 Bowery cor: Broome St: | New York City. POSTMARKS: Camden, N.J. | Aug 15(?) | 8 PM | 88; P.O.N.Y. | 8–16–88 | (?) | 88(?).

Camden Wednesday noon | Aug: 15 '88

Dear friend

Here is William Ingram's letter—forwarded at his request to you[22] —He comes to see me occasionally & is always welcome—John's good

22. When Ingram called on August 3, WW gave him a copy of *Specimen Days* for George Rush, Jr., who was in prison in Bucks County, Pennsylvania (CB). Ingram's

letter was rec'd this forenoon & is cheery & hospitable as always—Yes, dear friend, if I get able again to get about—& you settle down & the machinery moves regularly &c.—I may come to New York & see you all—We will see how the cat jumps—

I still remain in my sick room—tho' I have had no set back any thing worth mentioned—but remain very enfeebled & almost helpless in strength of legs & body, without improvement at all. This week so far the temperature has been just right here—My little booklet November Boughs is ab't done—will make 140 pages—I have for the concluding one a disjointed paper on "Elias Hicks"—the publication will be delayed yet a number of weeks—I am sitting up in my big arm chair writing this—am comfortable—Best love to you all.

Walt Whitman

1773. *To Richard Maurice Bucke*

ADDRESS: Dr R M Bucke | Asylum | London | Ontario Canada. POSTMARKS: Camden, N.J. | Aug 22 | 8 PM | 88; Lon(?) | Au 24 | 88 | Canada.

Camden | Wednesday Evn'g Aug: 22 '88

Am still keeping my room—Sunny & cool day very fine—the booklet slowly but surely advances to finish—& the Vol. of Complete Works is preparing to get on the stocks—

Walt Whitman

1774. *To Susan Stafford*

ADDRESS: Mrs: Susan Stafford | Kirkwood | (Glendale) | New Jersey. POSTMARK: Camden, N.J. | Aug 22 | 8 PM | 88.

Camden | Wednesday Evn'g: Aug: 22 '88

Still keeping in my sick room. Eva was here, with the little girl. Welcome. Harry is pretty well now. Herbert leaves London to-day in the ship "British Princess" for Philadelphia. My brother Eddy that was at

letter of August 10 reported how gratified Rush was to receive the gift and recounted in great detail the death and cremation of the "free thinker" William Cooper (Ohio Wesleyan).

Moorestown is now at Blackwoodtown.[23] Is well. I have just eat a hearty supper if that's any sign—

W W

1775. *To Richard Maurice Bucke*

ADDRESS: Dr R M Bucke | Asylum | London | Ontario | Canada. POSTMARK: Camden, N.J. | Aug 26 | 5 PM | 88.

Camden | Aug: 26 P M '88

Warm & pleasant—nothing very new or different—I enclose you a print of frontispiece under which is to go

The 70th year
taken from life.[24]

My *Complete Works*, ab't 900 pp Vol: will be put to press nearly contemporaneously with the *Nov. Boughs*—I can carry out the enterprises thro' Horace as if I could do it personally—perhaps better—At any rate I couldn't do it other how—Somehow strangely I don't recover strength or personal activity or any thing of that sort, the least particle—I have not left my sick room yet at all—am sitting here now—Agnes Traubel has just called—bro't some nice fruit—Mr Traubel *pere* called Friday—

1776. *To John Burroughs*

ADDRESS: John Burroughs | West Park Ulster Co: | New York. POSTMARKS: Camden, N.J. | Aug 31 | 8 PM | 88; N.Y. | 9–1–29(?) | 7 AM.

Camden Aug: 31 Evn'g '88

Horace Traubel bro't me the nice basket pears—& I have been eating—& Mrs. D[avis] has preserved a lot—best thanks—Tho' I don't get worse again I don't improve in strength, vim, &c. at all & hardly anticipate—My *Nov: Boughs* will be finished—& I shall have a big Vol. of all my stuff one Vol.—

Walt Whitman

23. On August 1 Louisa Whitman and Jessie placed Edward in the Insane Asylum at Blackwoodtown, New Jersey. The poet continued to pay his brother's expenses. On September 4 Mrs. Davis and Warren Fritzinger went to see Eddy: "He seems to be all right & as happy as is to be expected" (CB).

24. The frontispiece of *November Boughs*.

25. Scots: a little bit.

1777. *To Richard Maurice Bucke*

ADDRESS: Dr R M Bucke | Asylum | London | Ontario | Canada. POSTMARK: Camden, N.J. | Aug 31 | 8 PM | 88.

Camden Friday P M Aug: 31 '88

This is the paper *Nov: Boughs* is to be printed on—isn't it fine & thick? This is the (untrimm'd) size of page—the large book is thinner (same pulp) and a bittock[25] larger—all those matters are going smoothly—

Ab't me in physical improvement, strength &c. the stuck condition continues—perhaps when the weather grows cooler, I may be better—but I don't know but I am failing to anticipate any essential change—Your good letters come daily—y'r suggestions &c. will if possible be followed —rec'd to-day a basket of pears from John Burroughs—good weather—a rain in prospect—best wishes to the meter[26]—

Walt Whitman

1778. *To William Sloane Kennedy*

Camden Saturday Night | Sept: 1 '88

Dear W S K

Yours came right. I am still imprison'd in my sick room, yet sitting up & reading & writing & (in limits) talking & being talked to—It is all tedious & long drawn out—the worst no prospect of real improvement—I mean in any body or leg strength, wh' is very low indeed—but my spirits &c. sort o' fair—appetite & sleep not bad considering—I do not want any thing, comfort or necessity, I crave for—

I shall print the little booklet *November Boughs* 140 pp.—and at same time a big Vol. (900 pages) comprehending *all* my stuff—verses & prose —bound in one—Shall send you copies soon as ready—will be a few weeks yet—I hear from Dr B[ucke], O'C[onnor], and J[ohn] B[urroughs] —I get the Transcripts & thank for them—Traubel unspeakably faithful & kind[27]—

W W

26. Bucke and his brother-in-law William Gurd were attempting to perfect a water meter. While Bucke pursued his million-dollar rainbow, WW remained skeptical, sometimes to Bucke's annoyance.

27. In his letter of August 30 Kennedy had complained that Traubel did not keep him informed of WW's health: "It is cruel to keep a fellow ignorant" (Feinberg; Traubel, II, 243). In commenting on this letter to Traubel, WW noted the "querulous" tone: "It is always present in Kennedy: it breaks in upon his best harmonies" (II, 243).

1779. *To Richard Maurice Bucke*

ADDRESS: Dr R M Bucke | Asylum | London | Ontario | Canada. POSTMARK: Camden, N.J. | Sep 2 | 5 PM | 88.

Camden | Sunday 11 a m Sept: 2 '88

A perfect day—sunny cool—I felt easier this morning when I got up—(anticipate better feelings when the cooler weather comes—but we shall see)—Mr and Mrs Edward Coates have been over to see me—a cheery nice little visit—her atmosphere & talk were medicinal & inspiriting—he bo't the centennial ed'n—$10—I have had a good letter from O'Connor[28]—also f'm Kennedy—the little "Old Age's Lambent Peaks" appears in the just out *Century*—Maurice, I should like you to have my mare Nettie and phaeton (if it should come in) as pay for the $200 I owe you[29]—*I am deliberate ab't it*—the only thing is whether you could take them in—W'd that work well, & be desirable? Could you have any one who w'd take the mare & wagon & see them right to deliver to you? If so I wish it so—The vols: *Nov Boughs* and the big book will be good bits of typography & press work, I think—no special news ab't me—all comfortable—

Walt Whitman

1780. *To Mary Smith Costelloe*

ADDRESS: Mrs: Mary W. Costelloe | Llwynbarried House | Rhayader | Wales | via London | England. POSTMARK: Camden (?) | Sep 3 | 6 AM | 88.

Camden N J America | Sunday Evn'g Sept: 2 '88

Your good letter just rec'd[30] & here I am sending word back—Still imprison'd in my sick room—non-rehabilitated yet, but middling well for all that—my booklet *November Boughs* ab't finish'd—& a large Vol. comprising all my stuff begun—I am here just at sunset—Love to you all old & young—I sufficiently comfortable—

Walt Whitman

28. O'Connor wrote on August 31 (Feinberg; Traubel, II, 238–239). Traubel reports that "W. was very much moved by O'Connor's letter" (II, 238).

29. On September 4 Bucke wrote that WW owed him nothing—"(the balance is the other way)"—and suggested that he sell the house in Camden (Feinberg).

1781. *To Richard Maurice Bucke*

ADDRESS: Dr R M Bucke | Asylum | London | Ontario | Canada. POSTMARK: Camden, N.J. | Sep 3 | 8 PM | 88.

Camden | Monday Afternoon | Sept: 3 '88

All goes fairly with me. Yesterday & to-day I am perceptibly better —Cooler & signs of September—Still adhere to my 2d story room & the big chair—Have just had a call from the Phila. man of the N. Y. Herald who asks something of Elias Hicks (& the Nov: B)[31]—for the paper—wh' I promise to give—will send to-morrow. Your letters come & are welcomed. No news yet of Herbert Gilchrist but I expect him any moment—I have somewhere a printed slip of "Old Age's Lambent Peaks" & will yet send it—but I cannot lay my hand on it this moment—a cloudy rather pleasant day, almost cool—quiet—I reiterate the offer of my mare & phaeton[32]—

Walt Whitman

1782. *To Susan Stafford*

ADDRESS: Mrs: Susan Stafford | Ashland | Camden County | New Jersey. POSTMARK: Camden | (?) | 6 PM | (?).
TRANSCRIPT.

Camden Sept: 5 '88 P. M.

Dear friend

I am still here neither worse nor better—but keeping in my sick room & in the big old chair—have had something to see to in printing my books & it has probably done me more good than harm—& it all (the printing) has gone on & is going on satisfactorily—Herbert has arrived all right & is stopping over in Philadelphia—quite busy—he is to have a studio there & paint—rather thinks (but it has not yet been settled definitely) he has secured a studio already—He has been over to see me—a short visit this time—He looks hearty & handsome, red & fat & first rate—he will come down before long & see you & then tell you more fully

30. Mrs. Costelloe wrote from Wales on August 21 (Feinberg).
31. The Philadelphia representative of the *Herald* was C. H. Browning (Traubel, II, 146–147). See 1783.
32. This letter was written on the verso of Mrs. Costelloe's of August 21 (Feinberg).

his plans—wh' he did not to-day—but I believe he thinks stopping, working & painting here for a year to come—

I have not heard from any of you for quite a while—send me word how things are—tell me abt Debbys baby[33] & everything—George & Harry, as far as you know—& how are you yourself—I am sitting here alone up in my room, writing this—Mrs: Davis has been an hour or two ago out to the City Hall to pay my taxes (over $34)[34]—& some thief there stole a nice valuable silk sun umbrella from her—gone—Hope this will find you well —& God bless all—

Walt Whitman

1783. *To the Editor, New York* Herald *9.6. 1888*

ENDORSED: "Abstract printed this | A.M. (Sept. 17/88) | Habberton."

private

I send you the piece I spoke ab't on *Elias Hicks—the price is $15*[35]—

Walt Whitman

Sept 6 '88

1784. *To Richard Maurice Bucke*

ADDRESS: Dr R M Bucke | Asylum | London | Ontario | Canada. POSTMARK: Camden, N.J. | Sep 8 | (?) PM | 88.

Camden | Saturday Noon Sept 8 '88

Your good letters come daily—I had quite set on sending you the mare & phæton but when I saw (& saw clearly) the situation I resigned to give the scheme up & have sold the rig to Rev Mr Corning here (the Unitarian minister) for ab't enough for some bills needing payment[36]—O now I feel relieved—

33. Susan S. Browning, born November 17, 1886; see Charles L. Stafford, *The Stafford Family* (n.d.), 17.

34. According to CB, Mrs. Davis withdrew $50 from the bank in order to pay WW's city tax ($24.47) and culvert tax ($9.62).

35. A notice of *November Boughs* in the *Herald* on September 17 quotes one paragraph from WW's account of Hicks.

36. WW was paid $130 on September 7 by the Rev. J. Leonard Corning, a frequent visitor during the poet's illness (CB).

Nothing particularly different in my sickness—or if anything it is a mild suspicion of betterment—Tom Harned was here last evening, & Horace is most faithful & invaluable to me, comes every evening, & sees to the printing first rate—It is all going on favorably—Morse is in Chicago, working (moderately—writing some) & appears to be happy. Herbert Gilchrist has not been over here since—He has some plan or art-design I guess—mystified to me so far—Osler is still away—expect him back every day—Tennyson sent me his *Cordial best greetings* by H G—he is well—& I hear from Ernest Rhys—I am lately looking at Froude's 2d vol. ab't Carlyle "Life in London"—the refreshing natural old fault finder of everything & every person & writing, including his own utterances ("that cursed book" he calls the *Frederic*)—It is very moist & clouded & rather warm to-day—after two days and nights quite cold—but the *summer* season is over—I sit here the same—got down yesterday for five minutes but hitch'd back soon—Every body is good—"Whatever consists with thee," said Marcus Aurelius, "consists with me, O Nature."—Best luck to your meter scheme—Love[37]—

Walt Whitman

1785. *To Jacob Klein*

TRANSCRIPT.

Camden September 10, 1888

[WW informed Klein that he was sending *Leaves of Grass* and *Two Rivulets*.][38]

1786. *To Richard Maurice Bucke*

ADDRESS: Dr R M Bucke | Asylum | London | Ontario | Canada. POSTMARK: Camden, N.J. | Sep 10 | 8(?) | 88.

Camden | Noon Sept 10 '88

I rec'd a card f'm Rolleston, Ireland, that he had the first proofs of the German L of G. from the printing office—& wish'd me to communicate

37. Bucke on September 10 wrote that he hoped to receive soon autographed copies of *November Boughs* and *Complete Poems & Prose:* "I shall look upon them as the crown and summit of all my W. W. Collection—a collection by the way which gives me a lot of worry sometimes to think what I am eventually to do with it. I regard it as so precious that no ordinary disposition of it will do" (Feinberg).

38. On September 1 Klein, a St. Louis lawyer, wrote to Kennedy to inquire whether he should write directly to WW in order to obtain the 1876 edition of *Leaves of Grass*. Kennedy forwarded the letter to WW, who wrote "ans'd" on Klein's note (Barrett). See also 1793, and Traubel, II, 337.

with Dr Knortz[39]—Your letters reach me & are always welcome—I keep up—but gain not—am & have been reading the latter two Carlyle books (Froude and Cabot)[40]—not exactly you would say the cheery pabulum fit for me—raw, wet, cloudy weather here—H Gilchrist came this forenoon to inquire, but did not come up to my room—I guess Kennedy's MS is in abeyance yet[41]—the Japanee Hartmann is going to try some *essay-readings* (European, great but here in America almost unknown persons & art—productions &c)—good luck to him!—("God help all wanderers" said the cute Irish kitchen girl, giving out some bread & meat to the tramp at the gate the other day)—The strength of my arms & shoulders remains good—the mentality grip ditto—spirits fairly ditto—we think of binding Nov. Boughs in wine colored silesia (a sort of linen—cheap)—& entirely untrimm'd—

Walt Whitman

1787. *To Susan Stafford*

ADDRESS: Mrs Susan M Stafford | Kirkwood | (Glendale) | New Jersey. POSTMARK: Camden | Sep | 10 | 7 AM | N.J.

Mickle Street Camden | Monday P M Sept 10 '88

Your letter came in the noon mail & I will write a few lines—Glad to hear little Susie[42] is well & send her my love & hope she will grow on & up first rate—Yes, dear friend, come up & stay a little with us, & of course bring the chicken for me—it will be acceptable—Herbert was here this forenoon but did not come up to my room—though I was sure I would have been glad to see him & talk a bit—I think he has some scheme (painting most likely) on the carpet—At any rate I tho't he looks hearty & well—I am still kept in my sick room—don't get worse but don't gain any thing it seems—& I almost doubt if I ever will—weakness extreme—I have sold the mare & phæton—I sold her for a song—my brother Eddy is boarding at Blackwoodtown Asylum now[43]—my sister got quite dissatisfied with the Moorestown place—My books are being printed nicely—I have two on the stocks—one little one "November Boughs"—and one big

39. This is an accurate summary of Rolleston's note of September 1 (Barrett).

40. James Anthony Froude's *Thomas Carlyle; A History of the First Forty Years of His Life, 1795–1835* (1882) and *Thomas Carlyle; A History of His Life in London, 1834–1881* (1884), and James Elliot Cabot's *A Memoir of Ralph Waldo Emerson* (1887). For WW's evaluation of Froude, see Traubel, II, 251–252.

41. On September 2 Bucke inquired about Kennedy's projected book: "I fear

900 Vol. to contain all my works—you shall have them, when ready—Harry too—I send my love to Harry & to Eva & little Dora—it is a rainy, cloudy, coolish day, & I am sitting here alone in the big chair in better spirits & comfort than I deserve—

Walt Whitman

1788. *To Dr. Karl Knortz*

ADDRESS: Dr Knortz | 540 East 155th Street | New York City. POSTMARK: Camden, N.J. | Sep 10 | 8 PM | 88.

328 Mickle Street | Camden New Jersey
Sept: 10 '88

The enclosed card has just come from Rolleston—Delgany, County Wicklow, Ireland, I address him—I have had a hard time with sickness (another spell of war paralysis, the fifth or sixth time) all summer—the serious attack warded off again—but extreme weakness of legs and body remaining—Keeping me in my sick room so far—yet my usual mentality & good heart continued—

My little new 140 page $1.25 booklet "November Boughs" is finishing the print work & I shall send you a copy soon as it is done. I am to have all my books printed & bound in one large 900 page Vol. too, ("Walt Whitman Complete") soon ready—I am sitting in my room writing this, body almost paralyzed—

Walt Whitman

1789. *To William Ingram*

ADDRESS: Wm Ingram | Telford | Bucks Co: | Penn:. POSTMARK: (?)den, N.J. | Sep 13 | 8 PM | 88.

Camden—Thursday noon | Sept: 13 '88

Thanks, dear friend, & to dear Mrs: I[ngram]—the fruit came this forenoon by express—all safe—& the bottles of wine ditto—thanks. Beau-

publishers are not smiling upon him—fifty years from now they would be glad enough to get it" (Feinberg). Kennedy in his letter of September 4 (?) wrote that he was copying over his "Whitman MS. . . . I don't see much prospect of my book on you seeing the light soon" (Feinberg; Traubel, II, 263–264).

42. Mrs. Stafford's granddaughter, Susan Browning.

43. Eddy spent the day with WW on July 31, a scene touchingly described in Traubel, II, 66.

tiful perfect weather here. I am still kept in my sick room, (but no worse) —My book printing goes on smoothly—My "Notes," such as they are, on E[lias] H[icks]" among the rest—the bunch of golden rods on my table as I write[44]—

Walt Whitman

1790. *To Richard Maurice Bucke*

ADDRESS: Dr R M Bucke | Asylum | London | Ontario Canada. POSTMARK: Camden, N.J. | Sep 13 | 8 PM | 88.

Camden Thursday Evn'g | Sept: 13 '88

All continuing much the same. Perfect weather here to-day. Your letters come & help me—Still reading Froude's Carlyle, 2d Vol. (anything but cheery).[45] The printing goes on all right—a nice big basket of fruit from Mr. Ingram. Stedman's 13 pages of Ex[cerpts] from me in his "American Literature" (ab't 9th Vol) have been shown me[46]—good—Mrs. Davis's 2d boy Harry has come from California—

W W

1791. *To William J. Linton* [*9.13.1888*]

ADDRESS: W J Linton | p o box 489 | New Haven Conn:. POSTMARKS: Camden, N.J. | Sep 13 | 8 PM | 88; New Haven, Conn. | Sep | 14 | 8 (?)M | 188(?) | Recd.

Camden New Jersey

Dear friend,

If convenient please send me by mail the block of the wood engraving head—as I want to use it here at something I am printing[47]—

Walt Whitman
328 Mickle Street

44. This is WW's reply to Ingram's note of September 12 (Feinberg; Traubel, II, 320). On giving the letter to Traubel, the poet pronounced Ingram "the best salt of the earth."

45. Bucke replied on September 15: "No I would not recommend Froude's Carlyle to a man who needed cheering up. I read it a few years ago and it nearly gave me an attack of melancholia. I look upon that same Carlyle as being (or having been?) one of the worst 'Cranks' that ever lived. . . . I shall like to know C. by & by to see what he is like in the next world but I never expect to care much about him!" (Feinberg).

On September 14 Ingram wrote to Bucke that WW "looked bright & cheerful and in

1792. *To Ernest Rhys*

ADDRESS: Ernest Rhys, | [new address inserted]. POSTMARKS: Camden, N.J. | Sep 13 | 8 PM | 88; London, E.C. | A | 9 24 8 | 88(?).

Camden N J—U S America | Sept: 13 '88

Still kept in my sick room & the summer season is ab't over. I sit up all day, but feebleness & inability to get about possess me entirely.

My little 140 page *November Boughs* & the big 900 page Vol. *Complete* are nearly done. I will send them to you when ready—Gilchrist is here—

Walt Whitman

Y'r letter came—

1793. *To Jacob Klein*

ADDRESS: Jacob Klein | Attorney &c: | rooms 5, 6, & 7— | 506 Olive Street | St. Louis | Missouri. POSTMARK: Camden, N.J. | Sep 17 | 8 PM | 88.

Camden New Jersey | Sept: 17 '88

Dear Sir

Yours just rec'd—wh' I think I cannot better than send an authentic Vol: of L of G. wh' I forward by the same mail as this—the price is $3—send by p o money order.[48]

Walt Whitman

1794. *To Richard Maurice Bucke* *9.18–19. 1888*

ADDRESS: Dr R M Bucke | Asylum | London | Ontario | Canada. POSTMARK: Camden, N.J. | Sep 19 | 8 PM | 88.

Camden 9 P M Sept: 18 | '88

Some days now since I have written—but nothing notable or different—rather a bad dull time the last two days—indigestion—bad

good spirits." Bucke continued in his letter of September 17: "Still it is grand to see you keep up as you do—never giving up to the last [?]—I think it is immense, something for us all to be proud of and to take to heart—and the world *will* take all this to heart one day—and will be the better for it" (Feinberg).

46. Stedman sent the proofs to Traubel on September 8 (Traubel, II, 301). The article appeared in volume seven of *A Library of American Literature*, 501–513.

47. See 438. WW was to use Linton's engraving in *Complete Poems & Prose*.

48. It is clear from Klein's letter to Kennedy on September 1 that he was troubled by the latter's letter "Fraudulent 'Leaves of Grass'" in *The Critic* on June 2 (Barrett).

weather—muggy warm, the air a sort of diluted tar—a promise of better weather hence, this evening—Herbert Gilchrist here quite a long while this afternoon—talks well—says his price for that portrait of me is 300 pounds—studio (& address) 1708 Chestnut St. Phila—Harry Stafford here too to-day, he is hard at work (printing & his RR position)—looks well—physique—Horace regular—the books proceeding—Baker comes occasionally—no news yet of Ostler[49] here—

Wednesday noon Sept: 19 '88

Feeling perceptibly better—fair bowel motion—(I take calomel powders)—has been dark moist bad forenoon but just now the sun is out good—the enclosed letter is from Logan Smith[50]—& the *Herald* extract is from Habberton (staff H[erald])[51]—I am sitting here in my big chair pretty comfortable considering—as I close[52]—

Walt Whitman

1795. *To William Sloane Kennedy*

Camden Wednesday P M | Sept: 19 '88

Still here in my sick room. I sit up—occasional visitors—bad weather lately—I rec'd a note from Rolleston (Ireland) that he had got first proofs of the German trans of L of G—I sent word to Dr Knortz but no answer comes—I get word often from Dr Bucke—the printing of *November Boughs* and the complete Vol. proceeds fairly—I am feeling satisfactory. H. Gilchrist here yesterday—

Walt Whitman

Y'r letter arrives[53]—

49. For some reason WW had trouble with Osler's name as well as with Garland's (often Harland).

50. Logan Smith wrote a chatty letter from Wales on September 7 (Feinberg).

51. See 1783, and also Traubel, II, 347. About this time Bennett himself dropped a line to the poet: "Herald wanted to do you a favor by early notice of your new book. Sorry you didn't get the idea" (Feinberg). On September 23, in an article entitled "Walt Whitman's Words," a *Herald* reporter, probably John Habberton, quoted the following from his "notes of Whitman's opinions, which were revised by him": "I am an old bachelor who never had a love affair. Nature supplied the place of a bride, with suffering to be nursed and scenes[?] to be poetically clothed." WW denied that he had revised the

1796. *To Sidney H. Morse*

Camden Wednesday P M | Sept: 19 '88

Dear S H M

Am surviving yet & in good spirits (sort) after the past nearly four months—Am still imprison'd here in my sick room, unable to move around or get out at all—but have my brain power as before & right arm volition—(now reduced to them what great blessings they are!)—*November Boughs* is all done printed & press'd & waits the binding—will send you one as soon as I get it—then I am to have a *Complete* W W in one large 900 Vol. ($6) L of G, Spec. Days, & Nov. B—all & several condensed in one—this is now going through the presses—

Your bust of me still holds out fully in my estimation—I consider it (to me at any rate) the best & most characteristic, really artistic & satisfactory rendering of any—so tho't by me—the bust of Elias Hicks pleases & satisfies me first rate—goes to the right spot—the little arm chair statuette is here (as when you left it) & must not be forgotten[54]—it is valuable exceedingly—Horace is invaluable to me—I couldn't have done anything with the printing without him—Whether I shall get out of this *slough* remains uncertain—I am comfortable—Love to you & all inquiring friends—

Walt Whitman

1797. *To William D. O'Connor*

ENDORSED: "Answ'd Oct. 5, 1888." ADDRESS: Wm Douglas O'Connor | 1015 O Street | Washington | D C. POSTMARKS: Camden, N.J. | Sep 19 | 8 PM | 88; Washington, Rec'd. | Sep 20 | 7 AM | 88 | 1.

Camden Wednesday P M | Sept: 19 '88

"The same subject continued" was the heading of the old chapters' novelists, this is ab't my note—Am I right in predicating that all goes with

article (Traubel, II, 394, 425). Despite the inaccuracies, the poet found the piece "friendly"; see Traubel, II, 385, 389, 456–457, 470–471.

52. In his reply on September 21 Bucke observed: "We are talking of having a copy made (or get a casting) of your (Sidney Morse) bust and putting it in our new (big) amusement room (new building)—and hope we shall be able to manage it. . . . (the plan was to put Shakespeare there but as we cannot be sure of his likeness and can be of yours we thing of this change)" (Feinberg).

53. Kennedy wrote a joint letter to WW and Traubel on September 17, which included an announcement of Hartmann's appearance in *Narcisse* (Feinberg).

54. A photograph of the plaster model of this work is the frontispiece to Traubel's third volume.

you better than for some time? Somehow I hope so—I hear from Dr B[ucke]—& friends here come in a good deal—meantime I am anchor'd here in my big chair, quite immobile—The printing goes on fairly—

Walt Whitman

1798. *To Richard Maurice Bucke*

ADDRESS: Dr R M Bucke | Asylum | London | Ontario | Canada. POSTMARK: Camden, N.J. | Sep 22 | 8 PM | 88.

Camden Saturday noon | Sept. 22 '88

Still here in my big chair in the sick room yet—a coolish wave to-day, but pleasant enough—John Burroughs has been to see me, the good hearty affectionate nature-scented fellow, very welcome[55]—he left yesterday en route to visit Johnson (Century staff) at Sea Girt, on the N J sea coast—J B lodged at Tom Harned's, & T H and Horace liked him muchly—J B is not so hardy & brown & stout as formerly—that bad fiend insomnia haunts him as of old—he thinks himself it affects his literary power, (style, even matter)—Horace told him my half-suspicion that his association with the superciliousness & sort o' vitriolic veneering of the New York literati had eat into him, but he denied & pooh-pooh'd it—attributed it to his bad health, insomnia &c—said he knew himself he could not (or did not) write with the vim of his better days—(probably makes more acc't of that by far, than really *is*)—

I expect to get a specimen copy of *November Boughs* from the binder this evening—Shall not feel out of the woods & all safe, until I see the October *Century*, with my Army Hospital piece printed—accepted & paid for by them two years ago—as I consider myself obligated not to print from it until it has been *first* published by them—(But I have heard they give it—intend to—in the Oct. number)—

Afternoon—Horace comes with spec[imen] of *Nov: B* bound for sample—it is satisfactory—looks plain, larger than expected—I give an order or two changing the lettering on cover, &c.—the picture printing gives satisfaction—In fact *all will do*—("Only think" said the Irish girl "what

55. Burroughs was in Camden on September 19 and 20. In his journal he wrote of their farewell: "He presses my hand long and tenderly; we kiss and part, probably for the last time. I think he has in his own mind given up the fight, and awaits the end" (Barrus, 283).

56. On September 20 Bucke expressed great confidence in the meter—"we expect to

ye'd said if it was ever so worser")—I have been expecting Alma Johnston of N Y to-day (or yesterday)—but no sign—a dear & prized friend—"good roots" for the meter[56] (slang from N Y vagabonds, for favorable prophecy)—It gets cooler & I have donn'd my big blue wool overgown—as I end with love & thanks to you—

Walt Whitman

1799. *To Richard Maurice Bucke* 9.25–26. 1888

ADDRESS: Dr R M Bucke | Asylum | London | Ontario | Canada. POSTMARK: Camden, N.J. | Sep | 26 | 8 PM | 88.

Camden Sept: 25 '88

Of late I have two or three times occupied spells of hours or two hours by running over with best & alertest sense & mellowed & ripened by five years your 1883 book (biographical & critical) about me & L of G—& my very deliberate & serious mind to you is that you *let it stand just as it is*—& if you have any thing farther to write or print book shape, you do so in an *additional* or further annex (of say 100 pages to its present 236 ones)—leaving the present 1883 vol. intact as it is, any verbal errors excepted—& the further pages as (mainly) reference to and furthermore &c. of *the original vol.*—the text, O'C[onnor]'s letters, the appendix—every page of the 236 left as now—This is my spinal and deliberate request—the *conviction* the main thing—the details & reasons not put down.[57]

Sept: 26 noon

Dr Osler has call'd—evidently all right—I have a good deal of pain (often sort of spasmodic, not markedly violent) in the chest & "pit of the stomach" for the last three days. O says it is nothing serious or important—& prescribes a mustard plaster—lately we have a sort of cold wave & I shouldn't wonder if that was behind it—(I have the mustard plaster on now)—It is bright & sunny—rather cool—I have rec'd a long letter from Sidney Morse from Chicago[58]—no special news—Mr Sum-

astonish the Water Works people" (Feinberg).

57. Bucke replied on September 28: "I note all you say about my 'W. W.' Your wishes will be religiously respected. I did think of considerable changes (for I am certain the book will sell by & by) but was *never* set on them and less so lately. Yes, I shall leave it stand as it is and add under a later date what else I may have to say" (Feinberg).

58. Perhaps Morse's letter of September 2 (Traubel, II, 387–388).

mers, M P from England, has just call'd & we've had a talk[59]—a nice fellow (how much more & more the *resemblance* between the cultivated Englisher and Americaner)—I have been reading Miss Pardoe's "Louis XIIII"[60]—I wonder if as a sort of foil to the Carlyle reminiscences (T[homas]'s and J[ane]'s)—the same sort of business in another sphere & land—Your letters come & are always welcome—As I close I am sitting in my big chair in my room 1½ p m quiet & measurably comfortable—

Walt Whitman

1800. *To the Editor*, Century Illustrated Monthly Review

[*9(?).(?). 1888*]

TRANSCRIPT.

Camden

I sent the revised and added copy of the *Hospitals* article—also the signed receipt. Send me a line acknowledging them, as I have a little uncertainty ab't my P. O. messenger.

Walt Whitman

1801. *To the Editor*, Century Illustrated Monthly Review

[*9(?).(?). 1888*]

follow copy, punctuation &c—After reading first proof by copy, & correcting, please send me *a good second proof*. I send copy with it—Address *Walt Whitman 328 Mickle street, Camden, New Jersey.*

1802. *To Richard Maurice Bucke*

ADDRESS: Dr R M Bucke | Asylum | London | Ontario | Canada. POSTMARK: C[amde]n, N.J. | Oct 1 | 8 PM | 88.

Camden Oct 1 '88 noon

Yours of Sept: 28 came to-day—Well pleas'd that you seriously agree that *for good* you let the 236 page W W stand in its original present

59. William Summers came with a letter of introduction from Mrs. Costelloe dated September 1 (Feinberg); see also Traubel, II, 384–385, 390–391. Of Summers' article in *Pall Mall Gazette*, "A Visit to Walt Whitman," on October 18, WW observed: "It is good—pretty good: nothing to brag of, but passable" (Traubel, III, 14).

60. Julia Pardoe's *Louis the Fourteenth and the Court of France in the Seventeenth Century* (1855), 2 vols., now in the Feinberg Collection. WW made the same point on September 28 to Traubel: "Here is another world— . . . opposite to the gloominess, irascibility, of Carlyle and his extreme dissatisfaction with the condition of the world"

form, for any further addition to be followed by you. So I consider *that* settled—

I am some better (at any rate easier) than for three or four days past —have eaten & enjoy'd my to-day's breakfast heartier than for a week— (some oysters, coffee, Graham bread)—a sort of *nibble* of soreness & pain in my chest, diaphragm, throat, belly, &c. yet, but not pronounced as during the four previous days—quite a bowel movement yesterday—

Every thing much the same—I sit in the 2d story room—havn't been out its door in two weeks—not many visitors—have got a new stove, better & larger, for wood, the same style as the old one, but an improvement—I like it—

The just out *Century* for October has my Hospital article—relieving me greatly for I felt myself in honor to not publish my Last War Cases in *Boughs* till the *Century* piece had appear'd—now the coast is clear—the *Boughs* and the *Complete W W* are getting along—one delay & stoppage after another—but as there is no hurry it makes no difference—all is going along without fear—they are all printed & the sheets are at the binder's— & the printers and electrotypers' bills are all paid[61]—I will send you the earliest copies bound presentably—

Quite cool here—pleasant though—No news from O'C[onnor] for some time[62]—I suppose John B[urroughs] has got home now—He impress'd me as not being happy, physically & other—has bad insomnia— sorry, for I love him. Horace is faithful as ever—comes every day—Have not had any word lately from England—You must have had a quite *flurry* there[63]—perhaps the edges yet—I am watching the progress of the metre with interest—Love to Mrs B and all—

Walt Whitman

1803. *To William D. O'Connor*

ENDORSED: "Answ'd Oct. 5, 1888." ADDRESS: Wm D O'Connor | 1015 O Street | Washington | D C. POSTMARKS: Camden, N.J. | Oct 3 | 8 PM | (?)8; Washington, Rec'd. | Oct 4 | 7 30 AM | 88 | 6.

Camden Wednesday Evn'g | Oct: 3 '88

The doctor was here this afternoon & speaks encouragingly but I

(Traubel, II, 394). Carlyle's *Reminiscences* appeared in 1881.

61. According to WW's tabulations in CB the expenses in connection with the printing of *November Boughs* and *Complete Poems & Prose* in 1888 amounted to $705.26.

62. O'Connor had written to Traubel on September 28 asking whether Burroughs had any objections "to my speaking at Walt's funeral" (Traubel, II, 409–410). Understandably WW did not see this letter.

63. WW was probably referring to Bucke's accounts on September 24 and 27 of the "perfect babel" in connection with the Western Fair (Feinberg).

still keep in my sick room—My books are thro' the electrotyper & printer & are now in the binder—Soon as ready I shall send you—

Walt Whitman

1804. *To Mary Smith Costelloe*

ADDRESS: Mrs: Mary Whital Costelloe | 40 Grosvenor Road | the Embankment | London England. POSTMARK: Camden, N.J. | Oct 4 | 8 PM | 88.

Camden N J America | Thursday Evn'g Oct 4 '88

Still keeping my sick room but fair spirits & no worse—great debility of legs & without body strength & control—Book printing has proceeded & sheets now at bindery—will send you a copy of *Nov: Boughs* soon—Herbert Gilchrist comes occasionally—is well. Dr Bucke is well—busy—writes daily—Cold here—I have a new wood stove—better—Love to you, to y'r father & all—

W W

1805. *To William Sloane Kennedy*

ADDRESS: Wm Sloane Kennedy | Belmont | Mass:. POSTMARK: Camden, N.J. | Oct 4 | 8 PM | 88.

Camden Thursday Evn'g | Oct: 4 '88

Still here in my sick room—everything much the same—Book printing &c slowly proceeding—the sheets now in the bindery—Shall send you the little *Nov: Boughs* soon—a good visit f'm H Garland[64]—Cool & pleasant—I have a wood fire—Horace is here every day—continues invaluable.

Walt Whitman

1806. *To Richard Maurice Bucke*

ADDRESS: Dr R M Bucke | Asylum | London | Ontario | Canada. POSTMARK: Camden (?) | Oct 6 | 8 PM | 88.

Camden Saturday Noon | Oct 6 '88

Well I suppose you have just rec'd the little bound Vol. *Nov*

64. WW was "favorably impressed" with Garland's visit on September 26: "Garland has guts—the good kind: has voice, power, manliness—has chest-tones in his talk which attract me" (Traubel, II, 384).

65. For the negotiations with McKay, see Traubel, II, 427, 437, 510. The publisher agreed finally to take "one thousand copies of N. B. at thirty-one and a quarter cents" (510).

66. Forman on September 26 informed WW of George Eliot's change of mind about *Leaves of Grass* (Feinberg; Traubel, II, 433–434). After a discussion with Traubel,

Boughs—& I fancy you saying "It looks plain & common enough—not handsome or presentable evidently at first—but let us see what it has to give us for good—if any"—Dave McKay has taken the lot & will be the publisher[65]—& I am satisfied so—What it all results time will show—

A dark rainy day & I am sitting here as usual, nothing bad—in fact nothing very new—a bowel movement this forenoon—no breast &c aches at present, but they were bad & continued yesterday & night before last, dwelling left side, heart area. To-day I am feeling pretty fairly—Mr & Mrs Johnston, my N Y friends, call'd yesterday to see me—I had a letter from Buxton Forman[66] (wh' I will send you—Horace has it now)—sends authentic the anecdote we heard ab't of Geo: Elliot & L of G—I have rec'd a letter f'm Wm O Connor—his eyes are troubling badly—but he wields spirit & determination same as ever—am drawing to a close my perusing history Louis Fourteenth[67]—poor old *creetur* (as the old woman said to the Devil)[67.1]—Every thing quiet here to-day.

Walt Whitman

1807. *To John Burroughs*

ADDRESS: John Burroughs | West Park | Ulster County | New York. POSTMARK: Camden, N.J. | Oct 6 | 8 PM | 88.

Camden Oct 6 '88

Dear J B

I send you O'Connor's just rec'd, as I know you want to hear—Pretty much "the same subject continued" yet with me—I am still imprisoned in my sick room—good spirits & ab't the same mentality as ever—great blessings & remains & privileges—but after that is said pretty much every thing wreck'd else—

But I must not get into complaining—nor do I [fail?] there—Will send you *Nov. Boughs*, for it is done—In a month the big book—Best love—Send O'C's letter to Dr B[ucke][68]—

Walt Whitman

WW concluded: "George Eliot was a great, gentle soul, lacking sunlight" (II, 435).

67. Pardoe's book (see 1799).

67.1. Bucke notes this in *Walt Whitman*, 63, as one of the poet's favorite anecdotes.

68. Bucke noted receipt of O'Connor's letter on October 11: "He is a grand fellow that, the grandest of all your friends—a hero" (Feinberg). O'Connor's letter, dated October 5 according to Bucke, is apparently lost, but the contents are summarized in the following letter.

1808. *To William Sloane Kennedy*

Camden Sunday afternoon | Oct 7 '88

Curiously monotonous with me—I am still kept in the same sick room, unable to get out, even down stairs—don't seem to retrograde in some main respects—but little or no strength or the vim & go that underlie all going & doing—John Burroughs has been to see me, the dear good fellow, I was glad to have him, & his talk did me good—he is not very well, is troubled with persistent insomnia—works at physical labor (on his own land)—not much of late seasons on essay or book making—I had a letter day before yesterday from O Connor—he has great trouble with an affection of the eyes—one lid remains fallen, & the other eye sympathises with it—seems to be at his desk in the Life Saving Service office daily—I hear f'm Dr Bucke every day or so—T B Harned was here an hour ago—is well & busy—Horace Traubel is faithful to the utmost—I have not heard a word from Dr Knortz ab't that German translation being printed by publisher Schabelitz, Zurich Switzerland (I believe I told you Rolleston in Ireland sent me word he had rec'd first proofs)—I forward with this mail a copy of *November Boughs*—McKay will be the publisher this coming week—What has become of the W W plaster bust? Has it gone to Concord—or is going?[69] Sidney Morse is in Chicago—I remain in fair spirits & comfortable—am just going to have my dinner (I live neither abstemiously nor generously, two meals a day)—Splendid sunny October day—rather quiet—Love to you & yours—

Walt Whitman

1809. *To William D. O'Connor*

ENDORSED: "Answe'd Oct 9/88." ADDRESS: Wm D O'Connor | 1015 O Street | Washington D C. POSTMARKS: (?) | Oct(?) | 5 PM | 88; Washington, Rec'd. | Oct 8 | 2 AM | 88 | 9.

Camden Sunday Evn'g | Oct: 7 '88

Your welcome letter came—but I wish it had bro't me better news than that ab't the eyes—I still remain coop'd in my sick room—send you a copy of *November Boughs* same mail with this—Fine sunny Oct. weather now here—Am comfortable & send best love to you & dear N[elly]—

Walt Whitman

69. On October 9 Kennedy informed WW that Sanborn had accepted the Morse bust for the Concord School but had neglected to call for it (Feinberg; Traubel, II, 466).

70. Ingersoll's "Rome, or Reason? A Reply to Cardinal Manning" appeared in the October issue of the journal (394–414). For WW's reaction see Traubel, II, 452–453.

71. The slip announced the resignation of Dr. William Osler from the University of

1810. *To Richard Maurice Bucke*

ADDRESS: Dr R M Bucke | Asylum | London | Ontario | Canada. POSTMARK: Camden, N.J. | Oct 9 | 8 PM | 88.

Camden Tuesday noon | Oct: 9 '88

Middling comfortable & easy—take the bitter water—bowel movement this forenoon—weather sunny & cool—I keep a pretty good fire, oak wood—sleep fairly nights (from 12 to 5 must be unbroken in the main, when favorable)—for breakfast to-day 3 or 4 good stew'd oysters, some Graham bread toasted, & a cup of chocolate—ate pretty well (this & yesterday are favorable days)—In my eating neither at all ascetic nor sumptuous—pass two hours to-day putting my autograph to the poetic motto title to L of G. for the big book—Horace bro't the sheets (600 of them) f'm the bindery—David McKay has been over to-day—wants a different binding for N. B. wh' I agree to at his seeing to & expense—thinks the binding I have—like your copy—coarse & cheap—very likely—he paid me $106 royalty—I am satisfied with D McK—Have been looking over Cardinal Manning's & Col. Ingersoll's pieces in *N. A. Review*[70]—also Mrs. Carlyle's letters (for dessert)—quite a good many visits—a string indeed all day—

Our election trial is drawing near a verdict—as I see it, there are some things on each side—no great *enthusing* tho' they (the Rep[ublican]s) try to make it so—from the view of the *solidarity* of the common people *of all the globe*. I lean rather to the Cleveland side, (but I am sometimes squeamish even at that)—but it will be all right any how—Y'r welcome letter came yesterday—I enclose slip from to-day's *Phil. Press* ab't Dr Osler[71]—

Walt Whitman

1811. *To David McKay* [*10.11. 1888*][72]

ADDRESS: David McKay.

The plate is in Phila:—Horace knows where, but I do not—He will call & get it for you, or give you an order for it—If you know where H. is send *now* & get it—

Walt Whitman

Pennsylvania and his acceptance of a position at The Johns Hopkins University.

72. I have accepted the authenticity of the note by the first owner (W. A. S.): "Mr. D. McKay gave this Autograph to me Oct. 11/88, the day on which it was written & recd" (Syracuse). W. A. S. also noted: "The 'plate' mentioned is W. W.'s portrait as printed in November Boughs. This order is to get the plate to use in the Xmas No. of Pubr Weekly of 1888." See *Publishers' Weekly*, XXXIV (November 17–24, 1888), 47.

1812. *To Richard Maurice Bucke*

ADDRESS: Dr R M Bucke | Asylum | London | Ontario | Canada. POSTMARK: Camden, N.J. | Oct 14 | 5 PM | 88.

Camden Saturday P M | Oct: 13 '88

Yours came this mn'g—welcome as always—the photo has not come yet[73]—Thankful & even exulting that you are satisfied with *Nov: Boughs* inward & outward—It is upon the whole what I wanted & planned, especially the "Backwards Road" piece (as O'C[onnor] says "that's what I deliberately said, & I stand by it")—with that, & Nov. B. & probably all I have uttered, I have a considerate eye not at all to itself alone, but to its place with all the rest I have uttered, & also to the future & permanency—many sharp readers might not think so, but *I have*—Don't make much calculation of the complete Vol. It will be I hope a respectable looking piece of typography &c. but nothing to brag of—but it *authenticates* probably better than any thing yet—there were several errors hitherto—not serious perhaps but errors—all these have of course been corrected, & as I look over the pp. there appears not to be any typographical or any other blemish—(I am quite sure of that with L of G. throughout)—& there will be five or six likenesses from life—& autograph—Then this ensemble idea haunts me till I get it realized in an identity volume—

I am a little fearful ab't our dear O'C—eagerly look for word[74]—Matters so so with me—good bowel clearance to-day—word from my friend Linton[75] from Eng[land] to-day—he is well—Shall have some oysters for my dinner ab't 4—made my breakfast of a big roast apple & some Graham bread—the sun is out—

Walt Whitman

1813. *To John Burroughs, William D. O'Connor, and Richard Maurice Bucke*

Camden Monday noon | Oct 15 '88

I sit here to-day ab't the same—close by fire in my stove, as it is pretty cool, though pleasant and sunny—now here laid by in the fifth

73. According to his letter of September 30, Bucke had his picture taken because John H. Johnston had requested "a likeness of myself to be used in an article on 'Walt and his friends.' " He sent the portrait on October 11 (Feinberg).

74. On October 9 O'Connor wrote: "My eye is now under battery treatment (assault-and-battery treatment, you would think to look at it!)" (Feinberg; Traubel, II,

month—all my strength, all *bodily-ab't-going-ability* quite gone—Spend most of the time here in the big ratan-chair—yet good heart though (in emotionality & mental action)—no sign either of any change or improvement of strength recuperation—But we will see—"(Are we to be beaten down this way in our old age"?) *one of Carlyle's books.*

J B, I hope it is all going well with you—your little visit did me good —hope you will write me when you can—W O'C, have been thinking of that eye trouble—hope it has gone down or entirely over—Hope this letter from Mary Costelloe will interest you[76]—Show it to Nelly—in some respects it is a woman's letter, but I like it much—Doctor, the photo came this forenoon—it is one of the best I ever saw—Can you send one to J B and to W O'C?—Some of those photo places off one side appear to make the best pictures in the world—My printing matters (or rather *binding* ones) go on all right but slowly—

Walt Whitman

Please send to W O'C Washington—O'C, please send to Dr Bucke—

1814. *To William Sloane Kennedy*

Camden Tuesday Evn'g | Oct: 16 '88

Thanks for the *Thackeray* pamphlet,[77] (wh' I have been reading through this afternoon)—& the *Transcripts*—Pretty much the same sing song with me—no worse—no better—I am waiting with anxiety to hear from O'C[onnor]—the bad trouble with his eyesight—

Walt Whitman

1815. *To William Sloane Kennedy*

Camden Friday Evn'g | Oct: 19 '88

It is dark & I have had my dinner & am sitting by the fire & gas light—anchor'd & tied in my old big democratic chair & room, the same as all summer, now in the fall & soon the long winter & (if I live) probably

467).

75. Linton's letter of October 3 (Feinberg; Traubel, II, 473). See 1791.

76. Mrs. Costelloe's letter of October 1 (Feinberg; *Smith Alumnae Quarterly* [February, 1958], 87–88).

77. An article on Thackeray by Frederic R. Guernsey, who was on the staff of the Boston *Herald;* see Traubel, II, 492.

through all—I have been occupied most of the afternoon writing my autographs—there are to be 600 for the Edition of my complete writings —it will be ab't 900 pages, & include *all*—a last few ?[78] revisions (no changes at all, but a few misprints, brokennesses, & errors corrected)—will be an *authenticated* ed'n—You shall have one—I will send one when ready—It is slow, but I am in no hurry.

Y'r card came this P. M. but no *Trans*[*cript*] with notice yet[78.1]—(will doubtless come to-morrow)—No further word from O'C[onnor]. I wait with anxiety—I told you ab't my dear friend John Burroughs being here—he is now back at West Park[79]—I hear from Dr B[ucke] very often—welcome letters—have been reading Ellis's "Early English Metrical Romances" (Bohn's Ed'n)[80]—Miss Pardoe's Louis XIV, and several Carlyle books including Mrs. C's Letters—Symonds's "Greek Poets" &c —upon the whole, get along & baffle lonesomeness, inertia & the blues. God bless you & the wife—

Walt Whitman

1816. *To Richard Maurice Bucke*

ADDRESS: Dr R M Bucke | Asylum | London | Ontario | Canada. POSTMARK: Camden (?) | Oct 21 | 5 PM | 88.

Camden Sunday P M | Oct: 21 '88

Again "the same subject continued"—decidedly cold to-day—a good fire needed—I ate a good breakfast of stew'd chicken, brown bread, a roast apple & chocolate ab't 10—am writing & reading a little—friendly notices of Nov: B. in Bost: *Transcript* (by Kennedy)—& in to-day's Phila: *Press* (I don't know who)[81]—Probably you have got them sent you —if not say when you write & I will send—a friendly two or three sticks' full in N Y Herald three weeks ago[82]—did you get it? mostly ab't E Hicks —I suppose you got Mary Costelloe's letter to me, I had forwarded you—

No Ostler now over a week (is that a good sign of his verdict on me?)

78. WW's question mark.

78.1. Kennedy wrote on October 18 (Feinberg; Traubel, II, 507). This review of *November Boughs* appeared in the Boston *Transcript* on October 17 (reprinted in Traubel, II, 507–508), which also contained a long article by Hartmann.

79. Burroughs wrote from West Park on October 16 after his return from the seashore (Traubel, II, 493–494).

80. George Ellis' *Specimens of Early English Metrical Romances* first appeared in the Bohn edition in 1848. See Traubel, II, 23.

81. According to Traubel, the review in the *Press* was written by Melville Philips (II, 513).

82. See 1794.

83. In a form letter on October 19 J. L. and J. B. Gilder of *The Critic* asked for WW's "answer to the question raised by Mr. Edmund Gosse in his paper in the October

—bowel movements fair—no hitch in the progress of the big book, but slow—my dull indomitable inertia of body & brain tyrannic as ever—This enc: f'm *Critic* just rec'd—I have ans'd—sh[or]t letter may appear in next C[83]—

Walt Whitman

1817. *To David McKay*

Camd[en] Monday Evn'g Oct. 22 '88

Dave, I don't see how I can make the books bill a[ny] less than 33cts (& you to pay the binder)—th[ey] cost me more than that—& *that* was what—10cts. binding—I calculated from what Oldach sent specifically (though he now makes it more now)—I have to request you will sign the memorandum & send back to me by Horace—I send the order on Oldach[84]—

Walt Whitman

1817.1 *To Frederick Oldach* [*10.22. 1888*]

TRANSCRIPT.

Mr Oldach, give as he requests the "November Boughs" to Mr David McKay—and he will pay you the binding—except for 100 copies wh' I will pay you—

Walt Whitman

1818. *To Mary Smith Costelloe*

ADDRESS: Mrs: Mary Whitall Costelloe | 40 Grosvenor Road | the Embankment | London | S W | England. POSTMARK: Camden, N.J. | Oct 2(?) | 8 PM | 88.

Camden N J U S America | Tuesday Evn'g Oct 23 '88

Still imprison'd in the sick room—but keep up spirits & occupy

Forum, entitled 'Has America Produced a Poet?'—the question, namely, whether any American poet, not now living, deserves a place among the thirteen 'English inheritors of unassailed renown' " (Feinberg). WW sent his reply on October 20, which J. B. Gilder acknowledged on November 17 (Feinberg; Traubel, III, 124). WW's comments appeared on November 24. "It is nothing," WW observed to Traubel, "I sent it because it was in my head and they asked for it" (III, 124). See also Traubel, II, 517–518.

84. WW drew up documents that provided for the following: McKay was to receive 950 copies of *November Boughs* for $313.50; Oldach was to give the books to McKay, who was to pay for the binding—"except for 100 copies wh. I will pay you"; and McKay was to pay WW $313.50 by January 10, 1889, and had the right to print additional copies of *November Boughs* for three years on the payment of "twelve (12) cents royalty a copy," and WW was to have fifty copies "of the present batch . . . free for editors' copies" (Traubel, II, 516).

myself (or fancy I do)—Your kind good letter rec'd[85]—so glad to hear f'm you, & all the particulars—H Gilchrist seems to be thriving & happy—I hear often from Dr Bucke—I will send you forthwith my little *Nov: Boughs* wh' comes out in two or three days—The big Vol. (Complete Works) soon—

W W

1819. *To Hamlin Garland*

ADDRESS: Hamlin Garland | Jamaica Plain | Mass:.
POSTMARK: Camden | Oct 25 | 8 PM | 88.

Camden N J Thursday afternoon | Oct: 25 '88

Thanks for your kind letter[86]—I have just sent off the booklet to Mr H[owells] at Little Nahant—The doctor says I am perceptibly better (& I hope he talks true)—

Walt Whitman

1820. *To William Sloane Kennedy and John Burroughs*

Camden Thursday noon | Oct. 25 '88

First thank you for your good affectionate letter, inspiriting more than you knew—That seems to me too long, condensed, dwelling a pull proof reading work—pressing work too on the *delication* of the brain—I had a friend a woman of 30 a *counter* in the Redemption Bureau in the Treasury—told me she was "going to the devil, fast & steady" (her own description) from her dense brain-exhausting-dulling labors, till she adopted the plan of getting a 10 or 12 minutes' nap (sleep or even doze) at noon or one o'clock every day, just leaning down on her desk—fortunately

85. The letter of October 1.

86. On October 18 Garland informed the poet that he was about to begin a series of twelve lectures on "Walt Whitman's Message," and that "at the earliest possible moment I intend to get that article into shape concerning your work as a landscapist" (Feinberg; Traubel, II, 509). On October 24 Garland urged WW to send an autographed copy of *November Boughs* to William Dean Howells, who "spoke of you again with a good deal of feeling" (Feinberg; Traubel, II, 530). Howells reviewed the volume in *Harper's New Monthly Magazine* in February, 1889 (see 1897).

87. Kennedy wrote on October 20: "Mrs. K. is in Boston at a Symphony Concert and a precious ½ hour for my soul being at my disposal I feel a strong inner impulse to pour out here in the evening solitude, my heart to you in a genuine heart-letter of affection, welling up out of the deeps you long ago touched as no other ever did or can. Dear friend whom I have for so long admired, do you not feel that all is well with you & the great cause of freedom for which you have laid down yr life? I do. I feel somehow that the future is going to be with you, with us. Humanity is sweeping on into the larger light. To me who have drank at all fountains of literature the world over, & climbed the lonely

she *could* fall in her nap—wh' is the great part of it—at any rate it cured.[87]

I heard from Bucke to-day—he sends me the enclosed little slip from O'C[onnor][88]—the condition is bad, & I feel pretty gloomy ab't my best friend—yet he has great vitality & may tide over it—

Nothing very different with me—Dr Ostler (very 'cute, a natural physician, rather optimistic, but best so)—thinks I am either on a very good way, or substantially cured of this last attack—I only wish I could *feel* so, or even approximate it—But any how thank God so far my thoughts & mental power are entirely within my control—I have written a short letter to *Critic* (by their request) on the "Poet" question (wh' they may print)—My sister—George's wife—has just paid me a good cheery visit, (with some nice home made Graham biscuits)—So I get along well, am comfortable, have a fair appetite, & keep a good oak fire—Love—

Walt Whitman

Please send to John Burroughs with slip[89]—

1821. *To Richard Maurice Bucke*

ADDRESS: Dr. R M Bucke | Asylum | London | Ontario | Canada. POSTMARK: Camden, N.J. | Oct 26 | 8 PM | 88.

Camden Friday noon | Oct 26 '88

Yours came this morning, & I am satisfied & agreeable—Edward Wilkins (tell me more ab't him—is he a Canadian?) should understand that it is not a soft or profitable job, & some features not very nice either[90] —I have tho't of dispensing any caretaker, but I believe I get no nearer to even the *middling-get-along-condition-of-myself* before this spell—with a

peaks of thought in every land & age, your *Leaves of Grass* still towers up above everything else in grand aspiration, right philosophy, & the heart-beats of true liberty." Kennedy went on to complain that he was "really ill with hard work—nerves trembling, eye fluttering & above all sleepy" (Feinberg).

88. A brief note from O'Connor to Bucke on October 20 mentioned that "a month ago my right eye closed, and the lid had not yet lifted, spite of battery. So I am practically blind" (Pennsylvania).

89. On the verso of WW's letter Kennedy wrote to Burroughs on October 26: "What a good nice letter from the dear old fellow this is" (Pennsylvania; Barrus, 285).

90. On October 24 Bucke reported that he was sending Wilkins as a replacement for Musgrove: "He is a real good, nice looking, young fellow. I have known him some years—he is as good as he looks" (Feinberg; Traubel, II, 537). Wilkins (1865–1936) arrived in Camden on November 5 (*CB*). He stayed for a year, then returned to Canada to attend the Ontario Veterinary College in Toronto. After graduation in 1893 he moved to Alexandria, Indiana, where he married and spent the rest of his life. For this biographical information I am indebted to Bert A. Thompson, Director of Libraries at Kearney State College, Nebraska.

sort of prospect (if I live at all) of getting in a more immobile situation than ever—(am indeed in a pretty bad way now)—But you & Horace manage it, & I shall be docile—If E W is indeed the proper one & willing I shall be glad enough to have him—

I rec'd a nice letter f'm E C Stedman (44 East 26th St New York) this mn'g—He likes Nov. B. and has considerable to say of my "fame"—(I am not sure but we are to put E C S on our *list of real permanent friends & understanders*)[91]—

I suppose you have got (or will soon get) the Springfield *Republican* short notice of Nov: B[92]—I rec'd a note from Hamlin Garland, Jamaica Plain, Mass. asking me to send Nov. B. to W D Howells, wh' I did.

I am sitting in my big chair by the oak wood fire as I write—it is a darkish, damp, heavy-air'd day & I am not feeling my easiest—Mr Ingram has just been in & bo't a copy of Nov: B. for a Quakeress friend, & got some loose reading matter for a prisoner in jail I send to sometimes[93]—my head is weighty & sore to-day—

Dave McKay is behaving very well—he takes the whole ed'n, & pays me $313.50 on Jan 10 '89—& pays the binder—I retain 100 (printed 1100)[94]—Did I tell you I rec'd a strong affectionate literary & personal letter from Kennedy?—I repeat that last photo of you in hat &c. is one of the very best could be made—there is nothing better made here or in N Y—

Walt Whitman

1822. *To William D. O'Connor*

ENDORSED: "Answ'd Oct. 27/88." ADDRESS: Wm D O'Connor | 1015 O Street | Washington D C. POSTMARK: Camden, N.J. | Oct 26 | 8 PM | 88.

Camden Friday night | Oct: 26 '88

Am a little concern'd—not hearing from you for quite a while—hope that eye trouble has had a turn for the good[95]—Rec'd a friendly & cheering letter f'm E C Stedman this forenoon—As for me I get on ab't the same as of late—Keep my sick room yet, but mainly comfortable—

Walt Whitman

91. On October 25 Stedman wrote: "In many respects this collection (so strikingly and fittingly got up) is one of the most significant—as it is the most various—of your enduring works" (Feinberg; Traubel, II, 538).

92. The notice appeared on the editorial page on October 23. For WW's taste, "there's too much of the battered old veteran business" (Traubel, II, 538).

93. George Rush, Jr. (see 1772, *n.*22).

1823. *To Richard Maurice Bucke*

ADDRESS: Dr R M Bucke | Asylum | London | Ontario Canada. POSTMARK: Camden, N.J. | Oct 28 | 5 PM | 88.

Camden Sunday Evn'g | Oct: 28 '88

Am feeling fairly—all ab't same as before—am sitting here in the room—rain & cloudy weather—hysterical efforts to get up some excitement ab't Presidential election—hard go—I like McKay's binding & send you one—

Walt Whitman

1824. *To Richard Maurice Bucke*

ADDRESS: Dr R M Bucke | Asylum | London | Ontario | Canada. POSTMARK: Camden, N.J. | Oct 31 | 8 PM | 88.

Camden Wednesday noon | Oct 31 '88

Yours came yesterday evn'g—Mrs. Stafford here yesterday—Harry has the still same trouble with the throat—it gets neither worse [nor][96] better—H seems interested in what they call "politics"—he is I suppose greatly anxious ab't Harrison's election—the whole thing is mixed—I shall myself be content (following Epictetus's advice to those who watch the great games) with whoever the people *put in*—

Nothing new or special in my affairs—I sit here ab't the same—Mr Musgrove rec'd a note from our friend Harned this morning that after Monday next a new nurse & help carer for me w'd be install'd—M has always been kind & attentive to me—I suppose you have got the copy of Nov. B in McKay's style of binding—McK has been (is) off N Y & Boston ward "drumming"—is expected to come back to-day or to-morrow—Sorry indeed to hear such bad prospects of Pardee—I recd a few lines dated Oct 27 from O'C[onnor], also a postal from Mrs. O'C—the eye trouble still continued—lively letter in ab't the same as usual—kind, affectionate, & sparkling. Horace comes unfailingly & is a main reliance—

I feel half & half—pretty fair bowel movements—no Osler for ten days—bright & sunny to-day—Have been reading Matthew Arnold's

94. McKay had 950 copies to sell, 50 copies were distributed to reviewers, and WW retained 100 copies, some of which he sold but many of which he gave to friends.

95. O'Connor replied at length on the following day: "The pleasing little malady of the eyelid which has inspired me to much eloquent, though silent, profanity, is called *ptosis*, . . . and consists in a paralysis of the first nerve of the eyelid" (Feinberg).

96. WW wrote "than."

"Heine"—also George Elliot on same—both good (but probably not exhaustive)—

God bless you—

Walt Whitman

1825. *To Richard Maurice Bucke*

ADDRESS: Dr R M Bucke | Asylum | London | Ontario Canada. POSTMARK: Camden, N.J. | Nov 1 | 8 PM | 88.

Camden Thursday night | Nov: 1 '88

Had fine weather to-day. Much as usual with me—An elderly gentleman, an Iowan[97] just ret'g from Eng[land], told me at a dining party at Rossetti's a Frenchman told him of a review of L of G. ab't three or four months ago in Paris—the gent. said he could give me the date & name of magazine & if so I will tell you—Your letter came last evn'g—Have had beef & onions for my dinner—Ate with relish—

Walt Whitman

1826. *To Richard Maurice Bucke* *11.3–4. 1888*

ADDRESS: Dr R M Bucke | Asylum | London | Ontario | Canada. POSTMARK: Camden, N.J. | Nov 4 | 5 PM | 88.

Camden Saturday P M | Nov: 3 '88

Good breakfast at 9½ of chocolate, toasted Graham bread & broil'd chicken—enjoy'd all. Have rec'd a nice letter this mn'g f'm Mary Costelloe, return'd to London city—all well—Pearsall S[mith] well as formerly, (one eye sight however quite quench'd)—Rec'd also an acc't (in Pall Mall Gaz: Oct: 28) of a visit to me f'm the good fellow, Mr Summers, M P, I believe mention'd to you in letter months ago[98]—I will send the acc't to you—the two paper notices Boston *Transcript* & in the Phil: *Bulletin*, (of N B,) must have now reach'd you—they were sent.

Am pretty well, considering, but laggard & a dull headache most of the time—partial bowel action this forenoon—I don't get out of my room at all—the 6th month now—Mr Musgrove is kind active & considerate all through—dull, darkish, damp here to day—I sit here the same, the sash a little open'd—very moderate—

97. Charles Aldrich (see Traubel, III, 1–2). The "review" is probably Sarrazin's

Sunday noon Nov: 4—Bright, sunny, quiet day—am feeling ab't my easiest—fair bowel movement—the big book gets on—title page has been made of a big medallion profile of me, (lettering on it)—suits me—am thinking (composing it now) of a short concluding note at end—will see how I can get it in shape—

Tom Harned & his brother Frank & young Mr. Corning have just call'd & spent a short half hour (I don't know but I find myself *talking more* than I used to—talking perhaps more than ever)—I enclose you several letters (I send them as a foil, your duties & works there must be dry)—if you don't feel to read them, put it off for a better season, or put it aside altogether—I suppose Edward Wilkins will be here to-morrow—Mr M, my present nurse, is sort o' *vexed* ab't it all—he is a good fellow too, & I am almost glum ab't his going—I liked him well—Horace did not, & has not—H remains & is perfectly faithful & I depend on him more than words could describe—y'r letter came last evn'g.

Best love to you & yours—

Walt Whitman

1827. *To Richard Maurice Bucke*

ADDRESS: Dr R M Bucke | Asylum | London | Ontario Canada. POSTMARKS: Camden, N.J. | Nov 5 | 1 30 PM | 88; Philadelphia | Nov | 5 | 2 30 PM | 1888 | Transit.

Camden toward noon | Nov: 5 '88

Edward Wilkins has arrived here all safely & is welcome. With me the turn remains at favorable more than the other way. I suppose you have rec'd the letter sent last evn'g, with quite a budget enclosed—I am sitting here by the stove as usual—

Walt Whitman

1828. *To Richard Maurice Bucke* *11.6–7. 1888*

ADDRESS: Dr R M Bucke | Asylum | London | Ontario | Canada. POSTMARK: Camden, N.J. | Nov 7 | 1 30 PM | 88.

Camden Tuesday Evn'g Nov: 6 '88

Seems curiously quiet for election day, & has been all the time here

essay which appeared May 1 in *La Nouvelle Revue*.

98. See 1799.

—At my proposal Ed Wilkins went over to Phila: from 12 to 3 & took a note I sent to Tom Donaldson—(Ed says D treated him like a prince)—I am feeling better still—weather fine to day, sunny, rather warmish—I am trying to write a very short *concluding note* to the big book but it holds fire, don't suit me—& this is all that keeps matters back—but *n'importe*—we are in no way hurry—

Yours came to-day—it is indeed queer you don't hear from Wm Gurd at all ('twas me I should be uneasy)[99]—Tom Harned was here last evn'g—Horace too—a good deal ab't the election & "politics"—(the whole contest ab't high tariff & free trade is *too previous* & sophomorical at present—too abstract—But it will be a great point one of these days)—Whatever is done or happens at present the U S will prosper, grow, advance, in the nature of things, these ages—

Wednesday A M Nov. 7—Don't seem to be defined yet who is elected President—you will probably know before this reaches you—Fine weather still—I continue pretty well—No Osler for ten days—Ed Wilkins pleases me[1]—Did you get the Phil: *Times* Oct 27 with a quarter column notice of Nov. B?[2]—If not I will send it you—As I write I am sitting here as usual in the big chair by the stove—window a little open—every thing quiet & comfortable—

Walt Whitman

1829. *To Richard Maurice Bucke*

ADDRESS: Dr R M Bucke | Asylum | London | Ontario Canada. POSTMARK: Camden, N.J. | Nov 8 | 8 PM | 88.

Camden P M Nov: 8 '88

Yours of 6th just rec'd—still leaning to favorable—I have [just?] had a complete bath & flesh-rubbing—very good—Ed: W[ilkins] is very good and attentive to me—No visitors to-day yet—cloudy, damp, coolish weather—

As you see Harrison is probably elected—this one tack—but the ship will go on on her voyage many a sea & many a year yet—

Walt Whitman

99. Gurd, the coinventor of the meter, had gone to New York in order to obtain financial backing. On November 1 Bucke complained that he had "only written one letter in 2½ weeks" (Feinberg). On November 6 Bucke had heard from Gurd—"All is going fine with him and the meter" (Feinberg).

1. On November 9 Bucke commented: "I am real glad you seem pleased with Ed. W. I knew he would suit you or I would not have sent him so far—he was with me here a

1830. *To William D. O'Connor*

ADDRESS: Wm D O'Connor | 1015 O Street | Washington | D C. POSTMARKS: Camden, N.J. | Nov 9 | 8 PM | 88; Washington, Rec'd. | Nov 10 | 7 30 AM | 88 | 3.

Camden Nov: 9 night '88

I have had a pretty good week so far—am either throwing off (or easying) some of the worst bad subjections and *grips*—

My big book (collection of all) is all printed, & paid for & at the binders delaying for one or two little things—it is nothing more than you have seen—but I had a great desire for *all* to be combined, comprehended at one glance—and here it is—of course I shall send you a copy—

I am sitting yet in my sick room now in my usual big chair by the oak wood fire, & alone. I have plenty visitors enough & good ones—my appetite & sleep are fair—I have a new helper & nurse, a clean strong kind hearted young Kanuck man Dr. Bucke sent me—All indeed goes as well & comfortable as could be expected with me—And how with you? I think of you every day—& most all my friends coming here ask ab't you—I rec'd the letter last week & thankful & ask for more—I cannot say I enthuse on H[arrison]'s election—but I accept it—all right for what it goes—Dr. B. is probably coming this way in a week—Best love to you & to Nelly.

Walt Whitman

1831. *To Richard Maurice Bucke*

ADDRESS: Dr R M Bucke | Asylum | London | Ontario Canada. POSTMARKS: Camden, N.J. | Nov 10 | 8 PM | 88; Philadelphia, Pa. | Nov | 10 | 9 30 PM | 1888 | Transit.

Camden Saturday Evn'g | Nov: 10 '88

A little under to day, but feel clearer this evn'g. As I write the wind is blowing up quite a gale. Have finished the little beginning & end Notes I spoke of for the big book & sent to the printer—(I am a bit squeamish yet ab't them)—

Walt Whitman

long time and I know him well—he is just what he looks, a good, simple minded, quiet, honest country boy—just the kind you like" (Feinberg). On November 8 WW commented to Traubel: "I am coming to see that he is just the man I needed: he is my kind: he is young, strong" (III, 53).

2. Bucke termed the review, on November 9, "a middling notice—it is surprising to me how little the average reviewer sees" (Feinberg).

1832. *To Richard Maurice Bucke*

ADDRESS: Dr R M Bucke | Asylum | London | Ontario Canada. POSTMARK: Camden, N.J. | Nov 13 | 8 PM | 88.

Camden P M Nov: 13 '88

Sat in the bright warm sun an hour midday in the back room to-day—All continues fairly with me. Yours of 11th with parallel to Millet &c. rec'd. I shall look out for *the Nineteenth*[3]—Sent off the pesky little notes (more bother than they are worth)—the big book will now be stitched & bound—I came across a critique of John Burroughs in the old *Galaxy* magazine[4]—wh' I send you, tho' you probably had it before.

Walt Whitman

1833. *To William D. O'Connor*

ADDRESS: Wm D O'Connor | 1015 O Street | Washington | D C. POSTMARKS: Camden (?) | Nov (?) | 8 PM | 88; Washington, Rec'd. | Nov 14 | 7 AM | 88 | 1.

Camden P M Nov: 13 '88

A remarkably fine sunny day, & I went & sat in the warm bright *bask* of it from 12 to 1—Not much different in my condition—what there is, bends favorably. I am still imprison'd in my sick room—Please send the "Open Court"[4.1] (in the bundle) to Dr Bucke—Am comfortable & in good spirits—few visitors lately—

Walt Whitman

1834. *To Hamlin Garland*

ADDRESS: Hamlin Garland | Jamaica Plain | Mass:. POSTMARK: Camden | Nov 18 | 6 PM | (?).

Camden New Jersey | Nov: 18 '88

Thanks for the *Transcript* with notice, rec'd[5]—have much to say,

3. Bucke wrote enthusiastically on November 11 about an article by Julia Ady on "Jean-François Millet" in the September issue of *The Nineteenth Century*: "The parallelism in the lives of the two men (yourself & Millet) is wonderful." He proceeded to cite eleven parallels (Feinberg; Traubel, III, 93–94). See also Traubel, III, 88–90. WW, however, found Bucke's parallels "not convincing—no: only interesting" (III, 94).

4. See Traubel, III, 87.

4.1 *The Open Court* for November 8 (II, 1295–97) contained an article by Moncure D. Conway entitled "The Spiritualists' Confession."

5. Garland spoke of his review in the Boston *Transcript* on November 15 in letters dated November 9 (Feinberg; Traubel, III, 67) and November 16 (Feinberg; Traubel, III,

& thanks, but cannot write. I am getting along comfortably (considering what might be) & for the last ten days & now am easier. Big Vol. with my writings complete, ready in two weeks & shall send you a copy—

Walt Whitman

1835. *To Louisa Orr Whitman*

ADDRESS: Mrs: Louisa Whitman | Burlington | New Jersey. POSTMARK: Camden (?) | Nov 19 | 8 PM | 88.

Camden noon Nov: 19 '88

Dear Lou

I continue getting along pretty well considering—Eat my rations & sleep fairly—(the Graham biscuits taste good—have them most every meal—I only take two meals daily)—the publisher got an order for 250 copies *Nov: Boughs* yesterday from Scotland[6]—the enclosed (I send to George) was forwarded to me by Capt. Wright[7]—(I don't know what he wants George's address for—have not written myself)—Coolish, dark, rainy here to-day—I am sitting here yet by the stove in my sick room. The big book (all my writings collected complete) will be done in ab't a fortnight—I shall send you one—

Walt Whitman

1836. *To Josiah Child*

ADDRESS: Josiah Child | Care Trübner & Co: | 57 Ludgate Hill | London England. POSTMARK: Camden, N.J. | Nov 20 | 8 PM | 88.

Camden New Jersey U S America | Nov: 20 1888

I am not sure I receipted the balance $14.43—sent me Oct: 20, & safely reach'd me[8]—best thanks—I am in *good heart* here, but nearly altogether physically wreck'd (paralysis &c)—am living here in my little shanty by the Delaware river—Best remembrance to you—

Walt Whitman

114). WW commented to Traubel: "The Transcript piece has as a trifle a certain air almost of apology: but for that feature I like it. We are forcing the enemy to listen to us" (III, 114). Bucke observed on November 22: "I do not know when I have read any thing that pleased me more—not I think since I read O'Connor's letter in N. Y. Tribune in the Osgood-Stevens affair" (Feinberg).

6. Alexander Gardner was the publisher; see Traubel, III, 113, and 1846.

7. Possibly Colonel John Gibson Wright, the commanding officer of George's regiment during the war; see 143, *n.*22, and 163.

8. On October 20 Child sent "on behalf of Trübner & Co a draft for $14.43 for 39 copies of 'Democratic Vistas' which is all your commission stock they had left on hand" (Feinberg). For a complete record of WW's dealings with Trübner see 891.

1837. *To William D. O'Connor*

ADDRESS: Wm D O'Connor | 1015 O Street | Washington D C. POSTMARKS: Camden, N.J. | Nov 20 | 8 PM | 88; Washington, Rec'd. | Nov 21 | 7 AM | 88 | 3.

Camden Nov: 20 '88

Still ab't holding my own & comfortable—nothing very new or notable—The *Transcript* I send with Hamlin Garland's notice of *Nov: Boughs*—Still keep my sick room—Clear sunny cool to-day. How are you getting along?—The pub'r yesterday had an order for 250 copies Nov: B. for Scotland—

W. W.

1838. *To Harry Stafford*

Camden | Nov: 21 P M '88

Dear Hank

Yours of 20th rec'd this morning & is quite a surprise to me, & a little *not understandable*[9]—But you will tell me plainer when you come up & see me Saturday—Don't do any thing too hastily, & from great excitement—I shall look for you Saturday—If any thing prevents your coming, write me & write fully.

I am much the same—rather easier if any thing the past two weeks—but the bad pall-weight & inertia, (like a sluggish, sleepy, tired, great weight, as of heavy irons on me, body & spirit) seem to be on me all the time—& appear destined for life. Still keep the sick chair & sick room—(now going into the sixth month)—The big book, (my whole works in one Vol.) will be bound now in a week or ten days—I suppose Eva bro't you the little *Nov: Boughs*—Things go on comfortably with me—Eat & sleep fairly—spirits good yet—Sunny cold weather here—Herbert comes quite often—Two visitors (ladies, strangers) just here to see me—love to you, dear boy, & to Eva and Dora—

Walt Whitman

9. Unfortunately Stafford's letter is not known.
10. With a letter of introduction dated August 31 from Dowden (Feinberg;

1839. *To Edward Dowden*

TRANSCRIPT.

328 Mickle Street | Camden New Jersey
U. S. America | Nov 21, 1888.

My dear friend,

Again a few lines to you. The past summer & fall have laid me up again, & I am now entering the sixth month of confinement in my big chair & sick room—commenced early in June—abt the sixth *whack* (as I call it) from my old obstinate war-paralysis—from the overstrain'd work & excitement of Secession years, 1863, 4 & 5. I am now staving it off and on, but it is a serious siege & I do not really look for it being raised anything like really—I am in good spirits & comfortable enough. Mr Fry[10] (of England bro't a note from you) call'd upon me yesterday—and I sent you by him my new little book *November Boughs* (but it will be a week before he sails home). I have also a big 900 page Vol. nearly ready, combining all my writings, last revisions, &c.—I will send you a copy—Do you see anything of Rolleston? If so I send him my affectionate remembrances—I am sitting by my oak-wood fire writing this (cold but sunny weather here)—Spend most of my time alone—a few visitors—get along better than you might suppose. Love & thanks to you, my friend, & best best regards to my Irish friends all.

Walt Whitman

1840. *To Richard Maurice Bucke*

ADDRESS: Dr R M Bucke | Asylum | London | Ontario Canada. POSTMARK: Camden, N.J. | Nov 22 | 8 PM | 88.

Camden Evn'g Nov: 22 '88

Not much difference—if anything duller & some depression to-day. Clear weather & unmistakably cold. I sit crouch'd by the fire—No word from you for three days—An Englishman, Lewis Fry, MP. for Bristol, call'd, bringing two fine tall daughters. I am just writing to Mary Costel-loe.

Walt Whitman

Traubel, III, 146–147), Lewis Fry called on November 20. WW was much impressed with this "good Liberal" (Traubel, III, 137). Dowden acknowledged receipt of *November Boughs* on June 26, 1889 (Feinberg).

1841. *To Mary Smith Costelloe*

ADDRESS: Mrs: Mary Costelloe | 40 Grosvenor Road | the Embankment | London England. POSTMARKS: Camden, N.J. | Nov 22 | 8 PM | 88; Philadelphia, Pa. | Nov 22 | 8 PM | Paid.

Camden N J U S America | Nov: 22 '88

Keeping on ab't the same. Still in my sick room—less well to-day, but have had a fair fortnight. Clear & cold weather. I double-up here by the stove—Suppose you rec'd the *Nov: Boughs*—I expect Dr Bucke before long.

Walt Whitman

1842. *To Richard Maurice Bucke*

ADDRESS: Dr R M Bucke | Asylum | London | Ontario | Canada. POSTMARK: Camden, N.J. | Nov 24 | 8 PM | 88.

Camden Saturday noon Nov: 24 '88

Cold the last two days & this morning a continued snow storm, quite brisk—well I laid in a cord of oak wood yesterday & am keeping up a good fire—had my breakfast at 9½—three or four oysters, some Graham bread, a cup of coffee & a bit of stew'd blackberries—(the b[read] bro't up yesterday by Mrs. Stafford, sent by her daughter Debby)—I am ab't the same—rather leaning to the easier condition of the last ten days, (with spells of *down*)—tho' this is the news of this mornings paper—

> —Walt Whitman is gradually growing feebler, and has been confined to his room for the last few days by a heavy cold. He has done little work since completing his last book "November Boughs."
>
> *Phil: Record Nov 24*[11]

As I write Ed W[ilkins] is making up the bed—he is a good nurse to me & does well—I believe the big book is ab't done, & soon the binders will go at it—All I have meant in it is (as I have before told you) to make the completed, authenticated (& personal) edition of my utterances—a system of which L of G is the centre & source—Shall of course send you

11. The clipping was mounted in the letter at this point.

12. Frederic Henry Hedge's *Prose Writers of Germany* (1856).

13. Bucke reported on November 22 that Pardee "is bad—very sick indeed—mind very feeble" (Feinberg).

one of the earliest copies—tho' you may be here personally & receive one—wh' will be better still—

Have spent a couple of hours with Addington Symonds's "Greek Poets" and the Bible—full of meat to me, both of them—Have read Boswell's Johnson—also a long collation & brief Biog: of Kant in Prof: Hedge's "Prose Writers of Germany" (a big valuable book)[12]—

1.40 P M—Yours of 22d just come—Sorry, sadly sorry, ab't Pardee[13] —the direction is *Hamlin Garland, Jamaica Plain, Mass:*—I have not heard lately from O'C[onnor]—Have had a *currying* & bath—the sun came out an hour ago, but has gone under & every thing looks glum & cloudy—good blazing sputtering oak fire—

Walt Whitman

1843. *To Richard Maurice Bucke*

ADDRESS: Dr R M Bucke | Asylum | London | Ontario Canada. POSTMARK: Camden, N.J. | Nov 27 | 8 PM | 88.

Camden noon Nov: 27 '88

We have had (glum & dark yet) a severe storm & blow & destruction hereabout but I believe I am as serene as ever & getting on comfortably—had a present of some plump sweet partridges[14]—& half one for my breakfast—went well—I suppose you rec'd the *Critic*[15] and *American* sent last night—I believe the books, printing &c. are going to eventuate satisfactorily from my point of view & plans—no cyclone of success—but no special mishap—wh' is a great victory considering my wreck'd bodily condition—

Walt Whitman

1844. *To Frederick Oldach* [*11.27. 1888*][16]

TRANSCRIPT.

To Mr. Oldach 1215 Market St Phila:

Yes—the fixing up of the sheets—placing of the plates, &c &c—all right and the paper-bound specimen satisfactory—But I think you can do it *better* for me—*try*—

14. The partridges were sent by William H. Blauvelt of Richfield Springs, New York; see *CB*, and Traubel, III, 189.
15. See 1816.
16. Traubel transcribed this letter on the day it was written (III, 188).

I want fifty (50) copies bound in good strong paper covers—w'd it do in some handsome *marble* paper? W'd that be better? (I leave mainly to y'r taste & judgment)—if you have anything better as *strong* backs (stitching &c) as can consistently be made—uncut & untrimm'd like this sample (I like this sample even as it is pretty well)—
☞ *I will send you the label to put on the backs—I am now having them printed*—(will also have the 550 copies in handsome costlier stiff bindings afterwards.)

Walt Whitman
328 Mickle St Camden

1845. *To Richard Maurice Bucke* *11.30–12.1. 1888*

ADDRESS: Dr R M Bucke | Asylum | London | Ontario | Canada. POSTMARK: Camden, N.J. | Dec 1 | 8 PM | (?).

Camden Nov: 30 1888

A bad spell again—Wednesday was the worst—the light indeed was faintly fluctuating several times—but here I am yet—poor enough now but less *non*-myself—Osler was here last evening—He does not apparently think any thing serious—at least nothing new—nothing but we knew before—The worst is this inveterate horrible costiveness—then the water works give me great annoyance & trouble—my strength, equilibrium, power to stand up of my own volition & mastery are quite gone—Ed is very good—I gave him your little message[17]—he has just helped me to the closet, where I tried an injection of soaped warm water but no result at all—One thing is I have not eaten any thing for three days —to day three or four mouthfuls & a cup of coffee for breakfast—At present moment I am sitting in the big chair at the stove alone writing—weather cloudy half-&-half—not cold—

Your good letter came this morning—I am having some copies of the big book covered in paper & I will send you one, (perhaps two or three) at once—as there is some delay ab't the permanent binding—Yes I shall be hard to suit with the binding of the b[ig] b[ook]—As I finish the sun bursts out as if it meant to stay awhile strong & clear—I am going to stretch out on the bed (rest, *tide over*, *lay fallow*, & such—are probably my best remedies to meet these spells)—

17. Bucke wrote on November 28: "Remember me to Ed. Wilkins, tell him that every thing goes quietly along here since he left us" (Feinberg).

Saturday, sunset. Dec 1—Last night bad & sleepless—up forty to fifty times—water-works irritation, scalding—I have been lying on the bed most of the time, but am now sitting here by the stove—declining light—rather pleasant weather—not cold—no word of O'C[onnor]—

Walt Whitman

1846. *To William Sloane Kennedy, John Burroughs, William D. O'Connor, Richard Maurice Bucke* *12.3–4. 1888*

ADDRESS: Wm Sloane Kennedy | Belmont | Mass:.
POSTMARK: Camden, N.J. | Dec 4 | 8 PM | 88.

Camden Night Dec: 3 '88

This is the title-page of a small ed'n of *Nov: B.* in Scotland I tho't might amuse you[18]—My physical trouble has veer'd quite entirely lately, or more truly added to, & is now that senile botheration from prostrate or enlarged or inflamm'd gland, bladder business, diabetes—or other worse or less worse form of ailment—Dr Osler was here this afternoon, & is to bring over a surgeon expert on 5th P M for more concise examination—It has resulted the last four nights in quite no sleep, wh' is a pretty bad factor in my complication—

Have succeeded in a cheap & initiatory dress (binding) for the big book—(trilogy the proof reader at the office calls it)—wh' I am now only waiting the hard press'd binders (at present) to achieve & put in form, & I will send you one—each of you dear ones for Christmas—(& good much may it do you)—The more elaborated court dress with frills, yet waits before desperate vacancy & uncertainty—

Dec: 4 10 a m—have finish'd my breakfast—two or three nice stew'd oysters—some coffee & Graham bread—better to-day—a fair night this last, & fair sleep—The gland suffering or whatever it is—the distressing recurrent stricture-like spasms ab't from three to ten minutes almost continuously the last five days & nights—have let up—& the parts at present seem to be assuming something like normal condition—I am sitting in my big chair by the fire, the stove—it is sharp & cold, bright & sunny—Ed Wilkins (my young Kanuck, my nurse & helper, Dr B. sent) has just come in to tell me the result of an errand—& so monotonously my thread winds on—

18. The letter was written on a proof sheet of the title page of the Scottish edition of *November Boughs.*

My friends Mr & Mrs: Harned have a new:born son[19]—every thing working well—poor Dave McKay (he appears to be a good husband &c) has had a dreadful time with serious sickness of wife—pronounc'd out of danger yesterday—Horace continues helpful & faithful—Love to you all & as I finish this scrawl glad to give you as I write the assurance of my comfortableness—

Walt Whitman

Kennedy, please send this to John Burroughs—J B, please send to O'Connor—O'C, please send to Dr Bucke—my Ed W. has gone to the printer & binders for me & I sit here alone, slight headache.—

1847. *To Richard Maurice Bucke*

ADDRESS: Dr R M Bucke | Asylum | London | Ontario Canada. POSTMARK: Camden, N.J. | Dec 4 | 8 PM | 88.

Camden Evn'g: Dec: 4 '88

Yours of 2d rec'd—all goes along—a bad week past—(a combination of prostrate gland trouble & diabetes coming to the front)—Shall tell you more when Osler's mate[20] gives his verdict to-morrow—Had a better night this last than for a week—Fine weather here, day & night superb—God bless you all—

Walt Whitman

1848. *To Frederick Oldach*

TRANSCRIPT.

Camden, Evn'g: Dec: 4, '88.

Mr. Oldach | Binder

Sir, I will have 150 (not 50 nor 100) copies bound in the style I like—as sample.—I send 100 autograph sheets—(50 were sent before.) I send 100 labels—(50 were sent before.) The sample made up is herewith—partly as sample which all copies will be compared strictly by—and partly to put in *the right page for "Specimen Days" title back'd with the copyright line*, wh' in present is out (the printer's fault) endangering our copyright. Please see the right ones get in these copies.

Walt Whitman.

19. Herbert Spencer Harned.
20. Dr. Wharton (see 1849).

1849. *To Richard Maurice Bucke*

ADDRESS: Dr R M Bucke | Asylum | London | Ontario | Canada. POSTMARK: Cam(?) | Dec 5 | 8 P(?) | 88.

Camden 5½ P M | Dec: 5 '88

Drs: Osler and Wharton have been here—it is as we tho't the enlarged prostrate gland incident is senilia—A short visit not much talk —Wharton was very good—what gravity there may be in it time &c will show—At present it causes me any am't of annoyance & sometimes severe continued pain—Last night was kind of half and half—had some sleep—have had my supper (some rice pudding, stew'd apple, & a cup of tea)—

The big book is being bound, the cheap form—I will see ab't the postage—I want you to have three or four copies at once—& I shall decide whether to send by express, or p o—Did I send you the slip enclosed? I don't know how, but it got left out "Sands at Seventy"[21]—No word yet f'm O'Connor—You will get a letter sent to the fellows, to reach up with you ab't four days yet[22]—(nothing of any acc't)—poor Kennedy works like a house a fire—sends me a letter occasionally—the *Transcript* paper regular —Mild & pleasant here—I am sitting in the room alone finishing this—

Walt Whitman

1850. *To Richard Maurice Bucke*

ADDRESS: Dr R M Bucke | Asylum | London | Ontario | Canada. POSTMARK: Camden (?) | Dec 6(?) | 8 PM | 88.

Camden 2½ p m | Dec: 6 '88

Probably the two or three letters lately from me have sketch'd in the situation—Last night middling fair—the bulk, say from 12 to 4½, I must have slept hardly disturb'd—wh' was doing well—rose late—Ed comes in & makes the fire—had a few mouthfuls of breakfast—very light —an hour later a bowel action pretty moderate—rather less irritation & smartness &c than previous days—

I am sitting now in my big chair by the fire more negatively comfortable than you w'd suppose—Sunny, rather windy, pretty sharp cold—Mrs. Harned & the new born boy are getting along so far splendidly—H. was here last evn'g—he has lost two cases (rather notable here)—two tavern

21. WW enclosed "Shakspere-Bacon's Cipher," as Bucke noted on December 7 (Feinberg; Traubel, III, 269); it was included in *Good-Bye My Fancy* (1891).

22. See 1846.

keepers charged with selling liquor sunday—I keep on having applications for autographs, & to read *MS* poems—have had five the last two days—cannot give any attention to them—generally dont read them thro—I have heard from Edw'd Carpenter—a young Englishman, a friend of his, has just call'd—C is well, & occupied ab't the same as before—(rather wishes to come to America, & the mate & wife he has been living with wish the same for themselves.)

After 4—have been lying on the bed an hour or so—Sitting here now alone—quiet & cold & near sunset—wind shakes the window sashes—here comes my dinner—

Walt Whitman

1851. *To Edward Carpenter* *12.6–7. 1888*

ADDRESS: Edward Carpenter | Millthorpe | near Chesterfield | England. POSTMARK: Camden, N.J. | Dec 7 | 8 PM | 88.

Camden N J U S America | Evn'g: Dec: 6 88

Dear Edward Carpenter

I will send a line to you even if but for good love & memories to you—for I have them always for you—Was prostrated down with ab't the sixth recurrent attack of my paralysis again and iron-bound constipation early last June & have been kept ever since in my sick room & am so yet—with even other troubles, a bladder affection, enlarged prostrate glands—a pretty complete physical wreck. Still I keep up a good part of the time—have bro't out a little book "November Boughs" wh' I send a copy to you same mail with this—Also am finishing a big Vol. comprehending all my stuff, poems & prose, makes ab't 900 pages—A good young friend, Horace Traubel here, has help'd me between the printing office, bringing & carrying proofs, &c, so that I have ab't finished these jobs ready for binder—I am still at 328 Mickle Street—have not been out doors for over six months—hardly out my room—Have a good young strong & helper & nurse, Ed Wilkins—But get along better than you might think for—Your friend Mr Williams call'd to-day—Herbert Gilchrist is here at 1708 Chestnut, Philadelphia—he is well & doing well—The Staffords are ab't as usual—they come up here & see me

23. Carpenter replied at length on December 27 after receiving *November Boughs*, which he reviewed in *The Scottish Art Review* in 1889 (Feinberg).

Friday noon, Dec: 7

I am up, had a partial bath, a bit of breakfast & am now sitting my big chair by the oak wood fire finishing this—fine sunny cold weather—considerable bladder troubles, pains, &c. Send me soon the Misses Fords' address & I will send Nov: Boughs—Love to them—Love to you, dear friend[23]—

Walt Whitman

1852. *To Richard Maurice Bucke* *12.7–[8].1888*

ADDRESS: Dr R M Bucke | Asylum | London | Ontario | Canada. POSTMARK: Camden, N.J. | Dec 8 | 8 PM | 88.

Camden | Evn'g—Dec: 7 '88

Am better & less better from time to time—worse the afternoon & evn'g—or the reverse—But I feel better of the bladder trouble, wh' has been my worst affliction this past week—the voiding of water is more normal—& I have good or partially good nights, the last three, & prospect forthcoming, wh' is a great blessing to me. I am in good spirits—Ed has gone to the p o for me—Horace comes in & tells me the binder Oldach promises some finish'd copies (cheap binding) of the big book next Monday (10th)—So Tuesday I will send you one by mail—T B H[arned] comes in a few moments—Mrs: H gets on first rate—& the baby is immense—

Saturday noon

Had a pretty fair night—the painful irritation, spasms, &c have mainly stopt & I am feeling decidedly easier, freer—rose ab't 1½ hours ago—have had my partial bath, & quite a decided breakfast—have rec'd a note from Dr Osler, proposing that a recommended Dr Walsh shall come over daily & sort o' take charge[24]—Of course I shall be glad to see Dr W—but I am in hopes the worst of the gland ailment is over—& that Osler looking in every week as hitherto will do well enough—yours of 6th rec'd & welcomed—I am getting along better than you might suppose—To have the trilogy definitively done is a very great relief, for I had quite set my heart on putting it in shape & completion, wh' is now done, thanks, deepest

24. In several letters Bucke insisted that WW should be seen daily by a young doctor since Osler was too busy to attend the poet every day. Dr. Walsh was the brother of William Walsh, of Lippincott's (Traubel, III, 242).

thanks, to Horace Traubel—As I finish towards 4 the day has pass'd fairly well with me, & prospect good for night—

Walt Whitman

1853. *To Richard Maurice Bucke*

ADDRESS: Dr R M Bucke | Asylum | London | Ontario Canada. POSTMARK: Camden, N.J. | Dec 9 | 5 PM | (?).

Camden P M Dec: 9 '88

Am getting along favorably. Last night good considering. Drs: Osler and Walsh here at noon—pronounce every thing getting along well. I send you N Y *Tribune* of to-day with notice.[25] T B H[arned] and Miss Corning just in. Cloudy & rain—

Walt Whitman

1854. *To William D. O'Connor*

ENDORSED: "Answ'd Dec. 10/88." ADDRESS: Wm D O'Connor | 1015 O Street | Washington | D C. POSTMARK: Camden, N.J. | Dec 9 | 5 PM | (?).

Camden P M Dec: 9 '88

Have had a bad week, but am now much better—over it for this time, indeed—'Twas added to other things (as I believe I told you) a bladder &c. trouble—& giving for a while more annoyance & pain than any thing—The two doctors have just been. Love to you and Nelly—write, one of you, very soon—the Sunday Tribune, (N Y. to-day) has a short notice—

Walt Whitman

am now sitting alone in my big chair by the oak wood fire—comfortable—

1855. *To Richard Maurice Bucke*

ADDRESS: Dr R M Bucke | Asylum | London | Ontario | Canada. POSTMARK: C(?) | Dec 13(?) | 8 PM | 88.

Camden Thursday Evn'g | Dec: 13 '88

Well, dear friend, I have had another bad spell—perhaps the

25. A brief review of *November Boughs* appeared on this date.
26. Apparently WW had forgotten the postcard O'Connor wrote on December [10]

worst of all—a violent *whack* at what nervous power I had—but I am now up for a few moments & I write you to show you I *can* write—

I cannot medically describe the situation of the last four days but will ask definitely from Dr Walsh here who comes every day—& I like every thing except he gives me too much medicine—Ed is very faithful & watches me day & night—Not a word to me ab't O'C[onnor] rec'd[26]—I suppose Horace Traubel sent to you four copies of the big book in common binding by Canadian Express to-day—unpaid this end—write me what the freight & tariff—You ought to get them by Saturday 15th—I shall look till I get word of their reception—

Of course I have a good deal to say but must defer it & get back to bed where I have laid since Sunday last—extreme debility one thing—many points even too disagreeable [to write] ab't—But I think I am beginning to approximate myself—

Walt Whitman

1856. *To Richard Maurice Bucke* *12.16–17. 1888*

ADDRESS: Dr R M Bucke | Asylum | London | Ontario | Canada. POSTMARK: Camden, N.J. | Dec 18 | 6 AM | 88.

Camden Sunday night 9 oclock | Dec: 16 '88

Am sitting here a while to contrast the fearful tedium of lying in bed so long—eking a half hour more, to sit up here—though slowly & moderately, seems to me *I am decidedly better*, wh' sums all at present—seem to fall from one pit to a lower pit—what is to come remains to be seen—Dr Walsh (who is not very definitive) says it is an extreme case (this very last) of prostration & gastric trouble from indigestion—Monday, Tuesday & Wednesday last were worst—Tuesday was deathly—yesterday & to-day I begin at milk & broth & sit up more—feel pretty fair as I sit here this moment—have drink'd some sherry mix'd with milk—(wine, whey)—Hope you have rec'd the copies of the big book, sent by Canadian Express (sent last Thursday)—Hope you are not disappointed (or vex'd) at its looks—as it is, for all nine-tenths of L of G. are from normal al fresco genesis (beef, meat, wine, sunny, lusty) and three fourths of the rest of the trilogy ditto—it is fished out of one of Dante's hells, considering my physical condition the last three months—

Well, I will get to bed, with Ed's help—

in which he said: "I have been very sick and feeble for a month past, but am a little better. My eye got open at last, but is still bleary and bad" (Feinberg; Traubel, III, 288).

Monday afternoon Dec. 17—Fairly passable last night & some chicken broth for breakfast—anticipated a pretty good day & a good bath in the wash room, but not accomplish'd yet—Yours of 15th rec'd—Am sitting up—a dismal dark sticky rainy day—Suppose the big books must be to hand now—sweat easily, the least encouragement—quite great thirst—drink milk a good deal—have just eaten some vanilla ice cream—just rec'd an Italian (Palermo) paper[27]—& the Paris *Revue Independent* for Nov: with notice of L of G,[28] wh' I mail you—send me the synopsis when you have an opportunity—my head is in a sore poor condition—

Walt Whitman

1857. *To Richard Maurice Bucke*

ADDRESS: Dr R M Bucke | Asylum | London | Ontario | Canada. POSTMARK: Camden, N.J. | Dec 18 | 8 PM | 88.

Camden Tuesday afternoon | Dec: 18 '88

Sent you quite a letter & budget of papers last even'g—hope you rec'd them right—hope the big books have surely reach'd you all right by this time—I ought to be better than I am—but am feeling bad & sore & tired out—had a decided bowel movement this forenoon—appetite pretty good (I have just eaten some chocolate ice cream)—have not eaten any solid food for ten days—drink cold milk by preference—have much thirst—Dr Walsh comes every day, seems to watch carefully but gives no medicine—I like him & his ways—Have been sitting up here trying the morning newspaper—the utter fiasco of poor Lesseps[29]—the 81st birthday of Whittier—&c—have now been sitting up from three to four hours—have written to Kennedy—Yours of 16th rec'd & welcom'd—two sweet nice letters from 15 y'r girls—so good, so tasty—I must now get to bed to rest—

Walt Whitman

1858. *To William Sloane Kennedy*

Camden Tuesday P M | Dec: 18 '88

Thanks for the 13th note—write oftener—I have been thro an-

27. Perhaps a review of the translation *Canti Scelti* by Luigi Gamberale in 1887: see Gay Wilson Allen, *Walt Whitman Abroad* (1955), 187.

28. On December 19 Bucke noted that the article in *Revue Indépendante* contained eight pages of translations by Francis Vielé-Griffin and "no comment at all": "Translation not good (translator did not fully understand the English text)" (Feinberg). See also P. M. Jones, "Whitman in France," *MLR*, x (1915), 16–17.

29. Vicomte Ferdinand Marie de Lesseps (1805–1894), promoter of the Suez Canal, was later president of the French company constructing the Panama Canal. The New York *Tribune* on December 18 noted the defeat of the Panama Canal bill in the French Chamber of Deputies.

other very bad spell—ten days, two of them quite serious—but am somewhat better—am sitting up anyhow writing this, but my brain is flabby—my grip weak—The doctor speaks of a pronounc'd gastric trouble, from long indigestion—No I have no recollection of any "Solitude"[30]—have no doubt it is a total invention (not to use the word *fraud* wh' is perfectly proper)—my relations were never at all intimate with Lowell—there are a good many such—it might be worth while to stamp them peremptorily in future—I have included all my stuff in "Complete Vol," a big book authenticated by me now, rather cheaply bound & I w'd like to send a package of four or five copies (including one to you) by Express to you—one for Garland, one for Baxter and one for Mrs. Fairchild—all for Christmas presents—package to be prepaid—can you receive it & see they get to their destination?—Where shall it (the package) be directed to you, in Boston, if so?

I have seen the notice in the *Literary World*[31] & like it well enough—Dr Bucke (I hear from him often) likes it well—do you know its author? The Paris (France) *Revue Independent* magazine November has a notice L of G.—also something in a Palermo (Italy) paper—Dr B has them—No word now for quite a while from my dear O'Connor[32]—I am very uneasy ab't him—I have (did I tell you?) a good strong willing nurse, & good doctoring watch—I send my love & memories to Mrs: F., to Baxter, to Garland, to yourself, dear friend, & wife—& to Sanborn if you see him—I must now get to the bed—

Walt Whitman

1859. *To Richard Maurice Bucke*

ADDRESS: Dr R M Bucke | Asylum | London | Ontario Canada. POSTMARK: Camden, N.J. | Dec 19 | 8 PM | 88.

Camden P M Dec: 19 '88

Much the same—Suppose you get safely the letters sent f'm me every evn'g the last three. I am probably improving tho' very slowly—

30. On December 13 Kennedy inquired: "Did you ever write a production called 'Solitude.' It is credited to you by a pencil-script line in the Harvard College Library. I don't believe it is yrs, but that it is an imitation. It is unbound, abt ⅔ the size of this sheet, contains 16 pp. & has written on it in pencil 'Presented to the Library by Prof. Jas. Russell Lowell, 1860. Sept 26" (Feinberg).

31. A review of *November Boughs* appeared in *The Literary World* (Boston) on December 8. Bucke commented on December 16: "He [the author] is a good friend and has considerable insight into matters—is evidently *holding himself in* in the little col. and half article" (Feinberg).

32. But see 1855, *n.*26.

have some appetite—sitting up the last 4½ hours—last night fair—cold clear weather here—the last word I have f'm you is Sunday—did you get the letter written on Scot: pubr's blank title, by me?[33]

Walt Whitman

1860. *To Ellen M. O'Connor*

ADDRESS: Mrs: O'Connor | 1015 O Street | Washington D C. POSTMARKS: Camden, N.J. | Dec 19 | 8 PM | (?); Washington, Rec'd. | Dec 20 | 7 AM | 88 | 3.

Camden Evn'g Dec: 19 '88

Have had a pretty bad spell—nothing to brag of yet, but the doctor calls me better. Am very uneasy ab't William—have not heard now for many days—best love to him & to you.[34]

W W

1861. *To Richard Maurice Bucke*

ADDRESS: Dr R M Bucke | Asylum | London | Ontario | Canada. POSTMARK: Camden, N.J. | Dec 20 | 8 PM | 88.

Camden 10½ a m Dec: 20 '88

Am getting along—more favorably turning than the other—relish'd my mutton-broth & dry biscuit—& am sitting here by the stove—sharp cold & clear to day—Yours of 17th came this mn'g—so the books arrived at last—& you are contented & pleas'd—& the trilogy holds together & fuses, tho' various & paradoxical & rapidly twittering, (probably like Dante's filmy ghosts, rushing by with mere gibberish)—yes it is mainly all *autobiographic* environ'd with my time & deeply incarnated &

33. See 1846.

34. On the following day Mrs. O'Connor wrote at length of her husband's physical and emotional state: "I am sorry that I have not better news to give you of William. He has failed very much in the last six weeks, indeed I date the marked change for the worse from the paralysis of the eye lid, & that was the last of Sept. but a very marked change for the worse since Nov. 23d. No one is as well aware of it as I am, for I see him at his worst, as well as his best. I am his sole & only nurse, & help to dress, undress & bathe him, & he is under no restraint to say how he does feel to me, tho' he *always* puts the best face on things to every one, & is always ready to joke about himself & often makes me laugh when I am ready to cry. . . . Until lately, too, he has had the most wonderful courage, & would *not* give up, but it is not so all the time now. Still, there is one thing in his favor, (if one

tinged with it, & the moral begetting of it (I hope)—The first time soon write whether you get every thing letters & papers—I have written now every day the last five days & sent budgets of papers or magazines—wrote a line to Mrs. O'Connor last evn'g—If I hear any thing I will forward you —I am sitting up all day, yesterday & this—I believe I told you the bladder trouble appears to have subsided—

3 p m—I have just eaten some vanilla ice cream—McKay has out an ed'n with the *annex*, *Sands at Seventy*. I have one—it goes all right—sells the same $2—the postage on the big book is 38cts—I put four 10ct stamps—I sent one by p o to-day—(the last page contains "Old Age's Lambent Peaks")—I enclose two letters—one from Logan Smith—one from Algiers, Africa[35]—Love to you all & God bless you—

Walt Whitman

1862. *To Richard Maurice Bucke*

ADDRESS: Dr R M Bucke | Asylum | London | Ontario | Canada. POSTMARK: Camden (?) | Dec 2(?) | 12 | (?).

Camden 10 A M Dec: 21 '88

Every thing continues *not unfavorable* at least—had a fair night & have eaten my mutton-broth & toast with sort o' relish—I hasten to send off Mrs: O Connor's letter rec'd an hour ago, in hopes you will get it Saturday, P M—Bright and real cold here—as I sit, the great wolf skin is spread on the chair to protect my back & shoulders—comfortable—

Merry Christmas to you & all—

Walt Whitman

so regards it) & that is that he is still *determined* to live. I never saw such clinging to *this life*, in any one; & he still feels that if the right Doctor could be found that he could be made entirely well. He counted up the other day, & found that he had had *fifteen* doctors. . . . But his deepest unhappiness now is that he has not yet been able to get his article published which he wrote in defense of Donnelly [*Mr. Donnelly's Reviewers*]" (Feinberg).

35. Smith wrote a chatty letter on November 30 (Feinberg). Justin Huntly McCarthy (see 776) wrote to WW from Algiers on December 3, and noted the loss of his fiancée, an admirer of WW's poetry. In his grief he was reading WW's poems alone: "They are helping me, they are strengthening me & I wish to send you these few words of thanks & gratitude for the sake of my dead love & my living grief. Camerado, will you give me your hand across the sea" (Feinberg). See also Traubel, III, 334–335.

1863. *To William Sloane Kennedy*

Camden | Evn'g: Dec: 21 '88

Dear K

Yours came to-day & I have sent this evn'g: five copies of the big book by Express, unpaid, in a package, (nearly one foot thick, two broad, brown paper wrapt) to be call'd for at Adams's Central office, Boston—you ought to get it Saturday even'g or Monday—please pay the freight & I will return it you—There is no special hurry ab't delivering the books—the main thing is I want to be sure they get to their destined names—Each one is named on the wrapper—They are

Mrs Fairchild—yourself
Baxter
Hamlin Harland[35.1]
Frank Sanborn

I am getting better—slowly & little, but apparently *so*—the news from O'Connor is not good—Dr B[ucke] is all right—Merry Christmas—

Walt Whitman

1864. *To Ellen M. O'Connor*

ADDRESS: Mrs: O'Connor | 1015 O Street N W | Washington | D C. POSTMARKS: Camden, N.J. | Dec 2(?) | 8 PM | 88; Washington, Rec'd. | Dec 22 | 7 AM | 88 | 1.

Camden Evn'g Dec: 21 '88

Thanks for your good letter rec'd this forenoon—I sympathize with William as my brother in affliction, besides in soul—so wish I could show it practically—Very little by little & slowly, I seem to be improving—Ab't the worst is the forced confinement (now seven months) to indoors & the sick room—

Walt Whitman

1865. *To Richard Maurice Bucke* *12.21–22. 1888*

ADDRESS: Dr R M Bucke | Asylum | London | Ontario | Canada. POSTMARK: Camden, N.J. | Dec 22 | 8 PM | 88.

Camden | 1.30 P M Dec: 21 '88

I scribble away as perhaps you care to hear even minor affairs—

sent off Mrs: O'C[onnor]'s letter to me describing the situation wh' you must have rec'd—My poor dear friend Wm O'C—my brother in affliction —I have been out & had a thorough bath in the tub, (with Ed's assistance,) & complete clothe change, specially under—

Saturday 22d—9 a m—Feeling pretty well—& shall tackle my breakfast presently, had a fair night—sent big books off, (by express) to Boston yesterday afternoon to Kennedy, Baxter, Mrs. Fairchild, Harland & Frank Sanborn, (for Christmas presents)—yours of 20th rec'd this morning—

Noon—cold & bright—bowel movement, decided—(first in four days)—my brother George comes every day—bro't from Lou a good quilted lap robe to go over my knees & feet as I sit, very useful & acceptable—

Evn'g—Well I believe this has been, upon the whole, the nearest approximation for a tolerable day for six months and more—I am fearfully weak yet but *the feeling* & the comparative ease are like something toward sanity—I may fall back—but O that I can keep up the standard of to-day, moderate as it is—had my mutton-broth & couple of good raw oysters for my supper, 4¾, (no dinner)—as it is I am sitting by the wood fire—comfortable—Ed is snoozing on the couch—every thing is quiet—Christmas is near at hand & seems to be made extra much of here—Hope it will be a merry one with you all—

Walt Whitman

1866. *To Richard Maurice Bucke*

ADDRESS: Dr R M Bucke | Asylum | London | Ontario Canada. POSTMARK: Camden | (?) | 5 PM | (?); 8 | AM De | 25.

Camden 2½ P M Dec: 23 '88

Fair day—all quiet—Dr Walsh call'd—I sit here in the big chair hour after hour—hardly a noise or movement appears to disturb the day—Peace be with you all too—

W W

1867. *To Richard Maurice Bucke*

ADDRESS: Dr R M Bucke | Asylum | London | Ontario | Canada. POSTMARK: Camden | Dec 24 | 8 PM | 88.

Camden P M Dec: 24 '88

Continue easier & freer from the former afflictions—only ex-

35.1. Hamlin Garland.

tremely weak (but not so bad as ten days ago)—bowel action to-day—am sitting up (get up ab't 9 & take a partial bath—Ed makes a good fire all warm first)—perfect day, sunny, promising fine for to-morrow Christmas—I have just written a little (poem) piece & send it off to the *Critic* to-night[36]—Of course I will send it to you soon as it is printed—(a bit of a new tack, this time, something of the Dick Deadeye turn)—Yours came this mn'g & was welcome—I enclose a cheery letter from Ernest Rhys—it has done me good—Happy New Years to you, Mrs: B & all the childer—

Walt Whitman

1868. *To Ernest Rhys*

ADDRESS: Ernest Rhys | 11 Cowley Street | Westminster | London | S W | England.
POSTMARKS: Camden, N.J. | Dec 24 | 8 PM | 88; London S W | FO | Ja 3 | 89.

Camden New Jersey America |
Dec: 24 '88

Your cheery letter has come & does me good[37]—I have been sick many months & am yet confined & weak, but decidedly better—I want to send a package to Mr Pearsall Smith's by European Express with several big Vols. my "Complete works" including one copy for you & one for him—you shall have them—Harned, Kennedy, Dr B[ucke] & H Gilchrist are well. Write soon as you can—

Walt Whitman

1869. *To Katherine Johnston*

ADDRESS: Miss Kittie Johnston | 305 E. 17th Street | New York City.
TRANSCRIPT.

Camden Evn'g Dec: 25 '88

Thanks, dear Kitty, dear friend, dear girl, for the beautiful photo—it is indeed beautiful—Give my best love to your father & mother & sisters & Al & wife & Harold & Calder—I have had a bad sickness seven

36. "To the Year 1889" (later titled "To the Pending Year") appeared in *The Critic* on January 5, 1889; WW received $6 for the piece (*CB*).

37. Rhys's letter of December 12 was filled with vivid descriptions of his lectures and London scenes—as WW noted, a most delightful letter (Feinberg).

38. On December 17 Katherine, the daughter of John H. Johnston and his first wife Amelia, wrote to "My dear Uncle Walt": "We have once more a nest but need one dear person to make the family complete; this person is a Grandpa; won't you come and be one

months but am now some better—have sat up nearly all day, & eaten some dinner. Happy New Year to you and all[38]—

Walt Whitman

1870. *To David McKay* [*12.25(?). 1888?*]

Dave, I send a couple copies of my phiz, one for the children each —(If I knew their first names I w'd have written on)—

W W

Have just had my breakfast—hot buckwheat cakes with syrup & a cup of tea—*Merry Christmas to you & all*—

Walt Whitman

1871. *To Richard Maurice Bucke* *12.25–26. 1888*

ADDRESS: Dr R M Bucke | Asylum | London | Ontario | Canada. POSTMARK: Cam(?) | Dec 26(?) | 1 30 PM | 88.

Camden 6 P M Dec: 25 '88

Well Christmas has come & nearly gone—I hope you & all have enjoyed it—Superb weather here now two days—My fair feelings continue, & I have had quite a generous slice of turkey with some cranberries for my dinner an hour ago & a cup of coffee—the most of a meal for me for four months—

Every thing quiet here—some visitors, a young Englishman, Rathbone,[39] son of the man of the address on the "nude" I use in my printed piece—& several others—(some of whom I *declined*)—I rec'd a letter (enclosed) from John Burroughs this morn'g[40]—nothing very new —I wish you to tell me the tariff and freight of the four books, & whether they reach'd you in good order—I have been reading Tolstoi's "Sebastopol Sketches," Englished very well by Frank D. Millet, in a French translation —I found it very absorbing, sharp & hard—with a strongly eulogistic

to us? we would all be so happy if you came. There is a pretty park in front which is nice even in Winter; at night the electric lights are very pretty. Then in Summer you could walk in the park with us children as you used to do on 5th Ave. Do come, when ever it pleases *you* (but I want you *very, very* soon!)" (Feinberg). "Kitty" and her brother Harold were photographed with the poet in 1879 (*Corr.*, III, following 202).

39. Rathbone was the son of P. H. Rathbone whom WW quotes in *Specimen Days* (ed. Stovall, 495–496). See Traubel, III, 378–379.

40. Burroughs wrote a brief note on December 23 (Feinberg).

preface by W D Howells—a little book pub'd by Harpers—Horace bro't it to me—8½ Horace pays his welcome evening visit—

Wednesday 26th—10¾ A M

I continue fairly—have had my breakfast, & the fine weather continues—two welcome letters from you this morning's mail—I watch with interest the meter-Gurd fortunes & struggles—Well now for New years —& then 1889—God bless you & yours—

Walt Whitman

1872. *To Richard Maurice Bucke*

ADDRESS: Dr R M Bucke | Asylum | London | Ontario | Canada. POSTMARK: Camden, N.J. | Dec 27 | 8 PM | 88.

Camden 1 P M Dec: 27 '88

A change in the weather—cloudy & disposed to rain—very moderate temperature—I continue to feel fairly & what may be call'd improving —bowel movement this forenoon—I read letter from my young valued journalistic (German-educated & theosophistic) friend in Boston, Sylvester Baxter, wh' I include[41]—also copy *printed* of your letter on big book[42] —(I can send several copies if you want)—have rec'd yours of 24th, & note carefully what you say of food, alcohol, &c, and of the effete wretchedness—all thoroughly judged & true, & shall charge myself practically with it—certainly so—& glad to get it all—

As I write, the *Post* paper comes, with an item ab't my health &c, authentic[43]—& I enclose two more printed copies of the letter & send—I have rec'd from F B Sanborn & Kennedy,[44] acknowledging the big books. Rec'd y'rs of evn'g Dec. 25th—

3 P M—Passing an easier day upon the whole—have just eaten chocolate ice cream—read y'rs of 24th a second time—I guess I am getting along pretty well, considering everything—to have *the books* off my mind is a great relief—If I can now be freed of this gastric, head & feeble trouble—

Walt Whitman

41. Baxter thanked WW on December 25 for his copy of *Complete Poetry & Prose* and recommended that WW read Bellamy's *Looking Backward*, "a noble work, and delightful as well. It has made a profound impression and will do much towards realizing a grander future for our land" (Feinberg).

42. "For the elect, the few," WW had printed a broadside entitled "An impromptu criticism on the 900 page Volume, The Complete Poems and Prose of Walt Whitman, first issued December, 1888" (reprinted in Traubel, III, 397–398).

43. The article in the *Post* was a factual account of his recent illness written by the poet himself (Traubel, III, 396–397). Not surprisingly, he had thirty copies of the article to send to friends.

1873. *To David McKay*

TRANSCRIPT.

Camden, Dec. 27, '88.

I have no objection to this going in Miss Gould's little book—no objection at all, but no vehement desire either—If you can include it conveniently, do so; if not, not—I am feeling easier and freer the last four days.[45]

Walt Whitman.

1874. *To Richard Maurice Bucke*

ADDRESS: Dr R M Bucke | Asylum | London | Ontario Canada. POSTMARK: Camden, N.J. | Dec 2(?) | 8 PM | 88.

Camden P M Dec: 28 '88

Bright cold rather quiet day—I sit here the same—pretty good last night—no doctor now three or four days—a note from Mrs: Fairchild Boston rec'g the big book—my little poemet[46] will probably be printed Jan: 5—I will send you a copy at once—have been taking some ice cream & a cup of milk for my 1½ lunch—growing colder—

Walt Whitman

1875. *To Richard Maurice Bucke*

ADDRESS: Dr R M Bucke | Asylum | London | Ontario | Canada. POSTMARK: Camden (?) | Dec 29 | 8 PM | (?).

Camden noon Dec: 29 '88

Fine, still sunny day, not cold—continue ab't the same—pretty comfortable upon the whole—N Y Herald 23d last Sunday has a leading

44. On Christmas day Sanborn thanked the poet, and noted that he had two copies of the first edition of *Leaves of Grass*, given to him by Emerson and Sophia Thoreau (Feinberg; Traubel, III, 402–403). Kennedy wrote enthusiastically on the same day about the new book, which he personally delivered to Baxter, Garland, Sanborn, and Mrs. Fairchild (Feinberg).

45. McKay published Elizabeth Porter Gould's *Gems from Walt Whitman* in 1889. To Traubel WW observed: "These gems, extracts, specimens, tid-bits, brilliants, sparkles, chippings—oh, they are all wearisome: they might go with some books: yes, they fit with some books—some books fit with them: but Leaves of Grass is different—yields nothing to the seeker for sensations" (III, 395–396). See also Traubel, III, 405.

46. "To the Year 1889" (see 1867).

(book notice) two third column review of Nov: Boughs, mostly extracts —favorable more than any thing else[47]—glad you hit (fix) on the autobiographic underlying element of the collected Vol[48]—Was wondering whether *that* w'd be detected—did not say anything ab't it, but it has been in my mind of late y'rs unremittedly—of course not in the usual auto-writing style & even purposes, but with a freer margin—& I think if the book really grips, *that* will be what the good class literary detectives of the future will mainly settle & agree upon—Then I sh'd be tickled enough if I c'd think I had indeed skimm'd some of the *real cream* of the American History of the last 35 years & preserv'd it here—I have sent to some 20 of our friends & specialists home & abroad (wrapt in the *Post* item of last Thursday) the printed copy of y'r letter ab't it—(the "impromptu criticism")—I send you Kennedy's letter of 25th—y'rs of 26th came last evn'g[49]—

Yes, I shall *mind*—think I understand & accept the matter below it, & shall practically put it in action—as I finish I am sitting alone by my oak-fire—every thing still—& the sun out shining brightly—

Walt Whitman

1876. *To William Sloane Kennedy*

Camden P M Dec: 29 '88

Y'rs rec'd ab't the books—many, best thanks—have rec'd letters from Mrs: F[airchild][50] and F B S[anborn] acknowledg'g them. Also from Baxter—am slowly improving probably—am sitting here alone by oak-fire as I write—Just now comes a letter from Harland[51] receipting his book—Tell me in y'r next what was the express freight please—Dr B[ucke] writes most every day—O'C[onnor] is poorly but gritty.

Walt Whitman

47. The subtitle of the review was "Walt Whitman Unbosoms Himself About Poetry." WW considered the notice "very good: a very generous one" (Traubel, III, 410).

48. In "An impromptu criticism" Bucke wrote: "It is a gigantic massive autobiography, the first of its kind. . . ." For WW's guarded reaction to Bucke's assertion, see Traubel, III, 354–355.

49. Since Bucke's letter of December 26 is missing, it is not possible to explain WW's allusion in the following paragraph.

50. Mrs. Fairchild's letter was addressed to Kennedy (see 1885); WW was amused that she termed the book "sumptuous" (Traubel, III, 404).

51. Hamlin Garland.

1877. *To Richard Maurice Bucke*

ADDRESS: Dr R M Bucke | Asylum | London | Ontario Canada. POSTMARK: Camden, N.J. | Dec 3(?) | 5 PM | (?).

Camden P M Dec: 30 '88

Remarkably fine day—I hold ab't the same balance as before—sit here monotonously, try to interest myself reading, but don't succeed—the good Harned has been here bringing to-day's Tribune & a bottle of fine sherry—the baby flourishes, & Mrs: H was out-doors yesterday. Happy New Year—

Walt Whitman

1878. *To Richard Maurice Bucke*

Camden P M Dec: 31 '88

Our fine weather—upon the whole the finest December we ever had here—has changed, & to-day is dark & sulky & dripping—My fair feelings continue—the bowel action reasonable—&c. &c.—I enclose a sort of dedication for one of the Vol's. for you to keep for yourself—It ought to be inserted, cut & fitted properly by an expert—a book binder if you can have the deftness of such an one—When the books went I was unable to get up out of bed, & was in a horrible plight, with only the wish to get the Vols. sent to you while I c'd direct it—or I sh'd have written in then—I sent round to the printer's to get the corrections made & some more impressions struck off—but the types were distributed & I have not order'd them re-set—but will do so if you have the least wish—I will soon send you a few copies as they are, with the accented e in Goethe scratch'd out, (wh' is very easily done.)[52]

Y'r two letters came this morning—I am sitting here in the big chair —have eaten some ice cream & drank a cup of milk for my 2 o'c luncheon —Ed Wilkins is snoozing on the couch near—& so to-morrow begins with 1889 with us all[53]—

Walt Whitman

52. WW was referring to "An impromptu criticism."

53. According to my tabulation, based upon his letters and his entries in *CB*, WW's income in 1888 amounted to at least $925.04: royalties, $177.01; sales of books, $107.66; payments for articles and poems, $277.00; gifts, $224.37; and miscellaneous, $139.00. (The figures on book sales are to some extent conjectural, since I have had to assume he charged uniform prices for his various books.) It is probably of relevance to note that, beginning in 1888, WW's friends contributed regularly to a nursing fund; hence he did not receive quite so many gifts as in previous years. It is also of significance that as his health deteriorated, recordings in *CB* were less complete than hitherto. Thus there are very real discrepancies between amounts he deposited periodically in the bank and receipts of money from various sources.

1889

1879. *To Richard Maurice Bucke*

ADDRESS: Dr R M Bucke | Asylum | London | Ontario | Canada. POSTMARK: Camden (?) | Jan 2 | 6 AM | 89.

Camden P M Jan: 1 '89

Superb sunny day again & I am feeling all as right as could be expected—Still on mutton broth with toast & plenty of rice & a few mouthfuls of the stew'd mutton. As I told you, bowel action fair—A little of what I call cold in the head, but slight so far—Dr Walsh here last evn'g —he himself quite unwell—no Osler now for a fortnight—I enclose Mrs: O'C[onnor]'s card rec'd this mn'g—Ed: Stafford has been here—they are all well as usual & every thing goes on the same as of old—

So we have commenced on another year—& where it will take us, & *how*, are indeed mercifully hidden—for the *pique* of weaving & watching (with a gambler's uncertainty) makes the background & basis of the whole business—I have been reading "Goethe's & Carlyle's correspondence" wh' I find interesting—presents C in a different light from any other—

Walt Whitman

1880. *To Ellen M. O'Connor*

ADDRESS: Mrs: O'Connor | 1015 O Street N W | Washington | D C. POSTMARKS: Camden (?) | Jan 2 | 6 AM | 89; Washington, Rec'd. | Jan 2 | 12 M | 89.

Camden Evn'g: Jan: 1 '89

My best loving wishes for the New Year to you and William—O if deepest wishes & prayers c'd be realized!—For a week now I have been easier & freer, probably improving, though slowly—I & many are looking

1889

1. See 1872.
2. The card announced the child's birth on December 2, 1888 (Feinberg).

more than he knows toward W's prospects—Best love & sympathy to my dear friend—

Walt Whitman

1881. *To Richard Maurice Bucke*

ADDRESS: Dr R M Bucke | Asylum | London | Ontario | Canada. POSTMARK: Camden (?) | Jan 2 | 6 AM | 89.

Camden noon Jan: 2 '89

Every thing keeps on with even way. A slight head ache, or muddled condition. Y'r "impromptu criticism" letter *corrected* has been furnished me by the printer after all, & I will send you 15 copies[1]—The cards in the little envelope are my dear friend Mrs: Harned & the new baby boy's, *Herbert Spencer* H[arned][2]—both are flourishing tip-top. Tom H. comes every day—my brother George also—my sister Lou has just visited me this mn'g—Y'r letter came this mn'g—The Boston *Trans*[*cript*] (Kennedy) has a ¶ (Dec: 29) merely narrating that the big Vol. is printed & out—I have taken up & find myself curious enough, perhaps interested, to probably go thro' Tolstoi's "Confessions"—a strange product of our time, from Russia there—it is natural certainly, but morbific—a sort of Jack the Ripper treatment applied to himself—it is autobiographic of course—pathologic—

2.45 P M

It grows cloudy & cooler—have had my ice cream & milk—your good letter of Dec: 31 comes—yes "hurrah for 89!"—letter rec'd from J H Johnston—his new store Christmas sales reach'd $45000—I have just scribbled a little 10-line poemet I think I'll send to Century[3]—Am sitting here alone by the wood fire—

Walt Whitman

1882. *To Richard Maurice Bucke*

ADDRESS: Dr R M Bucke | Asylum | London | Ontario Canada. POSTMARK: Camden, N.J. | Jan 3 | 8 PM | 89.

Camden P M Jan: 3 '89

Y'rs of 1st comes—day fine—feeling fairly continued—sit here by the stove as I write—slightly sweating—send copies of the corrected letter

3. "Old Age's Ship & Crafty Death's" was accepted by *Century* and the poet paid $12 (*CB*). It appeared in February, 1890.

by this mail—Have written (perhaps I told you) another poemet & send it off to-night or to morrow to the *Century*—(shall send you a printed copy, & of the first one also)—It is near sunset as I close & all moves fairly—

Walt Whitman

1883. *To Sylvester Baxter*

Camden New Jersey | Evn'g Jan: 5 '89

I want to send at once my brief thanks & appreciation of y'r notice in the *Herald* of Thursday.[4] Such things coming to an old fellow after a hard journey make up for lots of knocks & botherations—God bless you, & indeed many thanks from me—

Walt Whitman

1884. *To Richard Maurice Bucke* *1.5–6. 1889*

ADDRESS: Dr R M Bucke | Asylum | London | Ontario | Canada. POSTMARK: Camden, N.J. | Jan 6 | 8(?) PM | 89.

Camden Saturday forenoon Jan: 5 '89

Fair yesterday—a little dull & tedious cribb'd up here so long, but got along—quite decided bowel action in the forenoon, & a good thorough hot-water bath (tub) in the afternoon—my diet continues the same, mutton broth (plenty of rice in it,) dry toast, and a cup of milk (or two, during the day) with some ice cream (wh' tastes good & welcome) ab't 1½ p m—I fancy I am growing very, very slowly to have more strength —but sit here pretty much the same—(I thoroughly believe in your diagnosis in letter of 24th)[4.1]—

This morning comes the Boston *Herald* of Jan: 3d with a splendid, nearly two-column criticism & setting forth of the big book, from Sylvester Baxter—wh' I think even you will applaud & be satisfied with—I will send the paper, but first wish to know if you have rec'd one from S B himself—(as I find I send sometimes what you have before)—

To-day opens dark & wet & lowering enough—no severe cold yet—I

4. See the next two letters.

4.1. On December 24, 1888, Bucke wrote: "O'C. has wonderful *grit* and will make a hard fight yet—We will continue to wish him God speed and ourselves hope for the best. Poor Mrs O'C. too, what noble courage and determination she has! She is as grand as he

still have signs of my "cold in the head" (not violent) yet—a letter from Kennedy—affectionate & devoted—sit here in the big chair three quarters idling—no emphasized physical uncomfortableness—

Sunday Jan 6

Lowering weather continued. A nice 20 minutes' call from Johnston the jeweler & Dick Hinton[5]—also f'm Tom Harned—am ab't the same—comfortable enough—as I sit Ed is making up the bed—& I am just going out to the wash-room—got in a cord of cut oak wood yesterday (ready therefore for a cold spell)—bowel action—Horace has just call'd—good luck to the meter—

Walt Whitman

1885. *To William Sloane Kennedy* *1.5–6. 1889*

Camden Saturday P M Jan: 5 '89

Nothing very notable or different. Your letters rec'd & welcomed —*Transcripts* also—hearty thanks for y'r services & promptness in conveying the books—yes I will leave you to pay express tax—but I had meant to refund—I have rec'd from every one letters of acknowledgm't &c. (Mrs: Fairchild's to you is here enclosed return'd)—Baxter's splendid notice & setting-forth of the book, in *Herald* of last Thursday, is rec'd, & seems to me the most complete & most friendly & penetrating (from the point of view of an absorber, believer & democrat) I have ever had—Dr Bucke will have a good time over it—I hear from B often—he is well, busied with his large family, with the Asylum, & with that *meter invention* I suppose you have heard of. O'Connor keeps on, but is badly off I fear. Burroughs is pretty well—We have had a long stretch of the finest weather, but to-day is dark & wet & glum enough—but I feel comparatively comfortable. I live on mutton-broth & milk & dry toast—sit up most of the day—have read Tolstoi & (it seems to me) all Carlyle's letters—& have enough. Much obliged with the *Trans*[*cript*] ¶ on big book[6]—

Sunday, Jan: 6

All continues well—glum weather, however—I am sitting here by the oak fire comfortable—

Walt Whitman

is, as grand as any" (Feinberg).

5. Hinton wrote about this visit in the New York *World* in April; see. 2007.

6. Kennedy's notice in the Boston *Evening Transcript* on December 29, 1888, was more of an (unpaid) advertisement than a review.

1886. *To John W. Tilton*[7]

ADDRESS: J W Tilton | Office John J. Winn | Attorney &c: | 60 Merrimack St. | Haverhill | Essex Co: Mass:. POSTMARK: Camden (?) | Jan 7 | 8 PM | 89.

Camden New Jersey | Jan: 6 '89

Y'rs of 3d recd here. The big book "Complete Works" &c: is $6. It contains "Democratic Vistas"—With four portraits extra on loose sheets it w'd be $6.50—If you desire it, send p o money order—& send word whether you prefer by mail or express—

Walt Whitman

I can send in a little paper bound Vol: "Dem: Vistas"—50cts—if wanted—

1887. *To Richard Maurice Bucke*

ADDRESS: Dr R M Bucke | Asylum | London | Ontario Canada. POSTMARK: Camden, N.J. | Jan 7 | 8 PM | 89.

Camden P M Jan: 7 '89

Every thing much the same—Y'rs of 4th rec'd—dark lowering weather—no Dr Walsh now four days (Is it a good sign?)—Any thing like strength is very slowly coming to me—but I fall back thankfully on being not such in a wretched way as three or four weeks ago—Ed W[ilkins] is well (but has disagreeable spells of heart burn)—

Walt Whitman

1888. *To Thomas B. Harned*

TRANSCRIPT.

Camden, Jan. 8, 1889

Tom, if you have it and you can, I wish you w'd fill my bottle again with that Sherry.

Love & respects to Mrs H. by no means forgetting Anna, Tommy & little Herbert.

Walt Whitman

7. Tilton (1844–1917) was a lawyer and book collector (Gohdes and Silver,

1889. *To Dr. Karl Knortz*

ADDRESS: Dr Karl Knortz | 540 East 155th Street | New York City. POSTMARK: Camden (?) | Jan 8 (?) | 8(?) | 89.

Camden New Jersey | 328 Mickle Street |
Jan: 8 '89

Dear Sir

Y'r note & German paper rec'd—Thanks—I wrote you (same address as this) some ten weeks ago, that Rolleston, Ireland, had rec'd first proofs of the translation of L of G. from Switzerland, & wished you to see them—I wrote to you to write & confer with him (R)[8]—but have no word f'm you—Did you receive my letter? or have you heard from R or from the proofs, or printer?—I fancy the trans: must be out, printed, by this time—I have nothing from R. now for a long, long while (with that exception)—

I am laid up in my sick room—essentially the sixth recurrence of my war paralysis—& have been (two or three spells serious) for over seven months—but am now some easier & freer. I am sitting up days most of the time—diet on mutton-broth & milk & toast bread—am very feeble, cannot get across the room without assistance—have a nurse, a good, strong Canadian young man—my mentality ab't the same as hitherto—have mean time bro't out "November Boughs," 140 pages, & a big Vol. 900 pages, my "Complete Works," every thing poems & prose—both Vols: at your service—Best wishes & thanks—(I believe you have my Mrs: Gilchrist book)—

Walt Whitman

1890. *To Richard Maurice Bucke* *1.8–9. 1889*

ADDRESS: Dr R M Bucke | Asylum | London | Ontario | Canada. POSTMARK: Camden, N.J. | Jan 9 | 8 PM | 89.

Camden Jan: 8 '89

Perfect weather here continued—I feel comparatively easier & freer also continued—sat for 40 minutes in the sun ab't 1, (in the back room, open window—Ed fixed it for me)—am still extremely weak—legs give out—

128*n*.).

8. See 1786 and 1788.

Dave McKay has been over here—pays me for 950 "Nov: Boughs" $313.50—and we try to fix on some style—(calf or more likely half-calf)—for the better binding of the big book—he & Horace & the binder (a Swiss, an expert journeyman) who made the present one—are commissioned by me to get up a good strong handsome cover &c & submit to me, soon—as purchasers are nibbling at Dave for it already—Boston & elsewhere—(but I shall not sell any for less than $6, even at present style)—have not rec'd any copies yet of Boston *Herald* Jan. 3 but expect some—(or perhaps one will be sent you f'm Boston—If no other way, I shall send you my copy)—the big book grows on me & satisfies me better—(Y'r "impromptu criticism" has been a 10-strike to me)—

Jan: 9 noon

All well—the weather-scene has changed completely—not cold, but dark & rainy & glum—Ed has been down to the bank to deposit my checks[9]—I am now sitting here alone by the stove—partial bowel action this forenoon—the room here is ab't the same in almost every respect, chair, bed, &c &c—they say I have not fallen away in flesh (ab't face &c) since my sick spell—my best strength is in my right arm, hand & side—I can get out of bed quite well now wh' I couldn't do (hardly at all) five weeks ago—no Dr Walsh for four or five days—God bless you & all—

Walt Whitman

1891. *To Edward Carpenter*

ADDRESS: Edward Carpenter | Millthorpe | near Chesterfield | England. POSTMARK: (?) | Jan (?) | 8 PM | 89.

328 Mickle Street | Camden N J U S America |
Jan: 11 '89

Dear Edw'd Carpenter,

Y'rs came yesterday with the draft $174.37—best & heart-felt thanks—it will help me deeply—You speak of the *original draft* sent me in May last—no such draft has been rec'd or seen or heard of by me, & must have been either lost or miscarried or something else—So I shall use *this* at once[10]—

9. He received $307.91 from McKay, $5.59 being deducted for an unspecified reason (CB).

10. WW explained the error at length (with many interpolations) in CB: "A *very bad* (never so bad before) lapse of my own memory. Edw'd Carpenter sent me a bank draft $174:37, last part of May, '88, wh' by Lou or Mrs: D[avis] I deposited (I was very ill at the time bedfast) in Bank July 2. Then in Jan: '89, not hearing of the first draft &

I am still cribb'd up in the sick room, now over seven months, but easier & freer of late—as I believe I told you in a letter three weeks ago[11]—am very weak & unable to get across the room without assistance —but have a good strong nurse—& good medical supervision—sit up most of the days.

I am wanting to envelope up & send some copies by Oceanic Express of my "Complete Works," a big 900 page Vol. (one copy for you), all directed to my friend R. Pearsall Smith, 44 Grosvenor Road, the Embankment, London—will send you word when I do so—also wish you to give me address of Misses Ford (give them my love) to whom I send a copy in same package—As I finish I am comfortable—sitting in my big chair here by the oak fire—

Walt Whitman

1892. *To Richard Maurice Bucke* *1.11–13. 1889*

ADDRESS: Dr R M Bucke | Asylum | London | Ontario | Canada. POSTMARK: Camden, N. J. | Jan 13 | 3 PM | 89.

Camden '89 | Jan: 11 P M

Nothing special to-day—weather fine, sunny—no doctor visiting—note f'm *Century* (Gilder) accepting my little poemet & paying—Yes I shall send it you when out—y'rs of 9th welcom'd—I show'd it to Ed—he is down splitting wood in his shirt sleeves.

Evening—I have pick'd up & been reading again Addington Symonds's "*Greek Poets*"—always fertile & interesting to me—The Boston *Herald* Jan: 3 has come, & I send it to you—Horace has been here—the *three* met at the binder's, & I am to have as designed by them a specimen of the good cover, &c. ready for my judgment this ensuing week—we will see—

Jan: 12—noon

Fine sunny day—Dr McAlister here (Walsh unwell)—good pleasant —young—Am sitting here in the monotonous same way by the fire, in the big chair—yours of 10th comes in the midday mail—a letter also from

fearing it lost, E C sent me *the same draft* in duplicate, & I forgetting all ab't the *first* (I had not rec'd it & supposing it lost) deposited it & was credited in Bank. Of course on presenting it for payment (to J M Shoemaker & Co. bankers) they spoke of the paid original draft, & I gave the Camden bank my cheque $174:37." See 1895, and Carpenter's reply on January 27 (Syracuse; Traubel, IV, 168–169).

11. See 1851.

Hamlin Garland, Mass—I still read the "Greek Poets"—S's attempt to explicate the "Prometheus" play puzzle (essentially insoluble, as probably all first class puzzles are) is one of the finest bits of writing & argument I know—(I take a *whack* at it several times)—

Sunday Jan: 13

Another fine sunny day—just right—Continue well considering—my breakfast mutton-broth & toast—now sitting in the big chair with wolf skin spread on the back of it & the woolen foot-cloth in front on the floor, with a lap-spread on my knees—reading the Sunday papers, &c—seems to me the sun & day never poured down so copiously & brightly—Love to you & all—

Walt Whitman

1893. *To Hamlin Garland*

ADDRESS: Hamlin Garland | Jamaica Plain | Mass:. POSTMARK: Camden (?) | Jan 12 | (?) PM | 89(?).

Camden Evn'g: Jan: 12 '89

Y'r welcome letter rec'd[12]—I saw Baxter's ardent & noble notice & am very grateful—am still cabin'd here in the sick room—don't feel particularly sick but the physical machine seems disabled & weakened almost to an extreme—can hardly move across the room without assistance—fortunately retain good spirits—fine sunny weather here—give my best respects to Mrs. Moulton, to Chamberlain[13] & to all my Boston friends—

Walt Whitman

1893.1 *To Thomas Donaldson*

ADDRESS: Thomas Donaldson | 326 N 40th Street | Philadelphia. POSTMARK: Ca(?) | Jan 14 | 8 PM | 89.

Camden N J— Jan: 14 1889

Received from Thomas Donaldson Ten Dollars for books—

Walt Whitman

12. In his undated letter Garland referred to the Bostonians mentioned in WW's reply (Lion; Traubel, IV, 78–79).

13. "Judge Chamberlain, of the Public Library," according to Garland's letter, but J. E. Chamberlin, of the Boston *Evening Transcript*, wrote on March 5 about a Whitman reading, and declared: "Neither you nor the Leaves of Grass are on trial any more" (Syra-

Dear T D

I am here imprison'd yet in my sick room—don't get any thing that can be call'd a set back (yet)—but physical weakness & disability remain fully the same as ever, & I can't get out, or even around the house—take no medicine—am free from any pronounc'd pain &c—Best love to you & all—

W W

What has become of Clayton Peirson,[13.1] the young fellow that came over to see me sixteen or eighteen months ago?

I have a copy of my big 900 Vol. "Complete Poems & Prose" (plain bound) for you—& I think Ed Wilkins will bring it over to you ab't noon to-morrow Tuesday—

1894. *To Richard Maurice Bucke*

ADDRESS: Dr R M Bucke | Asylum | London | Ontario | Canada. POSTMARK: Camden, N.J. | Jan 15 | 8 PM | 89(?).

Camden early P M | Jan: 15 '89

Nothing different—Fine sunny weather—Am sitting here by the oak-fire—Ed has gone over to Donaldson's with a copy of the big book I have sent him—quite alone—no visitors to-day—no doctors—Send you enclosed old letters—(may be uninteresting—if so throw 'em in the fire)—I suppose you have rec'd the Boston *Herald* with Baxter's notice—I am waiting to hear from the German translation (I fancy now out)—shall tell you soon as I hear—O that I could get out & bask in this copious sunshine of to-day—

Walt Whitman

1895. *To Edward Carpenter*

ADDRESS: Edward Carpenter | Millthorpe | near Chesterfield | England. POSTMARK: Camden, N.J. | Jan (?) | 8 PM | 89.

Camden N J U S America | Jan: 16 '89

I was too fast & all wrong abt the drafts. The *first* one was duly

cuse; Traubel, IV, 320–321).

13.1. According to an entry in CB on March 25, 1887, Clayton Wesley Peirson took WW's "'Day Book' to be re-bound—(is to make me a new one also)." At the beginning of his last "Day Book," the poet noted: "CWP is located (July 24 '90) at 3819 Lancaster av: Phila—real estate office."

rec'd (I was very ill at the time) & cash'd—Best thanks. The *second*, the duplicate, I have destroy'd—Remain here laid up in the old sick room, but sort of comfortable—just had a letter f'm the Misses Ford—Remembrances & love to you[14]—

Walt Whitman

1896. *To Richard Maurice Bucke*

ADDRESS: Dr R M Bucke | Asylum | London | Ontario | Canada POSTMARK: Camden (?) | Jan 18(?) | 8 PM | 89.

Camden Jan: 17 '89

Y'rs rec'd this morning—letter f'm Rhys also[15]—Kennedy has sent me a letter he receives from F. W. Wilson, Glasgow, to hurry up the copy for the book "W W the Poet of Humanity"—as he, Wilson, is ready (& even in a hurry) to publish it—I have heard from Karl Knortz, N Y, that he sent word to a German scholar friend at Zurich, Switzerland, to look after the proofs of the translation book (printed there by J Schabelitz, pub'r)—I have not heard f'm Rolleston, since he sent me word that he had rec'd the first proofs from Zurich—have rec'd a Springfield Republican with a long criticism of "Whittier, Whitman & Emma Lazarus" evidently by Frank Sanborn[16]—wh' I will send you in a day or two—

I am fairly—sitting here alone, as usual—dark, rainy, glum to-day, not at all cold—it is near noon—Mrs. Davis has been in for five minutes—I hear Ed down stairs somewhere practising on his fiddle—no doctor now this week yet—Tom Harned & Horace here last evn'g—

P M—So the day whiles on—no visitors—pass the hours I know not how, yet evenly & sort o' comfortably. Have rec'd a notice in San Francisco Bulletin wh' I will forward you—Have you rec'd two German papers with something in?—Still cloudy, lowering, rainy—near sunset.

Walt Whitman

14. On January 13 Carpenter sent WW a copy of his review of *November Boughs* that appeared in the April issue of *The Scottish Art Review*, and enclosed a gift of 22*s.* 6*d.* from an anonymous Belfast friend (Feinberg).

15. Rhys's letter of January 5, misdated 1888 by Rhys and by Traubel (III, 440–441).

16. The Springfield *Daily Republican* printed this unsigned review of the three poets on January 15.

17. *Poet-lore* printed a notice of *November Boughs* in its March issue.

18. It was the leading article in *The Critic*, and concluded: "On the whole, all these 'boughs' together make a very rich bouquet, tied at every twig with a love-knot for the

1897. *To Richard Maurice Bucke* *1.19–20. 1889*

ADDRESS: Dr R M Bucke | Asylum | London | Ontario | Canada. POSTMARK: Camden, N.J. | Jan 2(?) | 8 PM | 89.

Camden early P M Jan: 19 '89

I suppose you got the Springfield *Rep'n* with Sanborn's criticism—the San Franc: *Bulletin* with notice—& *Poet-lore*, the new magazine[17]—a fine sunny day here—somewhat cooler—much the same with me as of late, but I am getting fearfully *staled* with this long, long confinement—do not get any physical strength or improved ability—not a bit—

The *Critic* (Jan: 19) comes—has a notice of *Nov: Boughs*, perhaps the most eulogistic & sweeping yet[18]—I send it to you—I am alone—stir up the fire & put in some wood—as it grows colder—have my nice lunch of ice cream & a cup of milk—

Sunday Jan: 20

Cloudy & looks & feels like snow—The good bound big Vol. is not made by the binder yet—& goes over to the ensuing week. I shall have one for you—(I make no great calculations on satisfaction)—Send you enclosed Edward Carpenter's last[19]—no word from O'Connor. Horace rec'd a few words from John Burroughs—He is still at his place West Park on the Hudson—seems to be so-so in health &c. working &c—

I dig away at Symond's *Greek Poets*—very instructive & competent—his dissertations on the great poets I dwell on and again—he takes a stand on the modern, & then makes a world-criticism & dissection of them—very true & acceptable & convincing to me—Ed is off for a two hours or more excursion on foot—I sit here by the stove—very quiet to-day—Do you get *Harper's Monthly?* Look in Feb: number at Howells's *Editor's Study*[20]—at a guess—God bless you all—

Walt Whitman

reader, and full of the unction and eloquence of a most sweet personality." WW observed to Traubel: "I am even inclined to rate it above all the other things so far said of the book" (IV, 19).

19. Carpenter's letter of December 27, 1888 (Feinberg); see 1891.

20. Howells, as the review testifies, had mellowed toward WW's poetry over the years, perhaps under the influence of Hamlin Garland and his own developing sense of realism. WW termed Howells' notice "so-so" but "friendly" (Traubel, IV, 17). Bucke on January 22 noted receipt of WW's "good, heartily welcomed letter" and the various clippings. He also mentioned a "lovely" two-page review of *November Boughs* in *The Century Guild Hobby Horse* of January by Selwyn Image (Syracuse).

1898. *To William D. O'Connor*

ADDRESS: Wm D O'Connor | 1015 O Street N W | Washington | D C. POSTMARKS: Camden, N.J. | Jan 20 | 6 PM | 89; Washington, Rec'd. | Jan 21 | 2 AM | 89 | 9.

Camden Sunday Evn'g | Jan: 20 '89

Ab't the same with me. Am still imprison'd in the sick room—very tedious but I get along better than one m't fancy—snowing here as I write. Best love to you & N[elly][21]—

Walt Whitman

1899. *To William Sloane Kennedy and Richard Maurice Bucke*

Camden Jan: 22 '89

Still keep up & read & write ab't the same—but remain cribb'd in my room. Situation much the same & am ceasing to count for any thing seriously better—(only hug myself on the tho't it might be & has been much worse)—Sunny to day, & markedly cold—I have a good wood fire—

I send enclosed quite a budget of letters wh' explain themselves—I also send the French *Nouvelle Revue* of May last[22]—I shall send you & Dr B. copies of the German book soon as I get them—Have rec'd Wilson's (publisher's) letter[23]—I shouldn't wonder if he has been a little frighten'd by Alex: Gardner of Paisley, who had a small ed'n of *Nov: Boughs* (I hear we have quite a clientage in Scotland)—I have sent the *Complete Works* Vol. to Rolleston by mail—McKay has rec'd several orders, & is waiting for the better binding—I guess the N B has done & is doing fairly publisherially—I have just had a short visit from two young deaf mutes f'm Washington D C—Am feeling comfortable—I will keep you posted, & you must me—Best love & prayers—

Walt Whitman

Send this letter, with all enclosures, to Dr Bucke—also the French magazine—

21. Ellen O'Connor on the following day thanked WW for his "good words & wishes," but noted that William "had last week an ill turn, like that just a year ago, & he has not been down stairs since" (Feinberg).

22. Gabriel Sarrazin's "Poëtes modernes de l'Amérique: Whitman," in *La Nouvelle Revue* on May 1, 1888. Sarrazin himself, on January 6, informed WW that his essay had been abridged in the journal, and that the excised portions would be restored when printed

1900. *To William Sloane Kennedy* *1.22.* [*1889*]

Camden Jan: 22

Don't hurry ab't sending the French magazine to Dr B[ucke]—Do you read French?—If entirely convenient, give me a brief resumé of it, the Sarrazin piece (or the am't of it) when you write again—Who wrote that notice first page last *Critic?*[24] It penetrated & pleas'd me much.

Walt Whitman

1901. *To Deaf and Dumb Callers* *1.22. 1889*

Glad to see you—the doctor prohibits callers nearly altogether—but I suppose because they *talk* too much—wh' I find you do not—but I can only say Hail—& good bye—

Walt Whitman
Jan: 22 '89

1902. *To Richard Maurice Bucke*

ADDRESS: Dr R M Bucke | Asylum | London | Ontario | Canada. POSTMARK: Camden, N.J. | Jan 23 | 5 PM | 89.

Camden early P M Jan: 23 '89

Sunny fine day—have had a good bath—sent a letter with enclosures & French *Nouvelle Revue* (of May last, with long review) via Kennedy, to you—will probably come nearly as soon as this—also with this, a paper & facsimile I forget whether I gave you at the time—(All will do no harm if no good)—O'C[onnor] seems to be either partially or wholly bedfast—the enc's above alluded to contain a short vague p[ost] c[ard] from Mrs. O'C.[25]—nothing special in my condition—an indigestion spell, if any thing—I stop the ice-cream eating as I think it has some influence in that—am sitting here as usual by the wood fire—no doctors for some days—(just as well)—appetite & rest at night fair—my eyesight

in *La renaissance de la poésie anglaise* (Feinberg). See Roger Asselineau's article in WWR, v (1959), 8–11.

23. On January 21 Kennedy wrote about his manuscript and Howells' article (Feinberg). He agreed on January 29 with WW's speculation about Wilson (Feinberg).

24. The notice of *November Boughs* on January 19 (see 1897). As later letters indicate, WW had Kennedy's translation of Sarrazin's article set in type.

25. See 1898, *n.*21.

weakening perceptibly—spirits keep up better than one w'd suppose—Horace T[raubel] comes every even'g—the binder has promised to send the specimen of better binding to-night—

3½ P M—The day moves steadily on—pretty dull and heavy with me here—Mrs. Davis has been in to cheer me up & was very welcome—(she has that indefinite something *buoyancy of presence*)—Ed is down stairs practising on his fiddle—For a change I am going to stretch out on the bed, for a little while—I have got so that books & papers are no recreation to me, almost revolting—no letters to-day—no visitors—the days are perceptibly growing longer—Love & best wishes & God bless you all—

Walt Whitman

1903. *To William D. O'Connor*

ADDRESS: Wm D O'Connor | 1015 O Street N W | Washington | D C. POSTMARK: Camden, N.J. | Jan 24 | 10 AM | 89.

Camden Evn'g: Jan: 23 '89

Much the same with me in disabled cond'n, confinement to room, & paralysis—& do not anticipate improvement—only pray it may be no worse—wh' it has been & may be again—think of you every day as we all do—many inquiries ab't you—have a big Vol (my *Complete*) for you—expect Dr B[ucke] here in Feb:—

Walt Whitman

1904. *To Richard Maurice Bucke* *1.23–24. 1889*

ADDRESS: Dr R M Bucke | Asylum | London | Ontario | Canada. POSTMARK: Camden, N.J. | Jan. 24 8 PM | 89.

Camden '89 / Jan 23—after 9 P M

Horace has bro't the costlier binding specimen copy—a handsome substantial volume—not that I am overwhelmed or even entirely satisfied by it, but as I had not put my calculations high & was even expecting to be disappointed, I shall accept it, & have some bound after it—It is dark green, half calf, gilt top, rough bottom & front, plain & sufficiently rich, the stitching & all else strong & durable (as I am told)—price of binding

26. Bucke on January 26–27 was concerned that "$1.24 is a big slice off $6. The price of the book should have been more than $6. I would not have put it a cent below $10" (Syracuse; Traubel, IV, 50).

each copy $1.24[26]—back lettering simply "Walt Whitman's Complete Works," then half way down "Poems and Prose" and then at bottom "Edition 1889"—

I have felt easy & comfortable the last four hours—sent you a letter & papers by the 8 p m mail—also a few words to O'C[onnor]—Rec'd a letter from Rice asking me to write for the *N A Review*[27]—

Jan: 24

With me ab't "the same subject continued"—a partial bowel dejection this forenoon—cloudy, still, raw, coolish weather—I keep a good fire—quiet here—I have seen the Feb: Harper's, with Howells's notice of *Nov: Boughs*—it is friendlyish & sort o' caressing but perhaps guarded—I suppose you get the mag:—if not I will send you mine—Yours of 22 rec'd—(read the last *Critic's* notice again—I am not sure but it is the best of all)—I finish sitting alone in the room by the fire—the afternoon half passed, & all well—

Walt Whitman

1905. *To William D. O'Connor*

ADDRESS: Wm D O'Connor | 1015 O Street N W | Washington D C. POSTMARK: Camden, N.J. | Jan 26 | 8 PM | 89.

Camden Evn'g: Jan: 26 '89

Much "the same subject continued" with me—do not get out of the sick room yet, but comparatively free from pain & suffering—the doctors come rarely—spirits remain fair—Expect Dr B[ucke] here in ten days or so—Best love—

Walt Whitman

1906. *To Richard Maurice Bucke*

ADDRESS: Dr R M Bucke | Asylum | London | Ontario | Canada. POSTMARK: Camden, N.J. | Jan 27 | 5 PM | 89.

Camden 4 P M Jan: 27 '89

Quiet & comfortable & ab't the same—y'rs came yesterday—expect

27. On January 18 Rice requested "an article of two thousand words, or less," on "The American Ideal in Fiction" (Traubel, IV, 18). Rice died on May 16, 1889; see Traubel, V, 191, 193.

to see you now before long—have the letters come via Kennedy—& the French magazine with Sarrazin's piece?—Of the latter I wish you w'd give me the running am't in translation (no hurry)—Cloudy & rainy day—

Walt Whitman

1907. *To William Sloane Kennedy*

TRANSCRIPT.

Jan. 28, '89

Your letter and the translation have come and I thank you markedly. I have sent M. Sarrazin (his piece is a great steady trade-wind hurrying the ship into port) a copy of the big book. . . . Dr. Bucke makes a little fun of Howells's notice of *Nov: Boughs* in Feb. *Harper's* (the wonder is that it is so friendly and good). . . . I sit up all day and read and write (tho' both are getting almost loathsome), and keep fair spirits upon the whole.

1908. *To Richard Maurice Bucke*

ADDRESS: Dr R M Bucke | Asylum | London | Ontario | Canada. POSTMARK: Camden (?) | Jan (?) | 8 P(?) | 89.

Camden Jan: 29 '89

Am feeling pretty well considering. My obstinate spell of indigestion continues though—I take the Frederickshall water every morning—drink a cup of coffee every breakfast now—(after an abstinence of four or five months)—eat rather lightly—mutton broth yet—a few bits of the well-stew'd mutton, good graham bread toasted—only two meals—no ice cream lunch at 1½ as formerly, at all—in fact follow out the theory & advice (in general, in main) indicated by y'r letters of three or four weeks ago—appetite-relish pretty good—no bother with bladder troubles—seems to be fair skin condition, a little sweat perceptible most every day—no doctor at all now for a week or ten or more days (I think Walsh is ill)—

Have you rec'd the French magazine with Sarrazin's article, from

28. G. C. Macaulay's article "Walt Whitman" (see 1182).
29. On January 28 Mrs. O'Connor spelled out at length the gravity of William's

Kennedy? It seems to be one of the most ardent & penetrative, & eulogistic sort—I have sent him a copy of the big book by mail—Edward Carpenter has sent me the *Scottish Art Review* notice by him (E C) of *Nov: B*—I will send it you—Horace has it now—I have order'd 50 copies of the fine binding from the Phila: binder (Oldach)—shall keep one for you—30 or 35 will go to McKay on sale—I note what you say of Howells's opinion in Feb: *Harper's*—indeed it contrasts with such as Sarrazin's review in the *Nouvelle Revue* & in that *Nineteenth Century* piece (Dec: '82)—[28]

I receive word from O'Connor to-day from Mrs: O'C (enclosed) & it is rather gloomy. Of course he ought to have a good man nurse—needs that more than I do—poor dear friend—I fear more definitely physically wreck'd than ever—I am thinking ab't him all day—the impression I get is that *the meter is a success & a prospect*, but the work of such things is so slow & aggravating—sunny to-day, rather windy & cold—I am sitting by the oak fire—

Walt Whitman

1909. *To Ellen M. O'Connor*

ADDRESS: Mrs: O'Connor | 1015 O Street N W | Washington | D C. POSTMARK: Camden, N.J. | Jan 29 | 8 PM | 89.

Camden Evn'g Jan: 29 '89

Thanks for the letter giving me word abt Wm's present cond'n & hope indeed it will improve soon—Two months ago I was in a woful & horrible plight, bladder trouble, gastric malady & weak as a rag—& I have comparatively got over all & comparatively easier & freer—(tho' bad enough yet)—I expect Dr B[ucke] here next week but not certain—Best love & cheer to both.[29]

Walt Whitman

1910. *To Richard Maurice Bucke*

ADDRESS: Dr R M Bucke | Asylum | London | Ontario | Canada. POSTMARK: Camden, N.J. | Jan 31 | 8 PM | 89.

Camden Jan: 31 '89

A fine day, sunny, pleasantly cool. All well, here, ab't the same as

condition: "He feels discouraged for the first time, & says the outlook is very gloomy" (Feinberg).

of late. Y'rs of 28th came—am quite concern'd ab't the fire, & Ed is too—reads all ab't it with interest—has the *Revue* come yet? I told K[ennedy] he need not be any special haste, but must send it sure before long—he has made & sent me a fragmentary trans: of part that I have had my printer put in type & will soon (in probably three or four days) send you a copy—it is tip-top, warm & appreciative—

Ed & I are keeping the house to-day as Mrs: Davis has gone to Phila: to attend a law suit. She sued Wm Duckett,[30] the boy who was with us, for ab't 150, for his many months' board, (after waiting & being fooled eighteen months or more)—A lady has just call'd & bo't four copies *Nov: Boughs* & order'd more—a bowel dejection to-day (partial but definite)—am feeling pretty well considering to-day—(a suspicion of something like strength)—Tom Harned here last evn'g—good—that new baby must be splendid—Mrs: H is well—(she is a rare superior woman)—

The piece enclosed is Edw'd Carpenter's, as you will see[31]—(*Nov: B* is more likely to *be read* and *take* than any other of my books)—

3 P M—Mrs. D has just come back—the case is postponed—no trial yet—may come up to-morrow—fine day out & out—I am comfortable—good oak fire—

Walt Whitman

1911. *To William D. O'Connor*

ADDRESS: Wm D O'Connor | 1015 O Street N W | Washington | D C. POSTMARKS: Camden, N.J. | Jan 3(?) | 8 PM | 89; Washington, Rec'd. | Feb 1 | 7 AM | 89 | 4.

Camden Evn'g Jan 31 '89

Have had a favorable day in my condition—fine sunny pleasantly cool weather—hope much it has been easy with you—Dr B[ucke]'s establishm't has had a fire—one of the "cottages"—no loss of life or limb, but makes work & delay for him—A French periodical *la Nouvelle Revue* has given L of G. a mighty good notice wh' I shall soon send you a brief of trans:—Love & cheer to you—

Walt Whitman

30. WW was violently exercised about this "young scamp" and "young scoundrel"; see Traubel, IV, 64–66. However, on June 27 he lent Duckett $10 (CB, and see Traubel, V, 329–330). When the young man asked for $10 or $15 on December 20 (Feinberg), WW refused.

Walt Whitman
Sept: '87

Photograph of Walt Whitman by G. C. Cox (1887).

Walt Whitman 1887

"The Laughing Philosopher," photograph by G. C. Cox (1887).

Camden noon Dec: 29 '88

Fine, still sunny day, not cold—continue ab't the same—pretty comfortable upon the whole—N Y Herald 23d last Sunday Dec: has a leading (book notice) two third column review of Nov: Boughs, mostly extracts—favorable more than any thing else—
—glad you hit (fix) on the autobiographic underlying element of the collected Vol—Was wondering whether that w'd be detected—did not say anything ab't it, but it has been in my mind of late yr's unremittedly—of course not in the usual auto-writing style & even purposes but with a freer margin—& I think if the book really grips, _that_ will be what the good class literary detectives of the future will mainly settle & agree upon—Then I sh'd be tickled enough if I c'd think I had indeed skimm'd some of the _real cream_ of the American History of the last 35 years & preserv'd it here—I have sent to some 20 of our friends home & abroad & specialists (wrapt in the Post item of last Thursday) the printed copy of y'r letter ab't it (the "impromptu criticism")—I send you Kennedy's letter of 25th—Yr's of 26th came last ev'ng—yes, I shall _mind_—think I understand & accept the matter below it & shall practically put it in action—as I finish I am sitting alone by my oak fire—every thing still—& the sun out shining brightly—Walt Whitman

Letter (December 29, 1888).

328 Mickle street
Camden New Jersey
April 8 '89

The enclosed is Stedman's letter ab't the "Complete" I tho't you m't like to read—(T B Aldrich; also tho' short is very friendly & eulogistic—not sent here)——

—Nothing in my condition &c specially notable—but the pegs are gradually loosening, perhaps being slowly pull'd out—I have been kept in here now almost a year, (not been out doors once in the time—hardly out of the sick room)—but as before said I get along more comfortable (had lots of Doctors, but they have all vanished) than you might suppose—fair nights & tolerable days—Am busying myself with a new edn of L of G. with "Sands at 70" and "Backward Glance" all in one Vol. bound (in thinner paper) in pocket-book style, I have had a notion for, & now put out partly to occupy myself, & partly to commemorate my finishing my 70th year—Sit up mainly all day—at present (as so often told) in my big arm chair with the thick wolf skin spread on the back—writing this on the tablet on my lap—early afternoon—fairly comfortable—a good oak fire—raw & dark weather out—Love & good prospects to all

Walt Whitman

Letter (April 8, 1889).

Bust of Walt Whitman by Sidney H. Morse.

"Lear" photograph (1889?).

William D. O'Connor.

Richard Maurice Bucke.

To
Dr R M Bucke
of Canada
from his friend the author
of this Volume – with best love
– memories of many seasons,
jaunts, talks, enjoyments, physician's help & steady faithfulness thro' thick & thin –
May God bless you in yr
comings in & goings out Maurice,
– you & yours – is my prayer –
Walt Whitman
Camden N J – U S America
December 31 1888 –

Inscription to Richard Maurice Bucke.

Camden p m Jan: 1 '89
Superb sunny day again & I am feeling all as right as could be expected — Still on mutton broth with toast & plenty of rise & a few mouthfuls of the stew'd mutton. As I told you bowel action fair — A little of what I call cold in the head, but slight so far — Dr Walsh here last evng — he himself quite unwell — no Osler now for a fortnight — I enclose Mrs: O'C's card rec'd this mng — Ed: Stafford has been here — they are all well as usual & every thing goes on the same as of old — — So we have commenced on an other year — & where it will take us & how, are indeed mercifully hidden — for the pique of weaving & watching (with a gambler's uncertainty) makes the background & basis of the whole business — I have been reading "Goethe's & Carlyle's Correspondence" wh I find interesting — presents C in a different light from any other —
Walt Whitman

Letter (January 1, 1889).

My 71st year arrives; the fifteen past months nearly all illness or half illness — until a tolerable day (Aug: 6 1889) & convoy'd by Mr. B and Ed: W. I have been carriaged across to Philadelphia (how sunny & fresh & good look'd the river the people, the vehicles, & Market & Arch streets!) & have sat for this photo: wh- satisfies me.

Walt Whitman

Photograph of Walt Whitman by Gutekunst (1889).

Painting of Walt Whitman by John White Alexander (1889; reproduced by courtesy of The Metropolitan Museum of Art, Gift of Mrs. Jeremiah Milbank, 1891).

1912. *To William Sloane Kennedy*

Camden Feb: 1 '89

Y'rs of 29th Jan: rec'd & welcom'd as always[32]—I continue on much the same—the last two days I fancy a little plus, something like strength—have got so when negative favors (to be free from special botherations) quite set me up.

Had my breakfast & relish'd it—three or four hot stew'd oysters, a stout slice of toasted Graham bread, & a mug of coffee—My housekeeper Mrs: Davis is compell'd to be temporarily absent these two days & Ed my nurse gets my breakfast & gets it very well.

I get along here without any luxury or any special *order*, but I am satisfied & comfortable & often bless the Lord & congratulate myself that things are as well with me as they are—that I retain my mentality intact—that I have put my literary stuff in final form—that I have a few (but sufficient) real & competent & determined advocates & understanders & *bequeathers* (important as much as any thing)—

Cold weather to-day & I keep a good oak fire—At Dr B[ucke]'s there has been something of a conflagration—one of the detached dwellings burnt—no loss of life or limb—piles on more labor & delay on Dr however —I write a few lines every two or three days to O'C[onnor] & send Mrs: O'C the *Trans*[*cript*]*s*—

Enclosed find a proof of y'r condensed translation of Sarrazin (I don't mind its hasty, somewhat broken form) wh' read & correct if anything & return to me at once—& I will send you some impressions—I like it well—Best love to you—

Walt Whitman

1913. *To Richard Maurice Bucke* *2.2–3. 1889*

ADDRESS: Dr R M Bucke | Asylum | London | Ontario | Canada. POSTMARK: Camden | Feb 3 | 5 (?) M | 89.

Camden P M Feb: 2 '89

Y'rs of Jan: 31 have come (two)—yes I value Sarrazin's review the more & more I get at it—(Curious that there in feudalistic Europe we

31. Carpenter's review of *November Boughs* (see 1895, *n.*14.).

32. WW did not refer to Kennedy's comment on January 29 about his recent visit to Camden: "Don't you think you are sometimes a little cold and repressive? . . . I want y'r personal love; the book I write chiefly to gain that & if it tends to make hearty sympathy impossible I w'd rather pitch it into the sea" (Feinberg).

find fellows that give us all odds, & go all above & under *us*—we in practice, they in theory)—The easy handling & simple *insousiance* of incredible claims is the most remarkable of S's piece—

Mrs: Davis had a verdict yesterday ag't W H D[uckett] (for $190)[33] —I continue on ab't the same—small bowel dejections—(use the ordinary injection pipe)—weather turn'd to cold & cloudy—feels like snow—I write a few words to O'C[onnor] every other day or so—nothing further rec'd f'm there—

Evn'g: have had my dinner, stew'd chicken & roast apples—no visitors to-day—no doctors—Cold night in prospect—

Sunday noon Feb: 3

Night not so very cold—y'r photo came—it seems to me one of the best pictures ever made—Mr & Mrs: Harned paid me a nice visit this mn'g—(the madame is one of my favorites)—have had a call also from three y'ng men of Phila (artists I think)[34]—take y'r time leisurely in making the abstract of Sarrazin, with careful reference to the critical & general features—Am sitting by the oak fire as usual—have to-day's *Tribune* and *Press*—(send the former to O'C—think of him very often)—Burroughs is stopping temporarily (for a change I suppose) in Po'keepsie with (I suppose) his wife & boy—I enclose Edw'd Carpenter's last[35]—

Walt Whitman

1914. *To Richard Maurice Bucke* *2.4–5. 1889*

ADDRESS: Dr R M Bucke | Asylum | London | Ontario | Canada. POSTMARK: Camden, N.J. | Feb 5 | 8 PM | 89.

Camden Noon Feb: 4 '89

An incipient "cold in the head" (from an open sash behind me two hours yesterday toward evn'g forgotten)—may pass over lightly—may grow worse—(generally of late seems to settle on, merge in bladder trouble)—Otherwise matters much the same—partial bowel action (thankful for that)—half sunny weather this forenoon, rather cold—The "Magazine of Poetry" from you came—all looks better than I w'd have anticipated—pictures, print, paper very fair—I see I appear quite largely —good biographic sketch f'm y'r pen I accept & like well[36]—quite many

33. Mrs. Davis received $140 after paying her attorney's fee of $50 (*CB*).
34. One of the young men was Bilstein, a printer (Traubel, IV, 78).
35. Carpenter's letter of January 13 (Feinberg).

names I had not heard before—rather an apotheosis of good mediocrity isn't it? & why not?

Feb: 5 noon

Nothing special—I am sitting by the stove alone—partial bowel dejection an hour ago—no letters rec'd this morn'g—sell two copies *Nov: B* to-day—I send papers & p[ost] cards to O'C[onnor] every other day—nothing very late from him—cloudy dark raw here like snow in prospect—

McKay is going off "on the road" (book selling &c) in ab't a week—takes the new bound big book with him—wants of me, a formal pledge that there will be *no more complete works* like this issued by me—but I refuse—(altho' I feel confident there will not, yet I prefer to keep it open) —I sell the C W to McK h'f calf bound for $4—so you see I don't indeed make much—will soon send you a printed slip of the Sarrazin fragment as the proof from K[ennedy] has come in the 2 p m mail. It seems but a fragment, but a typical one—Y'rs came to-day. The sun is out shining at setting—

Walt Whitman

1915. *To Richard Maurice Bucke*

ADDRESS: Dr R M Bucke | Asylum | London | Ontario | Canada. POSTMARK: Camden, N.J. | Feb 6 | 8 PM | 89.

Camden Evn'g Feb: 6 '89

Nothing special to write about—I continue the same—I enclose in advance a slip—the only one I have—shall send you some more as I shall have some more in a day or two—(S[arrazin] takes 'em all down in my opinion)—

I have heard from Mary Costelloe—shall send you the letter—C is elected as a *progressist* to the London directory municipal gov't under the new L bill (very important & a sort both of home rule & imperium within imperium)[37]—Alys & the parents are junketing on the continent—Love—

Walt Whitman

36. The first issue of this new journal had a lengthy notice (14–23), with a foreword by Bucke, Frank Fowler's etching, and a photograph.

37. A summary of her letter of January 25–26 (Feinberg; *Smith Alumnae Quarterly* [February, 1958], 88).

1916. *To Susan Stafford*

Camden 328 Mickle Street '89 | Wednesday forenoon
Feb: 6

Quite sharp & cold this forenoon, & I am sitting by a good oak fire —Am still imprison'd in the sick room—Keep up spirits pretty fair, but weak as ever in my movements, & being kept indoor for most nine months begins to tell on me—I almost wonder I keep as well as I do—but I have been pretty low—the doctors—even Dr Bucke—gave me quite up more than once—They just kept life like a little light prevented from being all put out (& this was the reason why I often had to deny friends from seeing me)—& for a month or so I was in a horrible plight—a nuisance to myself & all—but my nurse (Ed Wilkins, the Canadian young man Dr. B. sent) stuck to me & it has sort o' pas'd over—or at any rate the worst of it—At present I sit here in the room—Mrs Davis has just been in & wishes to send her love to you, & says come up & see us—my mentality ab't the same as ever (tho' I get very soon sore & tired reading, or being talked to)—& not much show of being any better—thankful that things are as well as they are with me—for they might be much worse—

Susan, your good letter came this forenoon & I was glad enough to hear from you all—I thank you so much for it—I write all this rigmarole at once—Herbert paid me quite a visit last evn'g—I fancy he is doing well, & quite a fellow over there among the artists—I hear from Edw'd Carpenter—he always wishes to be remembered to you all, specially Ed —he seems to be well & doing well.

My books are all completed, these last editions, wh' is a great relief. Eddy my crippled brother is still at Blackwood—(I yesterday paid the three months board bill $45:50 there) he is well, & seems to be well off & satisfied—young Harry Bonsall[38] died there three or four weeks ago—my sisters at Greenport L I and Burlington Vermont are ab't as usual—my brother & sister Lou are well at Burlington this state—I think quite often of Harry, & wish you would send this letter over to him without fail the first chance you get—it is written largely to him—I have what I call *sinking spells* in my sickness, & I had one the day he last visited me—Love to you & George, Ed, Van, Deb & Jo and all—

W W

38. See 1014.

1917. *To Harry Stafford*

ADDRESS: Harry Lamb Stafford | RR Station | Marlton | New Jersey. POSTMARK: Camden, N.J. | Feb 6 | 8 PM | 89.

Camden Feb: 6 '89

Am here yet, dear Hank, in the same place &c after passing a good hard shaking (& not out of it yet)—but somewhat better—Have written & sent your folks at Glendale a longish letter wh' I want you to have, as it is meant as much for you—I have finished all my books &c. and feel better. Best love—

Walt Whitman

1918. *To Richard Maurice Bucke*

ADDRESS: Dr R M Bucke | Asylum | London | Ontario | Canada. POSTMARK: Camden (?) | Feb 8 | 12 M | 89.

Camden Friday forenoon | Feb: 8 '89

I write mainly to send the card of Mrs: O'C[onnor], just rec'd[39]—gloomy prospect enough—Nothing new with me—have just had my breakfast, mutton broth with plenty of rice, & cup of chocolate—(ate & drank all)—Sent you several slip abstracts of the Sarrazin article—Harned paid Ed [Wilkins] up yesterday—he is well—Cold & half cloudy weather—I am sitting by the stove—thinking a good deal ab't O'C—

Walt Whitman

1919. *To John Burroughs* *2.8. [1889]*

TRANSCRIPT.

February 8.

Dear JB

Nothing very special with me—bad enough yet and imprison'd in the room and chair, but easier and freer of the intestinal and bladder troubles and fearful weakness of ten weeks ago—At present I am sitting by the oak fire in my big chair, well protected—as it is bitter cold the last two days and now here—

39. In her note of February 7 Mrs. O'Connor requested WW to let Bucke know that William "is failing" (Feinberg).

The news from O'Connor is bad, and worse—he is confined to the house and seems to be failing. . . . Most probably I shall continue ab't the stage I am at present—maybe some time, but the future will eventuate itself, and it will of course be all right. I continue almost totally disabled from getting around, can hardly get across the room—have a good stout nurse, Ed Wilkins f'm Canada—no serious pain in particular—good heart yet—eat and sleep fairly—so you see it is not so bad as might be—(and perhaps will be yet)—

I enclose a piece you might like to see[40]—Dr B[ucke] is expected here in a week or ten days—I suppose you hear f'm Horace Traubel and that keeps you posted. H. T. has been and is invaluable to me—my books are all printed etc. (I have a big book, complete poems and prose for you)—

Love to you and 'Sula and Julian—

Walt Whitman

1920. *To William D. O'Connor*

ADDRESS: Wm D O'Connor | 1015 O Street N W | Washington D C. POSTMARK: Camden, N.J. | Feb 9 | 8 PM | 89.

Camden Friday P M | Feb: 8 '89

Am thinking a good deal ab't you to-day—have rec'd the card N[elly] sent & it has rous'd my tho't's & sympathies greatly—Nothing new or special in my condition—Love to you & N—

Walt Whitman

1921. *To Richard Maurice Bucke* *2.9–10. 1889*

ADDRESS: Dr R M Bucke | Asylum | London | Ontario | Canada. POSTMARK: Camden, N.J. | Feb 10 | 5 PM | 89.

Camden Feb: 9 '89

All goes well & as usual—A sunny day, pleasant, fairly cool—bowel dejection—have been thinking a good deal of O'Connor—sent to him a letter & papers last night—

Y'rs of 7th has come by the 2 p m mail—you have of course by this time the printed slip-sheet of the Sarrazin trans: by K[ennedy] & it is good

40. Undoubtedly a copy of Kennedy's translation of Sarrazin.

—but I suspect there is plenty left of the S review, more that I sh'd like well to have—if (quite when opportune) you feel to make such additional trans: do so—but do not bother or hurry ab't it—but you probably have trans: & I shall get it to-morrow—Upon the whole I opine S's piece is the best we have rec'd in Europe—& that's saying a good deal. I have sent you six copies the S piece—Would it facilitate any when you come, (& supposing the leave obtained)—if you went directly from London to Washington, to see & be a few hours with O'C?—or is it best to come to Phila: & go hence to W?

Sunday p m Feb: 10

Still all well, I believe—Horace last evn'g bro't over four copies of the "Complete" in their good half-calf binding—they are superb, the best part being the *substantiality*, with the rich plainness of the look of them, one is for H himself with a dedication (wh' I have written in just now) & one I keep for you—Look for word f'm Mrs: O'C to morrow.

I enc: Mary Costelloe's letter,[41] tho' I dare say you have every minute occupied—

Walt Whitman

1922. *To William D. O'Connor*

ADDRESS: Wm D O'Connor | 1015 O Street N W | Washington | D C. POSTMARK: Camden, N.J. | Feb 10 | 5 PM | 89.

Camden Sunday afternoon | Feb: 10 '89

Hope you have as fine & sunny a day in Wash'n as we are having here—Send you my love & tho'ts as ever—Am myself imprison'd here in the big chair—yet all sort o' comfortable with me—

Walt Whitman

1923. *To William Sloane Kennedy*

Camden P M Feb: 11 '89

Much the same subject continued. I am still confined to the room & chair—eat & drink moderately—my meals mostly mutton-broth with bits of the well-stew'd meat & Graham bread & sometimes roasted apples or a

41. Her letter of January 25–26 (see 1915).

cup custard—appetite fair—of course monotonous here (it is getting to be the ninth month)—but I am comparatively comfortable & get along better than you w'd suppose—snowing to-day, half-melting when it falls—

You got the printed slips of the Sarrazin tran[slation] I sent?—Dr B[ucke] has the magazine—he has been forced to delay his jaunt this way —& now names the 18th inst. to start hither—he may go directly to Wash'n to see O'C[onnor]—with a possibility of it being further put off—

O'Connor is badly off—worse—& I am much worried ab't him—he is laid up, mainly bed fast, in his house—very bad, at my last acc'ts four days since, from Mrs O'C—

I hear that the German (partial) tran: is advertised in the German papers—so we will soon get the book here—& I will send you one when I get some—Pray you don't mind any little proof lapses in the S. trans: (if any)—it is a wonderfully *consoling* piece to me—coming from so evidently a fully equipt, sharp-eyed, sharp-nosed, sharp-ear'd Parisian Frenchman—running the critical leads the very deepest—& here what he reports—I have rec'd a good long warm flattering letter from Addington Symonds from Switzerland with a large photo head[42]—the best photo I ever saw—

Best love

Walt Whitman

1924. *To William D. O'Connor* *2.11. [1889]*

ADDRESS: Wm D O'Connor | 1015 O Street N W | Washington D C. POSTMARK: Camden (?) | Feb 11 | 8 PM | 89.

Camden Evn'g Feb: 11

Quite disappointed in not getting any word from N[elly]—every thing continuing same as of late—rec'd a good letter from Addington

42. The letter of January 29, a truly "warm" one, was signed "your true respectful and loving disciple" (Feinberg; Traubel, IV, 126).

43. *The Atlantic Monthly*, LX (1887), 275–281, contained a judicious review of *Anne Gilchrist*, but the writer took exception to her enthusiasm for WW's creed: "But we think she was wrong, fundamentally, in her philosophy; for materialism, however far it may be developed, never has accounted, and never can account, for the sons of God" (280). WW considered the review "malodorous" (Traubel, IV, 289).

44. Quoted from Rolleston's letter of February 2 (Feinberg). On January 7 Rolleston informed the poet that he had just returned the proofs to the publisher and that he would send on thirty copies of the German translation (Feinberg).

45. The notice appeared on February 9 and was written by Francis M. Larned (Traubel, IV, 447–448). WW pronounced it "a noble piece indeed: that man knows, understands!" (IV, 189). Larned's review was eulogistic, though not especially perceptive

Symonds, Switzerland—the German version (Zurich) is out, published —snow all day here—

Walt Whitman

1925. *To Richard Maurice Bucke* *2.11–12. 1889*

ADDRESS: Dr R M Bucke | Asylum | London | Ontario | Canada. POSTMARK: Camden, N.J. | Feb 12 | 8 PM | 89.

Camden | *Monday P M Feb: 11*, '89

Quite a steady snow to-day, half melting after it falls—I have written to Kennedy—nothing to-day (to my disappointment) from Mrs: O'C[onnor]—Knortz says the German trans: (Zurich) is out—advertised there—but I have not seen any thing of it—Your MS trans: of Sarrazin rec'd, & it completes much to me—letter with it—thanks—Have you the *Atlantic* magazine Aug: 1887, or w'd you like a second, with the notice of Mrs: Gilchrist—in which I & mine are spoken of quite largely?[43]—If not I will send you a copy I see I have in the rubbish—Rec'd yesterday a good warm letter f'm Addington Symonds from Switzerland (anent of *Nov: Boughs*, wh' he has, & dwells on)—also a photo, large, head of S. himself & very fine—

Tuesday Feb: 12

A short note from Rolleston, Ireland, acknowledging his "Complete" —He says "I like much your one volume plan—It's a book one can walk about in, as in a great land, & see things of inexhaustible meaning & promise."[44]

The Chicago *Morning News* Feb 9 has a long review (anent of Nov. B) wh' may probably have to go in range with Sarrazin's[45]—may even satisfy you—I will send you one—Sun shining to-day here, but the youngsters out with skates & sleds—

—the response of an idolator who admired the person as much as the poet: "With 'November Boughs' the work of Walt Whitman may be considered finished. The age of the poet (he was born in 1819), his infirmity, the suggestive title of the volume, and the character of its contents all indicate that it is the final word, the last farewell, of one who awaits death with the tranquil mind and the clear vision of the prophet. . . .

"It is impossible to contemplate the life of this man, with a thorough knowledge of his work or even with an imperfect realization of it, without experiencing a feeling of profound and reverential respect. But we are too near him now to get other than an imperfect view of him: his personality is so great that it crowds the narrow field of our vision; to be adequately grasped and appreciated he must be seen in the perspective of at least one hundred years. His figure then will be sharply outlined against the background of history, and the future will see with unshaded eye and in a light softened and tempered by time that of which the present can get but a partial view." (For Larned's notice I am indebted to the Newberry Library.)

Am thinking much of O'C—I enclose Symonds's letter—So far my "cold in the head" shows in a stuff'd & heavy half-dizzy feeling (nothing intense) in the said head & in occasional soreness in neck & shoulder joints.

Walt Whitman

1926. *To Ellen M. O'Connor*

ADDRESS: Mrs: O'Connor | 1015 O Street N W | Washington D C. POSTMARK: Camden (?) | Feb 12 | 8 PM | 89.

Camden Tuesday Evn'g | Feb: 12 '89

Soon as convenient send me a word or two, as I am thinking & worried—Send the Transcript to Dr B[ucke] (the one I mail to-night same as this)—the last date fixed by Dr B starting hither was 18th (next Monday)—Ab't as usual with me—(but my head dizzy with a "cold" in it)—Best love as always to you and W[illiam]—

Walt Whitman

1927. *To Richard Maurice Bucke*

ADDRESS: Dr R M Bucke | Asylum | London | Ontario | Canada. POSTMARK: Camden, N.J. | Feb 13 | 8 PM | 89.

Camden P M Feb: 13 '89

I send Mrs: O'C[onnor]'s letter rec'd this morn'g—welcomed tho' it has not (only indirectly) what I mostly wanted, all ab't, mainly & detailedly O'C's condition & every thing relating to *him*—(a good strong man nurse he evidently needs at once—my poor lamented friend—it is hard, hard)[46]—

I send Rolleston's short note—What I am specially tickled ab't is that a big five pound book (40 cents postage) goes safe & sure to Co[unty] Wicklow Ireland f'm Jersey here. I also enc: Jo: Gilder's invitation letter, just rec'd. Of course I make no response[47]—

Things nearly the same—not one even of my tolerable days—my head is uncomfortable, half aching & half-deaf—sunny & cold weather—yes, I

46. Mrs. O'Connor's letter of the preceding day, written while she was "nearly blind from loss of sleep," was filled with (understandable) self-pity (Feinberg). This letter to Bucke was written on the verso of Mrs. O'Connor's.

will send "Magazine of Poetry" back—Horace ask'd last evn'g of y'r definitive date of coming, with reference to fixing for y'r lecture—I am sitting here stupidly all day by the stove—

Walt Whitman

1928. *To William Sloane Kennedy*

ADDRESS: Sloane Kennedy | Belmont | Mass:.
POSTMARK: Camden (?) | Feb 14 | 8 PM | 89.

Camden Evn'g Feb: 14 '89

Y'rs came to-day, welcome—I send "Magazine Poetry" only half thinking it may be a sort of curiosity to you—Mail it to Dr B[ucke] as he owns it & wants it back—O'C[onnor] is still room-fast & badly off—I am fearful of the worst luck (of wh' a long miserable helpless lingering condition is perhaps worst)—Sunny & cold here—I am ab't as usual—a cold in the head—

Walt Whitman

I've sent a Sarrazin to Baxter & to Harland.[48]

1929. *To Dr. Karl Knortz*

ADDRESS: Dr Karl Knortz | 540 East 155th Street | New York City. POSTMARKS: Camden (?) | Feb 14 | 8 PM | 89; R | 2–15–89 | 6–1A—N Y.

328 Mickle Street | Camden N J p m
Feb: 14 '89

Y'r card came yesterday—Rolleston has rec'd in Ireland my big Vol. (complete works)—I send one to you today by express—it includes *Nov. Boughs* & all—send me card when it comes safe.

I hear from Dr Bucke often, he expects to come here next week—my friend O'Connor is very ill at Washington—

I am imprison'd in the sick room now in the ninth month, entirely disabled in movem't—pretty good heart tho'—

Walt Whitman

47. Gilder on February 12 requested a piece for *The Critic* from WW to honor the seventieth birthday of Lowell on February 22 (Feinberg).
48. Hamlin Garland.

1930. *To William D. O'Connor*

ADDRESS: Wm D O'Connor | 1015 O Street N W | Washington D C. POSTMARK: Camden, N(?) | Feb 15 | 8 PM | 89.

Camden Feb: 15 '89

Am sitting by the oak fire all day—no visitors or letters—but sort o' get along with my papers & books—Kennedy, Boston, sends kindest inquiries ab't you with sympathy & greeting—My friend Horace Traubel has been all day *numbering* in red ink the small ed'n of big books.

Walt Whitman

1931. *To Frederick Oldach* [*2.15. 1889*][48.1]

TRANSCRIPT.

Mr. Oldach, Bookbinder 1215 Filbert St. | Phila.

Please put a plain strong binding on this Vol: will cost me ab't 50 or 60 cts—want something *will last hard usage*, especially *a good durable back*—No particular fancy or beauty expected. I leave it to you what style. The label for back-lettering will be found pinn'd enclosed in front of the Vol:—

W. W.
328 Mickle Street
Camden

1932. *To Charles W. Eldridge*

ADDRESS: Charles W Eldridge | P O box 1705 Lawyer | Los Angeles Cal:. POSTMARK: Camden, N.J. | Feb 16 | 8 PM | 89.

Camden N J Feb: 16 '89

Am still here, pretty well considering but rigorously imprison'd in the sick room—good heart but entirely disabled—printing my final & complete editions all done—The news fr'm Wm is bad (I get word from N[elly] occasionally)—he is room-fast & weak—sits up part of the time, but does not write—I think hourly ab't him—it is gloomy—am uncertain

48.1. Traubel made a transcription of WW's note on the day it was written (IV,

whether you know ab't him or not. I expect Dr B[ucke] here next Wednesday.

Walt Whitman

1933. *To William D. O'Connor* *2.16–17.* [*1889*]

ADDRESS: Wm D O'Connor | 1015 O Street N W | Washington D C. POSTMARK: Camden (?) | Feb 17 | 5 PM | (?).

Camden—Feb: 16—Forenoon

Had my breakfast abt 9¼—mutton-broth, (some small bits of well stew'd meat) with Graham bread toasted & coffee—eat & drunk with relish—N[elly]'s card came—hope there may be many such *reasonable* nights—& days too—McKay has just come back f'm a book-tour in Boston and N Y—he sold 27 of the big books—& of *Nov. Boughs* over 700 have been sold—

Sunday Feb: 17

Rain & dark weather same as yesterday—alone here trying to interest myself in *Tribune* and Phil: *Press* to day's. I expect Dr B[ucke] Tuesday evn'g or Wednesday next.

Walt Whitman

1934. *To Mary Smith Costelloe*

ADDRESS: Mrs: Mary W Costelloe | 40 Grosvenor Road | the Embankment | London | S W | England. POSTMARKS: Camden, N.J. | Feb 18 | 8 PM | 89; Philadelphia, Pa. | Feb 18 | 11 PM | F D.

Feb: 18 1889 | 328 | Mickle st:
Camden New Jersey | U S America

Nothing special or very different—continue laid up & imprison'd in sick room—y'rs of a week ago rec'd & welcom'd—I want to send over some copies of my big book (works complete) one for you of course, & think of enveloping them stoutly & sending by ocean express—(to be call'd for there, or perhaps sent by local express)—& may send the parcel if you are willing—congratulate Mr. C on his success[49]—

Walt Whitman

156).

49. See 1915.

1935. *To William D. O'Connor*

ADDRESS: Wm D O'Connor | 1015 O street N W | Washington | D C. POSTMARK: Camden (?) | Feb 18 | 8 PM | 89.

Camden Feb: 18 '89

He [Traubel] or I will send you word of Dr B[ucke]'s visit here & whether & when if he comes to Wash'n—He comes with two or three others, (on that invention the *meter*) & puts up at Dooner's Hotel. I expect him by Wednesday—

All goes as usual with me—am feeling pretty well—to-day the third of rain & dark cloudiness—I send you the *Critic* to-morrow—a bundle of papers to-night—nothing particular—Love & prayers—

Walt Whitman

1936. *To William D. O'Connor*

ADDRESS: Wm D O'Connor | 1015 O Street N W | Washington D C. POSTMARK: Camden (?) | Feb 19 | 8 PM | 89.

Camden Feb: 19 '89

Am sitting as usual by the oak fire alone rather monotonous here after long confinement—sharp cold to-day—Dr B[ucke] may be a day or so later in coming—I expect him now 21st or 22d—Have rec'd a long criticism (markedly favorable) in London *Pall Mall Gaz:* Jan 25[50]—& another shorter *Echo* London, Jan: 26—Pretty fair with me, but "cold in the head" obstinate—Best love to you and N[elly]—

Walt Whitman

1937. *To Richard Maurice Bucke* *2.19–20. 1889*

ADDRESS: Dr R M Bucke | Asylum | London | Ontario | Canada. POSTMARK: Camden (?) | Feb 20 | 8 PM | 89.

Camden Feb: '89 19th—9 P M

Horace call'd to say you w'd not start till Monday next—All right

50. The *Pall Mall Gazette*'s notice of *November Boughs* was entitled "The Gospel

—nothing since f'm O'C[onnor], wh' is the most pressing matter with me now—I fear he is having a bad bad time—& think of him much—Nothing very different or new in my affairs—my "cold in the head" still hangs on—some twinge of bladder trouble, but nothing serious—upon the whole am getting along pretty fairly I fancy—have a fancy, contemplation, of a small special edition of L of G with Annex & "Backward Glance," all bound in pocket-book style pretty well, probably morocco, edges cut pretty close—Have rec'd the *Pall Mall*, Jan: 25, with a long favorable notice of *Nov. Boughs*—I sh'd send it now, but have lent it over to McKay to look at—shall keep it for you—no rec't yet of the German trans: book—Dr Karl Knortz has an office at 19 Dey St: New York not far from P O & wants you to stop & see him when you can.

Wednesday 20th—Sunny & cool & fine to-day—My brother Jeff from St Louis (topographical engineer) here—(as he grows older, we look curiously alike—you would know he was my brother)—he is not well, stomach & throat botheration—goes back to St Louis to-night—

Horace came last night with the tel[egram] that you w'd not start till next Monday—bowel action this mn'g—am sitting as usual by my stove —The enc: is f'm Ernest Rhys to me, nothing particular, but E R always cheery & welcome[51]—I guess A Gardner, publisher, Paisley, Scotland, must have sent copies of his little ed'n *Nov: B.* around to English and Scotch editors—very good—I have sent y'r Sarrazin abstract to be put in type—Shall give it to you to read proof—no hurry—it is in some resp[ect]s the best thing said ab't us—

Walt Whitman

1938. *To William D. O'Connor*

ADDRESS: Wm D O'Connor | 1015 O Street N W | Washington D C. POSTMARKS: Camden (?) | (?) | 8 PM | 89; Washington, Rec'd. | Feb 21 | 7 AM | 89 | 3.

Camden Feb: 20 '89

Have had a telegram f'm Dr B[ucke] that he will not start f'm Canada till next Monday—I am getting along fairly—physicalities &c. from fair to middling for an old man & whack'd & paralyzed at that—

My brother Jeff the civil engineer is here f'm St Louis—goes back this evn'g—is half unwell (stomach & throat)—Sunny & cold here—

Walt Whitman

According to Walt Whitman."

51. Rhys wrote from Wales on February 2 (Feinberg).

1939. *To John Burroughs*

ADDRESS: John Burroughs | 314 Mill Street | Po'keepsie New York. POSTMARKS: Camden, N.J. | Feb 22 | (?) PM | 89; Poughkeepsie, N.Y. | Feb | 23 | 1 AM | 1889.

Camden Feb: 22 '89

Y'r welcome letter rec'd this mn'g[52]—I am still here in good heart enough but almost entirely physically disabled—tied here to room & chair—The news from O'C[onnor] is no better—eyes given out, stomach, strength, bladder &c. in bad way.

I expect Dr B[ucke] to leave Canada next Monday for here—will send you a copy of the big book by express to West Park next week (or early in March)—Best love to you & 'Sula & Julian—

Walt Whitman

1940. *To William D. O'Connor*

ADDRESS: Wm D O'Connor | 1015 O Street N W | Washington D C. POSTMARK: Camden (?) | Feb 22 | 8 PM | 89.

Camden Feb: 22 '89

Snow & dark weather here, & rather cold (but I have just got in a *fourth* cord of oak)—rec'd a letter from John Burroughs—he is at Po'keepsie at present temporarily with his wife & boy & rather blue in health & emotionality (& heart as I call it)—N[elly]'s card came—I am sitting here doing nothing—no Dr B[ucke] yet—he leaves Canada Monday next—I shall seize the first chance to send you the big (complete works) book—

Walt Whitman

1941. *To William Sloane Kennedy*

Camden Feb: 24 '89

The "Magazine of Poetry" reach'd Dr B[ucke] all right—I expect

52. Once again Burroughs wrote, on February 21, in a depressed mood, as he looked back on "old times" in Washington, and lamented: "My life now seems very pale & poor compared with those days. There are but two things now from which I derive any satisfaction—Julian & that bit of land up there on the river bank [he wrote from Poughkeepsie]" (Yale; Traubel, IV, 297). WW could not understand why Burroughs romanticized the Washington days, but he would not agree to Traubel's (obvious) deduction that perhaps Mrs. Burroughs was, as O'Connor suggested, "a devil" (IV, 298).

53. *Mr. Donnelly's Reviewers* was issued posthumously.

him here by Wednesday next—(he expects to practically start that *meter* company & manufacturing)—O'C[onnor] is still very ill—he is yet eager that his late essay backing the pro-Bacon anti-Shaksperean argument sh'd be publish'd[53]—I hope so too—

Nothing very new with me—Am somewhat worse, (side-pains day & night)—There is a good notice in London *Pall-Mall* Jan: 25—Sunny & very cold here—

Walt Whitman

1942. *To William D. O'Connor*

ADDRESS: Wm D O'Connor | 1015 O Street N W | Washington D C. POSTMARK: Camden, N.J. | Feb 24 | 5 PM | 89.

Camden noon Feb: 24 '89

Sitting here by the oak fire dawdling over the Sunday's *Tribune* and the Phil: *Press*—my physical condition rather worse—a depression the last three days & nights—nothing very new—sunny & very cold here—some strangely favorable notices ab't my books lately, (Paris, London & Chicago)—I expect Dr B[ucke] here Tuesday evn'g—Best love to you and N[elly]—

Walt Whitman

1943. *To William Sloane Kennedy*

Camden Feb: 25 '89

Yours of 22d rec'd[54]—I send the little German trans: from Zurich (At y'r leisure, give me a sort of English abstract of Knortz's and Rolleston's prefaces in front)[55]—I am quite unwell—Dr B[ucke] will probably be here to-morrow evn'g—I have rec'd a letter f'm Sarrazin Paris[56]—he has the big "complete" book—his book (with L of G. &c article) will be out soon & he will send me one, wh' I will lend you—I suppose you rec'd the Dr B trans: of S I sent—

Walt Whitman

54. Kennedy informed WW that he was sending his manuscript to Gardner because he was dissatisfied with Wilson: "He acts like an imbecile to me" (Feinberg).

55. WW received the book of translations by Knortz and Rolleston, *Grashalme*, on February 25 (CB). Kennedy sent the requested translation on February 27 (Yale; Traubel, IV, 381; reprinted in Traubel, IV, 382–385).

56. Sarrazin on February 14 thanked WW for the copy of *Complete Poems & Prose*, and expressed his "admiration . . . with all my love for one I considered, from my first reading of him, as one of the best and the greatest men of the time" (Lion).

1944. *To William D. O'Connor*

ADDRESS: Wm D O'Connor | 1015 O Street N W | Washington D C. POSTMARKS: Camden, N.J. | Feb 26 | 8 PM | 89; Washington, Rec'd. | Feb 27 | 7 AM | 89 | 7.

Camden Feb: 26 '89

Fine sunshiny cold day—Dr Bucke is here, got in to-day all right —crowded with the *meter* company & capital & manufactoring matter— wants to come over to W[ashington] & see you, & probably will—but no day yet fixed—Rather miserable with me, constipation, cold in the head & now a bad *spleen* trouble (enlargement &c)—Have rec'd the German trans: L of G. (200 pp)—Shall I send you one?

Walt Whitman

1945. *To William D. O'Connor*

ADDRESS: Wm D O'Connor | 1015 O Street N W | Washington | D C. POSTMARKS: Camden, N.J. | Feb 27 | 8 PM | (?); Washington, Rec'd. | Feb 28 | 8 AM | 89 | 1.

Camden Feb: 27 '89

So-so with me—not as well even as usual—Dr B[ucke] is full of *the meter* business (the invention patented & company forming)—Am sitting here alone by the oak fire—dark & rain & hail all day—

Dr B will probably come on to W[ashington] (some days hence) in the morning & leave the same evening—Always best sympathy & love to you & N[elly]—

W W

1946. *To William Sloane Kennedy*

Camden Feb: 28 '89

The word f'm O'C[onnor] to-day is more favorable—has at times the use of his eyes—can eat & keep his food—& some general "let up"— Dr B[ucke] is here full of the water-meter enterprise—Keeps him busy enough (that's what he came for)—So so with me—pain steady left side —(spleen trouble Dr says)—I suppose you rec'd the German "Grashalme"—

Walt Whitman

57. A detailed and touching account of the visit to O'Connor appears in Traubel, IV,

1947. *To William D. O'Connor*

ADDRESS: Wm D O'Connor | 1015 O Street N W | Washington | D C. POSTMARKS: Camden, N.J. | Feb 28 | 8 PM | 89; Washington, Rec'd. | Mar 1 | 8 AM | 89 | 4.

Camden Feb: 28 '89

Glad & thankful indeed for N[elly]'s card to-day, of y'r partial "let up" on y'r afflictions & pray it may expand into a favorable & lasting gain —Dr B[ucke] is here quite overwhelm'd with his water-meter starting organization &c—I do not see much of him—Rather poorly with me (the spleen malady added to the others)—Quite possibly Dr B may come on hence on Saturday (2d) returning thence at night—

Walt Whitman

1948. *To John Burroughs*

ADDRESS: John Burroughs | West Park | Ulster Co: New York. POSTMARK: Camden, N. J. | Feb 28 | 8 PM | 89.

Camden Feb: 28 '89

Rather better word f'm O'C[onnor] to-day—the latest days bring a slight "let up" on his condition—eyes better at intervals but bad enough yet—Dr Bucke is here very busy with the water-meter business & starting it practically—all going fairly considering—Dr B expects to go to W[ashingto]n briefly—Not well with me, a bad trouble of spleen malady it seems—The little German translation is out—Shall I send you one?

Walt Whitman

1949. *To William D. O'Connor*

ADDRESS: Wm D O'Connor | 1015 O Street N W | Washington D C. POSTMARK: Camden (?) | Mar (?) | 8 PM | 89.

Camden March 1 '89

The situation ab't the same, weather sunny & fine—Dr B[ucke] expects to go on to W[ashingto]n in the 8.20 train to morrow, Saturday, & see you midday or soon after[57]—Horace Traubel, a young friend, & invalu-

252–263.

able help (printing &c) is going with him, to return in the latter afternoon train. I am sitting here by the fire comfortable.

Walt Whitman

1950. *To William D. O'Connor*

ADDRESS: Wm D O'Connor | 1015 O Street N W | Washington D C. POSTMARK: Camden, N.J. | Mar 3 | 5 PM | 89.

Camden March 3 '89

Am feeling better all day from the encouraging & sunny news my young friend Horace Traubel brings back to me of you—God grant it may all be fulfill'd, & I have great trust it will. H T will send hence (March 4) two copies of my big book by express, one for you & one for Nelly—yours has the German booklet also—if you want more of the Sarrazin trans: I can send them—I have not yet seen Dr B[ucke] but it is sure he & H T had a happy & *illuminating* visit—

Walt Whitman

1951. *To William D. O'Connor*

ADDRESS: Wm D O'Connor | 1015 O Street N W | Washington | D C. POSTMARKS: Camden, N.J. | Mar 4 | 8 PM | 89; Washington, Rec'd. | Mar 5 | 10 AM | 89 | 4.

Camden March 4 '89 | P M

Hope you have better weather in y'r Washington spree &c than we here—dark, rainy, half fog, & every way mean & untravelable here—I am still buoyed with the favorable news they bring from you—Dr, Horace & Wm Gurd (the inventor) here this afternoon—every thing goes favorably with the meter enterprise.

I am sitting here by the fire & gaslight, near 7—don't you get these cards early forenoon?—

W W

58. For an account of the lecture, see Traubel, IV, 287–288. After reading Bucke's address WW observed: "I must confess he has plastered it on pretty thick: . . . plastered it on not only a good deal more than I deserve but a good deal more than I like" (IV,

1952. *To William D. O'Connor*

ADDRESS: Wm D O'Connor | 1015 O Street N W | Washington | D C. POSTMARK: Camden, N.J. | Mar 5 | 8 PM | 89.

Camden March 5 '89

Suppose you & N[elly] have rec'd y'r big books by this time—I can hardly tell why, but feel very positively that if any thing can justify my revolutionary attempts & utterances it is such *ensemble*—like a great city to modern civilization, & a whole combined clustering paradoxical identity a man, a woman—

Rather dull here with me, no mail to-day, & I am sitting here alone, wearied with the very sight of papers & books—Dr B[ucke] was in here an hour ago—

Walt Whitman

1953. *To William D. O'Connor*

ADDRESS: Wm D O'Connor | 1015 O Street N W | Washington | D C. POSTMARK: Camden, N.J. | Mar 6 | 8 PM | 89.

Camden March 6 '89

Bright & sunny & just right temperature to-day—Dr B[ucke] has been in for half an hour—the prospects of the *meter* inauguration & practically being made & marketed are good—one thing & another delaying as was to be expected—but I guess it will all finâle in an extensive accepted & actual & prosperous thing—So mote it be—Dr gave his piece (abt L of G &c) last evn'g to the "Ethical Society" Phila: marked success[58]—Not physical comfortable to-day, bad head & trouble with the spleen—still here in the big arm chair with the big wolfskin back—

W W

N[elly]'s card came this P M[59]—

1954. *To John H. and Alma Calder Johnston*

TRANSCRIPT.

Camden, N. J., March 7, 1889

I am still quite bodily helpless—imprison'd the same in my 2d

292).

59. Mrs. O'Connor's card of March 5 acknowledged receipt of WW's book (Syracuse; Traubel, IV, 292).

story sick room . . . but get along sort o' comfortable. Dr. Bucke is here on his meter invention . . . O'Connor is rather easier (but pretty sick).

Walt Whitman

1955. *To William D. O'Connor*

ADDRESS: Wm D O'Connor | 1015 O Street N W | Washington | D C. POSTMARK: Camden, N.J. | Mar 7 | 8 PM | 89.

Camden March 7 '89 | 6:50 P M

Have come thro' the monotonous day much the same as usual—sold two big books to-day—Dr B[ucke] in for an hour, busy yet with the meter—every thing moving slowly, but no serious impediment—

Sitting here alone by gas light—dinner an hour or so ago—breakfast at 9½ a m—mostly free from serious pain—

Walt Whitman

1956. *To William D. O'Connor*

ADDRESS: Wm D O'Connor | 1015 O Street N W | Washington | D C. POSTMARK: Camden, N.J. | Mar 8 | 8 PM | 89.

Camden March 8 '89

Rather a bad day with me but the sunniest cheeriest look outside—Dr [Bucke] is somewhere over at Phila: with a party testing the meter at some office at experts—no doubt the m[eter] will stand that & every other test—

Alone all day & in the room—one of the watermen came to see me yesterday afternoon & told me all ab't the river & ferry (of wh' I knew so much & was fond—b[u]t now kept from a year & more)—

Love to you and N[elly]—

Walt Whitman

1957. *To Ellen M. O'Connor* *3.9–10. [1889]*

ADDRESS: Mrs: E M O'Connor | 1015 O Street N W | Washington | D C. POSTMARKS: (?) | Mar 10 | 5 PM | 89(?); Washington, Rec'd. | Mar 11 | 2(?) AM | 89 | 7.

328 Mickle Street Camden | March 9 P M

Y'r card came this mn'g & makes me gloomy all day[60]—was hop-

60. On March 8 Mrs. O'Connor wrote that two days earlier William "had *five* of

ing from Dr's and Horace's acc't's there would likely be a good, a long continuation of "let up" and easier time—& hope indeed when this comes, there will be again—

Matters here ab't "the same subject continued" as my former writing —I don't see much of Dr B—he is engrossed with the meter business—& has many acquaintances & invitations—& much to do any how—expects to return to Canada early the coming week.

Sunday noon March 10

A raw not clear day—Dr B and Horace call'd—nothing specially new—much sympathy for Wm & prayers & hopes he is better much—Dr B is probably to return home within a day or so—much depends on him there—I am suffering among the rest with a bad obstinate lingering cold in the head—sitting here alone by the stove as I write—Best love—

Walt Whitman

1958. *To William D. O'Connor*

ADDRESS: Wm D O'Connor | 1015 O Street N W | Washington | D C. POSTMARKS: Camden, N. J. | Mar 11 | 8 PM | 89; Washington, Rec'd. | Mar 12 | 7 AM | 89 | 7.

Camden Evn'g: March 11 '89

Disappointed in not getting any word f'm you to-day—sit here as usual alone—often thinking—Dr [Bucke] was in for half an hour—ab't a continuation every way with me—I sent a big book to Stedman to-day—O I hope & pray to get good news from you to-morrow—

Walt Whitman

1959. *To William D. O'Connor*

ADDRESS: Wm D O'Connor | 1015 O Street N W | Washington D C. POSTMARKS: Camden, N.J. | Mar 12 | 8 PM | 89; Washington, Rec'd. | Mar 13 | 7 AM | 89 | 7.

Camden Evn'g March 12 '89

Sunny & fine here—& ab't the same as usual with me—several orders more for the big book—hope you are over & resuscitated & comfort-

those epileptic seizures . . . going from one to another without recovering consciousness" (Syracuse; Traubel, IV, 309).

able again from the attacks of six days ago—have an idea you have a good doctor (Dr Hood) wh' is a great point—Lawyer Harned & Dr [Bucke], & Horace are just off to a swell supper.

W W

1960. *To William D. O'Connor*

ADDRESS: Wm D O'Connor | 1015 O Street N W | Washington D C. POSTMARKS: Camden (?) | Mar (?) | 8 PM | 89; Washington, Rec'd. | Mar 14 | 7 AM | 89 | 7.

Camden March 13 '89

Dr B[ucke] still here but expects to go in a day or two—the meter enterprise goes on swimmingly—N[elly]'s card rec'd & welcom'd this forenoon.[61] I am sitting here by the stove as usual—have just sent over five big books to McKay, on order—Fine & sunny here. (Spring is creeping along rapidly). F'm fair to middling with me—barring bad cold in the head & stupid monotony—

Walt Whitman

1961. *To William D. O'Connor*

ADDRESS: Wm D O'Connor | 1015 O Street N W | Washington | D C. POSTMARK: Camden, N.J. | Mar 14 | 8 PM | 89.

Camden March 14 '89

N[elly]'s card came this mn'g & has given me comfort all day with its favorable tidings[62]—sent it to Dr B[ucke] (whom I have not seen for two days)—Miss Eliz: P Gould of Boston call'd to-day—quite pleasant. (Some few of my most determined friends & understanders appear to be in Boston)—Rather dull with me to-day—

W W

1962. *To William D. O'Connor*

ADDRESS: Wm D O'Connor | 1015 O Street N W | Washington | D C. POSTMARK: Camden, N.J. | Mar 15 | 8 PM | 89.

Camden March 15 '89

Dull & rather bad day with me—so I fear I cannot write any thing

61. Mrs. O'Connor reported on March 12 that "Wm. has recovered his mental balance, & is once more rational" (Syracuse; Traubel, IV, 335).

62. She informed WW that "Wm. is gaining, but is very weak" (Syracuse; Traubel, IV, 342).

cheering—but I send in a Dublin magazine a criticism worth reading[63]—Dr B[ucke] is here yet—Hope this will find you gaining & comfortable.

Walt Whitman

1963. *To William Sloane Kennedy*

Camden Evn'g March 17 '89

Matters not very different—the *Transcripts* rec'd—read & sent to O'Connor—O'C had a very bad spell ag'n since I wrote you ab't him (epileptic fits)—but was better three days ago, but weak & in bed—Dr B[ucke] here yet—

I sit here alone same as ever, in my big old chair with the thick wolf-skin back—Mrs Spaulding call'd to-day.[64]

Walt Whitman

1964. *To William D. O'Connor*

ADDRESS: Wm D O'Connor | 1015 O Street N W | Washington | D C. POSTMARKS: Camden (?) | Mar 17 | 5 PM | 89 ; Washington, Rec'd. | Mar 18 | (?) AM | 89 | 7.

Camden Evn'g March 17 '89

Pleasant visit f'm Mrs: Spaulding of Boston, friend of L of G. & of me—I rather think Dr [Bucke]'s meter business will be practically started, & will be a success—Horace Traubel will be Secretary.

Things with me abt same—I sit here in my big chair alone most of the time, as ever, same old monotonous story—yet I keep a good front I hope—

Walt Whitman

1965. *To William D. O'Connor*

ADDRESS: Wm D. O'Connor | 1015 O Street N W | Washington | D C. POSTMARKS: Camden (?) | Mar 18 | 8 PM | 89; Washington, Rec'd. | Mar 19 | 7 AM | 89 | 5.

Camden Evn'g March 18 '89

Sunny mild March day—Dr B[ucke] leaves at 8—will be due home

63. *Dublin University Review* for November 1886 contained an article by W. B. Yeats on "The Poetry of Sir William Ferguson" (Traubel, IV, 347).

64. Mrs. A. H. Spaulding on March 27 expressed extravagant gratitude for the visit (Feinberg). On one of her calling cards the poet wrote: "dear friend of L of G & me—a middle-aged lady—I sh'd say—*one of the real circle*" (Feinberg).

in London ab't noon to-morrow—The practical outset of the meter enterprise collapsed at the last moment for the want of capital investors[65]—

N[elly]'s card came this mn'g—I am easier to-day—Hope the cold in the head is "petering out"—

W W

1966. *To William D. O'Connor*

ADDRESS: Wm D O'Connor | 1015 O Street N W | Washington D C. POSTMARK: (Cam(?) | Mar (?) | 8 PM | 89.

Camden March 19 '89

Have rec'd the *Saturday Review* with notice (bad enough, yet essentially taking back their old insults & charges) in wh' y'r name & Dr B[ucke]'s are flung about[66]—will probably send it to you to-morrow—(Horace T has taken it away temporarily—Nothing new with me—if anything different it is I am feeling easier—a dark half raining warmish day here—with me sitting the same alone in big chair—sleep & eat fairly yet—Best love—

Walt Whitman

1967. *To Richard Maurice Bucke*

ADDRESS: Dr R M Bucke | Asylum | London | Ontario Canada. POSTMARK: Camden, N.J. | Mar 19 | 8 PM | 89.

Camden Evn'g March 19 '89

Rec'd the *Saturday Review* with notice of Nov: B. wh' I will send you soon (thro' O'C[onnor])—Nothing different to write ab't—am rather easier in head &c.—a dark half rainy day not cold—sold two books to-day[67]—am sitting here as usual in the big chair dawdling over the papers &c—Rather wonder I feel as well & hearty even as I do—

Walt Whitman

65. For details of the "collapse," see Traubel, IV, 370–371, 402–403.

66. *The Saturday Review of Poetics, Literature, Science, and Art* on March 2 was not nearly so intemperate as WW alleged; it would have none of the excesses of O'Connor and Bucke, but the final paragraph was not without point: "No; let us, if it be ours to lecture on poetry, hold up Walt Whitman as much as any one pleases for an awful example of the fate that waits, and justly waits, on those who think (idle souls!) that there is such a thing as progress in poetry, and that because you have steam-engines and other things which Solomon and Sappho had not, you may, nay must, neglect the lessons of Sappho and Solomon. But let us none the less confess that this strayed reveller, this

1968. *To Arthur Newton Brown*

ADDRESS: Arthur Newton Brown | U S N Library | Annapolis | Md:. POSTMARK: Camden, N.J. | Mar 20 | 8 PM | 88(?).

328 Mickle street | Camden New Jersey
March 20 '89

Dear Sir

Am not definitely certain f'm yours of 18th (rec'd—thanks) whether you request the new big 900 vol. complete poems & prose works —If I were I sh'd send it at once—The price is $6—please if you wish that send me the am't in p o order, & I will immediately dispatch the Vol. by express.[68]

Respectfully &c:

Walt Whitman

1969. *To William Sloane Kennedy*

328 Mickle Street Camden | P M March 20 '89

Y'rs came in mid-day mail—thanks—Dr B[ucke] went back to Canada Monday night—the practical outsetting of the meter enterprise collapsed at the last hour—(but it is settled that it is a genuine & valuable invention)—O'C[onnor] recuperated from the epileptic fits, & at last acc'ts was in bed very weak, but quite over them, & what could be call'd (mildly) improving—you know he has no use at all of the lower legs (knees to feet) from what appears to be absolute paralysis, abnegation—

The *Saturday Review* (March 2) has a rather curious *hot & cold*—*I would but dare not* sort of notice of *Nov: B.* & me, in wh' O'C's and Dr B's names are toss'd ab't superficially & with attempted sarcasm—(You are invited to see what *you* may be destined to)—Horace T continues faithful & regular—was in here two hours ago—I sympathize too with Mr & Mrs Sanborn[69]—I count on Burroughs coming out from his hole yet[70]—Lawyer

dubiously well-bred truant in poetry, is a poet still, and one of the remarkably few poets that his own country has produced." An earlier notice of WW appeared in the journal on May 2, 1868 (287, *n.*76).

67. WW sent Miss Langley, a bookdealer in Reading, England, *Leaves of Grass* and *Specimen Days* for "Mrs: General Faber" (CB), ordered by Miss Langley on March 9 (Feinberg).

68. See 1978.

69. On March 18 Kennedy wrote that Sanborn's twenty-three-year old son had committed suicide (Feinberg).

70. A reference to Burroughs' depressions (see 1939).

Harned & wife have just call'd on me, both welcome (they have fine children & sometimes bring them)—I am sitting here yet as one held by a heavy chain or coil—Yes wonder I get along as I do, as well upon the whole, for I understand how *much worse* all might be—Love to you & to Mrs. K—

Walt Whitman

1970. *To William D. O'Connor*

ADDRESS: Wm D O'Connor | 1015 O Street N W | Washington | D C. POSTMARK: Camden (?) | Mar 20 | 8 PM | 89.

Camden Evn'g March 20 '89

When the *Saturday Review* comes, soon as after convenient send to Dr B[ucke]. I rec'd note from Kennedy to-day—nothing special—he seems to be hard employ'd, long hours (proof reading, big house)—

Dull times with me—constipation & inertia at the fore, & both big—have had my dinner & relish'd it—a dark wet day & evening—a comfortable oak fire—

Walt Whitman

1971. *To Richard Maurice Bucke*

ADDRESS: Dr R M Bucke | Asylum | London | Ontario Canada. POSTMARKS: Camden (?) | Mar (?) | 6 (?) | 8(?) ; Philadelphia, Pa. | Mar | 21 | 7 30 PM | 1889.

Camden March 21 '89

Noon—Feeling pretty well—dark & rainy (the third day)—News not favorable from O'C[onnor] as you will see by enc'd card[71]—I write a few lines every day to him & send Mrs. O'C the Boston paper. The "process" plate (considerably reduced) of that ¾ pict: McK[ay] got in N Y. is good, & I shall use it in book before long—Shall send it you (probably several impressions) soon as I have them printed nicely—definite bowel action this forenoon—the *Sat: Review* (March 2) has either gone to you, or will soon go (A rather curious notice)—I havn't seen

71. Mrs. O'Connor's card of March 20 noted no significant change in William's condition (Feinberg).

Lawyer Harned since you went[71.1]—Horace was in this forenoon—faithful & invaluable as ever—Mrs: Davis has come in for a few moments to see if I am "all right"—Ed has been making up the bed.

Toward sunset

Had a good thorough bath this afternoon, hot water—my "cold" has not altogether withdrawn—I feel it in the head perceptibly enough an hour or two now and then—heavy sloppy muddy day—I almost envy your having such lots to do, responsibilities & strong & well & energetic to do 'em—My *lassitude* is one of the worst points in my condition—but whether Sidney Morse's man's answer (when reproach'd for drunkenness) "Suppose 'twas so intended to be," was right or no—Mrs: Davis's woman's remark is "So it really *is* any how"—& answers all philosophy & argument (up to a certain line you probably say)—Well I will adjust myself for dinner, & hope you & Mrs B & all are having good times—& send my love to all—

Walt Whitman

1972. *To William D. O'Connor*

ADDRESS: Wm D O'Connor | 1015 O Street N W | Washington D C. POSTMARKS: Camden, N.J. | Mar 21 | 6 PM | 89; Washington, Rec'd. | Mar 22 | 7 AM | 89 | 7.

Camden March 21 '89

Am feeling pretty well, but it is now the third dark rainy muddy half-raw day—Have just written to Dr B[ucke]—Hope & pray this will find you better—Have just had a bath & some massage—sitting now in the big chair & wolf skin, sort o' comfortable—Best love to you & N[elly]—

W W

1973. *To William D. O'Connor*

ADDRESS: Wm D O'Connor | 1015 O Street N W | Washington | D C. POSTMARK: Camden (?) | Mar 2(?) | 8 PM | 89.

Camden March 22 '89

Sunny and beautiful & sufficiently mild to-day—Am feeling fairly.

71.1. A fib or a lapse of memory; see 1969. Harned attempted to make the legal arrangements for the manufacture of Bucke's meter.

N[elly]'s card came this mn'g,[72] & I sympathise profoundly with you—hope & pray this will find you comparatively easier & better—Have just a letter from Dr B[ucke]—they went hence to New York a day & night, saw J H Johnston—appear to have made some beginning at practically launching the *meter*. The 4th Vol. American Supplement to *Enc*: *Brit*: (p. 772) has a statistical rather friendly notice ab't me &c[73]—Love—

W W

1974. *To Richard Maurice Bucke*

ADDRESS: Dr R M Bucke | Asylum | London | Ontario Canada. POSTMARK: Camden, N.J. | Mar 22 | (?) PM | 89.

Camden March 22 '89

Sunny & fine & mild to-day—am fairly well—O'C[onnor] is still weakly, badly, vomiting &c—a card from Mrs O'C to day—Yours of 20th rec'd—A long visit from T B H[arned] last evening—talk'd of the meter—plans of launching it here &c.—The 4th Vol. (p 772) of the American Supplement *Brit*: *Encyc*: has a pretty good statistical & friendly notice of me—

W W

1975. *To William Sloane Kennedy*

Camden March 22 '89

Sunny & beautiful to-day here. I am fairly well considering—News *not* of favorable or improving character from O'C[onnor]—has great weakness & fits of vomiting—Dr B[ucke] has got safely home in Canada & resumes his work—the meter project will yet be launched, & go—the last Vol. 4th American Supplement to *Enc*: *Brit*: page 772 has a notice &c of me—

W W

72. According to the note of the preceding day O'Connor's health remained unchanged (Feinberg).

73. Of the article WW commented: "It seems to me here is one of the best brief statements of us—if not the best—that has ever been made. It is true it is severely toned down, but then it is carefully put together: every word tells" (Traubel, IV, 430). (The account of WW appears in the fifth volume of the 1891 reprint of the supplement to the

1976. *To Richard Maurice Bucke* *3.23–24.1889*

ADDRESS: Dr R M Bucke | Asylum | London | Ontario | Canada. POSTMARK: Camden (?) | Mar 24 | 5 PM | 89.

Camden Saturday March 23 '89

Noon—another sunny beautiful day—am in fair order (for me)—secretions & excretions not to be complained of—have just sold a big book & got the money for it—Horace has been in this mn'g—I sent word to McKay (who wants more big books—he has had 45) that I w'd let him have the sheets entire with autograph & plates for $3.33 a set, he to bind them—(this charge I have to pay of $1.28 for binding the vol. half chokes me)—I must get more out of it[74]—The proposed ed'n of L of G. with Annex & Backward Glance (ab't 420 pp) is *to be*—bound (probably) in handsome morocco, pocket-book style, six or eight portraits, & autograph—$5—(shall probably bring it out to commemorate my finishing my 70th year)—a little inscription on title—

Afternoon—another big book sale—T B Aldrich, Boston, who sends $25 for it!—Ed has resumed his flesh-brushing & half-massage on me—had a spell two hours ago—

Sunday 24th—Bright fine weather continued (couldn't be finer)—Hope you have it too & enjoy it—& deeply hope O'C[onnor] is easier & comfortable. Had my breakfast ab't 9, hot oysters & chocolate & Graham bread—McK[ay] declines my proposition—I am sitting here in the big chair—bowel action an hour ago—hope to get downstairs few moments to day—

Walt Whitman

1977. *To Thomas Bailey Aldrich*

328 Mickle street | Camden New Jersey | March 24 '89

Thanks for the money & order wh' were duly rec'd—I have sent the book to you by express, & when you get it safely please send me a card notifying me. Am laid up here disabled & paralyzed, but getting along, & comfortable enough. Best love to you & yours[75]—

Walt Whitman

ninth edition.)

74. Bucke on March 27 observed bluntly: "The price of the book once established cannot well be changed and if McK[ay] paid $3.33 and $1.28 for binding—$4.61—he would have too little profit" (Syracuse).

75. Aldrich acknowledged receipt of the book on March 25 (Feinberg). Aldrich's check for $25 is in the Houghton Library.

1978. *To Arthur Newton Brown*

ADDRESS: A N Brown | Library | Naval Academy | Annapolis Md:. POSTMARK: Camden, N.J. | Mar 2(?) | 5 PM | 8(?).

March 24 '89—328 Mickle st: | Camden New Jersey

According to y'r request I have sent the Vol. (same as this address) by express—When safely rec'd w'd you kindly send me a card notifying me? Pay rec'd. Thanks.

Walt Whitman

1979. *To William D. O'Connor*

ADDRESS: Wm. D O'Connor | 1015 O Street N W | Washington | D C. POSTMARKS: Camden (?) | Mar 24 | 5 PM | 8(?); Washington, Rec'd. | Mar (?) | 2 AM | 89 | 7.

Camden March 24 '89

Another beautiful sunny day. Rec'd a kind letter from T B Aldrich Boston—he buys the big book (sending $25 for it)—Am feeling well (for me)—pass my whole time in the room & chair & bed—wonder I keep up & as good trim & spirits—but believe *I do*—no doctors now for over a month—No visitors to day—no mail—have flesh rubbing & massage daily —Best love to you & N[elly][76]—

Walt Whitman

1980. *To William D. O'Connor*

ADDRESS: Wm D O'Connor | 1015 O Street N W | Washington | D C. POSTMARKS: Camden (?) | Mar 25 | 8 PM | 89; Washington, Rec'd. | Mar 26 | 7 AM | 89 | 7.

Camden March 25 '89

All the same with me—O how I hope this will find you better. Have just had my massage treatment. Is beneficial. An old farmer & his son from Long Island to see me to-day—quite a curiosity—Best love to you & N[elly]—

W W

76. On March 23 Mrs. O'Connor reported that "William has had two epileptic attacks" (Feinberg).

77. Dr. Bucke wrote candidly on March 23: "We must make up our minds to his

1981. *To Richard Maurice Bucke*

ADDRESS: Dr R M Bucke | Asylum | London | Ontario Canada. POSTMARK: Camden, N.J. | Mar 26 | 8 PM | 89.

Camden March 26 '89

Fine weather continued—a little cooler. The news ab't O'C[onnor] in y'r letter & Dr Hood's strikes in & gloomily—& has depress'd me all day[77]—

Much the same with me—feeling fairly, physically—Getting ready for L of G. ed'n to commemorate 70th year finish—have paid the binder's (Oldach) bill for calf bind'g $65.28 & also bill for the ¾ portrait "process" 10.50—McKay was here yesterday—promis'd to come 28th & pay me the 1st Dec. '88 statement (wh' is not yet paid)—have also to pay other bills just come in, wh' I will now be enabled to do—

W W

1982. *To William D. O'Connor*

ADDRESS: Wm D O'Connor | 1015 O Street N W | Washington | D C. POSTMARKS: Philadelphia (?) | Mar 26 | 11 PM | 89; Washington, R(?) | Mar 27 | 7 AM | 89 | 7.

Camden March 26 '89

Have been hoping all day I sh'd get some word & relieving word from you—but nothing—Can only write my sympathy & hope & love—& write on in the dark. Nothing new with me—Sitting here seeking to while away the hours—

Walt Whitman

1983. *To Richard Maurice Bucke*

ADDRESS: Dr R M Bucke | Asylum | London | Ontario | Canada. POSTMARK: (?) | Mar 27 | 8 PM | 89.

Camden March 27 '89

The news is pretty gloomy yet from O'C[onnor] as you see from

death or *worse*—for should he live much longer his life would necessarily become a burden to himself and others" (Syracuse). He enclosed a letter from Dr. T. B. Hood, O'Connor's physician, written on March 19 (Traubel, IV, 426).

the enclosed card[78]—Ab't the same with me as hitherto of late. Cloudy & dull weather. Horace has been in this forenoon—Ed has just been making up the bed &c—I am sitting here in the big chair back'd with the old wolf-skin—not cold to-day, (but half raw)—Six letters rec'd by mail, & five of them autograph applications! (Did I acknowledge the Bury English paper July 13 1880 with y'r California &c narrative wh' I peruse & over again with greatest interest?)[79]

Evn'g—All fair as usual—bowel action—the daylight grows apace—it is 7 & I have just lighted the gas—very quiet—even dull as I write—this goes in the Phila: P O soon after 8 P M—when does it reach you?

I see in this evng's news death of John Bright[80]—a grand star quench'd—Herbert Gilchrist here this afternoon—he says there is late news of Tennyson's bad illness—I havn't seen it—

Walt Whitman

1984. *To Richard Maurice Bucke*

ADDRESS: Dr R M Bucke | Asylum | London | Ontario | Canada. POSTMARK: Camden, N.J. | Mar 28(?) | 6 AM | 89.

Camden | March 28 '89

Every thing keeps on ab't the same as of late. Somewhat of a lull in O'C[onnor]'s sufferings—Y'r letter came at noon—(a beautiful bunch of flowers from Mrs. Spaulding, Boston, same time—they are scenting the room as I write.) Horace and Mr Blake, Unitarian minister f'm Chicago, here this mn'g—pleasant visit—a spell of my currying (massage) f'm Ed at noon to me—(generally have two spells in the twenty four hours, one at bed time)—am getting ready for the special L of G. ed'n I spoke of—

Horace has just gone over to the printer's & paper supplier's—Dave McKay has been over to day—paid me the royalty $55.64 cts. for sales of L of G. and S D on the last six months—& $100 on acc't of big books he has had & sold[81]—write out on a slip all the typo: errors in L of G.—Annex—& Backward Glance—you find—& send me at early convenience—I ask you to write a line to D McK. to let me have a few copies (whatever I require) of your book in sheets, you waiving the royalty—I of course paying him the cost price—

W W

78. The card of March 26 was terse and poignant: "It is most sad & pitiful, & I am glad you can't see him" (Feinberg).
79. Bucke forwarded the article on March 22 (Syracuse).
80. The English statesman and admirer of Lincoln (1811–1889).
81. The receipt and the financial statement appear in Traubel, IV, 440 (Pennsyl-

1985. *To William D. O'Connor*

ADDRESS: Wm D O'Connor | 1015 O Street N W | Washington | D C. POSTMARK: Camden (?) | Mar 29 | 6 AM | 89.

Camden March 28 '89

Thanks for the card from N[elly]—so glad even that it is well as it is.[82] Every thing goes on with me same as before—McKay has just been here & paid me $55.64 for royalties of last six months—I am going to print a small special ed'n of L of G. with Sands at Seventy & Backward Glance as epilogue & am busying myself at it (to commemorate my finishing my 70th year)—Best love—

W W

1986. *To Richard Maurice Bucke*

ADDRESS: Dr R M Bucke | Asylum | London | Ontario Canada. POSTMARK: Camden (?) | Mar 29 | 8 PM | 89.

Camden March 29 '89

A long & good letter f'm Stedman[83] & a present of the big vols: (all yet printed, 7) of his "American Literature" in wh' I appear (with good wood-eng[raving] portrait)—My condition ab't same—bowel action—sit here same pretty dull & stupid—weather fair—cooler—A letter f'm Kennedy—y'rs came—Ed has rec'd a big veterinary book—seems inclined to that study & "business"—

W W

1987. *To William D. O'Connor*

ADDRESS: Wm D O'Connor | 1015 O Street N W | Washington D C. POSTMARK: Camden, N.J. | Mar 29 | 8 PM | 89.

Camden March 29 '89

A long & good letter to-day f'm Stedman—he also sends me the

vania).

82. Mrs. O'Connor's note on the preceding day was encouraging: "Wm. has had the best day to-day of any since the attacks last Sat[urday]" (Feinberg).

83. See 1990. Kennedy wrote on March 28 about the account of WW in Appleton's *New Dictionary of American Biography* (Feinberg).

vols: so far pub'd of "American Literature." (I can see the effect of y'r talks with C[84])—Also letter f'm John Burroughs[85]—they are all back to his own house at West Park—& well—J B has another vol: being set up—Am anchor'd here as usual by the stove—Cooler but bright—

Walt Whitman

1988. *To Richard Maurice Bucke*

ADDRESS: Dr R M Bucke | Asylum | London | Ontario Canada. POSTMARKS: Camden, N.J. | Mar (?) | 5 PM | 89; London | AM | Ap 2 | 89 | Canada.

Camden March 31 '89

Just a word any how. Nothing new or different—Pretty dull—my cold in the head rampant—I am trying to while the day with the *Press* and N Y *Tribune*—Mr and Mrs Harned to call on me—

Walt Whitman

1989. *To William D. O'Connor*

ADDRESS: Wm D O'Connor | 1015 O Street N W | Washington D C. POSTMARKS: Camden, N.J. | Mar 31 | 5 PM | 89; Washington, Rec'd. | Apr 1 | 2 AM | 89 | 7.

Camden March 31 '89

Thanks for N[elly]'s card & am cheer'd much[86]—Have been looking at some vols: Stedman's great "American Literature"—It is a deep mine & probably best of that sort of thing—Much the same with me as before—A lady has just made & sent me in some ice cream, of which I took moderately (if you ever have trouble with qualmish revolting stomach, try ice cream—I have more than once found it a great help)—

Walt Whitman

84. Stedman; why WW used the initial *C*, not *E*, I do not know. On March 2, when Traubel and Bucke visited him, O'Connor said: "I have had many talks with Stedman and have, I am confident, broken down most of his remaining prejudices against Walt" (Traubel, IV, 256).

85. On March 28 Burroughs mentioned his new book: "A collection of Indoor Essays; rather a piece of bookmaking—not much worth" (University of Kansas; Traubel, IV, 449).

1990. *To Edmund Clarence Stedman*

ADDRESS: Edmund C Stedman | 3 east Fourteenth Street | (C E Webster Publisher's) | New York City. POSTMARK: Camden (?) | Mar 31 | 5 PM | 89.

328 Mickle Street | Camden New Jersey
March 31 '89

Thanks, my dear E C S, for the box of noble books with the endless mines in them—& double thanks for the loving cheering (I fear flattering) long letter, wh' has done me good, & I have read twice—My friendly & liberal presentation 7th Vol. is thoroughly appreciated by me —& the picture is certainly printed at its best—The whole presentation indeed is by far the best of that sort I ever received. I wish to convey my best regards to the printers, proof-readers & print-plate presser &c[87]—

I have been specially laid up for nearly a year almost entirely disabled —imprison'd in sick room—last fall & during winter sometimes low, serious, but just now easier, comparatively free from pain—getting along better than you might suppose.

Our dear friend O'Connor is very ill at Washington (lower legs paralyzed, & lately attacks of epilepsy)—Burroughs is pretty well—is at his place West Park Ulster Co: with his wife & boy (with a book in press, I believe)—Best regards & love to you & yours—Have put off this letter of thanks & good wishes waiting for a day I sh'd feel pretty well to write it in, but such day lagging I delay no longer—

Walt Whitman

1991. *To William D. O'Connor*

ADDRESS: Wm D O'Connor | 1015 O Street N W | Washington D C. POSTMARKS: Camden, N.J. | Apr 2 | 8 PM | 89; Washington, Rec'd. | Apr 3 | 7 AM | 89 | 7.

Camden Evn'g April 2 '89

A word for you only as the young man is waiting to go to P O—All ab't same with me—Wretched f'm cold in the head—Raining hard—Love to you & N[elly]—

W W

86. According to the message of March 29, William was somewhat improved (Syracuse; Traubel, IV, 451).

87. Stedman, who termed himself on March 27–28 "one of your most faithful lovers," gushed about the *Complete Poems & Prose*: "There is no book just like this, & there never will be" (Feinberg; *Life and Letters of Edmund Clarence Stedman* [1910], II, 120–122). WW received more space in *The Library of American Literature* than any other poet. Stedman printed Linton's wood engraving of the poet. See 981 for WW's earlier reaction to Stedman's criticism.

1992. *To Richard Maurice Bucke*

ADDRESS: Dr R M Bucke | Asylum | London | Ontario Canada. POSTMARKS: Camden, N.J. | Apr 5 | 6 AM | 89; N.Y. | 4–5–89 | 10 30 AM | 2.

Camden April 4 '89

The "cold in head" still grips me. As I write the sun shines out clear & inspiriting—y'r letter comes—Ed has been down to the bank to deposit some cheques for me[88]—My sister from Burlington[89] has just been here & the sweetest young 16 y'r girl that exists—most magnetic & attractive & blended—I am sitting here in the big chair & every thing goes on ab't the same as ever.

Walt Whitman

1993. *To William D. O'Connor*

ADDRESS: Wm D O'Connor | 1015 O Street N W | Washington | D C. POSTMARK: Camden (?) | Apr (?) | 6 (?) | 8(?)

Camden April 4 '89

Interest myself (partially) with the 7 vols. I have rec'd of Stedman's "Am: Literature"—some new things & some older. Grant's & Sherman's &c. quite fascinate me.[90] (I am in the 7th Vol. & at better presentation, picture &c. than you might fancy)—Am still under my "cold in the head" *misery* (to use the word of the Virginia blacks—& a very fitting one in this case)—Best love.

Walt Whitman

1994. *To Richard Maurice Bucke*

ADDRESS: Dr R M Bucke | Asylum | London | Ontario Canada. POSTMARK: Camden (?) | Apr 7 | 5 PM | 89.

Camden April 7 '89

Y'r letters arrived & welcome—My card yesterday f'm Mrs:

88. The checks amounted to $196.64 (CB).
89. Louisa Orr Whitman.
90. The selections from Grant and Sherman appear in *The Library of American*

O'C[onnor] speaks of our dear friend as having *a good night* previous—& sitting up next forenoon—Nothing new with me—Horace, Tom, Mrs: H[arned] and Mr Morehouse[91] have just call'd—My cold in the head still on—cloudy & raw weather—Am sitting here in the big chair alone—have had two moderate sweating spells past two days—

Walt Whitman

1995. *To William Sloane Kennedy*

Camden April 7 '89

Much the same with me (a long bad cold in the head)—I hear often from Dr B[ucke]—The latest news from O'C[onnor] is of being a little easier—(but he is very ill)—Rough weather here—

Walt Whitman

1996. *To William D. O'Connor*

ADDRESS: Wm D O'Connor | 1015 O Street N W | Washington D C. POSTMARKS: Camden, N.J. | Apr 7 | 5 PM | 89; Washington, Rec'd. | Apr 8 | 2 AM | 89 | 7.

Camden April 7 '89

Hope this will find you at ease & comfortable—With me every thing continues on much the same—am slowly getting on with the new (pocket-book) ed'n L of G. with Annex bits & Backw'd Glance at end—My cold in the head still keeps on & pretty bad—have just had several visitors—

Walt Whitman

1997. *To Susan Stafford*

ADDRESS: Mrs: Susan Stafford | Kirkwood | (Glendale) | New Jersey. POSTMARK: Camden, N.J. | Apr 7 | 5 PM | 89.

Camden April 7 '89

Quite a while now since I have seen or heard of any of you—How are you all—George, & Ed & Harry & all?

Literature, VII, 573–580, and 550–555, respectively.

91. Moorhouse or Morehouse, a Unitarian minister in Camden (Traubel, v, 4, 508).

I am here coop'd up just as closely & helpless as ever—don't get my health or strength an atom more—Sit up most of the time days here in the great arm chair with the old wolf-skin spread back—trying to pass away the time (& succeeding after a fashion) but some days very low indeed.

Love to you all—

Walt Whitman

1998. *To Richard Maurice Bucke*

ADDRESS: Dr R M Bucke | Asylum | London | Ontario Canada. POSTMARK: Camden, N.J. | Apr 8 | 8 PM | 89.

Camden April 8 '89

Shall send you Stedman's letter in a day or two—it is well worth reading—Nothing very new—As I smell the fumes of the cooking while I write, thankful that they do not seem utterly welcomeless to me as so much (books, magazines &c) do. Well, here comes my dinner—

W W

1999. *To William Sloane Kennedy, William D. O'Connor, and Richard Maurice Bucke*

ENDORSED: "Kennedy please send all to | Wm O'Connor | & O'C please send on | to Dr Bucke."

328 Mickle Street | Camden New Jersey | April 8 '89

The enclosed is Stedman's letter ab't the "Complete" I tho't you m't like to read—(T B Aldrich's also tho' short is very friendly & eulogistic—not sent here)—

Nothing in my condition &c specially notable—but the pegs are gradually loosening, perhaps being slowly pull'd out—I have been kept in here now almost a year, (not been out doors once in that time—hardly out of the sick room)—but as before said I get along more comfortably than you might suppose—had lots of Doctors but they have all vanished—fair nights & tolerable days—Am busying myself with a new ed'n of L of G. with "Sands at 70" and "Backward Glance" all in one Vol. bound (in thinner paper) in pocket-book style, I have had a notion for, & now put out partly to occupy myself, & partly to commemorate finishing my 70th year—

Sit up mainly all day—at present (as so often told) in my big arm chair with the thick wolf skin spread on the back—writing this on the tablet on my lap—early afternoon—fairly comfortable—a good oak fire—raw & dark weather out—Love & good prospects to all—

Walt Whitman

2000. *To Dr. Karl Knortz*

TRANSCRIPT.

Camden, N. J. April 8, '89

The enclosed was brought this morning by the carrier. Suppose you received some copies of the "Grashalme," as I did from Rolleston.

Am still laid up here by disablement and paralysis—am confined entirely to my room and mostly to my chair. I received your acknowledgment of the big book "Complete Works."

Dr. Bucke is well—hard at work managing the big Insane Asylum at London, Ontario, Canada. My dear friend O'Connor is very ill at Washington. Am sitting here in big arm chair (with great wolf skin spread back) as I write—raw dark day—keep up pretty good spirits.

Walt Whitman

2001. *To William D. O'Connor*

ADDRESS: Wm D O'Connor | 1015 O Street N W | Washington | D C. POSTMARKS: Camden, N.J. | Apr 8 | 8 PM | 89; Washington, Rec'd. | Apr 9 | (?) AM | 89 | 7.

Camden April 8 '89

Have been trying to while the last two or three hours with the labors, good & ill fortunes &c (well told) of antiquarian Lord Elgin[92] in Greece nearly 100 years ago. Hope this idle card will find you resting & easy—nothing new with me—

Walt Whitman

2002. *To Richard Maurice Bucke*

ADDRESS: Dr R M Bucke | Asylum | London | Ontario Canada. POSTMARK: Camden (?) | Apr 11 | 8 PM | 89.

Camden April 11 '89

Y'r cheery little letter has just come—have just finished & sent to

92. Thomas Bruce, earl of Elgin (1766–1841).

the printer a little two page preface (so to call it) that has to be eked out in the Backward Glance for 70th y'r ed'n L of G—

Am having bad hours (& now seven or eight days) with the damnable cold & constipation leagued—

W W

2003. *To William D. O'Connor*

ADDRESS: Wm D O'Connor | 1015 O Street N W | Washington D C. POSTMARKS: Camden, N.J. | Apr 11 | 8 PM | 89; Washington, Rec'd. | Apr 12 | 8 AM | 89 | 7.

Camden April 11 '89

Splendid sunny perfect weather here—I sit with my window open —friendly notices from Chicago[93]—Am busying myself with a special L of G. ed'n (to be trimm'd close & bound pocket book style) to include Sands at 70 and "Backward Glance"—Am quite miserable from the join'd cold & constipation ruling me now over a week—A good letter just from Dr B[ucke]—

Walt Whitman

2004. *To Richard Maurice Bucke*

ADDRESS: Dr R M Bucke | Asylum | London | Ontario | Canada. POSTMARK: Camden, N.J. | Apr 14 | 5 PM | 89.

Camden April 14 '89

Fine sunny weather—nothing special in my health—(if any difference am suffering less from the join'd "cold in the head" & constipation firm)—am sitting here in the big chair—have been trying to eke out a two-page preface for the new reprint of Backw'd Glance of 70th y'r ed'n of L of G. & shall send off to the printer what I have, hit or miss—

Sleep at night pretty well—appetite poor—Did you get the letter (via O'C[onnor]) containing Stedman's? Have not heard from O'C for a week —am a little anxious—Harned & Mrs. H here & little Tom—Horace faithful as always—Ed all right—the doctors all abstinent—havn't had a call for two months—Signs of spring—longer days—presents of little

93. William W. Payne forwarded on April 7 his review of *November Boughs* in the Chicago *Evening Journal* of March 16 (Feinberg).

94. See 2011 and 2006.

95. See 1999.

bunches of flowers—had a letter from our friend R P Smith—England (enclosed)—The letter from Kennedy also enclosed[94]—I have made no answer or opinion to him ab't it—

God bless you & all—very partial sort o' restricted bowel actions, ab't every other day—seem natural—took a calomel powder night before last—often the Frederickshall water—

Walt Whitman

2005. *To William D. O'Connor*

ADDRESS: Wm D O'Connor | 1015 O Street N W | Washington | D C. POSTMARKS: Camden (?) | Apr 14 | 5 PM | 89; Washington, Rec'd. | Apr 15 | 8 AM | 89 | 7.

Camden April 14 '89

Fine sunny coolish day—Ab't same as before with me—(fancy less *rub-a-dub* in my brain from the "cold in the head" & constipation coalition)—Hope to hear (& good news) f'm you to-night or to-morrow—Have you rec'd mine, & Stedman to me enclosed, I sent you via Kennedy?[95] Have just written to Dr B[ucke]—Best love to you and N[elly]—

Walt Whitman

2006. *To William Sloane Kennedy*

Camden April 16 '89

Nothing very different or new in my affairs—the past ten days bad rather—sort of suspicion of lull to-day—y'r last rec'd—have no opinion or comment or suggestion to make[96]—did you receive (& send on to O'C[onnor]) my letter with Stedman's enc'd? Am sitting here alone as usual.

Walt Whitman

2007. *To Richard Maurice Bucke*

ADDRESS: Dr R M Bucke | Asylum | London | Ontario Canada. POSTMARK: Camden, N.J. | 16 Apr | 8 PM.

Camden April 16 '89

Cloudy raw weather—(may be part of my glum condition)—No

96. This was a cold rejoinder to Kennedy's announcement on April 8 that Gardner was going to publish "Walt Whitman, Poet of Humanity" "in 2 vols." WW offered no opinion about Gardner's request to delete "the censor's list of objectionable passages" in the Osgood edition (Feinberg).

word from O'C[onnor] now for a week and over—write a card to him to-night, & to Kennedy—Good words &c from big printed quarters (N Y *World* and *Herald*)[97]—if I get them will send you—

W W

2008. *To William D. O'Connor*

ADDRESS: Wm D O'Connor | 1015 O Street N W | Washington | D C. POSTMARKS: Camden, N.J. | 16 Apr | 8 PM; Washington, Rec'd. | Apr 17 | 7 AM | 89 | 7.

Camden April 16 '89

Much disappointed the last two days at not getting word f'm you. Pray this may find you comfortable. Nothing new or different with me—have had bad ten days, head, stomach, &c—Suspicion however of slight lull to-day—Some good words of me in big printed quarters (such as N Y *World*, *Herald*, &c)—Sit here in big chair ab't same—Love to you and N[elly]—

W W

2009. *To Richard Maurice Bucke*

ADDRESS: Dr R M Bucke | Asylum | London | Ontario Canada. POSTMARK: Camden (?) | 17 Apr | (?) PM.

Camden April 17 '89

Y'rs came—welcome—I send some papers—the "sayings" of the Japanee[98] make Horace frantic angry—they are invented or distorted most horribly—I take it all phlegmatically—Dark, heavy, raw day, & my feelings ab't same.

Love—

Walt Whitman

97. Richard Hinton's three-column article "Walt Whitman at Home" appeared in the New York *World* on April 14. WW observed to Traubel: "It seems like three crowded columns of gush. . . . It may seem ungracious . . . to say so (for Dick is my friend and means me well) but his piece impresses me most by its emptiness—impresses me as a big tumor or boil, much swelled, inflamed, bulging, but nothing after all" (Traubel, v, 40, 48). Hartmann's article "Walt Whitman. Notes of a Conversation with the Good Gray Poet by a German Poet and Traveller" appeared in the New York *Herald* on April 14. For WW's reactions, see 2009 and 2026; also Traubel, v, 33–36, 38–39. Bucke prepared a correction for the *Herald* which was not printed (Traubel, v, 136).

2010. *To William D. O'Connor*

ADDRESS: Wm D O'Connor | 1015 O Street N W | Washington | D C. POSTMARK: Camd(?) | 17 Apr | 8 PM.

Camden April 17 '89

A heavy saturated leaden day—& my condition ab't the same. N[elly]'s card came yesterday—my best prayers for more mark'd improvement—I have just sent off books bo't in England—one Dr B[ucke]'s book specially sent for[99]—I have just finished my supper: dinner.

Love—

Walt Whitman

2011. *To Mary Smith Costelloe*

ADDRESS: Mrs: Mary Whitall Costelloe | 40 Grosvenor Road | the Embankment | London England. POSTMARKS: Camden (?) | Apr 19 | 8 PM | (?); Philadelphia, Pa. | Apr 20 | 4 PM | Paid.

Camden N J U S America | April 19 '89

Am still anchor'd here in my second story in Mickle street—not much different, yet every month letting the pegs lower—Have not sent the big books (complete ed'n) but shall soon.

Fondest love to little Rachel & the newcomer too—I rec'd the good letter f'm y'r dear father, also Mrs S[mith]'s card[1]—Is his address still at 44? I am preparing a new ed'n of L of G. & shall send you one.

Walt Whitman

2012. *To Richard Maurice Bucke*

ADDRESS: Dr R M Bucke | Asylum | London | Ontario Canada. POSTMARK: Camden (?) | Apr 22 | 8 PM | 89.

Camden April 22 '89

The best news to-day is the saving of those 750 Danmark voyag-

98. Hartmann; see preceding note.

99. He sent Bucke's biography and two copies of *November Boughs* to Miss Langley (*CB*).

1. Writing on March 31, Smith informed WW of events in the family: Alys was to attend Bryn Mawr College in the fall, Logan was studying at Oxford, and Mrs. Costelloe had a second child (Feinberg). His wife Hannah wrote on March 13 to WW about her granddaughter's birth (Feinberg; *Smith Alumnae Quarterly* [February, 1958], 88). Mrs. Smith was no admirer of the poet, who said of her: "She still believes that the world is to be persuaded, driven into salvation. I do not—never did!" (Traubel, v, 53).

ers, wh' quite gives additional glow to this fine weather[2]—Y'r letter and Mrs: O'C[onnor]'s note rec'd—

I continue much the same—rec'd letter from Alys Smith, from Eng: from Mary's house—all ab't well—the new ed'n gets on slowly but fairly. Harned's fine baby here yesterday—splendid child—Ed has gone out for a stretch.

Walt Whitman

2013. *To William D. O'Connor*

ADDRESS: Wm D O'Connor | 1015 O Street N W | Washington D C. POSTMARK: Camden (?) | Apr 2(?) | 8 P(?) | 89.

Camden April 22 '89

Decidedly the best news to-day is the saving of the wreck'd Danmark's 750 passengers & crew—out from the very jaws of death!

Fine sunny weather here—Every thing continuing on the same with me—Letter from Dr B[ucke]. He has rec'd the S[tedman] letter & likes it well—I am entirely pleased with the presentation (selections & portrait) S makes of me—

Walt Whitman

2014. *To Alys Smith*

ADDRESS: Miss Alys Smith | 40 Grosvenor Road | the Embankment | London | S W | England. POSTMARK: Camden (?) | Apr 2(?) | 8 PM | 89.

Camden N J U S America | April 22 '89

Y'r welcome letter has come & Mary's word—my best love to all, not forgetting the dear little ones—

Nothing very new with me—am still a prisoner here in Mickle Street 2d story, sitting at this moment in the big ratan chair—are you (father, mother, &c) domiciled still at 44?—Yesterday here almost hot—

Walt Whitman

2. On April 22 the New-York *Tribune* reported that the passengers aboard the *Danmark* had been rescued by the *Missouri*. See also Traubel, v, 66.

3. Stedman was hurt because WW refused to disavow publicly Hartmann's report that the poet considered Stedman a "dancing master"; see Stedman's letter to Traubel (v, 68).

4. On April 25 the New-York *Tribune* reported that Captain Hamilton Murrell of the *Missouri* "now has the record of saving more human beings from death than any master of a ship in the past."

2015. *To Richard Maurice Bucke*

ADDRESS: Dr R M Bucke | Asylum | London | Ontario | Canada. POSTMARK: Camden (?) | Apr 25 | 8 PM | 89.

Camden April 25 '89

Not much difference—restricted bowel action, every day or two, (enough "to swear by")—still live on mutton-broth, Graham bread, coffee or tea, mainly—appetite fair—nights fair—no doctors, not one, now for two months—(is it a good sign?)—have taken a calomel powder three or four evn'gs ago, & shall probably take another to-night—write for me plainly the proper calomel prescription—*a trifle stronger dose if you think proper*—& send me in your next—(I think I w'd prefer to have it from Brown's place 5th and Federal)—

Pleasantish weather, a little raw and dusty—we need rain, & will probably soon have it—

Stedman is *mad* over that Japanee's item in the *Herald* of my (invented opinion) lines ab't him—he, S, has written to Horace T. in answer to H T's to him, disavowing the authenticity[3]—Much *furore* & newspaper reporting here in Phila: over Capt: Murrell of the Missouri the last three days[4]—I see by the slip in this mn'g's *Phil: Record* a great change, wh' see.[5] I had not heard of it before—

All y'r letters come & are welcome. The enc: card rec'd from Mrs: O'C[onnor] to day[6]—New ed'n of L of G. progressing—Horace was here to-day—My "cold in the head" still adheres to me—Ed is well—Am sitting here in the big chair alone comparatively comfortable—Best love to you & all—

Walt Whitman

2016. *To William Sloane Kennedy*

Camden April 25 '89

Y'r card just rec'd[7]—papers come regularly—thanks—Nothing very different with me—Still imprison'd—my dilapidation not mending

5. The item, pasted on the letter, referred to a government proclamation that would prevent Canada from being "a haven" for American criminals.

6. Mrs. O'Connor reported on April 24 that William was still "very sick & weak since I wrote you . . . 'throwing up' at all times of day & night" (Feinberg).

7. On April 24(?) Kennedy wrote: "Your Homeric lines on the dandelion ["The First Dandelion"] . . . are as immortal as those of Burns or Wordsworth on the daisy" (Feinberg). Kennedy's card of April 18(?) was unenthusiastic about Stedman's book: "Good for cross-road school-houses, I suppose" (Feinberg).

(slowly gradually worse if any thing, but not much change)—am preparing my (to me) most satisfactory new really complete ed'n L of G. including "Sands" and epilogue "Glance"—will send you one—Am sitting here in the big chair sort o' comfortable—alone all day—O'C[onnor] still very sick—Dr B[ucke] well & busy—

Walt Whitman

2017. *To Susan Stafford*

ADDRESS: Mrs: Susan Stafford | Kirkwood | (Glendale) | New Jersey. POSTMARK: Camden (?) | Ap(?) | 8 PM | 89.

328 Mickle St: Camden | April 25 '89

The spirit seems to move me to write you a line even if no account —Here I am yet the same cribb'd up in chair & room, & little or no prospect—yet sort o' cheery hearted & comfortable (it might be worse, you know)—How are you all & getting along—George & Ed & Harry & Van & Deb?—Mont was here Sunday & very welcome—I hear often from Dr B[ucke]. Herbert is all right—

Walt Whitman

2018. *To William D. O'Connor*

ADDRESS: Wm D O'Connor | 1015 O Street N W | Washington | D C. POSTMARKS: Camden (?) | Apr 26 | 8 PM | 89; Washington, Rec'd. | Apr 27 | 6 AM | 89 | 7.

Camden April 26 '89

Deeply hope this will find you easy & comfortable—N[elly]'s card rec'd yesterday—weather rainy wh' we wanted—temperature mild—I have a big bunch of lilacs on the table near, (from my yard)—Have been looking over some vols: Stedman's big "Am: Literature"—seems to be all admirably done—I was reading Paul Jones's report to Congress (on his fight with the Serapis)[8]—it all came back to me.

Love always—

Walt Whitman

8. Stedman's *The Library of American Literature*, III, 380–387.

9. On April 24 Bucke wrote of "the John Hopkins Hospital. Walt, if I were in your fix I would think seriously of going there for the next six months or a year . . . as a private patient. . . . I do not suppose the expence would be much more than the present

2019. *To Richard Maurice Bucke* 4.27–28.1889

ADDRESS: Dr R M Bucke | Asylum | London | Ontario | Canada. POSTMARK: Camden, N.J. | Apr 28 | (?) PM | 89.

Camden April 27 '89

Y'r good letter rec'd—ab't the Balt. Hospital idea it does not at present come to me any thing like decidedly—but will probably have some more definite feeling soon[9]—the cloudy & rainy spell continued to-day—quite a sort o' bowel movement this forenoon—(took a cal[omel] powder last night & some bitter water this morning)—rare egg, fried, Graham b'd and coffee for breakfast—am to have three or four rare stew'd oysters for my supper ab't 5—(I eat no dinner)—all goes sort o' comfortable—gloomy & rainy enough out tho'—mild rather—

Sunday afternoon April 28

Well it just looks out like clearing & sunshine—so mote it be—Nothing very different with me—my head &c: the "cold" & stuffy (is it catarrh?) heavy, deaf, half-ache feeling—have been trying to interest myself in the *Press* and the *Tribune* to-day—poor work—rather dull to-day, (& indeed these days)—

Yes the sun comes out stronger—promising great things for the New York show, wh' seems to be much made of all around here[10]—I enc: two or three cards &c: (like the dinner givers put on some extra dishes, even if not much appetizing in them they fill up)—the new ed'n of L of G. will have six little portraits in—all goes on smoothly—am sitting here by a pretty good fire as it is coolish—Best love to you all—

Walt Whitman

2020. *To William D. O'Connor*

ADDRESS: Wm D O'Connor | 1015 O Street N W | Washington | D C. POSTMARKS: Camden (?) | Apr 28 | 5 PM | 89; Washington, Rec'd. | Apr 29 | 2 AM | 89 | 7.

Camden Sunday afternoon | April 28 '89

Clearing up & sunshine as I write—good *roots* for the N Y show—(on which great calculations on)—Nothing new with me, nor better

subsidy but if it is we can easily get more money" (Feinberg; Traubel, v, 84). Bucke wrote about the subject to Traubel on the same date (Feinberg; Traubel, v, 84).

10. The three-day celebration of the centennial commemorating the inauguration of George Washington.

nor worse—no visitors or mail—pretty heavy dull day (but not at all on those acc'ts)—Am sitting here in the big bare-wood chair as usual—Best love—

Walt Whitman

2021. *To Richard Maurice Bucke*

ADDRESS: Dr R M Bucke | Asylum | London | Ontario Canada. POSTMARK: Camden, N.J. | May 1 | 8 PM | 89.

Camden May 1 '89

Well the N Y show goes over to-day in a blaze of glory, & Barnum's great circus comes in here at noon & exhibits to night—(Ed goes—I am favorable)—& besides Dr Baker "graduates" this afternoon—you know he is my first nurse—last June—& Osler makes the address—indeed I believe *two* of 'em—things ab't same as before with me—

Walt Whitman

2022. *To Richard Maurice Bucke*

ADDRESS: Dr R M Bucke | Asylum | London | Ontario | Canada. POSTMARK: Camden (?) | May 3(?) | 6 AM | 89.

Camden May 2 '89

Feeling ab't fairly—weather not unpleasant, cloudy, & a little cool—am sitting here by the oak fire—a middling fair bowel action an hour ago, I go out to the closet myself & return—Horace has been in—the L of G. pocket-book ed'n is getting along—(probably the press-work to-day—also some of the plates at the plate press)—Well the big N Y show seems to have all pass'd over successfully—to me *the idea* of it is good, even grand, but I have not enthused ab't it at all—(may be a whim, but the most insignificant item in the whole affair has been Harrison himself, President for all he is)—So the circus here was a success last night—Ed enjoy'd it hugely—& I suppose Dr Baker has gone off (to Minneapolis)

11. Whittier's "The Vow of Washington" appeared in the New York *World* and elsewhere on May 1.

12. Wyatt Eaton's "Recollections of Jean François Millet" in *Century* (90–104). For WW's comments, see Traubel, v, 123–124, 133–134.

immediately after his graduation—Mrs. Davis was there—Osler spoke well & was treated to great applause—all this in the Phila: Academy wh' must have look'd gayly—

I have been looking over the May *Century*, the *Book News* and the *Critic* (so I may be supposed to be posted with current literature)—read Whittier's long N Y centennial ode[11]—also Wyatt Eaton's reminiscences (interesting) of J F Millet[12]—the "cold in the head" still upon me palpably—stew'd chicken, Graham bread & coffee for my meals lately—Ed gives me a good *currying* every evening—Sleep fairly—Sun bursting forth as I write—the great long *burr-r-r* of the Phila. whistles from factories or shores often & plainly here sounding, & I rather like it—(blunt & bass)—some future American Wagner[13] might make something significant of it—Guess you must have all good times there—occupied & healthy & sufficiently out door—I refresh myself sometimes thinking (fancying) ab't you all there—I enclose Mrs. O'C[onnor]'s yesterday's card—I send card or something every evn'g—Love to you, Mrs B & the childer—

W W

Y'rs of April 30 rec'd—

2023. *To William D. O'Connor*

ADDRESS: Wm D O'Connor | 1015 O Street N W | Washington | D C. POSTMARKS: Camden (?) | May 3 | 8 PM | 89; Washington, Rec'd. | May 4 | 7 AM | 89 | 7.

Camden May 3 '89

Matters going on much the same with me—N[elly]'s card came yesterday[14]—Coolish weather—am sitting here by the oak fire alone—trying to interest myself with the morning papers & Harper's *Weekly*, &c—My young friend Horace Traubel comes in (as every day) & manages all the printing affairs as I wish & direct—Best love to you & N—

Walt Whitman

13. For WW's response to Wagner, see my *Walt Whitman's Poetry: A Psychological Journey* (1968), 175–177.

14. According to her note on April 30, there had been "a let up for nearly 48 hours, but the old trouble vomiting, in addition to all the others, has come on again" (Feinberg).

2024. *To Dr. Karl Knortz*

TRANSCRIPT.

Camden, May 4, '89.

Am continuing on here much the same imprisoned in my room and chair and locomotion quite out of the question—mentality and brain action (while easily tired and sore at the best) remain, the muscles, especially my right hand and arm, good—spirits, sleep etc. fair—and the main elementary functions active at least half (or even plus half) to keep off so far my complete down fall.

I believe I told you I am preparing a small handsome pocket book bound edition of L. of G. including the "Sands at 70" and "Backward Glance," as a sort of commemorating my completion of 70th year (May 31, 1889). Shall send you a copy when out. Sarrazin's book is out in Paris —"La Renaissance de la Poésie Anglaise 1798–1889." Papers on Shelley, Wordsworth, Coleridge, Tennyson, Robert Browning and W. W. A handsome 279 pp. book in the beautiful easy handy French style.

Your postal card of two weeks since received—have not heard anything more of "Grashalme" or Rolleston—hear frequently from Dr. Bucke —my dear friend O'Connor at Washington very ill yet—Wm. Walsh on the *Herald*, and Julius Chambers on the *World* are friendly to me—I am sitting in my big rattan chair by the oak fire writing this—sit here this way nearly all day—a young man, friend Horace Traubel (of German stock) comes in every day, is very faithful and kind and serves as medium to the printers. Write—

Walt Whitman

2025. *To Gabriel Sarrazin*

TRANSCRIPT.

Camden New Jersey U S America | May 4 '89

The book "Poésie Anglaise" safely rec'd—thanks & thanks again. I am still laid up here lame & paralyzed—Kept in for a year but getting along (as we call it) better & gayer heart than you might suppose. Am

15. The inscribed copy is now in the possession of Sarrazin's son; see *WWR*, v (1959), 10.
16. *The Literary News*, x (May, 1889), 180–181.
17. On May 6 Kennedy observed that he thought he had the only copy of Hartmann's criticism (see 1619), but apparently there was a duplicate. He was ready to

preparing an ed'n of Leaves of Grass to be put in pocket book binding, with fuller text, & shall send you one when ready.[15] For this time I send loving wishes & an old fellow's benison.

Walt Whitman

2026. *To William Sloane Kennedy*

Camden May 4 '89

Sarrazin's book has come "La Ranaissance de la *Poésie Anglaise* 1798–1889—Paris—35 quai des grandes Augustine"—279 pp. handy beautiful French style, paper—Nothing very different in my affairs—the N Y *Literary News* for May has a notice[16]—did you see that infernal farrago of my *opinions*!! in the Herald three Sundays ago by that Japanee?—S[tedman] is quite mad I hear[17]—O'C[onnor] is no better.

Walt Whitman

2027. *To Richard Maurice Bucke* *5.4–5.1889*

ADDRESS: Dr R M Bucke | Asylum | London | Ontario | Canada. POSTMARK: Camden, N.J. | May 5 | 5 PM | 89.

Camden May 4 '89

Sarrazin's book (from him from Paris) has come, & looks wonderfully inviting all through but is of course sealed to me[17.1]—I enclose a slip of title detailedly, as you may want to get one from New York—(but of course you can have my copy as much as you want)—I have written to Knortz (540 East 155th St New York)—& a card acknowledging reception to S, Paris—

Fine & sunny here—am rather heavy-headed—& *hefty* anyhow to-day —nothing specially to particularize—ate my breakfast, (mutton broth & Graham bread with some stew'd apple,) with ab't usual zest—(nothing at all sharp, but will do, & even thankful it's as well as it is)—The "Literary News" (N Y) book &c monthly, May, has a good two page biography & notice—wh' I send (or will send soon)—Did you get a letter in wh' I

remove the Hartmann section from his manuscript. The letter concluded: "Regards to yrself & the senior members of our masculine-comrade-family—the three or four when you write 'em" (Feinberg).

17.1. The presentation copy to WW, inscribed April 19, is now in the Feinberg Collection.

asked you to write out & enclose in my letter for Dr Brown, (apothecary here) a proper calomel powder prescription a *little stronger* (if you thought right)—did you get the letter?—Did you send your WW book to Sarrazin?

Sunday May 5

Fine & sunny to-day—feeling fairly—all going smoothly—In general ab't the world, I guess we are now floating on *dead water* in literature, politics, theology, even science—resting on our oars &c. &c.—criticising, resuming—at any rate *chattering* a good deal (of course the simmering, gestation, &c. &c. are going on just the same)—but a sort of *lull*—a good coming summer to you & Mrs. B & all of you—

Walt Whitman

2028. *To William D. O'Connor*

ADDRESS: Wm D O'Connor | 1015 O Street N W | Washington | D C. POSTMARKS: Camden (?) | May 5 | 5 PM | 89; Washington, Rec'd. | May 6 | 2 AM | 89 | 7.

Camden May 5 '89

The Frenchman Sarrazin's book came yesterday "Poésie Anglais" —tantalizing me a good deal, as I can just glean enough for a whiff only—Nothing special to write ab't in my affairs—dull here—fine & sunny too—Love to you & N[elly] & prayers for your ease & comfortableness—

Walt Whitman

2029. *To Richard Maurice Bucke*

ADDRESS: Dr R M Bucke | Asylum | London | Ontario Canada. POSTMARK: Camden, N.J. | May 6 | 8 PM | 89.

Camden May 6 '89

Splendid sunny weather—nothing specially new—good bowel action—wrote you at some length last evn'g ab't Sarrazin's book rec'd—y'r good letter this mn'g—have tho't no more definitely of the Baltimore Hospital scheme[18]—am sitting here as usual comfortable enough—my sister Lou just been here, has been down to see my bro: Eddy—he is all right—

Walt Whitman

18. See 2019.

2030. *To William D. O'Connor*

ADDRESS: Wm D O'Connor | 1015 O Street N W | Washington | D C. POSTMARK: Camden, N.J. | May 6 | 8 PM | 89.

Camden May 6 '89

How is it with you today, dear friend?—I deeply hope easy & comfortable—is so with me considering every thing—Superb sunny day here & young Summer advancing—Mrs: D[avis] has bro't up a great bunch of fresh lilacs—beautiful—am cogitating of a strong out-door push *chair* to get out in, to be propell'd by my good hearty Canadian nurse—Will send you what comes of it all—Best love to you & N[elly]—

Walt Whitman

2031. *To Richard Maurice Bucke*

ADDRESS: Dr R M Bucke | Asylum | London | Ontario Canada. POSTMARK: Camden (?) | May 8 | 8 P(?) | 89.

Camden May 8 '89

The word from O'C[onnor] is bad as you see by the enclosed card —in some respects the worst yet—I am feeling badly depress'd ab't it to-day as you may think—Otherwise nearly the same as usual—fine sunny weather—Horace and Ed are going over to Phila: on a hunt for the *out-door chair* suitable for me—the pocket-book ed'n L of G is progressing fairly—Wm Ingram has just call'd—he is well—stays mostly at his farm —the 1 p m whistle is sounding burr-r-r over the Delaware—the sun is pouring down almost hotly out (O that I could be out & move in it) & my dear O'C is there in W[ashington] may-be unconscious—may-be passing from life—meanwhile—thought o'ertoppling all else—my old nurse Musgrove has just been in to see me, I have a friendly feeling toward him—Tom Harned was here last evn'g—He is busy—is always good to me—

Walt Whitman

2032. *To William Sloane Kennedy*

Camden May 8 '89

Y'rs of 6th rec'd—thanks—yes, I am agreeable to your sending S[tedman] my former letter, (& rather advise it)[19]—Bad, bad word from

19. Letter 1619.

O'C[onnor] (f'm the wife) to day, & I am gloomy—Dr B[ucke] writes me every day & cheerily—Horace & my nurse Ed have gone prospecting to Phila: for a strong suitable *out-door chair* for me to be pull'd or push'd out.

Walt Whitman

2033. *To Richard Maurice Bucke*

ADDRESS: Dr R M Bucke | Asylum | London | Ontario Canada. POSTMARKS: Camden, N.J. | May 01 | 6 AM | 89; (?) | 5–10–89 | 10 30 AM.

Camden May 9 P M '89

No word to-day from O'C[onnor] leaving me to gloomy apprehensions—Sunny & warm here & I am expecting an *out-door chair* to get forth in, under Ed's convoy. If the weather keeps good & no hitch in my condition, I shouldn't wonder if I got out that way, before you receive this—

Walt Whitman

2034. *To Ellen M. O'Connor*

ADDRESS: Mrs: O'Connor | 1015 O Street N W | Washington | D C. POSTMARK: Camden (?) | May 01 | 6 AM | 89.

Camden P M May 9 '89

Have been sitting here some time thinking of Wm—am deeply depress'd by y'r card of yesterday—but keep up hope—I continue ab't as before—Love to him & you as always—

Walt Whitman

20. Mrs. O'Connor wrote on May 9: "The sad end is come. William passed peacefully to rest at 2 A.M. this day. He failed very much the last week, & more on Sunday, & from that day on.

"It is sad because he so wanted to get well, & to the last thought he was going to recover.

"But he lies now the image of perfect rest & peace, & more beautiful than I ever saw him, & looks as he did when I knew him first so long ago, & the late loss of flesh in the face has brought back the very look of youth" (Feinberg).

On May 13 Bucke wrote to WW: "I believe, dear Walt, that it is all right and as it

2035. *To Richard Maurice Bucke*

ADDRESS: Dr R M Bucke | Asylum | London | Ontario
Canada. POSTMARK: Camden, N.J. | May 10 |
12 M | 89.

Camden May 10 '89

Our dear friend O'Connor died peacefully at 2 a m yesterday[20]—

Walt Whitman

2036. *To John Burroughs*

TRANSCRIPT.

May 10, 1889

Our dear friend O'Connor died peacefully at 2 a m yesterday.[21]

2037. *To Thomas B. Harned*

TRANSCRIPT.

May 10th, 1889.

Tom:

If you will, fill the brown bottle with sherry for me, and the small white bottle with Cognac. My dear friend O'Connor is dead.

Walt Whitman.

2038. *To William Sloane Kennedy*

ADDRESS: Sloane Kennedy | Belmont | Mass:.
POSTMARK: Camden, N.J. | May 10 | (?) | 89.

Camden May 10 '89

Our dear friend O'Connor died peacefully yesterday at 2 A M[22]—

Walt Whitman

should be—and I trust when I come to die myself, as I must and ought in a little while, that I shall say the same thing. 'We shall go to him though he will not come back to us' " (Feinberg).

21. Burroughs on May 11 expressed the sentiments of many of O'Connor's friends: "And it is sad to me to think that he has left behind him no work or book that at all expresses the measure of his great powers" (Feinberg).

22. On May 11–12 Kennedy responded: "How can we really believe in death? It is in yr writings, & there alone that *I* have found the deepest glimpses into death-realm. You have made it life-realm to me—given me an idea of it grand in mystic possibilities" (Feinberg).

2039. *To Richard Maurice Bucke* *5.[11]–12. 1889*

ADDRESS: Dr R M Bucke | Asylum | London | Ontario | Canada. POSTMARK: Camden, N.J. | May 12 | 5 PM | 89.

Camden | *Saturday—just after noon*

Of course the main tho't has been yesterday, & is to-day, the death of O'C[onnor]—I enclose the letter of Mrs: O'C rec'd yesterday—

(Another death here, old Mrs: Mapes, buried this afternoon)[23]—Y'r letters come & are welcom'd—(if you sent one with the calo[mel] prescription, however, it never reach'd me—it was but really rec'd two days since) —Am feeling sufficiently easy to-day—my out-door wheel chair has come & is very satisfactory (both to Ed & me) & I intended to get out this forenoon, but I took a rather laborious bath at 10½, & felt some exhausted, & shall probably get out a little this afternoon—pleasant weather, not quite so warm to-day, but has been markedly warm—fair bowel-action this forenoon—

Some of the friends here in Camden, (lawyers, a teacher or two, an editor, Tom Harned, & others)[24] have laid out a sort of *commemoration formal dinner* for my arriving my 70th year old terminus—a good dinner, tickets ($5), toasts, speeches, &c.—no wine—you have probably rec'd the newspaper item f'm Horace—I have let them go on their own way, as they have set their hearts upon it, & they are all quite fellows of love & respect —but I have definitely told them it is not certain I shall get there in *propria personae*—& if so (wh' I will if practicable) w'd only show myself & acknowledge the compliment wh' seems to be no more than decent—tho' the *jamboree* does not present itself as appropriate, or particularly encouragable to my mind—Well we shall see—The pocket-bound ed'n is getting on smoothly, & no mishap or hitch yet—the printed sheets are at the binder's—Horace sold a big book to-day & McKay another—

Sunday May 12 '89

Well I went out in the wheel chair yesterday afternoon & was probably out an hour & a half—every thing work'd well—the chair is a success & sits & goes easy—Ed of course propell'd me—Shall go out again to-day— the weather continues fine, very mild—I sweat quite freely—had some good asparagus for my breakfast (sent f'm my brother's garden, Burling-

23. Apparently the mother-in-law of the Mrs. Mapes who assisted Mrs. Davis. See *In Re*, 375–376.

24. The committee included Henry (Harry) L. Bonsall, Geoffrey Buckwalter, and

ton)—Harry Stafford was here yesterday, he is pretty thin, is still working managing the RR station at Marlton, N J—all the rest ab't as usual—Wm Ingram comes often.

Love to you & Mrs: B. and all—

Walt Whitman

2040. *To Ellen M. O'Connor*

ADDRESS: Mrs: O'Connor | 1015 O Street N W | Washington | D C. POSTMARKS: Camden, N.J. | May 12 | 5 PM | 89; Washington, Rec'd. | May 13 | 2 AM | 89 | 7.

Camden May 12 '89

After a great trouble, or death, a sort of *silence* & *not* trying words or to depict y'r feelings come to me strongest—But I will send a word any how to you, dear friend, of sympathy & how the death of William, for all I have for some time anticipated, comes very bitterly—

I am somewhat better, & late yesterday afternoon I was taken out & jaunted around for an hour—my first experience of out door for most a year, & it was very refreshing—then when I came back & up to my room I spent the sunset & twilight hour thinking in silence of W and you & old times in Wash'n—

Best love to you, & send me word when you can—

Walt Whitman

2041. *To William Sloane Kennedy*

TRANSCRIPT.

May 13, '89

Our friend has no doubt been buried by this—his death hour was peaceful. I think he must have been unconscious for a good while previous. The face and all looked peaceful and beautiful in death. Traubel has sent a short piece about him to the *Critic*.[25] I will send you (or word of) all I hear or get. I have been out to-day noon in wheel chair to the river shore as secluded as I could find and staid over half an hour.

Harned (Traubel, v, 145).

25. *The Critic* declined Traubel's obituary notice, and printed what WW called a "tame" one on May 18 (see 2045), which included extracts from O'Connor's letters to the magazine.

2042. *To Frederick Oldach*

328 Mickle Street | Camden May 16 '89

Dear Sir

This sample of your binding (old fashion'd pocket-book style with ordinary tongue or tuck-flap, all holding snug, but not too tight or stiff) is satisfactory & suits me best. The dark green morocco, if you have it already, will do—but if you have to get it get *a lighter green.* Bind the whole ed'n alike, no variety. Make a stout paper pocket—(see last page, as written on in sample)—In trimming the plates, &c. (if yet to be done) trim them, especially No: 1 and No: 4, leaving a little *more* white paper at bottom, & *less* at top—the trimming in this sample seems to me to be the very reverse—

The plates are all put in right in this sample—the stamp on cover is right—& altogether the job looks satisfactory. *I particularly want 50 copies (or 100) in a week.*

Walt Whitman

2043. *To John Burroughs*

ADDRESS: John Burroughs | West Park | Ulster Co: New York. POSTMARKS: Camden, N.J. | May 17 | 8 PM | 89; West Park | May | 18 | 1889.

Camden May 17 '89

As I write (noon) I have not heard a word since from Wash'n but of course our dear friend is buried & all has gone like tracks on the shore by sea waves washed away passing—

Much the same with me (gradually yielding)—One betterment—I get out in a wheel'd chair, often twice a day—am sitting here by the open window—perfect weather—best love—

Walt Whitman

2044. *To Richard Maurice Bucke*

ADDRESS: Dr R M Bucke | Asylum | London | Ontario Canada. POSTMARK: Camden, N.J. | May 19 | 5 PM | 89.

Camden May 19 '89

All goes much the same, & fairly. I have just sent to Mrs:

26. The obituary was written by a man named Hurd (Traubel, v, 195); see also 2249, *n.*85.

O'[Connor] a Boston *Transcript*, May 16, with a 20 or 30 line notice of O'C's death[26]—Have not seen yet any acc't of funeral—I get out a little every day in the wheel chair. The pocket-book ed'n will be bound & ready in a week—

Walt Whitman

2045. *To Richard Maurice Bucke*

ADDRESS: Dr R M Bucke | Asylum | London | Ontario | Canada. POSTMARK: Camden (?) | May 2(?) | 8 P(?) | 89.

Camden just after 11 a m | May 20 '89

A warm pleasant clouded day—am feeling fairly—bowel action an hour ago—have been, yesterday 3 hours, signing the autographs for the pocket-book ed'n L of G—the book will probably be a good job except the *press work* wh' dont suit me—the pictures appear to be all good—(I wanted to send off three or four copies to Europe, & am a little disappointed—I had even a tho't of sending it to the Paris Exposition—of course I shall send one to Sarrazin)—the *Critic* (18th May) has rather a tame obituary of O'C[onnor]—I send it to Mrs: O'C:—If you care to see them (the Boston *Trans*[*cript*] too) I will ask her to send them to you, to be returned to her—But there is nothing memorable—Horace wrote an obituary & sent but the C[ritic] declined it—

Horace has a situation in a bank Phila:, likes it I believe—hours &c: easy—Ed is well—is down stairs at his fiddle—I have rec'd a letter from Mrs: Costelloe herewith enc'd[27]—all well—was indoors all yesterday, in the room here—a bad night, last—have not used the cal[omel] powders any yet—I will keep them for specially bad spells—sweat freely—appetite good enough—a rare fried egg, graham bread, coffee, & some stew'd rhubarb for breakfast—eyes bad—rain falling copiously as I write—sitting here alone 2d story room—the complimentary dinner (in wh' of course I shall not join—it will be quite a feat to be wheel'd there, & show myself—if I do that) is smoothly moving—It is now noon & after, & I, thanks to Ed, have had my *currying* of half an hour, for an interregnum —rainy & warm—

Walt Whitman

27. Mrs. Costelloe wrote a lively letter on May 10 (Feinberg; *Smith Alumnae Quarterly* [February, 1958], 88).

2046. *To William Sloane Kennedy*

ADDRESS: Sloane Kennedy | Belmont | Mass:. POSTMARK: Camden, N.J. | May 2(?) | 8 PM | 89.

Camden p m May 21 '89

Y'rs rec'd an hour ago—Yes I sent Mrs: O'C[onnor] the longer obituary[28]—there is a sort of tame one, also sent to Mrs: O'C, in last Sat: *Critic*—(O'C was far too real, penetrating, far-reaching & non-conventional to have many or fussy obituaries)—Horace sent one to the C. wh' they declined. Have you sent the card f'm me (or was it letter?) ab't Hartmann's stuff, to Stedman?[29]

Yes indeed I value the Stepniak memorandum[30]—sh'l send it to Dr B[ucke]—Is it possible for you to come to the *dinner*, 5 p m 31st May?—It is all a venture of my friends here—of wh' I have nothing to do (rather disapprove)—am ab't same—get out in wheel chair—have just been curried & massaged—

Walt Whitman

2047. *To Richard Maurice Bucke* *5.[25]–26. [1889]*

ADDRESS: Dr R M Bucke | Asylum | London | Ontario | Canada. POSTMARK: Camden, N.J. | May 26 | 5 PM | 89.

Camden Mickle Street

Well, Maurice, every thing here goes on much the same, & fairly enough—As I write, it is abt 1 P M, Saturday, clear but not sunny & neither cool nor warm—I have just had a midday currying—partial bowel action two hours ago—feel middling (but cold in the head, or catarrh or gathering or whatever it is yet)—get out a little in the wheel chair—they are all going out, Mrs. D[avis] and all, to an East Indian ship for two or three hours this afternoon—I told Ed to go too as he was invited, (& he will go)—the ship is here from Bombay, & our sailor boys know some of their sailors—

We broke a big bottle of good wine yesterday & all of us (seven—me

28. Undoubtedly the excellent biographical account in the Boston *Evening Transcript* on May 16.

29. See 2032. On May 23 Kennedy said that he had decided not to send WW's letter to Stedman (Feinberg; Traubel, v, 221). WW was annoyed (v, 217).

30. Kennedy enclosed on May 18 an article in the Boston *Evening Transcript* of

at the head) drank health & respects to Queen Victoria—(it was her birthday you know—)

My big dinner (wh' however I shall probably not eat, and only be there a few minutes if at all) is coming on swimmingly they say—Herbert Gilchrist is to make the responsive speech to the British toast to friends—Col. Ingersoll's coming is uncertain—*not* Howells nor Burroughs nor Aldrich nor Kennedy to be here—no word yet f'm Stedman (Achilles laid up in his tent moody, am rather sorry, but am not to blame)—

Night—9½—Have been out twice to day in the wheel-chair—short excursions—T B H[arned] has been here this evn'g—150 dinner tickets taken now—y'r letter rec'd by H[orace]—(I have not seen it yet)—coolish temperature three days & now stopping sweat exudation & somewhat bad for me but well enough as I sit here alone, every thing quiet, but some sailors from the ship downstairs—

Sunday toward noon May 26

A clouded rather rawish day—Am going up to my friends Mr & Mrs: Harned's in an hour, in my wheel chair—to stay a few minutes, & probably get a drink of champagne—(of which H always has the best & treats me to galore)—Havn't now had such a tipple for a year.

Nothing particular to write—My head is a little heavy & thick—no pocket-book copies yet, but I count on them in a couple of days—All goes fairly as c'd be expected—

Walt Whitman

2048. *To Edward Carpenter*

ADDRESS: Edw'd Carpenter | Millthorpe | near Chesterfield | England. POSTMARK: Camden (?) | May 28 | 8 PM | 89.

328 Mickle Street | Camden New Jersey
U S America | May 28 1889

Thanks, dear friend, for your love & remembrance & faith & liberality—And thanks with same to Bessie & Isabella Ford & William & Ethel & Arthur Thompson—(The letter—somehow one of the best I ever

that date entitled "Stepniak at Home. | A Chat with the Famous Russian Nihilist about Emerson, Walt Whitman, George Eliot and Others . . ." There was one brief reference to WW: "Ah, here's another of my favorites (holding up a volume of 'Leaves of Grass;') an author who is not sufficiently appreciated in his own land." At this time Sergei Mikhailovich Stepnyak (1852–1895) was in exile in London after he had murdered General Mezentsev.

rec'd—goes to my heart—of May 18 with the draft 194:95 reaches me safely)[31]—

I am here yet, much the same, to say it summarily, fairly jolly—go out now sometimes in a wheel chair, exceptionally for an hour or two to the river shore when I feel like it—have a good strong young Canadian (Ed Wilkins) for my helper & nurse—have just had what I call my *currying for the mid-day*—& am probably getting along better than you all might suppose—fortunately my right & left arms are left me in good strength & volition, (in the terrible wreck & almost helplessness of the rest of the body)—There is somewhat against my wish & advice to be a sort of public & speechifying dinner &c. in compliment to my finishing my 70th year, here in Camden, towards even'g May 31—I will send you any acc't may be—

I have lately seen Herbert Gilchrist—he is well & flourishing—The Staffords are well & much the same—I have not sent your & the Misses Fords' big books (Complete Works) yet—Shall probably send in a box to Mrs: Costelloe, 40 Grosvenor Road, the Embankment, London, but I shall send you word when—You & the Fords & the rest have help'd me more than you know—Love—

Walt Whitman

2049. *To Richard Maurice Bucke*

ADDRESS: Dr R M Bucke | Asylum | London | Ontario | Canada. POSTMARK: Camden, N.J. | Jun 1 | 8 PM | 89.

Camden 1889 | *Saturday early P M June 1*

Well here I am, feeling fairly, commencing my 71st year. The dinner last evening came off & went off, all right, & was a great success—they say they had a mighty good *dinner* (nothing to drink but Appollinaris water)—I was not at the eating part, but went an hour later—Ed wheel'd me in the chair, & two policemen & two other good fellows just carried me from the sidewalk, chair & all as I sat, up the stairs & turning (which were fortunately wide & easy) to the big banquet hall & big crowd, where I was roll'd to my seat, & after being rec'd with tremendous cheering they bro't me a bottle of first rate champagne & a big glass with ice, (Tom Harned sent to his house for the wine)—The whole thing was

31. Carpenter sent the birthday gift of $194.95 (£40) on May 18 (Feinberg; Traubel, v, 256). On Carpenter's letter WW wrote: "Seems to me one of the leading best missives I ever had—goes to the heart." Traubel included it in *Camden's Compliment to*

tip top & luckily I felt better & more something like myself, and nearer chipper, than for a year—I made a short talk, wh' you will see in the paper I enclose[31.1]—also Herbert's speech—It was largely a home & neighbors' affair (wh' I liked) although there were (& speeches from) outsiders—The compliments & eulogies to me were *excessive* & without break—But I fill'd my ice-glass with the good wine, & pick'd out two fragrant roses f'm a big basket near me, & kept cool & jolly & enjoy'd all—

I suppose you have the pocket-book copy L of G wh' I mailed yesterday—have just sold one & got the 5 for it—Hamlin Garland has been to see me to-day—also Tom Harned—The Phila: papers have long reports —a little rainy & broken to-day, but pleasant—

Walt Whitman

2050. *To Horace Traubel*

ENDORSED: "Horace Traubel | Show this to T B Harned, Harry Bonsall & Buckwalter—& then to David McKay."

Sunday noon June 2 | '89

Horace, I was just thinking the *pamphlet* notion might be improved & expanded on by having a nicely 60 or 70 page (thick good paper, with portrait for front piece) *book*, trimmed & gilt edged—good job—bound in crepe—thick paper (like my Passage to India, robin-blue-egg color with white inside)—to be publish'd by Dave, & sold at 50cts retail —to be call'd

Camden's Compliment

to Walt Whitman on his finishing his 70th year.

putting in enough appropriate stuff to the occasion & latest developements —(if needed) to make out 60 or 70 pp—

Mention this to Tom, Harry Bonsall & Buckwalter—then see if Dave w'd undertake & publish it at his expense—I don't think it needed be stereotyped—print it f'm the types—1000 copies—Us here, Dr B[ucke], Tom, other Camdenites, Johnston in N Y, &c, to subscribe for 100 & pay the cash down when ready—

The more I think of it *this way*, the more I believe it worth doing, & that it will pay for itself, at least—& I think Dave will go in—(no great

Walt Whitman, 54.

31.1. Probably the Philadelphia *Press* of June 1, which reported the celebration at length and quoted WW and Gilchrist directly.

risk or money investment any how.) The whole thing of the dinner was such a success & really a *wonder* it ought to be commemorated—

W W

2051. *To Richard Maurice Bucke*

ADDRESS: Dr Bucke Asylum | London | Ontario | Canada. POSTMARK: Camden, N.J. | Jun 2 | 5 PM | 89.

Camden Sunday Evn'g June 2 | '89

All goes well—the *feeling pretty good* Friday evn'g continues. Suppose you rec'd the pocket-book b'd L of G—I sent you yesterday three or four papers with lengthy reports of dinner &c—Every body says it was a mark'd success—It is well toward sunset & I am going out for an hour in the wheel chair, (wh' proves a great comfort)—fine sunny weather—

Walt Whitman

2052. *To William Sloane Kennedy*

ADDRESS: Sloane Kennedy | Belmont | Mass:. POSTMARK: Camden, N.J. | Jun 4 | 8 PM | 89.

Camden P M June 4 '89

Your c[ar]d just recd—by this time you must have got papers I sent with report of dinner &c:—All was a great success, intense meaning & expression yet very quiet—I was there an hour & a half at the last (drank a bottle of champagne)—I felt unusually well, wh' has continued ever since, till to day, (not so well at present)—The idea now is to print all in a little book—Do you want further papers? If so I can send you. What do you mean by "the $4.99" on y'r card?[32] I have rec'd none—

W W

32. On June 3 Kennedy sent a brief notice of the birthday celebration from the Boston *Evening Transcript* and a check for $4.99, his facetious way of ordering the pocket-book edition of *Leaves of Grass* (Feinberg).

33. Johnston and Wallace sent the gift on May 21 (Feinberg and Bolton Public Libraries).

34. The Johnstown flood. In CB WW wrote on June 1: "The most pervading & dreadful news this m'ng is of the strange cataclysm at Johnstown & adjoining Cambria

2053. *To J. W. Wallace*

ADDRESS: J W Wallace | 14 Eagle Street | Haulgh | Bolton England. POSTMARK: Camden, N.J. | Jun 4 | 8 PM | 89.

328 Mickle Street | Camden New Jersey
U S America | June 4 '89

The good letter, the £10 & the photos: reach me safely—& most affectionate responses & wishes to you & Dr J[ohnston] & "the boys" all[33] —(Note a paper with report of public dinner, sent to J)—If different f'm last acc'ts I am rather better—get out almost daily in the open air, push'd on a wheel'd chair by a stout Canadian friend, my nurse—We are all gloomy from the great cataclysm west[34]—

Walt Whitman

2054. *To Richard Maurice Bucke* *6.4–5. 1889*

ADDRESS: Dr Bucke | Asylum | London | Ontario | Canada. POSTMARK: Camden (?) | Jun 5 | 8 PM | 89.

Camden 1889 | *June 4 1 p m*

Suppose you got the papers &c: with report of the dinner, speeches, &c:—quite a success, a great crowd, mark'd enthusiasm & yet a sort of Quaker (even Greek) *no-excess*, no hifalutin over all—the project now is to have all, speeches, &c: printed in full in a handsome 72 page booklet (50cts) pub'd by Dave McKay—

Suppose you got the pocket-book b'd copy of L of G—Felt better than usual & very phlegmatic (fortunately) Friday evn'g—& ever since—not quite so well to-day—weather heavy, damp, cloudy to-day—have been feasting on strawberries (a big basket f'm my sister Lou, the best I ever saw)—We are all gloomy here, f'm the dreadful cataclysm in Cambria county, Penn:—the more we hear, the worse & more destructive & deadly it proves—

County, Penn: by wh' many thousands of people are overwhelm'd, kill'd by drowning in water, burnt by fire, &c: &c:—all our hearts, the papers & the public interest, are fill'd with it—the most signal & wide-spread horror of the kind ever known in this country—curious that at this very hour, we were having the dinner festivities &c—unaware." Browning, now the Philadelphia representative of the New York *World*, was instructed by Julius Chambers to ask WW for "a threnody on the Johnstown dead," which became "A Voice from Death" (Traubel, v, 266).

June 5 11 a m

Have just come out of the bath room—feeling fairly, leaning toward better, to-day—breakfast of rice-&-mutton soup, & asparagus galore—fine sunny day, not warm—A long good letter (Chicago) from a western soldier boy of twenty four years ago,[35] was with me a good deal, bringing back hospital & war scenes of long ago—have not heard f'm Mrs: O'C[onnor]—send her the Boston or other paper 'most every day—have rec'd a good letter & gift from two friends in Bolton, England[36]—did I tell you I rec'd a handsome birthday gift (all lump'd) from Edward Carpenter, two sisters named Ford (Leeds), & others? Good wishes to Mrs: B. and all the childer—Y'rs ab't the ball &c: rec'd[37]—I believe Herbert G. expects to return to London next September. Ed and Horace well—I go out in the wheel chair—

Walt Whitman

2055. *To Richard Maurice Bucke*

ADDRESS: Dr Bucke | Asylum | London | Ontario | Canada. POSTMARK: Camden, N.J. | Jun 6 | 8 PM | 89.

Camden P M June 6 '89

Y'rs comes to day—As you ought to have rec'd the papers, & something may have happened with them, I send others with this mail—Nothing especial or new—Have the last two hours (& just sent off) been writing "Voice f'm Death," the Cambria Co[unty] Cataclysm here, wh' they last night sent for (& off'd $25 for)—to appear I believe in N. Y. World of to-morrow[38]—

Walt Whitman

35. Milford C. Reed wrote to the poet on June 1: "Do you remember the young man of the 5th U S Cavalary who you used to visit in Armory Square Hospital and the many times you used to take me into a Restaurant and give me a good square meal. I suppose you done that to so many you would hardly remember me by that. for all Soldiers know[n] to you looked upon you as their friend, for you ever wore your heart on your sleeve to Old Soldier boys. You used to call me Cody then. . . . In the years gone by I have often passed through Camden, and had I have known it was your home I should surely have stopped to see you, that I might once more have crasped you by the hand and looked into that kindly face and fought over our battles (once again) in Washington" (Feinberg). WW's reply on June 9 is lost. Reed also wrote to the poet on May 26, 1863 (Yale).

36. See the preceding letter.

2056. *To Richard Maurice Bucke* 6.8–9.1889

ADDRESS: Dr Bucke | Asylum | London | Ontario | Canada. POSTMARK: Camden, N.J. | Jun 9 | 5 PM | 89.

Camden 1889 | *Saturday noon June 8*

Suppose you got the little poem in N Y World June 7 I sent—It was specially requested by the editor & written in an hour & a half & sent on to N Y by mail the same evn'g 6th—I believe I told you I am to get $25 for it—We are all here yet under the depression of the fearful cataclysm, so deadly, so near—

Cloudy & dull weather—bowel action to day—Y'rs rec'd—I see you like the pocket-b'k ed'n of L of G—yes, I am satisfied with it, everything but the press work—McK[ay]'s current ed'n, including Annex, is well printed—McKay is to start off on a long business & drumming tour west—goes in three weeks, will be away two months—

My worst present botheration is this catarrhal or head gathering, half ache, half heavy weight & discomfort—fortunately I sweat pretty easily & often—I fancy it is good for me—weather variable—coolish just now. I enclose a letter to me from John Burroughs—and one from an old soldier boy[39]—lately rec'd—

Sunday, 9th A M

Rather a warm night—temperature changed greatly at evn'g—but I must have slept fairly—warm to-day here—breakfasted on rice-&-mutton-broth & asparagus & some Graham bread & coffee—fair bowel action this forenoon—rather "under the weather" yesterday & this forenoon, (but of course it will move off cloud like)—

A good Illinoisian & wife came to see me last evening—bo't a big book—(enthusiastic ab't L of G.)—rec'd a letter f'm Mary Costelloe—all well—

I am writing a little—"poemets"—one yesterday[40]—what names (if

37. According to Bucke's letter on May 28, the annual ball at the asylum took place on May 30. On June 2 he observed: "There is nothing in God's world more absurd than these balls & parties at which one sits up all night pretending to have a good time and (without any pretence) has a very bad time for some days afterwards" (Feinberg).

38. "A Voice from Death" appeared on the first page of the New York *World* on June 7.

39. Burroughs' letter of May 11 (Feinberg; Traubel, v, 179–180) and Reed's of June 1 (Feinberg).

40. WW sent "My 71st Year" on June 9 to Richard Watson Gilder of *Century*, where it appeared in November. He received $12 (CB). On June 11 he sent "Bravo, Paris Exposition!" to the New York *Herald* and requested $10. When it was returned he sent it, on June 13, to the New York *World* and asked $6 (CB). It was finally published in *Harper's Weekly*; see 2114.

any) in Canada send me them of great wealthy public bequeathors or benefactors, like our Girard and Johns Hopkins? I want to make a piece ab't 'em & put names in—

Towards noon—sun out—a fine June day—

W W

2057. *To Louisa Orr Whitman*

Sunday forenoon June 9 '89

Lou, I rec'd the aspargus, strawberries &c, by Charley—have had some of the a[sparagus] for my breakfast—very good—thanks.

I w'd like you to put a *strong middling deep pocket* (one at least either on the right or left side) with a button at top—I am so in the habit of carrying things in my pocket—(no hurry at all for the gown)[41]—

Am a little "under the weather" yesterday & to-day but will pass over —Judge Garrison yesterday bo't twelve books (6 L of G. & 6 Nov. B) & paid the money.[42] To-day quiet & warm & dull here muchly—I am sitting up in the 2d story room alone—door & windows open—Did you or George get my little poem in N Y World Friday mn'g last, or Camden Courier same evn'g?—If not I will send you one—

W W

2058. *To Thomas Donaldson*

ADDRESS: Thomas Donaldson | 326 N. 40th Street | Philadelphia. POSTMARK: Camden, N.J. | Jun 9 | 1889 | 5 PM.
TRANSCRIPT.

328 Mickle Street | Camden N. J. June 9 '89

Dear Tom

That cheque for me from Irving—is it for me personally—if so, send it over to me, as I am in want of money.[43]

I am ab't as usual—

Walt Whitman

41. Louisa "bro't my new blue gown" on June 11 (CB).
42. Judge Charles G. Garrison had been a speaker at the birthday celebration (*Camden's Compliment to Walt Whitman*, 34–36); he paid $19.50 for the volumes (CB).
43. Henry Irving and Bram Stoker sent gifts of $50 and $25, respectively, to WW

2059. *To Thomas B. Harned*

TRANSCRIPT.

June 9, 1889

Have had such a good time with the Champagne you sent me, must at least thank [you] for it. I drank the whole bottle (except a little swig I insisted on Ed taking for going for it) had it in a big white mug half fill'd with broken ice, it has done me good already (for I was sort of "under the weather" the last 30 hours.)

Walt Whitman

2060. *To Mary Smith Costelloe*

ADDRESS: Mrs: Mary W Costelloe | 40 Grosvenor Road | Westminster Embankment | London England. POSTMARK: Camden, N.J. | Jun 14 | 8 PM | 89.

Camden New Jersey U S America | June 14 '89

Thanks for letters—& papers too—We are all (Dr. B[ucke] particularly) more interested in movements & your fortunes &c: there than you suppose[44]—I am getting along the same, fairly—get out daily in the wheel chair—write a little—Keep up pretty good spirits—cloudy rainy warm weather—Love to you, Alys, Mr S[mith] & all, not forgetting the little girls.

Walt Whitman

2061. *To Richard Maurice Bucke* *6.14–16.1889*

ADDRESS: Dr Bucke | Asylum | London | Ontario | Canada. POSTMARK: Camden, N.J. | Jun 16 | 5 PM | 89.

Camden 1889 | Friday noon June 14

Cloudy warm pleasant—feeling fairly (the main bother is this catarrhal, or whatever it is, head malady, quite bad much of the time)—

through Donaldson; see Traubel, v, 271. Donaldson informed WW on September 16 that he had deposited the sum and would bring a check to Camden (Feinberg). WW received the money on October 1 (CB), and sent receipts to Donaldson through Wilkins on October 16 (Donaldson, 98).

44. Almost always WW sent Mrs. Costelloe's letters to Bucke.

Herbert Gilchrist here last evening—bowel action sufficient & regular at present—go out in my wheel chair toward latter part of afternoon—

Saturday, toward sundown—A brisk rattling thunder shower—(will probably change the temperature)—have relish'd my supper, a bit of beef steak & some bread pudding—if it were not for this "cold in the head" I w'd feel quite tolerable—rainy & warm & no getting out for me in the wheel chair to-day—n'importe—thankful for feeling as well as I do—

Sunday 16th near noon—Have had a bath, & am going in wheel chair to Harned's, to lunch, & spend a couple of hours—(The family goes off in the mountains next Wednesday)—Pleasant here, but pretty warm—y'rs rec'd—have been reading the N Y and Phil. Sunday papers—sitting here in 2d story, Mickle—alone—Best love to all—

Walt Whitman

2062. *To William Sloane Kennedy* [*6.17.*] *1889*

Camden Monday 9 A M | '89

Am sitting here just ended my breakfast, an egg, some Graham bread & coffee—all wh' I relish'd—rec'd my morning mail, & send you this f'm Dr B[ucke][45]—with my scribbling on back—fine sunny day, moist enough (plenty of rain lately here) & pretty warm—was out last evening (sunset) two hours down to the Delaware shore, high water—sky & river never look'd finer—was out also at one p m to my friend Harned's to drink a bottle of champagne—(lunch, or dinner, but I ate nothing)—So you see I am getting around sort o' in my wheel chair—Have written a little the last two weeks—& sent off—Some accepted & paid, some rejected[46]—& so we are well in for another summer—I want to get out somewhere (sea side or mountains) but it is a fearful job for me to be moved from my habitat & ways here—As things are I depend on inherited impetus mainly, & humor everything or rather let it go.

Walt Whitman

45. WW's letter was written on the verso of Bucke's of June 15 (Ohio Wesleyan). On June 12 Kennedy had informed the poet of a "condition" he had established with Gardner, who was to publish his Whitman study: "that my corrections on proofs shd be followed. I only *surmised* that he *might* be mean enough to go ahead without me. But I have no *real ground* to think so" (Feinberg).

46. See 2056.

2063. *To William Carey*

ADDRESS: Wm Carey | *Century* office Union Square | New York City. POSTMARKS: Camden, N.J. | Jun 17 | 8 PM | 89; D | 6–18–89 | 8 A | N.Y.

328 Mickle Street | Camden New Jersey |
June 17 '89

Will you (or Mr Cox the photographer, he having copyright) loan for me to a N Y party the negative plate of the photo head (with hat) I call "the laughing philosopher"—to "process" for me? Answer me here[47]—

Walt Whitman

2064. *To G. C. Cox*

ADDRESS: Mr Cox | Photographer | Broadway & Ninth st: | New York City.

Camden New Jersey | June 23 '89

If convenient please give the bearer, for the Photo: Process Co: for me, the negative of the photo: my head (with hat) I call "the laughing Philosopher"—to be carefully cared-for & return'd to you in a month or less.

Walt Whitman

2065. *To Richard Maurice Bucke*

ADDRESS: Dr Bucke | Asylum | London | Ontario Canada. POSTMARK: Camden, N.J. | Jun 23 | 5 PM | 89.

Camden noon June 23 '89

Sunny, cool, first rate day—Every thing much the same in my condition &c. Have heard nothing f'm Mrs: O'C[onnor] at Wash'n—go down by the river most every day in the wheel chair & sit an hour when the weather is agreeable—The two principal summer months now July & August to confront—what they will bring we shall duly see—

W W

47. Traubel wanted to use the photograph in *Camden's Compliment to Walt Whitman* (Traubel, v, 268). Carey on June 18(?) requested additional information (Feinberg; Traubel, v, 305). On June 21 Carey informed Traubel that "Mr. Cox will make no objection as the picture is for Mr. Whitman" (Feinberg; Traubel, v, 312). Apparently Traubel was to go to New York with the following letter and pick up the negative (v, 314). The photograph is reproduced in this volume.

2066. *To Richard Maurice Bucke* [*6.29*]–*30.* [*1889*]

ADDRESS: Dr Bucke | Asylum | London | Ontario | Canada. POSTMARK: Camden, N.J. | Jun 30 | 5 PM | 89.

Camden Saturday afternoon

Hot unpleasant weather—under a bad spell (caving in feeling generally)—this is the third day—Still I get out in the wheel chair—was out to the river at sunset yesterday an hour—sleep & eat fairly yet—(made my breakfast of a dish of raspberries and Graham bread)—pulse fair—we have a good letter from Sarrazin wh' you will see in the pamphlet—(did I mention Rossetti's?)[48]—Horace delays a little, to get these slow letters wh' probably is all right—even better—(tho' I wanted the pamphlet to be out *at once*)—Nothing very new or significant—a little German review in paper f'm Berlin[49]—now sent by me to Mr Traubel to English it—will send it to you soon—Horace wishes me to say he will attend to having the little L of G bound as you desired, & send—Sylvester Baxter here yesterday—talk'd political reform & socialism strong—is going down to Kentucky (for the Boston *Herald*)—ask'd me as he left what word or message I had to give him—I said (a la Abraham Lincoln) there was a queer old Long Islander in my boyhood who was always saying "*hold your horses*"—(I like S B well—he is a good fellow, & a good friend.)[50]

Sunday 30th 10–11 a m—Rather pleasanter, cloudy, warm yet—bad spell continued—have had my breakfast, a rare egg, some Graham bread and cocoa & am sitting here alone—been looking over the Sunday paper—rather quiet day—T B Harned stays the coming week up in the mountain country—have myself no great desire to go country ward for a few weeks—Love to you all—

Walt Whitman

48. Letters from Sarrazin and Rossetti appear in *Camden's Compliment to Walt Whitman*, 49–50.

49. On June 16 Eduard Bertz (1853–1931) sent WW an article he had published in the *Deutsche Presse* of June 2 (Feinberg; Traubel, v, 330–331). On July 2 WW sent Bertz *Complete Poems & Prose*, and on July 7 a copy of Bucke's book (*CB*). Bertz thanked the poet on July 20–22; he stated that he preferred Freiligrath's translations to those of Rolleston and Knortz, and called attention to his own book *The French Prisoners* (1884), "the story of a friendship between a German boy and a young French soldier," with a chapter motto from *Leaves of Grass* (Feinberg). In 1905 Bertz published *Walt Whitman; ein Charakterbild.*

50. See Traubel, v, 326–327.

51. *Liberty* had a brief obituary for O'Connor, reprinted in Traubel, v, 333–334.

2067. *To Ellen M. O'Connor* 7.2. [*1889*]

ADDRESS: Mrs: O'Connor | 1015 O Street N W | Washington | D C. POSTMARKS: Camden (?) | Jul 2 | (?) PM | 89; Washington, Rec'd. | Jul 3 | 7 AM | 89 | 5.

Camden July 2d Evn'g

Havn't heard f'm you since dear W[illiam]'s death—Suppose you are in O St. for the present—I send you "Unity" and "Liberty"[51]—I send U to Eldridge and Burroughs—

Nothing markable in my condition—am doubtless declining—suppose you get the papers I send—Hot weather. Best love always—

Walt Whitman

2068. *To Richard Maurice Bucke*

ADDRESS: Dr Bucke | Asylum | London | Ontario Canada. POSTMARK: Camden, N.J. | Jul 3 | 8 PM | 89.

Camden July 3 noon '89

Easier slightly—continue to eat & sleep fairly—weather continues rainy warm unhealthy (now 4th day)—fair bowel action every 2d or 3d day—havn't taken any medicine in a long time—(no doctors here 3 or 4 months)—sent the big b'k to my late German friendly critic, Edw'd Bertz, Potsdam[52]—As I conclude the sun shines out—Wrote yesterday to Mrs. O'C[onnor] & sent "Unity"—

Walt Whitman

2069. *To Richard Maurice Bucke* [*7.*]*5–7. 1889*[53]

ADDRESS: Dr Bucke | Asylum | London | Ontario | Canada. POSTMARK: Camden (?) | Jul 7 | 5 PM | 89.

Camden 1889 | [*July*] *5 P M*

Fine weather, sunny, not hot & I feel well for me—good sound

Traubel wrote another obituary for *Unity*, XXIII (June 29, 1889), 138.

52. See 2066, *n*.49.

53. WW misdated this letter consistently for three days. July 7 fell on Sunday, June 7 on Friday. Mrs. O'Connor sent an eleven-page letter to WW on July 3, about which he expressed doubts to Traubel on July 6 as to sending it to Bucke (V, 352). For additional confirmation of the date, see Traubel's account of the poet's activities from July 5 to 7 (V, 347–353).

WW rightly foresaw that Bucke would seize upon the following section in Mrs. O'Connor's letter: "I have had several most *vivid* dreams of you, so distinct that all the next day I felt as if I had been with you; & I wonder whether my 'astral body' went to you, or yours came to me. A day or two before William passed away he awoke from a nap & asked me 'if Walt had gone?' I said you had not been here, but he repeated the question, & then I said yes, you had gone" (Feinberg). See 2073.

sleep last night & rest & quiet (bad enough the previous day & night)—appetite, bowels &c: fair continued—have rec'd a letter f'm Mrs: O'C[onnor]—enclosed—y'rs come safely—the "Camden Compliment" little book copy goes into the printer's (Ferguson's) hands to-day I believe—is to be frontispieced by a photo (wh' I do not like but the others do, & this is not *my* funeral) of Morse's bust (wh' I *do* like)—There is a good deal in the text wh' will please you I guess—

[July] 6—Fine weather—sun shining—bad spell resumed—got out in the wheel chair last sunset to river side (full tide, fine)—nearly two hours—sat there by the edge in my chair—saw the sun set over Phila:—

[July] 7—Sunday forenoon—Fine sunny weather continued—bad spell quite decided—rec'd y'r prescription, & shall use it this noon—thanks—Ed is just making up the bed—nothing very new—McKay goes off (for 4 or 5 weeks) on a business & drumming tour west—quiet forenoon here—

Walt Whitman

2070. *To William Sloane Kennedy* 7.7. [*1889*]

Camden Sunday aft'n July 7

Nothing very new or different—Keep up—go out in the wheel chair—a bad spell the last week & now (gradually declining)—a letter f'm Mrs O'C[onnor] Wash'n. She is gloomily, poorly left without means.[54] The little dinner book is being put in type—

W W

2071. *To Richard Maurice Bucke*

ADDRESS: Dr Bucke | Asylum | London | Ontario | Canada. POSTMARK: Camden, N.J. | Jul 10 | 8 PM | 89.

Camden noon July 10 '89

Fearful heat here now a week & at present looks like continued—thro' wh' tho' I get along better than you m't suppose. Am taking the tonic

54. Kennedy wrote on July 9 of Mrs. O'Connor: "The wife of such a Philip Sidney of a man as O'C demands chivalrous treatment if we w'd emulate the virtues of *him*. So I think & shall act" (Feinberg).

55. Traubel brought the poet a copy of Mrs. Ward's translation of *Amiel's Journal:*

—it (or something) relieves me the last two days of the worst of the weakness, caving-in & head inertia—but I feel it, the dose, for an hour after taking in my head & stomach very perceptibly & very uncomfortably —bowel action yesterday & also this forenoon, quite good—Ed stands it first rate—a note f'm Kennedy this mn'g, enclosed—nothing notable—he is half ill tho' this summer—nothing ab't his book—the printers are working at Horace's dinner book—

Have been dipping in the new French book Amiel's *Journal Intime* translated by Mrs: Humphrey Ward. He is evidently an orthodox conservative determined to stand by his (moth-eaten) colors, tho' modern science & democracy draw the earth from under his very feet—He is constantly examining, discussing *himself*, like a health-seeker dwelling forever on his own stomach—I heard it was a great book & going to be *established*—but I say *no* to both—he is one of those college pessimistic *dudes* Europe (& America too) sends out[55]—

I am sitting here in my big chair—every thing still—just drank a great drink of iced lemonade (pleasant but non-healthy)—After a New York boy's slang, I conclude by sending you *good roots*—

Walt Whitman

2072. *To Louisa Orr Whitman*

Camden | Friday Evn'g July 12 '89

Dear Lou

Your card rec'd to day—Nothing particular or very new with me —Hot and oppressive here eight or nine days & I have been under the weather probably from it as much as anything—Keep up ab't the same tho'—am taking a tonic dose (iron & strychnia I fancy) prescribed by Dr Bucke to stave off the terrible weakness & faintness—& it does so—but it costs as much as it comes too—So far I eat & sleep pretty well, wh' of course is the greatest help—Got a card f'm Hannah, & have written to her this evn'g—I send my best love to Amy and Warren—I wish I had something to send them—They are getting printed in a little book the speeches &c at my birth-day dinner & I will send you one when out—& one to Emma too[56]—

I havn't been out this is the fourth day in the wheel chair but shall

The Journal Intime of Henri-Frederic Amiel (London, 1889) on July 7 (Traubel, v, 353). On July 26 WW commented: "It is very introspective—very full of sin—of looking sinwards—a depressing book, in fact" (v, 393).

56. Louisa Whitman's sister, Emma Dowe, and her children, Amy and Warren (see 823). For Amy's recollections of WW, see *WWR*, XIII (1967), 73–79.

resume in a day or two—I am sitting here in the old den in Mickle st second story near sunset quite comfortable—

Walt Whitman

2073. *To Richard Maurice Bucke*

ADDRESS: Dr Bucke | Asylum | London | Ontario | Canada. POSTMARK: Camden (?) | Jul 13(?) | 8 (?) | 89.

Camden Saturday noon July 13 '89

Cloudy (rainy last night)—Still hot—Still eat & sleep fairly—take the tonic—y'r letter ab't Mrs O'C[onnor] rec'd—doubt whether it w'd suit her—such a plan—am not moved to it favorably[57]—Most things are bad enough with me, but I am blessed thankful they are no worse & that I get along as well as I do—Am getting along better than you suppose—rec'd a letter (I enclose it) from John Burroughs.[58] His address for twelve days will be Hobart N Y. The printing of Horace's little book is progressing—I am writing nothing—stretch'd out on the bed half the time fanning away the flies &c—not down ill but not far from that—some blackberries & a rare egg for my breakfast—

Sunset—Have had my supper & relish'd it—send this hence Camden (to Phila) 8 P M July 13—see & itemize to me, when it reaches you—over an hour's rain latter afternoon—I am feeling fairly—sweating—Well we must have a turn in the temperature presently—perhaps to-night—Best regards & love to Mrs B and all—

Walt Whitman

2074. *To Richard Maurice Bucke*

ADDRESS: Dr Bucke | Asylum | London | Ontario Canada. POSTMARK: Camden, N.J. | Jul 19 | 6 AM | 89.

Camden Evn'g July 18 '89

Nothing very new—I am dull—rather extra so in head, belly &c.—tho't it might be instigated by my tonic—& have intermitted it to-day

57. Bucke's letter is not extant, but WW summarized its contents for Traubel: "Doctor's last letter was written in a terrible strain: he proposes to me that, Mrs. O'Connor having no place her own now—nothing to do—that we somehow set up a bargain—that she keep house for me—that we go into alliance, get spliced" (v, 366). Bucke's reasoning was not an illogical deduction from Mrs. O'Connor's letter quoted in note 53. It would be interesting to know why WW chose the word "terrible" (terrifying?) to characterize Bucke's proposal.

58. Burroughs' letter of July 12 (Feinberg).

(for the first since you sent)—am sitting here after my supper, & shall go out in wheel chair to river side—y'r letters rec'd—weather pleasant.

Walt Whitman

2075. *To John Burroughs and Richard Maurice Bucke*

ADDRESS: John Burroughs | Hobart | New York.
POSTMARK: Camden, N.J. | Jul 19 | 8 PM | 89.

Camden noon July 19 '89

Pretty fair with me personally to-day—warm spell over two weeks but I keep up amid it (but every week or month a button or peg gives out—most of the time mildly—but I realize it well enough—my sight & hearing are quite markedly dulling)—warmth shaded a little to-day & cloudy any how—ate a rare egg & some Graham bread & coffee for my breakfast—eat two meals a day & moderate & plain, but relish them—sit here alone, as now, quiet & middling comfortable—rather an *un*fair night last (not common)—bladder botherations—bowel action this forenoon—I enclose Eldridge's rec'd to day, as you might like to know—Where & ab't Marvin I don't know—I will send you "Donnelly's Reviewers" right away[59]—I lent it to a friend & have just sent for it but could not get it this forenoon—Mrs: O'C[onnor] is yet at Wash'n, but expects to break up soon I think—

Y'rs rec'd & welcom'd as always—love to you & 'Sula & Julian—I have a big book (my "complete works" in one Vol. rather cumbersome) for you, John—send these (both) to Dr Bucke—

Walt Whitman

The "Donnelly" booklet comes now & I send it to you same mail with this—

59. On July 3 Mrs. O'Connor informed WW that she was sending him a copy of William's "last literary work," *Mr. Donnelly's Reviewers* (Feinberg). On August 27 Burroughs commented: "I read Williams pamphlet on Donnelleys Reviewers with melancholy enjoyment. It is very brilliant & effective, quite equal to his best work I think. If he had only left out some of his mud-epithets, or if he had only not claimed Montaignes Essays & Burtons Melancholy for Bacon! How such a claim as that does discredit the whole business. . . . Wm was fated to slop over in just this way, & to steel his reader against him" (Feinberg).

2076. *To Charles W. Eldridge*

TRANSCRIPT.

Camden, July 20, '89

Dear C. W. E.

Y'rs rec'd & welcomed, as always[60]—So you have flitted north on the Pacific Coast & settled in San Francisco. Good—no doubt—To use the N. Y. slang of low life I send you "good roots" for your new & future habitat—

I am still holding out here—probably better than you might suppose—but bad enough—physically almost completely disabled.

[WW also spoke of Dr. Bucke, John Burroughs, and the death of William D. O'Connor.]

Walt Whitman

2077. *To Richard Maurice Bucke*

ADDRESS: Dr Bucke | Asylum | London | Ontario Canada. POSTMARK: Camden, N.J. | Jul 21 | 4 30 PM | (?)9.

Camden Sunday P M July 21 | '89

Dull with me—am sitting quietly in my 2d story room—am not taking the tonic three or four days—easier in head—not writing lately—weather fluctuating, rainy & warm—tolerable to-day—eat blackberries most every day—Lawyer Harned out in the mountains—

Walt Whitman

2078. *To Ernest Rhys*

ADDRESS: Ernest Rhys | care Walter Scott, publisher | 24 Warwick Lane Paternoster | Row | London England. POSTMARKS: Camden, N.J. | Jul 23 | 8 PM | 89; Philadelphia, Pa. | Jul 23 | 11 PM | Paid.

Camden Evn'g July 23 '89

The Scottish Art Rev: with pictures has come safely[61]—thanks—I

60. On July 13 Eldridge informed WW that he had returned to the Internal Revenue Service and that he intended to remain in California (Feinberg).

61. Rhys's article "The Portraits of Walt Whitman" in the June issue (17–24) was slapdash journalism: Eakins became "Eadie."

62. WW made a similar observation in CB on July 19, "No sale worth mentioning of my books by myself."

63. WW sent the book July 23 to J. W. Wassall, of Chicago (CB), and Traubel sold two copies to "the Lychenheim boys" on July 16 (Traubel, v, 368, 371).

am here yet getting along fairly—seven weeks hot weather here—but I hug to my old den thro' all as the best I can do in my immobile condition —no sales of books[62]—love to all inquiring friends—am comfortable as I write—

Walt Whitman

2079. *To Richard Maurice Bucke*

ADDRESS: Dr Bucke | Asylum | London | Ontario Canada. POSTMARKS: Camden, N.J. | Jul 25 | 6 AM | 89; N.Y. | 7–25–89 | 1030 AM | 10.

Camden early P M 24th July | '89

Nothing special or new—Every thing going on the same & fairly —think quite a good deal of O'C[onnor] lately—breakfasted on an egg & some blackberries—have sent the little "Donelly" book to John Burroughs (at his request) at Hobart N Y. Have just sold to Chicago purchaser one of the big book (three the last week, but that is exceptional)[63]—

Walt Whitman

2080. *To Richard Maurice Bucke*

ADDRESS: Dr Bucke Asylum | London | Ontario Canada. POSTMARK: Camden, N.J. | Jul 25 | 8 PM | 89.

Camden | P M July 25 '89

Dull & quiet—Slightly more ill than usual—half cloudy & warmish—Kennedy's book is at sea again as you will learn by enclosed[64]—Herbert Gilc[hrist] comes frequently—often strangers, visitors, sometimes queer ones—

I get out in the wheel chair—was out last evening till dark—acts as sort o' pacifyer—The Staffords are well—

Walt Whitman

64. On July 24(?) Kennedy sent Gardner's letter of rejection—"the pultroon's letter"—and observed: "I guess we have to wait for the book & pub[lish] it here sometime. . . . I am going to let Fred [W] Wilson look at the MS again. He has never refused it, you know" (Feinberg). On August 4 he commented "I kind o' hope Fred. Wilson will tackle in some way my Whitman" (Feinberg). On September 5 he rationalized: Gardner "publishes highly respectable *religious* books (not our cosmic-pantheistic kind, of course)" (Feinberg)—a somewhat silly remark since Gardner was the English publisher of *November Boughs.*

2081. *To Richard Maurice Bucke*

ADDRESS: Dr Bucke | Asylum | London | Ontario Canada. POSTMARK: Camden, N.J. | Jul 26 | 8 PM | 89.

Camden dusk July 26 '89

A word first for Pardee—gone over then to the majority, where we are all steadily tending "for reasons"—blessed be his memory!

have just eaten my supper, stew'd chicken & rice—feel poorly these days & nights—a shade easier this evn'g—the heat I suppose has sapp'd & indigestion's talons are fix'd on me again—yours rec'd this P M—cooler —a rain in prospect—

Walt Whitman

2082. *To Richard Maurice Bucke*

ADDRESS: Dr Bucke | Asylum | London | Ontario Canada. POSTMARKS: Camden, N.J. | Jul 28 | 5 PM | 89; Buffalo, N (?) | Jul 29 | 1030 AM | 89 | Rec'd.

Camden P M July 28 '89

Wet, warmish, cloudy half dark to day—feeling fairly—bowel action & water-works action middling fair (sluggish & delayed)—peaches have come, good, & I eat them cut up & sugar'd—still stick to the mutton-rice broth—have been looking over the proofs of Horace's dinner book—(it is a cataclysm of praise &c:)—of course you will get one soon as printed—well some three or four weeks of hot weather yet, with perhaps of intervals even in that—

W W

2083. *To George and Susan Stafford*

Camden noon July 30 '89

Well, friends all, here I am yet (surely but rather slowly going down hill) not so much very different from of old, but *more so*—more lame & helpless in body, dimmer in sight & harder in hearing—yet in pretty good spirits—warm & wet weather here, & lots of it—stand it yet here, thro' the summer mostly because I have to & *can't help it*, but it is very oppressive & stale here much of the time—but it might be much much worse, & I get along—Mrs: D[avis] and Ed Wilkins (my nurse) are good & so far I get along fairly with appetite, grub & sleep wh' of course make the foundation of all—

Herbert comes over quite frequently, & is well & I guess doing well (I hear of you all by him—otherwise you might as well be at the antipodes) —Sickness & death are all around me here, & on the houses each side—I sit in the big chair all day & pass away the time as well as I can—

Dr B[ucke] is still in Canada—is well—I hear f'm him often—I had a letter from Ruth, enclosed, tho' I suppose she has written to you—I send my love to Harry—have not heard from or seen him in a long time—Love to you & George, and to Ed & Deb & Van & young Geo & to Jo—not forgetting the children—Lord bless you all—

Walt Whitman

2084. *To William Sloane Kennedy*

ADDRESS: Sloane Kennedy | Belmont | Mass:.
POSTMARK: Camden, N.J. | Aug 2 | 8 PM | 89(?).

Camden P M July 31 '89

Nothing of importance—Rainy rainy weather here night & day. To-morrow the beginning of the last month of hot summer—I have stood it pretty well here, & am fairly condition'd as I write this afternoon—I not only know but feel that even a fair nibble is better than no loaf of bread at all (wh' comes to the question sometimes)—Ah there comes the sunshine as I conclude—

W W

2085. *To Richard Maurice Bucke*

ADDRESS: Dr Bucke | Asylum | London | Ontario Canada.

Camden Aug: 2 '89

The sun is out—quiet & warm & very moist—nothing very new—Dull & rather poorly with me—I send two copies of the little new morocco bound ed'n of L of G. by this mail—is it that way you wanted? Yr letters come, always welcome.[65] Had a letter f'm Hamlin Garland—with first rate

65. There are no extant letters from Bucke to WW between July 14 and August 4.

carte photo:—notice a good portrait of Tennyson (in old age) in Aug: Century[66]—All well—

Walt Whitman

2086. *To Richard Maurice Bucke* *8.3–4.1889*

ADDRESS: Dr Bucke | Asylum | London | Ontario | Canada. POSTMARK: Camden, N.J. | Aug 4 | 5 PM | 89.

Camden New Jersey '89 | P M Aug: 3

Moist & warm continued, but the sun is out this afternoon—I am so-so—from sitting in the big chair (as now) to reclining on the bed, with palm leaf fan in hand—getting along fairly with all—I hope you will receive the two little L of G. sent by mail yesterday—Am slowly lazily occupying myself, (*must* have something to do, or pretend) with getting the photos: & prints of different stages on uniform sized cards or sheets, to be put in a good handsome fitting envelope (? perhaps album)—you shall receive one collected of all the portraits (there are 6 or 7 or more) soon as prepared—though you have them all now—

Sunday Aug. 4 towards noon—Fine & clear & quiet—feeling fair as usual—cut-up peaches, an egg, &c: for my breakfast—am sitting here alone in my big den—bowel action an hour ago—Mr Stafford here yesterday afternoon—they are all well—rec'd a long good letter from a German scholar, has been in America, writes English good, *Edward Bertz, Holzmark't Str. 18, Pots-dam, Prussia*—He bids fair to be, or rather is, one of the first class friends of L of G.—I have sent him (& he rec'd) the big vol. & your book—I send you a paper with interesting piece ab't Tennyson by Gosse—(a pleasant blanc-mange bit for the palate)[67]—

W W

2087. *To Ellen M. O'Connor*

ADDRESS: Mrs: O'Connor | 1015 O Street N W | Washington | D C. POSTMARKS: Camden, N.J. | Aug 4 | 5 PM | 89; Wash. D. C. Forwarded | Aug 5 | (?) 30 PM | 29.

Camden P M Aug: 4 '89

Nothing very new—have not left my Mickle St: quarters this

66. The frontispiece was an engraving by Thomas Johnson after a photograph by a Mrs. Carver.

67. Kennedy on August 4 (Feinberg) called WW's attention to Gosse's two-column article in the Boston *Evening Transcript* of the preceding day entitled "Tennyson at

summer (hardly *can*)—am feeling fairly to-day—my friend Traubel has written (at their request) & sent on to "*Liberty*" (Boston) a piece abt Wm wh' if they print I will send you[68]—I suppose you have heard from Ch's Eldridge at San Francisco (Revenue Ag't there)—Best love—

Walt Whitman

2088. *To Richard Maurice Bucke*

ADDRESS: Dr Bucke | Asylum | London | Ontario Canada. POSTMARK: Camden (?) | Aug 5 | 8 PM | 89.

Camden Aug: 5 '89

Feeling fairly—moist continued, less warm—Yes I like the Tennyson head in *Century* too (that T Johnson engraver is best of 'em all)—A T is getting splendid notices in the papers for his old birthday to-morrow, & deserves them—Mrs: O'Connor is at North Perry, Maine—I have just sent her a packet of papers there—

Walt Whitman

2089. *To Richard Maurice Bucke*

ADDRESS: Dr Bucke | Asylum | London | Ontario Canada. POSTMARK: Camden, N.J. | Aug 8 | 8 PM | 89.

Camden noon Aug: 8 '89

Feeling pretty well—sitting here in 2d story den—rec'd a letter from Logan Smith, they are all down in Surrey—Haslemere—all well—hope you have got the two copies little pocket bound L of G I sent—letter f'm you yesterday—Ed went over to "Chimes of Normandy" Eng: Opera last evn'g—good—Herbert Gil[christ] here last evn'g—superb weather here, this the third day.

Walt Whitman

Y'rs of 6th since rec'd that the two books have come—

Eighty."

Mounted on this letter are two newspaper clippings, one an article about the North Pole and the other an account of an insane asylum.

68. See Traubel, v, 492.

2090. *To Mary Smith Costelloe*

ADDRESS: Mrs: Mary Whitall Costelloe | 40 Grosvenor Road | the Embankment | London | England. POSTMARK: Camden, N.J. | Aug 8 | 8 PM | 89.

Camden Aug: 8 '89

Am feeling pretty well for me—good weather here—was yesterday over to Phila: to Gutekunst's to sit for big picture (at vehement request)[69]—went in large easy cab—every thing, river, ferry, Market & Arch streets & the vehicles & people *look'd so well & bright & prosperous & even gay*—thank Logan for his good letter & send this to him—H Gil[christ] was here last evn'g & has taken the letter away—Love to all—

Walt Whitman

2091. *To Richard Maurice Bucke*

ADDRESS: Dr Bucke | Asylum | London | Ontario Canada. POSTMARK: Camden, N.J. | Aug 14 | 8 PM | 89.

Camden Aug: 14 '89

Middling—nothing very new. Specimens of the photos: have come & I like pretty well a large half-size sitting figure—have requested some & shall reserve one for you when I get them—I send you another paper ab't the "elixir"—If you want any more send me word—if not, not—do you remember the *blue glass* furore of ten or twelve y'rs ago? My picture collation goes on[70]—I send papers &c: to Mrs: O'C[onnor] at North Perry, Maine. Y'rs of 12th has just come—

W W

2092. *To Richard Maurice Bucke* *8.16–18.1889*

ADDRESS: Dr Bucke | Asylum | London | Ontario | Canada. POSTMARK: Camden (?) | Aug 18(?) | 5 PM | 89.

Camden '89 | Aug: 16 near noon

Superb sunny day—poorly to-day & yesterday—brain & belly le-

69. WW was accompanied on this excursion by Buckwalter and Wilkins—"got along very well" (*CB*). On August 13 WW requested "specimens—big heads ('panel' size)—a big half-length, sitting, no hat, (big pict: but less than 'panel')—this 2d one I like—& a number of others." On August 23 he asked Gutekunst to copyright six of the

sions—eat little—am sitting in my big chair in 2d story room alone—moderately cool—y'r letters come[71]—some of the biggest officers land office at Washington spell it *adobie*, & I like it best—David McKay has just return'd—I have not seen him—Heard no word lately from Kennedy or Mrs: O'C[onnor] nor John Burroughs—Herbert Gil[christ] comes over quite often—Horace regularly, daily—Ed W[ilkins] keeps well—

Aug: 17—perfect day again—half-bad night last—ate an egg, Graham bread & cut-up peaches for breakfast—am sitting here—sufficiently cool—slightly clouded over—

Aug 18—Sunday, just after noon—fine weather continued—sitting here, pretty weak & ill, but had a fair night—have been looking over the proof slips of Horace's dinner book—curious—all honey & sweet meats—a nice girl has just bro't me a bouquet, a great fine tiger lily, in a lot of fluffy green sprigs, loose—queer & very pretty—

Am going to lie down on the bed—

Love to you—

Walt Whitman

2093. *To Richard Maurice Bucke*

ADDRESS: Dr Bucke | Asylum | London | Ontario Canada. POSTMARK: Camden, N.J. | Aug 22 | 8 PM | 89.

Camden P M Aug: 22 '89

Hot & oppressive weather—bad spell for me—one of the very bad ones (like when you were here fourteen mo's ago)—now the sixth day[72] —have a fine photo: for you. Shall I send it on, or keep it (as it is pretty big)—Herbert Gil[christ] here last evn'g—good visit—y'rs came—am sitting here alternating bet: ch'r & bed—

Walt Whitman

Sunset—am certainly easier—

photographs (CB). The "2nd" portrait is reproduced in this volume.

70. He was preparing a portfolio of self-portraits.

71. There are no extant letters from Bucke between August 4 and 25.

72. On the following day he wrote in CB: "Have had a bad week—one of the worst (tho't sometimes it might be the *close*)—but am a little easier to-day."

2094. *To Susan Stafford*

ADDRESS: Mrs: Susan Stafford | Kirkwood (Glendale) | New Jersey. POSTMARK: Camden, N.J. | Aug 22 | 8 PM | 89.

Camden P M Aug: 22 '89

Y'rs came this afternoon. Herbert was here last evn'g, very good visit—Hot weather here—Am pretty ill—one of my worst spells—now a week—half the time stretch'd out on the bed—half the time in my big chair as now—Love to you all—glad to hear f'm Harry—

Walt Whitman

2095. *To Richard Maurice Bucke*

ADDRESS: Dr Bucke | Asylum | London | Ontario | Canada. POSTMARK: Camden, N.J. | Aug 24 | 8 PM | 89.

Camden A M Aug. 24 '89

Am easier than during the week, but bad enough yet—Have made away with my breakfast (wet Graham toast, honey & tea) though—(living mostly on toast & tea the last three or four days)—am sitting here in the big chair, by window—cloudy & half rainy to-day—a jolly letter f'm Ernest Rhys f'm Wales, wh' I enclose—Y'rs rec'd this mn'g—thanks—was formally requested (did I tell you?) to write an article "Tennyson at 81" for the Oct. No. of the *N A Review*—by the new owners—but have been too ill to try it, & shall probably give it the go-by—(I don't know but I have said all I want to say ab't T any how)[73]—the sun out—& warm—It is ab't noon as I finish—I am feeling sort o' comfortable—Mrs: D[avis] and one of the boys[74] have gone over to Phila: wharf somewhere to see an old staunch ship the "Emily Reed," involved in their family history—Ed is here taking care—Luck & prayers.

Walt Whitman

73. See Traubel, v, 451.

74. Harry and Warren Fritzinger, children of a sea captain whom Mrs. Davis had nursed, were living in the Camden "shanty"; see Allen, 519.

75. Rhys's letter of August 14 was indeed a "jolly" and astute comment on Wales

2096. *To Ernest Rhys*

ADDRESS: Ernest Rhys | Care Walter Scott Publisher | 24 Warwick Lane Paternoster Row | London England. POSTMARK: Camden, (?) | Aug 2(?) | 6 AM | 89.

Camden New Jersey U S America | Aug: 25 '89

Y'rs f'm Wales came yesterday & was welcome (I have sent it to Dr Bucke, as he likes such)[75]—Nothing very significant—am still here in my *den* in Mickle street—Keep pretty good heart, but alternations of bad & less bad health (plenty of the former)—the summer is waning here, & I have pass'd along & through it better than was anticipated—Write often as you can—Gilchrist, Kennedy, Dr B. & Traubel well—

Walt Whitman

2097. *To Ellen M. O'Connor*

ADDRESS: Mrs: E M O'Connor | North Perry | Maine. POSTMARK: Camden, N.J. | Aug 27 | 8 PM | 89.

Camden Aug: 27 '89

Am getting along pretty fairly. Nothing very new or marked—Ups & downs—the *trend* steadily the latter way, as of course is to be expected. I believe I sent you "Poet-Lore" with the notice,[76] & I suppose you have rec'd it before this—send me word when you next write—also what if anything I can do, or get & send—don't be afraid to request me—I hear f'm Dr B[ucke] often—he is well & busy—Ch's Eldridge is in St Francisco, no d[oub]t as U S Revenue Ag't—I suppose you get the papers all right—the weather changes here cooler to-day—

Walt Whitman

2098. *To Richard Maurice Bucke*

ADDRESS: Dr Bucke | Asylum | London | Ontario Canada. POSTMARK: Camden, N.J. | Aug 27 | 8 PM | 89.

Camden Aug: 27 '89

Am pretty comfortable & easy upon the whole—breakfast, toast, honey & tea—have just written to Mrs O'C[onnor]—also an "autobiogra-

and Paris (Feinberg). Rhys replied to WW on September 11, and informed him of his study of Welsh poetry (Feinberg).

76. *Poet-lore* printed a review of *November Boughs* in March (147) and an account of the birthday banquet in July (348).

phic note" for Horace's dinner book, (a page, fine type)—bowel voidance this forenoon (first during a week)—sit here alone, ab't the same—the weather markedly changed cooler to-day—the Japanee Hartman call'd yesterday[77]—have been idly reading & scribbling a little to-day—one of my *let ups*—

Walt Whitman

Y'rs of 25th comes—shall be glad to see Dick Flynn[78]—

2099. *To John Burroughs*

ADDRESS: John Burroughs | West Park | Ulster County New York. POSTMARK: Camden, N.J. | Aug 28 | 8 PM | 89.

Camden Aug: 28 '89

Y'rs of yesterday has come & welcome—I am feeling fairly enough to-day, after one of my bad spells of ten days—weather cooler here—get out a little in propell'd wheel chair—was out last evening to sunset at river shore, (after some days interregnum)—Hear f'm Dr B[ucke] often—Mrs: O'C[onnor] is at North Perry, Maine, temporarily—I will send you Horace Traubel's dinner book soon as printed—Did you get the morocco-b'd L of G. I sent to Hobart?

W W

2100. *To The Editor*, Harper's New Monthly Magazine

TRANSCRIPT.

Camden, Aug. 29, '89

Y'rs of yesterday rec'd with picture suggesting piece (illustration in text). Will this do? I shall want proof (wh' don't forget)—the price is $25[79]—

Walt Whitman

77. There is (curiously) no record in Traubel of a visit from Hartmann on August 26.

78. WW met Flynn when he visited London, Ontario, in 1880 (976, *n.*57; 990). See also Traubel, v, 461.

79. On August 25 Alden, the editor of *Harper's New Monthly Magazine*, requested a poem (Feinberg). WW on August 30 sent "Death's Valley," and was paid $25 on September 1 (*CB*). The poem was to accompany an engraving of George Inness' "The

2101. *To Richard Maurice Bucke*

ADDRESS: Dr Bucke | Asylum | London | Ontario
Canada. POSTMARK: Camden (?) | Aug 29 | 8 PM |
89.

Camden Aug: 29 '89

Am writing this just before sunset—feeling pretty fair—been requested by Alden the editor to write a piece for Harper's Monthly, & shall send it off this evn'g—If printed I shall either send it you or inform you—Dick Flynn came last evn'g, & he & Ed: are off to-day in Phila—I believe Dick goes hence Saturday—shall probably send the picture by him—just had to pay nearly $40 for taxes to the banditti who *govern* our city here[80]—word from Burroughs yesterday—he is well—back in West Park—

Walt Whitman

2102. *To Richard Maurice Bucke* *8.30–31.1889*

ADDRESS: Dr Bucke | Asylum | London | Ontario |
Canada. POSTMARK: Camden (?) | Sep 1 | 5 PM |
(?).

Camden '89 | *Friday noon Aug. 30*

Another perfect sunny day—plenty warm enough—am feeling middling fair—toast, a rare fried egg, & cup of tea, for breakfast (demolished all)—the vibrating voices of the loud-crying peddlers in the streets, quite a musical study, some of them have wonderfully fine organs as they peal and drawl them along—& it is fine, healthy, strengthening, expanding, blood-circulating & blood-clarifying exercising, calling loudly out in the open air this way, throwing the voices out freely, slowly walking along—I almost envy them, (with their cabbages, fish or what not, & their old vehicles & nags.)

Dick Flynn & Ed are over in Phila—I sent Ed for the pictures again—I hope y'rs will come right—Dick is very quiet—we all like him here—he has left & will get there before this—I sent off the little piece to

Valley of the Shadow of Death" (1867); see LeRoy Ireland, *The Works of George Inness* (1965), 98–99. When the poem appeared in April, 1892, the frontispiece of the magazine was a photograph of Alexander's portrait of WW, and above the poem appeared a more recent sketch of the poet by the same artist. A partial facsimile of this manuscript appears in Traubel, v, 242.

80. WW paid a city tax of $25.28 on August 24 and a water tax bill for $8.40 on August 28. Of the former he wrote: "In Italy & Greece they have a dis-illegal banditti—here we have a regular legal one, & numerous & remorseless" (*CB*).

Harper's last evn'g—written in an hour—it is to accompany a fine engraving, "the valley of the shadow of Death"—I ask $25—(of course it may not suit them—we will see)—

Herbert Gil[christ] was here last evn'g. He is very good company—Horace was here—the dinner book will be soon out now—

Saturday—noon—Aug. 31—Suppose Dick has reach'd home by this time—give him my best regards & wishes—rather warmish weather (fine) here—I am middling fairly—have been writing this forenoon—Harper's has accepted the little piece & sent the pay & proof (not to be printed, I fancy, soon)—also just rec'd f'm *Century* a little eight line poemet proof, "My 71st Year" (I believe for Nov.)—I enclose Pearsall Smith's good letter rec'd last evn'g[81]—they have evidently great inward intestinal agitation & unsettledness in Great Britain, (we too here in America, but our belly is so large)—then the unsettledness on the Continent too—as dear Mrs G[ilchrist] said we are all "*going somewhere*" indeed—I suppose the dyspeptic Carlyle would say "Yes, to hell"—But per contra old black Sojourner Truth was always saying "God reigns yet I tell you"—

Walt Whitman

2103. *To Richard Maurice Bucke*

ADDRESS: Dr Bucke | Asylum | London | Ontario Canada. POSTMARK: Camden, N.J. | Sep 2 | 8 PM | 89.

Camden Evn'g Sept: 2 '89

Am feeling middling well—ab't as usual—sort o' busy all day—bowel action this forenoon—a long letter f'm Mrs: O'C[onnor] f'm North Perry, Maine—nothing special—am going out in the wheel chair for a short turn—

Walt Whitman

2104. *To William Ingram*

Camden P M Sept: 2 '89

Respects & good-will & good luck to you, dear friends both—Nothing very new or different with me—I have just finished my early supper (I

81. Smith's letter of August 13 (Feinberg).

82. In CB WW noted: "Rush call'd—look'd well—was very thankful, eulogistic, full-hearted—is just out of prison, is just off to his parents in the country." See 1772, *n.*22.

only eat two meals a day—no dinner)—mutton & rice broth, Graham bread & a cup of tea—relish'd all—

Rush was here to-day—his imprisonment over, & he goes right off to Concordville (is it?)—he looks well & was very thankful—had your names over & over again with thanks & blessings[82]—

I am writing for pub'n a little still—have had a bad spell last week & before—one of my worst—but am now ab't as usual considering *the steady downward trend*—Dr Bucke is well—I enclose some pictures.

Walt Whitman

2105. *To Richard Maurice Bucke*

ADDRESS: Dr Bucke | Asylum | London | Ontario Canada. POSTMARK: Camden, N.J. | Sep 4 | 8 PM | 89.

Camden near noon Sept: 4 '89

Fine weather—nothing very different or new—am feeling passably comfortable—rec'd y'rs of Dick Flynn's safe return & of y'r satisfaction with the picture! Did it come in good order? We too all like it well—T B [Harned] and Frank [Harned] and H Traubel and Herbert G[ilchrist] all here last evn'g—& Mr & Mrs Ingram this forenoon—

I am sitting as usual in the big chair in second story room as I write—was out in the wheel chair last evn'g—

Walt Whitman

2106. *To Richard Maurice Bucke* *9.6–8. 1889*

ADDRESS: Dr Bucke | Asylum | London | Ontario | Canada. POSTMARK: Camden (?) | Sep 8 | 5 PM | 89.

Camden 1889

Sept: 6—early P M—A warm rather oppressive day—these middle hours—not well—lying down a good deal—bowel action yesterday—y'rs rec'd—out to river side last evn'g by wheel chair—

Sept: 7—P M—ab't same—rather bad, but nothing extreme—had a

On February 13, 1890, Rush, apparently an entertainer, wrote to WW from Missouri; he characterized his imprisonment as "a gross injustice": "While Beer & music is yet one of my standards & enjoyed by all the West We dont have to go to Prison three years for enjoying theme out here" (Feinberg).

partially good night—a card from Kennedy, nothing very significant—good *memoriam* article in "Liberty" Boston Sept. 7, by Horace ab't O'Connor—I expect some copies & then I will send you one—Ed has been over to the big launch, the new war ship "Philadelphia" noon to-day—weather middling to-day, warmish, a little air—Horace's dinner book will be out next week—I am sitting here in big chair—alternate to bed—

Sept: 8—noon—a shade easier—rather extra breakfast, a rare fried egg, Graham toast, roast apple & tea—bowel action—cloudy, still day, not warm—T B H[arned] and Mr Green, English Unitarian preacher, just here—card f'm Kennedy enc'd: just rec'd—also an old letter f'm Dowden[83]—

Walt Whitman

2107. *To William Sloane Kennedy* *9.7–8.1889*

Camden 1889

Saturday Evn'g Sept: 7—Am having rather bad spells—had one ten or twelve days last of August—but then they ease up quite perceptibly—was easier for five days, & now am passing a rather depress'd time again—probably to be follow'd by a sort of let up—& that seems by long experience the routine of the matter—

Y'r card came to-day—welcome—Look for to-day's Sept. 7. "Liberty" (Tucker's paper)[84] for a very good little *memoriam* of Wm O'Connor, by my young friend Traubel here—Mrs: O'Connor is still at North Perry, Maine (& if convenient after you have got & read the "Liberty" I speak of, send it to Mrs: O'C—just the place, only, address)—

I hear from Dr Bucke often—he is well & busy at his Institution, London, Canada—I hear f'm my friends the Smiths and Mrs: Costelloe, in Eng:—Did you come across the French book, Sarrazin's, yet? "*Poetes Anglaise*" wh' I told you was out & I have had a copy—(it has been *out* ever since and is out now)—it seems to be *the most determined blow* we have had happen to us yet—

Traubel's dinner book (as I call it) is not out, printed yet, but will be very soon—& I will send you one.

83. Kennedy's card of September 5 and Dowden's letter of June 26 (Feinberg).

84. Benjamin R. Tucker, the editor of *Liberty*, was an old friend (see 1232).

85. On September 12 Sir Edwin Arnold (1832–1904) wrote from Washington, D. C., requesting permission to visit WW (Feinberg). (The Boston *Traveller* on October 5, however, reprinted a purported letter from Arnold to WW dated September 12, written from New York, in a flamboyant style not found in the actual letter.) For an account of Arnold's visit, see Traubel, v, 506, 509–510: "My main objection to him, if

Sept. 8—noon—A shade better, easier, to-day—am sitting here by the open window, pretty comfortable—Respects to Baxter & all & any of the boys, if you see 'em—the enc: letter to me is f'm Logan Smith, son, England—also an old slip song at one of the [wharves?] "circles" here—

W W

2108. *To Richard Maurice Bucke*

ADDRESS: Dr Bucke | Asylum | London | Ontario | Canada. POSTMARK: Camden, N.J. | Sep 14 | 8 PM | 89.

Camden as usual | *Saturday P M Sept: 14 '89*

The sun shining this afternoon & pleasant after four or five days of rain & gale, very bad around here and at sea but nothing specially alarming here—I am much the same—not feeling at all easy & free f'm disturbance—Sir Edwin Arnold[85] here yesterday afternoon ab't an hour—a tann'd English traveler—I liked him—an actor from Phila. theatre also here yesterday.[86]

I sit here in 2d story room, alone—rather expect to go out later in wheel chair, first time in ab't a week—Ed is well, went to see "Bohemian Girl" Eng: opera—Horace comes regularly—you will see Mrs. O'C[onnor]'s letter, just rec'd—y'rs come & welcomed always—I will keep you posted when any new little pieces of mine come out—

Walt Whitman

2109. *To William Sloane Kennedy*

ADDRESS: Sloane Kennedy | Belmont Mass:. POSTMARK: Camden, N.J. | Sep (?) | 8 PM | 89.

Camden Saturday Evn'g | Sept. 14 '89

Nothing particular or new in my affairs or condition—feel bad enough head, viscera &c:—Mrs: O'Connor leaves North Perry Monday next for Boston—address care Charles E Legg,[87] 146 Devonshire St—

objection at all, would be, that he is too eulogistic—too flattering." Arnold published his own version of the interview in *Seas and Lands* (1891), in which he averred that the two read from *Leaves of Grass*, surrounded by Mrs. Davis, knitting, a handsome young man (Wilkins), and "a big setter."

86. The actor, WW informed Traubel, was "a hearty fellow, too—Hanson, I think was his name" (v, 507).

87. Mrs. O'Connor's nephew, according to her letter of September 12 (Feinberg).

Doctor [Bucke], Mr Harned, Horace, &c well—the sun out this afternoon here, after a weeks absence & heavy storms[88]—

Walt Whitman

2110. *To Ellen M. O'Connor*

Camden P M Sept: 15 '89

Enclosed I send Wm's picture given by him to me when last here —not knowing whether you have one like it, or w'd wish to use it, or favor it—But it is the one I like best[89]—*Of course I want it return'd to me here without fail*—Have you rec'd the "Liberty" Boston, dated Sept. 7?—I requested one sent you at North Perry a week ago—If not reach'd you get one in Boston—there is a good *memoriam* of dear W (by Horace Traubel[90]—

Nothing new or significant particular with me—I continue pretty poorly & uncomfortable brain, eyesight & viscera—half-clear & warmish here, after the week's storm—Sir Edwin Arnold, the English poet, was here to see me, very cheery & eulogistic—aged ab't 40, quite a traveler, now bound (soon) to the Pacific & round the world—I enclose you a picture or two besides—the one in the hat I call "the laughing philosopher"—I am sitting here alone in my big ratan arm chair in my den—Supper soon—I only eat two meals (no dinner) but relish them—

Walt Whitman

2111. *To Richard Maurice Bucke*

ADDRESS: Dr Bucke | Asylum | London | Ontario Canada. POSTMARK: Camden, N.J. | Sep 18 | 8 PM | 89.

Camden noon Sept: 18 '89

Y'rs f'm "Star House" rec'd—I send herewith "Liberty" with Horace's piece ab't O'C[onnor]—Cloudy, dark, rainy here several days, & now

88. On September 5 Kennedy informed WW ("Dear Dad" was the salutation) that he was now reading "proof at Riverside Press." He noted on September 15 that his wife would visit WW shortly, and recommended Dumas' "D'Artagnon romances"—"Manly comradeship is the theme and love. But *especially comradeship* . . . yr calamus doctrine embodied in a faint & inferior degree" (Feinberg).

89. Mrs. O'Connor on September 12 asked WW's advice as to which picture of her husband she should submit to *Appleton's Encyclopedia.* She also described her anxiety: "I

—So-so with me—nothing I suppose very bad, but bad enough—am sitting here in my "den" as usual—growing cooler weather—a poor night last—indications that "fall" & even winter & the need of fire are approximating—havn't been out in the wheel chair some days—eat bread, honey, & drink tea—relish all—No sales of L of G—

Walt Whitman

2112. *To Ellen M. O'Connor*

ADDRESS: Mrs: E M O'Connor | care Charles E Legg | 146 Devonshire Street | Boston Mass:. POSTMARKS: Camden, N.J. | Sep 19 | 8 PM | 89; Boston | Sep 20 89 | (?) PM | 6.

Camden Evn'g, Sept. 19 '89

Nothing new or notable—have not heard for certain yet whether you are in Boston safe. Suppose so tho'—& that you rec'd the photo. of Wm: I lent—also the "Liberty" piece sent—(I sent one to C W E[ldridge])—much the same as when I wrote—not at my worst but bad enough—I sit here writing & reading in moderation—unable to move—

Walt Whitman

2113. *To Richard Maurice Bucke*

ADDRESS: Dr Bucke | Asylum | London | Ontario Canada. POSTMARK: Camden, N.J. | Sep 22 | 5 PM | 89.

Camden P M Sept: 22 '89

Quite cool here—I have an incipient fire to-day & yesterday. Am feeling as usual—middling fair—very quiet to-day. Quite a strong "last word" from J A Symonds f'm Switzerland—you will see it in Horace's book[91]—*that* will be out next week I guess—

Walt Whitman

dread, dear Walt, I can't tell any one how much I dread the going back home. I say *home*, but the sense of loneliness that overtakes me when I think of going is heart-sickening. And the uncertainty of all adds to it" (Feinberg).

90. Mrs. O'Connor on September 26 termed Traubel's note "*noble* and *generous*" (Feinberg).

91. Symonds' tribute to WW, dated September 3, was included among the postscripts in *Camden's Compliment to Walt Whitman*, 73. On September 21 the poet sent *Complete Poems & Prose* to Symonds (CB).

2114. *To Richard Maurice Bucke*

ADDRESS: Dr Bucke | Asylum | London | Ontario | Canada. POSTMARK: Camden, N.J. | Sep 25 | 8 PM | 89.

Camden | early P M Sept: 25 '89

Dark & rainy weather continued—mild cold—moderate bowel action—still eat mutton & rice broth, Graham bread, honey & tea. Am sitting here in the 2d story room, alone, trying to while away the day—But this is all the old, old story—Am feeling fairly to-day but dull, dull—I told you that Harper's Monthly (H M Alden editor) had accepted & paid for "Death's Valley," a little poemet to illustrate an engraving f'm a picture "the shadow of the Valley of Death" by the N Y painter Ennis (or Inness)[92]—the Harper's *Weekly* (John Foord editor) has accepted & paid for "Bravo! Paris Exposition!"[93]

Ed is making up the bed as I write—I have been anxious ab't the French elections—glad republicanism has done as well as it has (for want of better)—it is the *lodgement* of free institutions in Europe that pends—I enclose John Burroughs' last[94]—havn't heard f'm him since—thanks f'r y'rs[95]—

W W

2115. *To Richard Maurice Bucke* *9.27–28. 1889*

ADDRESS: Dr Bucke | Asylum | London | Ontario | Canada. POSTMARK: Camden, N.J. | Sep 28 | 8 PM | 89.

Camden noon Sept. 27 '89

Bright sunny day—quite cool—Ed has just built a fire—I am sitting here as usual in the big chair—suppose you get the *Harper's Weekly* I sent yesterday with my little poemet "Bravo Paris Exposition!" —Nothing very new or notable—bowel action—no medicines, no doctor-visits for a long time—Mrs: O'C[onnor] must be still in Boston, (she went temporarily thence to Nantucket but I guess has return'd)—I guess R P Smith has return'd to 44 Grosvenor Road, London—(I have sent of

92. George Inness' "The Valley of the Shadow of Death" (see 2100 and *n.*79).

93. WW sent "Bravo, Paris Exposition!" to *Harper's Weekly* on September 18 (*CB*); on the following day Foord accepted the poem and enclosed $10 in payment (Feinberg). It appeared on September 28. See also 2056, *n.*40.

94. Burroughs' letter of August 27 (Feinberg).

late by mail to him at Haselmere)—y'rs rec'd—welcomed—have not been out in wheel chair many days—shall probably get out this afternoon—

Sept. 28 noon—Sunny & cool continued. Am feeling fairly—John Burroughs is here this forenoon—has been at Asbury Park (a nice place on the Jersey sea shore) the last week, with his wife & boy—all well—the last two have gone back to Po'keepsie—& John jaunts on here, & to New York to-night, & back to West Park. J is well, & looks well, works in his vineyard & farm, & feels well[96]—Dr Brinton here last evn'g (with Horace)—talked interestingly of *Arabia* where he has lived lately—of the common people & their ways, looks, & life—the bulk of Arabs—

I have grapes quite copiously of late, & eat them—Shall send this off Saturday night—

Walt Whitman

letters to-day (28th) f'm Mrs. O'C and Kennedy—all well—

2116. *To Ellen M. O'Connor*

ADDRESS: Mrs: E M O'Connor | care Chs: E Legg | 146 Devonshire Street | Boston Mass:. POSTMARKS: Camden, N.J. | Sep 29 | 5 PM | 89; Boston | Sep (?) 89 | (?).

Camden Sept. 29 '89

Y'rs f'm Nantucket rec'd—the return'd photo: has come all right —John Burroughs was here yesterday & went back (via New York city) to West Park—his wife & boy to Po'keepsie—Matters ab't as usual with me—am sitting in big chair in my den as I write—

Walt Whitman

2117. *To John Burroughs*

Camden Sept: 30 '89

So you didn't come back—I expected you, & Tom Harned & Horace too were here looking for you & were disappointed. The 9th Vol of

95. On September 20 Bucke confided to WW that he might resign his position if the meter proved successful. Of WW's health he wrote: "I have great hopes that you may have some comfort in your life yet—and beyond—beyond? Yes, we shall have good times yet—the old times were good but the new times shall be better" (Feinberg). The poet, interestingly, never responded to Bucke's cosmic exuberance.

96. For Burroughs' account of his visit, see Barrus, 289.

the big "American Literature" from Stedman came this morning—I see you appear in it with a good portrait & ten pages of text, well selected—all very good & generous I say—and deserved—O'Connor is also in the book—

Nothing very new in my condition—am sitting here in big chair in den alone—cloudy day, portending more rain—

Love to 'Sula and to Julian—I see you are extracted from & biographised in "Harpers Fifth Reader" too[97]—

Walt Whitman

2118. *To O. O. Hemenway* [*9.30.1889*]

ADDRESS: O. O. Hemenway | Pittsfield | Ill:.
POSTMARK: Camden, N.J. | Sep 30 | 8 PM | 89.

Walt Whitman has rec'd y'r letter & request—Yes he can send you two copies fullest & latest ed'ns "Leaves of Grass"—The price of the two $4 (2 each) (p o order preferred) address here

328 Mickle Street, Camden,
New Jersey—

2119. *To William Sloane Kennedy*

ADDRESS: Sloane Kennedy | Belmont | Mass:.
POSTMARK: Camden, N.J. | Sep 30 | (?) PM | 89.

Camden Sept: 30 '89

Y'r letters & the papers rec'd—best thanks—I am much as usual —sit here in the old den in the arm chair, altogether disabled—John Burroughs has been here—& return'd to his farm, West Park N Y—is well—dark & rainy here continued long—Mrs: O'C[onnor] must now be there in B[oston] again—A unitarian minister to see me yesterday, they all come here—

Walt Whitman

97. Harper & Brothers sent the new *Fifth Reader* to WW on September 25 (Feinberg).

98. *The New England Magazine* was launched in September and included Sylvester

2120. *To Richard Maurice Bucke*

ADDRESS: Dr Bucke |Asylum | London | Ontario Canada. POSTMARK: Camden (?) | Oct 3 | 8 PM | 89.

Camden Oct 3 after dark | '89

Nothing special—sunny & coolish—I have fire—good bowel action yesterday—

Have been reading Sarrazin in full—it is both immense & definite—have we had any thing up to it yet?—& to think it comes from Paris!

W W

2121. *To Richard Maurice Bucke*

ADDRESS: Dr Bucke | Asylum | London | Ontario | Canada. POSTMARK: Camden (?) | Oct 5(?) | 8 PM | 89.

Camden Saturday noon Oct: 5 '89

Sunny & coolish & fine—have a good oak fire—I think the press work of Horace's dinner book must have been done yesterday or day before, & the binding will follow soon & you shall have it.

There is quite a (I suppose they claim first class) pretensive magazine "The New England Monthly"[98] out in Boston & Horace has been formally invited to write them a ten page article ab't me, (life, works, L of G. &c I suppose of course) wh' he is going to do—$25 pay—nothing new or special with me, condition &c—the old dulness & heaviness—head, (catarrhal?) & bladder—have laid in a cord of good hard dry oak, all sawed—eat pretty heartily—nights so-so—havn't been out for a fortnight—Are you interested in this All-Americas' Delegates' visit here & convention at Washington?[99]—their trip R R, 50 of them, between five & six thousand miles in U S without change of car interests me much—it is the biggest best thing yet in recorded history—(the modern *is* something after all)—They say this racket is in the interest of *protection*—but I sh'd like to know how it can be prevented f'm helping free trade & national brotherhood—You fellows are not in this swim I believe—but you tell the Canadians we U S are "yours faithfully" certain, & dont they forget it—

Walt Whitman

Baxter's article on Bellamy's *Looking Backward.*

99. The International Congress of American States opened in Washington on October 2; the delegates began a grand tour of the United States two days later.

here enclosed is an old letter of Kennedy—may interest you—may not—

2122. *To William Sloane Kennedy*

Camden New Jersey Evn'g, Oct. 7 '89

Here yet holding the fort, gradually being sapp'd no doubt but fair spirits yet—Y'rs rec'd & always welcomed[1] (I enclose Dr Bucke's letter to me, mentioning y'r last wh' I lent him)—Nothing specially new or significant with my condition or literary matters—the proceedings of the Birth Day Dinner not yet bound but I believe have gone to press—& I will send you one soon as ready—

Walt Whitman

2123. *To Richard Maurice Bucke*

ADDRESS: Dr Bucke | Asylum | London | Ontario | Canada. POSTMARK: Camden, N.J. | Oct 8 | 8 PM | 89.

Camden Oct 8 '89

Y'rs of 6th rec'd—Did you get the Harpers' Weekly Sept. 28 with my little "Bravo, Paris Exposition!" I sent? Nothing very new—I am poorly & depress'd enough—(a very near relative has been seriously ill—last news better)[2]—had very good buckwheat cakes for breakfast—cold & sunny—am sitting alone here in chair as usual—

W W

2124. *To Richard Maurice Bucke*

ADDRESS: Dr Bucke | Asylum | London | Ontario Canada. POSTMARK: Camden, N.J. | Oct 10 | 8 PM | 89.

Camden Oct. 10 '89

Y'rs of 8th rec'd—weather pleasant here—nothing very new—shall send you the sheets of the "Dinner book" soon as I get them (or

1. Kennedy's letter of October 3 was addressed to "Dear Old Quaker Friend of the horse-taming sea-kings of Long Island." Among other things in his affected prose he asked, "How is it with you? Do you get any Emersonian soul-baths?" He continued: "I have not seen a *man* for *two* years. I begin to think they are scarce, scarce, scarce. Dr. Bucke seems to me one. . . . Query: if I want to see an heroic man, why don't I become one myself? Perhaps I am, unbeknownst!" (Feinberg).

Horace will)—the press work seems to have been delayed, but I believe it is now done—McKay was here yesterday—p'd me $88.56 royalty &c (the past six months)—will send the N[ew] E[ngland] Magazine—the carpenter &c here to-day making repairs, shores, &c—(the old shanty some danger of sagging, tumbling &c.)[3]

Walt Whitman

2125. *To William Sloane Kennedy*

Camden Oct. 10 '89

Y'rs of 9th just come—Whittier's poetry stands for *morality* (not its *ensemble* or in any true philosophic or Hegelian sense but)—as filter'd through the positive Puritanical & Quaker filters—is very valuable as a genuine utterance & very fine one—with many capital local & yankee & *genre* bits—all unmistakably hued with zealous partizan anti-slavery coloring. Then all the *genre* contributions are precious—all help. Whittier is rather a grand figure—pretty lean & ascetic—no Greek—also not composite & universal enough, (don't wish to be, don't try to be) for ideal Americanism—Ideal Americanism would probably take the Greek spirit & law for all the globe, all history, all rank, the $^{19}/_{20}$ths called evil just as well as the $^{1}/_{20}$th called good (or moral)[4]—

The sense of *Mannahatta* means *the place around which the hurried (or feverish) waters are continually coming or whence they are going*—

Walt Whitman

2126. *To Richard Maurice Bucke*

ADDRESS: Dr Bucke | Asylum | London | Ontario | Canada. POSTMARK: Camden, N.J. | Oct 12 | 8 PM | 89.

Camden toward noon Oct. 12 '89

Horace was here last evn'g—the dinner B[ook] it seems was not put to press yet f'r some reason, but was to be *this forenoon*—

2. The entry in *CB* for this date reads: "Letter f'm C L H[eyde]. Hannah very ill jaundice—next day letter, 'much better'—sent $6."

3. The work was completed on October 19. WW paid $33.40 to the carpenter, William H. Johnson, whom he termed a "scamp & fraud" (*CB*).

4. Kennedy requested on October 15 permission to quote WW's comments on Whittier; the poet wrote on Kennedy's letter: "Don't know ab't this—wasn't indited for publication" (Feinberg).

Miss Gould's little "Gems from W W" is out, (a finished specimen any how)—it makes a neat looking little oblong booklet—what it may am't to we will see—

The most uncanny item of my news is that Ed is going to leave here & go back to Canada (London I believe) for the purpose of finishing his veterinary studies—

I am ab't as usual (my *less* uncomfortable feet foremost) to-day—bowel evacuation—breakfast an egg & bread & honey—

Mrs. O'C[onnor] seems to be in Boston yet—I guess fairly well—weather fine here to-day—Harry Stafford was here[5]—he is well—Kennedy is busy at MS of *Whittier's life* (something of a pot boiler I fancy f'r him) —nothing lately f'm Mrs. Costelloe or the Smiths—New York Johnston was here(returning f'm Templars' racket at Washington)—I am going to try & get out in the air in wheel chair to-day—

Love to all—

Walt Whitman

2127. *To William Sloane Kennedy*

ADDRESS: Sloane Kennedy | Belmont | Mass:. POSTMARK: Camden, N.J. | Oct 13 | 5 PM | 89.

Camden Oct: 13 PM '89

Nothing important—y'rs rec'd & welcomed—Dr B[ucke] writes me frequently—still anchor'd in my big chair—visitors & correspondence —inertia & lassitude & paralysis—slowly hardening & defining deafness & (more slowly) blindness—I send the little pocket-book ed'n L of G. Remember me to Baxter[6] when you see him (& to all inquiring friends)—I keep up pretty good heart—

Walt Whitman

2128. *To Richard Maurice Bucke*

ADDRESS: Dr Bucke | Asylum | London | Ontario | Canada. POSTMARK: Camden, N.J. | Oct 15 | 8 PM | 89.

Camden Oct: 15 noon '89

Well, Maurice, you must have rec'd Horace's "Camden's Compli-

5. Stafford visited the poet on October 9 (*CB*).
6. Kennedy on October 10 mentioned Baxter's recent article on WW in the Boston

ment" sheets, as he sent them to you last evn'g, as soon as he could get a copy f'm the printing office—I have just been looking over them—a curious & interesting collection—a concentering of praise & eulogy rather too single & unanimous & honeyed for my esthetic sense—(for tho' it has not got around, *that same esthetic* is one of my main governments, I may candidly say to you)—

I am sitting here alone & pretty dull & heavy—fairly, though, I guess —bowel movement—rainy, raw, dark weather—oak wood fire—nothing further ab't Ed's leaving here, but I suppose he intends leaving—he is here yet—We have got along very well indeed—A book rec'd f'm Edwd Carpenter "Civilization, its cause & Cure"[7] (the *disease* part of all)—few visitors lately—a steady shower of autograph applications by mail—carpenter & mason here propping up this old shanty—it was giving out & down—I have been reading (4th time probably) Walter Scott's "Legend of Montrose" and other of his Scotch stories—Dave McKay sent them over—Mary Davis is good to me, as always—had a pretty fair night, (Ed generally gives me a good currying before)—had an egg, cocoa & bread & honey for breakfast—

Walt Whitman

2129. *To Mary Smith Costelloe*

ADDRESS: Mrs: Mary Whitall Costelloe | 40 Grosvenor Road | the Embankment | London | S W | England.
POSTMARK: Camden, N.J. | Oct 15 | 8 PM | 89.

Camden New Jersey U S America |
Oct: 15 '89

Feeling a sort of impalpable *nudge* I send a line but what for I don't know, for there is nothing to write ab't—only the fact of writing to you if that is anything—Here I am in my den as for a year & a half, but not so much different or given out yet—My sleeping & appetite yet hold fair—you know I am along now in my 71st—Love to you all—

Walt Whitman

Herald (Feinberg).

7. The title of Carpenter's book was *Civilization: Its Cause and Cure; and Other Essays.*

2130. *To Richard Maurice Bucke*

ADDRESS: Dr Bucke | Asylum | London | Ontario | Canada. POSTMARK: Camden (?) | Oct 17 | 6 AM | 89.

Camden Oct: 16 '89

Noon—Sunny splendid day—have had a good bath &c.—feeling so-so—Ed has gone over to my friend Tom Donaldson's[8]—D seems to take a fancy for Ed & he reciprocates—I am sitting here in the den in my big chair—Ed is leaving here soon Londonward—is there any special thing you want to commission him to get or bring for you?

McKay has gone off on a short drumming trip to New York and Boston—y'rs rec'd last evn'g—mutton & rice broth, Graham toast & tea for my breakfast—

3½ p m Sun & splendor continued—no visitors—no letters—Kennedy sends Boston Transcript regularly—I sent it on to Mrs O'C[onnor] in Wash'n—but she is now in Boston—Ed still over in Phil—have been looking over Horace's book further—some pages are very inspiriting & encouraging especially Sarrazin's and Symonds'—but the main wonder-fact of it all is that L of G. seems quite decidedly to have, or begin to have, a real and "respectable" and outspeaking clientelage—

Am having a pretty comfortable day—they have hung an electric at the corner above & it glints in here like moonlight after dark, very pretty. I sit in the dark & enjoy it. God bless you all in your risings up & lyings down—

Walt Whitman

2131. *To William Sloane Kennedy*

ADDRESS: Sloane Kennedy | Belmont | Mass:. POSTMARK: Camden, N.J. | Oct 17 | 8 PM | 89.

Camden New Jersey | Oct: 17 '89

Thanks for the nice currants (I have had some for my breakfast) & the good little calamus confections by mail. Thanks to the dear western

8. Donaldson has a lengthy report of his conversation with Wilkins on this date (98–102). Wilkins took to Donaldson receipts for gifts from Henry Irving and Bram Stoker (see 2058).

9. On October 15 Kennedy sent currant jam and calamus caramels made by a young lady (Feinberg).

10. On October 18 WW sent a cluster of poems entitled "Old Age's Echoes" to Alden of *Harper's New Monthly Magazine* and asked $100 (CB). On October 24 Alden rejected the work: "It is too much of an improvisation for our use. I had it set up, hoping

girl[9]—Nothing notable with me—am much the same—in good spirits—If you come across a spare number of y'r new "Transatlantic Magazine" Boston send me—Sunshiny here to day—

Walt Whitman

2132. *To Richard Maurice Bucke* *10.18–[19]. 1889*

ADDRESS: Dr Bucke | Asylum | London | Ontario | Canada. POSTMARK: Camden (?) | Oct 19 | 8 PM | (?).

Camden Oct: 18 toward noon '89

Feeling middling—am scribbling a little—I believe the ensuing *Century* is to print my little poemet "My 71st Year"—& I think of sending off a piece to Harpers—(sent it off Friday evn'g—w'd make a page)[10]—fine sunny weather, now the third day—A young rather green fellow, Charles Sterrit, came over here as candidate for my new nurse & helper—could not tell only from practical trial—is to come Monday—what slight impression I had was rather pleasant—we are all sorry Ed is going—every thing has been smooth & good without anything—no hitch or anything of the kind—bowel action this forenoon—pretty fair I guess these late & current days—am sitting here in my den, alone as usual—have rec'd the Boston "*Transatlantic*," it is like *Harper's Weekly* in form, & semi-monthly—Y'r letters come—thanks—O how beautiful it looks out—the sun shining clear—& the active people flitting to and fro—

9 P M—am sitting here alone—comfortable enough—Ed has gone over to the theatre with one of Mrs. D[avis]'s boys—Alys Smith (the dear handsome gay-hearted girl) has come back and was here this afternoon—all are stout & well & hearty over there in London—Mary least so, but she not ill—I guess "society" (a great humbug) is a bad strain on her, & the responsibility of household & two little children—& Mary is not a rugged girl—

Saturday, P M—ab't same—right as can be expected—have rec'd Arnold's printed letter in Lond. *Telegraph* & will send you by-and-by—A

that, seeing it in type, I might come to a more favorable impression of its form. The thought is worthy of a more careful texture in its parts & of a more shapely embodiment as a whole. I am not criticising. Criticism has no place in the poet's world. I am writing only as a Magazine editor with reference to Magazine requirements" (Lion). On November 3 WW sent the piece, now called "Old Age Echoes," to *Nineteenth Century* and asked £20; the editor, James Knowles, returned the manuscript on February 21, 1890 (Feinberg). The "3 or 4 sonnets poemets," as the poet characterized the work in CB, were eventually published separately. "To the Sun-Set Breeze" appeared in *Lippincott's Monthly Magazine* in December, 1890; WW received $60 (CB).

is on the Pacific *en route*—Horace comes regularly—the nurse-dislocation bothers us (but all goes into a life time)—Love to you all—

Walt Whitman

2133. *To Richard Maurice Bucke*

ADDRESS: Dr Bucke | Asylum | London | Ontario Canada. POSTMARK: Camden, N.J. | Oct 21 | 8 PM | 89.

Camden Oct: 21 P M '89

Ed has left—goes in the 4.15 train—I send you by him a parcel of portraits—tell me if they reach you in good order—Am feeling in one of my easier spells just now—the man who was to come to-day has *not* put in an appearance[11]—I am sitting here as usual—Mrs: D[avis] is just making up the bed—cloudy raw to-day—don't be uneasy ab't me in any respect—nature has not only endowed me with immense emotionality but immense bufferism (so to call it) or placid resignation to what happens—

W W

2134. *To Richard Maurice Bucke*

ADDRESS: Dr Bucke | Asylum | London | Ontario Canada. POSTMARK: Camden, N.J. | Oct 22 | 8 PM | 89.

Camden P M Oct: 22 '89

Fine sunny weather continued—Warren Fritzinger, one of Mrs D[avis]'s sailor boys, is acting as my nurse & helper—I have just had a good massage—get along fairly—send you the London *Telegraph* with Sir E A[rnold]'s letter. Y'rs rec'd—Suppose Ed is there all right by this time—Shall I send you my N Y *Critic* after rec'd? You shall have the 1872 ed'n L of G. & I think I have Harrington for you too[12]—

W W

11. Charles Sterrit (see the preceding letter).

12. Bucke specifically requested on October 18 the rare 1872 book and a copy of O'Connor's novel of 1860, *Harrington* (Feinberg).

2135. *To Richard Maurice Bucke*

ADDRESS: Dr Bucke | Asylum | London | Ontario | Canada. POSTMARK: Camden (?) | Oct 23 | (?).

Camden early P M Oct: 23 '89

Quite a spiteful east wind snow storm all this forenoon (it melted as it fell)—have some fulness & pain in head but am getting along fairly—bowel action (middling)—I have been sitting here, trying to interest myself in the mn'g papers—have three of them—& my mail—hasty note frequently f'm Kennedy (one enclosed)—McKay sent over yesterday for one of the big books (the "complete") for a customer—McK has them from me for $4—I suppose you got Tennyson's "Throstle" I sent[13]—(rayther funny)—y'r letter just rec'd—you must have all had a jolly time Delaware ward & there—where is Pardee?[14] & how is he developing? tell the boy I have not forgot him—Best love & respects to Mrs. B too—

Is Beemer there yet! & how is he? if there give him my love. W F (Warren Fritzinger) has just (1 p m) given me a good currying (with a horse brush) & will give me another ab't 9½—they are very acceptable to me—sting a little & make my flesh all red—

One of the Cambridge, Mass: College fellows has just sent to get L of G, the pk't b'k ed'n[15]—sent the money—several have been b't there before—I shall have some adv: circulars printed soon, & will send you some—It is stormy looking enough out, n e wind, but the snow fall stopt & no signs of it on the ground—Love to you & God bless you all.

Walt Whitman

2136. *To Richard Maurice Bucke*

ADDRESS: Dr Bucke | Asylum | London | Ontario Canada. POSTMARKS: Camden, N.J. | Oct 24 | 4 30 PM | 89; N Y | 10–24–89 | 11 PM | (?).

Camden Oct: 24 '89

A fine sunny cold day, but n e wind—Y'rs rec'd this mn'g—I send you papers this mn'g—(a mistake that they *were sent*, Horace had them)—am feeling middling—appetite good—sleep not bad—(must have a

13. Apparently a parody of Tennyson by Gosse.
14. Bucke's son, apparently named after his friend Timothy Blair Pardee, who died in July (see 2081).
15. The book was sent to Edmund B. Delabarre (CB).

quite uninterrupted nap of say four hours f'm 12 to 4 nearly every night) —an egg (fried very rare) with Graham br'd for my breakfast—tea, cocoa or coffee—no medicine or spirits at all—bad or half-bad head *muss* (? catarrhal—?[16] cold in head feeling) 5/6ths of the time—& more or less bladder trouble same—not so weak as four months ago—

W W

2137. *To Richard Maurice Bucke* *10.26–27. 1889*

ADDRESS: Dr Bucke | Asylum | London | Ontario | Canada. POSTMARK: Camden, N.J. | Oct 27 | 5 PM | 89.

Camden Saturday Oct: 26 P M '89

Am so-so—Sitting here as usual—had the old half-trembling sapless leafless tree in front cut down & the walk brick-paved over this forenoon (was afraid it w'd fall & perhaps hurt some one)—all done by a stout young black man in less than two hours—$2½—(& I gave him a glass of sherry)—was satisfied with the whole job—goodbye old tree—how long shall I linger behind?—("Why cumbereth it the ground?")[17]—*Harpers Monthly* man *rejects* my poem—says it is too much an *improvisation*[18]—An Englishman (in an eulogium with the money) sends a letter rec'd this mn'g for a pk't-b'k L of G[19]—Alice Smith, the dear delicate cheery girl, is over this afternoon & pays me a good long sunshiny visit—I have been down in the little front room for a change—dark cloudy half raw weather—inclined to rain—

Evn'g—8½—moderate & rainy—Tom Harned here—Horace too—Have been reading J T Fields's "Yesterdays with authors"[20]—read the Hawthorne piece, every line—then the others—full of letters, good idea —*If any one throws up to you the praise (or sweetness or eulogium) of your W W book—let him read these two pieces ab't Hawthorne and Dickens*—gossipy but very interesting this book of Fields—an sweating moderately to-night—

Sunday forenoon Oct. 27—Rainy & dark—buckwheat cakes & honey & coffee for breakfast—a fairly good night—sitting here alone by stove—bowel action at 10—head mussy (?catarrhy) sore & aching, half uneasy

16. WW's question marks.
17. An almost identical entry appeared in CB on this date.
18. See 2132.
19. Walter Delaplaine Scull, a young English artist, sent $6 for the book on Oc-

—reading the Sunday Phil. *Press*—this enclosed piece is (I suppose) in Nov. *Century*[21]—as I take it Mrs. O'C[onnor] is yet in Boston—

Walt Whitman

2138. *To Mary Smith Costelloe* [*10.27. 1889*]

ADDRESS: Mrs: Mary Whitall Costelloe | 40 Grosvenor Road | the Embankment | London | S W | England. POSTMARK: Camden, N.J. | Oct 27 | 5 PM | 89.

Camden New Jersey U S America

Nothing very new or different, Alys comes often & is as welcomed as sunshine—I am sitting here in my den as ever—dark & rainy to-day & yesterday—My Canadian nurse & friend has left me—(he had a good chance to go into veterinary studies, finish & practice.) I am getting along better than you might imagine—a bad physical brain probably catarrhal—& hopeless locomotion—are my set fiends—fair spirits, appetite & nights however—

Walt Whitman

2139. *To Richard Maurice Bucke* *10.27–28. 1889*

ADDRESS: Dr Bucke | Asylum | London | Ontario | Canada. POSTMARK: Camden, N.J. | Oct 28 | 8 PM | 89.

Camden '89

Sunday night—Oct: 27—Strange I did not get word by to-night's mail of the arrival of Ed or y'r picture-packet I sent—due by noon 21st—& y'r letter 25th, rec'd to-night—a dull day no visitors—I wriggle f'm the chair to the bed—read & write &c &c—but keep up pretty good spirits—will see what to-morrow brings forth—

Oct: 28—It is near noon—Yrs of 26th rec'd—Give my best remembrance and love to Pardee, to Maurice,[22] and to Dr Beemer—want to hear soon as Ed W arrives whether the packet of pictures reaches you in good order—you will see Tennyson's "Throstle" in one of the papers I sent—I

tober 14 (Feinberg).

20. *Yesterdays with Authors* appeared in 1872 and was reprinted in 1886.
21. WW enclosed a reprint of "My 71st Year" with corrections (Feinberg).
22. I have not been able to identify the person referred to.

send you last *Critic*—(I think there is more *piled on* & more honey plaster'd, on Fields's Hawthorne and Dickens papers in the "Yesterdays" than I said—they are both good tho')—

I enclose a "Viking Age" notice[23]—my tho't is we are (myself among the rest) more *genesis'd* f'm those far-back Danes and Norwegians than we have any idea of, or have allow'd for—Dull and heavy & alone yesterday & to-day—head in a rather bad way—dark & half-rainy weather continued—am writing a little but not feeling ab't it—is now 2 P M—no Horace yesterday—

Walt Whitman

2140. *To Richard Maurice Bucke* *10.28–29. 1889*

ADDRESS: Dr Bucke | Asylum | London | Ontario | Canada. POSTMARK: Camden, N.J. | Oct 29 | 8 PM | 89.

Camden Monday night Oct. 28 '89

Horace has been in & bro't a copy of the actual finish'd bound "Camden's Compliment" book—& I suppose you will have some copies sent on to you to-morrow (before this gets to you I fancy)—It looks very well—& it has seem'd to me as I have just been looking over it *an almost incredible book*—deliberately I never expected to live to read such explicit things ab't L of G—probably the last pages are the most curious & incredible—Have had some New England (Fall River, Mass) visitors this afternoon, who bo't books (two ladies & one man)—cloudy & moderate to-day all—

Tuesday 29th—began sunshine but soon clouded and rain-looking—a rare egg, Graham bread & tea for my breakfast—extra bad fulness & uncomfortableness in head—Sitting here alone as usual—good letter (enclosed) f'm Pearsall Smith[24]—had a good currying (kneading) ab't 1—a letter f'm Kennedy this midday mail, but no news of Ed's arrival safe in Canada—

23. A three-column review from the Philadelphia *Press* of Paul B. Du Chaillu's *The Viking Age;* the reviewer was probably Melville Philips.

24. Smith's letter of October 13, in which he informed WW that "Mary is under a nervous break-down—not suffering much but compelled to great quiet" (Feinberg). On October 26 Mrs. Costelloe told WW that she was going to Spain, since her health had not improved (Feinberg).

25. On October 31 WW noted in CB: "Sister Han has had a bad spell illness—jaundice—is now easier." About this time he received a letter from Heyde about Hannah's indisposition and his (usual) economic problems (Trent). WW was probably referring to this letter when he wrote in CB on November 8—"Snivelling letters continued (apparently

The Unitarians are having a sort of general convention in Phila—& Tom Harned and Horace are interested & attending—Unpleasant this ab't Mary Costelloe's ailing health & strength—I think quite a good deal ab't it —my sister at Burlington Vermont is sick—makes me sombre[25]— (primp'd here like a rat in a cage) sometimes the old Adam will burst forth—perhaps does good to let out the gall for a little—have been reading a book ab't Voltaire—I wonder if some of his causticity han't got in me—

Walt Whitman

2141. *To Richard Maurice Bucke*

ADDRESS: Dr Bucke | Asylum | London | Ontario | Canada. POSTMARK: Camden, N.J. | Oct 30 | 8 PM | 89.

Camden Oct: 30 '89—near noon

Still cloudy, dark & threatening rain—My sister Lou this forenoon with a nice chicken & some Graham biscuits—Warren (my nurse, my sailor boy) drove her out in a little wagon to the cemetery "Evergreen" where my dear mother & Lou's baby children are buried—as she wanted to go out there to see to the graves—Ab't the same as usual with me —have been sitting here trying to interest myself in the morning papers—Tom Harned took 200 of the little book & has sold 100 of them already—they have not yet been delivered—Horace told me last night yours had *not* yet gone—I urged him to see they were sent forthwith—(there is a good deal in the little book—partly as a *curio*—partly as a memento of L of G. history)—

P M—Of course still sitting here—"potter" around, bathe or partially bathe, hitch around, &c: &c: to while away time—have quite a mail of papers &c: sometimes the queerest letters imaginable—No news yet of Ed's arrival & y'r reception of the packet of pictures—A friend has just been in with a lady's album for autograph—

These two scraps I cut from Boston Transcript just rec'd[26]—Ken-

endlessly) f'm the miserable whelp C L H[eyde] (he knows I can't help myself—I never answer them—I feel as if I could crush him out like an offensive bed-bug wh' he is)." The invective continued on November 18: "He is the worst nuisance & worriment of my illness —Keeps me back, (his damnable letters) ab't the worst factor of all time—always whining & squeezing me for *more money*—damn him—he ought to be crush'd out as you w'd a bed-bug." On December 19 WW sent $10 to Hannah "(5 for C)," and, apparently in response to two letters from Heyde in December (Trent), almost hysterical in their pleas for money, forwarded $2 on December 31 (*CB*).

26. The clippings from the *Evening Transcript*, mounted on the letter, dealt with a proposed Goethe monument in New York's Central Park and the life of Emin Bey.

nedy's letter enclosed—(Mrs: K lately visited me—very pleasant & good)[27]—

Walt Whitman

2142. *To Richard Maurice Bucke*

ADDRESS: Dr Bucke | Asylum | London | Ontario | Canada. POSTMARK: Camden (?) | Oct (?) | 8 PM | 89.

Camden Oct: 31 '89

"The same subject continued"—good bowel passage last evn'g—my sailor boy nurse (Warren Fritzinger, he is just making up the bed) had a letter from Ed this morning—so he got there all right any how—buckwheat cakes & honey for my breakfast—Did you not see (he got £250 for it) Tennyson's "Throstle" & a burlesque of it in one of the papers I sent you? Gosse I sh'd call one of the amiable conventional wall-flowers of literature (see Thackeray—"Yellowplush" I think)[28]—We too have numbers of good harmless well-fed sleek well-tamed fellows, like well-order'd parlors, crowded all over with wealth of books (generally gilt & morocco) & statuary & pictures & bric-a-brac—lots of 'em & showing first rate—but no more real *pulse and appreciation* than the wood floors or lime & sand walls—(one almost wonders whether literary, even Emersonian, culture dont lead to all that)—

Toward noon weather here turns to rain—bet'n 12 and 1 had a good massage, pummeling &c.—bath also—have had a visit f'm some of the Unitarian conference—y'rs of 29th rec'd—my head, hearing, eyes, bad to-day, yet I am feeling pretty fairly—a present f'm R P Smith of a cheque for $25 to-day—sent him the pk't-b'k morocco ed'n L of G—Mrs: Davis off to-day to Doylestown, Penn: (20 miles f'm here) to visit & comfort a very old couple—returns to-night—my sailor boy has just written to Ed & has gone to the p o to take it—it is towards 3 P M & dark & glum out & I am alone—have a good oak fire—am sitting here *vacant* enough, as you may fancy (but it might be worse)—have myself for company, such as it is, any how—God bless you all—

Walt Whitman

27. The Kennedy letter of October 27 was filled with an account of Mrs. Kennedy's visit: "She was *finally* converted by the impression made by your personal presence. Says she felt that strange thrill (caused by yr great magnetism) that so many others have felt" (Feinberg).

28. WW was equally caustic in remarks to Traubel: "Gosse is a type of the modern

2143. *To Richard Maurice Bucke* *11.1–2. 1889*

ADDRESS: Dr Bucke | Asylum | London | Ontario | Canada. POSTMARK: (?) | 8(?).

Camden '89

Friday 8 P M Nov. 1—Been in the room here of course all day—y'rs rec'd—of Ed's safe arrival—& call on you—is the packet of prints in good order? I have sent letter & some prints to R P Smith, Eng:—send you papers & letters quite freely but not much in either—Have been looking over Nov. *Century*—lots of *poetry!* in it—a good wood eng: (T Johnson) of Esop, f'm photo of pt'g by Velasquez (Spain)—wonderfully good, I look'd at it, frontispiece, for ten minutes[29]—By what the fellows (experts) tell me who have travel'd in Spain I guess there is no portrait-painting existing any better than V's—

Nov. 2 toward noon—cloudy & dark & rain looking—buckwheat cakes & honey for breakfast—bowel action—Herbert G[ilchrist] here last evn'g—rec'd f'm *Century* (& sent back) proof of my little 8 line poemet "Old Age's Ship & Crafty Death's"—Have you rec'd the dinner books? How does that print of Morse's bust seem to you?[30]

½ past 2—still dark & raining—had a good *pummeling* an hour ago—& shall have another at 9 evening—My sailor boy is first rate at it—he gives me the best curryings of all—goes into it (as the great painter Corot demanded his pupils to go to work) with *conscience*—Am sitting here the same—weather temperature mild—(I am half sweating a good deal of the time)—

God bless you all—

Walt Whitman

2144. *To Richard Maurice Bucke*

ADDRESS: Dr Bucke | Asylum | London | Ontario | Canada. POSTMARK: Camden (?) | Nov 5 | 8 PM | 89.

Camden Monday noon Nov 4 '89

Fine sunny day—perfect temperature—bowel action—Alys Smith here last evn'g, (a beautiful holly branch with red berries & green leaves),

man of letters—much-knowing, sharp witted, critical, cold,—bitten with the notion that to be smart is to be deep" (v, 494); and "He is the cheapest of the present essay writers over there in England" (v, 505).

29. "Head of Æsop, by Velasquez."

30. The frontispiece of *Camden's Compliment to Walt Whitman.*

a nice long visit—Mary C[ostelloe] not at all as well as c'd be expected—(her letter to me enclosed)[31]—She is going off to Spain and France on a half-jaunt half-racket (by advice of the doctor)—also rec'd a good letter from Ernest Rhys (wh I will send you)[32]—by this time E R is back in London—I don't hear any thing of Mrs. O'Connor but I suppose she is yet in Boston—I hear often (& very welcome) f'm Kennedy—Tom Harned was here—he has sent off the *Compliment* to nearly a dozen people (purchasers) in parcels of f'm one or two copies to a dozen—all like it—(T H you know signed to take & pay for 200 copies to McK[ay])—

The big general *Unitarian Conference* in Phila: is over—had lots of speeches, discussions, *advices* pro & con &c: I suppose all part of the *great intestinal agitation* that seems to be perhaps the great feature of the civilized world old & new our times—& no or few markedly individualized specimens (perhaps a good mark—"happy is that era, country, that has no history")—have sent off the little MS cluster "Old Age Echoes" to English "Nineteenth Century"[33]—if not rejected I will of course send you a slip—I am sending a *Compliment* to Sarrazin and to Bertz, Berlin—Of course, very dull & stupid with me here, but I guess every thing going with me fairly *considering*—Am sitting here alone in my den by the oak-wood fire alone as usual—my sailor boy is off to the dentist, for a long bad job with teeth—Fair appetite & night's rest continued—Fair spirits &c—In fact congratulating myself I get along as well as I am & do—

Walt Whitman

2145. *To Richard Maurice Bucke*

ADDRESS: Dr Bucke | Asylum | London | Ontario | Canada. POSTMARK: Camden, N.J. | Nov 6 | 8 PM | 89.

Camden Wednesday Nov: 6 AM '89

Feeling fairly—bright sunny day—cool—was out yesterday ab't 2 in wheel chair (first time in three weeks) but it was markedly coolish, & I didn't feel to stay out long—had turn'd cool since noon—send you French paper *Le Temps* with "Bravo! Paris Exposition"—I am still scribbling a

31. Her letter of October 26 (Feinberg).

32. On October 23 Rhys sent "another shaft of imagination to you sitting solitary perchance in Mickle St.! With all desires, that you may have poet's thoughts still to drive off pain, & indeed everything that you yourself desire!" (Feinberg).

33. See 2132, *n.*10.

34. On November 6 Bucke with his usual bluntness wrote: "I am exceedingly sorry for Mrs Costelloe but the fact is the life she went in for (an attempt to carry all London on her back) was simply suicidal. Should she fully recover from this breakdown (as I

little—y'rs (two) came last evn'g—thanks—We have sent the *Compliment* to most of the foreign friends—am a good deal exercised ab't Mary Costelloe[34]—I too feared a sort of collapse or break-down—(am a little fearful that the Spanish journey & racket will feed the enemy as much as it saps him)—

2 P M—Have had a strong currying & pummeling—good—quiet election yesterday & quiet to-day—(Harrisonian-Republicanism is losing its grip as is to have been expected)—the party-politics business here is a sad muddle every way. Scrawl just rec'd fr'm Kennedy—enclosed—

Walt Whitman

2146. *To William Sloane Kennedy*

ADDRESS: Sloane Kennedy | Belmont | Mass:. POSTMARK: Camden, N. J. | Nov 6 | 8 PM | 89.

Camden Nov: 6 P M '89

All fairly well with me—Sunny bright cool weather—y'rs rec'd[35] —let the MS: lay by then & mellow & round & be added to (& be yet rounded if fate ordains)—settle on the few matters you w'd expect & bend to them & enrich & fortify them, & prune (perhaps) the rest, & sort 'em out—I hear fr'm Buck[e] often, he is well & busy—Was out yesterday, (after the week's embargo) in my wheel chair, too cold. Best respects to Mrs. K—

Walt Whitman

2147. *To Ellen M. O'Connor*

ADDRESS: Mrs: E M O'Connor | care C E Legg 146 Devonshire St: | Boston Mass:. POSTMARKS: Camden (?) | Nov 7 | 8 PM | 89; Boston | Nov 8 89 | 2 PM | 4.

Camden New Jersey | Nov: 7 p m '89

Am still here & getting along fairly—have not heard fr'm you for a long time—Of course hope all goes well with you—Horace Traubel still

trust and think she will) she will no doubt be wiser and do better in future" (Feinberg).

35. Kennedy wrote on November 5: "Fred. Wilson writes me that if he publishes I must pay cost of production. I can't, so I write him to return the MS. to me. I must wait till I get able" (Feinberg). Bucke, to whom WW sent Kennedy's note, promised on November 8 that if the meter paid off he would "ad[vance] the funds required, for I am [most?] anxious to have K's book pub[lised] and so made safe" (Feinberg). On January 28, 1891, Kennedy informed Bucke that Wilson had not returned his manuscript: "He has about $200 at least subscribed. I recently wrote him again, asking him if he wd like to bring out the 1st half, & let the Concordance slide" (Feinberg).

helps me faithfully—Dr Bucke is well & busy—Send me word of y'r movements & health. Affectionate respects as always[36]—

Walt Whitman

2148. *To Richard Maurice Bucke*

ADDRESS: Dr Bucke | Asylum | London | Ontario | Canada. POSTMARK: Camden, N.J. | Nov 9 | 8 PM | 89.

Camden Saturday Noon Nov: 9 '89

Y'rs rec'd—Ab't same as usual with me—Dark & glum & rainy to-day—have been scribbling a memorandum of what I saw (ab't 1831) of *Aaron Burr*, New York—(I wrote one three y'rs ago, but seem to have lost it, the MS)[37]—he was one of our most important & curious 1776–1836 characters—died in the last mention'd year—

1 p m Have had a good kneading massage & back rubbing &c—very helpful—

F B Sanborn has sent a letter to Horace, wh' H will some day tell you more fully ab't, but S don't want it published (? at present)—is ab't Edw'd Emersons sneaking lying *note* anent of me in his late b'k ab't R W E[38] —B[39] is cool & collected & conservative but I consider him a real honest permanent friend of self & L of G—

3½ P M—Still glum & rainy, pouring down hard now & most dark—Of course have been in all day occupying the big arm chair—dull enough, & yet, better perhaps than you might suppose (this *vigorous* pummeling treatment is a sort of salvation)—have been looking (2d time) again at the *Hawthorne* in Fields's "Yesterdays"—H seems to have been quite a good deal of what we Unionists & Anti-Slaveryites call'd a *copperhead*—yet somehow we take to such characters—not pure silver or gold—quite mixed, even questionable—like Burns, Mary Stuart, Aaron Burr, (perhaps Shakspere)—Lord bless you—

Walt Whitman

36. On the following day Mrs. O'Connor reported that she hoped to see WW "next week" (Feinberg).

37. See Traubel, III, 138–139.

2149. *To Richard Maurice Bucke*

ADDRESS: Dr Bucke | Asylum | London | Ontario | Canada. POSTMARK: Camden, N.J. | Nov 12 | 8 PM | 89.

Camden just P M Nov: 12 '89

Bright sunny day—y'rs came last evn'g—expect Mrs. O'C[onnor] now, en route for Wash'n—Shall try to get out in wheel chair a little to-day—nothing very different in my affairs or condition—pretty dull & heavy as I sit here mostly alone (left to latent resources, but somehow get along)—

Evn'g—Had a good hearty *massage* at 1 & went out in wheel chair soon after 2—quite a jaunt—went to the bank—went down to the river side—sun, river & sky fine—sat 15 minutes in the Nov. sun—find my head & bodily strength pretty low yet (no improvement)—I like my sailor boy nurse—I cannot move without his help—my grub to-day rice-and-mutton broth, bread, and stew'd prunes—appetite fair—feeling pretty fair as I sit here just after 6—(it is dark here now by 5)—bowel action not bad—this head botheration (heaviness, stuffiness, half ache) unintermitted—at times quite bad—but consider myself blessed to have it all as well as I do —You fellows in the Asylum must have gay times—God bless you all—

Walt Whitman

2150. *To Richard Maurice Bucke*

ADDRESS: Dr Bucke | Asylum | London | Ontario Canada. POSTMARK: Camden, N.J. | Nov 13 | 8 PM | 89.

Camden Evn'g Nov: 13 '89

Mrs: O'C[onnor] has been here most of the day (returns to Wash'n Friday or Saturday ensuing)—looks better a good deal than I anticipated—*is* pretty well for her—a very good visit & talk—all the *particulars* of last hours of O'C, and then the funeral—& many things—but especially the evidence & presence of my dear friend Mrs: O'C herself[40]—

W W

38. Edward Emerson's *Emerson in Concord: A Memoir* refers to WW in a note (228*n.;* reprinted in Traubel, v, 172). For WW's reaction, see Traubel, v, 176, 178–179.
39. Sanborn.
40. WW gave her $10 (CB).

2151. *To Richard Maurice Bucke* *11.13–14. 1889*

ADDRESS: Dr Bucke | Asylum | London | Ontario | Canada. POSTMARK: Camden (?) | Nov 14 | 8 PM | 89.

Camden 1889

Nov: 13 7½ p m—Rainy & dark all day—moderate temperature—ab't as usual with me—bowel action this mn'g—stew'd oysters, Graham bread, apple sauce & coffee for my 4½ supper—great show of all-color'd chrysanthemums this season hereabout—you must have a splendid show of them—the yellow (canary) & white in a bunch are my favorites—but all are beautiful & cheery—I told you (in a p[ost] card) of Mrs: O'C[onnor]'s visit here—

Nov: 14 11 a m—Fine bright sunny forenoon—I suppose Mrs. O'C will return to Wash'n to-morrow—She is lodging with a friend in Phila—I am sitting here as usual—no letter mail yesterday & this forenoon, (except my usual daily stranger's autograph application)—pretty dull with me these days—yet I think I keep fair spirits (a blessed hereditament probably fr'm my dear mother—otherwise I sh'd *go up* forthwith)—am interested in that program of lectures, concerts, balls, &c: for the patients there—good, good[41]—

1¼ P M Have had a good massage, & now I am going out in the wheel chair—the sunshine bright & alluring indeed. The Lord be with you—

Walt Whitman

3½—have been out a little while in the wheel chair & returned—all right—

2152. *To Richard Maurice Bucke*

ADDRESS: Dr Bucke | Asylum | London | Ontario | Canada. POSTMARK: Camden, N.J. | Nov 16 | 8 PM | 89.

Camden Saturday noon Nov: 16 | '89

Bright sunny cold day—feeling fairly—bowel action—an egg, Graham toast, stew'd peaches & cocoa for breakfast—reading & scribbling

41. According to Bucke's letter on November 5 he was giving a series of lectures to students on such topics as "Melancholia" and "Mania" (Feinberg).

41.1 Included in *Three Tales* (1892), with "The Ghost" and "The Carpenter."

42. WW sent the poem (later entitled "A Christmas Greeting") to Foord of

aimlessly—a lull in visitors, mail &c—Mrs. O'C[onnor] must be in Washington D C same address—Wm left two great boxes of MSS wh' she is to overhaul—he had for many years been at intervals on a story "*the Brazen Android*"[41.1]—quaint and old & mystic—was once sent out & partly set in type (by the *Atlantic*) & then recall'd by O'C—

I am sitting here as usual (the same old story)—have a good oak-wood fire—am ab't to have my *currying*—makes a good midday break indeed—very sunny out—

W W

Sat: Evn'g—6½—Mrs: O'C did not go—leaves Monday—has been over here a couple of hours—is having a nice visit to Phila—Alys Smith & a fellow student girl have been here this evn'g—good visits, talks &c—

Clear weather continued—Y'rs rec'd & welcomed—Am feeling fairly —*Suspicion* of more strength in me—splendid effect f'm electric light shining in on big bunch of snowy white chrysanthemums—Love—

W W

2153. *To Richard Maurice Bucke*

ADDRESS: Dr Bucke | Asylum | London | Ontario | Canada. POSTMARK: Camden, N.J. | Nov 19 | 8 PM | 89.

Camden Evn'g Nov. 19 '89

Feeling fairly—dark wet day—bowel action—have just written (a ten or twelve line welcome sonnet to Brazil) "A north Star to a South" & send it off to Harper's Weekly[42]—Y'rs just rec'd—Sold a big book & [sent] it off by express to Maine[43]—dull & stupid as can be here—Capital massages tho' rough & rasping as I can stand like the ones ordered by my old Washington physician in '73—went up to Tom Harned's & took a glass of champagne—H full of work (making money too)—the new baby growing & splendid—

I forget whether you ever got the really good & full edition of *Robert Burns*—Globe edition, 636 pages 16mo (or 12mo), Macmillan pub'r, Alexander Smith editor—if not get one—the common cloth bound is 3s 6d sterling—Burns shows deeply (they all do) how the personnel, the for-

Harper's Weekly and asked $10. When it was rejected, he sent the manuscript on December 4 to S. S. McClure (see 2161), who paid $11 and printed it in *McClure's Magazine* on December 25 (CB).

43. See the following letter.

tunes, ups & downs & concrete & worldly & physiological facts are *indispensable* to getting really in his meaning & works—

Walt Whitman

2154. *To R. F. Wormwood*

ADDRESS: R F Wormwood | Fryeburg | Maine. POSTMARK: Camden, N.J. | Nov 19 | 8 PM | 89.

328 Mickle Street | Camden New Jersey | PM Nov: 19 '89

Yours with $5 recd. with order—thanks—I send you the Complete Works, big Vol, (with the little poemet you requested) by Express—If not delivered to you, please send or inquire at the Express office in y'r place. Please kindly send me word without fail (a P O card will do) soon as you get the book right. The price is $6 (not 4.40)—

Walt Whitman

There are several portraits in the book I send—If you want further pict: I will send—

2155. *To Richard Maurice Bucke*

ADDRESS: Dr Bucke | Asylum | London | Ontario | Canada. POSTMARK: Camden, N.J. | Nov 21 | 8 PM | 89.

Camden Nov: 21 '89

Cloudy now the third day—Nothing very new—my little poemet (welcoming Brazil republic) return'd from Harper's Weekly rejected—I am feeling fairly—the *suspicion* (not at [all] decided) of fairer strength continued—the bad weather however has kept me in the last four days—rest &c: last night satisfactory—rare fried eggs, Graham bread, stew'd prunes & tea for my breakfast—am sitting here (same, same old story) in the big rocking chair alone in den—the elder of the two young sailor men,

44. See 2168, *n.*66.
45. Her card of November 20 noting her arrival in Washington (Feinberg).
46. This letter is not known.

Harry Fritzinger, has just been up to see me—I like the two fellows, & they do me good (his brother Warren is my nurse)—I sent you "the American" with the notice of Sarrazins book in it[44]—Send me word if you get the bundle safe—the Boston *Transcript* has printed a good little notice of the *Compliment* wh' I have given to Horace, as he likes to collect all such—I enclose Mrs: O'C[onnor]'s card just rec'd[45]—She has in view to get an appointment as woman clerk in some Dep't there, & will probably get such—Donnely's (Cryptogram) pubrs have issued a little livraison of favorable criticisms—& sent me one—Shall I send it to you? or have you rec'd one? I send another piece ab't Dr Sequard—it is just past noon & I am ab't having my currying.

God bless you all—

Walt Whitman

2156. *To Ellen M. O'Connor*

ADDRESS: Mrs: E M O'Connor | 1015 O St N W | Washington | D C. POSTMARKS: Cam(?) | Nov 24 | 5 PM | 89; Washington, Rec'd. | Nov 25 | 2 AM | 8(?) | 6.

Camden Saturday P M Nov: 23 '89

Dear Nelly O'Connor

A fine sunny day here & I am feeling fairly—have just had a good stout currying & kneading & it fits my case—am going out for half an hour in the wheel chair, the sun is so inviting—rec'd your postal card—I enclose Dr B[ucke]'s letter, just come[46]—I too think at least a volume ought to be & probably might be well collated & printed of dear W's MS—

Evn'g—Am sitting here alone by oak fire—went out in the wheel chair & enjoy'd it—sales of my books sparse but give me a little to do, & a sufficient sustenance, little but will do—just had a letter f'm Wiesbaden ab't the German L of G.[47]—very eulogistic &c—one of the best criticisms is f'm France—by a Parisian, Gabriel Sarrazin, if ever printed (translated) I will send to you—

God be over you & bless you—

Walt Whitman

47. Rolleston wrote from Wiesbaden on November 10 and enclosed a clipping from the *Piccadilly* of October 31, an account of the German acceptance of the Knortz-Rolleston translation (Feinberg).

2157. *To Richard Maurice Bucke*

ADDRESS: Dr Bucke | Asylum | London | Ontario | Canada. POSTMARK: Camden, N.J. | Dec 3 | 8 PM | 89.

Camden Dec: 3 '89

Y'rs of 1st rec'd & welcomed—Much the same as of late continued with me—I saw the Ill: London News portrait—not satisfactory[48]—have sent off the little "Northern Star-Group to a Southern" (welcome to Brazilian Republic)[49] wh' if printed I will see that you get copy—rec'd a good letter f'm Ed: Wilkins—(think it very likely that veterinary business is a good move for Ed: in the future)—lots of bad or half-bad weather here—but I go out a little in the wheel-chair—was out yesterday—have just had my mid-day currying—The enclosed printed bit ab't Edw'd Carpenter comes f'm Chicago[50]—(If you write to E C & choose, you can send it to him)—the other is f'm Mrs: O'C[onnor] who is back in her old quarters in Wash'n[51]—I see you are busy enough—& fulfilling it all—I almost envy you.

Walt Whitman

2158. *To S. S. McClure*

328 Mickle Street | Camden New Jersey | Dec: 4 '89

Dear Sir

Can you use this poemet[52] in your cluster? It would probably do to go out just as well during the week immediately preceding Christmas—The price is $11 (ten for the little piece & one for printing the slips)—Your notes rec'd: thank'd for, & I may send you some thing—

Respectfully

Walt Whitman

48. The *Illustrated London News* included on November 16 a two-page supplement containing M. Klinkicht's engraving of WW after a photograph by Sarony. A column devoted to WW in the same issue concluded that he was not "a great author, or a good writer in point of literary skill."

49. See 2153 and 2158.

50. Caroline K. Sherman on November 27 sent WW her article on Carpenter entitled "He's an English Thoreau," which appeared in the Chicago *Herald* (Feinberg).

2159. *To Richard Maurice Bucke*

ADDRESS: Dr Bucke | Asylum | London | Ontario | Canada. POSTMARK: Camden, N.J. | Dec 8 | 6 PM | 89.

Camden Saturday 1 P M Dec: 7 '89

Bright sunny perfect day—have just been out an hour or two, a drive in a smooth cab in the rural roads & to Harleigh Cemetery—enjoy'd it well—was out early last evn'g to Tom Harned's to supper & to meet Prof: Cope[53] & others—Herbert Gilchrist there—am feeling fairly, but extremely lame & feeble—get out largely for the change wh' is important —Short jaunts, & the eating & drinking in moderation (I have not forgotten)—So Jefferson Davis is dead—the papers to day are full—he stands, will remain, as representative for a bad *even foul* move—& himself a bad & foul move—that's the deep final verdict of America's soul—had my *currying* &c: to-day (since above written)—last night & to-day perfections of weather, sky, &c.—I stopt the chair last evn'g & look'd at the full moon & clouds & brightness a long time—

Am sitting here alone in my den—one bunch of flowers on the table at my left & another on the right—& Warren my nurse downstairs practicing a violin lesson. Prof: Cope (above) gave a lecture last evn'g in Unitarian Ch. here on the "Descent of Man"—(a pretty formidable theme)—they say a good lecture—I came home here at 8—can't find a cutting f'm the London "Piccadilly"[54] I desired to enclose—so I put in an old letter f'm Kennedy[55]—Regards & love to you & Mrs: B & all—

Walt Whitman

Alys Smith here to-day—Mary's trouble is f'm *the eyes*—

51. Mrs. O'Connor's letter of November 29 (Feinberg).
52. "A Christmas Greeting."
53. Edward Drinker Cope (1840–1897), a naturalist and editor of *American Naturalist*.
54. WW forgot that he had sent Rolleston's letter and the clipping to Mrs. O'Connor (see 2156, *n.*47).
55. Kennedy's letter of January 11, 1888 (erroneously dated 1887 by Kennedy) (Feinberg).

2160. *To Mary Smith Costelloe*

ADDRESS: Mrs: Mary Whitall Costelloe | 40 Grosvenor Road | the Embankment | London England. POSTMARK: Camden (?) | Dec 8 | (?) PM | 89.

Camden New Jersey U S America | Saturday Evn'g Dec: 7 '89

Finest sort of weather, sun, skies &c here days & nights—I was out last evn'g to supper and stopt my chair to have a good long look at the skies & full moon—Alys has been here to-day with a young woman chum —on their way to Milville—Nothing to write about but feel pretty well & tho't I w'd write. The news (the papers full) is of death of Jeff Davis— that ends it—or seems to—Love & respects to father & all, not forgetting the girls.

Walt Whitman

2161. *To Richard Maurice Bucke* *12.9–[10]. 1889*

ADDRESS: Dr Bucke | Asylum | London | Ontario | Canada. POSTMARK: Camden, N.J. | Dec 11 | 6 AM | 89.

Camden Dec 9 '89

9 P M—Rather dull & stupid but all the organs, secretions &c: fairly condition'd I guess. The enclosed is f'm Rolleston who is or has been in Germany, (seems to have a magnetic draw thither)—My poemet greeting Brazil U S is bo't by McClure's newspaper syndicate & will be printed in them at Christmas—he has sent the pay for it (I told you it was rejected by Harper's Weekly)—you must have just rec'd my adv: circulars,[56] I sent four—(you can have any more you want)—damp & dark, & very mild here—I have had a bath, & am sitting here alone—Warren my nurse has gone off to get a violin lesson—Horace has been here this evn'g —I have rec'd the 10th & concluding Vol. of Stedman's "American Literature" collect—good I fancy—

Tuesday, 1 P M—Fine sunny day—just had a good currying & pum-

56. Circulars to advertise *Complete Poems & Prose* ($6), *Leaves of Grass* ($5), and *Portraits from Life* ($3). The advertisement appeared in *Camden's Compliment to Walt Whitman;* a facsimile of WW's draft of the circular appears in Traubel, v, 242.

57. Bucke had written on December 8: "I have spent part of the day looking over L. of G. and I wish I could tell you, or convey to you in the faintest way, the deep down

meling—fair bowel action this forenoon—so far so good—am going out in the wheel-chair—I believe nothing more this time—God bless you all—

Walt Whitman

2162. *To David McKay*

TRANSCRIPT.

Camden New Jersey Dec. 11 '89

Received $12 (twelve dollars) from David McKay for three copies Complete Works, (tally bill Nov. 6)—

Walt Whitman

the "Carol for Harvest 1867" is on page 278 under title of "the Return of the Heroes"—

I continue much the same, but palpably slowly declining—have just sold a little 8 line bit "Christmas Greeting" ie: (welcoming Brazil republic) to S S McClure N Y for his syndicate—will tell Horace to call—Love to the young ones—

2163. *To Richard Maurice Bucke*

ADDRESS: Dr Bucke | Asylum | London | Ontario Canada. POSTMARKS: Camden, N.J. | Dec 13 | 8 PM | (?); London | AM | De 16 | 89 | Canada.

Camden Evn'g Dec: 13 '89

Continuing fairly—have been out in the wheel chair I guess two miles—Sunny mild weather here—So Browning is dead—as it has happen'd I never read him much—(Does he not exercise & rather worry the intellect—something like a sum in arithmetic?)—Am sitting here alone as usual in my den—all right I guess[57]—

Walt Whitman

emotions that that book excites in me. There is nothing stirs me up like it. Sometimes as I read it I feel as if my whole previous life were rolling en masse through me, and as if at the same time vast vistas were opening ahead which I longed and yet half dreaded to enter. The profound religious sentiment which that book is destined to develope in the human heart when it becomes once assimilated by (incorporated into) the life of the race is, I think, simply inconceivable at present" (Feinberg).

2164. *To William Sloane Kennedy*

ADDRESS: Sloane Kennedy | Belmont | Mass:. POSTMARK: Camden, N.J. | Dec 13 | 8 PM | 89.

Camden Evn'g Dec: 13 '89

All goes on the same & fairly. Have been out in the sun & mild temperature a good part of afternoon. Sent on a little poemet (welcoming Brazilian Republic) to McClure's N Y Syndicate—& rec'd money for it. So Browning is dead—(I have never read much B & don't have any inherent opinion)—How are you & Mrs: K?

Walt Whitman

2165. *To Ellen M. O'Connor*

ADDRESS: Mrs: E M O'Connor | 1015 O Street N W | Washington | D C. POSTMARKS: Camden, N.J. | Dec 18 | 6 PM | 89; Washington, Rec'd. | Dec 19 | 11 AM | 89.

Camden Dec: 18 1889

Matters (pretty monotonous of course) are going on with me much the same as hitherto—(of course palpably physically *declining*)—Rec'd a letter, (I suppose you got one too) with the announcement of marriage between Chas: W Eldridge and Emily Louisa Brown at San Francisco, Dec: 5—(nothing but the printed announcement)—Also to-day a letter f'm John Burroughs f'm Poughkeepsie, where they are all, (wife boy & he) wintering, housekeeping—J B not either exactly well or ill, but has met a bad financial set-back & loss—$1000 or more—the little boy well & growing.[58]

Dr Bucke is well & busy—writes me every two or three days—Horace Traubel was here last evn'g as usual (always welcome)—he is well—is a clerk in a bank in Phila—Am sitting at present alone in my den—shall have a good stout currying & pummeling (massage) in a few minutes—a dark rainy day out, with indications of fog—& what's the news with you? & how are matters shaping? I enclose one of my late circulars as it may have a wisp of interest to you. The translation of (partial) L of G. is well

58. This is an adequate summary of Burroughs' letter of December 17 (Feinberg).
59. Mrs. O'Connor replied on December 21: she had visited William's grave and "plucked a few leaves [of ivy] for *you*" (Feinberg).

rec'd in Germany. So Browning is dead & Whittier is 82—Love & God bless you[59]—

Walt Whitman

2166. *To Richard Maurice Bucke* *12.18–21. 1889*

ADDRESS: Dr Bucke | Asylum | London | Ontario | Canada. POSTMARK: Camden, N.J. | Dec 22 | 5 PM | 89.

Camden Dec: 18 '89

3 P M—Every thing, feelings, appetite, bowels, vim, &c: continuing on much the same, monotonously but I guess fairly—Have written to Mrs: O'C[onnor]—no news from her lately—Rec'd word f'm John Burroughs (wh' I enclose)—also f'm Rhys[60]—have had a good currying bout —I sometimes fancy I get the *vitalest* ones I ever had f'm my present nurse—young & strong & magnetic he is—

Dark and rainy here now & yesterday not cold—not many visitors—no book sales—suppose you got a bundle of circulars just sent—have just rec'd the news of my friend Chas: W. Eldridge's marriage at San Francisco—(g't chum of O'C[onnor] in war time in Wash'n—of mine also)—

20th—toward noon—feeling so-so—dark & rainy—sold one of the big books yesterday[61]—heard f'm E C Stedman—he is quite prostrated ill nervous lassitude &c: am sorry—y'r letter rec'd—you must have lively times there at the Asylum—Wm Ingram here quite a long visit this forenoon—Herbert G[ilchrist] last evn'g—plenty callers—temperature continues moderate—was out afternoon an hour in wheel chair—

Saturday noon Dec: 21

Bright sunny day & fair temperature—am ab't same as usual—The Harleigh Cemetery Supt. has just been here—they propose to give me a lot, & I wish to have one in a small side hill in a wood—& am going out soon to locate it—am impress'd pleasantly with the Supt: Mr Wood[62]—nothing special—Merry Christmas to you, Mrs: B & the childer—

Walt Whitman

60. Burroughs' letter of December 17 and Rhys's of December 7 (Feinberg).
61. Sent to Mrs. E. C. Waters, who paid $6.40 (*CB*).
62. J. B. Wood wrote about the cemetery plot on December 24 (Feinberg).

2167. *To Rudolf Schmidt*

ADDRESS: Rudolf Schmidt | Blaagaardsgade 16 B | Copenhagen N | Denmark. POSTMARKS: Camden, N.J. | Dec 24 | 8 PM | 89; London | AM | Ja 2 | 90(?); OMB. 1 | 4–1–90 | (?).

Camden New Jersey U S America |
Dec: 24 '89

Still (after a sort) *hold possession of the ship*—but my grasp growing fainter & my eyes dimmer—Wish to specially write to thank you for kindness[63]—Y'r proof just rec'd by Horace Traubel—To-day a fine sunny day & I have been taken out two hours on a drive—enjoy'd all—the sun most of all—been to a cemetery to select a lot.

Walt Whitman

2168. *To Richard Maurice Bucke* *12.25–26. 1889*

ADDRESS: Dr Bucke | Asylum | London | Ontario | Canada. POSTMARK: Camden, N.J. | Dec 26(?) | 8 PM | 89.

Camden '89

Dec. 25 6 p m—have been out to-day in the wheel chair—& down to the kitchen at the table for my supper—now sitting as usual up in my den—J A Symonds from Switzerland has sent the warmest & (I think sh'd be call'd) the most *passionate* testimony letter to L of G. & me yet[64]—I will send it to you after a little while—

Yesterday went out (two hours drive) to the Harleigh Cemetery & selected my burial lot—a little way back, wooded, on a side hill—lot 20 x 30 feet—think of a vault & capping all a plain massive stone temple, (for want of better descriptive word)—Harleigh Cemetery is a new burial ground & they desire to give me a lot[65]—I suppose you rec'd the *Critic*[66]—

Dec 26 noon Perfect sunny day—Tom Donaldson here last evn'g—

63. Schmidt was quoted in *Camden's Compliment to Walt Whitman*, 53–54.

64. Symonds' letter of December 9 was indeed "passionate": "I cannot even attempt to tell yourself (upon this page of paper with this pen in my hand), what it is that makes me ask you now to bless me. . . . Perhaps we shall yet meet [after death]: . . . I shall ask you about things which have perplexed me here—to which I think you alone could have given me an acceptable answer. . . . I cannot find words better fitted to express the penetrative fate with which you have entered into me, my reliance on you, & my hope that you will not disapprove of my conduct in the last resort" (Feinberg). What WW failed to see was that Symonds, who was preoccupied with his study of sexual inversion, was trying to ask the questions he finally posed nine months later; see 2278.

sold a little pocket-book L of G. to-day, & got the money[67]—am feeling fairly (inclined to heavy) to-day—plain indications of rheumatism in my right arm—both my parents had r but not yet in me—Shall have a currying & then get out in the wheel chair—

Walt Whitman

Sudden death of a special friend & neighbor I have known from her 13th—a fine young handsome woman—typhoid—buried to-day—

2169. *To Richard Maurice Bucke*

ADDRESS: Dr Bucke | Asylum | London | Ontario Canada. POSTMARKS: Camden, N.J. | Dec 29 | 5 PM | 89; London | AM | De 31 | 89 | Canada.

Camden Sunday Evn'g | Dec: 29 '89

Much the same things &c: continued—feeling dull & stupid—dark bad weather—my nurse is laid up sick—Tom Harned here—no serious defection in sleep, appetite or bowel ability—We have had five splendid days till now—

Walt Whitman

2170. *To Edward Wilkins*

Camden N J—U S A | Night Dec: 31 '89

Dear Ed

Y'r letter came this forenoon & am glad you keep well & are satisfied at y'r occupation[68]—No doubt it will turn out well as it is a good business & with ordinary luck will return a handsome income—& besides it is y'r own choice & satisfaction—wh' is a great point—Nothing very

65. Almost the same information appeared in the Camden *Post* on December 26 in a paragraph probably written by WW: "He resolutely passed by all the show parts and lawns, and chose a place back on a woody side hill, . . . where a solid gray stone monumental vault will be constructed" (clipping mounted in CB).

66. *The Critic* of December 21 contained an extract from Harrison S. Morris's article in *The American* entitled "Whitman's 'Indescribable Masculinity,' " a review of Sarrazin's book by his American translator.

67. A "morocco b'd L of G to Alma Johnston N Y. Paid 5" (CB).

68. On December 24 Wilkins informed WW that he had left Camden because he was unhappy with his Camden friends and because he wanted to enter the "Veterinary business" (Feinberg).

new or different here—If you were to come here (& pleas'd w'd I be to see you, boy) now, you w'd see me seated by the oak wood fire in the big ratan chair with the gray wolf-skin spread on the back, & the same old litter of papers & MSS & books around on the floor in the same old muss—I don't get any worse but no improvement in health or strength either—but I keep pretty good spirits & eat & sleep fairly yet—Have my daily curryings, & get out often in wheel chair—Warren has had a couple or three days sickness—the doctor was a little afraid of typhoid fever, but it seems to have pass'd over, & he is getting ab't the same as before—Mrs: D[avis] is well—I send you a paper—hear from Dr B[ucke] often—he is well & busy —Warren is learning the fiddle—he is getting along well—takes lessons of Watson.

Good bye for the present, Ed, & my remembrances & love to you, boy—

Walt Whitman

2170.1 *To David McKay* [(?).(?). *1889?*][69]

David McKay | bookseller, |
9th st. opp: P O Phila:

Dave,

Please send me over by bearer, twelve copies Leaves of Grass, (with the Annex)—

Walt Whitman

the pocket-b'k copy I send is a present to you from me—

69. Since the note refers to WW's two recently published books, it seems logical to assign it to 1889.

According to my tabulation, based upon his letters and his entries in *CB*, WW's income in 1889 amounted to at least $1,447.91: royalties, $626.47; sales of books, $245.89; payments for articles and poems, $95.00; and gifts, $480.55. (The figures on book sales are necessarily to some extent conjectural, since I have had to assume that he charged uniform prices for his various books.) The entries in *CB* in 1889, like those in 1888, are not complete, as discrepancies between amounts deposited in the bank and notations of receipts of money are commonplace.

Appendix A

A LIST OF MANUSCRIPT SOURCES AND PRINTED APPEARANCES

The locations of the manuscripts transcribed in this volume appear in the following list, through abbreviations explained in the list of abbreviations in the Introduction. If the version in this edition is based upon a printed source, or is derived from an auction record, the fact is indicated by the word TEXT. Unless otherwise indicated, the manuscripts have not previously appeared in print. I record all earlier printed appearances through the abbreviations CT (Complete Text) and PT (Partial Text). The locations and printed appearances, if any, of draft letters are also noted. Occasionally the location of a letter is followed by a reference in parentheses to an envelope in another collection. In this way I have, artificially, restored the manuscript to its original state.

This list is followed by a list of the institutions and individuals whose manuscripts are represented in this volume, in order that scholars may readily tell which letters are to be found in a given collection.

Letters

1373. TEXT: Anderson Galleries, May 13, 1916.
1374. Berg.
1375. Feinberg.
1376. Feinberg.
1377. Berg.
1378. Berg.
1379. Feinberg.
1380. Brown University.
1381. Princeton University.
1382. Feinberg.
1383. Doheny. CT: Barrus, 259–260.
1384. Robert H. Taylor.
1385. Berg.
1386. Barrett. CT: *SB*, v (1952), 208.
1387. SOURCE: Stan V. Henkels, November 7, 1911.
1388. Berg.
1389. Trent. CT: Gohdes and Silver, 100.
1390. Roger W. Barrett, who supplied a typescript.
1391. Berg.
1392. TEXT: Barrus, 261.
1393. Trent. CT: Gohdes and Silver, 101.
1394. Barrett. CT: Donaldson, 108–109.
1395. Mrs. William R. Weber.
1396. Trent. CT: Gohdes and Silver, 101.

1397. Oberlin College.
1398. Berg.
1399. Hanley.
1400. Hanley. CT: *Letters of W. M. Rossetti* (1934), 184.
1401. Feinberg. CT: *Colophon*, n.s., II (1937), 202.
1402. Barrett. CT: Knortz, 95; *AL*, XX (1948), 160; *SB*, V (1952), 208.
1403. Feinberg.
1404. Trent. CT: Gohdes and Silver, 101.
1405. Feinberg.
1406. Huntington (New York) Public Library.
1407. Feinberg.
1408. Feinberg.
1409. Feinberg.
1410. Trent. CT: Gohdes and Silver, 101–102.
1411. TEXT: S. T. Freeman Company, March 18, 1913.
1412. Photostat in Feinberg.
1413. Hanley.
1414. Huntington. CT: *AL*, VIII (1937), 431; Nonesuch, 1045.
1415. Barrett.
1416. Feinberg.
1417. TEXT: Anderson Galleries, October 18, 1923.
1418. Barrett.
1419. Trent. CT: Gohdes and Silver, 102.
1420. Barrett. PT: *Pall Mall Gazette*, December 23, 1886.
1421. Trent. CT: Gohdes and Silver, 102.
1422. Trent. CT: Gohdes and Silver, 103.
1423. Trent. CT: Gohdes and Silver, 103. PT: Kennedy, 51.
1424. Barrett.
1425. Hanley.
1426. TEXT: *Rare Book Auction Dinner for German Refugees* (New York), December 8, 1938.
1427. Trent. CT: Gohdes and Silver, 103.
1428. Rutgers University.
1429. Feinberg. CT: *Colophon*, n.s., II (1937), 202. PT: *Pall Mall Gazette*, December 23, 1886.
1430. Trent. CT: Gohdes and Silver, 103–104.
1431. Berg.
1432. Trent. CT: Gohdes and Silver, 104.
1433. Pennsylvania (Envelope in Feinberg).
1434. Feinberg.
1435. University of Richmond.
1436. Berg.
1437. Hanley.
1438. Missouri Historical Society. CT: *Missouri Historical Society Bulletin*, XVI (1960), 111.
1439. Missouri Historical Society. CT: *Missouri Historical Society Bulletin*, XVI (1960), 111–112.
1440. Trent. CT: Gohdes and Silver, 104.
1441. Missouri Historical Society. CT: *Missouri Historical Society Bulletin*, XVI (1960), 112.
1442. Feinberg. CT: *Colophon*, n.s., II (1937), 202. PT: *Pall Mall Gazette*, December 23, 1886 (dated September 15).
1443. Missouri Historical Society. CT: *Missouri Historical Society Bulletin*, XVI (1960), 112.
1444. Whitman House, Camden. CT: *AL*, VIII (1937), 434 (dated 1888).
1445. Pennsylvania.
1446. Trent. CT: Gohdes and Silver, 104–105. PT: Kennedy, 50 (dated September 16).
1447. TEXT: Donaldson, 191.
1447.1 Northwestern University (Envelope in Missouri Historical Society).
1448. Feinberg.
1449. Feinberg. CT: *Colophon*, n.s., II (1937), 203. PT: *Pall Mall Gazette*, December 23, 1886.
1450. British Museum.
1451. Trent. CT: Gohdes and Silver, 105. PT: Kennedy, 50.
1452. William D. Bayley Collection, Ohio Wesleyan University.
1453. FACSIMILE: Donaldson, 46.
1454. DRAFT LETTER in Feinberg.
1455. DRAFT LETTER in Feinberg.
1456. Berg.
1457. Feinberg. CT: *Colophon*, n.s., II (1937), 203. PT: *Pall Mall Gazette*, December 23, 1886.
1458. Feinberg.
1459. Berg.
1460. Berg.
1461. Pennsylvania.

1462. Trent. CT: Kennedy, 50.
1463. Feinberg. CT: *Colophon*, n.s., II (1937), 203.
1464. Professor Gay Wilson Allen.
1465. Feinberg.
1466. Feinberg.
1467. Cornell University.
1468. Feinberg.
1469. Trent. CT: Gohdes and Silver, 105.
1470. Trent. CT: Gohdes and Silver, 105. PT: Kennedy, 51.
1471. TEXT: Anderson Auction Company, December 9–10, 1909.
1472. Trent.
1472.1 TEXT: C. Sadakichi Hartmann, *Conversations with Walt Whitman* (1895), 34.
1473. Feinberg.
1474. Feinberg. CT: *Colophon*, n.s., II (1937), 203–204.
1475. FACSIMILE (partial) and TEXT: *Pall Mall Gazette*, January 25, 1887. DRAFT LETTER (in Barrett).
1476. Feinberg.
1477. Yale.
1478. Feinberg.
1479. Berg.
1480. Trent. CT: Gohdes and Silver, 106.
1481. TEXT: *The Month at Goodspeed's*, VIII (September, 1936), 7.
1482. British Museum.
1483. Feinberg. CT: *Colophon*, n.s., II (1937), 204.
1484. SOURCE: William D. Morley, Inc., April 14, 1941.
1485. Feinberg.
1486. Feinberg.
1487. Trent. CT: Gohdes and Silver, 106. PT: Kennedy, 51.
1488. Trent. CT: Gohdes and Silver, 106–107.
1489. TEXT: Kennedy, 76–77. CT: *Poet-Lore*, VII (1895), 72–73; Nonesuch, 1045–46; Shephard, *Walt Whitman's Pose*, 10.
1490. TEXT: Kennedy's transcription in Trent; Anderson Gallery, November 25, 1927. PT: Kennedy, 51–52; Barrus, 263.
1491. Whitman House, Camden. CT: *AL*, VIII (1937), 431.
1942. Trent. CT: Gohdes and Silver, 107. PT: Kennedy, 52.
1493. Feinberg.
1494. Whitman House, Camden. CT: *AL*, VIII (1937), 431–432.
1495. Feinberg. FACSIMILE: Binns, 326. CT: *WWN*, IV (June, 1958), 89.
1496. Mrs. Doris Neale.
1497. Charles Norton Owen, who supplied a typescript.
1498. Trent. CT: Gohdes and Silver, 107–108.
1499. TEXT: Kennedy, 52–53.
1500. TEXT: Kennedy's transcription in Trent.
1501. Feinberg. CT: *Colophon*, n.s., II (1937), 204.
1502. Barrett. CT: *Princeton University Library Chronicle*, III (November, 1941), 6–7.
1503. Yale.
1504. TEXT: Typescript in Stanford University Library.
1505. Barrett. CT: Knortz, 95; Nonesuch, 1046–47; *AL*, XX (1948), 160.
1506. Feinberg.
1507. George McCandlish.
1508. Feinberg.
1508.1 TEXT: *The Collector*, LVII (1943), 38.
1509. Feinberg.
1510. Pennsylvania.
1511. TEXT: Kennedy's transcription in Trent.
1512. TEXT: *The Modern School*, VI (April–May, 1919), 127.
1513. Feinberg. CT: *Colophon*, n.s., II (1937), 204.
1514. Barrett. CT: *SB*, V (1952), 208–209. PT: Kennedy, 53.
1515. Yale.
1516. Feinberg.
1517. Whitman House, Camden. CT: *AL*, VIII (1937), 432.
1518. Trent. CT: Gohdes and Silver, 108.
1519. Trent. CT: Gohdes and Silver, 108.
1520. Feinberg.
1521. Feinberg.
1522. Feinberg.
1523. Trent. CT: Gohdes and Silver, 108.
1524. Feinberg.
1525. New York Public Library. DRAFT LETTER (in Feinberg).

1526. Trent. CT: Gohdes and Silver, 108–109.
1527. Yale.
1528. Feinberg.
1529. TEXT: Kennedy's transcription in Trent. PT: Kennedy, 53.
1530. Hanley. CT: Perry, *Walt Whitman*, 252–253.
1531. Feinberg.
1532. Trent. CT: Gohdes and Silver, 109.
1533. Feinberg.
1534. Trent. CT: Gohdes and Silver, 109. PT: Kennedy, 53–54 (dated April 27).
1535. TEXT: Catalog of J. F. Drake, 1931.
1536. Barrett. CT: Nonesuch, 1047.
1537. Feinberg.
1538. Barrett. CT: Knortz, 95; Nonesuch, 1047; *AL*, XX (1948), 160.
1539. TEXT: Baker & Brooks, February 9, 1944.
1540. TEXT: Kennedy's transcription in Trent.
1541. Draft letter in Yale.
1542. Feinberg. CT: *Colophon*, n.s., II (1937), 205.
1543. Trent. CT: Gohdes and Silver, 109–110.
1544. Feinberg.
1545. Trent. CT: Gohdes and Silver, 110.
1546. Boston Public Library. CT: *More Books*, XIII (1938), 191.
1547. Trent. CT: Gohdes and Silver, 110.
1548. Feinberg.
1549. Trent. CT: Gohdes and Silver, 110.
1550. Library of Congress. CT: *Visits*, 243.
1551. Library of Congress. CT: *Visits*, 243.
1552. Boston Public Library. CT: *AL*, VIII (1937), 432; Nonesuch, 1048.
1553. Columbia University. CT: Elizabeth Dunbar, *Talcott Williams* (1936), 197; *AL*, VIII (1937), 433.
1554. Feinberg.
1555. SOURCE: Catalog of J. F. Drake, 1927.
1556. Trent. CT: Gohdes and Silver, 110–111. PT: Kennedy, 54.
1557. Feinberg.
1558. British Museum.
1559. Trent. CT: Gohdes and Silver, 111.
1560. Feinberg. CT: *Colophon*, n.s., II (1937), 205–206.
1561. Trent (Envelope in Boston Public Library). CT: Gohdes and Silver, 111–112. PT: Kennedy, 54.
1562. Mark Twain Papers, General Library, University of California, Berkeley.
1563. TEXT: American Art Association, February 16, 1927.
1564. Barrett. CT: *SB*, V (1952), 209.
1565. Feinberg.
1566. Boston Public Library. PT: *More Books*, XIII (1938), 191.
1567. Trent. CT: Gohdes and Silver, 112–113.
1568. Yale.
1569. Yale.
1570. Barrett.
1571. Feinberg.
1572. Feinberg. CT: *Colophon*, n.s., II (1937), 206.
1573. Boston Public Library. PT: *More Books*, XIII (1938), 191.
1573.1 Feinberg.
1574. Feinberg.
1575. Boston Public Library.
1576. Rollo G. Silver. CT: *Colophon*, n.s., II (1937), 206.
1577. Trent. CT: Gohdes and Silver, 113. PT: Kennedy, 54.
1578. TEXT: Kennedy's transcription in Trent. CT: Kennedy, 55.
1578.1 Carl H. Pforzheimer Library.
1579. Trent. CT: Gohdes and Silver, 113. PT: Kennedy, 55.
1579.1 Pennsylvania.
1580. Trent. CT: Gohdes and Silver, 114. PT: Kennedy, 55.
1581. Trent. CT: Gohdes and Silver, 114.
1582. Boston Public Library. PT: *More Books*, XIII (1938), 192.
1583. Dr. R. J. H. DeLoach. PT: Barrus, 265.
1584. Feinberg. CT: *Colophon*, n.s., II (1937), 207.
1585. Feinberg.
1586. Berg.
1587. TEXT: Kennedy's transcription in Trent. CT: Kennedy, 55.
1588. James S. Wroth.

1589. Feinberg.
1589.1 Lion.
1590. Boston Public Library. PT: *More Books*, XIII (1937), 192.
1591. Trent. CT: Gohdes and Silver, 114.
1592. Feinberg.
1593. Feinberg.
1594. Berg.
1595. TEXT: Catalog of Thomas Madigan, 1930.
1596. Feinberg. TEXT: *Colophon*, n.s., II (1937), 207.
1597. TEXT: *Pall Mall Gazette*, August 30, 1887; *AL*, XXXIII (1961), 70–71.
1598. British Museum.
1599. William E. Barton Estate.
1600. TEXT: Kennedy's transcription in Trent. CT: Kennedy, 55.
1601. Iowa State Education Association (Envelope in Gilbert S. McClintock).
1602. TEXT: Dodd, Mead & Company, January, 1903.
1603. Trent. CT: Gohdes and Silver, 114–115. PT: Kennedy, 56.
1604. Professor Harold D. Kelling.
1605. Feinberg. CT: *Colophon*, n.s., II (1937), 207–208.
1606. Feinberg. CT: *Colophon*, n.s., II (1937), 208.
1607. Mrs. Barbara Halpern (Envelope in Feinberg). CT: *Colophon*, n.s., II (1937), 208–209.
1608. Trent. CT: Gohdes and Silver, 115. PT: Kennedy, 56.
1609. The New Jersey Historical Society. CT: *Proceedings of the New Jersey Historical Society*, LXXV (1957), 219.
1610. The Museum of the City of New York.
1611. Feinberg.
1612. Feinberg. FACSIMILE: George M. Williamson, *Catalogue of A Collector of Books, Letters and Manuscripts* (1903).
1613. SOURCE: American Art Association, December 12, 1934.
1614. Yale.
1615. Trent. CT: Gohdes and Silver, 115–116. PT: Kennedy, 56; Nonesuch, 1048.
1616. Boston Public Library. PT: *More Books*, XIII (1938), 192.
1617. Feinberg. CT: *Colophon*, n.s., II (1937), 209.
1618. Feinberg. CT: *Colophon*, n.s., II (1937), 209.
1619. Trent. CT: Gohdes and Silver, 116.
1620. Pennsylvania.
1621. Feinberg. CT: Barrus, 269–270.
1622. Trent. CT: Gohdes and Silver, 116.
1623. Berg.
1624. Berg.
1625. Barrett.
1626. Lion (Envelope in Widener Collection, Harvard).
1626.1 Feinberg.
1627. TEXT: Hallam Tennyson, *Alfred Lord Tennyson: A Memoir* (1897), II, 345; New-York *Tribune*, November 22, 1887.
1628. Berg.
1629. Trent. CT: Gohdes and Silver, 117.
1630. Trent. CT: Gohdes and Silver, 117–118. PT: Kennedy, 56.
1631. Barrett. CT: *Wake*, VII (1948), 13.
1632. Feinberg.
1633. Barrett.
1634. Feinberg (Envelope in Berg).
1635. Feinberg.
1636. Trent. CT: Gohdes and Silver, 118.
1637. Feinberg.
1638. Trent. CT: Gohdes and Silver, 118.
1639. TEXT: Swann Auction Galleries, April 4–5, 1951.
1640. TEXT: Swann Auction Galleries, April 4–5, 1951.
1641. The Phillips Exeter Academy.
1642. John S. Mayfield.
1643. Trent. CT: Gohdes and Silver, 119.
1644. Barrett.
1644.1 TEXT: Transcription in Feinberg.
1645. Feinberg.
1646. Yale. PT: Barrus, 271.
1647. Trent. CT: Gohdes and Silver, 119. PT: Kennedy, 57.
1648. Berg.
1649. Feinberg.
1650. Doheny.
1651. Feinberg. PT: *Harvard Studies and Notes in Philology and Lit-*

erature, XIV (1932), 23 (dated January 8).
1652. Berg.
1653. Feinberg.
1654. Trent. CT: Gohdes and Silver, 120.
1655. Berg.
1656. Trent. CT: Gohdes and Silver, 120.
1657. Mills College.
1658. Feinberg.
1659. New York Public Library.
1660. Trent. CT: Gohdes and Silver, 120.
1661. Feinberg.
1662. Feinberg.
1663. Feinberg.
1664. TEXT: *The Month at Goodspeed's*, VIII (1937), 190.
1665. Feinberg.
1666. Trent. CT: Gohdes and Silver, 120–121.
1667. Berg. CT: Nonesuch, 1049–50. PT: Barrus, 272.
1668. Feinberg.
1669. Trent. CT: Gohdes and Silver, 121.
1670. Trent. CT: Gohdes and Silver, 121.
1671. Feinberg.
1672. Berg.
1673. Trent. CT: Gohdes and Silver, 121–122.
1674. TEXT: Baker & Brooks Auction #106, February 9, 1944.
1675. Feinberg.
1676. Feinberg.
1677. Feinberg.
1678. TEXT: *In Re*, 389.
1679. Feinberg.
1680. Feinberg.
1681. DRAFT LETTER in Yale.
1682. Berg.
1683. Pennsylvania.
1684. Feinberg.
1685. Trent. CT: Gohdes and Silver, 122. PT: Kennedy, 57.
1686. Feinberg.
1687. Feinberg.
1688. Professor Harold D. Kelling.
1689. Trent. CT: Gohdes and Silver, 122. PT: Kennedy, 57.
1690. Trent. CT: Gohdes and Silver, 122–123. PT: Kennedy, 57–58.
1691. Feinberg.
1692. Mrs. Louis Broido.
1693. Feinberg.
1694. TEXT: *The Autograph*, I (November, 1911), 14.
1695. Berg.
1696. Pennsylvania.
1697. Feinberg.
1698. Berg. PT: Perry, *Walt Whitman* (1906), 257.
1699. TEXT: Stan V. Henkels, May 8, 1917.
1700. Feinberg.
1701. Feinberg.
1702. Berg.
1703. Feinberg.
1704. Yale. PT: Barrus, 274.
1704.1 Feinberg. CT: Traubel, I, 94.
1705. Feinberg. PT: *Harvard Studies and Notes in Philology and Literature*, XIV (1932), 11.
1706. Trent. CT: Gohdes and Silver, 123. PT: Kennedy, 58.
1707. Berg.
1708. Feinberg. CT: *Colophon*, n.s., II (1937), 209–210.
1709. Feinberg. CT: Traubel, I, 171.
1710. Berg.
1711. Feinberg. FACSIMILE: Traubel, I, 192.
1712. Feinberg.
1713. FACSIMILE: New York *Daily Graphic*, June 2, 1888.
1714. Berg.
1715. Trent. CT: Kennedy, 58.
1716. Feinberg.
1717. TEXT: Swann Auction Galleries, October 1, 1942.
1718. Feinberg.
1719. Berg.
1720. Feinberg.
1721. Feinberg.
1722. FACSIMILE: Binns, 326.
1723. Feinberg.
1724. Feinberg.
1725. Berg.
1726. Feinberg.
1727. Feinberg. CT: *Colophon*, n.s., II (1937), 210.
1728. Trent. CT: Gohdes and Silver, 124. PT: Kennedy, 58.
1729. Feinberg.
1730. Feinberg.
1731. Feinberg.
1732. Barrett.
1732.1 FACSIMILE: Julius Chambers, *News Hunting on Three Continents* (1921), 305.
1733. Feinberg.
1734. Berg.

1735. Feinberg. CT: *Colophon*, n.s., II (1937), 210.
1736. Feinberg.
1737. Feinberg.
1738. Trent. CT: Gohdes and Silver, 124. PT: Kennedy, 58.
1739. Berg.
1740. Feinberg.
1741. Barrett.
1742. TEXT: Barrus, 280–281.
1743. Feinberg. CT: *Colophon*, n.s., II (1937), 210.
1744. Feinberg.
1745. Feinberg.
1746. Feinberg.
1747. Berg.
1748. Pennsylvania.
1749. Feinberg.
1750. Feinberg.
1751. Feinberg. CT: *Colophon*, n.s., II (1937), 211.
1752. Feinberg.
1753. Feinberg.
1754. Feinberg.
1755. Hanley.
1756. Trent. CT: Gohdes and Silver, 124.
1757. TEXT: Typescript, prepared by Bliss Perry, in Berg.
1758. Feinberg.
1759. Feinberg.
1760. Doheny. PT: Barrus, 281.
1761. Feinberg.
1762. Berg.
1763. Feinberg. CT: *Colophon*, n.s., II (1937), 211.
1764. Feinberg.
1765. Berg.
1766. Feinberg.
1767. Feinberg.
1768. Feinberg.
1769. Feinberg.
1770. Whitman House, Camden. CT: *AL*, VIII (1937), 433.
1771. Feinberg.
1772. William D. Bayley Collection, Ohio Wesleyan University.
1773. Feinberg.
1774. Feinberg.
1775. Feinberg.
1776. Feinberg.
1777. Feinberg.
1778. Trent. CT: Gohdes and Silver, 124–125. PT: Kennedy, 58.
1779. Feinberg.
1780. Feinberg. CT: *Colophon*, n.s., II (1937), 211.
1781. Feinberg.
1782. TEXT: Transcription supplied by Professor Cora E. Stafford.
1783. Feinberg.
1784. Feinberg.
1785. SOURCE: Samuel T. Freeman & Company, May 3, 1921(?).
1786. Feinberg.
1787. Feinberg.
1788. Barrett. CT: Knortz, 93; *AL*, XX (1948), 161.
1789. Professor Harold D. Kelling.
1790. Feinberg.
1791. Yale.
1792. British Museum.
1793. Barrett.
1794. Feinberg.
1795. Trent. CT: Gohdes and Silver, 125.
1796. Feinberg. CT: *In Re*, 389–390.
1797. Berg.
1798. Feinberg. PT: Barrus, 284.
1799. Feinberg. PT: *In Re*, v; Shephard, *Walt Whitman's Pose*, 199.
1800. TEXT: Goodspeed's Catalog, #280, 1937.
1801. William E. Barton Estate.
1802. Feinberg.
1803. Berg.
1804. Feinberg. CT: *Colophon*, n.s., II (1937), 211.
1805. Huntington (New York) Public Library.
1806. Feinberg.
1807. Feinberg. CT: Barrus, 284.
1808. Barrett. PT: Kennedy, 58–59.
1809. Berg.
1810. Feinberg.
1811. Syracuse University.
1812. Feinberg.
1813. Feinberg.
1814. Trent. CT: Gohdes and Silver, 125–126.
1815. Trent. CT: Gohdes and Silver, 126. PT: Kennedy, 59.
1816. Feinberg.
1817. Pennsylvania. CT: Traubel, II, 516.
1817.1 TEXT: Traubel, II, 516.
1818. Feinberg. CT: *Colophon*, n.s., II (1937), 212. PT: *Smith Alumnae Quarterly* (February, 1958), 88.
1819. University of Southern California. CT: *The Personalist*, XXXVI (1955), 369–378.

1820. Pennsylvania. CT: Barrus, 285. PT: Kennedy, 59–60.
1821. Feinberg.
1822. Berg.
1823. Feinberg.
1824. Feinberg.
1825. Feinberg.
1826. Feinberg.
1827. Feinberg.
1828. Feinberg.
1829. Feinberg.
1830. Berg.
1831. Feinberg.
1832. Feinberg.
1833. Berg.
1834. University of Southern California. CT: Hamlin Garland, *Roadside Meetings* (1931), 141.
1835. Barrett.
1836. Feinberg.
1837. Berg.
1838. Feinberg.
1839. TEXT: Edward Dowden's transcription in Berg.
1840. Feinberg.
1841. Feinberg. CT: *Colophon*, n.s., II (1937), 212.
1842. Feinberg.
1843. Feinberg.
1844. TEXT: Traubel, III, 188.
1845. Feinberg.
1846. Feinberg. PT: Kennedy, 60–61.
1847. Feinberg.
1848. TEXT: Traubel, III, 232.
1849. Feinberg.
1850. Feinberg.
1851. Hanley.
1852. Feinberg.
1853. Feinberg.
1854. Berg.
1855. Feinberg.
1856. Feinberg.
1857. Feinberg.
1858. Photostat in Feinberg.
1859. Feinberg.
1860. Berg.
1861. Feinberg.
1862. Feinberg.
1863. Barrett.
1864. Berg.
1865. Feinberg.
1866. Feinberg.
1867. Feinberg.
1868. British Museum.
1869. TEXT: Copy in Feinberg.
1870. Mrs. Charles Gridland.
1871. Feinberg.
1872. Feinberg.
1873. TEXT: Traubel, III, 395.
1874. Feinberg.
1875. Feinberg.
1876. Trent. CT: Gohdes and Silver, 127.
1877. Feinberg.
1878. Feinberg.
1879. Feinberg.
1880. Berg.
1881. Feinberg.
1882. Feinberg.
1883. FACSIMILE: *L'Ane d'Or*, V (1926), 57; Jean Catel, *Walt Whitman—La naissance du poète* (1929), 304.
1884. Feinberg.
1885. Trent. CT: Gohdes and Silver, 127–128. PT: Kennedy, 61.
1886. Trent. CT: Gohdes and Silver, 128.
1887. Feinberg.
1888. TEXT: Stan V. Henkels, May 8, 1917.
1889. Barrett. CT: Knortz, 93; *AL*, XX (1948), 161–162.
1890. Feinberg.
1891. Hanley.
1892. Feinberg.
1893. University of Southern California. CT: Hamlin Garland, *Roadside Meetings* (1930), 141.
1893.1 Feinberg.
1894. Feinberg.
1895. John Z. Katz.
1896. Feinberg.
1897. Feinberg.
1898. Berg.
1899. Feinberg.
1900. Trent. CT: Gohdes and Silver, 128–129.
1901. Feinberg.
1902. Feinberg.
1903. Berg.
1904. Feinberg.
1905. Berg.
1906. Feinberg.
1907. TEXT: Kennedy, 61.
1908. Feinberg.
1909. Berg.
1910. Feinberg.
1911. Berg.
1912. Photostat in Feinberg. PT: Kennedy, 61–62.
1913. Feinberg.
1914. Feinberg.
1915. Feinberg.

1916. Feinberg.
1917. Feinberg.
1918. Feinberg.
1919. TEXT: Barrus, 286–287.
1920. Berg.
1921. Feinberg.
1922. Berg.
1923. Photostat in Feinberg. PT: Kennedy, 62.
1924. Berg.
1925. Feinberg.
1926. Berg.
1927. Feinberg.
1928. Trent. CT: Gohdes and Silver, 129.
1929. Barrett. CT: Knortz, 94; *AL*, XX (1948), 162.
1930. Berg.
1931. TEXT: Traubel, IV, 156.
1932. Feinberg.
1933. Berg.
1934. Feinberg. CT: *Colophon*, n.s., II (1937), 212.
1935. Berg.
1936. Berg.
1937. Feinberg.
1938. Berg.
1939. Knox College.
1940. Berg.
1941. Trent. CT: Gohdes and Silver, 129.
1942. Berg.
1943. Trent. CT: Gohdes and Silver, 129–130. PT: Kennedy, 62.
1944. Berg.
1945. Berg.
1946. Trent. CT: Gohdes and Silver, 130.
1947. Berg.
1948. Doheny.
1949. Berg.
1950. Berg.
1951. Berg.
1952. Berg. PT: Emory Holloway, *Free and Lonesome Heart* (1960), 202.
1953. Berg.
1954. TEXT: American Art Association, February 26, 1930.
1955. Berg.
1956. Berg.
1957. Berg.
1958. Berg.
1959. Berg.
1960. Berg.
1961. Berg.
1962. Berg.
1963. Trent. CT: Gohdes and Silver, 130.
1964. Berg.
1965. Berg.
1966. Berg.
1967. Feinberg.
1968. Feinberg.
1969. Barrett. PT: Kennedy, 62.
1970. Berg.
1971. Feinberg.
1972. Berg.
1973. Berg.
1974. Feinberg.
1975. Trent. CT: Gohdes and Silver, 131.
1976. Feinberg.
1977. Harvard.
1978. Syracuse University.
1979. Berg.
1980. Berg.
1981. Feinberg.
1982. Berg.
1983. Feinberg.
1984. Feinberg.
1985. Berg.
1986. Feinberg.
1987. Berg.
1988. Feinberg.
1989. Berg.
1990. Huntington. CT: *AL*, VIII (1937), 434–435; Nonesuch, 1051.
1991. Berg.
1992. Feinberg.
1993. Berg.
1994. Feinberg.
1995. Trent. CT: Gohdes and Silver, 131.
1996. Berg.
1997. Feinberg.
1998. Feinberg.
1999. Feinberg. PT: Kennedy, 62.
2000. TEXT: Knortz, 94; *AL*, XX (1948), 162.
2001. Berg.
2002. Feinberg.
2003. Berg.
2004. Feinberg.
2005. Berg.
2006. Trent. CT: Gohdes and Silver, 131.
2007. Feinberg.
2008. Berg.
2009. Feinberg.
2010. Berg.
2011. Feinberg. CT: *Colophon*, n.s., II (1937), 205 (dated 1887).

2012. Feinberg.
2013. Berg.
2014. Feinberg. CT: *Colophon*, n.s., II, (1937), 212–213.
2015. Feinberg.
2016. Trent. CT: Gohdes and Silver, 131–132.
2017. Feinberg.
2018. Berg.
2019. Feinberg.
2020. Berg.
2021. Feinberg.
2022. Feinberg.
2023. Berg.
2024. TEXT: Knortz, 92; *AL*, XX (1948), 163.
2025. Bernard Sarrazin. TEXT: *WWR*, V (1959), 9.
2026. Trent. CT: Gohdes and Silver, 132. PT: Kennedy, 63.
2027. Feinberg.
2028. Berg.
2029. Feinberg.
2030. Berg.
2031. Feinberg.
2032. Trent. CT: Gohdes and Silver, 132. PT: Kennedy, 63.
2033. Feinberg.
2034. Berg.
2035. Feinberg.
2036. TEXT: Barrus, 288.
2037. TEXT: *The Modern School*, VI (April–May, 1919), 127; Nonesuch, 1052.
2038. Morgan. CT: Kennedy, 63.
2039. Feinberg.
2040. Berg.
2041. TEXT: Kennedy, 63.
2042. Feinberg. CT: Traubel, V, 190.
2043. Dr. R. J. H. DeLoach. PT: Barrus, 288.
2044. Feinberg.
2045. Feinberg.
2046. Brooklyn College.
2047. Feinberg.
2048. Hanley.
2049. Feinberg.
2050. Feinberg.
2051. Feinberg.
2052. Feinberg.
2053. Library of Congress. CT: *Visits*, 243–244.
2054. Feinberg.
2055. Feinberg.
2056. Feinberg.
2057. Barrett.
2058. Paul J. Eisel, who supplied typescript.
2059. TEXT: Stan V. Henkels, May 8, 1917.
2060. Feinberg. CT: *Colophon*, n.s., II (1937), 213.
2061. Feinberg.
2062. William D. Bayley Collection, Ohio Wesleyan University.
2063. Feinberg.
2064. Feinberg. CT: Traubel, V, 316.
2065. Feinberg.
2066. Feinberg.
2067. Berg.
2068. Feinberg.
2069. Feinberg.
2070. FACSIMILE: Gay Wilson Allen, *Walt Whitman* (1961), 124.
2071. Feinberg.
2072. Barrett.
2073. Feinberg.
2074. Feinberg.
2075. Feinberg.
2076. TEXT: American Art Association, February 13–14, 1924.
2077. Feinberg.
2078. British Museum.
2079. Feinberg.
2080. Feinberg.
2081. Feinberg.
2082. Feinberg.
2083. Feinberg.
2084. Feinberg.
2085. Feinberg.
2086. Feinberg.
2087. Berg.
2088. Feinberg.
2089. Feinberg.
2090. Feinberg. CT: *Colophon*, n.s., II (1937), 213.
2091. Feinberg.
2092. Feinberg.
2093. Feinberg.
2094. Feinberg.
2095. Feinberg.
2096. British Museum.
2097. Berg.
2098. Feinberg.
2099. Dr. R. J. H. DeLoach.
2100. TEXT: Anderson Galleries, October 18, 1923.
2101. Feinberg.
2102. Feinberg.
2103. Feinberg.
2104. Professor Harold D. Kelling. FACSIMILE: *Occasional Notes*, Norlin Library, University of

Colorado, IV (May, 1964), 2–3.
2105. Feinberg.
2106. Feinberg.
2107. Feinberg. PT: Kennedy, 63.
2108. Feinberg.
2109. Feinberg. PT: Kennedy, 63.
2110. Berg.
2111. Feinberg.
2112. Berg.
2113. Feinberg.
2114. Feinberg.
2115. Feinberg.
2116. Berg.
2117. Vassar College. PT: Barrus, 290.
2118. Barrett.
2119. William D. Bayley Collection, Ohio Wesleyan University.
2120. Feinberg.
2121. Feinberg.
2122. Trent. CT: Gohdes and Silver, 132–133.
2123. Feinberg.
2124. Feinberg.
2125. Berg. PT: Kennedy, 64.
2126. Feinberg.
2127. Trent. CT: Gohdes and Silver, 133.
2128. Feinberg.
2129. Feinberg. CT: *Colophon*, n.s., II (1937), 213.
2130. Feinberg.
2131. Trent. CT: Gohdes and Silver, 133. PT: Kennedy, 64.
2132. Feinberg.
2133. Feinberg.
2134. Feinberg.
2135. Feinberg.
2136. Feinberg.
2137. Feinberg.
2138. Barrett.
2139. Feinberg.
2140. Feinberg.
2141. Feinberg.
2142. Feinberg.
2143. Feinberg.
2144. Feinberg.
2145. Feinberg.
2146. William D. Bayley Collection, Ohio Wesleyan University.
2147. Berg.
2148. Feinberg.
2149. Feinberg.
2150. Feinberg.
2151. Feinberg.
2152. Feinberg.
2153. Feinberg.
2154. Feinberg.
2155. Feinberg.
2156. Berg.
2157. Feinberg.
2158. Louis E. Stern Estate.
2159. Feinberg.
2160. Feinberg. CT: *Colophon*, n.s., II (1937), 214.
2161. Feinberg.
2162. Mrs. Ward Greene, who supplied a transcription.
2163. Feinberg.
2164. William D. Bayley Collection, Ohio Wesleyan University.
2165. Berg.
2166. Feinberg.
2167. Royal Library of Copenhagen. CT: *Orbis Litterarum*, VII (1949), 60.
2168. Feinberg.
2169. Feinberg.
2170. Trent. CT: Gohdes and Silver, 134.
2170.1 Feinberg.

Collections

Professor Gay Wilson Allen, 1464.
Barrett Literary Manuscripts Collection, University of Virginia, 1386, 1394, 1402, 1415, 1418, 1420, 1424, 1475 (*draft*), 1502, 1505, 1514, 1536, 1538, 1564, 1570, 1625, 1631, 1633, 1644, 1732, 1741, 1788, 1793, 1808, 1835, 1863, 1889, 1929, 1969, 2057, 2072, 2118, 2138.
Roger W. Barrett, 1390.
William E. Barton Estate, 1599, 1801.
Henry W. and Albert A. Berg Collection, New York Public Library, 1374, 1377–1378, 1385, 1388, 1391, 1398, 1431, 1436, 1456, 1459–1460, 1479, 1586, 1594, 1623–1624, 1628, 1648, 1652, 1655, 1667, 1672, 1682, 1695, 1698, 1702, 1707, 1710, 1714, 1719, 1725, 1734, 1739, 1747, 1757 (*transcription*), 1762, 1765, 1797, 1803, 1809, 1822, 1830, 1833, 1837, 1839 (*transcription*),

1854, 1860, 1864, 1880, 1898, 1903, 1905, 1909, 1911, 1920, 1922, 1924, 1926, 1930, 1933, 1935–1936, 1938, 1940, 1942, 1944–1945, 1947, 1949–1953, 1955–1962, 1964–1966, 1970, 1972–1973, 1979–1980, 1982, 1985, 1987, 1989, 1991, 1993, 1996, 2001, 2003, 2005, 2008, 2010, 2013, 2018, 2020, 2023, 2028, 2030, 2034, 2040, 2067, 2087, 2097, 2110, 2112, 2116, 2125, 2147, 2156, 2165.

Boston Public Library, 1546, 1552, env. 1561, 1566, 1573, 1575, 1582, 1590, 1616.

British Museum, 1450, 1482, 1558, 1598, 1792, 1868, 2078, 2096.

Mrs. Louis Broido, 1692.

Brooklyn College, 2046.

Brown University, 1380.

Mark Twain Papers, General Library, University of California, Berkeley, 1562.

Columbia University, 1553.

Royal Library of Copenhagen, 2167.

Cornell University, 1467.

Mrs. Charles Cridland, 1870.

Dr. R. J. H. DeLoach, 1583, 2043, 2099.

Estelle Doheny Collection of the Edward Laurence Doheny Memorial Library, St. John's Seminary, 1383, 1650, 1760, 1948.

Paul J. Eisel, 2058.

Charles E. Feinberg Collection, 1375–1376, 1379, 1382, 1401, 1403, 1405, 1407–1409, 1412, 1416, 1429, env. 1433, 1434, 1442, 1448–1449, 1454 (*draft*), 1455 (*draft*), 1457–1458, 1463, 1465–1466, 1468, 1473–1474, 1476, 1478, 1483, 1485–1486, 1493, 1495, 1501, 1506, 1508–1509, 1513, 1516, 1520–1522, 1524, 1528, 1531, 1533, 1537, 1542, 1544, 1548, 1554, 1557, 1560, 1565, 1571–1572, 1573.1, 1574, 1584–1585, 1589, 1592–1593, 1596, 1605–1606, 1611–1612, 1617–1618, 1621, 1626.1, 1632, 1634–1635, 1637, 1644.1 (*transcription*), 1645, 1649, 1651, 1653, 1658, 1661–1663, 1665, 1668, 1671, 1675–1677, 1679–1680, 1684, 1686–1687, 1691, 1693, 1697, 1700–1701, 1703, 1704.1, 1705, 1708–1709, 1711–1712, 1716, 1718, 1720–1721, 1723–1724, 1726–1727, 1729–1731, 1733, 1735–1737, 1740, 1743–1746, 1749–1754, 1758–1759, 1761, 1763–1764, 1766–1769, 1771, 1773–1777, 1779–1781, 1783–1784, 1786–1787, 1790, 1794, 1796, 1798–1799, 1802, 1804, 1806–1807, 1810, 1812–1813, 1816, 1818, 1821, 1823–1829, 1831–1832, 1836, 1838, 1840–1843, 1845–1847, 1849–1850, 1852–1853, 1855–1857, 1859, 1861–1862, 1865–1867, 1869 (*transcription*), 1871–1872, 1874–1875, 1877–1879, 1881–1882, 1884, 1887, 1890, 1892, 1893.1, 1894, 1896–1897, 1899, 1901–1902, 1904, 1906, 1908, 1910, 1913–1918, 1921, 1925, 1927, 1932, 1934, 1937, 1967–1968, 1971, 1974, 1976, 1981, 1983–1984, 1986, 1988, 1992, 1994, 1997–1999, 2002, 2004, 2007, 2009, 2011–2012, 2014–2015, 2017, 2019, 2021–2022, 2027, 2029, 2031, 2033, 2035, 2039, 2042, 2044–2045, 2047, 2049–2052, 2054–2056, 2060–2061, 2063–2066, 2068–2069, 2071, 2073–2075, 2077, 2079–2086, 2088–2095, 2098, 2101–2103, 2105–2109, 2111, 2113–2115, 2120–2121, 2123–2124, 2126, 2128–2130, 2132–2137, 2139–2145, 2148–2155, 2157, 2159–2161, 2163, 2166, 2168–2169, 2170.1.

Mrs. Ward Greene, 2162.

Mrs. Barbara Halpern, 1607.

T. E. Hanley Collection, University of Texas, 1399–1400, 1413, 1425, 1437, 1530, 1755, 1851, 1891, 2048.

Harvard University, 1977.

Henry E. Huntington Library, 1414, 1990.

Huntington (New York) Public Library, 1406, 1805.

Iowa State Education Association, 1601.

John Z. Katz, 1895.

Professor Harold D. Kelling, 1604, 1688, 1789, 2104.
Knox College, 1939.
Library of Congress, 1550, 1551, 2053.
Oscar Lion Collection, New York Public Library, 1589.1, 1626.
George McCandlish, 1507.
Gilbert S. McClintock, env. 1601.
John S. Mayfield, 1642.
Mills College, 1657.
Missouri Historical Society, 1438–1439, 1441, 1443, env. 1447.1.
Pierpont Morgan Library, 2038.
Mrs. Doris Neale, 1496.
New Jersey Historical Society, 1609.
Museum of the City of New York, 1610.
New York Public Library, 1525, 1659.
Northwestern University, 1447.1.
Oberlin College, 1397.
Ohio Wesleyan University, William D. Bayley Collection, 1452, 1772, 2062, 2119, 2146, 2164.
Charles Norton Owen, 1497.
University of Pennsylvania, 1433, 1445, 1461, 1510, 1579.1, 1620, 1683, 1696, 1748, 1817, 1820.
Carl H. Pforzheimer Library, 1578.1.
Phillips Exeter Academy, 1641.
Princeton University, 1381.
University of Richmond, 1435.
Rutgers University, 1428.
Bernard Sarrazin, 2025.
Professor Rollo G. Silver, 1576.
University of Southern California, 1819, 1834, 1893.
Professor Cora E. Stafford, 1782.
Stanford University Library, 1504 (*typescript*).
Louis E. Stern Estate, 2158.
Syracuse University, 1811, 1978.
Robert H. Taylor, 1384.
Trent Collection, Duke University, 1389, 1393, 1396, 1404, 1410, 1419, 1421–1423, 1427, 1430, 1432, 1440, 1446, 1451, 1462, 1469–1470, 1472, 1480, 1487–1488, 1490 (*transcription*), 1492, 1498, 1500 (*transcription*), 1511 (*transcription*), 1518–1519, 1523, 1526, 1529 (*transcription*), 1532, 1534, 1540 (*transcription*), 1543, 1545, 1547, 1549, 1556, 1559, 1561, 1567, 1577, 1578 (*transcription*), 1579, 1580–1581, 1587 (*transcription*), 1591, 1600 (*transcription*), 1603, 1608, 1615, 1619, 1622, 1629–1630, 1636, 1638, 1643, 1647, 1654, 1656, 1660, 1666, 1669–1670, 1673, 1685, 1689–1690, 1706, 1715, 1728, 1738, 1756, 1778, 1795, 1814–1815, 1876, 1885–1886, 1900, 1928, 1941, 1943, 1946, 1963, 1975, 1995, 2006, 2016, 2026, 2032, 2122, 2127, 2131, 2170.
Vassar College, 2117.
Mrs. William R. Weber, 1395.
Whitman House, Camden, 1444, 1491, 1494, 1517, 1770.
Widener Collection, Harvard University, env. 1626.
James S. Wroth, 1588.
Yale University, 1477, 1503, 1515, 1527, 1541 (*draft*), 1568–1569, 1614, 1646, 1681 (*draft*), 1704, 1791.

Appendix B

A CHECK LIST OF WHITMAN'S LOST LETTERS

It is sometimes of importance to biographers and critics to know about letters WW wrote, even though the letters themselves are not extant. The entries in this check list include (1) the date, (2) the name of the recipient of WW's letter, and (3) the source of information which makes possible the reconstruction, unless the source is the *Commonplace-Book* (Feinberg). Many of the dates are approximate because the information is based upon a letter addressed to WW, which simply informs us that the poet had written before the correspondent had replied. I have indicated the date and present location of correspondence addressed to WW. Allusions to lost letters in WW's own correspondence are designated WW and followed by the appropriate letter number. Auction records which contained no text are incorporated into this list, since the letters as of the moment are "lost." The abbreviations are explained in the table of abbreviations in the Introduction.

1886

March 27. To John Burroughs. Formerly in the possession of Charles H. A. Wager (1935).

April 13(?). To Hiram Corson. Letter from Corson, April 26 (Feinberg; Traubel, I, 287).

April 26. To William D. O'Connor. Letter from O'Connor, May 25 (Syracuse; Traubel, IV, 283).

April 28. To Richard Maurice Bucke. Letter from Bucke, May 13 (Feinberg).

About May 15. To Roden Noel. Letter from Noel, May 16 (Feinberg; Traubel, I, 394).

May 25. To Richard Maurice Bucke. Letter from Bucke, June 9 (Barrett).

June 5. To George M. Major. Envelope in Feinberg.

June 12. To an unidentified correspondent. Formerly in Hanley.

June 29. To Hannah Heyde, enclosing $5.

July 13. To G. M. Williamson. Letter from Williamson, July 17 (Feinberg).

About July 16. To G. M. Williamson. WW's notation on envelope of letter from Williamson, July 17 (Feinberg).

July 22. To William Walsh, *Lippincott's Monthly Magazine*, sending "My Book and I."

July 27. To the Editors, *The Critic*, sending "A Thought on Shakspere." Envelope in Feinberg.

August 5(?). To Hannah Heyde, enclosing $5.
August 6. To James Redpath, of *The North American Review*, enclosing "Robert Burns as Poet and Person."
August 25. To O. S. Baldwin, sending "Lafayette in Brooklyn."
September 14. To Hannah Heyde, enclosing $5.
September 15. To the Editor, *Harper's New Monthly Magazine*, sending "Some War Memoranda. Jotted Down at the Time."
September 19. To Harry Stafford. WW 1448.
October 5(?). To James Redpath, of *The North American Review*, sending "Some War Memoranda. Jotted Down at the Time."
About November 13. To James Wilkie. WW's notation on letter from Wilkie, November 13 (Feinberg).
December 22. To Hannah Heyde, enclosing $10.
December 22. To Mary Van Nostrand, enclosing $10.
About December 31. To R. Brisbane. Letter from Brisbane, February 1, 1887 (Syracuse; Traubel, IV, 266): "Your two postals . . ."

1887

About January 18. To Herbert Gilchrist. WW's notation on letter from Gilchrist, January 6 (Feinberg).
February 2. To Ernest Rhys.
February 3. To Ernest Rhys.
February 4. To Henry B. Lovering, concerning WW's pension.
February 17. To Richard Maurice Bucke. Letter from Bucke, February 20 (Feinberg).
March 4. To Thomas Loskey(?), acknowledging receipt of five shillings.
March 8. To Ernest Rhys, sending preface for English edition of *Specimen Days.*
March 8. To Samuel Hales, acknowledging receipt of £2.12.6.
March 8. To the Editor, Newcastle-on-Tyne *Chronicle*(?), acknowledging receipt of money.
March 10. To John Hay. Envelope in Library of Congress.
March 15. To Ernest Rhys, sending "Additional Note" for *Specimen Days.*
April 29. To Frederick A. Stokes. Letter from Stokes, April 30 (Feinberg).
May 2. To James Knowles, Editor of *Nineteenth Century*, sending "November Boughs."
May 11. To Ernest Rhys. Letter from Rhys, May 24 (Feinberg; Traubel, III, 59).
May 22. To the Editor, *The Critic*(?), sending "Poet's 68th Year."
May 24. To the Editor, Philadelphia *Press*, sending "Poet's 68th Year."
May 31. To William Walsh, *Lippincott's Monthly Magazine*, sending "November Boughs."
About June 3. To John W. Wroth. WW's notation on envelope of Wroth's letter, June 2 (Feinberg).
June 8. To Mrs. Walter Browne, sending photograph "for Elizabeth Burroughs."
June 9. To Richard Maurice Bucke. Letter from Bucke, June 12 (Feinberg).
June 23. To S. S. McClure, sending "The Dying Veteran."
July 3. To the Editor, *Century Magazine*, sending "Twilight."
August 6. To the City Surveyor, Camden. Letter from the Office of the City Surveyor, August 9 (Feinberg).
September 6. To Henry M. Alden, Editor of *Harper's New Monthly Magazine*, sending "Shakspere-Bacon's Cipher."
October 12. To Sylvester Baxter, sending "Shakspere-Bacon's Cipher."
October 12. To the Editor, [London?] *Athenaeum*, sending "Shakspere-Bacon's Cipher."
October 12. To the Editor, Philadelphia *Press*, sending "Shakspere-Bacon's Cipher."
October 12. To the Editor, Springfield *Daily Republican*, sending "Shakspere-Bacon's Cipher."
October 12. To the Editor, Washington *Star*, sending "Shakspere-Bacon's Cipher."
October 20(?). To Richard Maurice Bucke. WW 1619.
October 28. To Charles W. Eldridge. WW 1623.

November 1. To Ernest Rhys. WW 1625.

December 7. To *Munyon's Illustrated World*, sending poem in honor of Whittier, probably "As the Greek's Signal Flame."

About December 10. To Thomas Jefferson Whitman. Letter from Jeff, December 11 (Feinberg).

December 14. To the Editor, New York *World*, sending "As the Greek's Signal Flame."

December 17. To John Greenleaf Whittier. Traubel, I, 127.

December 22. To Hannah Heyde, enclosing $10.

December 22. To Mary Van Nostrand, enclosing $10.

1888

January 14. To Sidney H. Morse.

March 2. To Harry Stafford.

March 11. To the Editor, New York *Herald*.

April 1. To the Editor, New York *Herald*, sending a bill for $40.

About April 1. To Thomas J. McKee. Letter from McKee, April 7 (Feinberg).

April 3. To Samuel Hollyer, sending a photograph to be etched.

April 6. To Harry Stafford.

April 7. To the Editor, New York *Herald*.

April 8. To William D. O'Connor. Letter from O'Connor, May 16 (Syracuse; Traubel, IV, 244).

April 9. To the Editor, *Century Magazine*, sending "Old Age's Lambent Peaks."

April 9. To the Editor, *Lippincott's Monthly Magazine*, sending "A Carol Closing Sixty-Nine."

April 23. To William D. O'Connor. Letter from O'Connor, May 16 (Syracuse; Traubel, IV, 244).

May 11(?). To Francis Vielé-Griffin. Traubel, I, 137.

May 18. To Mary Smith Costelloe. Traubel, I, 171.

May 28. To William Walsh, Editor of *Lippincott's Monthly Magazine*, requesting return of "A Carol Closing Sixty-Nine." Traubel, I, 223.

May 30. To George Ferguson.

June 24. To Hannah Heyde. Traubel, I, 374.

About July 12. To Thomas Jefferson Whitman. Letter from Jeff, July 14 (Feinberg).

July 15. To Sylvester Baxter. WW 1744.

July 15. To an old New York Broadway driver. WW 1744.

July 15. To Thomas Donaldson. Envelope in Hanley.

About July 18. To Charlotte Fiske Bates. Letter from Miss Bates, July 19 (Feinberg).

July 23. To Richard Watson Gilder. Traubel, II, 28.

July 29. To Richard Maurice Bucke. Traubel, II, 54.

August 8. To Hannah Heyde. Traubel, II, 107.

August 29. To Ingersoll Lockwood. Traubel, II, 216.

About September 1. To Sidney H. Morse. Traubel, II, 387.

September 4. To Hannah Heyde. Traubel, II, 255.

September 19. To Sidney H. Morse. Traubel, II, 347.

October 11(?). To T. W. Mather, of the Sheffield Scientific School of Yale College. Traubel, II, 465.

October 20. To the Editors, *The Critic*. WW's annotation on letter from the Gilders, October 19 (Feinberg).

October 24. To Dr. W. A. Hawley, sending a book.

November 6. To Thomas Donaldson. WW 1828.

November 27. To William H. Blauvelt. Traubel, III, 189.

December 20. To Hannah Heyde, enclosing $10.

December 20. To Mary Van Nostrand, enclosing $10.

December 24. To the Editors, *The Critic*, sending "To the Year 1889" ["To the Pending Year"].

December 27. To Sylvester Baxter. Formerly in the possession of Owen D. Young.

1889

January 4. To the Editor, *Century Magazine*, sending "Old Age's Ship & Crafty Death's."

About January 20. To Joseph B. Gilder, of *The Critic*. Traubel, IV, 172.
January 22. To T. W. H. Rolleston.
About March 1. To Hannah Heyde. Letter from Charles L. Heyde, March 2 (Trent).
March 3. To William Sloane Kennedy. Traubel, IV, 277.
About March 15. To Robert Pearsall Smith. Letter from Smith, March 31 (Feinberg).
March 20. To Richard Maurice Bucke. Envelope in Feinberg.
March 21. To the Editor, Harper Brothers, granting permission to print "O Captain! My Captain!" Traubel, IV, 392.
March 29. To John Burroughs. Traubel, IV, 448.
April 7. To Charles L. Heyde. Traubel, IV, 508.
April 16. To Hannah Heyde. Letter from Hannah, April 18 (LC).
May 8(?). To Katherine Johnston. Traubel, V, 149.
About May 13. To Hannah Heyde. Letter from Hannah, May 14 (LC).
May 25. To Herbert Gilchrist. Envelope in Feinberg.
June 9. To Richard Watson Gilder, Editor of *Century Magazine*, sending "My 71st Year."
June 9. To Milford C. Reed.
June 11. To the Editor, New York *Herald*, sending "Bravo, Paris Exposition!"
June 11. To William Sloane Kennedy. Formerly in the possession of Mrs. Frank J. Sprague.
June 13. To the Editor, New York *World*, sending "Bravo, Paris Exposition!"
June 18. To Herbert Gilchrist. Envelope in Feinberg.
June 27. To Julius Chambers. Traubel, V, 328.
July 2(?). To Eduard Bertz. Letter from Bertz, July 20–22 (Feinberg).
July 12. To Hannah Heyde. WW 2072.
July 30. To C. F. Currie(?), superintendent of the Blackwoodtown Asylum, sending a check for Edward's board.
August 11. To Hannah Heyde, sending money.
September 13. To Thomas B. Harned. Envelope owned by Richard Gimbel.
September 18. To the Editor, *Harper's Weekly*, sending "Bravo, Paris Exposition!"
October 1. To the Editors, *The Critic*, sending a photograph.
October 7. To Ernest Rhys. Letter from Rhys, October 23 (Feinberg).
October 9. To Charles L. Heyde, sending $6.
October 16. To Thomas Donaldson. Donaldson, 98.
October 18. To Henry M. Alden, Editor of *Harper's New Monthly Magazine*, sending "Old Age's Voices" ["Old Age Echoes"].
October 31. To Louisa Orr Whitman. Catalogue of American Art Association, November 5–6, 1923.
November 1. To Robert Pearsall Smith. WW 2143.
November 3. To James Knowles, Editor of *Nineteenth Century*, sending "Old Age Echoes."
November 19. To the Editor, *Harper's Weekly*, sending "A North Star to a South" ["A Christmas Greeting"].
December 19. To Hannah Heyde, enclosing $10.
December 19. To Mary Van Nostrand, enclosing $10.
About December 22. To Edward Wilkins. Letter from Wilkins, December 24 (Feinberg).
December 31. To Charles L. Heyde, enclosing $2.

Appendix C

A CALENDAR OF LETTERS WRITTEN TO WHITMAN

This Calendar includes extant letters written to WW. The following information appears in the entries: (1) the date; (2) the name of the correspondent, sometimes with a brief identification in order to indicate the nature of the correspondence; (3) the location of the letter, if known; and (4) appearance in print, if applicable. The letters to WW which are reproduced in this volume are marked WW with the appropriate letter number. Excerpts from many of these letters appear in the notes. Abbreviations are explained in the table of abbreviations in the Introduction.

1886

[January 2?]. From William Sloane Kennedy. Berg.

January 5. From William Michael Rossetti. CT: Traubel, II, 291.

January 11. From William Michael Rossetti. Feinberg.

January 21. From William D. O'Connor. Feinberg. CT: Traubel, III, 74–75.

January 25. From Herbert Gilchrist. Feinberg.

February 2. From John Newton Johnson. Feinberg.

February 5. From William Sloane Kennedy. Feinberg.

March 23. From William D. O'Connor. Syracuse. CT: Traubel, IV, 413–415.

March 26. From Hiram Corson. Feinberg. CT: Traubel, I, 286–287.

March 30. From Roden Noel. Feinberg. CT: Traubel, I, 432–433.

April 3. From John Burroughs. Feinberg. CT: Traubel, II, 549–550. PT: Barrus, 260–261.

April 9. From Moses A. Walsh (concerning the Wesley Water Cure). Feinberg.

April 12. From Smith & Starr, managers of the Salem (New Jersey) Opera House (proposing a Lincoln Lecture). Feinberg.

April 15. From Talcott Williams. Feinberg.

April 19. From William Sloane Kennedy. Feinberg.

April 26. From Hiram Corson. Feinberg. CT: Traubel, I, 287.

May 13. From Richard Maurice Bucke. Feinberg.

May 16. From Roden Noel. Feinberg. CT: Traubel, I, 394.

May 17. From Edward Carpenter. Feinberg.

May 17. From Dr. John Johnston. Feinberg.

May 17. From William Michael Rossetti. Feinberg.

May 22. From Ernest Rhys. Hanley.

May 25. From William D. O'Connor. Syracuse. CT: Traubel, IV, 283–285.

June 9. From Richard Maurice Bucke. Barrett.

June 11. From Talcott Williams. Feinberg.
June 14. From W. I. Whiting, for Scammel Brothers (noting auction prices for WW items). Feinberg.
June 14. From Lavinia F. Whitman (concerning Whitman genealogy). Feinberg.
June 17. From William Sloane Kennedy. Feinberg.
June 19. From Edward T. Potter. Syracuse. CT: Traubel, IV, 311–312.
June 28. From John Burroughs. Feinberg.
July 1. From William Sloane Kennedy. Feinberg.
July 5. From Gertrude Van Duren (ordering a book). Feinberg.
July 7. From W. L. Shoemaker, an admirer. Feinberg.
July 10. From William Sloane Kennedy. Feinberg.
July 13. From Samuel G. Stanley, a Brooklyn friend. Feinberg.
July 16. From Elizabeth J. Sharpe, a friend of the Staffords. Feinberg.
July 17. From George M. Williamson (offering to purchase some WW manuscripts). Feinberg.
July 18. From William Sloane Kennedy. LC.
July 19. From Charles Morris (requesting permission to include "Song of the Redwood-Tree" in *Half Hours with the Best American Authors*). Feinberg.
July 30. From Mary Grace Thomas, a student at Bryn Mawr College. Feinberg.
August 2. From William Sloane Kennedy. Feinberg.
August 17. From William D. O'Connor. Yale.
August 18. From William Sloane Kennedy. Feinberg.
September 10. From Herbert Gilchrist. Feinberg.
September 16. From James Matlack Scovel. Feinberg.
September 16. From William S. Walsh, of *Lippincott's*. Feinberg.
September 20. From Henry M. Alden, of *Harper's Monthly*. Feinberg. CT: Traubel, II, 226.
October 5. From James Redpath, of *The North American Review*. Feinberg. CT: Traubel, II, 226.
October 5. From Charles F. Wingate, secretary of The Twilight Club in New York. Feinberg.
October 16. From Herbert Gilchrist. Feinberg.
October 18. From W. I. Whiting (concerning a recent auction). Feinberg.
October 21. From Mary Smith Costelloe. Feinberg. PT: *Smith Alumnae Quarterly* (February, 1958), 87.
October 21. From Percy Ives, the artist. Feinberg. CT: *Detroit Historical Society Bulletin*, XVI (February, 1960), 9.
November 9. From Herbert Gilchrist. Feinberg.
November 9. From Thomas Jefferson Whitman. Feinberg. PT: *Missouri Historical Society Bulletin*, XVI (1960), 112.
November 13. From James Wilkie (enclosing a gift). Feinberg.
November 16. From William Michael Rossetti. Feinberg.
November 24. From Hamlin Garland. Feinberg. CT: Traubel, II, 160–162; Garland, *Roadside Meetings* (1930), 128–130.
November 26. From Ernest Rhys. Feinberg. CT: Traubel, IV, 228–230.
December 4. From Richard Maurice Bucke. Feinberg.
December 6. From Sylvester Baxter (concerning the pension). Feinberg.
December 10. From William D. O'Connor. Syracuse. CT: Traubel, IV, 128–130.
December 17. From Gerald Maxwell, a young admirer. Feinberg.
December 21. From John Burroughs. Yale. CT: Traubel, IV, 130–131.
December 21. From William D. O'Connor. Feinberg.
December 23. From Herbert Gilchrist. Feinberg.
December 25. From Morley C. Roberts. Feinberg. CT: Traubel, III, 466–467 (erroneously dated December 12).

1887

January 6. From Herbert Gilchrist. Feinberg.
January 11. From the Editor of the New Orleans *Picayune*. Location un-

known. CT: *Prose Works 1892*, 605.
January 15. From Alfred Lord Tennyson. Feinberg. WW 1476.
January 15. From Percy W. Thompson (requesting an autograph). Feinberg.
January 17. From Mary Smith Costelloe. Feinberg. PT: *Smith Alumnae Quarterly* (February, 1958), 87.
January 19. From Ernest Rhys (WW's notation: "a wonderful letter"). Feinberg.
February 1. From R. Brisbane. Syracuse. CT: Traubel, IV, 266–267.
February 3. From Henry Norman, of *Pall Mall Gazette*. Feinberg.
February 3. From Louis H. Sullivan. Feinberg. CT: Traubel, III, 25–26; Sherman Paul, *Louis Sullivan: An Architect in American Thought* (1962), 1–3.
February 11. From Charles W. Eldridge. Location unknown. CT: Barrus, 262–263.
February 12. From C. A. Spofford (requesting information about *Leaves of Grass*). LC.
February 15. From Ernest Rhys. Morgan.
February 16. From Joseph B. Marvin. Syracuse. CT: Traubel, IV, 412.
February 20. From Richard Maurice Bucke. Feinberg.
February 28. From Daniel G. Brinton. Feinberg.
March 11. From Mrs. William Hawley Smith. Feinberg.
March 12. From John Hay. Location unknown. CT: Traubel, III, 91–92.
March 13. From Annie Fields (extending an invitation on behalf of an unnamed committee). Feinberg.
March 16. From Edward W. Bok (concerning a memorial for Henry Ward Beecher). Feinberg.
March 17. From Joseph B. Gilder. Barrett. CT: *The Princeton University Library Chronicle*, III (November, 1941), 6.
March 24. From John H. Johnston. Feinberg. CT: Traubel, II, 431.
March 29. From Ernest Rhys. Barrett.
March 31. From Herbert Gilchrist. Feinberg.
April 8. From James Grant Wilson. Feinberg. CT: Traubel, II, 135.
April 9. From William Sloane Kennedy. Feinberg.
April 19. From William Carey, of *The Century Magazine* (requesting an autographed copy of "O Captain! My Captain!"). LC.
April(?) 19. From Charles L. Heyde. Trent.
April 20. From Edward Carpenter. Feinberg.
April 25. From Major James B. Pond. Feinberg.
April 28. From Ernest Rhys. Location unknown. CT: Traubel, IV, 487–489.
April 30. From Frederick A. Stokes, a publisher. Feinberg.
May 15(?). From Dr. John Johnston and James W. Wallace. Typescript in Bolton (England) Public Libraries.
May 19. From James Knowles. Feinberg. CT: Traubel, I, 28.
May 24. From Ernest Rhys. Feinberg. CT: Traubel, III, 59–61.
May 27. From Herbert Gilchrist. Feinberg.
June 1. From George M. Williamson. Barrett.
June 2. From John W. Wroth (concerning his trip West). Feinberg.
June 12. From Richard Maurice Bucke. Feinberg.
June 13. From Fred G. Kitton (asking for WW's impressions of Charles Dickens). Feinberg.
June 16. From Aldred Emery. LC.
June 16. From William Sloane Kennedy. Boston Public Library.
June 18. From Sylvester Baxter. LC.
June 21. From Sylvester Baxter. Feinberg. CT: Traubel, II, 305.
July 7. From Grace Ellery Channing. Feinberg.
July 9. From Cassius M. Clay (acknowledging receipt of a book and including an address he delivered at Yale). Feinberg.
July 29. From William F. Channing. LC.
July 31. From Nugent Robinson, of *Once A Week*. Feinberg. CT: Traubel, II, 220 (dated July 30).
August 1. From William Morlow Fullerton (acknowledging WW's gifts). Feinberg.
August 2. From Sylvester Baxter. Syr-

acuse. CT: Traubel, II, 378–379.
August 2. From Ellen M. O'Connor. Feinberg.
August 2. From Louisa Snowdon. Location unknown. CT: Traubel, IV, 233–234.
August 3. From Hampton L. Carson, of the Constitutional Centennial Commission (requesting a patriotic poem for the occasion). Feinberg.
August 5. From Percy Ives. Feinberg. CT: *Detroit Historical Society Bulletin*, XVI (February, 1960), 10.
August 8. From Louisa Snowdon. Syracuse. CT: Traubel, IV, 233–234.
August 9. From the City Surveyor of Camden. Feinberg.
August 10. From James Redpath (requesting an article for *The North American Review*). Historical Society of Pennsylvania.
September 2. From Walter Lewin (enclosing his article on WW in current *Murray's Magazine*). Feinberg.
September 10. From John H. Johnston. Feinberg.
[September 12]. From Sidney H. Morse. Feinberg.
September 24. From James Matlack Scovel (asking WW to write on the Irish question). LC.
October 8. From Sylvester Baxter. Location unknown. CT: Traubel, II, 299–300.
October 10. From Herbert Gilchrist. Feinberg.
November 3. From A. H. Spaulding (reporting his defense of WW's "Children of Adam" before a Boston literary society). Feinberg.
November 15. From Alfred Lord Tennyson. Location unknown. WW 1627.
November 16. From Herbert Gilchrist. Feinberg.
November 18–22. From William Sloane Kennedy. Feinberg.
November 30. From M. H. Spielmann. Feinberg. CT: Traubel, II, 232–233.
December 5. From William Sloane Kennedy. Feinberg.
December 11. From Julius Chambers. Location unknown.
December 11. From Thomas Jefferson Whitman. Feinberg.
December 25. From Sidney H. Morse. Feinberg.
December 30. From Mrs. Anna M. Kerr (recalling old Brooklyn days). Feinberg.

1888

January 2. From William Sloane Kennedy. Feinberg.
January 3. From William D. O'Connor. Feinberg.
January 4. From Ernest Rhys. Feinberg.
January 4. From Ellen Terry. Feinberg. CT: Traubel, I, 5.
January 10. From William Sloane Kennedy (misdated 1887). Feinberg.
January 11. From William Sloane Kennedy (misdated 1887). Feinberg.
January 13. From John Burroughs. Feinberg.
January 13. From John Greenleaf Whittier. Feinberg. CT: Traubel, II, 8.
January 23. From James Gordon Bennett. LC.
January 26. From Ernest Rhys. Syracuse. CT: Traubel, IV, 47–48.
January 30. From Ellen M. O'Connor. Feinberg.
January 31. From Charles H. Buck (requesting an autograph). Feinberg.
January 31. From Sidney H. Morse. Feinberg.
[February 8?]. From William Sloane Kennedy. Feinberg.
[February 10?]. From Richard Maurice Bucke. Berg.
February 12. From Richard W. Colles. Syracuse. CT: Traubel, IV, 141–142.
February 13–15. From William Sloane Kennedy. Berg.
February 16. From Mrs. Talcott Williams. Feinberg.
February 17. From Herbert Gilchrist. Feinberg.
[February 20?]. From Richard Maurice Bucke. Feinberg.
February 20. From Ernest Rhys. Feinberg. PT: Barrus, 273*n*.
February 21. From Richard Maurice Bucke. Feinberg.

February 22. From Sidney H. Morse. Feinberg.
[February 25]. From William Sloane Kennedy. Feinberg.
February 26. From Sidney H. Morse. Feinberg.
March 1(?). From William Sloane Kennedy. Yale.
March 2. From Judah B. Voorhees, of the Society of Old Brooklynites. Feinberg.
March 3. From Charles T. Sempers, a Harvard student. Feinberg.
March 4. From Charles T. Sempers. Feinberg.
March 6. From W. J. Hemsley (enclosing a sonnet). Feinberg.
March 7. From Ernest Rhys. Lion. CT: Traubel, IV, 46–47.
March 8. From John R. Witcraft, a young admirer. Barrett.
March 11. From Richard Maurice Bucke. Feinberg.
March 13. From Ellen M. O'Connor. Feinberg.
March 14. From Sidney H. Morse. Feinberg.
March 20. From Henry H. Collins, an admirer. Feinberg.
March 24. From John W. Wiggins, of the Society of Old Brooklynites. Harvard.
March 29. From William Sloane Kennedy. Feinberg.
April 3. From Ernest Rhys. Feinberg. CT: Traubel, II, 30–31.
April 7. From James Gordon Bennett. Feinberg.
April 7. From Thomas J. McKee. Feinberg.
April 13. From Sheridan Ford. Syracuse. CT: Traubel, IV, 496–497. PT: Kennedy, 96; Barrus, 273.
April 14. From William D. O'Connor. Syracuse. CT: Traubel, IV, 497–499.
April 19. From Hamlin Garland. Feinberg.
[April 22]. From William Sloane Kennedy. Feinberg.
April 25. From Richard Maurice Bucke. Yale.
April 26. From Francis Vielé-Griffin. Location unknown. CT: Traubel, I, 119.
April 28. From O. G. Hempstead & Son. Location unknown. CT: Traubel, I, 93.
May 4. From James Gordon Bennett. Yale.
May 13. From William Harrison Riley. Feinberg.
May [15?]. From Dr. John Johnston and James W. Wallace. Typescript in Bolton (England) Public Libraries.
May 16. From William D. O'Connor. Syracuse. CT: Traubel, IV, 244–247.
May 21. From Ernest Rhys. Feinberg. CT: Traubel, I, 292–293.
May 30. From Ernest Rhys. Feinberg. CT: Traubel, II, 31–32.
May 31. From F. S. Ryman (birthday greetings). Feinberg.
May. From Ingersoll Lockwood (sending *The American Bookmaker* for August 6 with an article on WW and a portrait by Frank Fowler). Feinberg.
June 7. From Ernest Rhys. Feinberg. CT: Traubel, II, 33.
June 7. From George M. Williamson. Feinberg.
June 8. From William Sloane Kennedy. Feinberg.
June 11. From Edmund Blake (requesting an autograph). Feinberg.
June 11. From John Burroughs. Feinberg. CT: Traubel, I, 418–419; Barrus, 274–275.
June 13. From William D. O'Connor. Syracuse. CT: Traubel, IV, 499–500.
June 13. From Lt. Percy Thompson (requesting an autograph). Feinberg.
June 15. From Richard Maurice Bucke. Feinberg.
June 15. From Sidney H. Morse. Feinberg. CT: Traubel, I, 405–406.
June 16. From Elmer B. Lane (requesting an autograph). Feinberg.
June 18. From William Hosen Ballou (concerning WW's pension). Feinberg.
June 20. From Robert Pearsall Smith. Feinberg.
June 23. From Charles F. Sloane, a young admirer. Feinberg.
July 2. From Reginald A. and Katie E. Beckett, two fervid English socialists. Feinberg.
July 8. From Herbert Gilchrist. Feinberg.
July 9. From Richard Maurice Bucke. Feinberg. PT: Traubel, II, 17.

July 9. From William Sloane Kennedy. Feinberg.
July 9–10. From Ernest Rhys. Feinberg.
July 11. From Richard Maurice Bucke. Feinberg.
July 12. From William D. O'Connor. Feinberg.
July 13. From Sylvester Baxter. Feinberg. CT: Traubel, II, 192–193.
July 14. From Thomas Jefferson Whitman. Feinberg.
July 16. From John Burroughs. Feinberg.
July 19. From Charlotte Fiske Bates. Feinberg.
July 22. From Richard Maurice Bucke. Feinberg.
July 24. From Richard Maurice Bucke. Feinberg.
July 24. From C. Sadakichi Hartmann. Feinberg.
July 24. From M. H. Spielmann. Feinberg. CT: Traubel, II, 104.
July 24. From Susan Stafford. Feinberg.
July 25. From William Carey. Feinberg.
July 25. From William D. O'Connor. Feinberg. CT: Traubel, II, 176–177 (dated July 26).
July 27. From Richard Maurice Bucke. Feinberg.
August 3. From William D. O'Connor. Feinberg. CT: Traubel, II, 101–102.
August 4. From John Baker (about WW's illness). Feinberg.
August 4. From Richard Maurice Bucke. Feinberg.
August 7. From Richard Maurice Bucke. Feinberg. PT: Traubel, II, 114.
[August 7]. From Jessie E. Taylor. Feinberg. CT: Traubel, II, 450–451.
August 8. From Richard Maurice Bucke. Feinberg.
August 10. From Richard Maurice Bucke. Feinberg.
August 10. From William Ingram. William D. Bayley Collection at Ohio Wesleyan University.
August 11. From Richard Maurice Bucke. Feinberg.
August 15. From C. H. Browning, of the New York *Herald*. Feinberg. CT: Traubel, II, 146–147.
August 15. From Richard Maurice Bucke. Feinberg. CT: Traubel, II, 147–148.
August 17. From Richard Maurice Bucke. Trent.
August 21. From Mary Smith Costelloe. Feinberg.
August 21. From John Herbert Clifford (acknowledging receipt of a book). Feinberg.
August 24. From Richard Maurice Bucke. Feinberg.
August 25. From Richard Maurice Bucke. Feinberg.
August 27. From Richard Maurice Bucke. Feinberg.
August 28. From Richard Maurice Bucke. Feinberg.
August 28. From Charles L. Heyde. Trent.
August 29. From Charlotte Fiske Bates. Feinberg. CT: Traubel, II, 263.
August 29. From Richard Maurice Bucke. Feinberg. PT: Traubel, II, 228.
August 30. From Richard Maurice Bucke. Feinberg. CT: Traubel, II, 242.
August 30. From William Sloane Kennedy. Feinberg. CT: Traubel, II, 243.
August 31. From Edward Dowden. Feinberg. CT: Traubel, III, 146–147.
August 31. From William D. O'Connor. Feinberg. CT: Traubel, II, 238–239.
September 1. From Mary Smith Costelloe. Feinberg.
September 1. From T. W. H. Rolleston. Barrett.
September 2. From Richard Maurice Bucke. Feinberg.
September 2. From Sidney H. Morse. Feinberg. CT: Traubel, II, 387–388.
September 3. From Richard Maurice Bucke. Feinberg.
September 3. From Mrs. C. F. Stowe, a loving admirer. Feinberg.
September 3. From Mrs. Mary B. N. Williams. Feinberg.
September 4. From Richard Maurice Bucke. Feinberg.
September 4(?). From William Sloane Kennedy. Feinberg. CT: Traubel, II, 263–264.

September 7. From Logan Pearsall Smith. Feinberg.
September 7. From Richard Maurice Bucke. Feinberg.
September 8. From Richard Maurice Bucke. Feinberg.
September 9. From Richard Maurice Bucke. Feinberg.
September 10. From Richard Maurice Bucke. Feinberg.
September 11. From Richard Maurice Bucke. Feinberg.
September 12. From Richard Maurice Bucke. Feinberg.
September 12. From William Ingram. Feinberg. CT: Traubel, II, 320.
September 14. From Richard Maurice Bucke. Feinberg. CT: Traubel, II, 337–338.
September 15. From Richard Maurice Bucke. Feinberg.
September 17. From Richard Maurice Bucke. Feinberg. PT: Traubel, II, 374.
September 17. From William Sloane Kennedy to WW and Traubel. Feinberg.
September 18(?). From James Gordon Bennett. Feinberg.
September 19. From Richard Maurice Bucke. Feinberg.
September 20. From Richard Maurice Bucke. Feinberg.
September 21. From Richard Maurice Bucke. Feinberg.
[September 21]. From Mrs. C. S. Haley, a gushing admirer. Feinberg.
September 22. From Richard Maurice Bucke. Feinberg. PT: Traubel, II, 378.
September 23. From Julius Chambers. Feinberg.
September 24. From Richard Maurice Bucke. Feinberg.
September 26. From H. Buxton Forman. Feinberg. CT: Traubel, II, 433–434.
September 26. From Richard J. Hinton. Feinberg.
September 27. From Richard Maurice Bucke. Feinberg.
September 27. From Charles William Dalmon, an English sailor. Feinberg.
September 28. From Richard Maurice Bucke. Feinberg. PT: Traubel, II, 417.
September 30. From Richard Maurice Bucke. Feinberg.
October 1. From Richard Maurice Bucke. Feinberg.
October 1. From Mary Smith Costelloe. Feinberg. PT: *Smith Alumnae Quarterly* (February, 1958), 87–88.
October 1. From Herbert P. Horne. Feinberg. CT: Traubel, II, 528.
October 3. From Richard Maurice Bucke. Feinberg.
October 3. From William J. Linton. Feinberg. CT: Traubel, II, 473.
October 5. From Richard Maurice Bucke. Feinberg.
October 9. From Richard Maurice Bucke. Feinberg.
[October?] 9. From William Sloane Kennedy. Feinberg. CT: Traubel, II, 466.
October 9. From T. W. Mather. Feinberg. CT: Traubel, II, 465.
October 9. From William D. O'Connor. Feinberg. CT: Traubel, II, 467.
October 11. From Richard Maurice Bucke. Feinberg. PT: Traubel, II, 474.
October 11. From Ernest Rhys. Feinberg.
October 16. From Jerome Buck. Feinberg. CT: Traubel, II, 501.
October 16. From Richard Maurice Bucke. Feinberg.
October 16. From John Burroughs. Location unknown. CT: Traubel, II, 493–494.
October 18. From Hamlin Garland. Feinberg. CT: Traubel, II, 509.
[October 18]. From William Sloane Kennedy. Feinberg. CT: Traubel, II, 507.
October 19. From Jeannette L. and Joseph B. Gilder. Feinberg.
October 19. From Charles L. Heyde. Trent.
October 20. From Josiah Child. Feinberg.
October 20. From William Sloane Kennedy. Feinberg.
October 21. From Richard Maurice Bucke. Feinberg.
October 21. From Logan Pearsall Smith. Feinberg.
October 23. From Richard Maurice Bucke. Feinberg. PT: Traubel, II, 533–534.

October 24. From Richard Maurice Bucke. Feinberg. CT: Traubel, II, 536–537.
October 24. From Hamlin Garland. Feinberg. CT: Traubel, II, 530.
October 24. From Susan Stafford. Feinberg.
October 25. From Richard Maurice Bucke. Feinberg.
October 25. From Edmund Clarence Stedman. Feinberg. CT: Traubel, II, 537–538.
October 26. From W. C. Angus. Location unknown. CT: Traubel, IV, 198–199.
October 27. From Charles L. Heyde. Trent.
October 27. From William D. O'Connor. Feinberg.
October 28. From Richard Maurice Bucke. Feinberg.
October 30. From Sidney H. Morse. Feinberg.
October 31. From William H. Blauvelt. Location unknown. CT: Traubel, III, 8.
October. From Charles L. Heyde. Trent.
[October?]. From Louisa Orr Whitman. Trent.
November 1. From Richard Maurice Bucke. Feinberg. PT: Traubel, III, 12.
November 1. From William D. O'Connor. Feinberg. CT: Traubel, III, 9–10.
November 3. From Wellesley Sayle. Feinberg.
November 4. From Richard Maurice Bucke. Feinberg. PT: Traubel, III, 36.
November 6. From Richard Maurice Bucke. Feinberg. PT: Traubel, III, 56.
November 8. From Richard Maurice Bucke. Feinberg.
November 9. From Richard Maurice Bucke. Feinberg.
November 9. From Hamlin Garland. Feinberg. CT: Traubel, III, 67.
November 11. From Richard Maurice Bucke. Feinberg. PT: Traubel, III, 93–94.
November 14. From Richard Maurice Bucke. Feinberg.
November 16. From Richard Maurice Bucke. Feinberg.
November 16. From Hamlin Garland. Feinberg. CT: Traubel, III, 114.
November 17. From Joseph B. Gilder. Feinberg. CT: Traubel, III, 124.
November 22. From Richard Maurice Bucke. Feinberg. PT: Traubel, III, 167.
November 25. From Richard Maurice Bucke. Feinberg.
November 26. From James Matlack Scovel (concerning a meeting with Maurice Barrymore). Feinberg.
November 28. From Richard Maurice Bucke. Feinberg.
November 28, Evening. From Richard Maurice Bucke. Feinberg.
November 28. From C. W. Moulton (requesting permission to publish WW's poems in *The Magazine of Poetry*). Feinberg.
November 29. From George E. Dixon (requesting an autograph). LC.
November 30. From Logan Pearsall Smith. Feinberg.
November. From Charles L. Heyde. Trent.
December 1. From Herbert Gilchrist. Feinberg.
December 2. From Richard Maurice Bucke. Feinberg. PT: Traubel, III, 249.
December 3. From Richard Maurice Bucke. Feinberg. CT: Traubel, III, 248–249.
December 3. From Justin Huntly McCarthy. Feinberg.
December 6. From Richard Maurice Bucke. Feinberg.
December 7. From Richard Maurice Bucke. Feinberg. CT: Traubel, III, 269–270.
December [10]. From William D. O'Connor. Feinberg. CT: Traubel, III, 288 (erroneously dated December 9 by O'Connor).
December 11. From Richard Maurice Bucke. Feinberg.
December 12. From Ernest Rhys. Feinberg.
December 13. From William Sloane Kennedy. Feinberg.
[December 13]. From William Sloane Kennedy. Feinberg.
December 15. From Richard Maurice Bucke. Feinberg. PT: Traubel, III, 391.

December 15. From Samuel Hollyer. Feinberg.
December 16. From Richard Maurice Bucke. Feinberg.
December 16. From Thomas Tylston Greg. Location unknown. CT: Traubel, III, 432–433.
December 17. From Katherine Johnston. Feinberg.
December 19. From Richard Maurice Bucke. Feinberg.
December 20. From Richard Maurice Bucke. Feinberg.
December 20. From Ellen M. O'Connor. Feinberg.
December 21. From Richard Maurice Bucke. Feinberg.
December 21. From George M. Williamson. Feinberg.
December 23. From Richard Maurice Bucke. Feinberg.
December 23. From John Burroughs. Feinberg.
December 24. From Richard Maurice Bucke. Feinberg.
December 25. From Sylvester Baxter. Feinberg.
December 25. From Richard Maurice Bucke. Feinberg.
December 25. From William Sloane Kennedy. Feinberg.
December 25. From Franklin B. Sanborn. Feinberg. CT: Traubel, III, 402–403.
December 27. From Edward Carpenter. Feinberg.
December 27. From Joseph B. Gilder(?). Feinberg.
December 30. From Elizabeth and Isabella Ford. Feinberg.
December 30. From Sophia Kirk, an admirer. Feinberg.
December 31. From Richard Maurice Bucke. Feinberg.

1889

January 1. From O. F. Hershey, a Harvard student ("You are no stranger but an ever present comrade"). Feinberg.
January 4. From Edwin C. Gellett (sending a pamphlet). Feinberg.
January 5. From Ernest Rys. Feinberg. CT: Traubel, III, 440–441 (misdated 1888 by Rhys and Traubel).
January 5. From Logan Pearsall Smith. Feinberg.
January 6. From Gabriel Sarrazin. Feinberg.
January 7. From Mary Ashley. Location unknown. CT: Traubel, IV, 5–6.
January 7. From T. W. H. Rolleston. Feinberg.
January 8. From Frederick York Powell. Feinberg.
January 9. From Richard Maurice Bucke. Feinberg.
January 9. From O. W. True, an admirer. Feinberg.
[January 11]. From Hamlin Garland. Lion. CT: Traubel, IV, 78–79 (dated January 10).
January 13. From Edward Carpenter. Feinberg.
[January 13]. From Karl Knortz. Feinberg.
January 18. From Richard Maurice Bucke. Trent.
January 18. From Charles Allen Thorndike Rice. Location unknown. CT: Traubel, IV, 18.
January 21. From William Sloane Kennedy. Feinberg.
January 21. From Ellen M. O'Connor. Feinberg.
January 22. From Richard Maurice Bucke. Syracuse.
January 25. From Richard Maurice Bucke. Feinberg.
January 25–26. From Mary Smith Costelloe. Feinberg. PT: *Smith Alumnae Quarterly* (February, 1958), 88.
January 26–27. From Richard Maurice Bucke. Syracuse. PT: Traubel, IV, 49–50.
January 27. From Edward Carpenter. Syracuse. CT: Traubel, IV, 168–169.
January 28. From Ellen M. O'Connor. Feinberg.
January 29. From William Sloane Kennedy. Feinberg.
January 29. From John Addington Symonds. Feinberg. CT: Traubel, IV, 125–126. PT: Barrus, 290–291 (dated July 29).
January. From Horace C. Simmons (requesting a list of WW's publications for Miss Langley, a bookseller). Feinberg.
February 2. From Ernest Rhys. Feinberg.

February 2. From T. W. H. Rolleston. Feinberg.
February 3. From Richard Maurice Bucke. Lion.
February 7. From Ellen M. O'Connor. Feinberg.
February 12. From Joseph B. Gilder. Feinberg.
February 12. From Ellen M. O'Connor. Feinberg.
February 14. From Gabriel Sarrazin. Lion.
February 15(?). From Richard Maurice Bucke. Location unknown. PT: Traubel, IV, 163.
February 21. From John Burroughs. Yale. CT: Traubel, IV, 297.
February 22. From William Sloane Kennedy. Feinberg.
February 25. From Margareta L. Avery, WW's cousin. LC.
[February 25]. From William Sloane Kennedy. Feinberg.
February 27. From William Sloane Kennedy. Yale. CT: Traubel, IV, 381.
March 2. From Charles L. Heyde. Trent.
March 2. From Ernest Rhys. Hanley.
March 4. From Gleeson White (requesting information for an English magazine for girls). Feinberg.
March 5. From J. E. Chamberlin, of the Boston *Evening Transcript*. Syracuse. CT: Traubel, IV, 320–321.
March 5. From Ellen M. O'Connor. Syracuse. CT: Traubel, IV, 292.
March 5. From Huntington Smith (requesting permission to quote from WW's books). Feinberg.
March [6?]. From William Sloane Kennedy. Location unknown. PT: Traubel, IV, 292.
March 8. From Ellen M. O'Connor. Syracuse. CT: Traubel, IV, 309.
March 9. From Miss E. Langley (a book order). Feinberg.
March 12. From Charles L. Heyde. Trent.
March 12. From Ellen M. O'Connor. Syracuse. CT: Traubel, IV, 335.
March 13. From Ellen M. O'Connor. Syracuse. CT: Traubel, IV, 342.
March 13. From Hannah W. Smith. Feinberg. CT: *Smith Alumnae Quarterly* (February, 1958), 88.
March 17. From W. S. Walsh, of the New York *Herald*. Location unknown. CT: Traubel, IV, 372.
March 18. From William Sloane Kennedy. Feinberg.
March 18. From Frank H. Williams. Syracuse. CT: Traubel, IV, 388.
March 20. From Richard Maurice Bucke. Syracuse.
March 20. From Ellen M. O'Connor. Feinberg.
March 20. From *The Mail and Express*, New York (asking WW's opinion of George Washington). Feinberg.
March 21. From Richard Maurice Bucke. Syracuse.
March 21. From Ellen M. O'Connor. Feinberg.
March 21. From J. W. Wallace. Feinberg.
March 22. From Richard Maurice Bucke. Syracuse.
March 23. From Richard Maurice Bucke. Syracuse. PT: Traubel, IV, 425–426.
March 23. From Ellen M. O'Connor. Feinberg.
March 24. From Richard Maurice Bucke. Feinberg.
March 25. From Thomas Bailey Aldrich. Feinberg.
March 25. From Richard Maurice Bucke. Syracuse.
March 26. From Richard Maurice Bucke. Syracuse.
March 26. From Ellen M. O'Connor. Feinberg.
March 27. From Richard Maurice Bucke. Syracuse.
March 27. From Ellen M. O'Connor. Feinberg.
March 27. From Mrs. A. H. Spaulding. Feinberg.
March 27. From the Photo Engraving Office (acknowledging receipt of $10.50 from WW). Feinberg.
March 27–28. From Edmund Clarence Stedman. Feinberg. CT: *Life and Letters of Edmund Clarence Stedman*, II, 120–122.
March 28. From Richard Maurice Bucke. Syracuse.
March 28. From John Burroughs. University of Kansas. CT: Traubel, IV, 448–449.

[March 28]. From William Sloane Kennedy. Feinberg.
March 29. From Ellen M. O'Connor. Syracuse. CT: Traubel, IV, 451.
March 30. From Richard Maurice Bucke. Syracuse.
March 31. From Robert Pearsall Smith. Feinberg.
April 1. From Richard Maurice Bucke. Syracuse.
April 2. From Richard Maurice Bucke. Syracuse.
April 3. From Richard Maurice Bucke. Syracuse.
[April 3]. From Hamlin Garland. Feinberg. CT: Traubel, IV, 491–492.
April 4. From James Gordon Bennett. Yale.
April 4. From Richard Maurice Bucke. Syracuse.
April 4. From Henry A. Holmes, a composer (ordering books). Feinberg.
April 6. From Richard Maurice Bucke. Feinberg.
April 7. From William W. Payne, of the Chicago *Evening Journal* (enclosing his review of *November Boughs*). Feinberg.
April 8. From William Sloane Kennedy. Feinberg.
April 9. From Richard Maurice Bucke. Feinberg.
April 9. From D. H. Kenaga. Feinberg.
April 12. From Richard Maurice Bucke. Feinberg.
April 13. From Richard Maurice Bucke. Feinberg.
April 14. From Richard Maurice Bucke. Feinberg.
[April 14?]. From Karl Knortz. Feinberg.
April 18. From Hannah Heyde. LC.
April [18?]. From William Sloane Kennedy. Feinberg.
April 22–24. From Ernest Rhys. Feinberg.
April 24. From Richard Maurice Bucke. Feinberg. CT: Traubel, V, 84.
[April 24?]. From William Sloane Kennedy. Feinberg.
April 24. From Ellen M. O'Connor. Feinberg.
April 27. From Will Carleton (ordering a book). Feinberg.
April 28. From Alice Hicks Van Tassel, great grandniece of Elias Hicks (acknowledging receipt of *November Boughs*). Feinberg.
April 28. From William Sloane Kennedy. Feinberg.
April 30. From Ellen M. O'Connor. Feinberg.
May 6. From William Sloane Kennedy. Feinberg.
May 9. From Ellen M. O'Connor. Feinberg.
May 9. From James L. Sill (concerning O'Connor's death). Feinberg.
May 10. From Richard Maurice Bucke. Feinberg. PT: Traubel, V, 181.
May 10. From Mary Smith Costelloe. Feinberg. PT: *Smith Alumnae Quarterly* (February, 1958), 88.
May 11. From John Burroughs. Feinberg. CT: Traubel, V, 179–180.
May 11. From George Hall, an English curate and "a humble and obscure lover of yours" (enclosing an article on WW). Feinberg.
May 11–12. From William Sloane Kennedy. Feinberg.
May 12. From John B. Barnhill (requesting a manuscript relating to Tolstoi and Sir Walter Scott). Feinberg.
May 12. From Richard Maurice Bucke. Feinberg.
May 13. From Richard Maurice Bucke. Feinberg.
[May 13]. From William Sloane Kennedy. Feinberg.
May 14. From Hannah Heyde. LC.
May 14. From Fred S. Ryerson (concerning O'Connor's death). Feinberg.
May 15. From Richard Maurice Bucke. Feinberg.
May 16. From William Sloane Kennedy. Feinberg.
May 18. From Richard Maurice Bucke. Feinberg.
May 18. From Edward Carpenter. Feinberg. CT: Traubel, V, 256. PT: *Camden's Compliment to Walt Whitman*, 54.
May 18. From William Sloane Kennedy. Feinberg.
May 19. From an unsigned Australian admirer. Feinberg.

May 21. From J. W. Wallace. Feinberg, and typescript in Bolton (England) Public Libraries.
May 22. From George W. Childs. Feinberg. PT: *Camden's Compliment to Walt Whitman*, 64.
[May 23]. From William Sloane Kennedy. Feinberg. CT: Traubel, v, 221.
May 24. From Laurence Galimberti, a young Italian laborer. Feinberg.
[May 24]. From William Sloane Kennedy. Feinberg.
May 27. From Julius Chambers. Feinberg. CT: *Camden's Compliment to Walt Whitman*, 67.
May 28. From Richard Maurice Bucke. Feinberg.
May 28. From Hamlin Garland. Feinberg.
May 28. From Henry Latchford, of the Chicago *Evening Journal* (birthday greetings). Feinberg.
May 30. From Richard J. Hinton. Feinberg. PT: *Camden's Compliment to Walt Whitman*, 68.
June 1. From W. J. O'Reardon (birthday greetings). Feinberg.
June 1. From Milford C. Reed, a Civil War veteran. Feinberg.
June 2. From Richard Maurice Bucke. Feinberg.
June 3. From Richard Maurice Bucke. Feinberg.
June 3. From William Sloane Kennedy. Feinberg.
June 4. From Richard Maurice Bucke. Feinberg.
June 5. From Richard Maurice Bucke. Feinberg.
June 7. From Charles L. Heyde. Trent. CT: Gohdes and Silver, 229–230 (dated "June 89").
June 9. From Richard Maurice Bucke. Feinberg.
[June 10?]. From Elizabeth A. Cottell, an English admirer. Feinberg.
June 12. From William Sloane Kennedy. Feinberg.
June 15. From Richard Maurice Bucke. Ohio Wesleyan University.
June 16. From Eduard Bertz. Feinberg. CT: Traubel, v, 330–331.
June 16. From Richard Maurice Bucke. Feinberg.
June [18?]. From William Carey. Feinberg. CT: Traubel, v, 305.
June 26. From Edward Dowden. Feinberg.
July 3. From Ellen M. O'Connor. Feinberg.
July 8. From Rudolf Schmidt. Feinberg.
July 9. From William S. Kennedy. Feinberg.
July 12. From John Burroughs. Feinberg.
July 12. From A. Gardner(?). Feinberg.
July 13. From Charles W. Eldridge. Feinberg.
July 14. From Richard Maurice Bucke. Feinberg.
July 20–22. From Eduard Bertz. Feinberg.
July 21. From Charles W. Sparkes, an English priest. Feinberg.
[July 24]. From William Sloane Kennedy. Feinberg.
[July 25]. From William Sloane Kennedy. Feinberg.
August 1. From Ellen M. O'Connor. Feinberg.
August 3. From Walter B. Whitman, a cadet at Annapolis. Feinberg.
August 4. From Richard Maurice Bucke. Feinberg.
August 4. From William Sloane Kennedy. Feinberg.
August 13. From Robert Pearsall Smith. Feinberg.
August 14. From Ernest Rhys. Feinberg.
August 25. From Henry M. Alden. Feinberg.
August 25. From Richard Maurice Bucke. Feinberg.
August 27. From John Burroughs. Feinberg.
August 28. From John Oliver (protesting WW's description of religion as "bloodless"). Feinberg.
September 1. From O. W. True, a somewhat incoherent admirer. Feinberg.
September 3. From Richard Maurice Bucke. Feinberg.
September 5. From William Sloane Kennedy. Feinberg.
September 9. From Richard Maurice Bucke. Feinberg.
September 11. From Ernest Rhys. Feinberg.

September 12. From Sir Edwin Arnold. Feinberg.
September 12. From Ellen M. O'Connor. Feinberg.
September 15. From William Sloane Kennedy. Feinberg.
September 16. From Thomas Donaldson. Feinberg.
September 19. From the Reverend J. Leonard Corning (thanking WW for photographs). Feinberg.
September 19. From John Foord, editor of *Harper's Weekly*. Feinberg.
September 19. From Fanny M. Grundy, an English admirer. Feinberg.
September 20. From Richard Maurice Bucke. Feinberg.
September 21. From Mary A. Fisher (requesting that WW give a reading for the benefit of the Home-Hotel Association for needy authors and artists). Feinberg.
September 21. From Susan Stafford. Feinberg.
September 25. From Marjorie Cook, an eleven-year-old girl. Feinberg.
September 25. From Harper & Brothers (sending the *Fifth Reader*). Feinberg.
September 26. From Ellen M. O'Connor. Feinberg.
September 28. From Richard Maurice Bucke. Feinberg.
October 1. From Louis S. Kelley (an autograph request). Feinberg.
October 3. From William Sloane Kennedy. Feinberg.
October 8. From Richard Maurice Bucke. Feinberg.
October 8. From Charles W. Eldridge. Feinberg.
[October 10]. From William Sloane Kennedy. Feinberg.
October 10. From William P. McKenzie, a young admirer who sent his first book. Feinberg.
October 11. From A. K. McIlhaney, a school principal ("planting a tree and naming it in honor of you"). Feinberg.
October 13. From Robert Pearsall Smith. Feinberg.
October 14. From Walter Delaplaine Scull, an English artist (ordering a book). Feinberg.
October 15. From William Sloane Kennedy. Feinberg.
October 16. From Richard E. Labar, a young admirer. Feinberg.
October 18. From Richard Maurice Bucke. Feinberg.
October 18. From William Sloane Kennedy. Feinberg.
October 23. From Ernest Rhys. Feinberg.
October 24. From Henry M. Alden. Lion.
October 25. From Richard Maurice Bucke. Feinberg.
October 26. From Mary Smith Costelloe. Feinberg.
October 27. From William Sloane Kennedy. Feinberg.
October 27. From James W. Wroth (noting receipt of WW's photographs). Feinberg.
October 29. From Richard Maurice Bucke. Feinberg.
October 30. From Richard Maurice Bucke. Feinberg.
October. From Charles L. Heyde. Trent.
[October?]. From Hamlin Garland. Feinberg.
November 5. From Richard Maurice Bucke. Feinberg.
November 5. From William Sloane Kennedy. Feinberg.
November 6. From Richard Maurice Bucke. Feinberg.
November 8. From Richard Maurice Bucke. Feinberg.
November 8. From Ellen M. O'Connor. Feinberg.
November 9. From Alys Smith. Feinberg.
November 10. From Jessie Louisa Whitman. Feinberg.
November 10. From T. W. H. Rolleston. Feinberg.
November 18. From Charles Aldrich (requesting an autographed copy of "O Captain! My Captain!" for the Iowa State Library). Feinberg.
November 20. From S. H. Grey, a Camden lawyer (acknowledging receipt of books). Feinberg.
November 20. From Ellen M. O'Connor. Feinberg.
November 27. From Caroline K. Sherman (sending a clipping of her article on Carpenter). Feinberg.

November 29. From Ellen M. O'Connor. Feinberg.
December 3. From Richard Maurice Bucke. Feinberg.
December 3. From S. S. McClure (requesting that WW give his ideas on "To lift, how little howsoe'er, the hearts of toilers struggling here"). Feinberg.
December 7. From Ernest Rhys. Feinberg.
December 8. From Richard Maurice Bucke. Feinberg.
December 9. From John Addington Symonds. Feinberg.
December 13. From Harrison S. Morris (concerning his translation of Sarrazin). Feinberg.
December 15. From S. Weir Mitchell. Feinberg.
December 17. From John Burroughs. Feinberg.
December 18. From James W. Wroth (Christmas greetings). Feinberg.
December 20. From Richard Maurice Bucke. Feinberg.
December 20. From William H. Duckett (requesting a loan). Feinberg.
December 21. From Ellen M. O'Connor. Feinberg.
December 22. From Richard Maurice Bucke. Feinberg.
December 24. From Richard Maurice Bucke. Feinberg.
December 24. From J. B. Wood, of Harleigh Cemetery. Feinberg.
December 24. From Edward Wilkins. Feinberg.
December 27. From Charles L. Heyde. Trent.
December 27. From William Sloane Kennedy. Feinberg.
December 30. From Elizabeth Porter Gould (expressing regret that her verses were not included in *Camden's Compliment to Walt Whitman*). Feinberg.
December 31. From Dr. John Johnston and J. W. Wallace. Typescript in Bolton (England) Public Libraries.
[December 31]. From F. W. Ream, an admirer (New Year's greetings). Feinberg.
December. From Charles L. Heyde. Trent.
[1889]. From Hamlin Garland (concerning an article about WW, information for which he was collecting after the poet's birthday celebration; see Traubel, v, 291). Feinberg.

Appendix D

CHRONOLOGY
OF WALT WHITMAN'S LIFE AND WORK

1819	Born May 31 at West Hills, near Huntington, Long Island.
1823	May 27, Whitman family moves to Brooklyn.
1825–30	Attends public school in Brooklyn.
1830	Office boy for doctor, lawyer.
1830–34	Learns printing trade.
1835	Printer in New York City until great fire August 12.
1836–38	Summer of 1836, begins teaching at East Norwich, Long Island; by winter 1837–38 has taught at Hempstead, Babylon, Long Swamp, and Smithtown.
1838–39	Edits weekly newspaper, the *Long Islander*, at Huntington.
1840–41	Autumn, 1840, campaigns for Van Buren; then teaches school at Trimming Square, Woodbury, Dix Hills, and Whitestone.
1841	May, goes to New York City to work as printer in *New World* office; begins writing for the *Democratic Review.*
1842	Spring, edits a daily newspaper in New York City, the *Aurora;* edits *Evening Tattler* for short time.
1845–46	August, returns to Brooklyn, writes for *Long Island Star* from September until March.
1846–48	From March, 1846, until January, 1848, edits Brooklyn *Daily Eagle;* February, 1848, goes to New Orleans to work on the *Crescent;* leaves May 27 and returns *via* Mississippi and Great Lakes.
1848–49	September 9, 1848, to September 11, 1849, edits a "free soil" newspaper, the Brooklyn *Freeman.*
1850–54	Operates printing office and stationery store; does free-lance journalism; builds and speculates in houses.
1855	Early July, *Leaves of Grass* is printed by Rome Brothers in Brooklyn; father dies July 11; Emerson writes to poet on July 21.
1856	Writes for *Life Illustrated;* publishes second edition of *Leaves of Grass* in summer and writes "The Eighteenth Presidency!"
1857–59	From spring of 1857 until about summer of 1859 edits the Brooklyn *Times;* unemployed winter of 1859–60; frequents Pfaff's bohemian restaurant.
1860	March, goes to Boston to see third edition of *Leaves of Grass* through the press.
1861	April 12, Civil War begins; George Whitman enlists.
1862	December, goes to Fredericksburg, Virginia, scene of recent battle in which George was wounded, stays in camp two weeks.

1863 Remains in Washington, D. C., working part-time in Army Paymaster's office; visits soldiers in hospitals.

1864 June 22, returns to Brooklyn because of illness.

1865 January 24, appointed clerk in Department of Interior, returns to Washington; meets Peter Doyle; witnesses Lincoln's second inauguration; Lincoln assassinated, April 14; May, *Drum-Taps* is printed; June 30, is discharged from position by Secretary James Harlan but re-employed next day in Attorney General's office; autumn, prints *Drum-Taps and Sequel*, containing "When Lilacs Last in the Dooryard Bloom'd."

1866 William D. O'Connor publishes *The Good Gray Poet.*

1867 John Burroughs publishes *Notes on Walt Whitman as Poet and Person;* July 6, William Michael Rossetti publishes article on Whitman's poetry in London *Chronicle;* "Democracy" (part of *Democratic Vistas*) published in December *Galaxy.*

1868 Rossetti's *Poems of Walt Whitman* (selected and expurgated) published in England; "Personalism" (second part of *Democratic Vistas*) in May *Galaxy;* second issue of fourth edition of *Leaves of Grass*, with *Drum-Taps and Sequel* added.

1869 Mrs. Anne Gilchrist reads Rossetti edition and falls in love with the poet.

1870 July, is very depressed for unknown reasons; prints fifth edition of *Leaves of Grass*, and *Democratic Vistas* and *Passage to India*, all dated 1871.

1871 September 3, Mrs. Gilchrist's first love letter; September 7, reads "After All Not to Create Only" at opening of American Institute Exhibition in New York.

1872 June 26, reads "As a Strong Bird on Pinions Free" at Dartmouth College commencement.

1873 January 23, suffers paralytic stroke; mother dies May 23; unable to work, stays with brother George in Camden, New Jersey.

1874 "Song of the Redwood-Tree" and "Prayer of Columbus."

1875 Prepares Centennial Edition of *Leaves of Grass* and *Two Rivulets* (dated 1876).

1876 Controversy in British and American press over America's neglect of Whitman; spring, meets Harry Stafford, and begins recuperation at Stafford farm, at Timber Creek; September, Mrs. Gilchrist arrives and rents house in Philadelphia.

1877 January 28, gives lecture on Tom Paine in Philadelphia; goes to New York in March and is painted by George W. Waters; during summer gains strength by sun-bathing at Timber Creek.

1878 Spring, too weak to give projected Lincoln lecture, but in June visits J. H. Johnston and John Burroughs in New York.

1879 April to June, in New York, where he gives first Lincoln lecture, and says farewell to Mrs. Gilchrist, who returns to England; September, goes to the West for the first time and visits Colorado; because of illness remains in St. Louis with his brother Jeff from October to January.

1880	Gives Lincoln lecture in Philadelphia; summer, visits Dr. R. M. Bucke in London, Ontario.
1881	April 15, gives Lincoln lecture in Boston; returns to Boston in August to read proof of *Leaves of Grass*, being published by James R. Osgood; poems receive final arrangement in this edition.
1882	Meets Oscar Wilde; Osgood ceases to distribute *Leaves of Grass* because District Attorney threatens prosecution unless the book is expurgated; publication is resumed in June by Rees Welsh in Philadelphia, who also publishes *Specimen Days and Collect;* both books transferred to David McKay, Philadelphia.
1883	Dr. Bucke publishes *Walt Whitman*, a critical study closely "edited" by the poet.
1884	Buys house on Mickle Street, Camden, New Jersey.
1885	In poor health; friends buy a horse and phaeton so that the poet will not be "house-tied"; November 29, Mrs. Gilchrist dies.
1886	Gives Lincoln lecture four times in Elkton, Maryland, Camden, Philadelphia, and Haddonfield, New Jersey; is painted by John White Alexander.
1887	Gives Lincoln lecture in New York; is painted by Thomas Eakins.
1888	Horace Traubel raises funds for doctors and nurses; *November Boughs* printed; money sent from England.
1889	Last birthday dinner, proceedings published in *Camden's Compliment to Walt Whitman.*
1890	Writes angry letter to J. A. Symonds, dated August 19, denouncing Symonds's interpretation of "Calamus" poems, claims six illegitimate children.
1891	*Good-Bye My Fancy* is printed, and the "death-bed edition" of *Leaves of Grass* (dated 1891–2).
1892	Dies March 26, buried in Harleigh Cemetery, Camden, New Jersey.

Index

Index

"Abraham Lincoln," 21
Academy, The, 18*n*, 103
Achilles, 341
Adler, Felix, 166
Ady, Julia, 234*n*
Æsop, 393
"After the Dazzle of Day," 144*n*
Alden, Agnes Margaret. Letter to, 38
Alden, Henry M., 48*n*, 119*n*, 122, 368*n*, 376, 384*n*, 425, 427, 429, 439, 440
Alden, John, vii
Alden, John B., 32*n*
Aldrich, Charles, 230*n*, 440
Aldrich, Thomas Bailey, 309, 310, 318, 341, 437. Letter to, 309
Alexander, John White, 20, 369*n*. Letter to, 20
Allen, Gay Wilson, vii, viii
"America," 144*n*
American, The, 401, 409*n*
American Bookmaker, The, 432
American Naturalist, 403*n*
Amiel, Henri Frédéric, 355
Angus, W. C., 435
Anne Gilchrist, 44*n*, 57*n*, 65*n*, 79, 82, 85, 88, 91, 101, 139*n*, 265
Appleton, Messrs., 57
Appleton, Professor W., 151*n*
Appleton's Encyclopedia, 374*n*
Armory Square Hospital, 346*n*
"Army and Hospital Cases," 38, 40–41, 42, 43, 51, 192, 194*n*, 214, 216, 217
Arnold, Sir Edwin, 373, 374, 385–386, 440
Arnold, Matthew, 229–230
As a Strong Bird on Pinions Free, 41*n*
Ashbee, C. R., 29
Ashley, Mary, 436
"As I Ebb'd with the Ocean of Life," 5, 6
"As I Sit Waiting Here," 145*n*
Asselineau, Roger, 273*n*
"As the Greek's Signal Flame," 136, 426
Athenæum, The, 18*n*, 425
Atlantic Monthly, The, 287, 399
Aurelius, Marcus, 207
Avery, Margareta L., 437

"Backward Glance O'er Travel'd Roads, A," 36*n*, 222
"Backward Glance on My Own Road, A," 36*n*
Bacon, Francis, 25*n*, 29, 118, 169*n*, 186*n*, 295, 357*n*
Baker, John, 433
Baker, Nathan M., 173*n*, 174, 180*n*, 182, 212, 328–329
Baldwin, O. S., 425
Baldwin's Monthly, 48*n*
Ballou, William Hosen, 432
Baltimore *Sun*, 19*n*
Barnhill, John B., 438
Barnum, Phineas Taylor, 328
Barrett, Clifton Waller, vii
Barrett, Roger W., viii
Barrett, Wilson, 73
Bartlett, Truman Howe, 57*n*
Barton, William E., viii
Bates, Charlotte Fiske, 192, 426, 433
Baxter, Sylvester, 65–66, 94, 97, 100, 103, 105, 106, 114, 131, 132, 136, 182, 242, 252, 253, 256, 258, 262, 263, 268, 269, 289, 352, 373, 378*n*, 382, 425, 426, 429, 430, 431, 433, 436. Letters to, 56, 93, 102, 110, 114, 125, 262
Beare, J. I., 159*n*
Beckett, Katie E., 432
Beckett, Reginald A., 189*n*, 432
Beecher, Henry Ward, 430
Beemer, Dr., 387, 389
Bellamy, Edward, 256*n*, 379*n*
Bennerman, Mr. Letter to, 171
Bennett, Mr., 20*n*
Bennett, James Gordon, 143–144, 183, 431, 432, 434, 438. Letter to, 181
Bertz, Eduard, 353, 362, 394, 427, 439
Bey, Emin, 391*n*
Bible, 86*n*, 239
Biddle, Mrs. Noble T. Letter to, 62
Bilstein, Mr., 280*n*
Blaine, James G., 178
Blake, Rev., 312
Blake, Edmund, 432
Blake, William, 5
Blauvelt, William H., 239*n*, 426, 435
Blodgett, Harold W., 119*n*
Bok, Edward W., 430
Bonsall, Henry (Harry) L., 282, 336*n*, 343
Book News, 329
Booth, Edwin, 125*n*
Borton, Walter, 32
Bosis, Adolfo de, 38
Boston *Advertizer*, 109*n*, 137*n*
Boston *Evening Transcript*, 1, 68, 112, 155, 157, 158, 169, 203, 223, 224, 230,

234, 243, 261, 263, 268*n*, 279, 338, 339, 340*n*, 362*n*, 384, 391, 401
Boston *Herald*, 1, 85, 101*n*, 109*n*, 131, 132, 169, 262, 263, 266, 267, 269, 352, 382*n*
Boston *Record*, 109
Boston *Traveller*, 372*n*
Boswell, James, 165, 170, 239
Brainerd, Erastus. Letters to, 113, 115
"Bravest Soldiers, The," 145*n*
"Bravo, Paris Exposition!" 376, 380, 394, 427
Bright, John, 312
Brinton, Dr. Daniel Garrison, 67*n*, 377, 430
Brisbane, R., 425, 430
"Broadway," 145*n*
Broido, Mrs. Louis, viii
Brown, Arthur Newton. Letters to, 305, 310
Brown, Emily Louisa (Mrs. Charles W. Eldridge), 406
Brown, Leonard M., 57*n*, 156*n*. Letter to, 132–133
Brown, Dr. Morgan, 127, 325, 332
Browne, Mrs. Walter, 425
Browning, C. H., 155, 205, 345*n*, 433
Browning, Deborah Stafford, 78, 79, 185, 191, 206, 238, 282, 326, 361
Browning, Joseph, 78, 146, 163, 167, 191, 282, 361
Browning, Robert, 330, 405, 406, 407
Bruce, Thomas, Earl of Elgin, 319
Bryn Mawr College, 39*n*, 323*n*
Buchan, Peter, 98*n*
Buchanan, Robert, 75
Bucke, Charles H., 431
Bucke, E. Pardee, 387, 389
Bucke, Jerome, 434
Bucke, Richard Maurice, 2, 4, 18, 24, 25, 26, 28, 31, 32*n*, 34, 35*n*, 36, 39, 41, 42, 44, 49, 53, 55, 59, 65*n*, 68*n*, 69, 74, 77, 80, 87, 91, 100, 103, 110, 114, 116, 117, 119, 120, 121, 122, 125, 126, 128, 129, 132, 137, 138, 140, 141, 143, 144, 146, 149, 150, 151, 152, 157, 159, 162, 167, 168, 173, 176, 177, 186, 189, 190, 203, 212, 214, 218, 219, 220, 224, 226, 227, 233, 234, 235*n*, 238, 249, 252, 254, 258, 263, 273, 274, 275, 276, 277, 278, 279, 282, 284, 288, 289, 291, 292, 293, 294, 295, 296, 297, 298, 299, 300, 301, 302, 303, 304, 305, 306, 307, 308, 317, 319, 320, 321, 323, 324, 326, 330, 334, 340, 343, 349, 350, 355, 358, 361, 367, 368, 371, 372, 374, 380, 382, 395, 396, 401, 406, 410, 424–441. Letters to, 70–71, 75, 80–81, 87, 91, 107, 112, 118, 134–135, 139, 142–144, 146–147, 150–154, 156–158, 160–161, 163–165, 168, 171–184, 186–208, 210–212, 214–219, 221–225, 227–234, 237–281, 283–285, 287–289, 292–293, 304, 306–309, 311–314, 316–325, 327–329, 331–377, 379–405, 407–409
Bucke, Mrs. Richard Maurice, 80, 307, 329, 346, 356, 387, 403, 407
Buckwalter, Geoffrey, 336*n*, 343, 364*n*
Buel, C. C., 40
Burns, Robert, 55, 325*n*, 396, 399
Burr, Aaron, 396
Burroughs, John, 18, 20*n*, 26, 28, 36, 45, 82*n*, 87, 91, 116*n*, 117, 128, 129, 141, 142, 150, 162, 187, 188, 203, 214, 224, 234, 255, 263, 271, 280, 294, 305, 314, 315, 341, 347, 353, 356, 358, 359, 365, 369, 376, 377, 378, 406, 407, 424, 427, 428, 429, 431, 432, 433, 434, 436, 437, 438, 439, 441. Letters to, 21–22, 26, 53, 59, 70–71, 75, 80–81, 82, 87, 91, 110, 118, 128, 139, 149, 167–168, 185–186, 195, 202, 219, 222–223, 226–227, 241–242, 283–284, 294, 297, 335, 338, 357, 368, 377–378
Burroughs, Julian, 140, 141, 186, 280, 284, 294, 315, 357, 377, 378, 406
Burroughs, Ursula, 22, 140, 186, 280, 284, 294, 315, 357, 377, 378, 406
Burton, Robert, 357*n*
Bushell, W., 25

C., V. S. Letter to, 172
Cabot, James Elliot, 208
"Calming Thought of All, The," 145*n*
Camden *Courier*, 94*n*, 348
Camden *Post*, 150, 256, 258, 409*n*
Camden's Compliment to Walt Whitman, 343, 344, 345, 352, 354, 355, 356, 360, 368, 370, 372, 375, 379, 380, 381, 382–383, 390, 391, 393, 394, 395, 401, 404*n*
Camelot Classics, The, 23*n*
Canning, George, 18
Canterbury Poet Series, The, 22*n*
Carey, William, 123, 124, 430, 433, 439. Letters to, 122, 124, 130, 351
Carleton, Will, 438
Carlyle, Jane, 216, 221, 224
Carlyle, Thomas, 207, 208, 210, 216, 223, 224, 260, 263, 370
Carnegie, Andrew, 83*n*, 85, 86, 87, 88, 116*n*, 147, 161, 173*n*. Letter to, 146
"Carol Closing Sixty-Nine, A," 145*n*, 161, 426
"Carol of Harvest, for 1867, A," *see* "Return of the Heroes, The"
"Carpenter, The," 24*n*, 398*n*
Carpenter, Edward, 17, 21, 23, 27*n*, 31, 90, 244, 271, 277, 278, 280, 282, 346, 383, 402, 428, 430, 436, 438. Letters to, 29–30, 77, 89–90, 244–245, 266–267, 269–270, 341–342
Carson, Hampton L., 431
Carver, Mrs., 362*n*

Century Club (New York), 141, 142, 147, 150
Century Guild Hobby Horse, The, 271n
Century Illustrated Monthly Magazine, 1, 20, 21, 41, 42, 43, 51, 55, 86, 108, 118, 124, 161, 191–192, 194*n*, 204, 214, 217, 261, 262, 267, 329, 347*n*, 362, 363, 370, 385, 389, 393, 425, 426. Letters to, 37, 38, 40–41, 216
Chamberlain, Judge, 268
Chamberlin, J. E., 268*n*, 437
Chamberlin, Jessie C. Letter to, 60
Chambers, Julius, 136, 330, 345*n*, 427, 431, 434, 439. Letters to, 136, 155, 181
Chandler, Arthur D., 86
Channing, Grace Ellery, 118, 196, 197, 430
Channing, Dr. William F., 18, 103, 195, 196, 430. Letter to, 106
Charlton, Jay, *see* J. C. Goldsmith
Chatto & Windus, 43, 53*n*. Letters to, 53, 59
Chicago *Evening Journal*, 320*n*
Chicago *Herald*, 402*n*
Chicago *Morning News*, 287
Child, Josiah, 434. Letter to, 235
Childs, George W., 25*n*, 116*n*, 439. Letter to, 15
"Christmas Greeting, A," 399, 400, 402, 404, 405, 406, 427
Civilization: Its Cause and Cure; and Other Essays, 383
Clay, Cassius M., 430
Clemens, Samuel, 125*n*. Letter to, 101
Cleveland, Grover, 121, 221
Clifford, John Herbert, 433
Clito, 73
Coates, Edward, 204
Coleridge, Samuel Taylor, 330
Colles, Richard W., 57*n*, 431. Letters to, 44–45, 54, 145
Collins, Henry H., 432
Consuelo, 107
Contemporary Club, 67, 147, 150. Letter to, 150
Contemporary Review, The, 34*n*
"Continuities," 145*n*
Conway, Moncure D., 40, 79, 116*n*, 132, 234*n*. Letter to, 76
Cook, Kenningale. Letter to, 19–20
Cook, Marjorie, 440
Cooper, William, 201*n*
Cope, Edward Drinker, 403
Corbin, Abigail Burroughs, 139
Corbin, Hiram I., 139*n*
Corning, Miss, 246
Corning, Rev. J. Leonard, 206, 231, 440
Corot, Jean Baptiste Camille, 393
Corson, Hiram, 59*n*, 424, 428
Cosmopolitan, The, 119*n*, 161, 164. Letter to, 160
Cosmopolitan Club (Philadelphia), 161
Costelloe, Benjamin F. W., 28*n*, 31, 120, 281, 291
Costelloe, Mary Smith, 32, 67*n*, 89, 98, 111, 116, 120, 153, 158, 163, 169, 189*n*, 190, 197, 198, 216*n*, 223, 224, 230, 237, 281, 285, 324, 339, 342, 347, 372, 382, 385, 391, 394, 395, 403, 426, 429, 430, 433, 434, 436, 438, 440. Letters to, 28, 31, 39, 42, 48, 51–52, 55, 58, 62, 67, 73, 76, 99–100, 104, 106–107, 121–122, 126–127, 129–130, 176, 178, 181, 183, 186, 196, 204, 218, 225–226, 238, 291, 323, 349, 364, 383, 389, 404
Costelloe, Rachel, 98, 99, 104, 111, 122, 126*n*, 153, 323
Cottell, Elizabeth A., 439
Cox, G. C., 83*n*, 88, 101, 118–119, 122, 124, 125, 131, 132, 134, 351. Letters to, 101, 123, 351
Cridland, Mrs. Charles, viii
Critic, The, 1, 43, 60, 68*n*, 76, 112, 128, 130, 153, 211*n*, 225, 227, 239, 254, 271, 273, 275, 289*n*, 292, 337, 339, 340, 386, 399, 408, 424, 425, 426, 427. Letters to, 33, 58, 61, 79, 96, 131
Currie, C. F., 427

Dalmon, Charles William, 434
Dart, Mrs., 139
Davidson, Thomas, 118*n*
Davis, Jefferson, 403, 404
Davis, Mary O., 17, 21, 65, 72, 73, 88, 90, 94, 107, 112, 123, 127, 132, 138, 146, 151, 154, 158, 162, 180, 200, 202, 206, 210, 266*n*, 270, 274, 278, 279, 280, 282, 307, 329, 333, 340, 361, 366, 383, 385, 386, 392, 410
Davis, Warren, 161
"Dead Emperor, The," 144*n*, 184*n*
"Death of Abraham Lincoln, The," *see* Lincoln Lecture
"Death's Valley," 368, 369–370, 376
Delabarre, Edmund B., 387*n*
DeLoach, Dr. R. J. H., viii
Democratic Vistas, 74, 81*n*, 176*n*, 179, 182, 183, 235*n*, 264
Deutsche Presse, 352*n*
Dick & Fitzgerald. Letter to, 152
Dickens, Charles, 82*n*, 388, 390
"Dismantled Ship, The," 144*n*
Dixon, George E., 435
Donaldson, Thomas, 24, 28, 101*n*, 183, 232, 269, 384, 408, 426, 427, 440. Letters to, 23, 24, 27, 41, 50, 53, 268–269, 348
Donnelly, Ignatius, 118*n*, 130, 168, 171*n*, 172, 185*n*, 187, 194, 357, 359, 401
Dowden, Edward, 30*n*, 32, 34, 44, 54, 372, 433, 439. Letters to, 46, 237
Dowe, Amy Haslam, 355

Dowe, Mrs. Frances E. (Emma), 355
Dowe, Warren, 355
Doyle, Peter, 174
Dublin University Magazine, 19*n*
Dublin University Review, 27*n*, 31*n*, 303*n*
Du Chaillu, Paul B., 390*n*
Duckett, William H., 16, 35, 53, 72, 82, 88*n*, 92*n*, 278, 280, 441
Dumas, Alexandre, 374*n*
"Dying Veteran, The," 63*n*, 102, 104, 425

Eakins, Thomas, 132, 134, 135, 143, 147, 154, 157, 160, 163, 176*n*
Eaton, Wyatt, 329
Echo (London), 292
Edel, Marie L., 148*n*
Eisel, Paul J., viii
Eldridge, Charles W., 45, 68*n*, 71*n*, 86*n*, 106, 110, 129, 353, 357, 367, 375, 406, 407, 425, 430, 439, 440. Letters to, 79, 87, 91, 103–104, 117–118, 290–291, 358
Elgin, Lord, *see* Thomas Bruce
Eliot, George, 219, 230, 341*n*
Elkton (Maryland) *Cecil Democrat*, 19*n*
Ellis, George, 224
Emerson, Edward, 152*n*, 396
Emerson, Ellen, 152*n*
Emerson, Ralph Waldo, 4, 21, 69–70, 120, 135, 257*n*, 341*n*, 380*n*, 392
Emerson, Mrs. Ralph Waldo, 152*n*
Emery, Alfred, 430
Encyclopædia Britannica, 308
Epictetus, 229

Faber, Mrs., 305*n*
Fairchild, Mrs. Charles (Elizabeth), 57*n*, 95, 100, 102, 109*n*, 136, 249, 252, 253, 257, 258, 263
"Fancies at Navesink," 23, 100
"Father Taylor and Oratory," 37, 43
Fawcett, Edgar, 149
Feinberg, Charles E., vii, viii
Ferguson, George, 354, 426
Ferguson, Sir William, 303*n*
Fields, Annie, 430
Fields, James T., 388, 390, 396
"First Dandelion, The," 144*n*
Fisher, Mary A., 440
"Five Thousand Poems," 68*n*, 78*n*
Flynn, Richard, 368, 369, 371
Foord, John, 376, 398*n*, 440
Ford, Elizabeth, 29, 77, 107, 245, 267, 270, 341, 346, 436
Ford, Isabella, 23*n*, 29, 77, 107, 245, 267, 270, 341, 346, 436
Ford, Sheridan, 163, 432
Forman, H. Buxton, 129, 165*n*, 219, 434
Fortnightly Review, The, 40*n*, 119*n*, 125
Forum, 225*n*
Fowler, Frank, 281*n*, 432
Fox, George, 191
Freiligrath, Ferdinand, 352*n*
Fritzinger, Harry, 210, 366, 400–401
Fritzinger, Warren, 366, 386, 387, 391, 392, 393, 394, 397, 400–401, 403, 404, 407, 410
"From Montauk Point," 144*n*
Froude, James Anthony, 207, 208, 210
Fry, Lewis, 237
Fullerton, William Morlow, 109, 430
Furness, Horace Howard, 15*n*, 25*n*

Galaxy, The, 234
Galimberti, Laurence, 439
Gamberale, Luigi, 248*n*
Gardner, Alexander, 272, 293, 295*n*, 321*n*, 350*n*, 359*n*, 439
Garland, Hamlin, 158*n*, 167, 218, 228, 236, 239, 249, 252, 253, 257*n*, 258, 268, 271*n*, 289, 343, 361–362, 429, 432, 434, 435, 436, 438, 439, 440, 441. Letters to, 226, 234, 268
Garrison, Judge J. F., 348
Gellett, Edwin C., 436
Gems from Walt Whitman, 382
Gerstenberg, A., 62*n*
Gilchrist, Anne, 16, 18, 21, 45*n*, 91, 92*n*, 287, 370
Gilchrist, Beatrice, 16
Gilchrist, Grace, 16
Gilchrist, Herbert, 16, 18, 21, 30, 34, 46, 47, 51, 54*n*, 64, 72, 82, 85–86, 92, 94, 95, 97, 98, 99, 100, 102, 103, 105, 107, 108, 110, 111, 116, 117, 119, 120, 121, 122, 123, 124, 126, 128, 130, 132–133, 138, 167, 169, 186, 190, 191, 199, 201, 205, 207, 208, 211, 212, 218, 226, 236, 244, 254, 282, 312, 326, 341, 342, 343, 346, 350, 359, 361, 363, 364, 365, 366, 367, 370, 371, 393, 403, 407, 425, 427, 428, 429, 430, 431, 432, 435. Letters to, 44, 49, 57, 78–79, 127–128, 156, 162–163, 189
Gilder, Jeannette L., 1, 58*n*, 118, 224*n*, 434. Letters to, 68, 88
Gilder, Joseph B., 1, 86, 87, 154, 224*n*, 267, 288, 427, 430, 434, 435, 436, 437. Letters to, 45, 68, 76
Gilder, Richard Watson, 1, 25*n*, 26, 82*n*, 173*n*, 347*n*, 426, 427. Letters to, 55, 85
Girard, Stephen, 348
Gladstone, William, 55*n*
Goethe, Johann Wolfgang von, 129, 259, 260, 391*n*
Goldsmith, J. C. ("Jay Charlton"), 40
Goldy, Ruth Stafford, 30, 361
Good-bye My Fancy, 242*n*
Gosse, Edmund, 224*n*, 362, 387*n*, 392

Gould, Elizabeth Porter, 257, 302, 382, 441. Letter to, 96
Gower, Lord Ronald, 62*n*
Grant, Ulysses S., 57*n*, 316
Grashalme (German translation of *Leaves of Grass*), 129, 207–208, 212, 220, 265, 269, 270, 272, 286, 287, 293, 295, 296, 297, 298, 319, 330, 401, 406–407
Greek Poets, 224, 267, 268, 271
Green, Rev., 372
Greene, Mrs. Ward, viii
Greg, Thomas Tylston, 436
Grey, Samuel H., 440
Grundy, Fanny M., 440
Guernsey, Frederic R., 223*n*
Gunther, Mr. Letter to, 25
Gurd, William, 232, 256, 398
Gutekunst, 364

Habberton, John, 206, 212
"Halcyon Days," 144*n*
Hales, Samuel, 425
Haley, Mrs. C. S., 434
Half Hours with the Best American Authors, 38
Hall, George, 438
Halleck, General Henry Wager, 56–57
Halpern, Mrs. Barbara, viii
Hamlet's Note-book, 24, 26, 29, 187
Hanson, Mr., 373*n*
Harkness, Dr. Jack, 199
Harleigh Cemetery, 5–6, 403, 407, 408
Harned, Anna, 130, 134, 264
Harned, Frank, 182, 231, 371
Harned, Herbert Spencer, 242, 243, 245, 259, 261, 264, 278, 324 , 399
Harned, Thomas B., 88*n*, 129, 134, 150, 156, 159, 161, 165*n*, 166*n*, 178, 179, 180, 187, 192, 207, 214, 220, 231, 232, 242, 245, 254, 259, 261, 270, 278, 283, 302, 306, 307, 308, 314, 317, 320, 324, 333, 336, 341, 342, 343, 350, 352, 358, 371, 372, 374, 377, 388, 391, 394, 399, 403, 409, 427. Letters to, 130, 133, 165, 182–183, 264, 335, 349
Harned, Mrs. Thomas B., 129, 134, 160, 169, 170, 174, 176, 242, 243, 259, 261, 264, 278, 280, 306, 314, 317, 320, 341
Harned, Thomas B., Jr., 134, 264, 320
Harney, Rev. G. L., 197*n*
Harper & Brothers, 427, 440
Harper's Bazar, 86*n*
Harper's Fifth Reader, 378
Harper's New Monthly Magazine, 48*n*, 51, 119*n*, 122, 148*n*, 226*n*, 256, 271, 275, 276, 369–370, 376, 388, 425. Letter to, 368
Harper's Weekly, 86, 347*n*, 376, 380, 385, 399, 400, 404, 427
Harrington, 386
Harrison, Benjamin, 196, 229, 232, 233, 328, 395
Hartmann, C. Sadakichi, 108, 110, 136, 192, 208, 213*n*, 224*n*, 322, 325, 331, 340, 368, 433. Letter to, 61
Harvard Monthly, 143
Harvard Signet Society, 143*n*
Hastings, Warren, 18
Hawley, Dr. W. A., 426
Hawthorne, Nathaniel, 388, 390, 396
Hay, John, 55*n*, 75, 83*n*, 425, 430
Hedge, Frederic Henry, 239
Hegel, G. W. F., 381
Heine, Heinrich, 55
Hemenway, O. O. Letter to, 378
Hempstead & Son, O. G., 170*n*, 432. Letter to, 168
Hemsley, W. J., 432
Hershey, O. F., 436
Heyde, Charles L., 381*n*, 390*n*, 427, 430, 434, 435, 437, 439, 440, 441
Heyde, Hannah, 51, 179, 282, 355, 380, 391, 424, 425, 426, 427, 438
Heywood, Ezra H., 157
Hicks, Elias, 79, 141, 151, 163, 164, 165, 182, 184, 189, 191, 194, 198, 199, 201, 205, 206, 210, 213, 224
Higginson, Thomas Wentworth, 86*n*
Hinton, Richard J., 263, 322*n*, 434, 439
History of King Arthur, *see Romance of King Arthur, The*
Hollyer, Samuel, 197, 426, 436
Holmes, Henry A., 438
Homer, 325*n*
Hood, Dr. T. B., 302, 311
Hopkins, Johns, 348
Horne, Herbert P., 127, 434
Houghton, Mifflin and Company, 25*n*. Letter to, 148
Howells, William Dean, 125*n*, 148*n*, 228, 256, 271, 275, 276, 277, 341
"How I Made a Book," 36, 37, 39
"How Leaves of Grass Was Made," 36*n*, 37
Hugg, Judge, 88*n*
Hughes, Harry D. Letter to, 67
Hurd(?), Charles E., 338*n*

Image, Selwyn, 271*n*
Ingersoll, Robert G., 142*n*, 164, 172*n*, 221, 341
Ingram, William, 154, 200, 210, 228, 333, 337, 371, 407, 433, 434. Letters to, 120, 158, 209–210, 370–371
Innes, George, 368*n*, 376
"Interpolation Sounds," 198*n*
Ireland, LeRoy, 369*n*
Irving, Henry, 41*n*, 348, 384n
Ives, Percy, 429, 431

Jaffe, Harold, vii
James, Henry, 30*n*
James, William, 143*n*
Johns Hopkins Hospital, 327, 332
Johnson, John Newton, 94, 103, 107, 158*n*, 159, 428
Johnson, Robert Underwood, 214. Letter to, 133
Johnson, Dr. Samuel, 165, 170
Johnson, Thomas, 362*n*, 363, 393
Johnson, Walt Whitman, 95
Johnson, William H., 381*n*
Johnston, Albert, 74, 86, 124, 254
Johnston, Alma Calder, 86, 119, 124, 215, 219, 254, 409*n*. Letters to, 73, 200–201, 299–300
Johnston, Amelia (Mrs. John H.), 254*n*
Johnston, Dr. John, 3, 96, 345, 346, 428, 430, 432, 441. Letter to, 95
Johnston, John H., 82*n*, 84, 143, 160*n*, 200–201, 222*n*, 254, 261, 263, 308, 343, 382, 430, 431. Letters to, 74, 84, 86, 118–119, 124, 165–166, 299–300
Johnston, Katherine, 427, 436. Letter to, 254
Johnstown Flood, 345, 346, 347
Jones, John Paul, 326
Judge, W. Q., 57*n*

Kant, Immanuel, 239
Katz, John Z., viii
Kelley, Louis S., 440
Kelling, Professor Harold D., viii
Kenaga, D. H., 438
Kennedy, William Sloane, 1, 15, 31, 34, 41, 43*n*, 53, 56*n*, 77, 87, 91, 102, 110, 117, 128, 134, 139, 140, 141, 142, 150, 157*n*, 160, 162, 166, 167, 204, 208, 228, 243, 253, 254, 256, 258, 261, 263, 270, 273, 276, 277, 278, 281, 284, 287, 290, 306, 313, 321, 322, 341, 355, 359, 365, 367, 372, 377, 380, 382, 384, 387, 390, 391–392, 394, 395, 403, 427, 428, 429, 430, 431, 432, 433, 434, 435, 436, 437, 438, 439, 440, 441. Letters to, 25, 27, 28, 33–36, 39–44, 47, 50, 52, 57–58, 60, 65–66, 68–72, 74–75, 78, 80–81, 83–89, 91–95, 97–100, 103, 105–109, 112, 114, 118–119, 122, 125–128, 131–132, 135–137, 140, 144–147, 149–150, 152, 157–159, 163–165, 168–169, 173, 179, 184, 193, 203, 212, 218, 220, 223–224, 226–227, 241–242, 248–249, 252, 258, 263, 272–273, 276, 279, 285–286, 289, 294–296, 303, 305–306, 308, 317–319, 321, 325–326, 331, 333–335, 337, 340, 344, 350, 354, 361, 372–374, 378, 380–382, 384–385, 395, 406
Kensington Museum, 121, 126
Kerr, Mrs. Anna M., 431
Kerswell, R. W., 64
Kinnear, Dr., 115*n*
Kirk, Sophia, 436
Kitton, Fred G., 430
Klein, Jacob. Letters to, 207, 211
Klinkicht, M., 402*n*
Knortz, Karl, 32*n*, 36, 129, 208, 212, 220, 270, 287, 293, 295, 331, 352*n*, 401*n*, 436, 438. Letters to, 31, 77, 90–91, 101, 209, 265, 289, 319, 330
Knowles, James, 90*n*, 385*n*, 425, 427, 430

Labar, Richard E., 400
"Lafayette in Brooklyn," 48*n*, 425
Lane, Elmer B., 432
Langley, Miss E., 305*n*, 323*n*, 436, 437
Lanier, Sidney, 87*n*
Larned, Francis M., 286*n*
Latchford, Henry, 439
Lazarus, Emma, 270
Lazarus, Josephine, 173*n*
Leaves of Grass, 33, 34, 50, 69–70, 117, 150, 153–154, 164, 215, 219, 227*n*, 230, 247, 299, 347, 362, 379, 384, 390, 391, 396, 408
  First edition, 32*n*, 257*n*
  Fifth edition, 386
  Sixth edition, 25*n*, 53, 54, 62, 75, 106, 137, 152, 204, 207, 211
  Seventh edition, 19–20, 29*n*, 38, 41*n*, 45, 59, 71, 86, 108*n*, 145, 147, 172, 312, 321*n*
  Eighth edition (*Complete Poems & Prose*), 181, 200, 201, 202, 203, 204, 209, 211, 213, 217, 218, 221, 222, 224, 225, 226, 231, 232, 233, 234, 235, 236, 237, 238, 239–240, 241, 242, 243, 244, 245, 247, 248, 249, 250, 252, 254, 255, 256, 258, 259, 261, 262, 263, 264, 265, 266, 267, 269, 271, 272, 274, 275, 276, 281, 282, 283, 284, 285, 287, 289, 290, 291, 294, 295, 298, 299, 300, 301, 302, 304, 309, 310, 312, 318, 319, 323, 336, 342, 347, 353, 357, 359, 362, 387, 399, 405
  Eighth edition (with *Sands at Seventy* and *A Backward Glance*), 293, 309, 311, 312, 313, 317, 318, 320, 323, 324, 325, 326, 327, 328, 330, 331, 333, 336, 338, 339, 343, 345, 347, 352, 361, 362, 363, 368, 378, 382, 387, 388, 392
  German translation, *see Grashalme*
Legg, Charles E., 373, 375
Leisure Moments, 67
Lesseps, Vicomte Ferdinand Marie de, 248
Lewes, George Henry, 129
Lewin, Walter, 103*n*, 431
Liberty, 353, 363, 372, 374, 375
"Life," 145*n*
"Life and Death," 145*n*

Life of Samuel Johnson, 239
Lincoln, Abraham, 21, 89, 148*n*, 352
Lincoln Lecture, 19, 22, 24, 25, 26, 27, 28, 35, 75, 78, 79, 80, 81, 83, 84–85, 86, 87, 88
Linton, William J., 222, 315*n*, 434. Letter to, 210
Lippincott Company, J. B., 156*n*
Lippincott's Monthly Magazine, 43, 55, 91*n*, 99, 100, 127, 153*n*, 157, 161, 385*n*, 426
Literary News (New York), 331
Literary World, The, 249
Lloyd, Rev. William, 149
Lockwood, Ingersoll, 426, 432
Loftus, J. P. Letter to, 137
Logue, Mr., 154
London *Illustrated News*, 402
London (Ontario) *Advertiser*, 151, 153
London *Piccadilly*, 401*n*, 403
London *Telegram*, 385, 386
Longfellow, Henry Wadsworth, 49
Loskey(?), Thomas, 425
Louis the Fourteenth and the Court of France, 216, 219, 224
Lovering, Henry B., 56, 65–66, 425
Lowell, James Russell, 83*n*, 148*n*, 249, 289*n*
Lychenheim, 358*n*

McAlister, Dr. Alexander, 267
Macaulay, Thomas Babington, 18
McCandlish, George, viii
McCarthy, Justin Huntly, 251*n*, 435
McClintock, Gilbert S., viii
McClure, S. S., 108, 399*n*, 404, 405, 406, 425, 441. Letters to, 102, 104, 114, 119, 402
McClure's Magazine, 399*n*
McIlhaney, A. K., 440
McKay, David, 124, 172, 219, 220, 221, 228, 229, 235, 236, 242, 251, 266, 272, 277, 281, 291, 293, 302, 306, 309, 311, 312, 313, 336, 343, 345, 347, 354, 365, 381, 383, 384, 387, 394. Letters to, 170, 221, 225, 255, 257, 405, 410
McKee, Thomas J., 161, 426, 432
McKenzie, William P., 440
McKinsey, Folger, 19*n*
Magazine of Art, The, 148*n*
Magazine of Poetry, The, 280, 289, 294
Major, George M., 424
Malet, Sir Edward, 62*n*
"Mannahatta," 144*n*
Manning, Cardinal Henry Edward, 221
Mapes, Mrs. Mary E., 336
Marvin, Joseph B., 75, 357, 430
Mather, T. W., 426, 434
Maxwell, Gerald, 429
Mayfield, John S., viii
Merrill, W. R., 97
Metropolitan Museum of Art, 20*n*
Millet, Frank D., 255
Millet, Jean François, 166, 234, 329
Mr. Donnelly's Reviewers, 294*n*, 357, 359
Mitchell, Dr. J. K., 187, 188, 189, 192
Mitchell, Dr. S. Weir, 25*n*, 187*n*, 441
Moll, Mrs. June, vii
Montaigne, Michel Eyquem de, 357*n*
Morehouse, Mr., 317
Morris, Charles, 429. Letter to, 38
Morris, Harrison S., 409*n*, 441
Morse, Sidney H., 92, 93, 95, 97*n*, 99, 103, 105, 107, 108, 110, 111, 112, 119, 120, 121, 124, 126*n*, 127, 132, 133, 134, 135, 136, 137, 139, 140, 150, 151, 156, 158, 159, 160, 163, 189, 207, 213*n*, 215, 220, 307, 354, 393, 426, 431, 432, 433, 435. Letters to, 154, 213
Morton, Levi Parsons, 196
Moulton, C. W., 435
Moulton, Ellen Louise Chandler, 165, 166, 167, 268
Moyne, Ernest J., 19*n*
Munyon's Illustrated World, 136*n*, 141*n*, 426
Murray's Magazine, 431
Murrell, Captain Hamilton, 325
Musgrove, W. A., 182*n*, 190, 227*n*, 229, 230, 231, 333
"My Book and I," 36*n*, 43, 55, 58, 63*n*, 66, 424
"My Canary Bird," 144*n*
"My 71st Year," 347*n*, 370, 385, 427
"Mystic Trumpeter, The," 67*n*

Nation, The, 17, 43, 139, 141
Neale, Mrs. Doris, viii
Nencioni, Enrico, 159*n*
Newcastle-on-Tyne *Chronicle*, 425
New England Magazine, The, 379, 381
"New Orleans in 1848," 64
New Orleans *Picayune*, 429. Letter to, 64
Newport, David, 151*n*
New York *Commercial-Advertiser*, 24*n*
New York *Evening Sun*, 83*n*, 89
New York *Herald*, 1, 5, 127*n*, 136*n*, 143–144, 146, 149, 151, 153, 155, 156, 157, 158, 159, 160, 161, 162, 164, 167, 170, 180, 198, 199, 200, 205, 212, 224, 257–258, 322, 325, 330, 331, 347*n*. Letters to, 136, 206
New York *Mail and Express*, 437
New York Times, 83*n*, 100, 149*n*
New York *Tribune*, 124, 130, 131*n*, 134, 235*n*, 246, 248*n*, 259, 280, 291, 295, 314, 327
New York *World*, 1, 118, 322, 328*n*, 330, 345*n*, 346, 348, 426, 427
Nicolay, John G., 55*n*
Nineteenth Century, The, 23, 91, 234, 277, 385*n*, 394

Nineteenth Century Club, 142*n*
Noel, Roden, 137*n*, 424, 428
Norman, Henry, 62, 430. Letter to, 63
North American Review, The, 36, 39*n*, 43, 48*n*, 55, 221, 275. Letter to, 61
"North Star to a South, A," *see* "Christmas Greeting, A"
Norton, Charles Eliot, 125*n*
Nouvelle Revue, La, 231*n*, 272, 273, 276, 277, 278, 286
November Boughs, 22, 46, 53, 55, 56, 77, 100, 117, 123, 151, 159, 160, 162, 173, 176, 177, 178, 179, 180, 183, 187, 188, 189, 190, 191, 192, 193, 194, 195, 196, 197, 198, 199, 200, 201, 202, 203, 204, 205, 206*n*, 208, 209, 211, 212, 213, 214, 217, 218–219, 220, 221, 222, 224*n*, 226, 228, 229, 232, 235, 236, 237, 238, 241, 244, 245, 246*n*, 258, 265, 266, 270*n*, 271, 272, 275, 276, 277, 278, 281, 282, 283, 287, 289, 291, 293, 304, 305, 320*n*, 323*n*, 348, 367*n*
"November Boughs," 99, 100, 105, 127, 425
Nuova Anatologia, 159*n*

"O Captain! My Captain!" 148, 427, 430, 440
O'Connor, Ellen M., 2, 136, 151, 162, 164, 173, 174, 177, 195, 223, 229, 233, 246, 251, 253, 260, 272, 273, 277, 279, 283, 284, 285, 286, 287, 288, 290, 291, 292, 294, 295, 296, 297, 298, 299, 300, 302, 304, 306, 307, 308, 310, 313, 314, 315, 316–317, 321, 322, 323, 324, 325, 326, 329, 332, 334, 336, 338–339, 340, 346, 351, 353, 354, 356, 357, 363, 364, 365, 367, 368, 370, 372, 373, 376, 377, 378, 382, 384, 389, 394, 397, 398, 399, 401, 402, 407, 431, 432, 436–441. Letters to, 112, 115, 151, 155, 250, 252, 260–261, 277, 288, 300–301, 334, 337, 353, 362–363, 367, 374, 375, 377, 395–396, 401, 406–407
O'Connor, William D., 5, 26, 27, 37*n*, 43, 44, 52, 53, 59, 60, 68–69, 71, 73, 74, 75, 77, 78, 79, 81, 87, 94, 95, 97*n*, 100, 106, 108, 109, 110, 114, 115, 118, 125, 126–127, 128, 132, 135, 136, 139, 140, 142, 143, 147, 149, 151, 153, 156, 157, 158, 160, 163, 164*n*, 167, 169*n*, 174, 186, 187, 194, 203, 204, 215, 217, 219, 220, 222, 223, 224, 227, 229, 239, 241, 243, 247, 249, 250, 252, 253, 258, 260–261, 263, 271, 273, 275, 277, 279, 280, 281, 283, 284, 285, 286, 288, 289, 305, 306, 308, 309, 311, 312, 315, 317, 319, 320, 321, 322, 326, 330, 331, 333, 334, 335, 336, 337, 338, 339, 340, 353, 358, 359, 363, 372, 374, 375, 378, 386*n*, 397, 399, 401, 406*n*, 407, 424, 426, 428, 429, 431–435. Letters to, 15, 17–19, 23–24, 26, 29, 43, 45, 54–55, 129, 134, 141, 143–144, 162, 164, 166, 169–173, 175, 177, 184, 188–189, 193, 195–197, 213–214, 217–218, 220, 222–223, 228, 233–234, 236, 241–242, 246, 272, 274–275, 278, 284–287, 290–304, 306–308, 310–311, 313–324, 326–329, 332–333
O'Dowd, Bernard, 3
Oldach, Frederick, 225, 245, 266, 277, 311. Letters to, 225, 239–240, 242, 290, 338
"Old Age Echoes," 385*n*, 394, 427
"Old Age's Lambent Peaks," 161, 204, 205, 251, 426
"Old Age's Ship & Crafty Death's," 261, 262, 267, 393, 426
"Old Salt Kossabone," 144*n*
Oliver, John, 439
"Orange Buds by Mail from Florida," 145*n*
O'Reardon, W. J., 439
O'Reilly, John Boyle, 57*n*, 100, 102
Osgood, James R., 235*n*
Osler, Dr. William, 51*n*, 147*n*, 174, 175, 177, 179, 187*n*, 207, 212, 215, 221, 224, 227, 229, 232, 240, 241, 242, 243, 245, 246, 260, 328, 329
"Out of May's Shows Selected," 145*n*
"Out of the Cradle Endlessly Rocking," 5, 67*n*
"Over and Through the Burial Chant," *see* "Interpolation Sounds"
Owen, Charles Norton, viii

Paget, Wal, 148*n*
Pall Mall Gazette, 52*n*, 55*n*, 62, 63, 85*n*, 102*n*, 127*n*, 128, 148*n*, 216*n*, 230, 292, 293, 295
Palmer, Courtland, 141. Letter to, 142
Panama Canal, 248*n*
Pardee, Timothy Blair, 119*n*, 143, 144, 146, 178, 229, 239, 360
Pardoe, Julia, 216, 219, 224
"Passage to India," 343
Path, The, 57*n*
"Paumanok," 144*n*
Payne, William W., 320*n*, 438
Peirson, Clayton Wesley, 269*n*
Pepys, Samuel, 124, 129
Philadelphia *Bulletin*, 230
Philadelphia *Daily News*, 113, 115
Philadelphia *Press*, 24, 25*n*, 28, 36*n*, 62*n*, 64, 67*n*, 96–97, 115, 135, 221, 224, 280, 291, 295, 314, 327, 389, 390*n*, 425. Letter to, 35
Philadelphia *Public Ledger*, 15*n*, 149*n*
Philadelphia *Record*, 325
Philadelphia *Times*, 232
Philips, Melville, 224*n*, 390*n*

Poems by Walt Whitman (Rossetti's edition), 53*n*
Poems of Walt Whitman. [Selected.], The, 22*n*, 53*n*
Poet as a Craftsman, The, 32*n*
Poet-lore, 271, 367
"Poet's 68th Year, A," 96, 425
Pond, Major James B., 91, 430. Letter to, 84, 86
Posnett, Hutcheson Macaulay, 42*n*
Potter, Edward T., 34*n*, 429. Letters to, 138, 185
Powell, Frederick York, 436
Powell, Rosamund E., 65*n*, 156
"Prairie Sunset, A," 144*n*
Price, Mrs. Abby H., 65*n*
Price, Arthur. Letter to, 65
Price, Helen E., 65
Prometheus, 268
Providence (R. I.) *Journal*, 109*n*
Publisher's Weekly, 221*n*

Queries to My Seventieth Year," 145*n*
Quigley, Mr., 164

Radical, The, 92*n*
Rathbone, Mr., 255
Rathbone, P. H., 255*n*
Ream, F. W., 441
Redpath, James, 21, 48*n*, 55, 425, 429, 431. Letters to, 36, 37, 39
Reed, John H., vii
Reed, Milford C., 346, 347, 427, 439
Reminiscences of Abraham Lincoln, 21, 32
Reminiscences of Walt Whitman, 33*n*
"Return of the Heroes, The," 405
Review of Reviews, The, 1
Revue Indépendante, La, 248, 249
Rhys, Ernest, 32, 68–69, 72, 74, 78, 81, 94, 99, 107, 114, 120, 126, 127–128, 130, 132, 133, 134, 135, 136, 137, 139, 140–141, 144, 145, 146, 147, 149, 150, 151, 152, 153, 156, 160, 163, 168, 172, 189, 190, 192, 207, 254, 270, 293, 366, 394, 407, 425–441. Letters to, 22, 52, 66–67, 98, 117, 192–193, 211, 254, 358–359, 367
Rice, Charles Allen Thorndike, 22, 32, 36*n*, 48*n*, 275, 436
Riley, William Harrison, 432
"Robert Burns," 55
"Robert Burns As Poet and Person," 39*n*, 43, 55, 425
Roberts, Morley C., 429
Roberts, R. D., 29
Robinson, Nugent, 430
Rogers, Elizabeth W., 163
Rolleston, T. W. H., 27*n*, 31, 207, 209, 212, 220, 237, 265, 270, 272, 287, 288, 289, 295, 319, 330, 352*n*, 401*n*, 403*n*, 404, 427, 433, 436, 437, 440
Romance of King Arthur, The, 66–67
Romsey, Mr., 39
Rossetti, Dante Gabriel, 32
Rossetti, William Michael, 18, 29*n*, 32, 44, 49, 52*n*, 115*n*, 163, 352, 428, 429. Letter to, 30
Rowlandson, H. (T. W. H. Rolleston), 27*n*
Rowley, Charles, 80
Royal Academy, 120, 121
Rubens, Peter Paul, 157*n*
Ruff, Josephine, 80*n*
Rush, George, Jr., 200*n*, 228*n*, 371
Ruskin, John, 33, 34, 122
Ryerson, Fred S., 438
Ryman, F. S., 432

S., W. A., 221*n*
Saint Botolph Club, 140*n*
Saint-Gaudens, Augustus, 83*n*, 87
Saintsbury, George, 30*n*
Sanborn, Franklin B., 70, 140*n*, 152*n*, 220*n*, 249, 252, 253, 256, 258, 270, 305, 396, 436
Sand, George, 107
San Francisco *Bulletin*, 270, 271
Sappho, 304*n*
Sarony (photographer), 402*n*
Sarrazin, Bernard, viii, 330*n*
Sarrazin, Gabriel, 98*n*, 230*n*, 272*n*, 273, 276, 279, 281, 283, 284–285, 286, 287, 289, 293, 295, 298, 330, 331, 332, 339, 352, 372, 379, 384, 394, 401, 409*n*, 436, 437. Letter to, 330–331
Saturday Review of Politics, Literature, Science, and Art, The, 304, 305, 306
Sayle, Wellesley, 435
Schabelitz, J., 220, 270
Schmidt, Rudolf, 439. Letter to, 408
Scott, Walter (publisher), 22, 52, 74, 98, 103*n*, 117, 176, 192, 358, 367
Scott, Sir Walter, 86*n*, 383
Scottish Art Review, The, 244*n*, 270*n*, 277, 358
Scovel, James Matlack, 15, 16, 29, 88*n*, 429, 431, 435
Scribner's Magazine, 15
Scull, Walter Delaplaine, 388, 440
Sempers, Charles T., 143*n*, 432
Sequard, Dr., 401
Shakespeare, William, 43, 70, 118, 127, 187*n*, 213*n*, 295, 396
"Shakspere-Bacon's Cipher," 119, 243*n*, 425
Sharpe, Elizabeth J., 429
Shaw, George Bernard, 127*n*
Shelley, Percy Bysshe, 165*n*, 330

Shephard, Esther, 106*n*
Sheridan, General Philip Henry, 198, 200
Sheridan, Richard Brinsley, 18
Sherman, Caroline K., 402*n*, 440
Sherman, William Tecumseh, 316
Shiells, Robert, 124
Shivers, Dr. C. H., 16
Shoemaker, W. L., 429
Shoemaker & Company, J. M., 267*n*
Sidney, Sir Philip, 354*n*
Sill, James L., 438
Silver, Rollo G., viii, 19*n*
Simmons, Horace C., 436
Sloane, Charles F., 432
Smith, Alexander, 399
Smith, Alys, 17, 28, 39, 42, 48, 52, 80, 92, 98, 99, 104, 107, 111, 120, 122, 126, 130, 163, 170, 181, 186, 281, 323*n*, 324, 349, 385, 388, 389, 393, 399, 403, 404, 440. Letter to, 324
Smith, Hannah W., 168, 323, 324, 437
Smith, Huntington, 437
Smith, Logan, 89
Smith, L. Logan. Letter to, 137
Smith, Logan Pearsall, 31, 48, 52, 58, 76, 92, 120, 126, 129, 165, 169, 194, 212, 251, 363, 364, 373, 434, 435, 436. Letters to, 104–105, 116
Smith, Robert Pearsall, 17*n*, 31, 55, 58, 80, 82, 87, 88, 89, 98, 99, 100, 107, 121, 126, 127, 128, 130, 140, 151, 163, 168, 178, 181, 186, 218, 230, 254, 267, 281, 321, 323, 324, 370, 372, 376, 382, 390, 392, 393, 404, 427, 432, 438, 439, 440. Letters to, 81, 92, 111, 120–121, 126, 169–170, 190
Smith, Mrs. William Hawley, 430
Smith & Starr, 428
Snowdon, Louisa, 431
Socrates, 74*n*
Solomon, King, 304*n*
"Some War Memoranda. Jotted Down at the Time," 48*n*, 51, 61, 425
"Song of the Redwood-Tree," 38*n*, 429
Sonnenschein & Company, 99
"Soon Shall the Winter's Foil Be Here," 5, 144*n*, 151*n*
Sparkes, Charles W., 439
Spaulding, A. H., 431
Spaulding, Mrs. A. H., 155*n*, 303, 312, 437
Specimen Days, 19, 23*n*, 29*n*, 66–67, 70*n*, 74, 117, 145, 171, 172, 200, 242, 255*n*, 312
Specimen Days in America, 63*n*, 80*n*, 99, 103, 105, 122, 125
Specimens of Early English Metrical Romances, 224
Spielmann, M. H., 431, 433. Letters to, 147–148
Spoffard, C. A., 430
Springfield *Daily Republican*, 102*n*, 228, 270, 271, 425
Stafford, Professor Cora E., viii
Stafford, Dora, 17*n*, 90, 201, 209, 236
Stafford, Edwin, 16, 21, 22*n*, 51, 64, 72, 80, 82, 98, 138, 146, 163, 185, 191, 194, 260, 282, 317, 326, 361
Stafford, Eva, 17*n*, 89, 111, 185, 201, 209, 236
Stafford, George, 16, 21, 35, 51, 64, 65, 72, 78, 79, 82, 89, 94, 98, 105, 107, 113, 138, 163, 185, 191, 206, 244, 282, 317, 326, 342, 359, 361, 362
Stafford, George, Jr., 80, 361
Stafford, Harry, 17*n*, 30, 51, 65, 78, 80, 82, 85, 90, 93, 113, 138, 139, 156, 163, 167, 201, 206, 209, 212, 229, 282, 317, 326, 337, 361, 366, 382, 425, 426. Letters to, 88–89, 111, 236, 283
Stafford, Montgomery, 80, 326
Stafford, Susan, 30, 44, 79, 127, 156, 163, 189, 229, 238, 283, 433, 435, 440. Letters to, 16–17, 19–21, 34–35, 51, 64–65, 72, 78, 82, 85, 90, 92–94, 97, 98, 105–106, 108–109, 113, 123, 138, 145–146, 166–167, 185, 190, 191, 199, 201–202, 205–206, 208–209, 282, 317–318, 326, 360–361, 366
Stafford, Van Doran, 80, 185, 282, 326, 361
Stanley, Samuel G., 429
Stead, William T., 1–2. Letter to, 116–117
Stedman, Edmund Clarence, 15*n*, 18, 32, 82*n*, 83, 118*n*, 124, 126, 164, 171*n*, 172*n*, 173*n*, 196, 197, 210, 228, 301, 313, 314, 316, 318, 320, 321, 324, 325, 326, 331, 333, 340, 341, 378, 404, 407, 435, 437. Letter to, 315
Stepnyak (or Stepniak), Sergei Mikhailovich, 340
Stern, Louis E., viii
Sterrit, Charles, 385
Stevens, Oliver, 235*n*
Stevenson, Robert Louis, 30*n*
Stoddart, Joseph M., 1
Stoker, Abraham, 41, 348*n*, 384*n*
Stokes, Frederick A., 425, 430
Stowe, Mrs. C. F., 433
Stuart, Queen Mary, 396
Suez Canal, 248*n*
Sullivan, Louis H., 430
Summers, William, 215–216, 230
Swinburne, Algernon, 63*n*, 119*n*, 121, 137*n*
Symonds, John Addington, 4, 30*n*, 32, 33, 35, 94, 119, 120, 121, 122, 125, 224, 239, 267, 271, 286, 287, 375, 384, 408, 436, 441. Letter to, 34

Taylor, Father Edward Thompson, 37
Taylor, Jessie E., 433
Taylor, Robert H., viii

Temple, Lady Mount, 170
Temps, Le, 396
Teniers, David, 157*n*
Tennyson, Alfred Lord, 58, 60, 70, 75*n*, 134, 141, 207, 312, 330, 362, 387, 389, 392, 430, 431. Letters from, 63–64, 131
"Tennyson at 81," 366
Terry, Ellen, 41*n*, 431
Thackeray, William Makepeace, 223, 392
"Thanks in Old Age," 135
Tharpe, Josephine M., 60*n*
Thayer, William R., 15n
"There Was a Child Went Forth," 6
Thomas, Mary Grace, 39*n*, 429
Thompson, Arthur, 341
Thompson, Bert A., 227*n*
Thompson, Billy, 27*n*
Thompson, Ethel, 341
Thompson, Percy W., 430, 432
Thompson, William, 29, 89, 165, 166, 341
Thoreau, Sophia, 257*n*
Thornton, Sir Edward, 49
"Thought on Shakspere, A," 43, 45, 424
"Throstle," 387, 389, 392
Tilton, John W. Letter to, 264
Time: A Monthly Magazine, 137, 139
To-day, 189
"To-day and Thee," 145*n*
"To Get the Final Lilt of Song," 145*n*, 160, 161, 164
Tolstoi, Leo, 255, 261, 263
Tooley, Sarah A. Letter to, 108
"To the Pending Year," 254*n*, 426
"To the Sun-Set Breeze," 385*n*
"To the Year 1889," *see* "To the Pending Year"
"To Those Who've Failed," 144*n*
Transatlantic Magazine, 385
Traubel, Agnes, 202
Traubel, Horace, 1, 2, 4, 18*n*, 136*n*, 142*n*, 158*n*, 160*n*, 168, 170, 171, 173*n*, 174, 178, 179, 180, 182, 186, 187, 191, 195, 196*n*, 200, 202, 203, 207, 212, 213, 214, 217, 218, 219, 221, 225, 228, 229, 231, 232, 242, 244, 245, 247, 256, 263, 266, 267, 270, 271, 274, 277, 284, 285, 289, 292, 293, 294*n*, 297, 298, 301, 302, 303, 304, 305, 307, 309, 312, 317, 320, 322, 325, 328, 329, 330, 333, 334, 336, 337, 339, 341, 346, 351, 352, 355, 356, 360, 363, 365, 367, 368, 370, 371, 372, 373, 374, 375, 377, 379, 380, 382, 384, 386, 387, 388, 390, 391, 395, 396, 401, 405, 406, 408. Letter to, 343–344
Traubel, Maurice, 202, 352
Trowbridge, John T., 50*n*, 69
True, O. W., 436, 439
Trübner & Company, 235*n*
"True Conquerors," 144*n*
Tucker, Benjamin R., 372
Turner, Joseph Mallord William, 33*n*
"Twenty Years," 147, 148
"Twilight," 108, 425
Two Rivulets, 25*n*, 53, 54, 137, 152, 207

Unger, Mr., 120
Unitarian Society, 78
"United States to Old World Critics, The," 145*n*
Unity, 353
Urie, Marie, 16

Van Duren, Gertrude, 429
Van Nostrand, Mary, 179, 282, 425, 426, 427
Van Tassel, Alice Hicks, 438
Velasquez, Diego Rodriguez, 393
Victoria, Queen, 341
Vielé-Griffin, Francis, 248*n*, 426, 432
Viking Age, The, 390
"Voice from Death, A," 345*n*, 346, 347, 348
Voltaire (François Marie Arouet), 391
Voorhees, Judah B., 432

Wagner, Richard, 329
"Wallabout Martyrs, The," 145*n*
Wallace, J. W., 3, 346, 430, 432, 437, 439, 441. Letters to, 96, 345
Walsh, Dr., 245, 246, 247, 248, 253, 260, 264, 266, 267
Walsh, Moses A., 428
Walsh, William S., 91*n*, 100, 245*n*, 330, 424, 425, 426, 429, 437
Walt Whitman, 32*n*, 65*n*, 159, 215, 216–217, 312, 332, 352*n*, 362, 388
"Walt Whitman, the Poet of Humanity," 33–34, 35, 36, 39, 40, 41, 42, 43–44, 52, 53, 68, 69, 77, 81, 94, 99, 139*n*, 140, 141, 144, 146, 149, 150, 152, 153*n*, 159, 162, 167, 208, 270, 273*n*, 279*n*, 321*n*, 350*n*, 355, 359, 395
"Walt Whitman at Camden," 52*n*
"Walt Whitman Calendar," 196–197
Walt Whitman Society, 108, 113, 122, 136
Ward, Mrs. Humphrey, 355
Washington, George, 327*n*
Washington *Star*, 114, 425
Wassall, J. W., 358*n*
Watson, Mr., 410
Weber, Mrs. William R., viii
Webster, C. E., 315
Wesselhoeft, Dr., 114
Westcott, Dr., 78*n*
Westminster Hotel, 82, 83, 87. Letter to, 83

Wharton, Dr., 242, 243
Wheeler, Dora, 83*n*, 133
"When Lilacs Last in the Dooryard Bloom'd," 5
White, Gleason, 437
White, R. G., 25*n*
Whiting, W. I., 32*n*, 428
Whitman, Edward, 73, 179, 201, 208, 282, 332, 427
Whitman, George, 47*n*, 50, 73, 167, 227, 235, 253, 261, 282, 348
Whitman, Jessie Louisa, 46, 47, 49, 51, 71, 83, 199, 202*n*, 440. Letters to, 47, 48, 72–73
Whitman, Lavinia F., 429
Whitman, Louisa Orr, 46, 47, 50–51, 73, 83, 167, 181, 202*n*, 227, 253, 266*n*, 282, 316, 332, 345, 391, 427, 435. Letters to, 199–200, 235, 348, 355–356
Whitman, Louisa Van Velsor, 3, 35*n*, 90, 188, 195, 391, 398
Whitman, Mannahatta, 46, 47, 48–49, 51
Whitman, Thomas Jefferson, 199, 293, 426, 429, 431, 433. Letters to, 46–51, 71, 83
Whitman, Walter B., 439
Whitman, Walter Orr, 35*n*, 391
Whitman, Walter (the father), 5, 90, 195
Whittier, John Greenleaf, 136, 141, 142, 164, 248, 270, 329, 381, 382, 407, 426, 431
Wiggins, John W., 432
Wilkie, James, 425, 429
Wilkins, Edward, 227, 231, 232, 233, 238, 240, 241, 243, 244, 245, 247, 253, 254, 259, 263, 264, 265, 267, 269, 270, 271, 274, 278, 279, 282, 283, 284, 307, 309, 312, 313, 316, 320, 324, 325, 328, 329, 333, 334, 336, 339, 340, 342, 345, 346, 349, 354, 355, 361, 363, 364*n*, 365, 366, 369, 372, 373, 376, 383, 384, 385, 386, 389, 390, 391, 392, 393, 402, 427, 441. Letter to, 409–410
Williams, Mr., 244
Williams, Francis ("Frank") H., 151*n*, 437
Williams, Mary B. N., 433
Williams, Talcott, 1, 24, 27, 81, 428, 429. Letters to, 27–28, 32, 66, 96–97, 115, 135, 155
Williams, Mrs. Talcott, 32, 81, 153, 431
Williamson, George M., 424, 429, 430, 432, 436. Letter to, 123–124
Wilson, Frederick W., 33*n*, 66*n*, 72, 81*n*, 139*n*, 141, 150*n*, 159, 160, 167, 270, 272, 295*n*, 359*n*, 395*n*
Wilson, General James Grant, 430. Letter to, 56
Wingate, Charles F., 429
Witcraft, John R., 432
"Woman's Estimate of Walt Whitman, A," 92*n*
Wood, J. B., 407, 441
Woodruff, Edwin H. Letter to, 59
"Word about Tennyson, A," 60, 63*n*
Wordsworth, William, 325*n*, 330
Wormwood, R. F. Letter to, 400
Worthington, Richard, 160
Wright, Colonel John Gibson, 235
Wroth, James Henry ("Harry"), 113
Wroth, James Stewart, viii, 441. Letter to, 113
Wroth, John W., 113, 425, 430, 440

Yeats, William Butler, 303*n*
Yesterdays with Authors, 388, 390, 396
"Yonnondio," 131

THIS BOOK is set in Monticello, a Linotype face designed after what was perhaps the first native American type face of real quality, cut by Archibald Binney probably in 1797. Printed on S. D. Warren Paper Company's University Text, the book was manufactured in its entirety by Kingsport Press, Inc.
The design and typography are by Andor Braun.